INSTRUCTOR'S MANUAL

to accompany the fourth edition of

METHODS AND MATERIALS FOR SECONDARY SCHOOL PHYSICAL EDUCATION

CHARLES A. BUCHER, A.B., M.A., Ed.D.

Professor of Education, New York University,
New York, N. Y.

CONSTANCE R. KOENIG, B.A., M.S. in Education

The Peabody Demonstration School of George Peabody
College for Teachers, Nashville, Tenn.

Prepared by

Myra F. Goldman

PREFACE

This instructor's manual, to be used with the fourth edition of *Methods and Materials for Secondary School Physical Education*, has been prepared in response to numerous requests for such an aid by colleagues in the fields of physical education, health, and recreation.

The number and wide variety of questions should provide instructors with a selection of questions suitable for either short quizzes or more comprehensive examinations. Questions are grouped by chapters so that examinations can be given over one chapter or a combination of several chapters.

The questions are predominantly best answer, multiple choice. Although multiple-choice questions take longer to prepare, they are generally regarded by educators today as providing the best type for examination purposes. They are easily graded and require a knowledge of facts on the part of the student to answer correctly. If the instructor desires to use essay questions, they may be found at the end of each chapter in the text. The number of questions vary from chapter to chapter, depending upon the length and type of material included in the corresponding text. A few chapters, because of their length, require more questions than others. .

The instructor will find that he can facilitate the scoring of his examination if he will provide an answer sheet and have the student black out the letter of the answer which the student feels is most nearly correct. Answer sheets can be easily prepared, and a key can be made for them by punching out the letters of the correct answers. The instructor can quickly score the examination by placing the key over the student's answer sheet.

It is expected that each instructor will use the questions in this manual according to his own needs. He should feel free to make such changes and additions as he feels are desirable, including corrections in the light of new findings. The examination should reflect the material for which the student is responsible and the degree of emphasis that the instructor has placed upon various areas. Some of the questions are concerned with generalities; others measure a greater depth of knowledge. It is not expected that the instructor will wish to use every question. The number of questions should be proportionate to the amount of time given the student to complete the examination.

We are deeply indebted to Myra F. Goldman for preparing the instructor's manual for the third edition. Although the fourth edition has been updated by the authors, this manual is still primarily the work of Miss Goldman.

Charles A. Bucher
Constance R. Koenig

CONTENTS

INTRODUCTION—THE SECONDARY SCHOOL'S QUEST FOR RELEVANCE

Write at the left the letter indicating the one *best* answer.

B 1. The new teaching technology was given its primary impetus by:
A. The flight of the Wright brothers
B. The Russian sputnik
C. Mission Apollo
D. Teacher militancy
E. The new student "left"

D 2. For the majority of people today's society is:
A. Characterized by activism
B. Characterized by militancy
C. Closed
D. Open
E. Characterized by tight money

A 3. A primary characteristic of this decade has been:
A. Increased suburbanization by the middle and upper classes
B. Increased urbanization by the middle and upper classes
C. Increased suburbanization by the lower socioeconomic groups
D. Increased industrialization of the suburbs
E. Increased employment opportunities for the urban poor

B 4. The average professional or skilled worker is finding that his working day is:
A. Shorter than in the past decade
B. Longer than in the past decade
C. About the same length as in the past decade

D This is a result of:
A. Machines taking over the work of men
B. The need to increase worker productivity
C. Domestic and foreign unrest
D. The need to keep abreast of technological advances

E 5. A hallmark of the "new" society is:
A. Vicarious recreation
B. Increased socialization
C. Lower-class social mobility
D. Lowered educational standards
E. Education for all

B 6. Changes in educational technology are taking place most rapidly on the:
A. Elementary school level
B. Secondary school level
C. Technical school level
D. Junior college level
E. College and university level

C 7. The earliest teaching machines were:
A. Talking typewriters
B. Videotape machines
C. Skinner boxes
D. Stop-action cameras
E. Teleprinters

D 8. Teaching machines:
A. Help to reduce the number of professional staff in a school
B. Eliminate the need for mass instruction
C. Enable a school system to increase class sizes
D. Help to individualize instruction
E. Are useful only in sciences and languages

E 9. Physical education has faced the challenge of the computer age by:
A. Making changes that parallel those made by general education
B. Contributing significant scholarly research on teaching machines
C. Developing programmed textbooks
D. Making full use of the conceptualized approach
E. Failing to keep up to date many new advances

A 10. A recent trend by suburban residents has been to:
   A. Defeat increased school-tax levies
   B. Approve increased school-tax levies
   C. Attempt to gain control of the schools
   D. Oppose the construction of educational parks
   E. Send their children to urban schools

   C This is a result of their desire to:
   A. Maintain land for recreational use
   B. End *de facto* segregation
   C. Force educational reform
   D. Attract the best teachers to the suburbs
   E. Challenge educational administration and structure

D 11. Old, overcrowded, and inadequately staffed schools are most likely to be found in:
   A. Rural areas
   B. Suburban areas
   C. Expanding communities
   D. Urban areas
   E. Housing development areas

B 12. One of the biggest problems faced by urban schools is:
   A. Bussing of students
   B. Obtaining qualified staff
   C. Overcrowding of classrooms
   D. Maintaining a good learning environment
   E. Community-public relations

A 13. The single most expensive item in new school construction is often:
   A. The physical education facility
   B. The modular architecture
   C. The science laboratory
   D. The computer center
   E. Language laboratory equipment

C 14. One of the most important things to today's youth is:
   A. Social activism
   B. Political militancy
   C. Asserting individuality
   D. Educational reform
   E. Elimination of crime

D 15. Today's adolescent reacts most favorably to:
   A. Traditional curricula
   B. Classical methodology
   C. Courses that do not employ teaching machines
   D. Courses that are involved with today's world
   E. Courses that tell what the world was like in the past

B 16. New technological devices in education:
   A. Help the student to adapt to education
   B. Help adapt education to the student
   C. Cannot cater to individual differences between students

   D. Conflict with the use of textbooks in the classroom
   E. Effectively stifle creativity

E 17. One of the most important tasks of the physical educator is to:
   A. Maintain traditional methodology
   B. Emphasize the "physical" part of the individual
   C. Oppose curriculum reform
   D. Plan the program
   E. Guide students

D 18. To appeal to today's youth, physical education should:
   A. Emphasize individual sports
   B. Teach more lifetime sports
   C. Be made an elective subject
   D. Become more intellectual
   E. Shift to a complete physical fitness emphasis

B 19. The recent trend toward teacher militancy has:
   A. Caused many National Education Association members to retire from teaching as a profession
   B. Resulted in some teacher gains in regard to class size and nonteaching duties
   C. Adversely affected working conditions
   D. Met with stern disapproval from professional organizations
   E. Caused a wide rift between teachers and administrators

A 20. Upward movement based on achievement is a characteristic of:
   A. Nongraded schools
   B. Flexible scheduling
   C. Modular scheduling
   D. Middle schools
   E. Core curricula

E 21. If a school building needs to expand to relieve overcrowding, and land space is not available, the school system might be advised to:
   A. Exercise the right of eminent domain
   B. Condemn surrounding properties to gain land
   C. Put the students on double sessions
   D. Use team teaching
   E. Construct subterranean facilities

B 22. Much of the current teacher militancy has been motivated by:
   A. A desire for professional recognition
   B. Student militancy
   C. Changing mores
   D. Changing communities
   E. Upward social mobility

E 23. Today's teacher:
   A. Has little time to participate in community affairs
   B. Is less flexible than were teachers of a decade ago

C. Has failed to broaden his scope of knowledge
D. Has proved unable to cope with the changes in education
E. No longer holds an "untouchable" place in society

A 24. Team teaching:
A. Has proved effective in physical education classes
B. Cannot be used with large classes
C. Is unwieldy to use at the secondary school level
D. Has no real implications for physical education
E. Is too traditional in approach for today's student

1   THE CHANGING COMMUNITY

Write at the left the letter indicating the one *best* answer.

D 1. The philosophy of a particular school program is greatly influenced by the:
   A. Size of the population
   B. Proximity of larger cities
   C. Local zoning ordinances
   D. Local community
   E. Available tax tables

B 2. The physical educator can best develop relevant physical education programs for his community by:
   A. Developing winning athletic teams
   B. Enlisting community support
   C. Offering a wide variety of activities
   D. Joining local social clubs
   E. Working through the school administration

E 3. The most important single factor in a community is its:
   A. Schools
   B. Population size
   C. Per capita income
   D. Educational philosophy
   E. People

A 4. In a sprawling community the after-school physical education program may be adversely affected by the:
   A. Need to transport pupils
   B. Diversity of available community recreation facilities
   C. Competition from other school clubs and activities
   D. Number of neighborhood recreation leagues
   E. Lack of school facilities

C 5. Community residents are probably less concerned with education in:
   A. A middle-class community
   B. A rural area
   C. An industrial community
   D. A small town
   E. An upper-class community

A 6. The three main types of local government are:
   A. Mayor-council; commission; city manager
   B. Commission; mayor; planning board
   C. City manager; planning board; mayor-council
   D. Planning board; commission; city manager
   E. Commission; city manager; city superintendent

E 7. The local administrative unit that determines school policies is the:
   A. Board of Examiners
   B. Parent-Teacher Association
   C. Planning Board
   D. Commissioner's Office
   E. Board of Education

   A The individuals that serve on these units are:
   A. Most often elected by the voters
   B. Elected by the teachers
   C. Political appointees
   D. Given these positions for life
   E. Nonresidents of the community

C 8. A current trend in the structure of school districts is toward:
   A. Construction of small, local high schools
   B. Construction of neighborhood high schools
   C. Consolidation
   D. Decentralization
   E. Vocational orientation

   B Such organization has implications for physical education because:
   A. Many small plants can be built
   B. Fully staffed plants can be created
   C. More physical educators can be hired
   D. Duplicate facilities are beneficial
   E. Each small school can have an autonomous program

E 9. The best physical education plants depend heavily on:
- A. Income from interscholastic athletics
- B. Teacher salary demands
- C. The quality of the program
- D. The number of persons on the physical education staff
- E. Community economic conditions

B 10. Opposition to rising school costs often comes from:
- A. Older individuals who no longer have children in school
- B. Parents of children who go to private schools
- C. Local businessmen
- D. Private home owners
- E. School board members

D These individuals may also influence the physical education program because:
- A. They consider it a frill
- B. Staff, facilities, and equipment are expensive
- C. They feel that the community can provide needed recreational experiences
- D. Certain activities are prohibited by some religious groups
- E. They do not feel that the program has a proved educational value

E 11. A group of people working to achieve a common goal is a (an):
- A. Ethnic group
- B. Sociological group
- C. Lobby
- D. Socioeconomic group
- E. Pressure group

B 12. Education is a function of the:
- A. Federal government
- B. State government
- C. City government
- D. Local community
- E. Individual school

C One responsibility of this organ is the:
- A. Hiring of teachers
- B. Setting of teacher salaries
- C. Setting of standards for various curricular areas
- D. Appointing of secondary school administrators
- E. Purchasing of supplies and equipment

D 13. Physical education may be successfully integrated with:
- A. Recreation only
- B. Health education only
- C. Neither health nor recreation
- D. Recreation and health
- E. Movement education only

A 14. An integrated physical education and recreation program:
- A. May help a school system save money
- B. Cannot be operable in a school situation
- C. Rarely receive community support
- D. Require vast expenditures of money
- E. May cause duplication of facilities

C 15. There is a trend in some states to:
- A. Eliminate school health education programs
- B. Cut back on school health services
- C. Require that health education teachers be certified
- D. Require that only doctors teach health
- E. Require that only school nurses teach health education

2 THE SCHOOL

Write at the left the letter indicating the one *best* answer.

E 1. In regard to the administration of education, a school district is responsible to the:
   A. Federal government
   B. Local community
   C. People
   D. Local government
   E. State

C 2. According to National Education Association surveys, the number of school districts in the United States is estimated to be about:
   A. 10,000
   B. 20,000
   C. 30,000
   D. 40,000
   E. 50,000

   B In comparison with the years 1948-1958, the above number is:
   A. Larger
   B. Smaller
   C. The same

   D This is because:
   A. There is a trend toward having smaller, more effective districts
   B. There is a trend toward having many overlapping districts
   C. The organization of new school districts has not kept pace with the population explosion
   D. There is a trend toward having larger, more effective districts

E 3. A school district is administered by the:
   A. People of the state
   B. District principal
   C. Superintendent of schools
   D. State commissioner's office
   E. School board

A 4. A secondary school physical educator teaching in an 8-4 school system would be in an organizational pattern known as the:

   A. Traditional high school
   B. Middle school
   C. Junior high school
   D. Combined junior-senior high school
   E. Unified school system

B 5. A school system has a middle school organizational pattern when:
   A. Grades three and four or four and five are grouped
   B. Grades five to eight or six to eight are grouped together and the junior high school is eliminated
   C. Grades eight and nine or eight to ten are grouped and the lower high school grades are eliminated
   D. Kindergarten to grade eight are in the elementary school and grades nine to twelve are in the high school
   E. Kindergarten to grade six are in the elementary school and grades seven to twelve are in the high school

   E This organizational pattern is frequently expressed by the numbers:
   A. 8-4
   B. 7-5
   C. 6-6
   D. 6-3-3
   E. 4-4-4

C 6. All of the following are common characteristics of a secondary school *except:*
   A. Guidance is offered by specially trained personnel
   B. Individual courses of study are planned for the students
   C. Teachers are generalists in subject matter fields
   D. Terminal education as well as college preparation is offered
   E. Extracurricular activities are a part of the program

D 7. The individual in charge of the supervision of a school system is the:
   A. District coordinator
   B. High school principal

C. President of the board of education
D. Superintendent of schools
E. Clerk of the works

B His responsibilities include each of these *except:*
A. Curriculum development
B. Syllabus construction
C. School organization
D. Personal recommendations
E. Publicity

A 8. The chief administrator of a school is the:
A. Principal
B. Attendance officer
C. Superintendent
D. Coordinator
E. School clerk

C One of the most difficult tasks for this individual is:
A. Establishing teacher-administrator relationships
B. Establishing parent-administrator relationships
C. Getting to know the pupils
D. Assuming a role in the community
E. Assuming a role in the Parent-Teacher Association

E 9. In large school systems, personnel supervision and direction for various academic areas are often the responsibility of the:
A. Principal
B. Assistant principal
C. Attendance officer
D. Faculty committee
E. Department head

A 10. Teachers are usually initially recommended for hiring by the:
A. Principal
B. Assistant principal
C. Faculty dean
D. Grade adviser
E. College adviser

D This recommendation is forwarded to the:
A. Department head
B. Curriculum specialist
C. Supervisory officer
D. Superintendent
E. Principal

B The above individual sends the recommendation for final action to the:
A. Superintendent
B. Board of education
C. School attorney
D. School clerk
E. School finance officer

D 11. The maintenance of playing fields and

marking of lines is often the responsibility of the:
A. Physical educator
B. Supervisor
C. Superintendent of buildings
D. Custodian
E. Principal

E 12. The individual vested with the responsibility for excusing students from physical education is often the:
A. Family physician
B. School guidance counselor
C. Physical educator
D. Attendance officer
E. School nurse

A 13. The individual who may be the most knowledgeable about student behavioral and emotional problems is the:
A. Guidance counselor
B. School physician
C. School nurse
D. Physical educator
E. Homeroom teacher

D 14. The voting public may be more willing to support school construction when the physical education facilities are:
A. Eliminated
B. Inexpensive
C. Designed for coeducational use
D. Designed for multiple use
E. Traditional in design

B 15. The three basic curricula offered on the secondary school level are:
A. General; required; vocational
B. Vocational; general; college preparatory
C. College preparatory; business; technical
D. Required; college board; technical
E. Distributive; special; general

C 16. A student generally starts to follow a prescribed course of study in grades:
A. Five and six
B. Six and seven
C. Seven and eight
D. Eight and nine
E. Nine and ten

E Some freedom of selection of courses is usually begun in grade:
A. Five
B. Six
C. Seven
D. Eight
E. Nine

A A chosen course of study is pursued in grades:
A. Ten to twelve
B. Nine to eleven
C. Eight to ten

D. Seven to nine

E. Six to eight

B 17. Policies in regard to various aspects of the physical education program, such as uniforms, excuses, and grading, are usually set by the:

A. Board of education

B. School administration

C. District principal

D. Physical education director

E. Physical education personnel

C 18. The physical educator can gain invaluable insights into his students by getting to know their:

A. Personalities

B. Friends

C. Parents

D. Hobbies

E. Interests

E 19. Good discipline in a physical education class is necessary for:

A. Good teaching

B. Respect

C. Rapport

D. Motivation

E. Safety

D 20. The true role of the director of physical education in some school systems is that of:

A. Supervisor of personnel

B. Master teacher

C. Fiscal manager

D. Administrative adviser

E. Athletic supervisor

A The scope of his responsibilities depends upon:

A. The size of the system

B. The size of the staff

C. Finances

D. Administrative support

E. The number of other administrators

B 21. The chairman of a physical education department is usually:

A. Elected by staff vote

B. Appointed by the superintendent

C. Voted upon by the board of education

D. Not involved in personnel evaluation

E. Given the title but not the responsibility

B 22. Two of the primary responsibilities of a new physical education teacher are to:

A. Develop pupil rapport and devise a program

B. Become a part of the department and of the school

C. Observe and teach

D. Assume a community role and join the PTA

E. Develop a winning athletic team and work toward tenure

C 23. Each of these is vital to an interscholastic athletic program *except:*

A. Challenging the athletically gifted

B. Enhancing school spirit

C. Keeping players scholastically eligible

D. Uniting the members of the school community

E. Educating through athletics

E 24. The physical educator must be particularly cognizant of the need to:

A. Emphasize the physical aspects of the program

B. Maintain good discipline

C. Produce winning athletic teams

D. Avoid speaking out in faculty meetings

E. Interpret his program to the public

3

THE NEW BREED OF STUDENT
IN TODAY'S SECONDARY SCHOOL

Write at the left the letter indicating the one *best* answer.

C 1. In the mid-1960's the number of students actually graduating from high school against the potential number of graduates was approximately:
   A. 50 out of 100   D. 80 out of 100
   B. 60 out of 100   E. 90 out of 100
   C. 70 out of 100

E 2. The number of handicapped persons needing special programs is approximately:
   A. One million   D. Four million
   B. Two million   E. Five million
   C. Three million

   A Out of this number the percentage actually benefiting from special programs is approximately:
   A. 50%   D. 20%
   B. 40%   E. 10%
   C. 30%

C 3. The number of stages of physical development through which the secondary school student passes is:
   A. Two   C. Four
   B. Three   D. Five

   D These stages are known as:
   A. Puberty, early adolescence, adulthood
   B. Puberty, adolescence
   C. Childhood, preadolescence, early adolescence, middle adolescence, late adolescence
   D. Preadolescence, early adolescence, middle adolescence, late adolescence
   E. Infancy, childhood, adolescence, adulthood

B 4. Sudden growth spurts in the secondary school student are caused by:
   A. Decreased hormone production
   B. Increased hormone production
   C. Changes in diet
   D. Decreases in caloric needs
   E. Increases in caloric needs

E 5. Boys experience a growth spurt at a different age from the age at which girls experience a growth spurt. The age differential is approximately:
   A. Six months   D. Eighteen months
   B. Three years   E. Two years
   C. One year

B 6. Not all boys or girls experience the growth spurt at the same time. The physical educator should take cognizance of this by:
   A. Scheduling coeducational dancing classes
   B. Distributing the students by height among squads
   C. Putting all students of the same height on the same squads
   D. Giving excuses from class to students whose physique embarrasses them
   E. Ignoring the emotional and physical problems caused by the growth spurt

D 7. Changes in the skeletal structure of youth also take place during the growth spurt. At this time bones change in:
   A. Length only
   B. Breadth and density
   C. Mass only
   D. Length, breadth, and density
   E. Length, density, and porosity

   A The physical educator's program during this stage of student development should include an emphasis on:
   A. Large-muscle exercises
   B. Strenuous activities
   C. Competition
   D. Fine motor coordinations
   E. Individual sports

C 8. The primary sex change for girls is the development of the:
A. Ovaries and urethra
B. Urethra and fallopian tubes
C. Ovaries and fallopian tubes
D. Fallopian tubes and testes
E. Testes and ovaries

E   This development signals the onset of:
A. Breast development
B. Menopause
C. Improved motor coordination
D. Decreases in physical strength
E. Menstruation

A 9. Secondary sex characteristics in boys include:
A. Development of a waistline
B. Breast development
C. Broadening of the hips
D. Decreases in physical strength
E. Slowing of the growth rate

B 10. A primary cause of acne in teen-agers is:
A. An increase in the perspiration rate
B. An increase in glandular activity
C. A change in dietary habits
D. A change in the circulatory system
E. A decrease in vital capacity

D 11. The body system that seems to attain fuller development first is the:
A. Circulatory   D. Nervous
B. Reproductive   E. Respiratory
C. Digestive

E 12. Young boys tend to perform better than girls in activities involving:
A. Accuracy   D. Intellect
B. Control   E. Balance
C. Agility

A 13. The percentage of teen-age deaths attributable to accidents is approximately:
A. 50%   D. 20%
B. 40%   E. 10%
C. 30%

C   Two thirds of this percentage is attributable to:
A. Falls in the home
B. Recreational mishaps
C. Motor vehicle accidents
D. Athletic injuries
E. Camping accidents

A 14. The most common physical defects in adolescents involve:
A. Vision, hearing, and posture
B. Teeth, tonsils, and glands
C. Focal infections, poor nutrition, and fatigue
D. Headache, fatigue, and weakness
E. Improper diet, rest, and exercise

D 15. Physical education programs for junior and senior high school students should emphasize:

A. Appreciation of physical activity
B. Body mechanics
C. Posture
D. Maintaining high levels of physical fitness
E. Remedial and corrective work

B 16. The three basic human emotions are:
A. Anger, fear, and joy
B. Fear, joy, and hate
C. Joy, hate, and passivity
D. Hate, passivity, and anger
E. Passivity, anger, and fear

E 17. Adolescent emotional responses are generally:
A. Unrecognizable   D. Infantile
B. Mature   E. Extreme
C. Stable

C 18. The physical educator can help students to find satisfaction and achievement through an emphasis on:
A. Team sports   D. Coeducational
B. Competition   activities
C. Variety   E. Lifetime sports

B 19. The adolescent's need for adventure can be partially satisfied through:
A. Creative rhythmic activities
B. Competition
C. Individual sports
D. Team sports
E. Self-testing activities

D 20. The physical educator can help students to gain self-reliance through:
A. Enforcement of adult-evolved rules and regulations
B. Formulation of strict codes of conduct
C. Elimination of the need for student responsibility
D. Assignment of leadership positions
E. Elimination of the need for student self-discipline

A 21. A fundamental social development objective of physical education is the development of:
A. Leadership qualities
B. Followership qualities
C. Clique formations
D. Peer groups
E. Heterosexual groups

C 22. Boys and girls are generally antagonistic to each other between the ages of:
A. Four and six
B. Seven and nine
C. Ten and twelve
D. Thirteen and fifteen
E. Sixteen and eighteen

A 23. Boy-girl antagonism tends to disappear when adjustment to the opposite sex is completed by the age of about:
A. Sixteen   D. Nine
B. Thirteen   E. Six
C. Ten

D This implies that the physical educator should plan to include in his program:
A. Posture work
B. Team sports
C. Games of low organization
D. Coeducational activities
E. Poise and balance activities

B 24. Early adolescents tend to:
A. Accept adult authority
B. Resent adult authority
C. Ask for adult help
D. Ask for adult advice
E. Be mature in their relationships with adults

C This has implications for the physical educator in regard to:
A. Class organization
B. Student motivation
C. Class management
D. Class leadership
E. Student evaluations

B This attitude of the early adolescent may cause problems in regard to:
A. Program planning
B. Teacher-student relationships
C. Student-student relationships
D. Class leadership
E. Student self-direction

E 25. A strong childhood intellectual power that seems to decline in adolescence is:
A. Reasoning   D. Concentration
B. Imagination   E. Memory
C. Creativity

D 26. When an adolescent is interested in a subject he tends to show an increase in the ability to:

A. Memorize
B. Ideate
C. Reason
D. Concentrate
E. Use logical thinking

B 27. Adolescent intellectual development has many implications for physical education. One of the most important is:
A. Program planning
B. Teaching methodology
C. Philosophy formulation
D. Ability grouping
E. Curriculum content

C 28. Written tests in secondary school physical education should include questions of the:
A. Multiple-choice type only
B. True-false type only
C. Essay type
D. Affective type
E. Matching type only

A 29. The program should introduce the student to:
A. Game strategy
B. Sports history
C. Team play
D. Game rules
E. New activities

D 30. A major responsibility of the physical educator is to:
A. Plan a good program
B. Decrease the time spent in student guidance
C. Allow students to take the responsibility for program planning
D. Set a good example for students
E. Teach

4

DEVELOPING GOALS— WHAT SHOULD PHYSICAL EDUCATION BE DOING FOR THE STUDENT?

Write at the left the letter indicating the one *best* answer.

A 1. Parent-teacher associations claim a national membership of approximately:
   A. Fifteen million
   B. Thirteen million
   C. Eleven million
   D. Nine million
   E. Seven million

D 2. Each physical educator must be able to understand and interpret the goals of:
   A. Education
   B. Education and physical education
   C. Parents and students
   D. Education, physical education, and students
   E. Education and the community

E 3. In setting objectives, the physical educator should be concerned with:
   A. The goals of the community first
   B. His professional goals first
   C. Student goals first
   D. Administrative goals first
   E. General education goals first

B 4. The educational objective of self-realization implies that physical educators should teach toward the development of:
   A. Creative thinking
   B. Healthful living
   C. Self-expression
   D. Physical fitness
   E. Emotional stability

C 5. The educational objective of human relationships implies that physical educators should teach toward the development of:
   A. The individual
   B. High competitive spirit
   C. Intragroup organization
   D. Worthy spectatorism

   E. Socialization

A 6. The educational objective of economic efficiency implies that physical educators should teach toward the development of:
   A. Knowledge of equipment
   B. Worthwhile use of leisure time
   C. Appreciation of the school plant
   D. A value system
   E. Objective judgment

E 7. The educational objective of civic responsibility implies that physical educators should teach toward the development of:
   A. Self-respect
   B. Leadership
   C. Cooperative relationships
   D. Recreational adjustment
   E. Team loyalty

B 8. Secondary school physical educational objectives should be drawn up to reflect the needs of the:
   A. Physical education program
   B. Students
   C. General educational program
   D. Physical educator
   E. Philosophy of the physical education department

C 9. A student who has developed the ability to deal with problems in an objective manner can be characterized as:
   A. Being self-sufficient
   B. Being socially minded
   C. Having a realistic attitude
   D. Having emotional stability
   E. Being flexible

E 10. A student who has developed a wide range of personal interests can be characterized as:
   A. Having emotional stability

B. Having value judgment
C. Having self-understanding
D. Being flexible
E. Being well-balanced

D 11. John is a high school senior, a physical education class leader, and a patrol leader in his scout troop. Several of the boys in his physical education class decide to sneak out of the gymnasium after attendance is taken, leave the school building, and then buy some beer to drink in the school parking lot. They ask John to help them carry out their scheme, but he refuses and convinces these boys to drop the plan entirely. John's actions were based on his desire to:
A. Understand the feelings of other people
B. Work out his own plans
C. Adjust to changes in a mature manner
D. Conform to the standards of acceptable behavior
E. Become more self-sufficient

C John may best be characterized as being:
A. Self-sufficient
B. Flexible
C. Socially minded
D. Emotionally stable
E. Secure

E 12. Coordinations, rhythm, accuracy, and poise are the concern of the:
A. Cognitive development objective
B. Personal-social development objective
C. Developmental goals of physical education
D. Physical development objective
E. Motor development objective

A 13. The physical development objective is concerned with:
A. Vitality, strength, endurance, stamina
B. Control, skill, proficiency, grace
C. Values, alertness, diagnosis, decision-making

D. Sportsmanship, courtesy, fair play, respect for authority
E. Balance, flexibility, mastery, objectivity

C 14. Knowledge of good health practices and understanding the rules and strategies of sports and games are part of the:
A. Developmental goals of physical education
B. Neuromuscular goals of physical education
C. Cognitive development objective
D. Physical development goals
E. Personal-social development goals

B 15. When cortical control of the body increases:
A. Physical fitness and motor ability increase
B. Coordination and skill increase
C. Heart rate and pulse rate increase
D. Ability to think and interpret increase
E. Judgment and confidence increase

A 16. Play is a (an):
A. Instinctive drive
B. Learned activity
C. Phenomenon limited to childhood
D. Stage of human development
E. Major objective of sound physical education programs

B 17. Each of the following is a desirable characteristic for a physical educator to develop *except*:
A. Specialized technical training
B. Uncontrollable competitive drive
C. Skill in activities
D. Suitable personality
E. Functional English usage

D 18. One of the major problems caused by large class size in physical education is:
A. High ratio of leaders to participants
B. Low ratio of equipment to participants
C. Maintenance of disciplinary standards
D. Low ratio of leaders to participants
E. High ratio of equipment to participants

5 RELEVANT HEALTH GOALS THAT CAN BE ACHIEVED THROUGH PHYSICAL EDUCATION

Write at the left the letter indicating the one *best* answer.

B 1. One important responsibility of the physical educator is to:
  A. Give students emergency health care
  B. Help students utilize school health services
  C. Diagnose and treat student health problems
  D. Help to control communicable diseases
  E. Excuse students from physical education when they are ill

A 2. Physical educators and school health educators can cooperate to:
  A. Improve student health knowledge, attitudes, and practices
  B. Give medical treatment when the school physician is not available
  C. Replace the school health services
  D. Show students how physical education and health education are different
  E. None of the above

D 3. The development of proper health attitudes depends primarily upon:
  A. Knowledge and application
  B. Need and worth
  C. Teaching and learning
  D. Interest and motivation
  E. Example and imitation

E 4. The most suitable approach to teaching proper health attitudes is a (an):
  A. Factual one   D. Negative one
  B. Illustrative one E. Positive one
  C. Informal one

C 5. Health teaching should be centered around:
  A. The school philosophy
  B. Teacher goals
  C. Student goals
  D. Physical fitness objectives
  E. Mental health objectives

B 6. A student who fails to receive proper rest and sleep, even though he has been exposed to and understands the need for it, does not have:
  A. Good health knowledge
  B. Good health practices
  C. Good health attitudes
  D. Good health
  E. Physical fitness

E 7. A secondary school physical educator who employs sound health practices would wish to include each of these activities in his program *except:*
  A. Tennis   D. Basketball
  B. Fencing   E. Boxing
  C. Trampoline

D 8. Students who have been ill and have returned to school:
  A. Should be excused from physical education
  B. Should not enter the locker or shower areas
  C. Should not participate in outdoor activities
  D. Should participate as their status warrants
  E. Should be placed in an adaptive program

B 9. An important prerequisite to participation in the physical education program for any student is a (an):
  A. Adequate level of fitness
  B. Medical examination
  C. Shower
  D. Complete freedom from disease
  E. Physical education uniform

B 10. Physical education can help to further health objectives if classes are of a manageable size. The number of students in a class preferably should not exceed:

A. Forty-five
B. Forty
C. Thirty-five
D. Thirty
E. Twenty-five

6 A RELEVANT PHYSICAL EDUCATION PROGRAM

Write at the left the letter indicating the one *best* answer.

D 1. The development of a sound physical education class program is based on student needs. These needs are:
   A. Organic
   B. Behavioral and psychosocial
   C. Physical, mental, and recreational
   D. Physical, mental, social, and emotional
   E. Physical, mental, social, emotional, and recreational

A 2. The physical education class program should include time for each of these *except:*
   A. Free play   D. Appreciation
   B. Strategies of sports   E. Skills
   C. Understanding

C 3. Physical education class instruction should:
   A. Stress game play
   B. Emphasize the perfection of skills
   C. Proceed from the fundamental to the complex
   D. Proceed from the complex to the fundamental
   E. Be concerned with teaching strategies

E 4. A certain secondary school physical educator is known for his sound program. When the students graduate from his school, they have reached certain standards of achievement in physical education and have mastered particular skills. These students may be said to be:
   A. Highly skilled
   B. Athletes
   C. Varsity-level competitors
   D. Knowledgeable about physical activity
   E. Physically educated

B 5. The percentage of time that should be spent on book and classroom work in physical education is approximately:

   A. 0% to 10%   D. 40%
   B. 10% to 20%   E. 50%
   C. 20% to 30%

A 6. Instruction in the subject matter of physical education can be meaningfully supplemented by:
   A. Textbooks   D. Physical activity
   B. Records   E. Longer class periods
   C. Instruction

C 7. The optimum number of class periods or the equivalent per week for a physical educator should be:
   A. Fifteen   D. Thirty
   B. Twenty   E. Thirty-five
   C. Twenty-five

E 8. Physical education classes should:
   A. Include only the physically fit
   B. Include varsity team members only when their sport is not in season
   C. Exclude students who have physical defects
   D. Exclude mentally retarded students
   E. Include all the students in the school

   C The reason for this is that:
   A. Varsity team members are in good condition when they are playing and do not need physical education at that time
   B. Students who are mentally retarded are hard to discipline
   C. Every student needs physical education
   D. Students with physical defects cannot participate fully
   E. The physically fit learn best

B 9. Secondary school students need:
   A. Fewer physical education class periods when they are in grade twelve
   B. A daily period of physical education
   C. To have their physical education class early in the day

D. To be able to elect to take physical education
E. More physical education class periods when they in grade ten

D 10. Adapted physical education programs are designed for:
A. Mentally retarded students only
B. Physically handicapped students only
C. Emotionally disturbed students only
D. Any student who cannot participate in the regular program
E. Any student who does not wish to participate in the regular program

A 11. Special provisions need to be made in physical education for approximately:
A. One in eight students
B. One in ten students
C. One in fifteen students
D. One in twenty students
E. One in thirty students

A 12. Scheduling for an adapted program depends on each of the following *except:*
A. Staff attitude
B. Finances
C. Facilities
D. Available staff
E. Educational philosophy

C 13. Voluntary all-school student participation is a characteristic of:
A. Interscholastic athletics
B. The regular physical education class program
C. Extramural programs
D. Team sports
E. Coeducational classes

B 14. The school physical education program includes the:
A. Class program only
B. Class program, adapted program, and intramural, extramural, and interscholastic athletics
C. Class program and intramural activities only
D. Class program and extramural activities only
E. Class program and interscholastic program only

E 15. The athletic program for junior high school students should include only:
A. Extramural activities

B. Intramural activities
C. Intramural and extramural activities
D. Interscholastic athletics
E. Intramural and extramural athletics

A This is because:
A. Many of these students are physiologically immature
B. Growth and development have been completed
C. The senior high school coaches need trained players
D. These activities help to motivate students to exercise regularly
E. The students are interested in and need such a program

D 16. The secondary school athletic program for girls should concentrate its main emphasis on:
A. Intramural activities only
B. Extramural activities only
C. Intramural, extramural, and interscholastic athletics
D. Intramural and extramural activities
E. Interscholastic athletics only

B This is primarily because:
A. Girls want this kind of program
B. Of their biological, psychological, and social characteristics
C. Of the current emphasis on Olympic development
D. Women physical educators are interested in coaching
E. Of the emphasis on spectator sports

D 17. The interscholastic program for boys must be:
A. A proved money-maker
B. A focal point of the school program
C. Geared to winning
D. Educational in nature
E. Begun at the junior high school level

A 18. High school interscholastic athletics should be:
A. Voluntary in nature
B. A part of the class period
C. Open only to the most highly skilled players
D. Expected to make a profit for the school athletic fund
E. Played for spectator appeal

7 DEVELOPING THE RELEVANT CURRICULUM

Write at the left the letter indicating the one *best* answer.

E 1. A curriculum is:
- A. A statement of philosophy
- B. A set of principles
- C. A series of objectives and goals
- D. All of the above
- E. A and C only

C 2. When units of study are required of all students, this is known as a (an):
- A. Elective program
- B. Problem-centered program
- C. Core program
- D. Core-elective program
- E. Curricular program

B 3. When staff and students work out program selections according to the needs of the group, this is known as a (an):
- A. Elective program
- B. Problem-centered program
- C. Core program
- D. Core-elective program
- E. Curricular program

A 4. The type of program to be used in a school is generally determined by a (an):
- A. Curriculum committee
- B. Student committee
- C. Administrative edict
- D. School superintendent
- E. Student-faculty committee

B 5. The order of steps in the construction of a curriculum is:
- A. Testing of students, analysis of data, construction of the curriculum
- B. Collection of data, analysis of materials, construction of the curriculum, adoption of the curriculum
- C. Evaluation of procedures, statement of philosophy, writing of principles, adoption of policies
- D. Writing of policies, forming of principles, formulation of objectives, construction of the curriculum
- E. Statement of philosophy, writing of operational procedures, development of objectives, construction of the curriculum

D 6. The guiding principles for the selection of activities for a physical education program are based upon:
- A. Balancing team and individual sports
- B. Mental and physical characteristics
- C. Balancing team, individual, and lifetime sports
- D. Physiological, sociological, and psychological characteristics
- E. Social and emotional characteristics

A 7. The most effective implement through which the goals of physical education are achieved is the:
- A. Teaching process
- B. Statement of philosophy
- C. Learning process
- D. Objective of the program
- E. Program's operating policy

E 8. None of the following are major goals of physical education *except:*
- A. Agility
- B. Accuracy
- C. Fencing
- D. Tumbling
- E. Physical fitness

C 9. None of the following are overall goals of physical education *except:*
- A. Improvement of speed in sprints
- B. Ability to score better in archery
- C. Development of accuracy
- D. Neuromuscular development
- E. Increased flexibility in tumbling

A 10. The amount of time to be devoted to each activity is determined on the basis of:
- A. Student needs and interests
- B. Teacher competency
- C. The length of the school year
- D. Administrative philosophy

E. The size of the staff

D 11. The choice of the teaching progression to be used is guided by:
  A. Program objectives
  B. Student needs
  C. The syllabus
  D. Unit goals
  E. Teaching philosophy

B 12. Goals are achieved by following a proper order of steps:
  A. Specific objective, objective, subobjective
  B. Objective, specific objective, subobjective
  C. Unit plan, objective, subobjective
  D. Yearly plan, specific objective, subobjective
  E. Procedure, objective, subobjective

E 13. A daily lesson plan contains:
  A. Unit outlines
  B. The four goals of physical education
  C. Unit goals
  D. The yearly outline in brief
  E. Step-by-step procedures

C 14. The effectiveness of the role of the student in program planning depends to a large extent on:
  A. Departmental philosophy
  B. Administrative dicta
  C. Teacher leadership
  D. Supervision
  E. Objectives and policies

B 15. Today's students react well to:
  A. Traditional approaches
  B. The conceptualized approach
  C. Highly structured programs
  D. Teacher-directed programs
  E. Programs that emphasize the physical

E 16. One material that will probably be used extensively in physical education facility construction in the future is:
  A. Masonite   D. Aluminum
  B. Concrete   E. Plastic
  C. Wood

A 17. Physical education curricula of the future will be founded on:
  A. Scholarly research
  B. Those of the past
  C. Those of the present
  D. A physical fitness emphasis
  E. A movement education emphasis

8 INNOVATIVE PROGRAMS IN SECONDARY SCHOOL PHYSICAL EDUCATION

Write at the left the letter indicating the one *best* answer.

B 1. The word innovation means to:
   A. Discard some aspect of the program
   B. Introduce something new or novel
   C. Retain the status quo
   D. Hire a new teacher
   E. Eliminate the program

C 2. The computer is related to:
   A. Basketball
   B. Programmed instruction
   C. Modular scheduling
   D. Teaching mathematics
   E. Bicycling

E 3. The quimmester program in Miami, Florida, utilizes:
   A. Two semesters
   B. Five weeks of physical conditioning
   C. The 5-5-5 administration plan
   D. Three semesters
   E. Five nine-week terms

A 4. The Fort Pierce Central High School Program is based on:
   A. Contracts
   B. Behavioral objectives
   C. Electives
   D. Performance objectives
   E. Modular scheduling

E 5. In Silverton High School in Colorado, the physical education program utilizes:
   A. The music facilities of the school
   B. The principal as a teacher
   C. The Dad's Club for tutorial assistance
   D. The local banks for fund raising
   E. The local environmental resources

D 6. At Ridgewood High School in Norridge, Illinois, physical education classes may vary in length from:
   A. Three to six modules
   B. Four to six modules
   C. One to three hours
   D. One to five modules
   E. Two to four hours

A 7. Independent study projects enable students to:
   A. Work on their own special projects
   B. Participate in the adapted program
   C. Play varsity sports
   D. Substitute shop for physical education
   E. Not have a physical education requirement

B 8. Performance objectives provide students in physical education with:
   A. An outline of the course
   B. A guide in respect to what is to be achieved
   C. A list of objectives for high school physical education from freshmen through the sophomore years
   D. The requirements for graduation
   E. The goals that physical education is trying to achieve in education

B 9. Paraprofessionals:
   A. Are parents who spend time in school with their children
   B. Assist the trained physical educator in the performance of his duties
   C. Have equal status with the professional physical educator
   D. Are paid the same salary as regular teachers
   E. Have usually pursued a four-year professional preparation program in physical education

B 10. The Trump Model Schools Program:
   A. Endorses the traditional approach to teaching
   B. Utilizes small and large group instruction
   C. Is based on Jahn's system of gymnastics
   D. Was developed in England
   E. Is teacher centered

9 INTERPRETING THE RELEVANT PROGRAM OF PHYSICAL EDUCATION

Write at the left the letter indicating the one *best* answer.

D 1. Physical education is:
   A. Well understood by the general public
   B. Respected by academic teachers
   C. Adequately interpreted to students
   D. Often misunderstood by persons outside the profession
   E. Clearly understood by the involved communities

C 2. The first step in a public relations program for physical education is to:
   A. Develop good community relations
   B. Develop good public relations with school alumni
   C. Develop good internal public relations
   D. Publish a statement of philosophy
   E. Develop winning athletic teams

B 3. Physical education will gain greater support if:
   A. Students like the physical educator
   B. The public is informed
   C. There are good facilities
   D. The physical educator joins community groups
   E. The physical educator is a good coach

B 4. The physical education public relations program should:
   A. Publicize the qualifications of the teacher
   B. Delineate a sound philisophy
   C. Present the physical educator's point of view
   D. Be entertaining
   E. Present the administrator's point of view

A 5. Surveys tend to show that most of the publicity in physical education is devoted to:
   A. Interscholastic athletics
   B. Intramural athletics
   C. The total physical education program
   D. The objectives of the physical program
   E. The importance of the program to the students

E 6. The number of public groups that need to be reached by physical education communications is:
   A. Two   D. Five
   B. Three   E. Six
   C. Four

B These public groups are:
   A. Youth, colleagues, school health personnel, parents, businessmen, the general public
   B. Youth, colleagues, administrators, parents, alumni, the general public
   C. Youth, colleagues, industry, the general public, parents
   D. Colleagues, businessmen, parents, alumni, industry
   E. Businessmen, industry, coaches, parents
   F. Administrators, colleagues, parents, youth
   G. School board, colleagues, administrators
   H. Youth, parents, the general public
   I. School board, parents
   J. Parents, the general public

A Of these individuals and groups, the best support for physical education should come from:
   A. Youth
   B. Colleagues
   C. General public
   D. Industry
   E. Administrators

C This is because:
   A. They are fellow educators and should support all of education

27

B. They pay the taxes that support education and should receive a return on their investment
C. They are directly involved in the program and will be asked, when they become adults, to support other programs
D. They are responsible for all phases of the physical education program and should support it
E. They want to live only in communities that have good schools with sound physical education programs

D 7. Excellent material usable for publicity purposes may be in the form of:
   A. Research studies
   B. Brochures
   C. Memoranda
   D. All the above
   E. A and B only

C 8. The most difficult communications medium for which to prepare publicity material is:
   A. Radio
   B. Newspapers
   C. Television
   D. Movies
   E. Public addresses

10 BECOMING A TEACHER

Write at the left the letter indicating the one *best* answer.

B 1. The personal qualities that administrators seem to regard most highly in a physical educator are:
A. Discipline, patience, and professionalism
B. Professionalism, promptness, and control
C. Understanding, professionalism, and control
D. Fairness, promptness, and discipline
E. Good appearance, good health, and good English

E 2. The personal qualities that students seem to regard most highly in a physical educator are:
A. Friendliness, patience, and skills
B. Good discipline, health, and fairness
C. Grading, understanding, and fairness
D. Good grader, skills, and friendliness
E. Patience, fairness, and understanding

A 3. To be able to conduct good skill demonstrations in class, a physical educator must:
A. Be highly skilled in a variety of activities
B. Have good posture
C. Wear neat clothing
D. Maintain good discipline
E. Know his students

E 4. In constructing his program the physical educator should:
A. Have a sound philosophy
B. Build in tight controls
C. Plan for his students
D. Consult with the administration
E. Plan with his students

D 5. A physical educator should have each of these emotional qualities to a high degree *except:*
A. Stability   D. Self-concern
B. Maturity   E. Consideration
C. Patience

C 6. A physical educator's ability to cope adequately with administrative details is a feature of his character known as the:
A. Emotional aspect
B. Administrative aspect
C. Intellectual aspect
D. Social aspect
E. Physical aspect

B 7. Before beginning to teach, prospective physical educators must obtain certification from the:
A. City
B. State
C. County
D. District supervisor
E. U. S. Department of Health, Education, and Welfare

A 8. The minimum stipulated age for becoming certified in many states is:
A. Seventeen   D. Twenty
B. Eighteen   E. Twenty-one
C. Nineteen

C 9. The number of general areas commonly included in certification regulations is:
A. Thirteen   D. Seven
B. Eleven   E. Five
C. Nine

D 10. Teachers who do not meet all requirements may sometimes be granted teaching certificates known as:
A. Life
B. Permanent
C. Tenure
D. Provisional
E. Probationary

B 11. The teacher's first introduction to his prospective employer is usually through:
A. An interview
B. A letter of application
C. A telephone call
D. The application form
E. A placement interview

C 12. Initial teaching contracts are generally signed by the teacher for:

A. Three years
B. Two years
C. One year
D. An unspecified number of years
E. A period just short of tenure

A 13. All the following are aspects of the management of a class *except:*
A. Self-evaluation
B. Motivation
C. Testing
D. Program planning
E. Parent conferences

D 14. Teachers share in the establishment of school policies:
A. Only in a small school
B. In very few schools
C. Only in a large school
D. In a democratically administered school
E. Only when they have achieved tenure

E 15. Teachers of other subject matter tend to evaluate the physical education program on the basis of:
A. Program content
B. Student progress
C. The athletic program
D. Teacher-teacher rapport
E. General attitudes toward the profession

B 16. Membership in professional organizations:
A. Helps the physical educator to gain tenure
B. Enhances the individual as a professional
C. Aids in the gaining of merit pay increases
D. Is unimportant at the local level
E. Does little for the individual teacher

A 17. A physical educator can help himself to develop as a professional through:
A. Graduate study
B. His program
C. Membership in social-professional organizations
D. Reading journals
E. Revisions in his philosophy

E 18. A physical educator is employed by:
A. The district supervisor
B. The school principal
C. An examining committee
D. A curriculum committee
E. A community's board of education

B 19. The number of principles in the Code of Ethics of the Education Profession is:
A. Five   D. Two
B. Four   E. One
C. Three

D 20. This Code was developed by the:
A. NEA
B. PTA
C. AAHPER
D. NEA and AAHPER
E. PTA and HEW

11 THE BEGINNING TEACHER

Write at the left the letter indicating the one *best* answer.

E 1. The two areas into which the beginning physical educator's problems seem to fall are:
   A. Personal and professional
   B. Personal and administrative
   C. Professional and administrative
   D. Supervisory and administrative
   E. Personal-professional and administrative

C 2. The average amount of time devoted by teachers during the school week to required nonteaching duties is approximately:
   A. Fifteen hours   D. One hour
   B. Ten hours   E. Thirty minutes
   C. Five hours

A 3. One of the most common problems for secondary school physical educators is:
   A. Discipline
   B. Class planning
   C. Locker room management
   D. Low economic conditions
   E. Student transiency

   D The above problem might be somewhat alleviated if the physical educator:
   A. Is paid enough
   B. Has an assistant
   C. Refuses to accept new students in the middle of a year
   D. Understands adolescent characteristics
   E. Does not have his students shower

B 4. One secret of success of beginning physical educators who establish good relations with colleagues is that they:
   A. Offer criticism
   B. Initiate the good relationship
   C. Offer advice to make themselves known
   D. Stay within their own department

   E. Remain away from the faculty room

C 5. New teachers often run into difficulties in regard to nonteaching duties because they:
   A. Accept too many assignments
   B. Accept too few assignments
   C. Are afraid to ask questions
   D. Don't understand their assignments
   E. Are inexperienced

B 6. In order to gain respect for their profession, physical educators should:
   A. Be physical educators first
   B. Be educators first
   C. Be administrators primarily
   D. Be autonomous within the school
   E. Try to break down the stereotype of the physical educator

   A This can be partially accomplished by:
   A. Doing a good job as a teacher
   B. Becoming highly skilled
   C. Learning to speak good English
   D. Attending solely to departmental matters
   E. Gaining promotions

E 7. One of the major reasons that girls' programs do not receive facility priorities is:
   A. Lack of an effective program
   B. Lack of staff
   C. Community apathy
   D. Student apathy
   E. Lack of administrative support

D 8. A common problem for beginning male physical educators seems to be:
   A. Poor beginning salaries
   B. Lack of equipment
   C. Inadequate facilities
   D. Overemphasis on interscholastic sports
   E. Overloaded teaching schedules

B 9. A common concern of the beginning physical educator's in regard to extra duties is that:
   A. Extra pay is not given
   B. They cut into teaching time

C. Free periods are eliminated

D. They take time away from coaching duties

E. The teacher is not prepared to handle them

A 10. In planning for a new gymnasium the physical educator should keep each of these factors in mind *except:*

A. His personal preferences

B. Space for spectators

C. The activities in the program

D. Safety

E. Number of students

C 11. When there is no locker room available and students have physical education uniforms, a last resort would be to:

A. Have them change clothes in a vacant classroom

B. Have them change clothes in a lavatory

C. Have them wear their uniforms under their clothing

D. Eliminate the uniform requirement

E. Eliminate the shower requirement

D 12. To be adequate, an auxiliary gymnasium should measure at least:

A. 20 × 40 feet   D. 40 × 60 feet

B. 20 × 60 feet   E. 60 × 80 feet

C. 20 × 80 feet

B 13. A good source of money for the purchase of physical education supplies and equipment is:

A. Alumni donations

B. School organizations

C. Local businessmen

D. Tax revenue

E. Requisitions

E 14. According to the AAHPER, the most common procedure for placement of students in physical education classes is by:

A. Homeroom

B. Ability

C. Track in the school

D. Age

E. Grade in school

C 15. The AAHPER has recommended that the number of students in a physical education class not to be allowed to exceed:

A. Forty-five   D. Thirty

B. Forty   E. Twenty-five

C. Thirty-five

D 16. The number of minutes of class time spent by boys in dressing and showering may range from:

A. Three to five

B. Six to seven

C. Ten to fifteen

D. Twelve to twenty

E. Sixteen to twenty-five

B 17. "Liability for personal or property injuries caused through the defendant's negligence" is descriptive of:

A. Negligence

B. Tort

C. Undue care

D. Legal liability

E. Proximate cause

C The number of elements of proof involved in the above action is:

A. Six   D. Three

B. Five   E. Two

C. Four

A 18. There can be no legal liability unless there is:

A. Negligence

B. Injury

C. A lawsuit

D. Prudence

E. Supervision

D 19. Teachers can be relieved of liability through the doctrine of:

A. *In loco parentis*

B. Tort liability

C. Act of God

D. *Respondeat superior*

E. Assumption of risk

12 THE PHYSICAL EDUCATOR AND TEACHING STYLE

Write at the left the letter indicating the one *best* answer.

E 1. Methods and materials courses in professional preparation programs are generally concerned with:
   A. Practice and perfection of individual teaching skills
   B. The development of a style of teaching
   C. Adolescent growth and development
   D. Planning equipment and facilities for teaching
   E. Patterns of class organization

B 2. Methods and materials courses are rarely concerned with:
   A. Correcting student errors in skill performances
   B. The individuality of the teacher
   C. Directing the practice of a skill
   D. Teaching specific skills
   E. Lead-up games

A 3. Teaching style is an observable phenomenon because:
   A. It is reflected in the physical educator's class management
   B. Ability groups are used exclusively by the physical educator
   C. It follows a traditional philosophy
   D. A textbook is followed explicitly
   E. It is adapted to the physical educator's teaching methodology

C 4. The autocratic physical educator may also be said to be:
   A. Democratic in style
   B. *Laissez-faire* in style
   C. Teacher-centered in style
   D. Skill-centered in style
   E. Methodology-centered in style

   B This physical educator states his objectives in terms of:
   A. The students   D. Progressions
   B. Himself   E. Outcomes
   C. Skills

A He states his program evaluation in terms of:
   A. What he has accomplished
   B. Student accomplishment
   C. The activities taught
   D. How well the unit plan was followed
   E. Student grades

E He usually expects his students to:
   A. Discipline themselves
   B. Work to their own peak capacity
   C. Assume leadership roles
   D. Be creative
   E. Perform to a common standard

A 5. The autocratic physical educator is chiefly interested in:
   A. Traditional methodology
   B. Educational innovation
   C. The individual student
   D. The affective areas of teaching
   E. Student needs

   D He feels this way because:
   A. He believes in being flexible
   B. He does not believe that only the cognitive area of learning is important
   C. He views skill ability as a phenomenon specific to the individual
   D. He feels that only proved methods work
   E. He wants to help his students become more inner-directed

   C In order to carry out this part of his philosophy, he:
   A. Provides many opportunities for student creativity and self-expression
   B. Tests new methods of teaching each year
   C. Demonstrates the skill performance techniques to be followed

33

D. Follows a problem-solving approach
E. Selects activities according to student interests

B He expects that his students will help further his philosophy by:
A. Assuming some of the responsibility for the class
B. Conforming to disciplinary and performance standards
C. Working on their own
D. Helping to plan the program
E. Helping to evaluate their own progress

C 6. The autocratic physical educator evaluates his students
A. On the basis of written tests only
B. Objectively
C. Subjectively
D. Through conferences
E. On the basis of skill tests only

E 7. The autocratic physical educator:
A. Selects intramural activities on the basis of student interest
B. Allows the intramural team members to play their own game
C. Welcomes all students to after-school activities
D. Cooperates willingly in the scheduling of after-school programs
E. Extends the class structure into the intramural program

B 8. The student-centered physical educator is often thought of as:
A. Autocratic
B. Democratic
C. *Laissez-faire*
D. Nonconforming
E. Traditionalist

C He states his objectives in terms of:
A. The program
B. Himself
C. His students
D. The administration
E. A traditional style

A He feels that his objectives have been met if:
A. His students find success
B. He has taught everything he planned to teach
C. The administration gives him a good evaluation
D. He does not have to adapt his methodology
E. He can evaluate himself highly

B 9. The student-centered physical educator:
A. Does not cater to individual differences
B. Is interested in the individual student

C. Prefers to demonstrate skills himself
D. Believes in a rigid teaching style
E. Motivates his students through fear of failure

E 10. The student-centered physical educator's classes are usually:
A. Rather loosely disciplined
B. Rather rigidly disciplined
C. Dull to watch
D. Unimaginative on the whole
E. Exciting to watch

A 11. The student-centered physical educator views innovations as:
A. Welcome challenges
B. A threat to his effectiveness
C. Something to be immediately adopted
D. Harmful to his program
E. An affront to traditional methodology

B 12. The student-centered physical educator welcomes student initiative:
A. Only in the intramural program
B. In all phases of the program
C. In none of the phases of the program
D. In the club program only
E. Only in the interscholastic program

D 13. Man's powers of reasoning and intuition are important to the:
A. Existentialist   D. Idealist
B. Realist   E. Pragmatist
C. Naturalist

C This philosophy places at the center of of the universe:
A. Experience
B. The laws of nature
C. Man
D. Society
E. The self

A It proposes that physical educators:
A. Encourage student initiative
B. Dominate when they coach
C. Be strongly teacher-centered
D. Have a rather loosely organized program
E. Provide few opportunities for student creativity

B 14. Science and mathematics are the core of the educative process for the:
A. Idealist
B. Realist
C. Pragmatist
D. Naturalist
E. Existentialist

E According to this philosophy, the best way to gain knowledge is through:
A. Experience
B. Ideation
C. The teacher-centered approach

D. The student-centered approach
E. The scientific method

A Under this philosophy the physical education program should:
  A. Help the student to learn to adjust to the world
  B. Help the student to learn to adjust to himself
  C. Be strongly student-centered
  D. Be strongly skill-centered
  E. Be strongly subjective in terms of student evaluations

E 15. Pragmatism is closely associated with:
  A. Gestalt
  B. Kierkegaard
  C. Kant
  D. Mann
  E. Dewey

B 16. The oldest philosophy known to the western world is:
  A. Existentialism
  B. Naturalism
  C. Pragmatism
  D. Realism
  E. Idealism

C 17. A physical educator begins to formulate a personal philosophy of physical education when he:
  A. Does his student teaching
  B. Starts his first year of teaching
  C. Studies principles and practices
  D. Decides to enter the profession
  E. Gains several years of experience

A 18. One of the major problems in student teaching is often the:
  A. Stylistic difference between the student teacher and the master teacher
  B. Lack of rapport between the student teacher and the master teacher
  C. Lack of rapport between the student teacher and the students
  D. Evaluative process
  E. Age of the master teacher

13 THE TEACHING-LEARNING PROCESS

Write at the left the letter indicating the one *best* answer.

B 1. Learning may be defined as:
A. The opposite of teaching
B. An observable change in behavior
C. A phenomenon restricted to the school years
D. Difficult to evaluate
E. A product of the environment

D 2. The four major areas of concern in the teaching environment are:
A. Heat, light, ventilation, and facilities
B. Control, guidance, security, and acceptance
C. Cooperation, competition, grouping, and rapport
D. Physical, emotional, social, and intellectual
E. Success, creativity, student needs, and student interests

E 3. Students function best in:
A. A single kind of learning situation
B. A teacher-centered learning situation
C. A teacher-dominated learning situation
D. A democratic learning situation
E. An indeterminate variety of learning situations

A 4. The educative process will be enhanced if each of the following is present *except:*
A. A drafty gymnasium
B. A well-ventilated locker room
C. Teacher-student rapport
D. Freedom of expression
E. Disciplinary standards

A 5. Effective learning cannot take place unless there is:
A. Teacher-student rapport
B. Skill teaching
C. A teacher-centered environment
D. A student-centered environment
E. An absence of environmental factors

C 6. The most desirable characteristic of a teacher, so far as students are concerned, is:

A. Patience
B. Firmness
C. Understanding
D. Knowledge
E. Skill

E 7. Teachers seem to prefer students who are:
A. Highly skilled
B. Compliant
C. Intelligent
D. Mature
E. Self-disciplined

B 8. A laissez-faire teacher:
A. Tends to be rather autocratic
B. Usually lacks class control
C. Demands rigid discipline
D. Generally has a well-structured program
E. Shares program planning with his students

D 9. The autocratic physical educator may sometimes be described as a:
A. Lax disciplinarian
B. Student guide
C. Warm teacher
D. Drill sergeant
E. Commander of respect

A 10. The current trend in education is toward a (an):
A. Individualized approach
B. Group approach
C. Laissez-faire approach
D. Autocratic approach
E. Skill-centered approach

C This helps to take learning from the:
A. Rote to the command stage
B. Skill to the performance stage
C. Command to the discovery stage
D. Inductive to the deductive stage
E. Nonmotivated to the motivated stage

E 11. Testing in physical education helps to determine:
A. The style of learning
B. Cognitive needs

36

C. Affective needs
D. The style of teaching
E. Individual activity needs

A 12. The percentage of intellectual ability attributable to heredity is approximately:
A. 70%   D. 40%
B. 60%   E. 30%
C. 50%

B 13. The disadvantaged are generally not prepared for the educative process because:
A. Schools do not know how to help them best
B. Their home situations do not stimulate learning
C. Teachers are not prepared to teach them
D. They are often migrants
E. They do not see the need for schooling

C 14. Far-reaching changes in the structure of the schools may be brought about by:
A. New professional preparation curricula
B. New secondary school curricula
C. Computers
D. Environmental changes
E. Taxation

D 15. In order to learn, an individual must be:
A. Taught
B. Capable
C. Verbally minded
D. Motivated
E. Creatively oriented

E 16. E. L. Thorndike contributed the:
A. Laws of growth
B. Laws of nature
C. Laws of exercise
D. Laws of memorization
E. Laws of learning

B They are listed as the laws of:
A. Readiness, effect, use
B. Readiness, exercise, effect
C. Exercise, effect, use
D. Incentive, response, effect
E. Exercise, effect, response

D When a student has received satisfaction in performing a skill correctly, this satisfaction is related to the law of:
A. Response   D. Effect
B. Exercise   E. Readiness
C. Use

D Drills in physical education are related to the law of:
A. Readiness   D. Exercise
B. Effect   E. Incentive
C. Use

C 17. Consistent performance of skills in physical education can be achieved by practice that leads to:
A. Learning   D. Associationism
B. Effectiveness   E. Goal attainment
C. Overlearning

B 18. The quarterback's ability to learn and comprehend all the facets of the game of football is related to:
A. The association theory
B. Gestalt psychology
C. Overlearning
D. Intellectual perception
E. Affective theories of learning

A 19. Movement education is closely related to the new learning approach called:
A. Problem-solving
B. Whole-part-whole
C. Traditionalist
D. Command-discovery
E. Democratic control

B The kind of learning that develops under this system is often termed:
A. Austic   D. Problematical
B. Heuristic   E. Theoretical
C. Verbalized

E 20. To perform fine motor skills the individual must have:
A. Leg strength
B. Shoulder girdle flexibility
C. Motor fitness
D. Physical fitness
E. Manual dexterity

C An example of a fine motor skill is:
A. Punting a football
B. Executing a lunge in fencing
C. Tying sneaker laces
D. Walking
E. Pitching a softball

B 21. Motor skill development depends on:
A. Motivation
B. Inheritance and learning
C. Inheritance only
D. Learning only
E. Physical fitness

A 22. The most important factor in the learning of skills is:
A. Motivation   D. Mental ability
B. Challenge   E. Reward
C. Physical ability

D This factor may be provided for:
A. By awarding high grades
B. Through the teacher's philosophy
C. By concentrating on endurance
D. Through the educational policies of the school
E. Either intrinsically or extrinsically

B Examples of this are:
A. Philosophy and program
B. Desire and praise
C. Weight training and football
D. The teacher-centered approach and the student-centered approach
E. Small classes and grouping

14 METHODS OF TEACHING

Write at the left the letter indicating the one *best* answer.

D 1. An educational setting is structured in accordance with:
   A. Techniques
   B. Stylization
   C. Educational philosophy
   D. Educational objectives
   E. Methodology

B One example of such a structure is:
   A. The unit plan
   B. The demonstration
   C. Deweyism
   D. Heurism
   E. Squad formations

E The use of a particular structure depends upon:
   A. Class size
   B. Equipment availability
   C. Staff requirements
   D. The nature of the physical educator
   E. The nature of the activity

C 2. Activities that take place in the water are termed:
   A. Synchronized swimming
   B. Recreational swimming
   C. Aquatics
   D. Boating
   E. Instructional

B 3. The nature of group goals is revealed best through:
   A. Autocratic group processes
   B. Democratic group processes
   C. Testing
   D. Evaluation
   E. Student conferences

A 4. The group for which a lecture in physical education would be the least appropriate consist of:
   A. Junior high school students
   B. Senior high school boys
   C. Senior high school girls
   D. High school sophomore girls
   E. High school boys

E 5. The choice of appropriate teaching methods is limited to:
   A. The director of physical education
   B. The school board
   C. The school principal
   D. The department chairman
   E. The physical educator

A Many of these choices are made on the basis of:
   A. Past experience
   B. Administrative philosophy
   C. Personal preference
   D. Desire to dictate
   E. Power to dictate

B 6. The approach usually used with good results in teaching team sports is:
   A. Part-whole
   B. Whole-part-whole
   C. Imagery-part-whole
   D. Skill-part-whole
   E. Play-drill-play

D 7. After the skills basic to a team sport have been learned, the class period should be concluded with a (an):
   A. Individual practice period
   B. Strategy session
   C. Filmed game
   D. Game situation
   E. Coaching session

C 8. Fundamental team sport skills should be presented:
   A. Only after individual sport skills have been mastered
   B. Only after physical fitness levels have been determined
   C. At the junior high school level
   D. At the senior high school level
   E. Only after lifetime sports skills have been mastered

E 9. Student creativity in team sports can be fostered by:
   A. Encouraging students to use new techniques

B. Modifying game situations

C. Having students try new positions

D. Coaching

E. Allowing students to create plays

A 10. Intellectual learning in team sports take. place through:

A. Discussion

B. Team organization

C. Demonstration

D. Drill

E. Criticism

C 11. The Lifetime Sports Foundation is an arm of the:

A. AAHPER

B. Recreation Federation

C. American Machine and Foundry Corporation

D. Minnesota Mining and Manufacturing Corporation

E. NEA

A The Foundation has developed instructional programs in:

A. Tennis, golf, bowling, badminton, archery

B. Dance, tennis, swimming, fencing, jogging

C. Swimming, golf, tennis

D. Jogging, isometrics, golf

E. Billiards, badminton, riding, archery, croquet

D 12. Folk and square dancing will be more appealing to the secondary school student if:

A. Classes are coeducational

B. Girls and boys are separated

C. Classes are taught by a woman physical educator

D. The work presents a challenge

E. The unit is used as a transition between two others

B 13. In general, students will be more highly skilled in rhythmic activities if:

A. A wide variety of material is presented

B. The amount of material covered is limited

C. They can see the material performed in movies

D. They present a public production each year

E. The teacher participates with the students

A 14. Swimming instuction is important in a secondary school program because:

A. There has been an upsurge of interest in water sports

B. Everyone should know how to swim

C. More high school swimming pools are being built

D. Swimming involves specialized skills

E. Most people live near water

E 15. Instructional standards for swimming are generally obtained from the:

A. AAHPER

B. NCAA

C. Water Safety Instructor Bureau

D. U. S. Pool Association

E. American Red Cross

C This group classifies swimmers as:

A. Novice, beginner, swimmer, advanced swimmer

B. Beginner, intermediate, advanced

C. Beginner, advanced beginner, intermediate, swimmer, advanced swimmer

D. Novice, intermediate, swimmer, junior lifesaver

E. Subjunior swimmer, junior swimmer, senior swimmer, senior lifesaver

B 16. The structure of gymnastics teaching generally follows:

A. AAU organization

B. Olympic outlines

C. Turnverein outlines

D. NCAA policies

E. Textbook guidelines

D 17. The balance beam helps girls to develop:

A. Physical fitness

B. Tumbling skills

C. Endurance

D. Poise

E. Strength

A 18. The number of gymnastic activities a single physical educator can effectively spot at a time is:

A. One

B. Two

C. Three

D. Dependent on class size

E. Dependent on the ability of the class

C 19. Track and field is especially appealing to secondary school students because:

A. Of the team effort involved

B. So many records can be broken

C. There is an activity for almost everyone

D. Supervision is not so strict

E. These classes are not highly structured

E 20. The value of low organization team games on the secondary level is that:

A. They present a unique challenge

B. They require intellectual responses

C. Student interest is usually maintained

D. Complex skills can be more easily developed

E. Everyone participates

15 METHODS AND MATERIALS FOR TEACHING THE ATYPICAL STUDENT

Write at the left the letter indicating the one *best* answer.

B 1. The culturally disadvantaged student is:
A. Always a city resident
B. Not a new educational phenomenon
C. A new educational challenge
D. Rarely educationally disadvantaged
E. Usually the most atypical of the students in a physical education class

D Culturally disadvantaged students now make up a percentage of the population of large cities estimated to be about:
A. 67%   D. 50%
B. 56%   E. 21%
C. 44%

B 2. Educational problems arise for the culturally disadvantaged student because:
A. He does not like school
B. He has not benefited from positive home influences
C. He does not know what courses to select
D. He does not benefit from peer group relationships
E. He cannot afford to purchase school supplies

E This causes the culturally disadvantaged student to:
A. Avoid doing his assignments
B. Attempt to develop confidence
C. Complete extra assignments
D. Become more self-motivated
E. Lose his aspirations

C 3. Conventional school curricula:
A. Help disadvantaged students to succeed
B. Properly discipline disadvantaged students
C. Are unrealistic in regard to disadvantaged students

D. Are easily modified to meet the needs of disadvantaged students
E. Help disadvantaged students to find vocational success

D 4. Remedial education for disadvantaged students:
A. Should make up the bulk of the secondary school program
B. Guarantees the meeting of educational needs
C. Guarantees the meeting of vocational needs
D. Makes a questionable contribution in many cases
E. Makes the teaching process much more difficult

E 5. The tracking system is often a part of the educational program known as:
A. Remedial education
B. Project Head Start
C. Upward Bound
D. Curriculum adjustment
E. Methodological modification

A The courses in such a program are oriented toward:
A. Vocational education
B. Higher education
C. Reading skills
D. Academic skills
E. Computer programming

C 6. The physical education program for disadvantaged students should be:
A. Highly competitive
B. Oriented toward rhythmics
C. Specially tailored
D. A time for free play
E. No different from usual programs

B This program should especially stress:
A. Leadership development
B. Physical fitness
C. Social and creative dance

D. The same things other programs stress
E. Self-discipline

E The program should especially cater to:
A. Health and hygiene needs
B. Competitive needs and interests
C. Coeducational activity needs and interests
D. Group needs
E. Individual differences

D 7. Disciplinary standards in physical education for disadvantaged students should be:
A. More rigid than for other students
B. Less rigid than for other students
C. The same as for other students
D. Tailored to these students
E. More flexible than for other students

A 8. The number of physically handicapped students served by the secondary schools is approximately:
A. 500,000   D. 2.5 million
B. 1 million   E. 3 million
C. 1.5 million

B 9. A physical handicap:
A. Is usually accompanied by a mental handicap
B. Is not necessarily accompanied by a mental handicap
C. Usually causes the student to develop some negative psychological traits
D. Usually causes the student to develop some negative social traits
E. Is usually congenitally caused

C 10. The physically handicapped student:
A. Is generally oversensitive
B. Is usually more severely handicapped than is apparent to the observer
C. Usually has to prove his abilities
D. Generally has more than one handicap
E. Cannot participate in regular physical education classes

E 11. If a physically handicapped student is placed in a regular physical education class:
A. He probably will not be able to succeed
B. He probably will be overly prone to accidents and injuries
C. The students in the class will probably resent him
D. The emotional and physical stress will probably be too great
E. He may be helped to gain a feeling of belonging

B 12. When a physical educator discovers that there is a physically handicapped student in a class, he should:
A. Diagnose the disability
B. Refer the student to a physician

C. Prescribe an exercise program
D. Determine the activities suitable to the student's needs
E. Excuse the student from vigorous activities

A 13. Blind students can enjoy participating in team sports if:
A. Cues are provided
B. The other students accept them
C. There are several other handicapped students in the class
D. The game does not involve running
E. They are physically fit

D 14. Where both an adapted and a regular program are provided:
A. The programs should be very different
B. It is not necessary to have any handicapped students in the regular class
C. Safety need not be so carefully watched
D. Both programs should be similar
E. Close supervision of the handicapped will not be so vital

A 15. The number of mentally retarded children and adults in the United States is now approximately:
A. 7 million   D. 4 million
B. 5 million   E. 3 million
C. 4.5 million

C Each year, the birth of mentally retarded babies increases this number by approximately:
A. 50,000   D. 200,000
B. 100,000   E. 225,000
C. 125,000

B 16. A leader in the field of mental retardation research is the:
A. Ford Foundation
B. Joseph P. Kennedy, Jr., Foundation
C. NEA
D. AAHPER
E. AMA

D 17. In motor development the age gap between normal children and retardates of the same chronological age is approximately:
A. Up to one year
B. Six months
C. Three to six years
D. Two to four years
E. One to two years

C 18. The quality most needed by the physical educator who teaches mentally retarded students is:
A. Skill
B. Confidence
C. Patience
D. Organization
E. Positive attitude

B 19. The greatest activity need of mentally retarded students is often:
- A. Rhythmic fundamentals
- B. Movement education
- C. Individual sports
- D. Games of low organization
- E. Lifetime sports

D 20. A student is often disruptive because he:
- A. Is mentally retarded
- B. Is physically handicapped
- C. Cannot adjust to school
- D. Cannot maintain good peer relationships
- E. Dislikes physical education

E 21. The physical educator can mitigate many of the problems caused by disruptive students if he:
- A. Controls his classes rigidly
- B. Is autocratic
- C. Sends these students to the guidance office
- D. Relaxes his discipline somewhat
- E. Plans for student success

B 22. The physical education experience sometimes hinders the classroom performance of the:
- A. Mentally retarded
- B. Poorly coordinated
- C. Culturally disadvantaged
- D. Emotionally disturbed
- E. Intellectually gifted

B This situation can be alleviated by:
- A. Asking the student to demonstrate a skill
- B. Praise and reinforcement
- C. Providing for trial-and-error learning
- D. Putting the student into a higher motor ability group to motivate him
- E. Increasing the skill challenges

D 23. The physically gifted student:
- A. Does not really need physical education
- B. Will be difficult to stimulate and challenge
- C. Is always a varsity athlete as well
- D. Usually has superior kinesthetic awareness
- E. Usually has little to learn in the way of new physical activities

C 24. The physically creative student:
- A. Usually has a well-developed kinesthetic sense in rhythmic activities only
- B. Must adapt to the activities included in the program
- C. Needs a structured physical activity program
- D. Does not usually have leadership capabilities
- E. Should be excused from physical education

16 METHODS AND MATERIALS FOR DEVELOPING PHYSICAL FITNESS

Write at the left the letter indicating the one *best* answer.

A 1. The President's Council on Physical Fitness and Sports was formed during the administration of President:
A. Eisenhower
B. F. D. Roosevelt
C. Truman
D. Kennedy
E. Johnson

    D "Physical Fitness" was added to the title under President:
A. Eisenhower
B. F. D. Roosevelt
C. Truman
D. Kennedy
E. Johnson

    E "Sports" was added to the title under President:
A. Eisenhower
B. F. D. Roosevelt
C. Truman
D. Kennedy
E. Johnson

B 2. A picture of the physical fitness level of each student, the class unit, and the school population is gained from:
A. Testing
B. Appraisal
C. Performance charts
D. Observation
E. Counseling

E 3. Established norms serve as:
A. Total pictures of the assessment phase of physical fitness
B. Definitive measures for all students
C. Techniques for determining developmental levels
D. Techniques for determining physical age
E. Comparative scoring devices

D 4. The Physical Fitness Test Battery for boys and girls was developed by the:
A. NEA
B. ACA
C. NCAA
D. AAHPER
E. AMA

C 5. Isometric exercises are used mainly to develop:
A. Endurance
B. Agility
C. Strength
D. Balance
E. Flexibility

    B This is achieved by:
A. Overcoming a resistant force
B. Contractions against an immovable force
C. Circuit training
D. Balance-beam walking
E. Calisthenic exercises

E 6. The value of isometrics lies in its ability to:
A. Help cut down on facilities
B. Eliminate the need for costly weight-training equipment
C. Replace a program of isotonics
D. Replace a program of conditioning exercises
E. Meet individual needs

A 7. The physical education activities that are conducted outside of regularly scheduled physical education classes may be properly termed the:
A. Noninstructional program
B. Intramural program
C. Extramural program
D. Club program
E. Interscholastic program

D 8. Dynamometers are:
A. Isometric exercisers

B. Similar in function to bicycle ergometers
C. Not properly a part of physical education equipment
D. Instruments that measure strength
E. Isotonic exercise devices

E 9. A complete exercise program plan for twelve- to eighteen-year-old girls is published under the title:
A. *Vigor*
B. 10BX
C. *Youth Physical Fitness*
D. *Physical Fitness*
E. *Vim*

B 10. The booklet *Vigor* may be obtained from the:
A. AAHPER
B. Superintendent of Documents
C. Queen's Printer and Controller
D. NRPA
E. Physical Fitness Association

17 AN INNOVATIVE PROGRAM FOR MOVEMENT EDUCATION IN THE SECONDARY SCHOOL

Write at the left the letter indicating the one *best* answer.

B 1. Movement education is:
  A. Synonymous with dance
  B. Not a recent development
  C. Used extensively on the junior high school level in the United States
  D. Used extensively on the elementary school level in the United States
  E. A recent innovation

E 2. Movement education theory may be traced historically to:
  A. Martha Graham
  B. The kinesiologists
  C. England
  D. The physiologists
  E. Rudolf Laban

B 3. The concepts of movement education were first introduced in the United States in the
  A. Early 1950's
  B. Late 1950's
  C. Mid-1960's
  D. Early 1940's
  E. Period just after World War II

A The principles were first taught on the:
  A. College level for women
  B. llege level for athletes
  C. College level for men
  D. Secondary school level for girls
  E. Elementary school level for all students

A 4. The teaching approach to movement education is:
  A. Intellectually oriented
  B. Conditioning oriented
  C. Based on the teacher-centered style
  D. Group instructional in nature
  E. Geared to the slow learner

C 5. Classes in movement education are:
  A. Loosely organized
  B. Generally undisciplined
  C. Highly structured
  D. Traditional in methodology
  E. Organized around competition

D 6. The first challenges presented to a student in a movement education class include:
  A. Locomotor movements
  B. Transitional skills only
  C. An emphasis on rhythmics
  D. The natural movements
  E. Circuit-training skills

B 7. In movement education, skill learning is developed through:
  A. Demonstration   D. Practice
  B. Exploration   E. Play
  C. Drill

E 8. Movement education is primarily concerned with:
  A. Sports skills
  B. Social development
  C. Emotional development
  D. Motor skill learning
  E. The body as a tool for movement

C 9. The key words in movement education are:
  A. Speed, timing, balance, rhythm
  B. Time, balance, leverage
  C. Force, time, space, flow
  D. Skill, practice, performance, perfection
  E. Problem, challenge, trial, skill

A 10. Movement education should:
  A. Be an ongoing part of the program
  B. Be used as a transitional device
  C. Not be used with boys
  D. Fill the entire class period
  E. Not be used on the secondary level

D 11. The role of the physical educator in movement education is to:

A. Explain sport skills
B. Demonstrate skills
C. Direct student drill
D. Stimulate student thinking
E. Correct errors in performance

B 12. Movement education is:
A. Speech-centered
B. Activity-centered
C. Teacher-centered
D. Demonstration-centered
E. Drill-centered

A 13. Movement education is often described as a means of:
A. Nonverbal communication
B. Choreographic communication
C. Modified communication
D. Adapted communication
E. Teaching dance

E 14. Movement education on the secondary school level serves each of the following *except* the:
A. Introduction of new skills
B. Correction of performance errors
C. Improvement of previously learned skills
D. Encouragement of student creativity
E. Making of highly skilled performers out of students with low motor ability

C 15. In a movement education program:
A. The performance of a skill is judged by a common single standard
B. Students work and react as a group
C. Each student sets his own goals
D. Student evaluations are made by the physical educator alone
E. Individual differences between students are not taken into account

18 RESOURCES AND MATERIALS FOR TEACHING

Write at the left the letter indicating the one *best* answer.

A 1. The teaching aids needing very careful scrutiny before use are:
   A. Record players
   B. Posters
   C. Magnetic boards
   D. Chalkboards
   E. Slides

D 2. Research seems to indicate that the supplementary teaching aid used with the most frequency in professional preparation programs is:
   A. The slide film
   B. Instructional television
   C. The wall chart
   D. 16 mm. film
   E. Chalkboard

E 3. The three broad categories of supplementary materials include:
   A. Reports, textbooks, charts
   B. Loop films, cartridge films, textbooks
   C. Journals, catalogs, advertisements
   D. Films, textbooks, charts
   E. Special aids, audiovisual aids, reading materials

B 4. One of the most complete physical education film rental services is located at:
   A. New York University
   B. University of Illinois
   C. Michigan State University
   D. Massachusetts Institute of Technology
   E. Carnegie-Mellon Institute

D 5. The supplementary aid that is spliced to provide continual projection is the:
   A. Magnetic tape
   B. Slide film
   C. Television tape
   D. Loop movie
   E. Cartridge film

A 6. Audiovisual materials provide:
   A. A variety to teaching
   B. A substitute for the teacher
   C. A means of testing students
   D. Entertainment for the students
   E. A means of killing time

A 7. A high school textbook in physical education is entitled:
   A. *Physical Education for Life*
   B. *Modern-Day Education*
   C. *Physical Fitness*
   D. *Foundations of Physical Education*
   E. *Administration of Physical Education*

19 CLASS MANAGEMENT

Write at the left the letter indicating the one *best* answer.

C 1. A fundamental step in effective class management is:
   A. Discipline
   B. Motivation
   C. Planning
   D. Incentive
   E. Efficiency

B 2. The major phases of class management are:
   A. Testing, teaching, evaluation
   B. Preparation, orientation, procedure
   C. Philosophy, objectives, curriculum
   D. Preparation, planning, procedure
   E. Orientation, teaching, evaluation

A 3. A physical education program is planned on the basis of:
   A. Departmental objectives and curriculum
   B. Instructional objectives and curriculum
   C. Individual objectives and curriculum
   D. Philosophy and goals
   E. Requirements and needs

E 4. Equipment and facilities should be checked against:
   A. Needs and utilization
   B. School population
   C. Incoming supply vouchers
   D. Repairs needed and executed
   E. The previous year's inventory

D 5. A detail that should be considered before school opens each year is the:
   A. Locker room
   B. Equipment and supplies
   C. Class lists
   D. Teaching schedule
   E. Student schedule

D 6. The assignment of physical education lockers:
   A. Should be made when students bring their uniforms
   B. Is generally a very simple procedure
   C. Can be extended over several class periods
   D. Should occupy no more than one class period
   E. Does not need to be made in the same manner for all classes

E 7. The amount of time usually allotted to changing into the physical education uniform is:
   A. Fifteen minutes
   B. Twelve minutes
   C. Ten minutes
   D. Seven minutes
   E. Five minutes

B 8. Accurate attendance records must be kept for each physical education class primarily because:
   A. Only in this way can accurate student evaluations be made
   B. The teacher has a legal responsibility for the group
   C. Most states require such records
   D. Equipment orders depend on an accurate census
   E. Staffing of the program depends on an accurate census

A 9. Temporary excuses from physical education:
   A. Should be authorized by the school health department
   B. Must be accepted by the physical educator when they are written by the parent
   C. Do not need to be honored unless they are written by a physician
   D. Should reduce the student's grade
   E. Should excuse the student from showers only

C 10. The maintenance of good class management demands that a physical educator be:
   A. Confident
   B. Calm
   C. Flexible
   D. Well disciplined
   E. Rigid

A 11. A 1964 survey indicated that the physical

education median class size in the junior high school was approximately:

A. Thirty-six   D. Twenty-five
B. Forty-six   E. Twenty
C. Thirty

C Senior high school median class sizes averaged approximately:

A. Fifty
B. Forty-five
C. Thirty-eight
D. Twenty-eight
E. Eighteen

D 12. The preferred way to group students in physical education skills is by:

A. Age
B. Height
C. Interest
D. Ability
E. Experience

B 13. If a physical educator is the sole member of his department and has forty-eight students in his volleyball class with two available courts, the grouping method he would probably choose consists of:

A. Two squads with twenty-four students each
B. Three squads with sixteen students
C. Four squads with twelve students each
D. Six squads with eight students each
E. Eight squads with six students each

E 14. A physical educator is the sole member of her department and has sixty students in a basketball class. There are six goals available. The grouping method she would probably choose consists of:

A. Two squads with thirty students each
B. Three squads with twenty students each
C. Four squads with fifteen students each
D. Five squads with twelve students each
E. Six squads with ten students each

20 INNOVATIVE PUPIL EVALUATION AND GRADING

Write at the left the letter indicating the one *best* answer.

B 1. The two general areas of evaluation for physical education are:
A. Physical skills and social development
B. Pupil evaluation and program administration
C. Activities and facilities
D. Leadership and administration
E. Pupil evaluation and class program

D 2. It is desirable that each student have a cardiovascular test:
A. At the beginning of a varsity sport season
B. At the end of a varsity sport season
C. At the beginning and end of a varsity sport season
D. Once a year
E. Before entering high school

B 3. Physical fitness tests should be given:
A. Once a year
B. Twice a year
C. Before the start of each new sport or activity
D. Whenever the situation demands it
E. At high school entrance and again at the conclusion of the senior year

A 4. Creative movement:
A. Can be subjected to teacher evaluation
B. Cannot be subjected to teacher evaluation
C. Can be reliably assessed according to group standards
D. Must be rated by a jury
E. Can be evaluated only by the performer

C 5. Attitudes and opinions can be determined by each of the following *except:*
A. Opinion polls
B. Surveys
C. Short-answer questionnaries
D. Objective tests
E. Knowledge tests

D 6. The goal of physical education that is least often evaluated is:
A. Physical development
B. Mental development
C. Emotional development
D. Social development
E. Skill development

C 7. Each of the following is a vital testing problem for the beginning physical educator *except:*
A. Selecting tests
B. Administering tests
C. Scoring tests
D. Keeping records
E. Using the results

A 8. When a test measures what it is supposed to measure, the test is:
A. Valid   D. Feasible
B. Reliable   E. Consistent
C. Objective

B 9. When a test repeatedly produces equivalent results, it is:
A. Valid   D. Feasible
B. Reliable   E. Consistent
C. Objective

C 10. When a test is free of subjective judgment, it is:
A. Valid   D. Feasible
B. Reliable   E. Consistent
C. Objective

C 11. Tests given at the close of a unit in physical education:
A. Serve as prognostic devices
B. Serve as diagnostic devices
C. Indicate achievement
D. Have little direct value for the student
E. Are motivators

B 12. Tests given in the middle of a unit in physical education:
A. Serve as prognostic devices
B. Serve as diagnostic devices
C. Indicate achievement
D. Have little direct value for the student
E. Are motivators

21 TEACHER AND PROGRAM EVALUATION

Write at the left the letter indicating the one *best* answer.

B 1. The teacher's personal record file in the administrative office holds information in the two general areas of:
   A. Teaching and student progress
   B. Personal and professional status
   C. Social and emotional stability
   D. Teaching and intellectual ability
   E. History and effectiveness

D 2. Some school systems require prospective teachers to take the:
   A. Graduate Record Examination
   B. Minnesota Teacher Attitude Inventory
   C. Rorschach Test
   D. National Teachers Examination
   E. Haverhill Evaluation Inventory

A 3. Student attitudes toward teachers may be assessed by the:
   A. Morris Trait Index
   B. Minnesota Teacher Attitude Inventory
   C. Minnesota Multiphasic Personality Inventory
   D. Beecher's Teaching Evaluation Record
   E. Scholastic Aptitude Test

D 4. Administrators may evaluate teachers by using the:
   A. Morris Trait Index
   B. Teacher Education Examination Program
   C. Rorschach Test
   D. Ohio Teaching Record
   E. Teaching Aptitude Test

B 5. A self-evaluation sheet for teachers is the:
   A. Morris Trait Index
   B. Haverhill Evaluation Inventory
   C. Thematic Apperception Test
   D. Ohio Teaching Record
   E. Beecher's Teaching Evaluation Record

D 6. Ratings should also be given for the teacher's:
   A. Class program
   B. Interscholastic program
   C. Administrative ability
   D. All of the above
   E. A and B only

C 7. Teacher evaluations should be done:
   A. At the end of the probationary period
   B. Just before tenure is granted
   C. Yearly
   D. After five years of experience
   E. When a teacher applies for a new position

METHODS AND MATERIALS FOR
SECONDARY SCHOOL PHYSICAL EDUCATION

METHODS AND MATERIALS FOR

SECONDARY SCHOOL PHYSICAL EDUCATION

CHARLES A. BUCHER, A.B., M.A., Ed.D.

Professor of Education, New York University,
New York, N. Y.

CONSTANCE R. KOENIG, B.A., M.S. IN EDUCATION

The Peabody Demonstration School of George Peabody College for Teachers,
Nashville, Tenn.

FOURTH EDITION

with 148 *illustrations*

THE C. V. MOSBY COMPANY

SAINT LOUIS 1974

FOURTH EDITION

Copyright © 1974 by The C. V. Mosby Company

All rights reserved. No part of this book may be reproduced
in any manner without written permission of the publisher.

Previous editions copyrighted 1961, 1965, 1970

Printed in the United States of America

Distributed in Great Britain by Henry Kimpton, London

Library of Congress Cataloging in Publication Data

Bucher, Charles Augustus
    Methods and materials for secondary school physical
education.

    1.   Physical education and training—Teacher training.
I.   Koenig, Constance R., joint author.   II. Title.
[DNLM: 1.   Physical education and training—In infancy
& childhood. QT255 B919m 1974]
GV361.B8 1974   613.7'07'12   73-11117
ISBN 0-8016-0872-4

PREFACE

The emphasis throughout the fourth edition of *Methods and Materials for Secondary School Physical Education* is upon **relevance**—relevance to our changing society, students, educational programs, and physical education offerings.

Regardless of what vocation a person follows—medicine, government, business, or whatever—he is well aware of the changes that are taking place in this country and the influence these changes are having upon his field of endeavor. This post–Vietnam War period, equal opportunity programs, activism among our youth, the nation's economy, the computer, space explorations, crime, poverty, and other developments are affecting his way of life.

Education, probably as much or more than any other field of endeavor, has felt the impact of the changes that are taking place. The stress on such developments as individualization of instruction, student involvement, innovative programs, equalization of opportunities for all students, and utilization of community resources is an indication of what is happening in our schools.

Physical education is also changing. Therefore, it is the purpose of this revision to show how the changes taking place in society and in education are affecting our programs in secondary schools and what should be done about them. To accomplish this task it has been necessary to take a new and hard look at our changing communities and schools, the new breed of student, innovative programs that exist in the United States and around the world, and the new methods and materials that are being utilized to bring physical education more in tune with the times.

The entire text has undergone revision in light of the need for a new and relevant physical education program. The reader will want to focus particular attention on the new chapter, Innovative Programs in Secondary School Physical Education. In addition, he will want to take special note of the major revisions in the Introduction: The Secondary School's Quest for Relevance, as well as in such chapters as The New Breed of Student in Today's Secondary School, A Relevant Physical Education Program, The Physical Educator and Teaching Style, and An Innovative Program of Movement Education for the Secondary School.

The college student preparing for a career in physical education, the physical educator in the field, educators in general, and other persons interested in this field of endeavor will find that this revised text will enlighten and assist them in bringing into being a more meaningful and relevant program of physical education.

Charles A. Bucher
Constance R. Koenig

CONTENTS

INTRODUCTION

THE SECONDARY SCHOOL'S QUEST FOR RELEVANCE

The secondary school is seeking relevance to the changing society of which it is a part. As a consequence, the educational program is characterized by reform and innovative ideas that fit the times in which we live. The student in junior and senior high schools, in his quest for identity and with different goals, values, and directions than students of the past, is demanding more involvement in planning the educational program that affects his future. The teacher, faced with change, is gradually attempting to use methods and a teaching style more appropriate to modern-day education. The special subject matter fields are changing, with stress being placed on such matters as the conceptual approach, utilization of community resources, and a greater concern for the present problems faced by society.

CHANGE—A PHENOMENON OF THE TIMES

• *Physical education has been slow to change.* In the past physical education has adhered primarily to its traditional approaches to curriculum content, scheduling, programming, methods of teaching, and grading practices. However, such recent developments as the elimination of required programs in some school systems, austerity budgets, reduction of personnel, and parental and student protests have resulted in the recognition of the need for change in physical education. Therefore, one of the major purposes of this revised

text is to help physical education to be more relevant to the times.

• *Change is a characteristic of modern-day education.* The changes taking place in education and in the secondary school are many and varied. The "open classroom," "voucher plans," "accountability," "free schools," "performance contracts," "twelve-month schools," and "career education" are terms that have become commonplace among those persons who are aware of the changes taking place as education strives to become more relevant.

Change is prevalent at all educational levels. The elementary school is changing in respect to the subject matter that is covered as well as the way it is taught. Colleges and universities are also changing their programs in order to better meet the needs of their students. Examples of innovations in higher education are "university without walls," delayed matriculation for students, admission to college after completion of the junior year in high school or to special programs after the sophomore year, and involvement of high school students in regular offerings on the undergraduate college level and in summer sessions. In addition, granting degrees at the end of three years, acceleration of the four-year degree, deceleration of the four-year degree, work-study programs, open admissions, and many other new programs are being utilized to meet the need of individual students.

Empire State College in Saratoga, New

3

York, is an example of an innovative college program where students enroll but do not attend classes. The faculty provides curricular guidance, study assignments, and suggested materials by mail, tape recordings, and television. Periodically, students confer with teachers at conveniently situated centers, attend seminars, and take tests.

• *Teachers must accept change.* Those of us who are teachers must face change today. We cannot escape it. The times demand it. Some reasons are: For the first time in our history we now have a youth culture with its own music, dances, and way of life. As adults we cannot become a part of it, although it is very important that we understand it. We are living in a period of great technological accomplishments, with men on the moon and space shuttles and interplanetary trips being planned for the future. We are living in a drug culture, a culture that has never before existed in the way it does today. We are living in an era of violence where physical attacks on public figures are prevalent and where the tragedy and disgrace of Vietnam rest heavily upon our shoulders. We live in a society characterized by urban growth and urban

Fig. 1. Teachers must accept change. (Manchester Public School, Manchester, N. H.)

problems that most of us never experienced in our earlier years—only 40% of us lived in the city in 1940. We live in a society where a black man looked into the future and said, "I have a dream," and his dream has yet to be realized. We live in a time where poverty, injustice, inequality, and other human ills exist. Change is needed since education can and must do something about these twentieth century conditions.

• *Change is essential to physical education.* Many of our programs, procedures, methods, and materials are as obsolete as the old Bentley and Pierce Arrow automobiles. We can no longer produce the responses that will enable us to survive. We have to innovate and develop programs that are up to date and relevant to today's society, education, and student. This means creative thinking, outstanding leadership, and teamwork that will help our students develop the resources and capacity to effectively express themselves. Progress will not be possible without change. One producer of change is research. Scholars in physical education and other disciplines have discovered new knowledge, which unfortunately has not been applied to our field of endeavor. The challenge is how can we close the gap between theory and practice. It must be done if we are to move ahead.

• *Physical education appears receptive to change today.* The profession is receptive to change today because of the pressures being exerted upon it. Pressures are being exerted on the one hand from dissatisfied parents, who feel their children are not getting much out of their classes, and on the other hand from frustrated students, who consider the schools too rigid and the program too boring. There are also pressures from the racial minorities, who believe the schools should help them more than they are at present. We recognize that these pressures are many times deserved and we believe in change.

Physical education is receptive to change because of economic necessity. Austerity budgets have forced retrenchments in many schools as a result of problems with the economy. Taxpayers and administrators are asking how more can be accomplished with fewer resources.

In being receptive to change, physical education should be aware of what the current reform movement is seeking. It is saying that we need such changes as greater flexibility and greater involvement of students in the planning of their own education. The reform movement also stresses that we need teaching based on scientific facts, new ways to enable students to learn on their own outside the classroom and gymnasium, and more productive use of the student's time and of educational facilities.

In meeting the demands of the reformers, some high schools are experimenting with *schools without walls* in order to permit students to learn from observation and apprenticeship in the "real world" (business offices, hospitals, industrial concerns, museums, and the like) for at least part of their secondary schooling. Some large high schools have created so-called *minischools*, schools within schools where a more personal approach and closer student-faculty relationships can be realized. Most schools are stressing accountability. Also, there is more concern as to what can be done about society's problems and how to better assure the student employment after graduation.

The emphasis on change in the area of methods of teaching includes a change from the traditional emphasis on the group to the present emphasis upon the individual, from a stress on the memorization of facts to an emphasis upon inquiry, from a sterile classroom climate to one where there is a zest for learning, from regularly scheduled classes to greater freedom for the student involving such things as independent study, and from teaching as telling to teaching as guiding. Physical education in the future will incorporate these changes and, in addition, will be based more on a scientific approach, such as the teaching of skills based upon sound principles of motor learning, more emphasis upon audiovisual aids, and greater stress on the individual whether he be normal or atypical.

• *Six major areas exist where secondary schools need to change in their quest for relevance.* Recently, a meeting representing a joint effort of the Office of High Schools of New York City Board of Education and the Chancellor's Center for Planning met in Princeton, New Jersey, and identified the problem areas where change needs to take place in secondary school education.* These areas indicate important considerations not only for education in general but also for physical education if programs are to be relevant to the times in which we live.

HUMANIZATION AND INVOLVEMENT. Our world and schools have become so large, complex, and remote that young people experience a powerless feeling, a feeling of inability to affect the course of their own lives. Unfortunately, many schools are impersonal, cold, and unresponsive to students as individual human beings. Change is needed to humanize our schools so that each student feels a sense of identity and belonging and is actively involved in the decision-making processes that affect him. Physical education programs need to be concerned with humanization and involvement processes.

NEW WAYS OF LEARNING AND DEVELOPMENT. Many secondary school students are deeply concerned about problems in the United States, such as poverty, race relations, war, environment, and urban life. At the same time, they feel the school does not focus its energies sufficiently on these significant problems. Methods of instruction are often outmoded, subject matter areas are too traditional in approach, some school practices are restrictive, and dynamic learning materials are not always available. Change is needed to utilize stimulating innovative methods and materials and to provide a broad range of

---

*The Task Force on High School Redesign of the Office of High Schools and the Chancellor's Center for Planning: Toward the 21st Century, New York, 1971, New York City Board of Education.

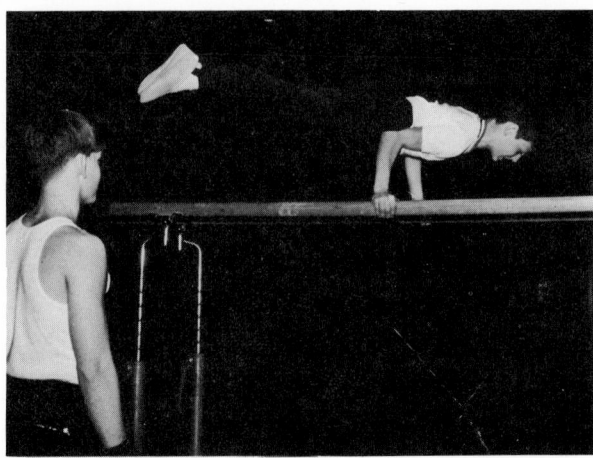

Fig. 2. Each student needs to feel a sense of identity and belonging. (Manchester Public Schools, Manchester, N. H.)

learning options. Physical educators must seek new ways to make their subject matter more exciting and useful to students and also relevant to the problems with which society is faced.

MAKING OPPORTUNITIES EQUAL. In order that students may have sufficient opportunities available to them, it is necessary that certain levels of skill, particularly in reading and quantitative thinking, be acquired. Change is needed to help all students achieve desirable levels of accomplishment. What is true of reading is also true of skills inherent in the teaching of physical education. Change is needed to help each student, whether normal, atypical, or somewhere in between, to achieve a level of skill appropriate to his individual physical resources that will provide him with the opportunities and vitality that can be enjoyed throughout a lifetime.

THE COMMUNITY AS SCHOOL. Education should not be confined to a school building. Change is needed whereby the resources of the community should also be utilized to expand and vitalize learning experiences under the auspices of the school, thus providing that both the resources of the community and of the school are included in the curriculum. Physical education has a wealth of community resources it can tap as part of its educational program.

SERVICE AND RESPONSIBILITY. Frequently, more walls than bridges arise between such groups as black and white, young and old, and student and teacher. Change is needed whereby young people, while establishing a sense of personal identity, at the same time develop a sense of common humanity. Experiences should be provided whereby young people develop abilities that balance rights and responsibilities and where they also acquire self-discipline. The gymnasium, playground, athletic field, and other physical education settings offer laboratories where service and responsibility may be learned.

MASTERING THE FUTURE. The many changes taking place in modern society result in young people finding it difficult to establish goals, career choices, and directions. Change is needed whereby the young people are better prepared for dealing with an unpredictable future. In part, this can be helped by giving each student some grasp of the vast opportunities of the world of work together with guidance in making wise career choices that will avoid psychological and occupational dead ends. Physical education should present a realistic picture to students concerning the career opportunities in its field of endeavor.

In the remaining pages of this chapter the changing nature of society, the community, education, the student, and physical education are discussed in greater detail.

CHANGE IN SOCIETY AND CULTURE

Our modern society is dynamic, flexible, demanding, and self-centered. The space age is freeing man from the confines of his own atmosphere and has permitted him to reach into outer space, even to the moon, and to probe the depths of the seas. This era has had an increasingly profound influence on society. The skilled working man has had to become a highly trained technician, and the professional has had to become a specialist. Widespread use of computers, the children of the space age, has increased the pace of life. More people need more education to understand and control the machines that are the core of modern life. Each highly complicated electronic vehicle that is launched into space or dropped into the sea is the result of increased technology and of the refinement of the machines of science, industry, and education.

Our world becomes more complicated year after year. Not only are there many problems that affect us domestically, such as the need for more education, increasing specialization among vocations, problems of the inner city and of the environment, and also a faster living pace, but there are also growing international problems.

Only a little over fifteen years ago, our world was a relatively uncomplicated place in which to live, become educated, and earn a living. There were brief periods of world peace, and domestic and international unrest were not in the forefront of the news. Students in high schools, colleges, and universities were willing to adapt themselves to required courses and curricula in order to have a job and a steady income. Today's youth, however, realize that schools and universities must change as the world changes and are calling for improvements in curriculum, faculty, and administration. The activism and mili-

tancy of the students have shown that they will no longer endure out-dated pedagogy. We have "new" secondary school students, and we are gradually giving them "new" secondary schools geared to the needs of tomorrow.

Today's secondary school students live in a computer-card world. They have never known international peace or domestic stability, but instead they are intimately familiar with a constantly fluctuating society, community change and upheaval, electronic marvels, and educational evolution. It is not technology per se that has brought about the changes in secondary schools but the effect technology and new developments have had on all the factors that combine to infuence and control secondary education. Society at large, the changing structure of communities, the student and his parents, educators, administrators, and the schools themselves are all intimate parts of educational evolution.

The structure of society is changing

Today's society is, for most people, an open one. People have become highly mobile, and more money is spent on more and more consumer goods and services. Ease of ownership of private automobiles has helped to motivate many families to travel extensively.

This last decade has been marked by increased suburbanization. Many persons have chosen to leave the cities to seek out the supposedly quieter, more stable, and relatively more peaceful life of the suburbs. Many former urbanites prefer to commute many hours to work rather than live in the crowded, industrialized cities. Many cities are now largely the domain of the lower socioeconomic groups who cannot leave because the suburbs cannot house or employ them or because they find that society has effectively closed the door on upward mobility.

The cities represent one of the nation's major problem areas. Transportation, crime, pollution, the high cost of welfare services, and inadequate housing are only a few of

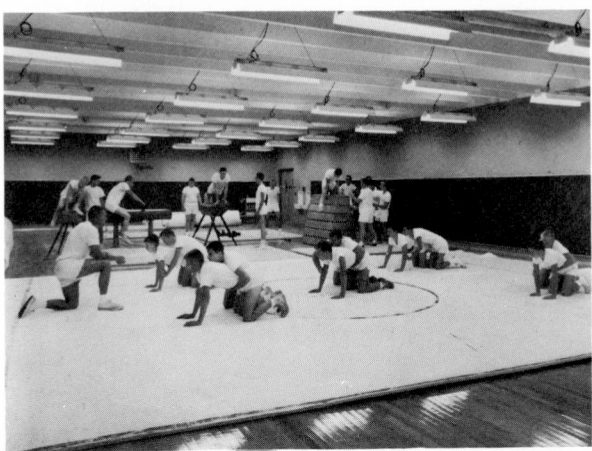

Fig. 3. Today's secondary school youth live in a computer-card world. (West High School, Davenport, Iowa.)

the critical areas where cities are suffering.

Society is concerned with its environment. The pollution of the air and the water, the destruction of our natural resources, overpopulation, and the increase of wastes have caused great concern among a large segment of population.

Society is also becoming more internationally minded. New communications media, such as Telstar and its sister satellites, have helped to bring the world and even the moon into every home. News is relayed, at the time it happens, from country to country, shrinking the size of the world and making international understanding a possibility. The youth of today are especially concerned with international understanding and are actively demonstrating this feeling through involvement, while in secondary schools, in United Nations Clubs and international relations clubs. Many older youth have turned to other humanitarian activities. Young people are opposed to war and actively demonstrate against it.

Our wealthy, knowledgeable, mobile, and highly automated society is still fighting the ills of poverty, discrimination, and unemployment. Many of our citizens in this affluent society live in poverty, lack money for adequate medical care, attend schools that do not meet their educational needs, and rarely venture outside their own neighborhoods. Additionally, lack of adequate education and training prohibits these individuals from obtaining employment.

The changing society and its impact on education

Education is one of the most important facets of modern life. There is an emphasis on providing education for everyone regardless of age or social class, and many more people than ever before are thinking in terms of continuing their education beyond secondary school. A minimal education, they realize, is of limited practical value in the demanding job market of the computer age. Our newly education-conscious society has helped to bring about the construction of many new community and junior colleges and technical schools, which in addition to "open" admissions in 4-year colleges and universities, are meeting the demand for "education for all."

It is at the secondary school level that the most startling educational changes are coming about. Some of the implications of the computer age for education have already been realized. The earliest teaching machines, in the form of manual Skinner boxes, have already been superseded by complex electronic devices such as talking typewriters, videotape and instant playback machines, recording and playback hardware, and the machinery specific to the language laboratory.

The use of electronic equipment has allowed the learner to proceed at his own pace in many curricular areas. Where electronic equipment is utilized, the teacher is freed to decrease mass instruction time while increasing individual instruction time. Thus the teacher can introduce new material more effectively and efficiently and can supplement group instruction with individualized machine instruction.

In many secondary schools scheduling of classes and room and teacher assignments are programmed by computers. Register keeping, once a time-consuming task, is also adaptable to computerization, giving the teacher additional hours of teaching time. However, the most profound influence of the computer age has occurred in the curriculum itself. Static and classic curricula have been forced to undergo extensive revision and continued evaluation. Not only the sciences but the languages and social sciences as well are updating all phases of their courses to meet the advancing tide of innovation such as programmed instruction.

Some secondary schools, however, do not have any of the hardware of the computer age, even though the computer has become increasingly important as an aid to education. Secondary schools that fail to keep up with modern educational methodology cannot hope to offer their students a competitive education by adhering to outdated educational processes. The full implications of the computer age for general education will not be known until society finds that it has exhausted the last frontiers of knowledge.

The changing society has had an impact on physical education

Physical education has so far failed to fully meet the challenge of today's world with its many innovations. While there are, and have been, many implications for physical education, they have not been utilized extensively in the teaching-learning process.

Researchers in physical education, for example, have used new electronic gadgetry, but only in a very limited fashion. The known effects of space and ocean exploration on the physiology and psychology of man have prompted much scholarly research by physical, behavioral, and social scientists. The knowledge they contribute holds many implications for changes in emphases in physical education curricula, but the challenge has not been fully met.

Our secondary school physical education programs too frequently lapse back into traditional patterns, apparently with no attempt to meet the computer age head on. Physical fitness has been emphasized for years. Movement education is being embraced as a "new" form of physical education. Unfortunately, some physical educators seem to be content to maintain the status quo while the rest of education passes them by.

Physical education needs to change. This could mean such things as programmed materials, greater utilization of textbooks to get at the knowledge and understanding in physical education, audiovisual aids, the full use of specially adapted teaching machines, a conceptual approach to physical education, new methods of teaching, and greater stress on the individual needs of each student.

CHANGE AT THE COMMUNITY LEVEL

A community is a place where people live and function as a largely homogeneous group, with their own schools, shops, and parks. It may be a section of a large city or an entire suburban town. While larger cities have traditionally been subdivided into wards or districts for political expediency, it is only recently that the citizens of these districts have begun to become more interested in assuming responsibility for the life of their community. Neighborhood groups in many large cities are currently seeking a greater voice in managing the affairs of their schools, especially those aspects related to curriculum and administration.

Educators as well as community members are aware of the climate that surrounds education and the educational systems of today. Many new or expanding communities attract home buyers or apartment renters by constructing carefully planned educational parks. These parks contain modern elementary and secondary schools as well as recreational facilities that are the core of these new communities and one of the vital forces of community life. Planning assures that these educational parks will fulfill community needs for years to come, in spite of the construction of additional dwelling units and resultant increases in school enrollments.

In still other newly developing suburban communities there has been no such careful planning. The need and demand for housing has far outstripped the supply of building lots, and recreational lands have been laid waste by housing developments. A secondary school student in such a community may have to commute many miles to a regional high school or attend a vastly overcrowded school in his own community.

The move to suburbia has not relieved the population density of the cities. More and more members of the lower socioeconomic groups move into the cities each day in search of adequate housing, higher paying jobs, and schools for their children. Their efforts are largely unrewarded. This great influx of people leads to crowded tenements and unemployment, and city schools that serve the lower socioeconomic groups are typically old, overcrowded, and inadequately staffed.

There is a rising civic interest in education and in providing a better education for all children regardless of where they live. It is hoped that the federal government will supply financial aid to the schools through its aid-to-education programs.

The changing community and education

Many suburbs boast futuristic secondary schools. Community planners and architects and builders specializing in school construction have developed new materials, new plant layouts, and new exteriors especially suited to modern-day secondary education. Geodesic domes and bubble-topped structures have made their appearance along with schools-in-the-round and schools that are completely submerged below the ground. These structures afford more flexibility, can accommodate more students, and are in general lighter and brighter than traditional architectural designs. Where building space has been at a premium, additions to existing secondary schools have been placed under athletic fields or under structurally sound portions of buildings. These subterranean structures are artificially lighted, soundproofed, and air-conditioned. The city of New York has recently opened several secondary schools that are above ground but windowless. These totally air-conditioned structures have several advantages such as helping keep out street noises that distract students from the learning process.

Other communities have supported the construction of rambling structures that have separate wings for science, mathematics, physical education, and the other divisions of the school. With such an arrangement students must walk farther between classes, but shop noises, for example, do not intrude on the quiet needed by students in language laboratories. This type of structure also allows needed sections to be opened for community use on evenings and weekends, while other sections of the school can remain closed.

Still other communities are involved in the process known as bussing. Both de facto and intentional segregation have created a plethora of unequal educational facilities in both suburbs and cities. Many larger suburbs have a divisional line between socioeconomic classes and have their own problems with ghettolike conditions. Civic concern, sometimes prodded by court order, may dictate that an equal number of students from all areas of the city or town attend each secondary school and that the school be made equal as possible in staff, equipment, and facilities. Many civic groups and parents' organizations have been opposed to bussing because some students must ride long distances on a bus between home and school twice each day. A rural school district in Colorado faced the problem of bussing realistically by installing audiovisual equipment and individual headphones in its school buses. Youngsters may choose from a wide variety of age-level instructional tapes on preassigned channels or select regular AM-band or live radio broadcasts on another channel, or they may choose not to listen at all. As a further option, this school district has installed three additional channels that students can reserve for their individual study of preselected tapes. When this specially equipped bus is not transporting students, it is used as a mobile classroom.

Innovations in the building of contemporary schools and the problems of providing an equal education for all students are not the only concerns of the various communities. Lay people today are calling for dedicated professionals to teach in their schools and dedicated people to administer them. Parent and community organizations are demanding adequately trained, professional educators who will devote themselves to understanding the needs of the communities in which they teach.

The influx of the culturally disadvantaged into the urban schools has created other unforeseen problems for school boards, administrators, and teachers. Frequent bussing of students and the lack of adequate staff in ghetto schools have created problems in giving the urban student an adequate education. Many urban schools find that obtaining and keeping qualified staff is their biggest problem. Experienced teachers are often unwilling to teach in difficult situations, and new teachers are ill equipped to cope with many of the problems that arise in the urban setting. This implies not only that our urban schools and school systems must prove that they are capable of providing for the educational needs of the city child but that they must also be able to staff their schools with qualified personnel who are willing and able to teach under adverse conditions.

The changing community and physical education

When new secondary schools are constructed the physical education facilities become a major concern because they are often the single most expensive item in the budget. Recent trends, however, have been to construct physical education facilities that can be opened to community use when school is not in session. A community is generally less than willing to pay for extensive and expensive facilities that will see only limited use.

The construction of new physical education facilities and the expansion of existing ones have met with community opposition in some cases. This resistance may be caused by parental interest in courses of an academic nature that help to determine college admission, the nationwide focus on science and mathematics, or general community apathy toward physical education as an important part of the curriculum. Affluent communities in which the citizenry has unlimited access to a variety of recreational facilities tend to oppose the added construction of secondary school physical education facilities beyond a bare minimum because they do not see any justified need for elaborate plants. Other communities view physical education as a frill added to the school curriculum. Opposition to modernization or expansion of physical education facilities may also come from administrators or school budget directors who either hold the same opinions as the community at large or who look with alarm on the necessary increase in personnel to staff any additional facilities.

Physical educators must be cognizant of

community needs and interests and must themselves elicit community support. This can be done only through the program that is offered and through the physical educator's willingness to become an active member of the community in which he teaches. Good community relations and eventually community support are developed and furthered in this way. When new facilities are proposed, the physical educator should take the initiative in making certain that the new physical education facility will be adequate and still modern many years into the future. He should take an active part in the planning and design of such facilities so that they can be used by the community as well as the school.

When completely new facilities for physical education are constructed, they often follow a rather unique but proved arrangement. Swimming pools and tennis courts are frequently placed under air-supported structures some distance from the main school building but close to playing fields. Additionally, communities have found that air-supported structures can, if planned well in advance, be converted to multiple use. For example, the tennis courts used in spring and summer may be flooded and used for ice skating in winter. The air-supported bubble over the swimming pool and tennis courts is often removed in warmer weather, and heating is easily piped in in colder temperatures. The gymnasium building itself, with lockers, office space, and possibly a classroom or two, will be erected adjacent to the other physical education facilities.

No longer are secondary schools built with a single open gymnasium that must be shared by both girls' and boys' classes. Modern construction almost always includes either two full-size gymnasiums or a single oversized facility that can be divided by a motor-driven door. Some of these large gymnasiums can be divided into four smaller rooms, affording adequate numbers of indoor stations for indoor seasons. Additional features of modern gymnasiums often include rooms for correc-

tives, weight training, and wrestling, as well as small dance studios adjacent to, but entirely separate from, the gymnasiums. Built-in sound systems and projection facilities are becoming more and more commonplace parts of new or modernized physical education facilities.

Outdoor facilities have also come in for their share of updating. New methods of seeding and new materials designed for outdoor use have facilitated rapid drainage after rainstorms and have helped to make such facilities as running tracks usable virtually the full year.

Not all secondary schools have new facilities, and not all secondary schools with inadequate and outdated facilities can look forward to community support for new facilities. Many secondary schools will have to struggle for many years with overcrowded and inadequate physical plants. Community character determines the educational support available, and the construction of new educational and physical education facilities depends on the community's educational outlook on the whole.

THE CHANGING STUDENT

The students who attend secondary schools today have never known a world at peace. Today's student lives in an open society that did not exist ten years ago. He is a questing individual whose environment includes many examples of moral decay, as evidenced by drug abuse, changing sexual mores, and an ever-increasing crime rate. Domestic and international ferment are facts of life for today's adolescent, who desperately needs guidance in coping with the world in which he lives.

Today's youth is concerned with his individuality and his place in the world as an individual. Social and political activism appeal to modern adolescents because they help him to establish himself as a part of society. Student militancy, especially among secondary school youth, is a recent phenomenon. Chief among the secondary school students' causes have been curriculum revisions and decreased administrative censorship of student publications. Where secondary school newspapers once reported only sterile school news, they now editorialize on national and world events and run feature articles concerned with the latest student causes the world over.

Today's adolescent is not content with mere obedience to parental controls; he actively seeks the freedom to direct the course of his own life. The new adolescent has had a profound effect on all of education, causing educators to take a new and hard look at educational methodology, procedures, objectives, and curricula. Discontent with what was not being taught has led to new, experimental curricula and new courses. Educators have been forced to realize that their programs of instruction lack the ability to teach the student about the world as it really is. The implications of this new voice for education has had a far-reaching effect that is only beginning to be felt.

The changing student and education

To today's adolescent, the individual and what becomes of him are extremely important. Within the environment of the school, those courses geared to today are the ones in which the adolescent is interested and from which he learns. The adolescent usually is not as interested in what the world was like yesterday as in what it is like today and what this means to him as an individual.

Education as a whole is beginning to develop courses that adolescents can understand and interpret for themselves. Those few courses that are not making use of the new media, new methodologies, and new curricula are in effect teaching the adolescent in a foreign language that he will never be able to understand.

Education is becoming profoundly aware of the student, of his individual needs, and of his creativity. Educators have begun to realize that creativity and individuality are enhanced when an individual takes on some of the responsibility for his own edu-

cational progress. Teaching machines, educational television, and language laboratories all cater to the differences of individuals, adapting education to the student rather than the reverse. Courses in history and languages, for example, which were once only dry textbook and memorization courses, have been made into living adventures through the use of individual instructional media.

Flexible and modular schedules have been developed that allow students to spend longer blocks of time in courses that stimulate and challenge them. Blocks of free time are arranged in some secondary schools so that students can pursue independent projects or participate in seminar or discussion groups. An increased emphasis on guidance and counseling in the secondary school has helped to uncover the real needs of students so that schedules and courses can be better adapted to them.

If a course does not interest today's adolescent, does not identify with him as an individual, or does not speak directly to him, he may endure it but will not attempt to pursue it beyond the formal requirements. Science clubs and language clubs usually enroll youngsters who attend them not because they must but because they have chosen to be there. They are motivated because their individuality is recognized and respected.

The changing student and physical education

To prosper in today's secondary schools, physical education must gain greater intellectual respectability and be recognized by the students as a worthwhile experience to them as individuals in today's world. Strong consideration should be given to providing physical education with a conceptual approach that will appeal to the individuality of the adolescent. At the same time, it must challenge his creativity.

The physical educator has typically been a sounding board for many students, and guidance of the student has been one of his meaningful tasks. Most physical edu-

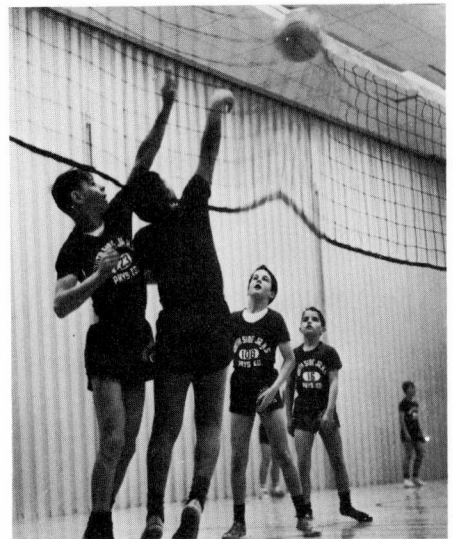

Fig. 4. Today's student presents a challenge to the physical educator. (Manchester Public Schools, Manchester, N. H.)

cators, however, have not capitalized on the rapport they have with students. The open society of today demands that secondary school physical education provide an outlet for excess energy and that it provide limitless opportunities for self-expression and creativity.

Today's student presents a challenge to the physical educator, not only in the area of understanding the student but also in regard to providing a program worthy of today's student. Physical education, through its use of traditional methodology, is presently guilty of failing to make a worthwhile contribution to today's youth. The average secondary school physical educator often is concerned with educating his students physically while losing sight of the mind the body houses.

To appeal to and motivate today's youth, one of the things physical education needs to do is shift more toward an intellectual emphasis and become a true part of the educational process. Years ago, young girls were dissuaded from seeking careers in physical education because the name of the field alone made their mothers think of gross musculature and possible mascu-

linization. Among some of today's adolescent girls this stereotype persists, and it persists basically because physical education in most of today's secondary schools is exactly the same as it was for their mothers years ago. Physical education does not, in many schools, answer the needs of today's youth of either sex.

New curricula in physical education and the use of new media and textbooks can help in bringing physical education up to date. Some schools have done just this, while others have utilized such methods as independent study, learning packages, and elective programs to make their programs more relevant to the times. Perhaps physical education will make its best move toward modernization by training teachers of physical education who can talk to adolescents in their own language, understand their world, and make physical education an essential and desirable part of their world.

CHANGE AND THE TEACHER

While the professions have for many years declined to align themselves with labor unions, such alignment has now become a fact in many cases. Frequently, newspapers carry items concerned with strikes and work stoppages by teachers. These tactics are not limited to the United States but are increasingly becoming an international phenomenon. The motives for walkouts are often centered around salary demands, but the desire for general improvement of the profession and the people served by it is also a strong motive, and it is sometimes the prime motive resulting in strikes by teachers.

Professional militancy can either devastate or enhance the process of general education. Where teacher strikes have occurred, teaching days have been lost and the educational continuity destroyed for the students. However, positive action has resulted from many of these walkouts. Some school systems have agreed to reduce the size of classes, decrease the amount of paper work required for teachers, and eliminate many nonteaching duties that cut into instructional time. Improved working conditions help to improve the effectiveness of the educator: smaller classes allow for more individualized instructions, and reductions in nonteaching assignments free the teacher to prepare and conduct more effective lessons. Of late, even the National Education Association has begun to approve of a greater degree of teacher militancy based on its analyses of educational gains made by these tactics.

The changing teacher and education

Today's teachers are more flexible, more knowledgeable, and more attuned to the whole panorama of education than any past generation of teachers. Much of this improvement, of course, has been born of the necessity to learn to cope with the new mathematics, the new social studies, and the new approaches to the other areas of the curriculum.

The teacher of today voluntarily attends in-service courses and seeks a higher education in quest of becoming a better educator. He is better read in all fields, attends more concerts and plays, and is more likely to participate actively in community affairs than was the teacher of ten years ago. Student militancy has motivated the teacher to speak out and be heard not only as a professional but as a citizen of the community. The educator does not hold the untouchable place in society that he once did, but instead he has gained the more important status of an equal citizen.

Within the confines of the school the teacher has been able to become more of an equal partner with administrators. It is the teacher who knows the educational pulse of the students most intimately, and the teacher in cooperation with the students can effectively help to translate their educational needs and interests to the administrators. Educators have had to drop their role of omnipotence in the light of the "new" student. They are now moving closer to the ideal of becoming guides through the educational process rather than retain-

ing their timeworn position as dictators of this process. The "new" teacher has accepted the student as an equal in the process of education.

The changing physical education teacher

The implications of teacher militancy for physical education parallel those for general education. Physical educators have traditionally taught larger-than-average classes and have been responsible for many nonteaching functions, such as proctoring of study halls, monitoring of the lunchroom, and supervising of buses. While teacher militancy has been effective as far as general educators are concerned, the nonteaching load of physical educators has not been lightened as much as it should be. Administrators tend to feel that someone must take on the nonteaching duties that abound in any school, and if paraprofessionals cannot be hired for these functions, they frequently devolve to the physical educator. These duties must be eliminated from the physical educator's routine so that he will be able to turn himself fully to the task of physical education.

Many secondary school physical educators have had to reexamine their roles in the light of student needs, but their adaptation to the "new" student has been somewhat slower than that of general educators. Physical educators have generally been able to maintain close contact with their students, but they have not as yet had to cope with the "new" student as well as a "new" type of physical education. Thus the physical educator will be one of the last members of the education profession to assume the new role of educational guide unless the field quickly accepts the challenge of formulating a modern approach to physical education.

There are, however, many encouraging developments among physical educators who are presently graduating from our colleges and universities. They are more scholarly, dedicated to the profession, and interested in changing the image traditionally reflected by the physical educator.

They are interested in research and applying research findings to their field of endeavor. For example, they are interested in utilizing sound principles of motor learning in the teaching of physical education skills. The new physical educators are not primarily interested in athletics and coaching but, instead, want to improve the teaching of physical education to the rank and file of the population. They understand the biological, psychological, and sociological worth of physical education to human beings and are dedicated to helping their students achieve a higher state of physical, mental-emotional, and social fitness.

POINTS TO REMEMBER

1. The implications of the space age for today's world
2. The effect of technology on education
3. The characteristics of the new society, the new communities, the new student, and the new teacher
4. The need for change and the need for relevance

PROBLEMS TO THINK THROUGH

1. What are the implications of programmed learning for physical education?
2. What constitutes a meaningful education for today's student?
3. How must physical education change in order to become more relevant to today's student?

CASE STUDY FOR ANALYSIS

Select one factor that has changed society greatly in the last ten years, such as technology. Analyze this change is it has developed and draw implications for physical education programs.

EXERCISES FOR REVIEW

1. Trace the growth of the computer age from 1957 to the present.
2. Show how changes in society have affected education and physical education from 1960 to the present.
3. Interview ten secondary school students to find out whether they think they are receiving a relevant education. Analyze their comments critically.
4. Compare your own secondary school experience with the new approaches to secondary school education.
5. Write an essay that shows how student militancy affects educational programs.

SELECTED READINGS

Alexander, William M., editor: The high school of the future, Columbus, Ohio, 1969, Charles E. Merrill Publishing Co.

Blubaugh, Ronald: School bells for migrants, American Education 4:5, 1968

DeBoer, John J.: The "new" English, Educational Forum 42:393, 1968.

Goodlad, John I., and Anderson, Robert H.: The nongraded elementary school, New York, 1963, Harcourt, Brace & World, Inc.

Hirsch, Werner Z.: Inventing education for the future, San Francisco, 1967, Chandler Publishing Co.

Hoffman, Milton: A new way of bussing students, American Education 4:14, 1968.

Oliva, Peter: The secondary school today, Cleveland, 1967, World Publishing Co.

Toffler, Alvin: Future shock, New York, 1970, Random House, Inc.

Van Til, William: Curriculum: quest for relevance, New York, 1971, Houghton Mifflin Co.

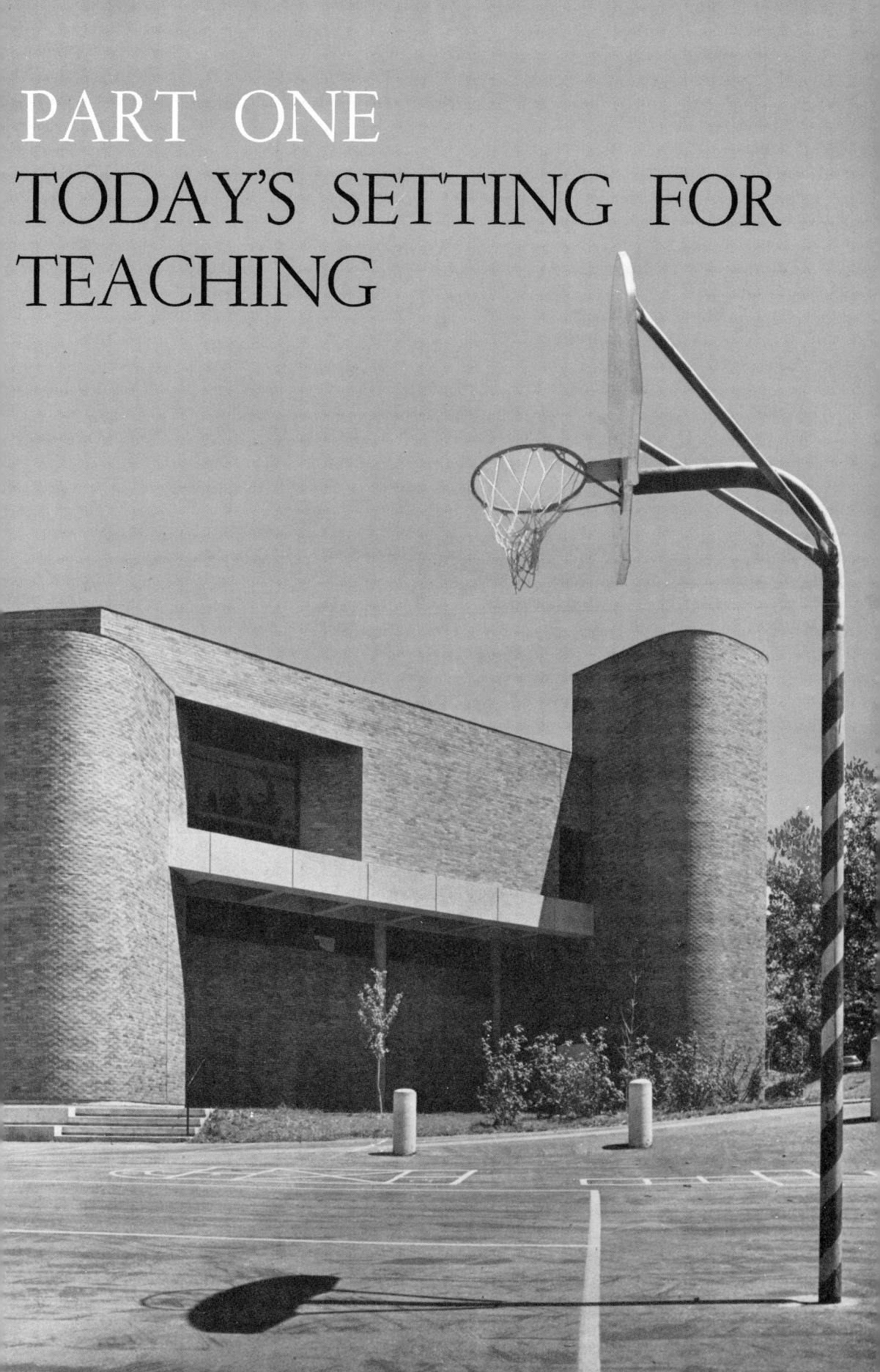

PART ONE
TODAY'S SETTING FOR TEACHING

1 THE CHANGING COMMUNITY

The vast changes taking place in our society and culture, which were discussed in the introduction, are leaving their imprint, to a greater or lesser degree, on each community in the United States. Some communities, because of their location, conservatism, or other factors, are changing more slowly than other, more progressive localities. However, most communities are different than they were only a few years ago.

The nation's economy has resulted in austerity school budgets with cutbacks in physical education, including athletic programs. Research conducted by the National Education Association has disclosed that many of the nation's largest school districts are operating under crisis conditions because of financial problems. The Vietnam war, international tensions, and domestic crises have contributed to a generation gap as well as to student activism at both high school and college levels. Students are requesting more involvement in school affairs and are questioning whether some educational requirements, including physical education, are necessary. As a result, some physical education programs are becoming voluntary rather than required.

The demand for an end to discrimination against minority groups has resulted in community discussions regarding such things as bussing, hiring of black teachers, and equal salaries and opportunities for women as well as men teachers. The population mobility has raised questions about what kind of educational program is needed for a nation on wheels. The alarming dropout rate in our schools, with large numbers of youth leaving with neither the skills nor the self-reliance needed for gainful and satisfying employment, has brought forth a recommendation to assign top priority to career education.

More community and parental concern for education has led to a demand for such things as greater accountability on the part of educators and such new developments as a voucher system to help upgrade educational programs. The computer age has been felt in each community, with such topics as moon landings, skylabs, and space travel being common topics of discussion. Computers also make school class scheduling and record keeping easier. In the large cities of the nation there has been a move to decentralize large cumbersome school districts and in their place make small community districts, which it is hoped will result in better administration and more lay involvement in the running of the schools.

The physical education program, as in many ways all education, reflects the community in which it exists. The community is that subdivision of people, homes, and businesses that make up a school district. It may coincide with the geographical limits of a city, town, or village, such as San Diego, California, or Denver, Colorado; or it may include two or more political subdivisions, such as the Bedford

School District, which includes the towns of Bedford, New Castle, North Castle, and Pound Ridge, New York.

In any event, the local community plays an important part in the philosophy and formulation of the school physical education program. A knowledge of the community is of importance to the teacher so that he or she may better prepare for the experiences to be encountered.

What is the structural organization of the community? What factors play a part in the financing of the schools? In regard to the schools, who is responsible to the citizens of the community? What influencing factors should be considered in establishing a philosophy of education? How is the physical education program affected by the community?

In this chapter these and other problems as they relate to the schools and specifically to physical education will be discussed so that teachers may be better able to understand and work with their particular situations.

COMMUNITY RELATIONS POLICIES FOR THE PHYSICAL EDUCATOR

The relations between the physical educator and the community are affected by many divergent interactions varying widely in scope, complexity, and intensity. The implications for the physical educator are of great depth and latitude, ranging from the seemingly innocuous task of answering the telephone to being able to effectively utilize public communications media. Because of the inherent dissimilarities in communities, any discussion here must be relatively broad in scope. Some policies that the physical educator should think about very carefully in his relations with the community in which his school is located include the following:

• *The physical educator should work closely with the community in goal setting, planning, and subsequent program evaluation.* Although the "how" of the school operation is essentially the responsibility of the professional physical educator, he

should constructively enlist the abilities, interests, and drives of persons in the community in respect to many school activities of which he is a part. By utilizing citizen cooperation at its highest level better programs can be developed, community needs can more readily be met, citizen involvement in activities such as parent-teacher associations and neighborhood clubs can be enhanced, and greater public interest can be gained.

• *The physical educator must be guided by the knowledge that public reaction to school personnel and practices creates the basis for community approval or rejection of many aspects of school affairs.* The physical educator should familiarize himself with the community's traditions, beliefs, resources, limitations, and, most importantly, its people. In working with the community, the physical educator must use integrity in all of his relations and must be efficient in his daily functions and services, for these have significant value.

• *The school, actively assisted by the physical educator, should offer learning opportunities that meet the needs of the community as well as its students.* Within legal limitations and within rules and regulations of the Board of Education, the physical educator should assist in making the school a community center by helping to provide recreational and educational activities for adults as well as children and youth. Furthermore, the physical educator should participate in community efforts and activities in the capacity of a resource person. Finally, the physical educator should utilize appropriate community facilities and resources to enhance his program of physical education in the school.

• *The physical educator should develop his program with the community in mind and flavor it with acceptable habits, customs, traditions, ideals, resources, and problems of the community.* In order to accomplish his task most effectively, the physical educator should familiarize himself with such things as the community's historical background, social pursuits, eco-

nomic status, political philosophy, leaders, and channels of organized communication.
• *In order to be most effective in community relations the physical educator must develop professional skills to make his role effective and his contributions as extensive as possible.* The physical educator should be capable of utilizing available communications media in his community, make adjustments and improvements to meet changing needs, maintain continual communication with various groups, and keep school and community leaders informed regarding his school and community activities.

COMMUNITY FACTORS INFLUENCING EDUCATION

There are many factors that have a bearing upon the school system and the program within the school. These factors could be termed external, in that they are related to influences outside the school and the teacher-pupil relationship. Their importance, however, cannot be overemphasized. In the pages that follow some of them will be discussed, and the implications they have for education and the possible means of working with them will be mentioned.

When developing a program for a particular community, it must be kept in mind that the community is the real focus of decision making. The program must be planned around the needs and interests of the community and the students. It further must be remembered that the school is only one community agency that contributes to the education of the children. Therefore, the physical education program must be related not only to the individual but also to the family and the community as well.

Economic conditions

One of the problems facing every community today is how to obtain enough money to close the gap between the amount and quality of education that is needed and the financial support that is available. The following factors that de-

termine the cost of education are listed by the National Education Association: the problem of securing an adequate number of teachers at salaries high enough to attract and hold them, the need for counseling and guidance, the need for adequate facilities, equipment, and the like, the need for enough classrooms to implement a modern program, and the need to lift poverty-stricken districts to a respectable level of support.

The community that is able and willing to meet these needs will have a sound educational system. In relation to physical education, this means well-planned physical plants—both indoors and out—and enough qualified personnel to administer a sound, safe, and varied class program, an inclusive intramural program, a full interscholastic program, and a practical adapted program.

In poorer areas many students have after-school jobs and, furthermore, because of crowded conditions cannot study at home. In this type of situation, nearly all educational experiences must take place in the school if they are to take place at all. Special dress or equipment requirements must be kept to a minimum because of the financial status of the families of most student. The physical facilities and equipment available will depend to some extent on what the community can afford to pay. In densely populated areas, the schools may be crowded. Program design must consider class size in order to achieve the maximum benefit within the limits of facilities and number of students. If there is not an overcrowding problem, many more options are open in choosing a curriculum. In the community that is not able to afford what it should have, there are lower salaries, larger classes, less equipment and supplies, fewer personnel, and limited intramural and interscholastic programs. Possible sources of revenue are indicated here:

1. Local property taxes. This source of revenue is reaching the breaking point, with many communities unwilling to approve the necessary funds for the con-

stantly rising costs of education. Recently, in one state approximately 45% of all referendums pertaining to the construction of new buildings or the addition or renovation of old ones were defeated during one year.

2. Other local taxes. Sales or other nuisance taxes are being used or considered in many communities. Opposition is so great that it is obvious that other sources must be found.

3. State aid. State aid as a reliable source has also reached a breaking point and certainly cannot be expected to offer much help to local communities under present tax structures.

4. Federal aid. Some educators see only two possible solutions: massive federal aid or a radical revision in state and federal tax structures. The subject of revenue sharing has been proposed as a possible solution to the problem.

The problem has no easy solution, but the implications for physical education, as for all education, are monumental. The economy of a community may have particular impact upon the physical education program. In an economically weak situation, the classes are apt to be overcrowded, with far too many students for an effective teaching-learning situation. There may be inadequate locker and shower facilities, as well as inadequate teaching stations both indoors and out. Equipment may be worn or inadequate, and new equipment may be difficult to obtain. In a situation where students may be employed after school, it may be difficult to operate an intramural program. Lack of staff may dictate that physical education personnel assume a variety of nonteaching duties, such as lunch hour supervision and study hall and bus duty. In a community where the schools enjoy strong economic support, the reverse will be true in proportion to economic standing in relation to school expenditures.

Religious groups

Fifty to one hunded years ago, religious groups had a great and direct influence upon the administration of a community's affairs, including the program in the schools. In recent years the separation of church and state has been greater, to a point where the influence of religious groups is less than it was before.

The church school has grown rapidly. Many children spend part or all of their school life without going to a public school. With conditions as crowded as they are in many public schools, this helps alleviate further overcrowding. Support for public education, however, is understandably less from this group.

A few religious groups frown upon certain activities that a school endorses. This may include social dancing, Saturday or Sunday athletic contests, and family-life courses. The attitude of some religious groups toward social dancing may cause students to drop out of this activity. Where a particular church has considerable influence, it may mean a complete breakdown of some parts of the program, even though they may be needed and wanted by the other students.

The prohibition on participation in athletics on the Sabbath may also affect planning of school activities in some parts of the country. In the realm of sex education courses, some religious groups have been outspoken opponents of incorporating courses of this kind in school programs.

In order to meet these religious problems, the physical educator must base the program on educationally sound principles. The teacher should be certain that the school administration is supporting the program. If a question arises, he should be prepared to explain his program with supportive evidence to representatives of the community's churches and to listen carefully for valid criticisms and suggestions for improvement.

Politics

In communities where school boards are appointed, merit and qualifications for the job may be taken into consideration. However, in other instances, appointments are made on the basis of political patronage. Where board members are elected, the entire voting community has a voice in who runs the schools. However, this system may also have drawbacks. Interested candidates who will do a good job run and often win election. However, aspiring politicians often run for the school board and then use their position as a stepping-stone in their careers. The process of education is frequently only a minor consideration to such politically motivated individuals. Further, in a community that favors one political party over another, the candidates of that party, rather than the best man for the job, may be elected.

Not only the school board but local politicians as well may have a voice in running the schools of a community. The local press and radio, through editorial comment, reflect local political views in regard to the schools. It is the school board, however, that hires and fires teachers, approves budgets, and decides on new construction. The teacher is ultimately responsible to the school board, which, as a group, is responsible to the community.

Strong support of a school board by the community will be reflected in the physical education program. Qualified staff will be hired, and they will teach in a healthful environment and, if satisfactory, be retained for further service. Budget requests and appropriations are most likely to be honored where the school board receives community support and in turn supports its teachers and their programs. Where the school board is ineffective and inefficient because it is politically maneuvered, all of education suffers.

Climate

Another consideration is the geographical location of the community. Planning must take the following aspects into consideration:

1. Amount of time it will be possible to be out-of-doors. It would be unreasonable to spend large amounts of money in equipping and maintaining an oversized gymna-

sium, to the detriment of the outdoor facilities, in southern California or Florida, where the amount of time spent out-of-doors will be much greater than that indoors. Conversely, in the northern states more time will be spent inside because of the weather.

2. Activities that will be of interest to local residents. The inclusion of and emphasis on skiing and ice skating in the program in northern states would certainly be understandable, while more emphasis on tennis would be reasonable in Arizona and Texas. This does not exclude ice skating from the program in the South or the Southwest, although facilities would have to be avaiable. The emphasis on winter sports in the South, however, would not approximate that in the northern section of the country.

It is necessary to determine the activities and interests of the community as they relate to the climate and make efficient use of funds in the light of it.

Sociological and cultural backgrounds

The composition of the community has a bearing upon the physical education program. The races or nationalities, wealth or lack of it, educational backgrounds, and ages of the residents are just a few of the sociological and cultural factors that should be considered when planning a program.

The program in a low socioeconomic area should include many opportunities for very active participation as an outlet for aggressive tendencies that may be more apparent in this type of area. In requiring proper gymnasium attire it is important to recognize that some pupils may not have the money to purchase sneakers or gym suits. It may be possible to stockpile uniforms as pupils outgrow them. It is necessary, however, to be tactful when making them available to pupils. It is also important that showers be taken because some of the pupils may not have other opportunities to take baths.

If the child resides in the ghetto, his play

space is usually limited to the streets and neighborhood playgrounds. It is up to the school to provide a well-rounded program of motor experiences for such students. If the parents of a child work and are poverty-stricken, there will be little money for recreational activities. If different ethnic groups are represented in the student body, new sports and activities may be included in the program in order to enhance a student's pride and respect for his own heritage. This is in keeping with making activities relevant to students' backgrounds. It makes much more sense, for example, than trying to teach deck tennis to ghetto children.

The community residents may be college graduates and fairly well-to-do. The physical education program should make use of the educational interests of these fathers and mothers to encourage support for programs, facilities, special equipment, and supplies. The program may include individual activities such as golf, tennis, and archery, since the students will probably be able to make use of these skills out of school.

The great problem of meeting the needs of children from varied backgrounds presents a challenge to the teacher in working not only with his or her pupils but with their parents as well. It is therefore important to know the parents of children in the community. Such knowledge could come from an anlysis of the following items concerning the parents: (1) interest in the parent-teacher association, (2) participation in various organizations that are important in the community (groups such as the League of Women Voters, garden clubs, and Junior League may indicate a higher educational background and socioeconomic status), (3) participation in hobbies and leisuretime activities (golf and tennis clubs and riding stables may indicate a higher socioeconomic area), (4) interest in school sports activities, which may indicate interest and potential support if properly channeled by the physical educator, and (5) the desire to conform (the danger lies in

the possibility of conforming to mediocrity).

Differences in taste, attitude, and race or nationality are minimized in the gymnasium and on the athletic field. Breaking down false beliefs, recognizing ability, and giving a feeling of belonging can be easily accomplished in the field of sports. The physical educator can help combat the harmful social and cultural variances within the community by means of a good program.

Attitude toward education

Is the community willing and able to support the schools? How have they voted in recent referendums relating to school expansion or expenditures? Do they regularly cut the school's operating budget? If they have, it is possible that the community is either unable or unwilling to meet desirable educational expenses.

A beginning physical education teacher should be conscious of the handicap of working where the equipment and supplies are old or in short supply, classes are overcrowded, or facilities are inadequate. The amount of relief that can be expected is largely dependent upon the attitude of the members of the community as evidenced by recent trends in voting on school budgets and referendums.

Another aspect worth noting is the degree of acceptance of educational trends approved and used in other communities or sections of the country. For instance, are antiquated strength tests, an excessive amount of formal work such as calisthenics, or heavy apparatus being used? Is the term "physical training" still used? The answers to these questions indicate attitudes of the community and schools that may have a part in the eventual success of the physical education program.

Consideration must be given to parents' ideas for their children's education in the design of any school program. All social groups have goals for their children, and these determine what programs the community will support and sanction. There is a need for clear lines of communication between curriculum planners and the community.

Pressure groups

A pressure group can be defined as an organization or group of people working to achieve a common goal. There are groups or organizations in every community that attempt to bring pressure to bear in order to elect a certain candidate, repair a street, reduce a tax, or perhaps change the physical education program. Examples of pressure groups are a dads' club desiring to sponsor a football league, a church group wanting to eliminate social dancing in the school, and a citizens' group trying to rally support for a school referendum.

Not all pressure groups try to tear down the program. In fact, quite the opposite is true. It is possible that one of the strongest allies in combating the goals of one pressure group will be another group. It is also true that many organizations believe they are helping the physical education program by their actions when in reality they are doing a great disservice to the students. For example, a fraternal organization that gives expensive prizes or awards or sponsors a football league at the elementary school level usually does so out of a desire to be of service to the community and the school. It is only by fostering an understanding of the possible harm that can be caused that the physical educator can effectively combat these influences.

When a physical education teacher is a member of the community, ideas are often discussed informally with him. This provides a good opportunity to encourage, dissuade, or rechannel a group of interested community members. Speaking at meetings, interpreting a good program, and sending home happy, understanding students are probably the best ways to combat undesirable group pressures.

COMMUNITY STRUCTURE

Through a knowledge of the composition and governing bodies of the community, the teacher will be better able to understand the problems facing the community. It is also true that any suggestions for improvement of the curriculum, school plant, facilities, number of personnel, or school philosophy will be more meaningful when they are based upon local community conditions. It is necessary, therefore, to investigate and obtain information about the community, evaluate these facts in the light of professional knowledge, and plan a course of action.

Size

Is the community a compact industrial area, such as Scranton, Pennsylvania, or does it sprawl over the countryside, as does Berkeley, California? The answer to this question has much significance for the school and the physical education program. In a compact area, for instance, there is little or no transportation problem. After-school activities such as intramurals and varsity team practice are not greatly affected, because public transportation is available to take students home. In the sprawling community, lack of public transportation can be a deterrent to the conduct of many activities. Solutions to these transportation problems may include convincing school authorities to provide extra transportation, enlisting the aid of the local parent-teacher association, and coordinating efforts with other departments, such as music or dramatics, thereby involving enough students to warrant extra transportation.

Another problem of community size involves future growth, particularly with regard to the current exodus to suburbia. Has the community reached its peak growth, or is it still expanding? Do facilities amply provide for the number of students they are now handling? What are the plans for the future regarding new facilities? Do these plans properly provide for physical education space, facilities, and teaching stations?

In an eastern community two elementary schools were constructed. It was expected that one of the schools would have a number of vacant rooms during its first two years of operation, while housing classes from kindergarten through grade 7. By the time of occupancy, however, there had been such an increase in the population that school authorities were unable to keep any rooms vacant. In each of the following three years, in fact, a grade was moved out of the school. After the completion of a new secondary school building, a community-wide realignment plan was effected. This plan enabled the schools to more adequately serve local residents.

Type

Are you going to teach in a predominantly residential community such as Darien, Connecticut, or Berkley, Michigan? If so, you may assume that the parents will take time to inquire about and be in on the planning for education. Active and interested parents are a great help to the school when they put their energies to work in helping the administrators and teachers. Interested parents can help the physical education program by supporting its activities, helping to obtain new facilities, equipment, and supplies, and gaining an understanding of the program. In an industrial community or in a culturally disadvantaged one, residents may be less inclined or may have less time to concern themselves with education. In Flint, Michigan, however, a public interest in education has brought more people into the schools at night than during the day.

Flint has developed the school-community idea to the point where each school has an evening center and most have gymnasiums that are at least 100 by 100 feet in area, as well as other community rooms. In addition to the evening recreation centers, there are a child health program, in-service training for teachers, an outdoor camp, Big Sister organization, adult education programs, tots and teens groups, a stepping-stone program, and other programs.

This program was begun in 1935 by the Mott Foundation in cooperation with the Flint Board of Education. Its purposes are threefold: (1) to make possible the maximum utilization of school buildings and school facilities as well as other community resources—personnel, material, and organizations; (2) to act as a pilot project in testing and demonstrating to the local board of education and other communities the possibilities of what may be accomplished; and (3) to stimulate, by demonstrating what can be done, constructive influences not only in this community but eventually in other parts of the state, the nation, and the world.

The values of the Flint program are obvious. Important also are the attitudes of the taxpayers when they are able to see and use the buildings for which they pay. Flint was blessed with the Mott Foundation, but most communities can achieve community-centered schools for very little extra cost.

You may find yourself in an industrial or business community like Flint, Michigan, but where the village, town, or city does not have a positive attitude toward education. There may be little room for playing fields and recreational areas. There may be a large populace of older residents who no longer have school-age children. The attitude of the public is of great importance because many residents may feel little sympathy for public school problems, particularly since most solutions to the problems involve an increase in taxes.

In addition to the older residents, there are those parents who send their children to private or parochial schools and who have no desire to pay twice for education. They must pay their taxes, which are used for public education, but they have a vested interest in minimizing these payments.

Although there are always many parents interested in the schools and their problems, the support of a majority of the population is necessary. This requires public interpretation. In Flint this positive attitude has been achieved through a community-centered program. In Norfolk, Virginia, an

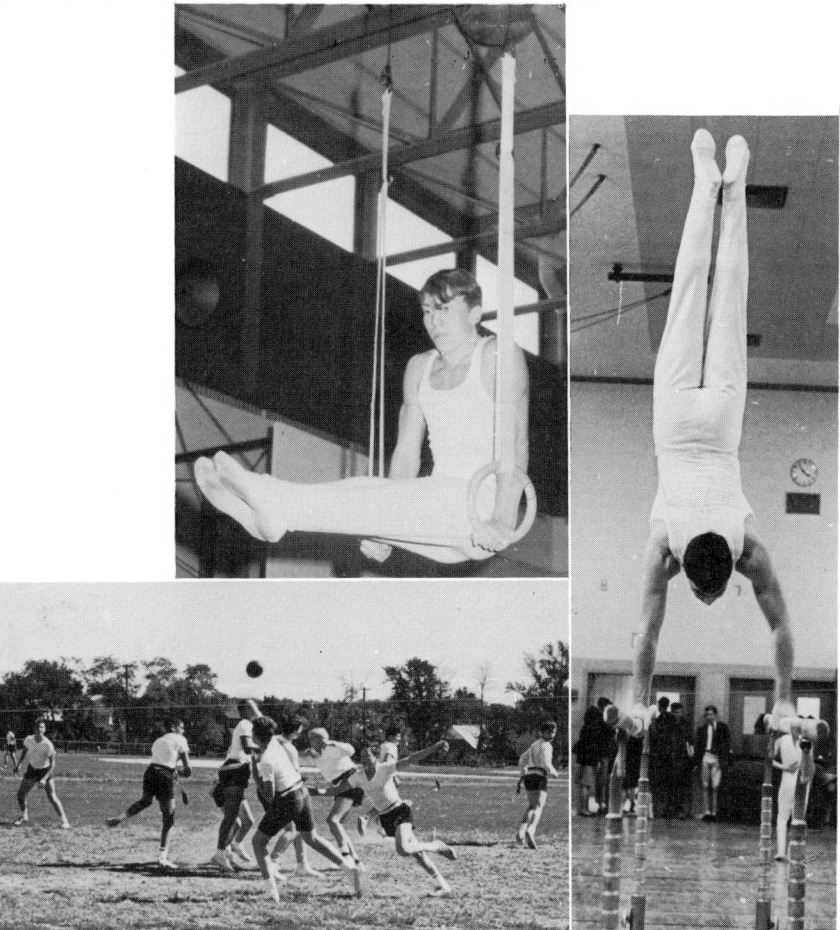

Fig. 1-1. Parents should be interested in their school physical education program and activities such as gymnastics and touch football.

interest has been manifested in education through a program of health instruction, activity instruction, and intramurals. This program developed because of close cooperation in the fields of health and physical education, which led to an integrated core of instruction.

If community support is not present, it is the responsibility of the school and of every individual in the school to foster it through careful planning.

Governing body

There are three main types of governing bodies that determine the form of local government: the mayor-council, the commission, and the city manager.

The *mayor-council plan* places primary control of administrative matters in the hands of an elected mayor. The council, elected by the citizens, handles local legislation. There are variations in the organization of this plan. Some communities have a dominant mayor, others divide the responsibilities of the mayor and the council relatively equally, and still others have a weak mayor, with the majority of the duties being handled by or through the council. The mayor-council plan is still the most prevalent. The majority of small cities use it in one form or another, as do such large cities as New York, Boston, San Francisco, and Detroit.

The *commission plan* has had its period

of growth and is now generally regarded as being in eclipse. The city of Galveston made this plan popular just after the turn of the century. There were five commissioners elected by the people. One was designated as mayor, but only for the purpose of presiding at the meetings. He had no veto power and only a proportionate share of the administration with the other commissioners. This type of plan is still used by some municipalities, but its popularity is on the wane.

The *city manager plan* is growing the most rapidly of any type of city government. In this plan, a career person trained in public administration is appointed by the council. He is responsible for the conduct of municipal administration. There are variations in this plan, such as that wherein the council keeps certain appointment rights. The majority of plans leave only two duties in the hands of the council: (1) the right to pass necessary ordinances and resolutions, and (2) the right to select the city manager. The trend in many municipalities is toward the city manager type of government.

The growth of the city manager plan has

numerous implications for education. The concentration of powers in a professional person (the manager is supposed to be nonpartisan and is generally chosen from an approved list) usually brings about wider use of modern administrative procedures, which generally are credited with unusually effective standards of modern administration.

The implications of the governmental structure, whether it is city, village, town, or other type, in your community for the school and the physical education program are numerous. Knowing it well will provide an understanding of the following:

1. The chain of responsibility—that is, who the local district leaders are and what they have to do with appropriated moneys
2. The use of modern governmental structure—that is, the degree to which the community is operating under an archaic form of patronage or an efficient modern structure that attempts to cut unnecessary costs and meet today's challenges
3. The pressure points in the community structure—that is, how public senti-

Fig. 1-2. Structure of town government.

ment for needed school expenditures can best be made known and brought to bear on local officials

It is your responsibility as a teacher as well as a member of the community to know as much as possible about your local government.

Board of education

The board of education, or school board or committee, as it is known in some areas, is the administrative unit whose responsibility it is to develop policies for the educational program in the local schools. Some communities have a single commissioner of education, but the vast majority of cities and districts retain the board plan. This is true in spite of the widespread movement to single-headed departmental control in such areas as police, fire, and health. This may be because of the reasonable success of the board plan and the caliber of board members, who are able to remain aloof from local politics. Whatever the reasons, the board plan appears to be here to stay, especially since most educators seem to prefer this type of administration.

A board of education may be financially independent, allowing it to fix its own tax rate within limits set by the state and to spend the money as it sees fit. In many cities of more than 25,000 people, as well as in some smaller communities, the boards are financially independent. When a board is fiscally dependent, it recommends the amount it needs to cover the cost of its budget, but the municipal administration decides upon the amount the board will receive. If the full amount is not given, the board must reduce, eliminate, or adjust budget items to fit the amount allotted.

It is important for the physical educator to keep the board aware of problems facing the teacher and to recommend some realistic solutions. It is necessary to channel this information through the principal, director or supervisor, or superintendent.

Composition. Boards of education for school districts evolve from acts of state legislatures. In most cities, boards are elected by the voters. There are places, however, where the mayor appoints members. Regardless of how they obtain their positions, their terms vary from one year to about four years. The usual term is three to four years. Terms are frequently overlapped to ensure continuity in membership.

Size. Boards of education are gradually diminishing in size, from the thirty- and forty-member boards of yesteryear to the five- and nine-member boards seen most commonly today. The number of board members ranges from three, who represent a small local district, to fifteen, who constitute the board in some large cities. The smaller boards of today seem to produce better results by working more efficiently and with greater harmony. As a rule, most members serve without compensation, although very nominal salaries are given in certain areas.

The National School Boards Association has indicated the following characteristics of school boards in forty-two cities throughout the nation having more than 300,000 population.

Most of these school boards have seven, five, or nine members, in that order. Three cities have boards with fifteen members. The composition of school board members (3% of whom are women and 13% of whom are Negroes) is broken down as follows: businessmen, 103; lawyers, 66; housewives, 51; physicians, 22; ministers, 11; and college professors, 8.

Most of the 137,000 members of the nation's 25,000 school boards are elected. Among the large cities, only Philadelphia, Pittsburgh, and Washington, D. C., choose boards through a committee of court judges. In Boston, Detroit, Los Angeles, and St. Louis, school boards are elected.

Duties. The board of education's responsibilities may be summed up as follows:

Establishes policies and legislates
    Curriculum—including physical education curriculum (in accordance with certain state regulations)
    School calendar—including time and days when

interscholastic contests may or may not be played

School entrance age—set by the state in some areas

Provides means for carrying out policies

    Prepares budget—including salary scale, arrangements for time off or extra pay for coaching, and policy regarding coaching duties

    Hires superintendent and other personnel (upon recommendation of the superintendent)

    Votes tax levies, if fiscally independent, or recommends adequate levies to those who have the fiscal responsibilty

    Plans and executes building and maintenance program (within limits mentioned above)—including new physical education plants and facilities

Sees that policies are efficiently carried out

    Visits schools

    Receives oral and written reports on progress

The board also represents the public in the preparation of its policies and budgets, interpreting to the public the needs of the school in terms of plant, facilities, and working conditions. Although there are some specific duties and responsibilities of boards of education and of superintendents, there is no exact line where the duties of the board end and those of the superintendent begin. This must be worked out together toward a common goal. The superintendent of schools, however, is the professional education leader, and members of the board of education are lay personnel. This, of course, has implications for the responsibilities of each.

There is a growing awareness among professional and lay leaders alike of the need for reform in repect to school board operations. Reforms have been advocated by such an important group as the New York Committee on Educational Leadership and are receiving support in some of the more progressive sections of the country. These reforms include (1) the transfer of all administrative functions that encumber school board operations to the superintendent of schools, (2) better procedures for screening school board members so that the "office seeks the man rather than the man seeking the office," (3) elimination of annual public votes on school budgets where required and substitution of budget hearings, and (4) improved procedures for selecting superintendents of schools.

ALLIED FIELDS

The fields of recreation and health are closely allied to physical education. The positions that are established to handle these responsibilities may or may not be within the department of physical education. It is obvious that cooperation is necessary regardless of the local structure. The city of Norfolk, Virginia, has shown how the objectives of education can better be reached through close cooperation in the fields of health and physical education. Flint, Michigan, has proved extensively the values of cooperation in the fields of recreation and physical education. The accomplishments made through mutual effort can be limitless when a community sets its mind to the task.

Recreation

Before discussing recreation, it is first necessary to define it. Recreation is a leisure-time activity—that is, an activity that is performed during nonworking hours. It is enjoyable and wholesome—something that contributes to one's satisfaction and happiness. It is voluntary—something in which the individual participates because he desires to do so.

There are many types of recreational activities. There are those that challenge the mind and those that challenge the body. There are those that call for cooperative effort and those that involve only the individual. Integrated physical education and recreation programs can be of great value to each other in at least the following ways: (1) programming, in which recreation programs are used as a testing ground for skills learned in physical education class; (2) extension of the intramural program; (3) facility construction, in which duplication is avoided by constructing one unit to serve both the school and after-school programs; and (4) economies, in which common use is made of personnel, supplies, and equipment.

There are different means of coordinating physical education and recreation. In one Minnesota city, the administration

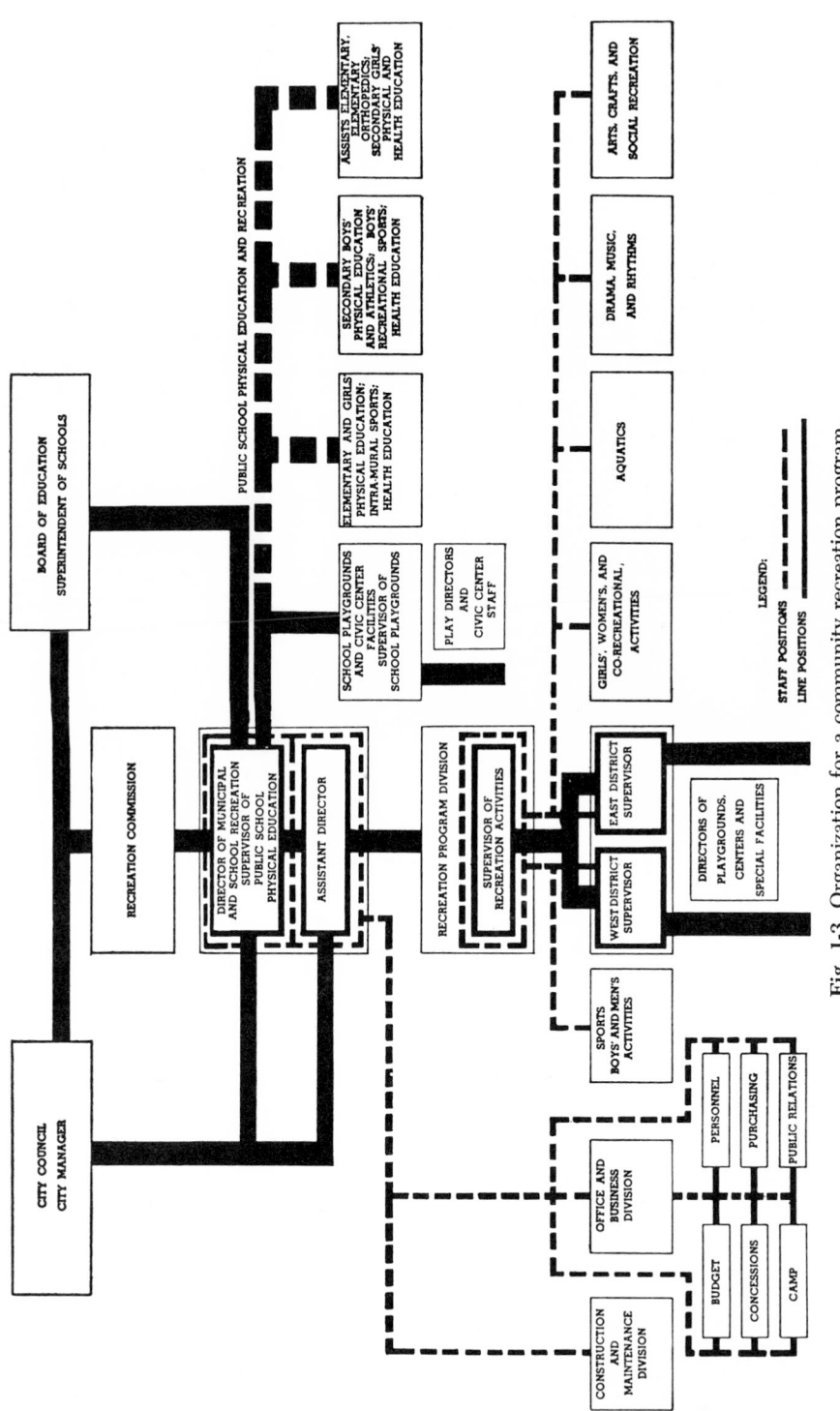

Fig. 1-3. Organization for a community recreation program.

of community recreation is vested in a board composed of one appointed representative from each city ward, one member-at-large, and three ex-officio members representing the school board, park board, and common council. In one California city the superintendent of recreation coordinates and administers the recreation program, and the costs are borne by the board of recreation, the board of education, and

NUMBER OF OCCASIONS OF PARTICIPATION IN OUTDOOR SUMMER RECREATION
1960 COMPARED WITH 1976 AND 2000 (BY MILLIONS)

Activity	1960	1976	2000
DRIVING FOR PLEASURE	872	1,341	2,215
SWIMMING	672	1,182	2,307
WALKING FOR PLEASURE	566	856	1,569
PLAYING OUTDOOR GAMES OR SPORTS	474	825	1,666
SIGHTSEEING	287	456	825
PICNICKING	279	418	700
FISHING	260	350	521
BICYCLING	228	297	452
ATTENDING OUTDOOR SPORTS EVENTS	172	252	416
BOATING OTHER THAN SAILING OR CANOEING	159	285	557
NATURE WALKS	98	153	263
HUNTING	95	123	174
CAMPING	60	113	235
HORSEBACK RIDING	55	82	143
WATER SKIING	39	84	189
HIKING	34	63	125
ATTENDING OUTDOOR CONCERTS, DRAMA, ETC.	27	46	92

ALL ACTIVITIES

1960	4,377
1976	6,926
2000	12,449

Fig. 1-4. The recreational activities that will be most popular among Americans in the year 2000. (A Report to the President and to the Congress by the Outdoor Recreation Resources Review Commission: Outdoor recreation in America, Washington, D. C., January, 1962, Superintendent of Documents.)

the city. In other areas similar plans are in effect, varying in many details except the important one, which is coordination, or cooperation.

Communities that have minimized the duplication of personnel and established a person or board responsible for recreation and physical education list the following values: (1) dollar savings, resulting from lack of duplication of facilities and use of the same personnel; (2) stronger programs, with continuity of school and out-of-school activities; and (3) greater participation, resulting in better understanding of programs and better public relations.

In some communities the recreation board and the school board have no administrative tie, and although they work together on particular activities or problems, they also have their differences, with no ready means of working them out. The importance of cooperation between physical education and recreation programs cannot be overemphasized.

Health

The fields of health and physical education share much in common, although they are two separate entities. It is only in recent years that the differences have become more commonly recognized. There were times when the job of health was everyone's job—from members of the mathematics department to the custodial staff—and so it was really no one's job. Today, some states have moved so far as to certify people in the field of health education, while other communities have put the responsibility in the hands of the director or supervisor of health and physical education. The degree to which this person is able to coordinate and guide is an important factor in establishing a good program. This is especially true when one realizes that a school health council may include any or all of the following: school principal, physician, dentist, nurse, health educator, teacher of physical education, teachers of biology and home economics, psycholo-

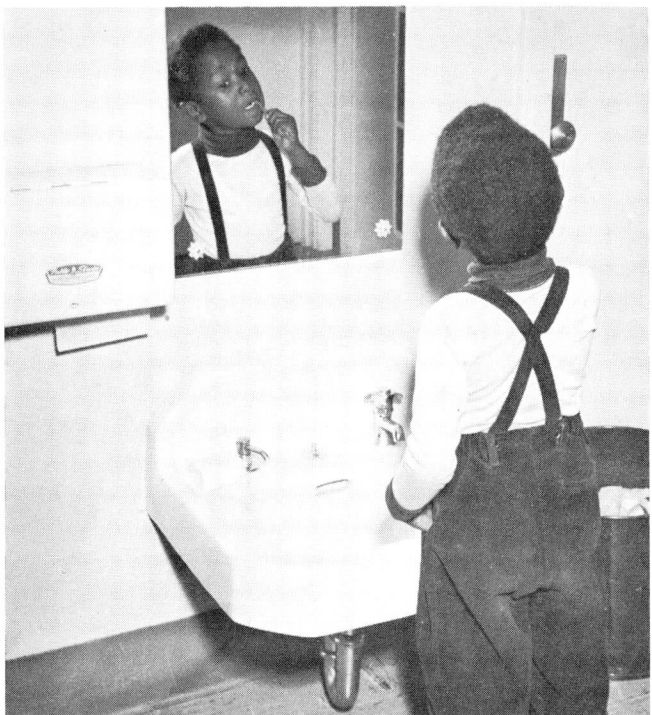

Fig. 1-5. Health education. (San Diego County Schools, San Diego, Calif.)

CHECKLIST OF SELECTED ITEMS FOR EVALUATING THE SECONDARY SCHOOL'S

PHYSICAL EDUCATION PROGRAM'S RELEVANCY TO THE COMMUNITY

1. The physical education program utilizes such community resources as facilities (parks, swimming pools, bowling alleys, and so on) as well as people with expertise in various physical education activities and such methodology as visual aids, curriculum development, and other areas in providing a rich experience for the students.
   YES ☐   NO ☐

2. Physical education takes into account the economic background of the community in planning activities (for example, weekend skiing trips may be too expensive).
   YES ☐   NO ☐

3. Physical education takes into account the physical needs of the residents of the community (physical fitness, nutritional needs, and skill levels).
   YES ☐   NO ☐

4. The physical education program takes into account the climate and other natural features of the community, making greatest use of the out-of-doors, providing seasonal activities, and the like.
   YES ☐   NO ☐

5. Physical education works cooperatively with closely allied community agencies such as Boys' Clubs, P.A.L., Y.M.C.A., Y.W.C.A., C.Y.O., Y.M.H.A., and Y.W.H.A.
   YES ☐   NO ☐

6. The physical education program provides for the interests and needs of people in the community with different ethnic backgrounds, in respect to its offering of games, dances, and sports.
   YES ☐   NO ☐

7. Physical education interprets articulately the value of its offering to the children and other residents of the community.
   YES ☐   NO ☐

8. Physical education works closely with the community's communication media to properly interpret the program, including the role of educational athletics in the school.
   YES ☐   NO ☐

9. Physical education interprets to the townspeople the athletic program and the proper behavior of spectators at sports contests in order to reflect favorably on the school.
   YES ☐   NO ☐

10. Physical education interprets to school authorities the need for community utilization of its facilities in order to further its objectives for the adult population.
    YES ☐   NO ☐

11. Physical education takes into consideration the attitude of the residents toward education and the level of aspiration for their children.
    YES ☐   NO ☐

12. Physical education takes into consideration such community problems as drugs, violence, and school dropouts in its curriculum planning.
    YES ☐   NO ☐

13. The physical education program takes into consideration the religious beliefs of the community in planning and carrying out its offering.
    YES ☐   NO ☐

14. Physical education provides a viable program, where feasible, during school vacation periods.
    YES ☐   NO ☐

15. Physical education provides advice and counsel for community physical fitness and athletic programs.
    YES ☐   NO ☐

16. Physical education does not yield to community pressures to utilize questionable professional procedures to develop outstanding athletic teams.
    YES ☐   NO ☐

gist, members of guidance staff, teacher for the physically handicapped, nutritionist, dental hygienist, custodian, student representatives, parent representatives, and representatives from community health organizations.

In some communities cooperative health services may be organized by a school health coordinating council. In other communities a joint cooperative plan involves the park board, board of education, board of health, and volunteer agencies. School health policies are formulated by the board of education and rendered by the town health department.

Coordination in the fields of health and physical education results in the following: (1) better total education—using coordinated means to reach the goals; (2) better program planning—avoiding duplication and providing more available hands to operate a complete program; (3) minimizing of clerical work in handling special problems, which is more economical and provides readily available records; and (4) more prompt and complete follow-up of remediable defects, through sound and convenient use of physical education and health personnel. Coordination and cooperation are obviously the key to better health and physical education programs.

STATE AND NATIONAL INFLUENCE

Education is a state function. The state legislature is responsible for education. Although most states follow similar administrative structures, they differ in details. In every state there is usually a commissioner or superintendent of education as well as a board of education.

State departments of education emphasize cooperative planning. They do not serve merely as law-enforcement agencies. Although most states have the power to change school districts, they prefer to leave as much choice as possible to the local districts; however, they will bring pressure to bear where necessary. They are always ready to provide consultant services to help in the solution of local problems.

Recently, at the request of an eastern city, the state department of education conducted a school survey in that city. The recommendations included in the survey covered many aspects of education. The imminent threat of the withdrawal of state aid was one of the factors that hastened the city's compliance with many of the basic recommendations made in the survey. In the field of physical education the survey resulted in the addition of teachers, an increase in allocation for supplies, and the expediting of plans for reconditioning and enlarging existing physical plants.

A knowledge of the minimum state standards will enable the beginning teacher to determine whether the school has provided the educational essentials. If the recommended standards have not been met, an attempt to make improvements should be made. Since one responsibility of state departments of education is to improve physical education programs, consultants are usually available to local schools and districts for (1) evaluation of program content, (2) assistance in curriculum revision, (3) guidance in problem situations, and (4) assistance in public relations. State department representatives will usually work to find ways of improving the profession, curriculum, standards, and facilities.

Since the Constitution of the United States does not carry any provision for federal education, the state has assumed the responsibility. The state has limited its own action primarily to guidance and the specification of minimum requirements, leaving a major part of the obligation of education in the hands of the local district and thus placing more responsibility on the physical educator to constantly interpret his program.

POINTS TO REMEMBER

1. There are different types of communities in which teachers work.
2. The nature of each type of community has many implications for physical education.
3. Many community factors—including economic conditions, religious groups, climate, sociological and cultural backgrounds, atti-

tude toward education, and pressure groups
—affect education and physical education.
4. The state departments of education serve
the local community through assistance,
guidance, and evaluation.
5. There is a vital need for cooperation between physical education, health, and recreation.

PROBLEMS TO THINK THROUGH

1. What are the advantages to the physical education department in a community where
the board of education is fiscally independent? Fiscally dependent?
2. What would you, as the physical educator,
do in a community where there is a movement to organize a Pop Warner Football
League?
3. What can you, as a physical educator, do to
combat the attitude of a community that
believes that taxes are too high and that the
physical education budget should therefore
be cut, since it is not a "solid" subject?
4. What are the implications for physical education in the drive to consolidate or cen-
tralize small school districts?

CASE STUDY FOR ANALYSIS

Select a community (where you live or where
you attended high school) and indicate the sources
of all money used for education. Would it be possible to secure additional money from the same
sources? Analyze other potential sources of financial aid and the effects of these new sources upon
the taxpayer and the schools.

EXERCISES FOR REVIEW

1. Describe the composition of the board of
education in your community and the powers and qualifications of the members.
2. What are the pressure groups in your community that may affect the physical education program?
3. List possible religious factors that could affect your program.
4. What effect does climate have upon the

physical education program in the secondary schools?
5. List five facets of a program of physical education that are successfully performed in
communities near your own.

SELECTED READINGS

Alexander, William M., editor: The high school
of the future: a memorial to Kimball Wiles,
Columbus, Ohio, 1969, Charles E. Merrill Publishing Co.
Bucher, Charles A.: Administrative dimensions of
health and physical education programs, includ-
ing athletics, St. Louis, 1971, The C. V. Mosby
Co.
Bucher, Charles A.: Administration of health and
physical education programs, including athletics,
ed. 5, St. Louis, 1971, The C. V. Mosby Co.
Callahan, Sterling G.: Successful teaching in sec-
ondary schools, Glenview, Ill., 1966, Scott,
Foresman & Co.
Conant, James B.: The American high school to-
day, New York, 1959, McGraw-Hill Book Co.,
Inc.
Hahn, Robert O., and Bidna, David B.: Second-
ary education: origins and directions, ed. 2,
New York, 1970, The Macmillan Co.
Morphet, Edgar L., and others: Educational or-
ganization and administration, Englewood Cliffs,
N. J., 1967, Prentice-Hall, Inc.
Morris, Van Cleve: Physical education and the
philosophy of education, Journal of Health,
Physical Education, and Recreation 17:21, 1956.
Mott Foundation: The Mott Foundation Program,
Flint, Mich., 1959, Board of Education.
Physical fitness elements in recreation—suggestions
for community programs, Washington, D. C.,
1962, President's Council on Physical Fitness
and Sports.
Simon, Herbert A.: Administrative behavior, New
York, 1957, The Free Press.
Thompson, James D., editor: Approaches to or-
ganizational design, Pittsburgh, 1966, Univer-
sity of Pittsburgh Press.
Van Til, William: Curriculum: quest for relevance,
Boston, 1971, Houghton Mifflin Co.
Van Til, William: Education: a beginning, Boston,
1971, Houghton Mifflin Co.

2 THE SCHOOL

Many changes that are taking place in our society and culture and that affect the educational programs in each community in this nation have been discussed. The school, as the hub of the educational program, should reflect societal changes that are meaningful and important to the students who attend these institutions. Furthermore, the school should work directly with the community, parents, and students in a manner consistent with the changes taking place. In order for teachers and school administrators to do this intelligently, the structure and role of the secondary school must be clearly understood.

The beginning teacher, particularly, in order to perform his or her role in the most effective way possible, should know and understand the way the school system is structured in the community, how the secondary school fits into this structure, the personnel who play key roles in the educational process, the facilities utilized, and the programs being offered. The lack of such knowledge and understanding can result in personnel problems, disregard for proper channels of communication, and failure to utilize important program resources or get innovative ideas accepted.

The school has the responsibility of educating tomorrow's citizens. Although the goals of education are similar, the means to the end will differ from one school system to another. In this chapter a picture will be presented of the organization and structure of schools, so that the beginning teacher of physical education can be better prepared

to take his or her place in the educational system.

As an additional aid, a checklist is provided at the end of the chapter in order to assist the reader in better understanding the modern secondary school.

STRUCTURE
School district

A school district is that subdivision that is responsible to the state for the administration of public education. Districts vary greatly in size and function. They may be formed on township and city lines, according to elementary or secondary levels, or using other divisions. The trend is away from having many, overlapping, ineffectual districts and toward the use of larger, more effective districts. The National Education Association reports that in the decade from 1948 to 1958 the number of school districts in the United States dropped from nearly 102,000 to 48,043. In recent years the number of school districts has been reduced; at the present time there are approximately 30,000.

Since public education is not mentioned in the federal Constitution, the state has assumed this obligation. Local school districts operate under authority granted by the state. The school district, which is administered by a board of education, is therefore legally responsible to all the people of the state, not to those of the school district only. The fact that a great amount of local freedom is allowed does not alter the legal responsibility. The school board's duties are explained in Chapter 1, on the community. The agents of the board, such as superintendents and principals, are the administrators who concern themselves directly with school problems. Their duties will be discussed in detail in this chapter.

The implications of district reorganization bode well for physical education. As districts become larger, their ability to support and maintain proper physical education plants, personnel, equipment, and supplies should increase—hence, the probability of a more comprehensive program.

School system

The size of the system dictates the number and type of duties its school administrators have. In a small system the superintendent performs many separate functions. In a larger system he is concerned primarily with coordination and public relations, while the many details are handled by assistant or deputy superintendents, department heads, subject supervisors, and principals.

The pattern of school organization at the elementary and secondary levels is in a period of transition. Some of the present patterns of school organization are as follows:

1. The traditional high school, or 8-4, system. Under this type of organization the four-year high school is preceded by the eight-year elementary school.

2. The combined junior and senior high school, or 6-6 or 7-5, plan. Under this type of organization the junior and senior high schools are combined under one principal.

3. The three-year junior high school, or 6-3-3, system. Under this plan the junior

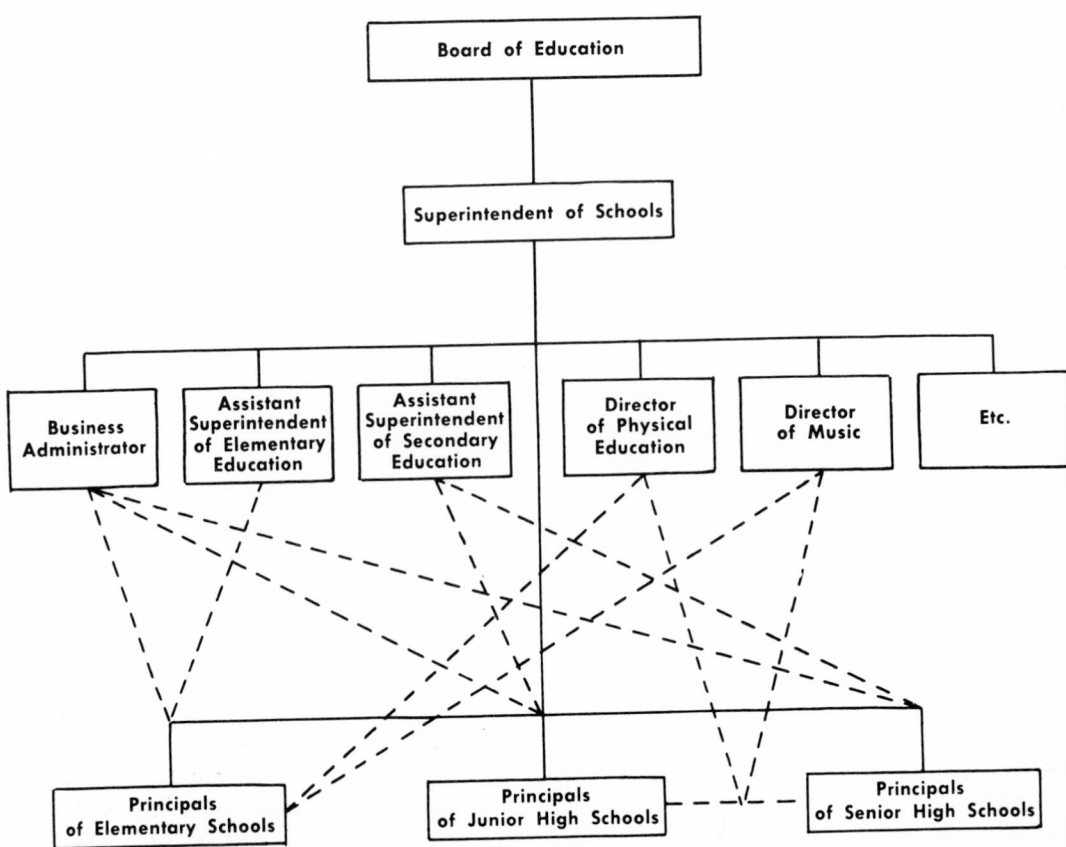

Fig. 2-1. Basic structure of a school district.

high school is grouped separately under one principal. Although the junior high school usually includes grades seven to nine, there are exceptions to this type of organization.

4. The four-year high school, or 6-2-4, system. Under this plan the four-year high school is similar to the traditional high school in organization, and the junior high school consists of two grades.

5. The middle school plan. This type of organization, such as the 4-4-4 plan, is a development that retains the old high school idea but groups the early elementary grades together, such as grades five to eight in one unit.

There are many arguments that can be set forth for each plan of school organization. The physical, psychological, and sociological aspects of the school setting and of child growth and development, the need for effective communication between schools, the range of subjects, the facilities provided, and the preparation of teachers are all pertinent to the type of administrative organization selected. One survey of 366 unified school systems with pupil enrollment of 12,000 or more, conducted by the Educational Research Service, showed that 71% of these school systems were organized on the 6-3-3 plan, 10% on the 8-4 organization, and 6% on a 6-2-4 pattern. Other patterns included 7-5, 6-6, 5-3-4, and 7-2-3.

Elementary school

In the elementary school the pupil is with one teacher most of each school day. The only change comes when a specialist handles the class for a period one or more times each week. These specialists may include the physical educator, music teacher, science teacher, art instructor, and an occasional resource person. In very small rural schools one teacher may instruct grades one through six—in the same classroom.

In some elementary schools all physical education is handled by the classroom teacher. In other situations a physical education teacher may meet with the elementary class weekly or biweekly and prepare a program for the classroom teacher to use during the intervening days. In other elementary schools the physical education specialist sees the children two or three times weekly.

Middle school

One pattern of organization being considered by many school systems is the middle school concept. Most simply stated, a middle school is for boys and girls between the elementary and high school years—grades six, seven, and eight, and sometimes five. New York City, for example, which has the nation's largest school system, eliminated junior high schools, replacing them with middle schools having a grouping by grades five to eight or six to eight. The secondary schools have become comprehensive high schools. Other places that have embarked on the middle school pattern are Bridgewater, Massachusetts; Bedford Public Schools in Mount Kisco, New York; Sarasota County, Florida; Saginaw, Michigan; Easton, Connecticut; and Independence, Ohio.

Some of the advantages of the middle school include the opportunity for more departmentalization, better stimulation of students, special teachers and special programs, and better student grouping.

Some of the disadvantages of the middle school include the lack of evidence to support its value, the social adjustment problems occurring when ninth graders are placed with twelfth graders, the possibility that youngsters in the middle school will be pushed too hard academically and socially, and the necessity of altering administrative techniques and procedures.

Secondary school

The junior high school is usually composed of grades seven, eight, and nine, and the senior high school is composed of grades ten, eleven, and twelve.

It is difficult to present a picture of a typical secondary school because of the variety in the size of the schools. They

Fig. 2-2. Elementary school program. (Madison Elementary School, Spokane, Wash.)

range from small rural schools with fewer than 100 pupils to large city schools that house student bodies numbering in the thousands. There are, however, certain *basic factors* that are true regardless of size or location:

1. Secondary education is usually coeducational.
2. Guidance is offered in most schools by specially trained personnel.
3. Extracurricular activities are an important part of the program.
4. Secondary schools are prepared to offer terminal education as well as college preparation.
5. Individual courses of study are prepared for the students.
6. Teachers are specialists in subject areas.

There are many *limiting factors to the small high school* that have brought about the present tendency toward centralization and consolidation. Some of them are listed below:

1. Meager curriculum offerings—inability to hire teachers for small groups of gifted children
2. Inadequate equipment—such as library, gymnasium, shops, laboratories, and so on—because of lack of funds for these expensive items
3. Inferior opportunities for social development—small number of children of comparable age and interests
4. Inferior staff—lower pay scale and living conditions as a result of lack of available funds

The *larger high schools* are generally able to offer a much more varied curriculum. Many educators have pointed to the necessity of challenging our gifted pupils and bringing along the slower ones. In the large high school the opportunity to meet these and other objectives is more readily available. Among recommendations for improving American secondary schools are the following:

1. More student involvement

Fig. 2-3. Physical education in the secondary school. (Mount Pleasant Senior High School, Wilmington, Del.)

Fig. 2-4. Physical education in the secondary school. (Mount Pleasant Senior High School, Wilmington, Del.)

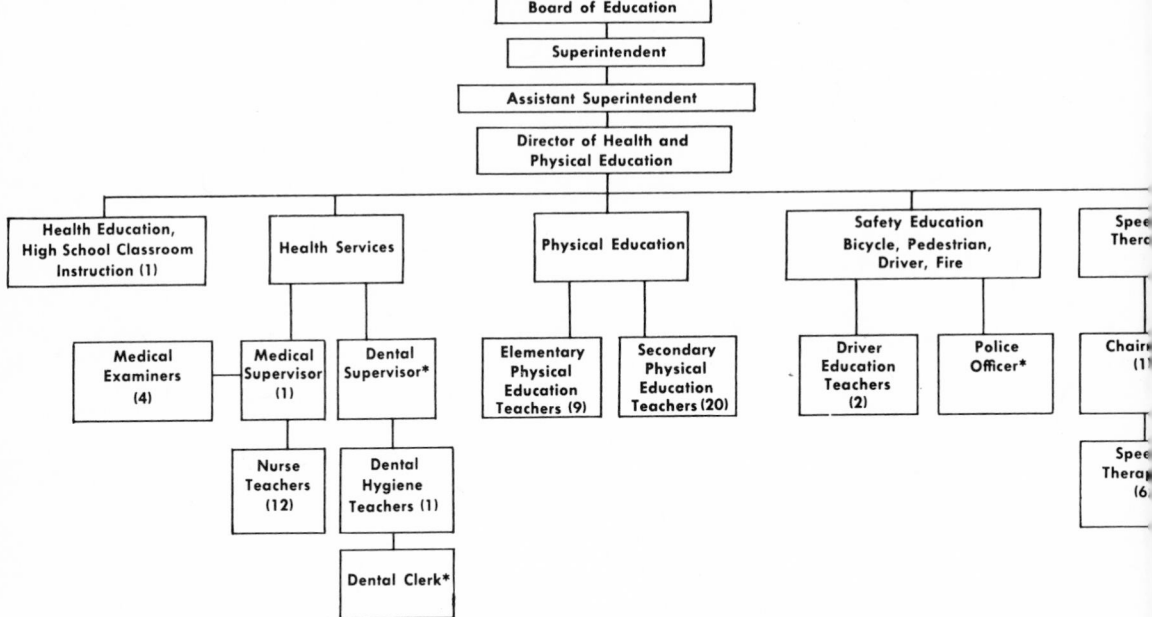

*Part time

Fig. 2-5. Administrative structure of a school district with a director of health and physical education.

2. Minischools
3. Use of paraprofessionals
4. Use of community resources
5. Teacher accountability
6. Flexible scheduling
7. Differentiated staffing
8. Individualization of programs
9. Self-paced instruction
10. Grouping according to ability

The opportunity to meet children's needs is greater in a larger school—one with a graduating class of at least 100 pupils. In a large school there are usually a sufficient number of gifted pupils to fill a special class. The more experienced and better teachers are attracted to the larger school by better salaries and working conditions. The curriculum is more varied because full-time teachers are hired to teach the slow readers and the languages, sciences, and other needed courses. Guidance personnel are also more readily available.

Specialists almost always handle the physical education program on the secondary level. In some junior high schools the arrangements are similar to the elementary

school procedure, but more and more schools are using physical educators to handle the entire program, as they do in senior high schools.

PERSONNEL

Responsibility for the operation of the local schools rests with the board of education. The board hires a professional educator to administer the school system. This practice is about 135 years old. It started when education grew to be more than could be handled by the existing town officials. Now, as then, administrators attempt to solve the ever-present problems of public education.

Superintendent

The chief school official hired to supervise a school system is the superintendent. In a small community he may double as the principal of a high school and may be referred to as the district supervising principal. In larger communities he has an office staff and possibly an assistant to handle his myriad responsibilities. In large cit-

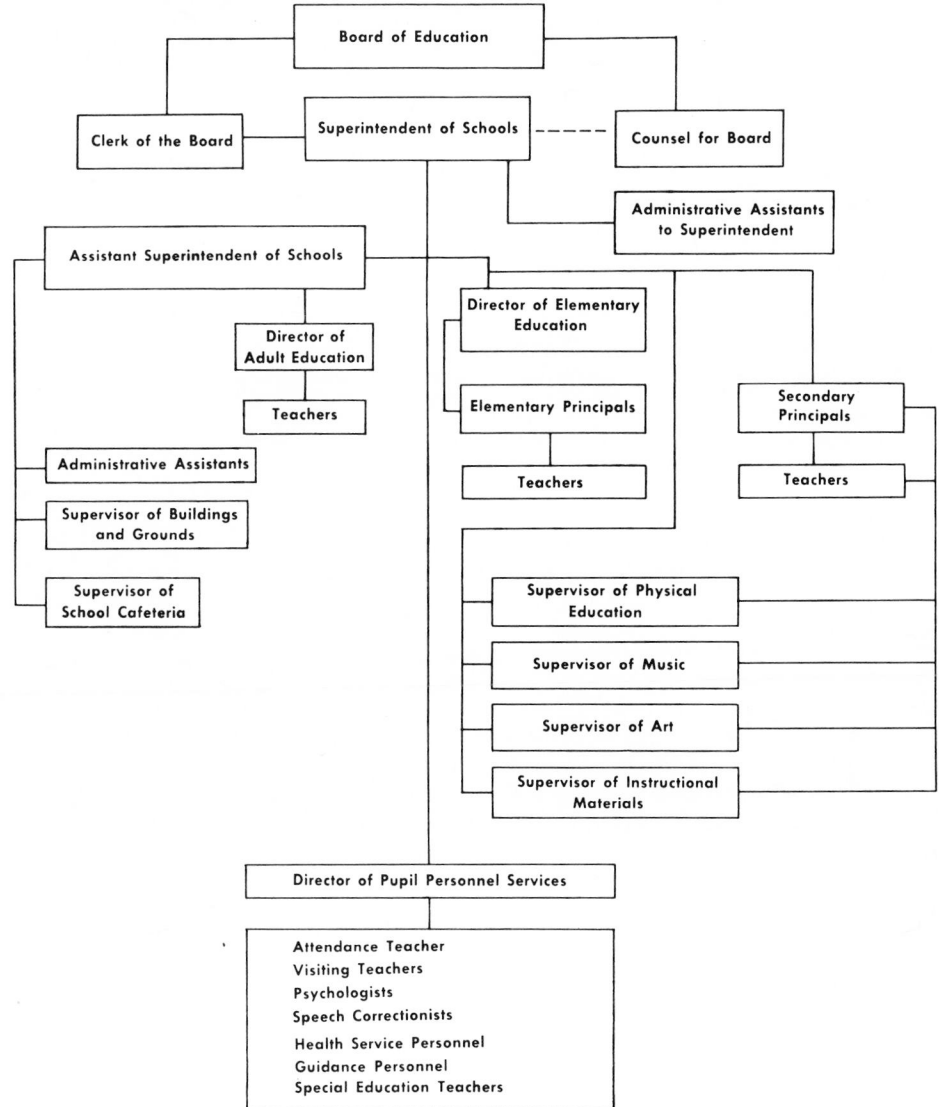

Fig. 2-6. Administrative structure of a school district with a supervisor of physical education.

ies or towns he has numerous assistants, deputies, or associates to assist in various duties (Fig. 2-1). Included in the superintendent's charge are these responsibilities:

1. School organization—establishes the school structure for the system
2. Curriculum development—establishes groups to conduct curriculum revisions in all areas
3. Personnel recommendations—recommends to the board those individuals needed to fill vacancies

4. Administration of all the school plants and facilities—supervises maintenance, construction, and repair of all plants and facilities
5. Budgetary recommendations—submits budget recommendations to the board of education
6. School-community relations—fosters good public relations through public appearances, meetings, and so forth
7. Advice—advises the board regarding policy changes, procedures, and prac-

tices, presenting educationally sound, workable suggestions

8. Publicity—keeps the board informed, giving reports on educational trends and notice of special school activities

To assist in these responsibilities and make recommendations to the superintendent there may be any or all of the following individuals as part of the administrative organization in the school system: assistants for secondary education and/or elementary education; business administrators; school health assistants; personnel assistants; public relations assistants; curriculum assistants; and directors of special areas such as art, music, library, industrial arts, physical education, and buildings and maintenance.

It takes dynamic, intelligent leadership to meet today's demands, increased as they are by student activism, greatly expanded programs, and new plants.

Principal

In each school within any system, the principal is the chief administrator. His duties vary, depending upon the size of the school. In a small building he may teach some classes in addition to his supervisory and administrative responsibilities. In larger schools he not only is relieved of his teaching duties but also has some administrative assistants. They may include an assistant principal, guidance personnel, department heads, deans of girls and/or boys, and a custodial head. (See Fig. 2-7.)

The principal's responsibilities are similar to the superintendent's. They consist of executing the educational policy as outlined by the superintendent, directing the instructional program, promoting harmony and a democratic feeling within the faculty, encouraging and directing good school-community relationships, and supervising the maintenance of the physical plant.

It is usually difficult for a principal to know all the pupils in a large high school, but as a rule the pupil-administrator relationship will be much better when the principal is able to know his pupils personally. Many administrators drop in at a rehearsal, team practice, or sports event not only to observe the teacher but also to let the students know that they are interested in their activities.

The principal also works closely with the parents. He plays an important role in the local parent-teacher association and in community affairs. He meets with parents to discuss student problems regarding college, grades, or discipline or acts as the intermediary to bring parents and teachers together to discuss these problems. The work is time consuming and tedious.

One of the responsibilities of a principal is to establish a democratic administration. This means that faculty members participate in the formulation of policies. Of course, it is the principal's decision to use or to discard any suggestions, but it is the successful and wise administrator who listens to faculty suggestions—whether in open meetings, through committees, or in personal conferences. Faculty committees are usually appointed by the principal to work with specific problems such as grading, graduation, discipline, and the honor society. The committees present their recommendations to the faculty and the principal, to be used in the formulation of school policies. A knowledge of the formation and the functioning of these committees can be invaluable to the new teacher. It is also important to know the function and frequency of staff meetings and the channels through which problems, questions, and innovating ideas may be presented. Knowing how to approach the supervisor can play an important part in the satisfactory adjustment of the beginning teacher.

Department heads

Depending upon the size of a school system, there may be heads of special subject matter areas. These heads assist the superintendent by coordinating the work of the teachers and programs in their special fields.

Similarly, in the larger high schools there

Fig. 2-7. Administrative structure of one secondary school.

are department heads to assist the principal in his duties. These people usually teach a number of classes, but their assignment also includes supervision, organization, and guidance. In smaller schools a department representative is often appointed by the principal to act as a liaison between the administration and the department when it is inconvenient to meet with the faculty as a whole.

In the field of physical education it is the usual practice in the larger school systems to have a director or supervisor who coordinates the work and supervises all the physical education teachers. In the smaller systems the superintendent or an assistant in charge of secondary or elementary education may supervise the physical education teachers.

Teachers

Teachers are hired by the board of education upon recommendation from the superintendent. A recommendation generally comes from a principal or department head.

In small schools a teacher may teach two different subjects, and possibly on two educational levels. This situation is not usually prevalent in larger schools. Physical education teachers on the secondary level usually teach physical education full time.

It is becoming more common to use specialists in health to handle all health instruction; however, in many systems the physical education teacher still doubles as the health teacher—and possibly as the driver education teacher, as well. Specific problems and details that the new physical education teacher must face are discussed in Chapter 11.

Custodians

Responsibility for the maintenance of the building rests with the principal. It is customary for a principal to delegate this responsibility to a head custodian. The importance of this aid to good teaching becomes very evident when the temperature is too high or seats are in disrepair and conditions are not satisfactory for effective learning. A means of communication from the teacher to the custodians is usually established so that these environmental factors can be quickly controlled and kept at optimum standards.

The school's custodians are often the physical educator's best friends and allies. Where they are treated with respect, the gymnasium and locker and shower rooms will be kept in spotless condition. Frequently, the custodians are also responsible for maintaining the playing fields and for marking lines. If the physical educator takes cognizance of these individuals, his work can be made much easier. Where good relationships exist, the custodians will go out of their way to help repair a piece of equipment, to build a special item, or to mow the field an extra time. Poor teacher-custodian relations can have disastrous effects on the entire physical education program.

Specialists

The size of a system usually determines how many specialists will be part of the professional staff and just what their duties will be.

Medical staff. A large system may have a full-time physician in charge of the nurses and part-time physicians who assist in the yearly examinations, follow-up of remediable defects, examination of athletic team participants, and the like. The medical staff in a smaller system may consist of a nurse who is assisted for a few hours weekly by a local physician.

Some schools authorize the nurse as the only person who can excuse a student from a physical education class for the day. She can assist the physical education department by observing and referring students who need advanced medical or dental treatment. She also has knowledge of those students in need of a modified program and can act as a liaison between the physical education department and the family physician. The school nurse is an invaluable resource person as a member of the physical education team.

Supervisory personnel. The range in this area will be from numerous assistants in the large system to a superintendent or supervising principal who is the primary supervisor in a small school.

Curriculum specialists. Responsibility for the curriculum may be placed in the hands of committees of classroom teachers, or it may be delegated to curriculum specialists.

Guidance specialists. Professional workers in guidance may include psychologists as well as other guidance personnel. Some students manifest various behavioral and/or emotional problems. The school guidance counselors have dossiers on each student and can guide the physical educator in the most effective way of handling a particular problem. The guidance people are usually backed up by school psychologists and social case workers, who may have, or who can obtain, further helpful information. The physical educator should seek the assistance of these people. A mishandled problem can create further problems, especially where a chronically disruptive pupil is concerned.

Because of their unique position in the school, the guidance counselors are often in a good position to observe and evaluate the physical education programs. They frequently hear the student's point of view in counseling interviews and can relate nonconfidential comments to the physical educator.

Business administrator. The details of business administration may be assigned either to an individual or to a staff responsible for the maintenance and repair of all plants, as well as the preparation and distribution of all supplies, texts, or equipment.

Cafeteria personnel. Supervision may be handled on an individual basis in each school, or it may be handled through a head dietitian responsible directly to the superintendent.

FACILITIES

An excellent educational program does not necessarily require an ideal plant, nor does an ideal plant guarantee a good program; however, they complement each other. School construction is a major problem in the United States. Since the physical education department is one of the most expensive items in the school, this problem is of particular interest to the physical educator. Multiple use of the physical education areas, such as the gymnasium, playing fields, and pool, undoubtedly engenders more support from the voting public for school construction. This implies the use of the facilities during evenings, weekends, holidays, and summers, in addition to school hours. Some communities that make extensive use of their school plants are Oakland, California; Spokane, Washington; and Norwich, Connecticut. Public reaction to educational expenditures is generally more favorable in such communities. This is undoubtedly true because many of the residents themselves are involved in the use of the school building, have a better understanding of where their money goes, and are therefore more inclined to support educational referendums.

Multiple use of facilities is not a panacea for education but has implications for the physical education teacher. Extensive use of facilities and proper interpretation to the public may help alleviate some of the problems relating to plant and facilities.

CURRICULA

Today's secondary schools vary greatly in the type of courses offered and in size and organization. If the trend toward centralization and consolidation of districts continues, it will help most schools to offer comprehensive programs and greatly raise the level of education.

There are three basic curricula offered on the secondary level. Some schools offer all three, which is a sound, comprehensive program. Others offer only one or two of these types.

General. The general curriculum is usually a terminal education program. It meets state requirements for graduation and covers the basic courses in English, history, science, mathematics, physical education, art, and music.

College preparatory. This program includes the same courses as above, at an advanced level, plus added units in any or all of the following subjects required for college entrance or used for advanced standing: foreign languages, sciences, mathematics, music, and art.

Vocational education. The vocational curriculum includes basic courses in English, history, practical mathematics, and physical education, as well as specialized courses in such vocational areas as bookkeeping, typing, welding, auto mechanics, food trades, and designing.

In most schools grades seven and eight follow the required courses; grade nine allows for some exploration; and the tenth, eleventh, and twelfth grades allow the student to follow his chosen course of study. This pattern is usually selected through the joint effort of the pupil, parents, and guidance personnel.

In some small schools the choice may be limited; therefore, a student may be forced into a pattern he would not select if given a choice. In some larger cities special schools meet the needs for special courses. In many cities there are schools that concentrate in a particular area, such as science, music and art, machine and metal trades, aviation, and food trades.

The type of course a student follows in high school has no bearing upon the amount of physical education required. It is generally accepted that this instruction is necessary for all students.

PHYSICAL EDUCATION IN THE SCHOOL

In order for beginning teachers to better meet their responsibilities, it is necessary to understand the place of the physical education department in the school and the responsibilities of the personnel in the department.

Structure

The positions of physical educators sometimes are more complicated than those of other teachers. As teachers, they will be under the direct supervision of the principal of the school. In many systems, however, there is a director or supervisor of physical education who represents the superintendent of school in his special area. One would expect this supervisor to have direct control over the members of his department. This is not usually the case. Although the director is responsible for the coordination of all physical education in the system, his or her role is primarily that of an advisor to the principal and superintendent. The relationship of physical edu-

cation instructors, their director, and the principal is a delicate one and should be understood by the new teacher so that he or she may avoid the obvious pitfalls. The beginning teacher should find out the chain of responsibilities in his system.

Personnel

In the field of physical education, the responsibilities of the personnel will depend upon the size of the system. In a small school one person may handle all the physical education duties from kindergar-

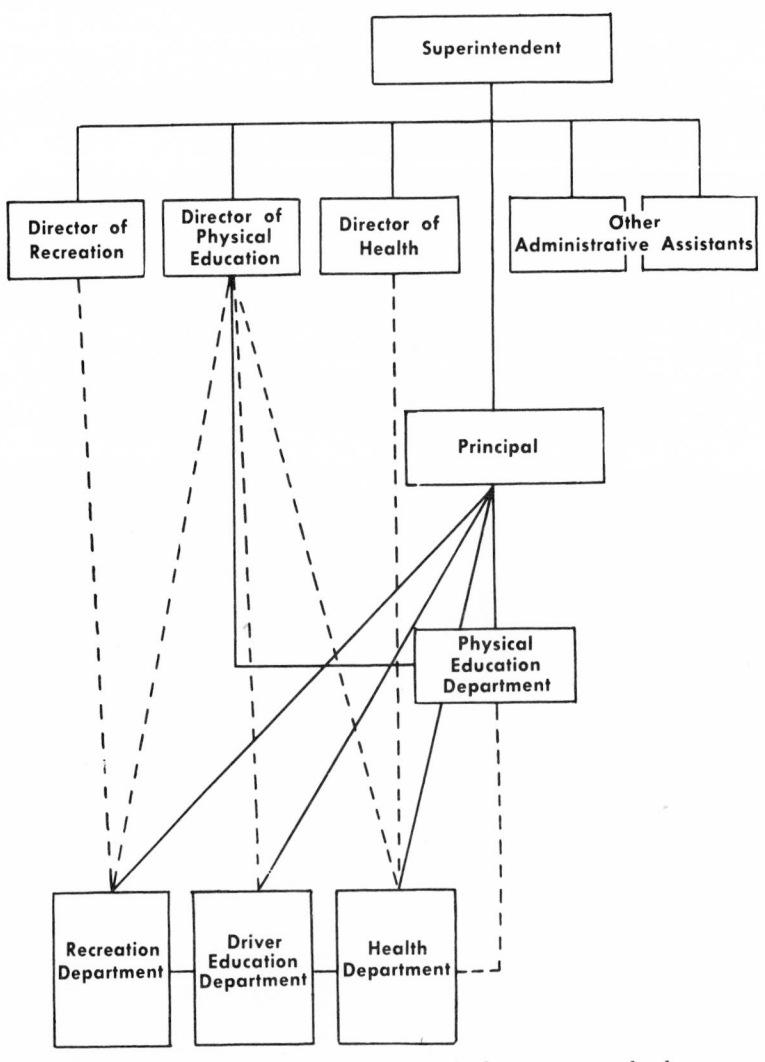

Fig. 2-8. Administrative structure of physical education in a school system.

ten through the twelfth grade. In other communities, the responsibilities may be divided by director, chairman, and teachers.

Director or supervisor. There is a trend that recognizes the necessity for one person to oversee and coordinate all physical education in a school system. In at least one state, a physical educator may become certified as a Director of Health, Physical Education, and Recreation. His responsibilities are to help establish policy; see that it is carried out; organize and administer girls' and boys' physical education programs at all levels; check facilities; coordinate programs; supervise teachers; help prepare the budget; organize all athletic programs, including scheduling—as well as arranging for officials, transportation, equipment, and insurance; and assume responsibility for all equipment and supplies. In some communities, these responsibilities are divided between the coach at the high school and an assistant or deputy superintendent.

The director's areas of responsibility include the following duties when he has been charged with administering the fields of physical education, health, and recreation.

General duties of the director

1. Implement standards established by the state department of education and the local board of education.

2. Interview possible candidates for positions in the special areas and make recommendations for these positions.

3. Work closely with the assistant superintendent in charge of business affairs, the assistant superintendent in charge of instruction, and subject matter and classroom teachers.

4. Coordinate areas of health, physical education, and recreation.

5. Supervise all inside and outside facilities and equipment and supplies concerned with special areas (this responsibility includes maintenance, safety, and replacement operations).

6. Maintain liaison with community groups—for example, hold educational meetings with doctors and dentists to interpret and improve the school health program, schedule school facilities for community groups, and serve on various community committees for youth needs.

7. Prepare periodic reports regarding areas of activity.

8. Coordinate school civil defense activities in some school systems.

9. Serve on the school health council.

Physical education duties of the director

1. Supervise total physical education program (class, adapted, intramurals, extramurals, and varsity interscholastic athletics).

2. Administer schedules, practice and game facilities, insurance, and equipment.

3. Maintain liaison with county, district, and state professional groups.

4. Upgrade program in general.

Health duties of the director

1. Supervise health services, including supervision of school nurse-teachers and dental hygiene teachers, coordination of the work of school physicians, preparation of guides and policies for the program of health services, organization of health projects, and obtaining of proper equipment and supplies.

2. Supervise health science instruction, including supervision of health education programs throughout the school system, preparation of curriculum guides and research studies, and upgrading of the program in general.

3. Promote healthful school living through general supervision of the school plant, attention to psychological aspects of the school program, and making of recommendations for improvement.

Recreation duties of the director

1. Supervise various aspects of recreation program, including, in addition to the school program, summer and vacation playgrounds, teen centers, and the like.

2. Obtain, where necessary, facilities, equipment, personnel, and supplies.

3. Plan and administer the recreation program.

Chairman. The chairman of a department is usually appointed by the principal or superintendent of schools. In some schools there is no formal department head; an individual is appointed by the principal to act as representative of the department. In most instances this person is the immediate supervisor of the physical education teachers. Part of his or her responsibilities may be to assist in the evaluation of a new teacher's performance. The person involved with this administration may teach a full program and receive extra compensation for duties rendered, may be relieved of some or all teaching responsibilities to allow time for administrative duties, or may merely be the department representative and have no supervisory responsibilities. He may be the athletic director, which means that he will arrange for and plan all interscholastic athletics. However, this may or may not be in addition to the responsibilities assigned to him as the department head.

Teachers. The teacher of physical education will handle the physical education classes, assist in curriculum evaluation, make suggestions for the improvement of the program, handle the intramural and interscholastic programs, and assume other obligations to the school that fall to the lot of every teacher.

In a small secondary school, the physical education program may be conducted by only one teacher for the girls and one for the boys. In such a situation, each teacher must assume total responsibility for all areas of the program, including teach-

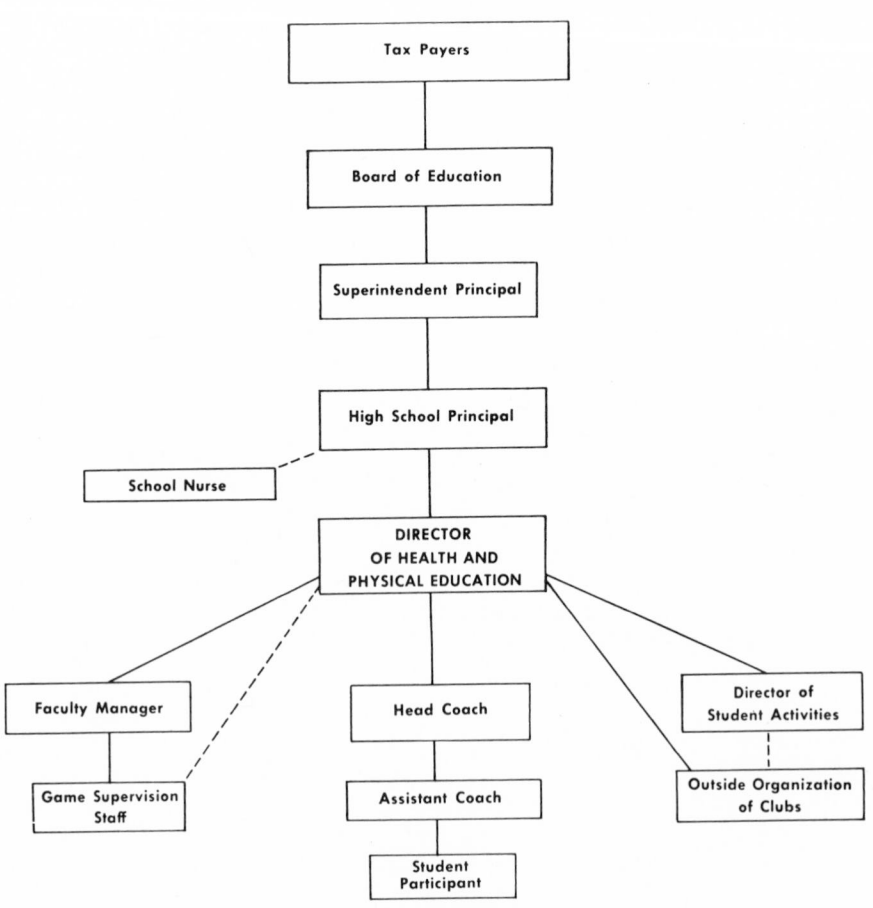

Fig. 2-9. Athletic organization chart in a secondary school.

ing, care of equipment, budget making, and directing intramural and extramural programs, as well as assuming any other responsibilities that may accure from being all things to all phases of the job.

In a large secondary school there are frequently several male and several female physical educators. One of these teachers may serve as department chairman and in turn be responsible to a supervisor of physical education who serves the entire school system. In this kind of hierarchy, each teacher is usually asked to assume the responsibility for a particular area, such as equipment maintenance or the ordering of library materials and audiovisual aids. This arrangement fragments the operation of the over-all program but frees each teacher to devote more time to teaching. Similarly, department chairmen and city supervisors can devote more time to serving as resource people and to general supervision of the program.

The new physical education teacher. Two of the main responsibilities confronting a new physical education teacher are to be accepted (1) as part of the total school and (2) as an important part of the physical education department.

1. Part of the total school picture. Some teachers look upon the physical education instructor with a certain amount of envy. Whose name is in the paper most often? To whom do almost all the children react favorably? Who is affectionately called "Coach"? Who is usually given the biggest hand when introduced in assembly? Who is most often called upon to assist the ad-

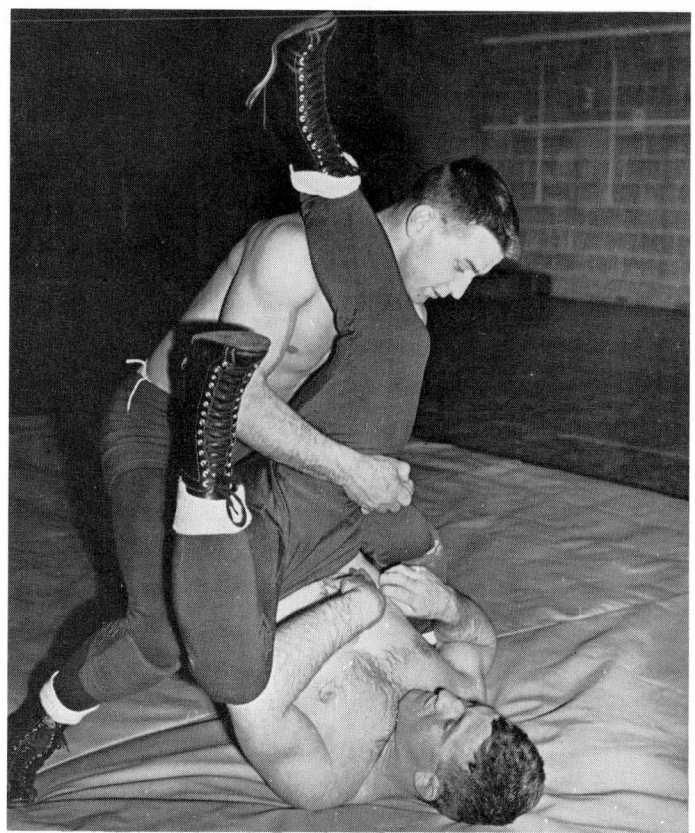

Phil H. Webber, Seattle

Fig. 2-10. Interscholastic athletics.

ministration? Many times it is the physical educator.

One way in which a physical educator may gain the respect of his colleagues is to do his share of the so-called boring, routine jobs that are so much a part of the school day. These may involve distribution of supplies, detention assignments, lunchroom duty, or graduation practice. It is well worth the effort to shoulder one's share of the day's responsibilities.

As a member of a school faculty, the physical educator should show an interest in school activities and projects of all kinds. There is always something to be done, such as helping with the annual concert, the dramatic presentation, or the magazine drive, as well as participating in parent-teacher association meetings, staff meetings, and even faculty social functions. The physical educator should know the teachers in his school so that they will have the opportunity to gain a new respect for and understanding of the physical education department. This could very well lead to a more honest evaluation of the physical education program and to new supporters for its rightful place in the school curriculum.

2. Member of the physical education department. As is true for any new faculty member, it is necessary for the physical educator to prove to his peers his capability, flexibility, and sincerity. To do this he must do his job as best he can and respect the experience and seniority of his colleagues. He should not be afraid to speak his mind but should remember that his colleagues have experienced what he has only studied. He should consider the whole picture, observe carefully and thoroughly, and have positive, realistic suggestions when discussing any facet of the program that he believes could stand improvement.

Interscholastic athletics

The interscholastic athletic part of the physical education program may involve controversy. It is unfortunately true that there are some coaches who go to extremes

in the handling of their teams. These men drive their teams unmercifully, attempt to pressure teachers to keep boys eligible, believe they have to win at any cost, and devote too much of their time and energy to their teams—to the detriment of their physical education classes. These people do not help to advance the cause of physical education.

It is important to have an interscholastic sports program in its proper place in the total program. It has great value in that it challenges the athletically gifted child, kindles and keeps aflame the spirit of a student body, and unites the members of a school and gives them a proud feeling of belonging, in addition to having many other worthwhile aspects. It is, however, only one part of a physical education program.

Interpreting physical education*

Too often the physical educator or coach is considered apart from the educational staff. The faculty is educating the child—the physical educator is exercising him.

The challenge of this attitude must be met by the physical educator. He must have a sound philosophy of education and an understanding of the place of physical education in the development and growth of the child. He must be exemplary in the performance of his duties. He should not be afraid to speak his mind at faculty gatherings; in fact, other faculty members should show that they are aware of and interested in the total education of the child. This interpreting of physical education must be directed not only to faculty members but to the community as a whole.

The physical educator has many means of interpreting the program at his disposal. Speaking at meetings of the Parent-Teacher Association, Rotary, Elks, Masons, Kiwanis, and other clubs is an accepted and effective method of presentation. Physical edu-

---

*See Chapter 9.

cation demonstrations, sports nights, and athletic contests can also afford good publicity.

The best selling point, however, is the student in the physical education class. If pupils understand why they spend hours on the playground or in the gymnasium, their reactions and comments at home are the best means of interpreting the program to parents. In order to accomplish this, however, students must receive more than a chance to play ball. There must be an understanding of the accumulated values of a well-rounded program. Students, then, can be the physical educator's best salesmen. If they are educated well, the opportunity to do an even better job will generally be forthcoming because of increased school and community support.

KEYS TO SUCCESS IN PHYSICAL EDUCATION

Indicated below are some characteristics of a secondary school that are essential for a sound education and physical education program.

Administrative philosophy and policies

The administrator of a secondary school may or may not view the physical education program with favor. His feeling of the worth of physical education in his school often has a very direct influence on the program. Where the administration values physical education, it will be easier to have homogeneous classes, and physical education will not be the last class to be scheduled. Where the administration is cooperative, the physical education program will be put on a par with academic courses. The administration often sets the policies in regard to uniforms, excuses, and the grading system. The teacher must abide by these policies. The administration also assigns extra duties to teachers. Where physical education is given its rightful place in the curriculum, the physical education teacher has a minimum of extra duties during the school day. Lack of homeroom duties means time to ready the equipment for the day. Lack of study halls and lunch duty frees the physical education teacher for teaching, and lack of afternoon bus duty allows time for the conduct of a good intramural program. In any case, the physical education program must be conducted within the existing administrative framework.

Use of the democratic process. The principal should use the democratic process in his relations with his staff as well as with the students and allow. them a voice in running the school.

Faculty relationships. The teachers should work together not only to coordinate subject matter but also to support and coordinate those special events that are so much a part of school life. The efforts of all teachers should be harmonized to culminate successfully in a music festival, school dance, general organization membership drive, athletic event, or other school-sponsored project.

The physical educator must strive to maintain cooperative relationships with the rest of the faculty. Social conversation with other faculty members allows for an interchange of ideas. Understandings are developed and concepts formed about other areas of the curriculum. It is also here that the physical educator can articulate the relationship of his program to the rest of the school. The physical educator should always maintain his professional ethics and refuse to discuss confidential information about students or to participate in a discussion that is concerned with gossip about students, other teachers, or the administration.

Teacher-parent relationships. When teacher-parent relationships are good, parents believe that they can approach their child's teacher to discuss any problem, and the teacher believes that he or she can call on parents for assistance when necessary. The relationship is one of mutual respect, providing the basis for a frank discussion between parent and teacher of problems and possible solutions.

Some secondary schools welcome par-

CHECKLIST OF SELECTED ITEMS FOR EVALUATING THE PHYSICAL EDUCATION PROGRAM'S RELEVANCY TO A MODERN SECONDARY SCHOOL

Educational philosophy

1. Educational philosophy of the school encourages innovation. YES ☐ NO ☐
2. Close school-community relationships are encouraged. YES ☐ NO ☐
3. Educational program is relevant to the times. YES ☐ NO ☐
4. Faculty and students are actively involved in the total educational program. YES ☐ NO ☐
5. Education is individualized for each student, including culturally disadvantaged, physically handicapped, mentally retarded, and so on. YES ☐ NO ☐
6. Worth of physical education program is recognized. YES ☐ NO ☐
7. Clear written statement of educational philosophy exists, with educational objectives enumerated. YES ☐ NO ☐

Administration

1. Administration represents a means to an end (an excellent educational program) rather than an end in itself. YES ☐ NO ☐
2. Administrative structure enhances and facilitates the implementation of the educational program. YES ☐ NO ☐
3. The school, including physical education, has a meaningful and accurate system of record keeping. YES ☐ NO ☐
4. School records are accurate and up to date. YES ☐ NO ☐
5. School is open to the community. YES ☐ NO ☐
6. Faculty and students play an important part in decision making and policy formation. YES ☐ NO ☐
7. School utilizes community resources. YES ☐ NO ☐
8. Adequate facilities, supplies, and equipment exist. YES ☐ NO ☐
9. Sufficient teaching stations exist to carry on a meaningful physical education program. YES ☐ NO ☐
10. Scheduling is done in an effective manner, including the utilization of flexible scheduling. YES ☐ NO ☐
11. Meetings are held regularly with the faculty to share new ideas and methods and discuss common problems. YES ☐ NO ☐
12. Students have representation at important administrative and faculty meetings. YES ☐ NO ☐
13. School facilities are utilized on a twelve-month basis. YES ☐ NO ☐
14. Facilities are designed to meet program needs, permit effective instruction, and ensure pupil safety. YES ☐ NO ☐
15. Community is kept informed concerning educational objectives. YES ☐ NO ☐
16. Equipment and supplies are checked periodically to ensure that adequate amounts are available and in good condition. YES ☐ NO ☐
17. Administration is democratic. YES ☐ NO ☐
18. School building is utilized to its maximum potential. YES ☐ NO ☐
19. Administration is receptive to innovative teaching techniques. YES ☐ NO ☐
20. Office practice is efficient and represents a valuable service in carrying out educational objectives. YES ☐ NO ☐
21. Administration understands the needs of physical education and its contribution to the achievement of educational goals. YES ☐ NO ☐
22. Channels of communication are readily available to faculty and students. YES ☐ NO ☐

Students

1. Students participate in curriculum planning. YES ☐ NO ☐
2. Students have the opportunity to evaluate the physical education program. YES ☐ NO ☐
3. Students are assigned to physical education classes on the basis of their physical development, needs, and achievement. YES ☐ NO ☐
4. Students find school and physical education a pleasurable and worthwhile experience. YES ☐ NO ☐
5. Students participate in a program that meets their individual needs. YES ☐ NO ☐
6. Students are properly grouped for activities according to ability and other relevant factors. YES ☐ NO ☐

7. Students have good rapport with teachers.   YES ☐   NO ☐
8. Students have opportunity to develop leadership potential.   YES ☐   NO ☐
9. Students are permitted to pursue individual dress and hair styles providing they do not interfere with the rights of other students or their own health, safety, and performance in school activities.   YES ☐   NO ☐

Teachers

1. Teaching assignments are made with regard to teacher's interests, strengths, and experience.   YES ☐   NO ☐
2. Opportunities are available to experiment with new teaching methods and materials.   YES ☐   NO ☐
3. Beginning teacher is provided with proper orientation to school and role to be played.   YES ☐   NO ☐
4. Evaluations of teachers are objective, with a view to improving teaching ability and service to students.   YES ☐   NO ☐
5. Accountability is required for outstanding teaching and service to students.   YES ☐   NO ☐
6. Salaries are given according to the role teachers play in the educational process.   YES ☐   NO ☐
7. Faculty meetings are attended regularly.   YES ☐   NO ☐
8. Leadership is provided for the community in teacher's specialty.   YES ☐   NO ☐
9. Excellent relationships exist with students.   YES ☐   NO ☐
10. Student leaders and paraprofessionals are utilized in order to develop leadership qualities of boys and girls and to devote more time to teaching.   YES ☐   NO ☐
11. Creativity is regarded as an important quality.   YES ☐   NO ☐
12. New developments in special field are well known, understood, and applied.   YES ☐   NO ☐
13. Harmonious working relationships exist with other members of the faculty.   YES ☐   NO ☐
14. Professional activity is recognized as being important.   YES ☐   NO ☐

Physical education program

1. Innovative ideas are utilized.   YES ☐   NO ☐
2. Students participate in the development and evaluation of the program.   YES ☐   NO ☐
3. Classes are of sufficient length to permit meaningful participation in scheduled activities.   YES ☐   NO ☐
4. Intramural program provides for maximum participation of all students.   YES ☐   NO ☐
5. Transportation is provided for athletic events.   YES ☐   NO ☐
6. Close working relationship exists between the physical education and health programs including school physician and health services.   YES ☐   NO ☐
7. Provision is made for individual differences.   YES ☐   NO ☐
8. Progression is a characteristic of the program, with a smooth transition from elementary to junior high school and from junior high school to senior high school.   YES ☐   NO ☐
9. Physical education is an integral part of the total educational offering.   YES ☐   NO ☐
10. Program evaluation is done periodically with necessary changes being made.   YES ☐   NO ☐
11. Program is relevant to the times, the student, and the role of education in modern society.   YES ☐   NO ☐

ents on visiting nights, host them at concerts and plays, and have strong parent-teacher associations. Other schools only see the parents when an urgent disciplinary matter is involved.

To know the parents helps the teacher to understand the child. By joining the parent-teacher association and attending its meetings and socials, the teacher is able to meet the parents in a relaxed and informal atmosphere. It is here that the teacher can explain his program and answer any questions the parents may have. The physical education program in a secondary school thrives on good public relations, and this starts with the parents of the community.

Teacher-pupil   relationships.   When teacher-pupil relationships are good, mutual respect exists between pupils and teachers. The teacher is aware of the need and the methods for earning this respect from his or her pupils and, therefore, is the one to foster this feeling. He or she is able to establish rapport with pupils, which greatly contributes to the success of his or her program.

Besides teaching his students, the physical educator must know and guide them and try to inspire them. In some schools, student respect for teachers is totally lacking, and good discipline is difficult at best to maintain. Safety alone requires that physical education classes be well disciplined. A new teacher must be especially cognizant of the fact that students will test him. They want to know how he will react to disrespect, horseplay in class, and bad conduct in general. Where the school administration has set strong behavior policies, the teacher will receive backing in maintaining these standards. Where behavior policies are weak, the teacher must set his own high standards and be consistent in applying them.

A martinet never develops close rapport with his students. The good disciplinarian who respects and knows his students as individuals will be able to develop good rapport. Discipline must be tempered with understanding and respect for the student.

Good teacher-student relationships also develop in, and are carried over to, areas outside the classroom. The teacher who attends football games and concerts and helps to chaperone dances and social affairs has the opportunity to develop a working and companionable relationship with his students. Students will respond in kind to respect, understanding, and interest.

POINTS TO REMEMBER

1. The structure of a school district
2. The personnel involved in education
3. The types and characteristics of secondary schools
4. The place of the physical education department in the total school picture
5. The new physical education teacher as a member of the department and the school

6. The problems inherent in a poorly conceived philosophy of interscholastic sports
7. The means of interpreting physical education to fellow teachers
8. The means of interpreting physical education to the public

PROBLEMS TO THINK THROUGH

1. What are the values of having a department chairman? How large should a department be to have a chairman?
2. What are some of the considerations that face a new teacher?
3. How may a coach avoid alienating members of the school faculty?
4. What are the advantages of a secondary school that has a graduating class of 100 pupils?
5. What value would a director or supervisor of physical education be to a school system?

CASE STUDY FOR ANALYSIS

Every teacher is responsible to his or her principal. Many physical education teachers are also supervised by a department chairman and/or a director or supervisor of physical education who represents the superintendent of schools. Analyze the chain of responsibility of all physical education teachers in a school system containing one senior high school, one junior high school, and four elementary schools. Consider possible friction points between the supervisory personnel. How can physical education teachers avoid difficulty in their relationships with their supervisors?

EXERCISES FOR REVIEW

1. What are the responsibilities of the superintendent of schools regarding physical education?
2. How may the physical education teacher best interpret his program to the general public?
3. To whom may the new physical education teacher turn for help and guidance? Indicate the specific areas needing assistance and the individuals who may be of greatest value.
4. Prepare a speech that you could use to interpret physical education to a parent-teacher association, men's club, or sports night dinner.

SELECTED READINGS

Blount, Nathan S., and Klausmeir, Herbert J.: Teaching in the secondary school, ed. 3, New York, 1968, Harper & Row, Publishers.

Bucher, Charles A.: Administration of health and physical education programs, including athletics, ed. 5, St. Louis, 1971, The C. V. Mosby Co.

Bucher, Charles A.: Foundations of physical education, ed. 6, St. Louis, 1972, The C. V. Mosby Co.

Calam, John, and Patenaude, John, The school

ain't what they used to be—and probably never were, Saturday Review, April 29, 1972, p. 52.

Callahan, Sterling G.: Successful teaching in secondary schools, Glenview, Ill., 1966, Scott, Foresman & Co.

Colo, Rosa Lee, and others: The beginning teacher, Today's Education 60:54, 1971.

Conant, James B.: The American high school today, New York, 1959, McGraw-Hill Book Co., Inc.

Hecht, George J.: What must be done to meet the needs of all American children, Parents 47:10, 1972.

Husen, Torsten: Does more time in school make a difference? Saturday Review, April 29, 1972, p. 32.

Oliva, Peter F.: The secondary school today, New York, 1967, World Publishing Co.

Resnik, Henry S.: The open classroom, Today's Education 60:16, 1971.

Van Til, William: Education: a beginning, Boston, 1971, Houghton Mifflin Co.

3 THE NEW BREED OF STUDENT IN TODAY'S SECONDARY SCHOOL

The number of pupils in public secondary schools is nearly nineteen million, or approximately 38% of the total figure for public school enrollment. The number of students graduating from public high schools each year is nearly three million. These students represent a new breed in our culture, with different values and personal philosophies of life than the students of ten or twenty years ago. Therefore, if a physical education program relevant to today's students is to be provided, it is imperative to know what today's students are like.

During the past fifteen years there have been at least four major changes in the world that have had a direct or indirect effect upon the high school student. The first change has been the growing power of the Soviet Union, particularly its achievements in space, with the growing concern in the United States that our school's technical and scientific offering must be improved. Second, the civil rights movement and the protests against discrimination have affected students by producing changes in the school curriculum as well as in the attitude of educators regarding their responsibilities in solving this problem. The third major change is that young people have grown to maturity with a keen awareness of social and political problems that prevail and the need to do something about them. Mass media have played a ma-

jor role in providing this generation with a social and political sophistication that previous generations did not have. The fourth change has occurred as a result of the Vietnam war, with young people taking a militant stand against further confrontations.

These four changes have had a marked effect upon today's secondary school student. Boys and girls are less concerned about material security and more concerned with basic human values. They resent the differences between what adults say and what they do. They want to participate more in deciding their own future. They are articulate and inclined to express themselves regarding how they feel about the major issues of the day.

Specifically, here are some characteristics of today's students.

• *Today's secondary school students want to be involved.* Boys and girls want a say in respect to the decisions that affect them. They want to participate in the curriculum they will follow, the rules and regulations that control their actions, and the matters that will affect their future. They want to have a voice in policy decisions, be on school committees, and evaluate courses and teachers.

• *Today's secondary school students are not inhibited.* They voice what they believe, which often is different from what adults believe. They want to know why they have to do certain things and why certain procedures and practices are followed.

• *Today's secondary school students have a new image of themselves.* Students recognize that they are human beings who have rights in this society and a say in what happens to them, what happens to their families, and what happens to their country. They are no longer content to let adults and others make decisions for them. They utilize their economic, political, and social power. They stress the individual and his value in society and the need for each person to have equal opportunities.

• *Today's secondary school students are antiestablishment.* They are skeptical of adults, of the school administration, of government, and of older people in general. They have seen the materialism, discrimination, pollution of the environment, war mongering, and other evils associated with past generations and want to bring about a change.

• *Today's secondary school students have different goals than do adults.* Students have different goals from adults, particularly in respect to such things as money, security, challenge, and position. According to a recent survey young people indicated that their three greatest sources of satisfaction listed in priority order are family, leisure, and occupation.

• *Today's secondary school students are educationally oriented in different ways.* Instead of memorization of dates, they want to know the reasons for the movements and events behind the dates, instead of merely knowing about historical events, to understand the underlying forces that resulted in these significant events.

• *Today's secondary school students are not part of the crowd.* Each student wants to be considered for his or her own self and talents. Girls, for example, want to have the same rights as boys. Students do not want to be treated in an impersonal manner and exposed to an impersonal curriculum. They do not want to be required to perform the same school tasks that other students, whose abilities, needs, and interests may be different than their own, are required to perform. Students feel they must be dealt with as they are and not as they are expected to be.

To illustrate what the secondary school student wants is shown by the demands of students as listed in a 1971 study conducted by a student task force in North Carolina. The survey covered students from representative high schools in the state. Their major demands included the following:

Administrators should maintain a constant dialogue with students.

Legitimate requests of students should be dealt with promptly and fairly.

Student dissent should be sanctioned if it is legitimate and does not disrupt the educational process.

Fig. 3-1. The new breed of student. (Ellensburg Public Schools, Ellensburg, Wash.)

Seminar sessions should be held regularly with students for discussion of current school problems.

Students should be permitted to form committees with powers to investigate and propose solutions to problems of unrest.

Students should be urged to respect the school as their institution of learning.

The local high school should be given responsibility for all rules and regulations.

Clear communication lines should be established between administration, faculty, and students.

Student government should be given as much responsibility as possible.

The principal should write a column in school newspaper as an avenue of communication.

As a result of these demands new and innovative methods and educational programs in North Carolina were established, students were given a voice in planning their own course of study, and they were appointed to committees and given a chance to revamp the grading system.

ANATOMY OF YOUNG PEOPLE'S CONCERNS

A survey of 200 college-bound young people upon graduating from high school revealed these feelings and facts about their educational and vocational plans and expectations; activities, achievements, and perceptions during secondary school; family background; and personal attitudes.

Educational and vocational plans and expectations
Choice of major field was influenced most by teachers, counselors, principals, and deans.
Most of the students surveyed plan to do graduate work.
When asked to give the one most important requirement of any job or profession they would consider entering, a large segment of the group, about one third, indicated they wanted an opportunity to be helpful to others and/or useful to society. Also, many indicated they would rather work with people than with things.
About one third of the sample would not be interested in participating in athletics in college.

Activities, achievements, and perceptions during secondary school
Most of the students attended public, coeducational high schools.
Art was the subject most enjoyed in high school.
Nearly one half of the students expressed some dissatisfaction with their high school studies.
Most of the students were not involved in extracurricular activities.
The most popular leisure-time activities included listening to popular music, attending movies, and reading.
Approximately one half of the students worked during their senior year.

Family background
Most parents of students are living together.
Parents' occupations listed according to frequency included: owner, manager, or partner of a small business; skilled worker or craftsman; salesman, bookkeeper, secretary; one of the professions; semiskilled worker; high level executive; service worker; unskilled worker, laborer, farm worker.
Parents' income listed according to frequency ranged from approximately $30,000 (about 5%) to less than $4,000 (about 6%). Most parents' income fell in the $8,000 to $20,000 range.

Student perceptions of parental attitudes
Parents place a high value on education.
Father is the authority in the home.
Interdependence and mutuality of family are stressed.

Personal attitudes
Although nonreligious, most students attend religious services on important holidays and profess religious faith.
About one half of the students would be disturbed about cheating but would not do anything about it.
Students favor a more liberalized curriculum.
Most students feel somewhat or quite dependent upon their parents.
About one third of the students feel women should be free to choose their own life style.
About one half of the students reported having a personal library of thirty-one or more books.
More than one half of the students felt that conscientious objectors should be excused from military service in wartime.
A majority of the students opposed capital punishment.
Most students have a strong positive regard for human life and express an antiwar sentiment.
More than one third of the students were concerned about the extent of poverty in the United States, and more than this about the lack of opportunities for nonwhites.
About one half of the students felt greatly disturbed about a growing preoccupation with material possessions and a lessening concern about human values.
Most students indicated their political views were either liberal or very liberal.

Most students agreed that the government should work for adequate medical care for all, yet at the same time felt that a welfare state tends to destroy individuality.

A survey of student and teacher attitudes in fifteen New York State high schools was conducted by the Human Affairs Research Center in Ann Arbor, Michigan. Approximately 2,500 students and 750 teachers were surveyed. About 11% of the students listed themselves as black and approximately 7% as Puerto Rican, but another 11% did not answer that question. About 3% of the teachers said they were black. The survey showed that schools fell into three categories: those that seemed responsive to students' needs, those that didn't, and those in between. One conclusion drawn from the the survey was that the more responsive the school, the better the teacher-student relationship as perceived by both students and teachers, and the better the overall morale. Some findings from the survey:

Students on the whole were negative about their teachers and felt great "underlying tension" toward teachers. This was especially true of black students, who felt better about the teachers in more responsive schools but even then had more negative attitudes toward them than did white students in the less responsive schools.

Students felt that rules were too strict and arbitrarily enforced, with black and Puerto Rican students seeing overt racism in the enforcement. Students recommended that there should be less discipline and more personal freedom.

Students viewed administrators as enormously powerful and neither accessible nor friendly.

Minority students felt left out of formal and informal student activities and relationships, but white students didn't see them as being left out.

White teachers and white students alike perceived no overt racism.

Many students found their school experience painful and unenjoyable, and minority students additionally felt a pattern of discrimination that denied them educational opportunity.

Teachers as a group have much the same attitude toward school, with no difference in values, perceptions of student-teacher relationships, and suggested directions for change.

In contrast to students, teachers see their students as friendly and are unaware of the youngsters' negative feelings.

Survey indicated that as a group, students feel powerless, although black and Puerto Rican students tended to feel powerful individually. Teachers were seen by students as powerful as a group, and principals most powerful.

Teachers felt their own group influential but felt powerless and isolated as individuals, viewing fellow teachers as unfriendly and unable to accept criticism.

Most students seemed to like the idea of a "student-controlled school" and favored more rather than less discipline.

Both students and teachers overwhelmingly preferred another type of hypothetical school where there was a great effort to involve students and teach courses that students thought were relevant. Minority students had some doubts, however, because they felt a mostly white middle class experimental school would not give them the skills they saw as necessary.

Teachers liked the idea of a "community involvement" school in which parents played a major role; apparently the teachers would welcome classroom assistants from the community. Black students liked it better than white, presumably reflecting community control sentiments that existed among their parents.

Another type of hypothetical school, the "job-related" school, emphasized work programs and outside jobs. Blacks and Puerto Ricans rejected this as not preparing them for the future, reflecting their misgivings about the purpose of schools.

The report concluded that any effort to make major changes in the organization of schools must be portrayed as a joint venture between teachers and students, perhaps cutting into the power of school boards and administrators.

The report proposes "minischools" of 150 to 200 students—perhaps to be established within an existing school building—in which there would be much closer teacher-student contact and students would participate much more in school and after-school activities.

The report recommended that students should help design the learning program; the teachers should run it.

The report recommended that students and teachers should be in on every policy decision, including curriculum, hiring and firing, budgets, and so on. Furthermore, the often submerged conflicts between the interests of teachers and students should be brought out in the open and aired.*

IMPLICATIONS OF SOCIETAL CHANGES FOR TEACHING IN SECONDARY SCHOOLS

Teachers in today's secondary schools face student populations quite different

---

*See checklist at end of chapter for implications for physical education of the new breed of student in the secondary school.

from those found many years ago. Both teen-agers and their environments have undergone extensive changes that need to be understood because of their implications for teaching.

National attention is being focused on this adolescent struggle for existence, and it is this increased interest in the teen-ager that has brought about further changes in his environment, other than the population increase. For example, the Children's Bureau in Washington, D.C., has studied teen-age living in both rural and urban communities and found that many changes have taken place. In New York, a research institute studied adolescents in terms of their buying power, for teen-agers have become a lucrative economic market and their trade is avidly sought by manufacturers. Teen-agers respond by lavishly spending their considerable allowances on cosmetics, clothing, and jewelry. They are spending more than thirty billion dollars per year at the present time. Students in several communities have evaluated their own secondary school curricula and suggested changes.

From these few examples it may be seen that today's student is being studied while he studies and is being influenced while he himself tries to exert influence. The student has achieved a unique importance in the structure of education, and it is this individual that the teacher must try to understand. The forces and pressures being exerted upon the adolescent while he is undergoing an important phase of personal growth and development all combine to make this a very difficult period of adjustment. The teacher must try to assist the student in every way possible.

What should a teacher expect to find in a secondary school population?

In a school of 500 students a teacher should be prepared to find 500 different

Fig. 3-2. The junior high school student. (Guymon Junior High School, Guymon, Okla.)

individuals, each one advancing through various stages of the adolescent process, and each one at a different level of development. While over 50% of the students may be college-bound, others require education to fit them immediately for life.

Secondary-school students will have a variety of cultural backgrounds and bring with them a vast assortment of needs, fears, hopes, abilities, and problems. Those individuals who require special attention—the mentally retarded, the culturally disadvantaged, and the physically handicapped—must be identified in order that programs may be tailored to meet their needs. At the present time the federal government is spending increased sums of money on special education programs for these individuals. Yet less than one half of the five million handicapped persons are receiving the special programs they require. Many of these students are still enrolled in public secondary schools. Physical educators have a very real responsibility for providing these students with an opportunity to develop their physical capacities equal to the opportunity provided for regular students. This may be done through the adapted program of physical education or through assignments within the regular class program. The individualization of teaching can best accomplish the goals.*

What is the role of the school?

The school must identify and recognize the individual nature of each student. It must strive to help all secondary school students to find themselves, for this is the central problem of adolescence. The development of self-esteem and the identification of the self are vital concerns of every teen-ager. Too often schools provide threats (through class distinctions and values and unrealistic standards of behavior) rather than reassurances to students. Too often schools demand conformity rather

than independence of thought and action. If the purpose of the school is to develop future worthy citizens, it must start by helping them to feel worthy and competent within themselves.

The physical education program provides excellent opportunities for the development of these needed competencies. The feeling of importance derived from team, group, or squad membership, the feeling of freedom of expression in movement, and the pride in accomplishment when points are scored for a team are all competencies that are natural outcomes of physical education activities. More important, however, is the recognition of the self as defined by a body concept developed through participation in a well-balanced program. Research indicates a close relationship between a body concept and a self-concept in terms of the confidence needed to face life. The individual who feels satisfied with his body in terms of its ability to move, to express, to attract, to feel, and to react is more apt to feel satisfied with his total adjustment to life. On the other hand, the unhappy student is frequently one who is dissatisfied with his own body image. Physical educators have a vital responsibility for the development of healthy attitudes toward the body and should therefore provide the necessary experiences through well-planned and well-executed programs.

Understanding the complex changes of adolescence is a large task, both for students and for teachers. The implications for teaching are many because of the relationship between the student's development and his achievements in education. It will be the purpose of the remainder of this chapter to describe the physical, social emotional, and intellectual changes that take place in the adolescent and also to indicate the specific implications for teaching physical education that these changes produce.

PHYSICAL DEVELOPMENT

The secondary school student passes through four stages of development gener-

---

*Chapter 15 discusses the different types of atypical students and the contribution that physical education can make to each.

Table 3-1. Stages of development[*]

	Girls	Boys
Preadolescence or childhood	11-13	13-15
Early adolescence	13-15	15-17
Middle adolescence	15-18	17-19
Late adolescence	18-21	19-21

[*]From Cole, Luella: Psychology of adolescence, New York, 1954, Rinehart & Co., Inc., p. 4.

ally labeled preadolescence, early adolescence, middle adolescence, and late adolescence. It should be understood that each individual develops according to his own growth pattern, but, in general, the stages may be identified at certain age levels.

The classification of adolescent development offered in Table 3-1 is a guide to the use of these terms throughout the discussions in this chapter of physical, emotional, social, and intellectual development.

Because of the complexity of adolescent physical development and the differentiation between boys and girls, it is necessary to consider each phase of their growth separately. Height and weight, skeletal changes, and primary and secondary sex changes will be discussed, with the differences in boys and girls explained at each level of development. The implications for physical education will also be included in the discussion.

Height and weight

Probably the most obvious physical changes during adolescence occur in height and weight. These changes can be accounted for by increased hormone production, which in turn causes the sudden growth spurt of the preadolescent and early adolescent period.

Girls eleven to thirteen years old become taller than boys of the same ages but then show slower increases in height until late adolescence. A rapid increase in weight also takes place at this time or following the growth in height. Girls are frequently heavier than boys at ages twelve to fourteen years, but with the onset of menstruation a leveling-off period occurs.

The sudden growth spurt in boys does not come until approximately two years after that of the girls, and it continues to a greater extent until around twenty years of age. Boys show an even greater increase in weight and also continue this gain for a longer period than do girls.

These changes have definite implications for the physical education program. First, boys and girls have a real concern for their physical development. Participation and total involvement in physical education activities provides an opportunity for them to forget their own self-concerns and to lose themselves in the enjoyment of the game.

Second, in regard to regular class activities in which height is an important factor, as in volleyball or basketball, it may be advisable to distribute the tallest boys and girls among the squads for the best playing results. Also, the coeducational program at the junior high level, where differences in sizes are most obvious, must be carefully organized to minimize any undue embarrassment experienced by both boys and girls. Dancing activities may be difficult to conduct because the boys are shorter than the girls, whereas relays, games of low organization, badminton, volleyball, and similar activities may have great success. However, it should be noted that in communities where social dancing is established and promoted for this age level, this activity will probably meet with success.

One of the most important factors that the physical education teacher should consider is the personal self-consciousness and embarrassment suffered by teen-agers in regard to their physical development. This is particularly true in physical education classes, where emphasis is placed on physical skills and bodily coordination. Students who are concerned with overweight or underweight conditions frequently seek excuses from class participation, showers, or exercise because of their discomfort, fatigue, and ineptitude. The teacher of physical education has a real opportunity for guidance in such cases by offering suggestions on healthful nutrition and proper exercise. A sincere interest and understanding of individual problems can direct the student's self-interest toward a solution of his problems and motivate him to put forth increased effort.

Skeletal changes

Some of the adolescent increases in height and weight may be attributed to inner changes in the skeletal structures (the bones), which cause differences in body proportions at this time.

The bones of the growing youth change in length and breadth as well as in density (mass). Studies of x-ray films show that a definite relationship may be found between skeletal age and age of puberty. In other words, a child's bony growth continues at approximately the same rate and time as other facets of his development and is complete when the sexual function is mature.

These skeletal changes cause differences in body proportions common in adolescence. The long bones of the arms and legs

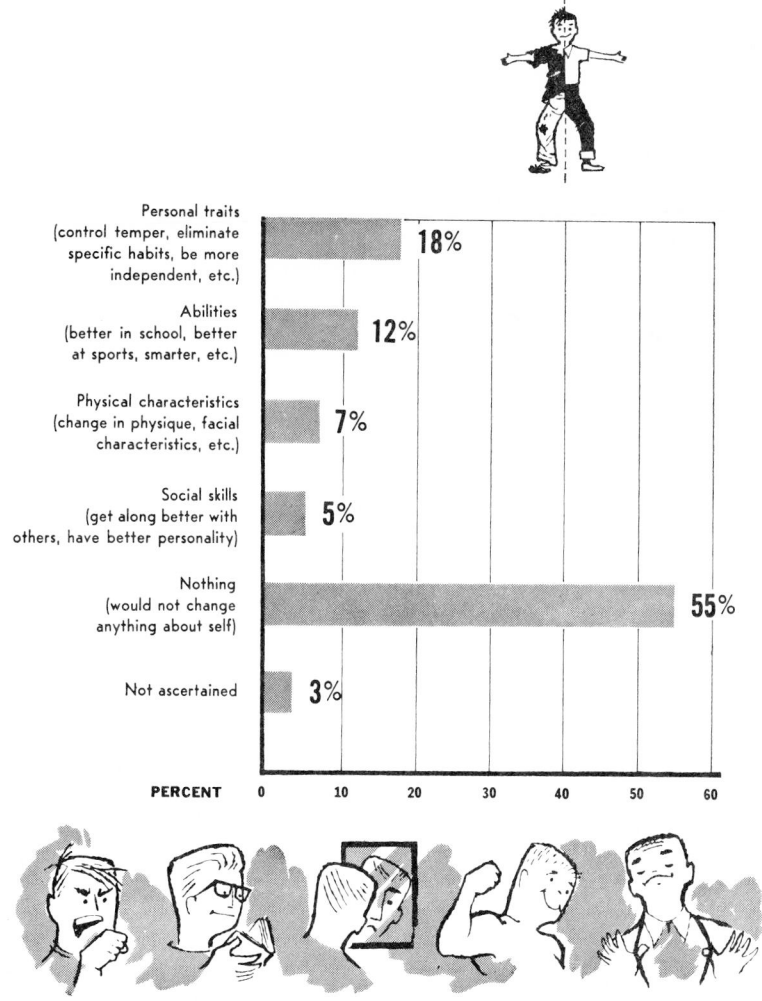

Fig. 3-3. What boys would like to change about themselves. Four out of ten boys would like to change something about themselves. (From Boys' Clubs of America: Report on the national survey of members aged 14 to 18—needs and interests of adolescent Boys' Club members, New York, 1960.)

are extended, with accompanying growth of the superimposed muscles. Facial contours change, and as the nose lengthens, the hairline changes and the second molars appear.

Several implications for physical education are involved here. With these constant changes occurring in their skeletal framework, adolescents need considerable exercise for their large muscles in order to maintain competent physical skills. The teacher must use caution, however, during strenuous activities and guard against fatigue and strain in this age group. Adolescents also need a broad understanding of the changes taking place in order to offset disappointment and discontent when skills suddenly seem less effective.

In relation to the competitive aspects of the intramural and interscholastic programs, especially among early adolescents, skeletal growth, muscle strain, and fatigue should be considered. Physical educators must, of course, follow state regulations in regard to competition, but in this connection it may be helpful to note what Kuhlen says:

> Excessive exertion, as is apt to occur in highly competitive sports, is probably bad hygiene at any age. It is desirable to play safe, to keep athletic competition at pubescence at a safe level, and organize teams so that no undue strain is placed on one individual and so that the beneficial effects to physical education will accrue to a larger number.[*]

Primary and secondary sex changes

Besides the sudden spurt in height and weight, the next most obvious adolescent change is in their sex characteristics. There are two levels of changes to be considered here: the primary sex changes, which involve the reproductive organs, and the secondary sex characteristics, which include those traits generally attributed to masculine and feminine appearances. Growth of facial hair on boys and breast

[*]From Kuhlen, Raymond G.: The psychology of adolescent development, New York, 1952, Harper & Brothers, p. 37.

development in girls are examples of secondary sex characteristics.

The primary sex change in girls is the development of the organs of reproduction (ovaries and fallopian tubes), which signal their maturation with the onset of the menstrual cycle. This signpost of adult function is of major importance to growing girls and usually occurs between the ages of twelve and fourteen years, although it may be earlier or later in a minority of cases.

The implications of this cycle in teaching physical education are many. In the first place it is essential that a healthy attitude toward menstruation be fostered by requiring all students to dress for classes and to participate in some, if not all, the activities. Girls should not be allowed to pamper themselves on these occasions but should learn to lead a regular, normally active life. There are, of course, exceptional cases—girls who are under a doctor's care and who may need rest at this time.

Instruction in proper hygiene and cleanliness, as well as in helpful exercise to relieve tensions, is another area wherein the physical education teacher can do great service to adolescent girls. Special provisions for showering may have to be made, however, to spare them real embarrassment. In schools where individual stall showers and dressing areas are provided there is no problem, but in other instances girls having their menstrual period may need to shower earlier or to substitute a sponge type of bath for a shower at the end of class.

The reproductive organs of boys (penis and testes) do not mature until approximately two years later than girls' reproductive organs, or around the ages of fourteen to sixteen years. Because growth of the male organs is external in nature, overdevelopment or underdevelopment is often a cause for much self-concern. Teachers should show care and understanding and should foster on the part of all students an attitude of acceptance of individual variations. Locker room antics and teasing about this personal characteristic can develop an unhealthy dislike for physical education and should not be permitted.

The main female secondary sex characteristic that develops in adolescence is the mammary gland. Other minor changes include growth of pubic and axillary hair, settling of the voice, and broadening of the hips. These changes begin the slow process of development at around ten years of age and continue long after the menarche.

In boys the changes termed secondary sex characteristics are similar to those of the girls: pubic and axillary hair, plus facial hair, as well as a deepening of the voice, broadening of the shoulders, and development of a waistline. These changes generally appear around the age of twelve years and continue into late adolescence.

The teacher of physical education should recognize the great importance these changes have in the minds of the students and the deep concern they feel about their growth and development. The teacher should help the students to understand the process of growth itself, and he should guide their thinking toward an appreciation of individual differences.

The teacher should also assist students in overcoming some of the problems that usually accompany sex changes. Acne, caused by the increase in glandular activity, and body odors, for example, may both be discussed by the physical education teacher, and hints may be given for improving these conditions. Group instruction on personal cleanliness and hygiene and individual, personal consultations in extreme cases are services that the teacher can perform for adolescents.

Other systemic changes

Other physiological systems undergo further development along with the previously mentioned areas of growth. The circulatory system, which includes the heart and blood vessels, continues to grow steadily during adolescence. This growth may be identified by a normal increase in blood pressures. However, the pulse rate seems to decrease in adolescence, although girls maintain a higher rate of speed than boys.

Respiratory system changes are also evident in adolescence, as seen by measurements of vital capacity. Large increases are registered in both boys and girls from ages ten to fourteen years, with a subsequent slowing down in girls' capacities, while boys' capacities continue to increase.

The digestive organs continue to grow during this time, necessitating more and more daily nourishment and thereby making greater demands on the adolescent body.

The nervous system is more fully developed before adolescence than the other systems, but there is thought to be an increase in the complexity of brain connections, with a subsequent increase in the types of thought processes. These developments continue until late adolescence.

Systemic changes should be considered as part of the total adolescent developmental picture, each having some bearing on the teaching program. In regard to the respiratory and circulatory changes, adolescent students should be watched carefully for signs of fatigue and exhaustion. Their appetites are usually large because of changes in digestion, but improper food habits are generally prevalent, and students need guidance in this respect. The further development of the nervous system, with increases in the types of thought processes, has implications for the knowledge and appreciation which adolescent students can now achieve. The teaching program may therefore be geared to more advanced aspects of strategy, rules, and philosophical ideas.

Basic motor skills

Consideration of the basic motor skills and their development during adolescence is a very important concern of the physical education teacher. The following observations seem to hold true:

1. Balance. Young boys perform better in this area than girls and continue their improvement of this skill in adolescence, while girls show little actual improvement.

2. Accuracy. Girls are usually better than boys in this skill throughout adolescent development.

3. Agility. Girls are more agile than boys until around thirteen years of age, at which time boys surpass the girls in this respect.

4. Control. Girls perform with more control than boys in early adolescence. The boys become superior after the age of fourteen.

5. Strength. Boys are always superior to girls in strength, but a greater degree of differentiation is seen with their maturity.

Basic motor skills are an essential part of the program in physical education. Therefore, changes in adolescent performance of these skills have definite implications for teaching. For girls emphasis should be placed on continuing improvement in balance, agility, control, and strength. Boys need to work, particularly in the early years, on accuracy, agility, and control, while in later years stress should be placed on their ability to achieve accuracy.

The differences in basic motor skill performances should be kept in mind when different aspects of the program are planned. With coeducational groups, for instance, activities requiring strength would not be chosen because of boys' superiority. When expected athletic perform-

Fig. 3-4. Motor skills—an essential consideration for the physical education teacher. **A,** Straddle vault. **B,** Uneven parallel bar frieze. **C,** Yoga handstand in free movement routine. **D,** Wolf vault. **E,** Flank vault. (Colorado Springs Public Schools, Colorado Springs, Colo.)

ances of students are estimated, these same skill differences and changes should be considered. The teacher should realize that a change in students' interest and satisfactions takes place as their motor skills change and develop. In motivating students, therefore, different techniques will be necessary at each age level.

Health aspects*

Although adolescence is sometimes described as one of the healthiest periods of life, a study† of illnesses and problems of secondary school students is quite revealing to teachers.

Figures gathered from nineteen clinics across the United States indicate that the most frequent diagnoses of adolescent patients include the following:

Obesity	74%
Acne	63%
Allergy	42%
Seizures	31%
Orthopedic problems	31%

The physical education program should consider what contributions it might make, through its curriculum, to alleviate the number one problem, obesity. At the same time, physical education teachers should realize that injuries, along with upper respiratory infections, are frequent problems for their students and consider what steps need to be taken to ensure student safety and freedom from exposure to disease.

It is also interesting to note that although the death rate among adolescents is low, accidents cause about 50% of their deaths, and two thirds of these are motor vehicle accidents. These statistics are particularly significant for teachers of driver training courses.

A comparatively new problem in high schools in the larger urban areas across the country involves pregnancy in high school girls. In many instances it is the girl's phys-

ical education teacher who first recognizes the symptoms, and therefore she should be aware of the type of help currently available in the schools for such students.

Although the health and vitality of adolescents are usually good, every teacher should be aware of other aspects of student life that may cause difficulties.

The physical education teacher should take advantage of every opportunity to offer guidance in health matters. The need for proper diet, rest, and exercise is easily related to athletic performance, and discussions of these factors can be very valuable. Guidance in proper body mechanics and posture, which is also a responsibility of the physical education teacher, is very important to adolescent health. Every program of physical education should contain a unit or series of classes devoted to postural studies for the identification of defects and improvement of postural conditions.

Fitness aspects

It is of utmost importance that physical fitness be an objective of the physical education program in junior and senior high schools. Students undergoing the constant process of change need to pay particular attention to achieving and maintaining a high level of fitness. It is at this stage in their development when a true appreciation of activity and fitness for its own sake is formulated. Fitness will be discussed further in Chapter 16. However, it should be emphasized here that the physical education teacher has a very great responsibility in this regard, for it is in this field alone where physical fitness may be promoted in the school.

The physical development of the adolescent is a very complex process. Its close association with the physical education program makes it essential that teachers understand thoroughly the various aspects of growth and development in order to meet the needs of the adolescent and help him to understand better the process that is taking place.

---

*See also discussion on health goals, Chapter 5.
†Gallagher, J. Roswell: Medical care of the adolescent, ed. 2, New York, 1966, Appleton-Century-Crofts.

EMOTIONAL DEVELOPMENT

The emotional development of the adolescent is just as complex as his physical development, but it is not as easily defined or measured because there is no exact pattern of development to follow. To discuss this phase of adolescence it will be necessary to picture briefly the basic human emotions and the adolescent adjustments and responses that are distinguishable from those of childhood and adulthood.

Basic human emotions. It must first be realized that the adolescent, like human beings of any age, experiences the three basic emotions—fear, anger, and joy—and their variations. It is in the stimulus exciting an emotion and in the response to a particular situation that the growing adolescent differs from other age groups.

Adolescent responses. Adolescent responses tend to be extreme in nature. Members of this age group are either highly excited or greatly depressed, and rapid changes of mood are typical. For this reason adolescence is sometimes described as a period of heightened emotionality.

Adolescents develop emotionally at the same time that physical, social, and intellectual maturation is taking place. Signs of extreme emotional responsiveness may be seen as early as the preadolescent stage, and the developmental process continues slowly, with completion in late adolescence. Boys mature approximately two years later than girls in this respect as well as in other phases of development.

The heightened emotional responses of adolescents can best be understood in terms of the changing needs that cause them and that in themselves form a pattern of emotional development. A study of these adolescent needs, therefore, is necessary in order to interpret their relationship to physical education.

Fig. 3-5. Swimming is an excellent activity for developing physical fitness. (Oconomowoc Senior High School, Oconomowoc, Wis.)

Adolescent needs

The emotions of adolescents are aroused in response to the adjustment needs peculiar to their stage of development. They must adjust to a changing physical state, to a heterosexual interest, and to an environment free from parental control. Other adolescent needs that must be satisfied are shared by all human beings. They include security, achievement, affection, adventure, and well-being. Adolescents, however, in satisfying these needs, find methods that are limited to their particular age group and that undergo changes as different stages of development are reached. It is this transition in satisfaction-producing factors that provides a clue to adolescent emotional development and that should be studied individually in respect to each student's needs.

Affection. The early adolescent seeks many friendships with individuals of the same sex, whereas in middle adolescence friendships for the opposite sex begin. These friendships become even stronger in late adolescence, while friends of the same sex continue to hold interest. Also in late adolescence relationships with adults are more friendly as authority relaxes, and eventually friendships with the same sex dwindle in number as they deepen in intensity.

Problems in regard to affection usually arise either from fears centered around the making or losing of friends or from conflicts with them. Still others may stem from a desire for continued affection from parents, which is in conflict with a simultaneous need for independence from them.

All teachers need to understand the basic problems faced by teen-agers in reference to their need for affection. Physical education teachers should provide many socializing situations in which friendships may be fostered and should further the process of adjustment to the opposite sex through co-educational activities.

Achievement. In early adolescence achievement is realized through success in many and varied interests and hobbies. In middle and late adolescence, as interests center upon fewer, more important areas, achievement is sensed through accomplishments in these areas. These later interests usually stem from the adult role that the adolescent determines is most suitable for him, and success is felt as this ideal approaches reality.

Problems of adolescents generally stem from lack of achievement in the areas of interest at each age level. For example, receiving good grades in school becomes a problem when an interest in a college education is aroused.

Teachers of physical education should realize that many students find satisfaction in superior performance and achievement in their field. For those students who have difficulty performing in physical education, the teacher should try to provide a program varied enough so that in some particular activity or sport a sense of accomplishment may be derived.

Adventure. In early adolescence the variety of interests in many different areas provides much satisfaction of the need for adventure. Striking out on one's own with the new freedom that this age permits provides much excitement in middle adolescence, and this same satisfaction is present in late adolescence.

The major problem occurs when satisfaction of this need for adventure is gained from improper experiences, as seen in the juvenile crimes of today.

In physical education this need for excitement and adventure may easily be satisfied through the challenge and thrills of sports and competition. The program should therefore be set up on a broad scale in order to provide satisfaction through after-school activities for as many students as possible.

Security. The early adolescent seeks security in his social world through the gang or crowd. The middle adolescent finds similar satisfaction in smaller groups or cliques, and the late adolescent begins to be satisfied with more adult relationships, having found security within himself.

The main problem that creates insecurity in the adolescent lies within himself. Because of the uncertainties life holds for him and the doubts he has of his own success, the adolescent does not dare to rely upon himself. Instead, he seeks security in whatever else he can find: the gang, the club, the world of books or music, or some other facet of life.

The physical education teacher has a very real responsibility toward the security of students in all activities. All students should feel at ease in the gymnasium, and this goal may be accomplished by giving concrete instructions and establishing definite procedures and regulations so that students will know exactly what is expected of them. This, together with consistency in handling routine procedures, discipline problems, and other everyday occurrences, ensures feelings of security in physical education.

Sense of well-being. A sense of well-being is brought about by adjusting the picture of the self through various mechanisms. Adolescents employ the same methods as all human personalities: rationalization, blame, compensation, and use of excuses, to name a few.

Superiority in physical pursuits provides one outlet for adjusting the self-picture of individuals who have difficulty in academic work. Students who can achieve in some area of physical education naturally augment their sense of well-being or sense of worth. Elementary classroom teachers have said that the key to all learning is making a child feel good about himself in regard to whatever he is trying to do. Surely this same principle applies to students of all ages.

Physical education teachers should be aware of the abnormal extremes to which human personalities may go when overrationalizing or overcompensating. When the teacher recognizes these extreme cases he should make the proper referrals to the school psychologist for study. In this way the teacher does a service to students who need help in regaining their sense of well-being.

Adjustment to physical change. The adjustment to the changing physical self has been discussed previously in this chapter. From the emotional standpoint it should be emphasized again that this is a source of great concern to all adolescents.

Adjustment to heterosexual interest. This discussion will be expanded in the section on social development, but the close relationship of heterosexual interest to emotional responses should be pointed out here. Many adolescent fears and worries center around this particular phase of

Fig. 3-6. Developing skill in soccer and other physical education activities helps the adolescent to develop a better self-image. (Walt Whitman High School, South Huntington Schools, N. Y.)

development, necessitating a real contribution on the part of the physical education program through coeducational activities to relieve tensions.

Freedom from parental control. In adolescence there is a particular need to gain freedom from parental control, yet the conflicts in treatment given adolescents by adults cause many problems.

At home adolescents begin to assume adultlike responsibilities in relation to doing household chores, baby-sitting, holding part-time jobs, and having an increased allowance. At the same time, however, they still are restricted in many things, such as using the family car, dating, and observing curfews. These discrepancies in treatment frequently seem senseless to the adolescent and are difficult to reconcile.

At school this dichotomy—treating adolescents partially as adults and partially as children—continues. Rules and regulations are established about smoking, dances, and conduct, while at the same time the students are allowed to run the school government, athletic organizations, and other school activities.

To help adolescents feel secure in themselves, without depending on parental or other adult controls, the physical education teacher should try to offer many opportunities for the development of self-responsibility, self-discipline, and self-reliance. This may be done through assignment of leadership positions and through class planning of rules and regulations of conduct. Students who are allowed to mutually formulate their standards of behavior better understand the necessity for having them and follow them more willingly.

An understanding of the many adolescent worries and needs helps the physical education teacher make provisions in the program to overcome these emotional difficulties. It is also important that additional problems be avoided in the school situation, and the teacher who understands possible areas of concern, such as security, is better able to provide a healthy teaching situation. Students who are emotionally upset learn little, and they need help in controlling emotional responses. It is the responsibility of teachers to assist them in achieving this goal.

SOCIAL DEVELOPMENT

Social development can be thought of in terms of the adolescent's relationships with friends of his own sex, with friends of the opposite sex, and with adults. In each of these areas different stages of growth are found, appearing later in boys than in girls, and to a different degree. The developmental process itself is based on the adolescent's desire to break away from his parents and to assume selfhood in his social world.

Relationships with his own sex

In early adolescence the individual finds a place in the social world by becoming part of a large group, which usually consists of age-mates of the same sex. This occurs with girls in junior high school, and somewhat later, perhaps in the ninth or tenth grade, with boys. Groupings usually evolve from similar school classes, neighborhoods, and social backgrounds. They provide standards of behavior, such as manner of dress and talk, as well as opportunities to learn how to act with people in different situations.

In middle adolescence the dictates of the peer groups continue to be strong. However, the crowds break down into smaller, more cohesive cliques that promote snobbishness and prejudices not usually found in the larger groupings. With girls these close friendships maintain an extreme importance that continues into the college years, while boys seldom rely as completely on friendships.

There are two important implications for physical education stemming from this phase of adolescent social development. One concerns leadership and the other, clique formations.

Because the development of *leadership* qualities is a fundamental phase of physical education, the program should provide many opportunities for promoting and guiding good leaders. The formation of leaders' clubs in junior and senior high school provides a structured situation wherein leadership qualities may be developed and practiced by many interested members. Learning to select good leaders may also be considered an outcome of physical education, and this factor should have carry-over value into out-of-school group activities.

Another phase of the physical education program that should have carry-over value in adolescent circles relates to the injurious aspects of *clique formations*. The socializing phase of physical education activities, such as the teamwork entailed, should point out the equalities of all individuals and promote consideration for and cooperation with people of all races and religions. The harmful effects of ostracizing a few people—so frequently found in small clique formations—should be discussed during class organization, with the hope that desirable extracurricular practices will be followed.

Relationships with opposite sex

In early adolescence, between the ages of ten and twelve years, boys and girls generally exhibit an antagonistic attitute toward one another.

In middle adolescence, girls of thirteen and fourteen, who are now developing physically, begin to take an active interest in boys, parties, and mixed social functions. Boys, however, remain uninterested in girls. Between fourteen and sixteen years of age boys return this interest in the opposite sex, and social activities consume a great deal of an adolescent's time and energies. It is usually at this point that pairs begin to develop. By the age of sixteen or seventeen, adolescent adjustments to members of the opposite sex are nearly complete.

The development of an interest in the opposite sex has two important implications in the physical education program: the planning of coeducational activities and the individual class program.

Coeducational activities for the early adolescent in junior high school should provide an opportunity for relaxed socialization, in which no undue embarrassment is felt. At this level boys and girls are at various stages of development, ranging from no interest to too much interest in the opposite sex. Activities should therefore be those already familiar to the students, such as badminton, volleyball, tennis, or recreational games. Knowing the activity helps the adolescent overcome the fear of socializing. Simple mass dancing activities may be successful when well organized and taught, particularly in communities that promote social activities in junior high school.

The senior high school coeducational program, on the other hand, may be instructional as well as recreational, and it should provide learning experiences that will have carryover value when students complete their education. Bowling, golf, and other individual sports may be introduced at this level if facilities permit.

The individual program of physical education must change somewhat along with this changing heterosexual drive. Younger girls love to play all kinds of games, but with physical development comes an increased desire for attractiveness, grace, poise, and balance, rather than extreme physical prowess. This aspect of their interests can and should be served in the teaching program, with dance and fitness activities stressing these goals. The motivation of boys does not change as much as that of girls because of their keen interest in competition and the stress placed on athletic achievements for popularity. This holds true for boys at all age levels, and the physical education teacher should capitalize on this natural motivational device.

Relationships with adults

Preadolescents usually accept adult authority, whereas early adolescents begin to be resentful. The latter try to assert themselves above such authority, except in cases of hero worship. In middle and late adolescence the students become more receptive to adult helpfulness and seek advice from those who represent fields in which they are strongly interested. Then at the end of adolescence adults are met on a more friendly basis, and the socially mature individual finds that he can enjoy casual friendship with everyone.

This change in the adolescent-adult relationship has two important implications for physical education. One concerns class management and the other, the problem of hero worship.

Because the younger adolescent tends to be resentful of adult authority, the physical educator should try to have members of a class manage themselves as much as possible. Through guided group planning the adolescent can set proper standards of behavior for himself and others, and therefore he has no reason to rebel. Students are then motivating themselves and providing self-direction—both of which are educational goals as well as developmental goals of adolescents.

In regard to the second factor, hero worship, it should be pointed out that in physical education, where an informal teacher-pupil relationship is likely to be maintained, hero worship and infatuations easily develop. This can become a serious problem for the student involved, for such strong feelings often become very time-consuming and thought-consuming, to the detriment of the individual. If such an attachment develops, the wise teacher remains objective and tries to be friendly and helpful and at the same time remote in his relationships with the student. Fortunately these infatuations are usually short-lived, and when they are properly handled no personal misunderstandings or ill-feelings result.

The social devolpment of the adolescent is of great importance both to him and to the school. The physical educator should assist in as many ways as possible in this development in all three aspects: relationships with friends of the same sex, with those of the opposite sex, and with adults.

INTELLECTUAL DEVELOPMENT

The adolescent does not go through a great intellectual growth spurt or change as in other phases of development. At this time there seems to be an expansion of powers, however, as well as an increase in capacities. The continuing growth toward intellectual maturity is extremely varied in individuals, with a high degree of this development being reached at any time between the ages of sixteen and twenty-five years. Boys and girls are alike in this respect, and the wide range of ages points out the individualized nature of intellectual growth.

Adolescent intellectual advancement may be discussed in reference to four general areas: memory, concentration, imagination, and reasoning power. The power of memory, which is so strong in childhood, seems to decrease in adolescence. Actually, however, it is the adolescent's lack of interest in making use of his capacity to memorize that causes this decline.

The powers of an adolescent to concentrate increase, particularly in regard to areas of work in which he is greatly interested. The adolescent's ability to use his imagination also increases at this time. Of greatest importance in relation to his schoolwork is the distinct increase in adolescent powers of reasoning and judging. It is this phase of intellectual development that distinguishes his growth away from his childish ideas and permits him to generalize from his experiences to formulate moral values and knowledge, together with a philosophy of life.

The importance of this intellectual development of adolescents to the physical education program lies in its relationship to teaching methods and the influences exerted by the teacher.

In regard to the first point, teaching methods, the teacher must be sure to consider the variation of intellectual abilities when presenting instructions and explanations. As students progress through high school, the material presented in physical education class should require more and

CHECKLIST OF SELECTED ITEMS FOR EVALUATING THE PHYSICAL EDUCATION PROGRAM'S RELEVANCY TO THE NEW BREED OF STUDENT IN THE SECONDARY SCHOOL

1. Activities are provided that will enable each student to be successful and feel that he has worth. YES ☐ NO ☐

2. Students are helped to relate to one another, to members of the opposite sex, and to adults. YES ☐ NO ☐

3. Students are provided an opportunity to have a say in the development of the physical education curriculum and consequently will be more highly motivated to participate in the program that is meaningful and interesting to them. YES ☐ NO ☐

4. Students are helped to understand the why of the activity as well as having the opportunity to participate in the activity. YES ☐ NO ☐

5. Students are grouped in classes according to their abilities. YES ☐ NO ☐

6. Teachers know each student and his problems and help him wherever possible in solving these problems. YES ☐ NO ☐

7. The community is involved in the physical education program, for example, father-son and mother-daughter activities. YES ☐ NO ☐

8. Instruction is provided in new sports, such as scuba diving, in which students have an interest. YES ☐ NO ☐

9. Students have a voice in policy-making decisions, are represented on important committees, and participate in the evaluation of courses and teachers. YES ☐ NO ☐

10. Physical education program is kept abreast of the changing times in society and the changing nature of students, with student needs being met in a realistic, meaningful manner. (Today, some students find their programs repetitious, time consuming, giving little emphasis to the unskilled, and so on.) YES ☐ NO ☐

11. The interests and needs of girls are taken into consideration. The program gives equal opportunities to both girls and boys. YES ☐ NO ☐

12. Opportunities are provided students for leadership roles. YES ☐ NO ☐

13. Students are represented at faculty meetings. YES ☐ NO ☐

14. The physical education program meets the needs of minority groups. YES ☐ NO ☐

15. Communication channels are available whereby students can submit their grievances to the administration. YES ☐ NO ☐

16. Intellectual as well as physical capacities of students are challenged. YES ☐ NO ☐

17. The curriculum provides for a sequential advancement from basic skills to more advanced skills. YES ☐ NO ☐

18. Individualistic hair styles and dress codes are permitted where they do not affect the health, safety, and performance of students. YES ☐ NO ☐

19. Physically handicapped, mentally retarded, emotionally disturbed, and culturally disadvantaged students are provided for in the physical education program. YES ☐ NO ☐

20. Sufficient variety and progression exist in activities to satisfy individual differences. YES ☐ NO ☐

21. The intramural, varsity athletic, and other extracurricular activities meet the needs of students. YES ☐ NO ☐

22. The program is designed to develop the optimum potential of each student. YES ☐ NO ☐

23. The objectives of the physical education program are clearly understood by students. YES ☐ NO ☐

24. Students have the opportunity to participate in activities where identification and acceptance are manifested. YES ☐ NO ☐

25. Students have the opportunity to participate in activities that will be of value to them not only now but also in the future. YES ☐ NO ☐

more reasoning power and judgment. Thought questions should be included in tests rather than simple true-false or multiple-choice types. Strategy and game concepts should become a part of the teaching program, for adolescents are now able to understand more fully this phase of physical education activities.

The teacher should also make use of teaching methods that promote creative thinking on the part of adolescent students. Units on modern dance obviously foster creative thinking in girls, but sports units for both boys and girls may be constructed to take advantage of improved adolescent powers of imagination and thinking. Students should have an opportunity to work out team plays in basketball, for example, or to develop their own exercise patterns, drill formations, or football plays. The teacher can use the problem-solving technique to accomplish this, asking the students to think out some specific solution to a given game situation.

The other important aspect of adolescent intellectual development that affects the physical education teacher lies in the student-teacher relationship. Because adolescence is the period in which adult attitudes, moral values, and a philosophy of life become formalized, the teacher of physical education should exemplify those ideals that are most suitable to mature living. For example, the physical education teacher should try to promote positive attitudes toward health and physical fitness: a desire to maintain good health, a desire to continue physical pursuits for enjoyment, and an appreciation for the outcomes of physical exercise. As an influence on adolescent moral values, on their concepts of right and wrong, and on their prejudices, which are now taking final shape, the physical education teacher should have clearly defined values that are consistently applied and worthy of imitation by the students. The ideals of respect for all individuals, no matter how different they may be, should be promoted in physical education, together with the real meaning of sportsmanship.

The philosophy of life that shapes an individual's outlook and actions is also formulated during adolescence. Religious doubts and philosophical questioning are increasing concerns of the adolescent. Physical education teachers never know when their actions, thoughts, or beliefs may be idealized or when guidance and advice may be sought. They must therefore be ready to serve and to answer students to the best of their abilities, and must recognize that many values are best learned from example.

POINTS TO REMEMBER

1. The process of adolescent physical development and the stages undergone are different in boys and girls, and each individual follows his own particular growth pattern.
2. The emotional responses of adolescents are different from those of adults because of their varying needs.
3. Social development in adolescence is recognizable by the changes in relationships with friends and adults.
4. Intellectual growth is experienced during adolescence and plays an important part in mature living.
5. The process of growth and development in adolescents has many implications for the physical education program.

PROBLEMS TO THINK THROUGH

1. How can we motivate high school girls in physical activities when social interests are uppermost in their minds?
2. How can we capitalize on the varying interests exhibited in junior high school students?
3. How can we promote and further good social relationships in junior high school students when heterosexual interests develop?
4. How can we develop in students an understanding of the physical growth that takes place during adolescence?
5. How can we develop good habits of cleanliness and proper hygiene techniques during early adolescence?
6. How can we prevent cliques from controlling or damaging class and afterschool activities?
7. How can we capitalize on the heightened interests and abilities of the older high school pupils?
8. How can we further the development of leadership techniques in students not usually given opportunities to demonstrate them?
9. How can we relieve extreme emotional tensions that develop during adolescence?
10. How can we promote attitudes of honesty, fair play, and consideration of others?

CASE STUDY FOR ANALYSIS

Tina was the rather unfortunate nickname given to a very large eighth grade girl, recently moved into a small community. Physical education classes met twice a week for all eighth grade girls and once a week with boys and girls together. Embarrassment over both her size and her lack of abilities in physical activities forced her to try every conceivable technique to be excused from class, especially the coeducational class, where she was completely ill at ease. How should Tina be motivated to enter into activities in order to derive the benefits she so badly needs?

EXERCISES FOR REVIEW

1. What points of good grooming should be emphasized with junior high school girls? Boys?
2. What steps should be followed in helping a student whose emotional adjustment is questionable, in a school where a nurse is not in daily attendance?
3. How would procedures regarding monthly periods be outlined to a class of seventh grade girls?
4. In what way could proper class and locker room management benefit the ostracized high school boy?
5. What adolescent individuals in the modern world of sports should be singled out as examples of athletic achievement?
6. What advice should be given the adolescent youth, ordinarily proficient in physical activities, who finds himself falling below par?

SELECTED READINGS

American Association for Health, Physical Education, and Recreation: The growing years—adolescence, fifth yearbook, Washingon, D. C., 1962, The Association.

Blumenfield, Warren S., and Remmers, H. H.: Sports preferences of high school students as defined by reported participation, Research Quarterly **36**:205, 1966.

Cordasco, Francesco, and Bucchioni, Eugene, editors: Puerto Rican children in mainland schools, Metuchen, N. J., 1968, Scarecrow Press.

Friedenberg, Edgar Z.: Coming of age in America, New York, 1965, Random House, Inc.

Friedenberg, Edgar Z.: The vanishing adolescent, Boston, 1959, Beacon Press.

Gallagher, J. Roswell: Medical care of the adolescent, ed. 2, New York, 1966, Appleton-Century-Crofts.

Gregory, Susan: Hey, white girl! New York, 1970, W. W. Norton & Co.

High school kids "turned off" by education, White Plains Reporter Dispatch, October 20, 1971, p. 10.

Morsbach, Mabel: The Negro in American Life, New York, 1967, Harcourt, Brace and World.

Murphy, Gardner: What can youth tell us about their potentialities? Bulletin of the National Association of Secondary-School Principals **50**: 10-24, 1966.

Oliva, Peter F.: The secondary school today, New York, 1967, World Publishing Co.

Rand, Lester: Teen-agers and money, National Education Association Journal **56**:34, 1967.

Schmuck, Richard: Concerns of contemporary adolescents, Bulletin of the National Association of Secondary School Principals **49**:19, 1965.

Some popular myths on youth (editorial), Wall Street Journal, June 28, 1971.

Strom, Susan: The schools and the pregnant teenager, Saturday Review, September 16, 1967, p. 80.

Ulrich, Celeste: The tomorrow mind, Journal of Health, Physical Education, and Recreation **35**: 17, 1964.

United States Department of Health, Education and Welfare: Dialogue on adolescence, Washington, D. C., 1967, U. S. Government Printing Office.

Youth's faith . . . (editorial), New York Times, May 8, 1970, p. 20.

PART TWO
THE RELEVANT
PROGRAM OF
PHYSICAL EDUCATION

4 DEVELOPING GOALS—WHAT SHOULD PHYSICAL EDUCATION BE DOING FOR THE STUDENT?

What are the objectives toward which physical education should strive in the secondary school? Will the selected goals, when achieved, contribute to the physical, mental, emotional, and social well-being of the student? What are the main contributions that physical education can make to the new breed of student who is attending junior and senior high schools of this country?

Thus far in this text we have considered the secondary school in a changing society, community, and school. We then looked at the new breed of student. A logical next step is to identify the goals and objectives that physical education hopes to achieve. In so doing, it is well to keep in mind four basic guidelines.

• *Goals must be clearly identified and should be understood by the student.* The goals toward which physical education is working should be clearly set forth and be understood and identified by the student. Surveys indicate that the purposes for which physical education programs exist are not always clear in the minds of students or are thought to have little value. This should not be the case. When a student takes physical education he should clearly understand at the outset the purpose of the program and the benefits and values he can expect to receive as a participant. In addition, the goals should have been so carefully thought through and se-

lected that the student will identify with them as being important to him now and in the future.

• *Goals should have scientific worth.* The physical educator should select goals that are backed by scientific investigation and that can be achieved. Unfortunately, some teachers make wild claims for physical education that they cannot prove scientifically or achieve.

• *Goals should be relevant to society, education, and the student.* The aims of physical education should reflect the changing society, education, and student discussed in the earlier pages of this text. Physical educators will be remiss if they fail to evaluate and select their goals with these changes in mind.

• *Goals should relate to the cognitive, affective, and motor domains.* Objectives of physical education should reflect directly or indirectly three domains, namely, the *cognitive*, with its emphasis upon knowledge and the development of intellectual abilities and skills; the *affective*, which relates to attitudes, values, interests, and appreciations; and the *psychomotor*, which refers to motor and manipulative skills. Furthermore, the interdependence of the three domains in relation to learning and the student should be recognized. For example, students do not think or behave without feeling. Instead, they respond as total organisms.

DEVELOPMENTAL OBJECTIVES OF PHYSICAL EDUCATION

ORGANIC

Proper functioning of the body systems so that the individual may adequately meet the demands placed upon him by his environment. A foundation for skill development.

Muscle Strength

The maximum amount of force exerted by a muscle or muscle group.

Muscle Endurance

The ability of a muscle or muscle group to sustain effort for a prolonged period of time.

Cardiovascular Endurance

The capacity of an individual to persist in strenuous activity for periods of some duration. This is dependent upon the combined efficiency of the blood vessels, heart, and lungs.

Flexibility

The range of motion in joints needed to produce efficient movement and minimize injury.

NEUROMUSCULAR

A harmonious functioning of the nervous and muscular systems to produce desired movements.

Locomotor Skills

Walking Skipping Sliding Leaping Pushing
Running Galloping Hopping Rolling Pulling

Nonlocomotor Skills

Swaying Twisting Shaking Stretching
Bending Handing Stooping

Game Type Fundamental Skills

Striking Catching Kicking Stopping
Throwing Batting Starting Changing direction

Motor Factors

Accuracy Rhythm Kinesthetic awareness
Power Balance Reaction time Agility

Sport Skills

Soccer Softball Volleyball Wrestling
Track & Field Archery Baseball
Basketball Archery Speedball Hockey
Fencing Golf Bowling Tennis

Recreational Skills

Shuffleboard Croquet Deck tennis Hiking
Table tennis Swimming Horseshoes Boating

INTERPRETIVE

The ability to explore, to discover, to understand, to acquire knowledge, and to make value judgments.

A knowledge of game rules, safety measures, and etiquette.

The use of strategies and techniques involved in organized activities.

A knowledge of how the body functions and its relationship to physical activity.

A development of appreciation for personal performance. The use of judgment related to distance, time, space, force, speed, and direction in the use of activity implements, balls, and self.

An understanding of growth and developmental factors affected by movement.

The ability to solve developmental problems through movement.

SOCIAL

An adjustment to both self and others by an integration of the individual to society and his environment.

The ability to make judgments in a group situation.

Learning to communicate with others.

The ability to exchange and evaluate ideas within a group.

The development of the social phases of personality, attitudes, and values in order to become a functioning member of society.

The development of a sense of belonging and acceptance by society.

The development of positive personality traits.

Learnings for constructive use of leisure time.

A development of attitude that reflects good moral character.

EMOTIONAL

A healthy response to physical activity through a fulfillment of basic needs.

The development of positive reactions in spectatorship and participation through either success or failure.

The release of tension through suitable physical activities.

An outlet for self-expression and creativity.

An appreciation of the aesthetic experiences derived from correlated activities.

The ability to have fun.

Fig. 4-1. Developmental objectives of physical education. (From Annarino, Anthony A.: The five traditional objectives of physical education, Journal of Health, Physical Education, and Recreation 41:25, 1970.)

STUDENTS AND PARENTS ARE CONFUSED

Many students and parents are confused about the real worth of games and sports as part of the school program. Over the years we have had the opportunity to discuss physical education with many people. Some of their comments reflect this confusion: "It's exercise done to command." "A matter of arms and legs and good intentions." "Something that entertains the students—a necessary evil." "A good device to keep the kids off the street." "Just an extracurricular activity—a frill, a fad." "It certainly isn't part of the educational program—merely an appendage." "Too much time should not be devoted to it—above all, don't take time away from learning science and mathematics."

If physical education and play do not mean more than these comments indicate, they should be abolished from the school program. After all, there are more than 100,000 leaders getting paid nearly one-half billion dollars annually in this specialized field today. Approximately sixty million school children are being exposed to their programs. Gymnasiums, swimming pools, playgrounds, and recreational facilities are being constructed at a cost of billions of dollars to taxpayers. An up-to-date gymnasium costs at least $300,000 and a seventy-five-foot swimming pool $75,000; even the basketball that the kids bounce up and down the floor costs $25. The average gymnasium is one of the most costly parts of the school building and takes up space equivalent to ten to fourteen classrooms. Why pay all these teachers, construct these expensive facilities, and take up valuable space unless they are going to produce results—unless they are an important phase of education?

Students and parents are demanding the answers to such questions. They have become vitally interested in education. For parents, this interest has mushroomed until today there are over fifteen million members of parent-teacher associations throughout the country. They want to make sure their children have the benefits of worth-while educational experiences. They vote money only for things they consider sound.

As these parents scan the educational programs of their communities, they should become increasingly aware that boys and girls do not learn, grow, and develop only during those hours spent at their desks in reading, writing, and working with paper and pencil. There are other times that may be even more important—time spent in taking a trip to the zoo, going to camp, making a doghouse, attending a dance, and YES, playing on the field, in the gymnasium, or in the swimming pool.

KNOWLEDGE OF OBJECTIVES— AN IMPORTANT CONSIDERATION

Upon the shoulders of the teacher of physical education rests the responsibility for interpreting to students, their parents, and the public in general the objectives of their specialized field. This responsibility cannot be met unless the teacher understands clearly the goals of education, students, and physical education. Furthermore, all these goals must be compatible with and must contribute to the educational development of each boy and girl in the secondary school.

Each student of physical education and each teacher in the schools should know the objectives they are trying to reach. These aims represent the worth of this specialized field, they show the contribution that can be made to young and old alike, and they provide a guide for action in our day-to-day programs.

It is impossible for a teacher of physical education to do a worthy educational job unless he or she knows the objectives of the field and how they fit into the total education picture. Trying to work without such vital information would be analogous to a carpenter's trying to build a house without blueprints to guide him.

THE DEVELOPMENT OF GOALS FOR THE PHYSICAL EDUCATION PROGRAM

The physical educator in the secondary school should use a logical, step-by-step approach for arriving at the goals he wishes to accomplish in his program. The following steps are suggested as a specific way in which goals may be determined. Each step is presented in a form of a question, and the questions proceed from general to specific considerations.

What is the purpose of education?

The physical educator should be aware of the purposes for which formal institutions of learning exist. This changing nation has basic objectives for educational programs that are well grounded in democratic ideals. Some of these objectives, discussed later in this chapter, were formulated by the Educational Policies Commission.

The physical educator should next determine how physical education can best help to accomplish the basic goals of education. Furthermore, he should recognize the place of physical education in the total sphere of general education. As will be discussed later, physical education makes a contribution to the physical, mental, emotional, and social development of the student.

What is the school's philosophy of education?

Physical education goals should be in keeping with the philosophy of education within the school where the physical educator works. Therefore, the physical educator should be familiar with the goals of education of his secondary school and relate them to his physical education program. A careful study of the school's goals should be made, and where there is doubt in regard to the school's philosophy, it should be clarified through discussions with the administration. Most schools have specific goals of accomplishment that have been put in writing. If not, there should be some research to identify existing goals. One school, for example, points out that it has as its goals the following: "To promote healthful living by developing physical fitness, emotional stability, and appreciation

of the ideals of good sportsmanship. . . . In our entire program we consciously support good physical and mental health habits, which are specifically taught in physical education, family living. . . . Through sports and other extracurricular activities we encourage participation in and enjoyment of rewarding recreational activities."

What are the needs and interests of the students?

The physical education program is for the students, and thus their needs and interests are a vital consideration. These needs and interests may be determined in a number of ways and by using a variety of resources, including school records, observation of students, talks with parents, making inventory of students' interests and suggestions, examining the literature that specifically relates to this subject, studying the professional research, and talking with specialists in the school program, such as the school physician, the nurse, and the guidance counselor. Any program that is developed should be compatible with the needs and interests of the students in a specific school. The procedure of studying students carefully should be a continuous one so that the goals are flexible and meet the changing needs of the students.

What are the influencing factors relating to such items as facilities, state regulations, and staff?

A basic premise for the development of physical education goals is that they must be established within the framework of factors that are essential for their accomplishment. For example, it would not be a worthwhile goal to indicate that each student should know how to swim, if there is no swimming pool or water available for such instruction, or if a state regulation does not permit the use of a trampoline, it would be foolish to list such an activity as a goal. Individualized instruction in many activities is not possible without adequate staff. In addition, there are other influencing factors, such as climate, local school regulations, equipment available, and administrative philosophy, that must receive the attention of the physical educator in the development of goals.

What does the nature of the community indicate is the type of program that is needed?

The community itself—its social, economic, political, and physical makeup—should play an important role in the development of goals. For example, Americans are becoming aware that a different type of education is needed in the "ghetto" and poverty areas of this country than in suburbia. The program must be geared to the boys and girls who dwell in these neighborhoods. The fact that they are physically, emotionally, socially, and educationally disadvantaged has implications for education. The fact that many of the students are anti-intellectual must be taken into consideration. Ethnic considerations are pertinent.

The physical education program has particular value and can make a valuable contribution to many boys and girls if it is related particularly to the conditions that exist in their communities and to the type of educational program needed to meet their needs and interests.

A consideration of the community is also important from the standpoint that its support and cooperation are needed if an excellent program of physical education is to be developed.

What is the physical educator's personal philosophy of education and physical education?

After all the previous steps have been taken into careful consideration, the physical educator should give thought to his own personal philosophy of education and physical education. His training, experience, and thought have resulted in a realization of what is valuable, what is educational, and the type of program that will make the greatest contribution to young people. When the first five steps, plus the

development of a personal philosophy, are synthesized, they should provide a valid formula that, when implemented, will result in an excellent physical education program.

OBJECTIVES OF GENERAL EDUCATION

The teacher of physical education must be concerned with general educational goals before thinking of the goals of his or her special field. Since physical education is a part of general education, it is important to understand the purposes of education—why schools, teachers, and curricula exist. Physical education is one part of the educational program, as is geography, science, mathematics, foreign languages, or art. Each field of specialization needs to keep its sights on the purposes of general education if it is to justify its rightful place in the schools. If each area of specialization in secondary education established its own objectives irrespective of the overall goals of education, chaos would result, and programs of education would probably conflict and become distorted, depriving the students of a well-balanced educational experience. Therefore, each area of learning must realize that it is a part of the whole, and that the whole is greater than the sum of its parts.

For purposes of this discussion the goals of general education set forth by the Educational Policies Commission* may be used. This influential policy-forming group pointed out that there are four major categories of educational objectives: (1) self-realization, (2) human relationship, (3) economic efficiency, and (4) civic responsibility.

The objectives of self-realization are concerned with helping the individual to become all that he is capable of becoming. For example, education should help each

---

*Educational Policies Commission: Policies for education in American democracy, Washington, D. C., 1946, National Education Association and American Association of School Administrators.

boy and girl to speak, read, and write effectively, to acquire fundamental knowledge and habits concerned with healthful living, and to develop ability to use leisure time in a wholesome manner.

The objectives of human relations are concerned with assisting the individual to fully understand and relate to his function as a human being working cooperatively with other human beings. Thus education should help to develop such things as an appreciation of the home, friendships, courtesy, the value of human welfare, and the ability to work harmoniously with one's fellowmen.

The objectives of economic efficiency relate to the individual as both a producer and a worker and also as a buyer and a consumer. Therefore, these objectives stress, on the one hand, such things as the importance of good workmanship, selecting one's vocation carefully, occupational adjustment, appreciation, and efficiency and, on the other hand, such things as consumer judgment, buying, and protection.

The objectives of civic responsibility pertain to the function of the individual in a law-abiding society. These goals apply to such things as the citizen's responsibility to his fellowmen, to his country, and to the world; his responsibility for being tolerant, scientific, critical, sympathetic, and cooperative as a member of a free society; and his responsibility for developing an unswerving loyalty to the democratic way of life.

The four categories of objectives outlined by the Educational Policies Commission point to the overall purposes of education. The goals of physical education, therefore, must be compatible with and reinforce these objectives. The education that takes place at the gymnasium, playground, dance studio, swimming pool, and other play facilities can contribute much to the accomplishment of these worthy objectives.

GOALS FOR SECONDARY SCHOOL STUDENTS

The teacher of physical education, in addition to understanding and appreciating the goals of general education, must also be familiar with the goals that are peculiar to boys and girls who are pursuing their secondary school education. General educational goals and physical education objectives must be interpreted and delineated in terms of what the student needs at each stage of development and at each educational level through which he passes. At the secondary level the teacher should be aware of the developmental goals that boys and girls are accomplishing and continually try to utilize the physical education program as a means of helping the young person to accomplish these worthy goals. Some of the developmental goals of the secondary school student include the following:

1. Understanding of self. He understands himself physically, mentally, emotionally, and socially—how each aspect of self is reflected in his personality, and how he should strive for integration of the various aspects of self so that he functions harmoniously as a whole.

2. Feeling of security. He has security because he has developed skills for such tasks as protecting himself against danger, earning a living, and meeting his physical needs. He has security within himself, and this sense of security embraces such conditions as being loved, possessing self-confidence, and having a feeling of belonging.

3. Realistic attitude. He has discovered his abilities and interests, has grown in understanding of himself, and knows his needs and capabilities. He is realistic in his self-appraisal and accepts himself for what he is. He deals with situations and problems with honesty and objectivity.

4. Self-sufficiency. He becomes increasingly self-sufficient. He develops skills and interests that free him from dependency on his family and group. He is increasingly able to make his own decisions, do original thinking, and work out his own plans.

5. Flexibility. He profits from the thinking and experiences of others and is tolerant and understanding of the feelings of other people.

Fig. 4-2. Organic development refers to the building of physical power in the student. Students pair up in teams to conduct exercises designed to build strong bodies. (South Camp Drake Junior High School.)

6. Social-mindedness. He establishes satisfying relationships with boys and girls his own age and with parents and adults, serves as a participating citizen in both school and community, learns about the social environment, gains experience in group living, and learns to respect the rights of others. He conforms to the standard of acceptable behavior.

7. Balance. He has a variety of interests —he is not interested in only one activity, such as basketball or reading, but develops a variety of interests that may include sports, drama, music, and history.

8. Sense of personal worth. He has self-respect and self-esteem. He has a sense of pride, achievement, mastery, usefulness, and success.

9. Emotional stability. He is able to control himself and adjusts to changes in a more mature manner.

10. Intellectual improvement. He develops basic mental skills, acquires knowledge, learns about the natural and physical environment, acquires better understanding of the scientific approach to learning, grows in ability to listen, read, think,

speak, and write, and is motivated by learning.

11. Value consciousness. He appreciates what is right and wrong and the importance of striving for excellence, scholarly behavior, and proper ethical conduct.

If the boy or girl in secondary school can achieve these developmental tasks before completing this phase of education, he or she will have gone a long way toward becoming an educated and well-adjusted person and thus lay the foundations for productive, happy, and healthful living. Physical education can play an important role in helping each young person to be successful in accomplishing these goals.

MAJOR OBJECTIVES OF PHYSICAL EDUCATION

The general objectives of physical education are usually stated in broad terms, with no distinction made for boys or girls. The physical education profession has selected, through its leading authorities, the general objectives of physical development, cognitive development, motor development, and personal-social adjustment.

Physical development

Physical development refers to the building of organic power through development of the various systems of the body. It is concerned with a state of vigorous health and physical fitness. Physical power is built into the individual partially through participation in a program of physical activities. Such participation, if engaged in wisely and adapted to the needs of the individual, results in the ability to sustain adaptive effort, to recover, and to resist fatigue. The value of this objective is that an individual will be more active, have better performance, and be healthier if the organic systems of the body are functioning properly. Physical activity helps these organs to function properly. Through vigorous muscular activity the heart provides better nourishment for the body and the person is able to perform work for a longer period of time with less expenditure of energy. Such a condition is necessary for a vigorous and abundant life. Throughout the entire day a person is continually in need of vitality, strength, endurance, and stamina—both to perform routine tasks and to meet emergencies. A well-planned physical education program can help equip the student with these essential items.

Motor development

Neuromuscular skills are concerned with proficiency in the performance of physical activities. They include the coordination, rhythm, accuracy, and poise that lead to excellence in executing various games, sports, and physical skills. Motor development is concerned with cutting down waste motion, with performing physical acts in a proficient, graceful, and esthetic manner, and with utilizing as little energy as possible in the process. This has implications for one's work, play, and any other activity requiring physical movement. This objective is sometimes referred to as "motor" development, a name that is derived from the relationship between a nerve or nerve fiber that connects the central nervous system, or a ganglion, and a muscle. As a consequence of the impulse thus transmitted, movement results. The impulse the nerve delivers is known as the motor impulse.

Motor, or neuromuscular, development is essential to physical education. With increased cortical control of the body there is less waste motion; consequently, coordination and skill are increased. Greater skill and proficiency and fewer errors mean more enjoyment of the activity and a greater desire to engage in it. It is human nature to like to do those things in which one excels. It is very important to the physical education profession, to the individual, and to society in general to develop many and varied skills in the individual. In this way, the desire and motivation will be present to spend time regularly in activities that will result in a more totally fit population.

Cognitive development

Cognitive development involves knowledge, judgment, and appreciation attendant on performing physical activities. It is concerned with an accumulation of knowledge essential to enriched living and the ability to think and to interpret situations continually encountered in day-to-day living. The accumulation of knowledge takes place when the person gains information concerning the body, the importance of exercise, the need for a well-balanced diet, and the values of good health attitudes and habits.

Cognitive development also includes knowledge of the importance of sanitation, factors in regard to disease prevention, community and school agencies that provide health services, rules and regulations in regard to various games and allied activities, techniques and strategies involved in organized play, human relations, and many other items useful in living a full life. The ability to think and to interpret situations is developed through many experiences in games and sports. These experiences foster a sense of values, alertness, the ability to diagnose a situation under tense conditions, the ability to make a decision quickly

Fig. 4-3. Gaining knowledge of out-of-door activities. (San Diego County Schools, San Diego, Calif.)

and wisely under highly emotional conditions, and the ability to interpret human actions. A body of knowledge is stored away so that it can be called upon at some future time to help in making discriminatory judgments, discerning right from wrong, and distinguishing the logical from the illogical.

Personal-social development

Personal-social development entails adjustment both to self and to others and development of desirable standards of conduct essential to good citizenship. It represents one of the main contributions of physical education to modern society. Through physical activities the individual, under qualified leadership, can be aided in making adjustments. Physical education carries its own drive. Most children and youth do not have to be motivated to engage in many of the activities that are offered. They want to participate as a result of their own free choice and as a result of an inner drive that propels them into action. Under such conditions rules can be established and a framework of conduct set forth, and the individual will conform in order to participate. Good human relations

are developed when there is respect for ability, one's desires are subordinated to the will of the group, aid is given to the less-skilled and weaker players, and the realization exists that cooperation is essential to the success of society. Physical education further aids in developing a feeling of belonging, regard for the rules of sportsmanship and fair play, courtesy, sympathy, truthfulness, fairness, honesty, and respect for authority. All are essential to good human relations—one of the most important keys to a peaceful and democratic world.

IS THERE A PRIORITY FOR OBJECTIVES OF PHYSICAL EDUCATION?

Leaders of physical education are beginning to ask such questions as: Is one objective of physical education more important than the others? Where should the emphasis in physical education programs be placed? Physical educators cannot do everything—what comes first? Does physical education have a master purpose? Is there a hierarchy of objectives?

Historically, we have seen where physical education in its early days was primarily concerned with organic development. However, at the turn of the century with the introduction of the "new physical education," other objectives more closely identified with general education, such as social development, were included. Today, there are varying viewpoints in regard to the question of priority of objectives.

A survey of selected leaders in the field of physical education, asking for their views as to a priority of objectives, resulted in some interesting information. Most professionals contacted felt that organic development and motor development are the objectives that should get highest priority. They listed such reasons as: they are most uniquely tied in with physical education, they are essential for fitness throughout life, they provide the impetus for the program, and they represent the objectives that can more readily be achieved. After organic and neuromuscular development, the leaders surveyed indicated that the most widely accepted objective in terms of importance is cognitive, mental, or interpretive development. The reasons listed for the importance of this objective included the fact that it is important to develop a favorable attitude toward physical education if any objective is to be achieved at all. Also included was the fact that education is primarily involved with developing a thinking, rational human being in respect to all matters, whether it be concerned with his physical development or other aspects of living. Social development ranked lowest in the survey. Reasons given to support this place on the priority listing were that all areas of education are interested in the social objective and that it was not the unique responsibility of one field, such as physical education. Therefore, the other objectives should receive a higher priority rating.

The survey of national leaders in physical education brought out another important consideration. Many professional leaders stressed the point that, with the national curriculum reform movement taking place today and with increased emphasis on educational priorities, physical educators should rethink their positions in regard to their place in the educational system. They should reexamine how they can contribute their greatest effort and make their greatest contribution in today's changing world.

Rosentswieg[*] conducted a study in which he had 100 college physical educators in the State of Texas rank ten objectives of physical education. Rosentswieg's findings showed that these 100 physical educators ranked the organic and neuromuscular objectives higher than all the rest. When the men physical educators were compared with the women physical edu-

---

[*]Rosentswieg, Joel: A ranking of the objectives of physical education, Research Quarterly **40**:783, 1969.

Table 4-1. Comparison ranking of objectives of physical education[*]

Objective	Ranking
Organic vigor	1
Neuromuscular skills	2
Leisure-time activities	3
Self-realization	4
Emotional stability	5
Democratic values	6
Mental development	7
Social competency	8
Spiritual and moral strength	9
Cultural appreciation	10

[*]From Rosentswieg, Joel: A ranking of the objectives of physical education, Research Quarterly **40**:783, 1969.

Table 4-2. Ranking of objectives by sex[*]

Objective	Ranking Males	Females
Organic vigor	1	2
Neuromuscular skills	2	1
Leisure-time activities	3	3
Self-realization	4	4
Emotional stability	5	5
Social competency	6	8
Democratic values	7	7
Mental development	8	6
Spiritual and moral strength	9	9
Cultural appreciation	10	10

[*]From Rosentswieg, Joel: A ranking of the objectives of physical education, Research Quarterly **40**:783, 1969.

cators, there was disagreement upon the primary objective of physical education. The statistical results of the study are illustrated in Tables 4-1 and 4-2.

LEADERSHIP—THE KEY TO ACCOMPLISHMENT OF PROFESSIONAL OBJECTIVES

Leadership is essential in the field of physical education if the goals that have been set for this profession are to be realized. The most elaborate facilities can be provided and the necessary materials can be at hand, but unless there are qualified leaders available, programs will fail. These leaders must have certain general and specific qualifications if they are to do an acceptable piece of work. Leaders will be better able to accomplish physical education objectives if they possess the following qualities:

1. Sound judgment, logical thinking, common sense, and the ability to discriminate right from wrong.

2. Functional use of written and oral English. Since the use of English is so essential in effectively presenting programs to the public, this qualification is required. In addition, because physical education leaders are emulated by the thousands of youths who engage in their programs, they must set a good example by using correct English.

3. Acceptable health. Leaders should be free from any physical or mental defects that would prevent successful leadership. Because of the important part a leader plays in shaping the lives of those under his leadership, persons with any health handicap that would adversely affect the consumer of the product should not be a part of this profession. Leaders should be

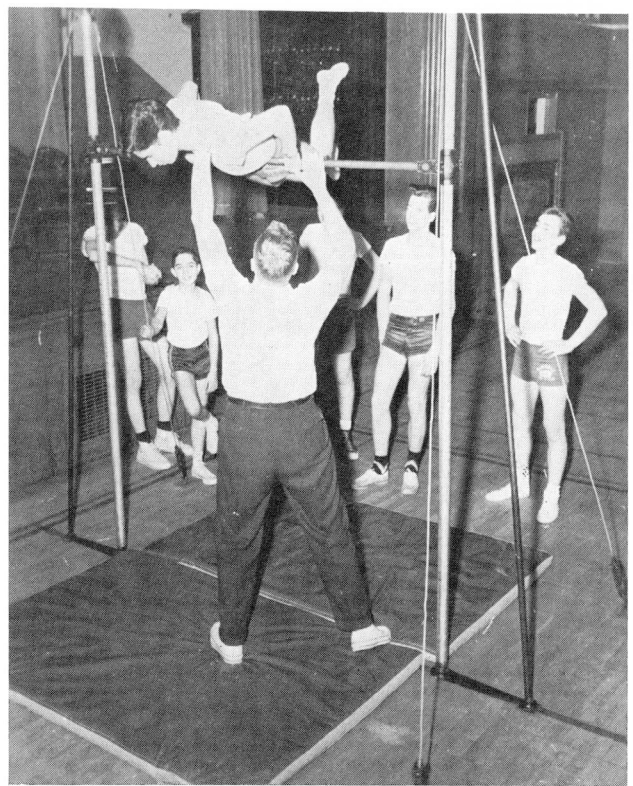

Fig. 4-4. Good leadership is essential to the accomplishment of physical education goals. (Hartsdale Public Schools, Hartsdale, N. Y.)

in a state of buoyant, robust health in order that they may carry out their duties regularly and effectively. They should be able to teach by doing and to participate in the activities they recommend to others. Good health is essential if this function is to be performed effectively. Most important, however, the physical education leader should be an example for the profession that stresses the importance of a healthy body.

4. Pleasant personality. Such traits as enthusiasm, friendliness, cheerfulness, industry, cooperation, dependability, self-control, integrity, and likeableness are essential to working with people in a manner that will ensure the success of the programs concerned.

5. Interest in and understanding of human beings. Leaders should be familiar with the needs of the atypical as well as the normal individual. They should be conscious of the interests and capacities of those with whom they will work. The leader should enjoy working with people. He or she should get along well with others, be interested in people, be able to obtain their respect, and be able to adapt to various social settings. Such qualities as patience, loyalty, tactfulness, sympathetic attitude, sincerity, friendliness, tolerance, reliability, and a good temperament are some of the essential attributes to develop if this qualification is to be met.

6. A sincere interest in the work. Leaders should be willing to contribute generously of time and effort to the advancement of the profession. Individuals must believe in what they are doing and conscientiously strive to promote their work so that more people may share its benefits.

7. Skill in many of the activities that constitute the program. Skill is essential in appreciating and demonstrating good performance, instilling confidence, knowing the work that constitutes the profession, and adequately interpreting the program to the public.

8. Technical training. Specialized training is essential for the field of physical education. An understanding of the fundamental sciences and of scientific principles in the areas of philosophy, administration, and methods and materials, in addition to many other areas of knowledge, is necessary to the development of physical educators.

The qualifications that have been listed are essential to one who desires to become a leader. Physical education work has appeal to many, but not all are qualified to become leaders in this endeavor. Only those who meet the essential qualifications should be considered. In the hands of good leadership, methods and materials may be used effectively and wisely.

Physical education leaders often remark that inadequate facilities are preventing them from doing a job, that it is impossible to have a good program without essential indoor and outdoor equipment, and that the program is not recognized because of these deficiencies.

Acres of beautiful green grass, spacious gymnasiums, and special equipment for sports and other physical education activities are very helpful. Other things being equal, they result in programs that better meet the needs and interests of the public than do programs that have poor resources. However, one must strive to do an effective job with what is available. Programs must be built on the status quo while effort is expended to obtain more and better facilities. Many needs can be satisfied by improvising and by obtaining auxiliary playing fields and space to tide over an emergency period. Doing an effective job with what is available is one of the best ways to stimulate good public relations to the point where additional facilities will be provided. The public must recognize the need for the program and how it is helping to build a better community. When the community is able to see how it can be further aided by additional facilities, the response will be greater. This will not be the situation if the leader exhibits apathy, indifference, and lassitude because ample resources are not provided.

There is an increasing need for better qualified leaders in physical education. There must be a stringent selective policy for all preprofessional students, and standards must be established that allow only qualified individuals to become members of the profession. Only in this way will it be possible to adequately meet the needs and interests of the public, obtain their respect and enthusiasm for this work, and realize the potentialities of this great profession.

The fact that many undergraduate students and leaders in physical education do not have sufficient knowledge of the many activities that comprise their programs presents a problem. This applies to any student recently graduated from college whose training did not cover the entire area he has been assigned to teach as well as to the person who has not received formal training in the work being done. Better professional preparation in our colleges and in-service education in the schools will help in solving the problem.

Another problem encountered by many professional leaders is that of large instructional groups. Under these conditions the ratio of leaders to participants is usually very low—a few leaders are responsible for many students. In order to do a good instructional job under such conditions, many important factors cannot be overlooked. There must be advance planning that takes into consideration all the equipment, visual aids, and other materials that will be needed. There must be good organization of the class, of materials, and of other essential items. Good teaching methods and proper techniques must be utilized. Safety precautions must be stressed. These items deserve attention even in smaller classes but must have special attention in large groups.

IMPORTANCE OF METHODS AND MATERIALS IN REALIZING PHYSICAL EDUCATION OBJECTIVES

Where do methods and materials fit into the total picture of leadership and teaching of physical education? The goals of physical education are worthy ones and should be accomplished in the most economical, thorough, and beneficial way possible. Since the activities that comprise physical education are the media through which the objectives are to be achieved, they should be taught by utilizing the best methods of organization and presentation that can be compiled. The methods and materials that are used should represent the experience and training of those who have worked with these activities for many years and who, through their training and experience, know the method that is most effective under various situations. The use of such methods and materials will result in the best teaching and learning situations, with consequent interest, acquisition of knowledge and skill, and proper attitudes on the part of the learner-participant. In this way individuals will experience the enriched living that members of this profession know will come from such activities. The consumers of the programs will find that their total fitness for living has increased, their relations with their fellowmen have been improved, their community has benefited, and they have developed their own personal skills and resources for leisure to an extent that was never before realized.

This book shows how activities may be presented with a minimum of equipment. Improvisations, sport and game variations, and teaching aids and materials that provide the best results under existing circumstances are set forth. The material allows for the presentation of activities in situations where limiting factors such as inadequate facilities are present. Also included are various techniques of presenting activities, teaching, and evaluating, as well as other aids that are useful in program development.

POINTS TO REMEMBER

1. An understanding of the goals of physical education
2. Importance of knowing the objectives of physical education

3. Scientific principles upon which physical education programs need to be based
4. The role of the leader in accomplishing the objectives of physical education
5. Importance of methods and materials in achieving the objectives of physical education

PROBLEMS TO THINK THROUGH

1. Why is a teacher who does not know the objectives of his or her profession somewhat like a ship without a rudder?
2. Why should the goals of physical education give support to and help accomplish general education goals?

CASE STUDY FOR ANALYSIS

Select a secondary school and study the program of physical education to determine how well this educational system is accomplishing the four major goals of our profession.

EXERCISES FOR REVIEW

1. Read four professional books in the field of physical education and list and discuss the goals of physical education as described by the authors.
2. Categorize the specific values of physical education under each of the four major objectives.
3. What knowledge should a student possess in regard to physical education?

4. Describe a physically educated boy and a physically educated girl.
5. Why is leadership so important in the achievement of educational objectives?

SELECTED READINGS

Annarino, Anthony A.: The five traditional objectives of physical education, Journal of Health, Physical Education, and Recreation 41:24, 1970.

Bloom, Benjamin S., editor: Taxonomy of educational objectives, Handbook I: Cognitive domain, New York, 1956, David McKay Co., Inc.

Bloom, Benjamin J., Hastings, J. Thomas, and Madaus, George F.: Handbook on formative and summative evaluation of student learning, New York, 1971, McGraw-Hill Book Co., Inc.

Gronlund, Normal E.: Stating behavioral objectives for classroom instruction, New York, 1970, The Macmillan Co.

Lessinger, Leon: Every kid a winner: accountability in education, Palo Alto, Calif., 1970, Science Research Associates.

Physical Education Association of Great Britain: The concept of physical education, British Journal of Physical Education 1:81, 1970.

Rosentswieg, Joel: A ranking of the objectives of physical education, Research Quarterly 40:783, 1969.

Tanner, Daniel: Using behavioral objectives in the classroom, New York, 1972, The Macmillan Co.

Van Til, William: Education: a beginning, Boston, 1971, Houghton Mifflin Co.

5 RELEVANT HEALTH GOALS THAT CAN BE ACHIEVED THROUGH PHYSICAL EDUCATION

The 1970's have seen greater concern for the need for health education in our schools. The pollution of the environment, the increased use of drugs among young people, the upsurge of venereal disease, and the extent of alcohol consumption among all age groups are a few of the critical health problems that have caused this increased concern.

State departments of education and health, voluntary and official health agencies, and other interested groups, individuals, and organizations are mobilizing their resources in an all-out effort to acquaint boys and girls with the need for good health and the practices necessary to achieve this goal. Physical education must also contribute to this important objective.

Physical education has a direct relationship to the health of secondary school boys and girls. The ultimate objective of any health program is to maintain and improve the health of the youngsters in the schools. This refers to all aspects of health, including physical, mental, emotional, and social. It applies to human beings regardless of race, color, economic status, creed, or national origin. The school has the responsibility to see that all students achieve and maintain optimum health, not only from a legal point of view but also from the standpoint that the educational experience will be much more meaningful if optimum

health exists. A child learns easier and better when in a state of good health.

The physical educator will find many teachable moments when it is possible to contribute to the achievement of health goals. The opportunity is provided to impart scientifically accurate information that will contribute to better health habits on the part of students when they ask: "Why will it be necessary to take showers?" "Must we bring clean towels?" "Why must uniforms be clean?" The physical educator is trained in the biological sciences. This foundational science information provides him with accurate factual information on various health subjects that have a direct bearing on the health of students.

The physical educator can see that the health services of the school and community are understood and utilized by the students in the physical education program, whether they involve emergency care, health appraisal, communicable disease control, or other health measures.

The physical educator should provide an environment that promotes health, growth, and learning. For example, he should cooperate with the custodian in providing safe and sanitary facilities that meet acceptable health standards; in providing proper ventilation, heating, and lighting in the settings for his activities; in seeing that all equipment is in a safe and clean condition; and in providing a proper social and emotional atmosphere for the conduct of his program. He should conduct regular inspections of facilities and equipment, institute rules that will promote safety in various activities, establish procedures to be followed in the event of illness or injury to participants, and provide proper insurance protection.

The physical educator should be cognizant of the health of students in the conduct of his program, being continually alert to their health practices and encouraging them to improve. He should take an interest in each student's total physical, emotional, social, and mental health.

Physical educators can help in the attainment of several specific objectives that the health program is attempting to accomplish in the schools. They are (1) to provide boys and girls with *health knowledge* that is reliable and based on scientific facts, (2) to help young people develop desirable *health attitudes,* and (3) to stimulate students to develop desirable *health practices.* This chapter outlines some specific ways in which the physical educator may help in the achievement of these worthy objectives.

HEALTH KNOWLEDGE

Physical educators have many opportunities to present and interpret scientific health data for purposes of personal guidance. Such information will help students to recognize health problems and to solve them by utilizing information that is valid and helpful. It also will serve as a basis for the formation of desirable health attitudes. In today's complex society there are many choices confronting a boy or girl in regard to factors that affect his or her health. A reliable store of knowledge is essential to making sound decisions.

Young people should know such things as how their bodies function, causes of infections, methods of preventing disease, factors that contribute to and maintain health, and the role of the community in the health program. Such knowledge will help boys and girls to live correctly, help them to protect their bodies against harm and infection, and impress upon them the responsibility for their own health and the health of others.

Presentation of facts about health varies with different age groups and educational levels. For young children in the early grades there should be an attempt to pro-

Fig. 5-1. The physical educator should be cognizant of the health of students. (Ellensburg Public Schools, Ellensburg, Wash.)

vide experiences that will show the importance of living healthfully. Such settings as the cafeteria, lavatory, and medical examination room offer excellent opportunities for such learning. When a boy or girl becomes a secondary school student, the underlying reasons for following certain health practices and ways of living can be presented. Some of the areas of health knowledge that should be understood by students and can be presented by physical educators include nutrition, the need for rest, sleep, exercise, and protection of the body against changing temperature conditions, contagious disease control, the dangers of self-medication, and community resources for health.

The following are a few areas of health knowledge that can be imparted by physical educators at the secondary school level:

1. Safety education as applied to physical education activities
2. Accident prevention as applied to physical education activities
3. Dangers of self-medication
4. How to dress for warmth, comfort, and protection
5. Sanitary practices involved in physical education participation
6. Available community health services
7. Organic systems of the human body
8. Good body mechanics
9. Physical limitation and fatigue
10. Effect of depressants upon the human body
11. Effect of stimulants upon the human body
12. Structures of the human body
13. How to safeguard eyes and vision
14. Physical defects and how to correct or live with them
15. Communicable and noncommunicable diseases and minor health disorders—how to prevent and control
16. Nutrition and weight control
17. Good grooming
18. Importance of an adequate and a balanced use of free time for relaxation and recreation

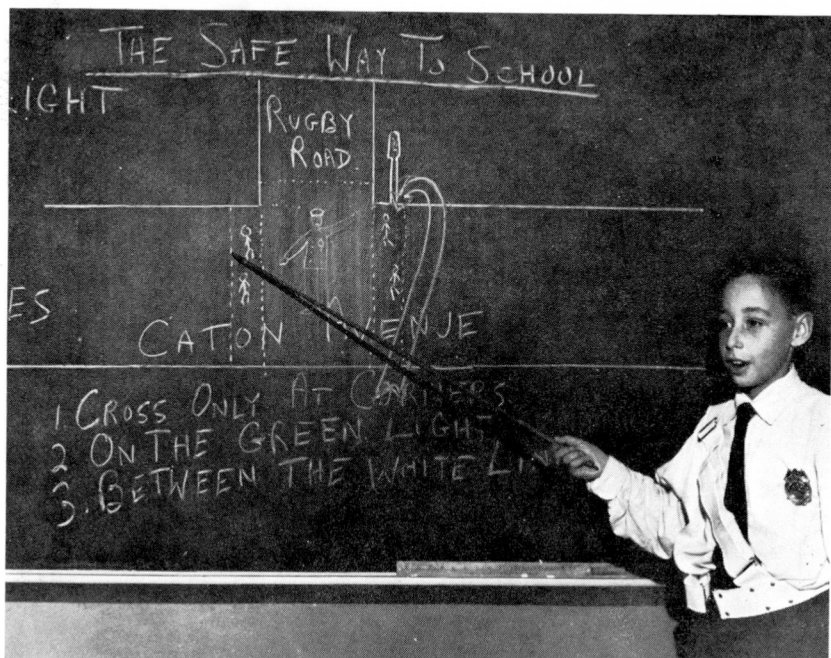

Fig. 5-2. Education should try to develop sound attitudes toward safety. (New York City Schools.)

19. Relationship between exercise and good health
20. Need for physical activity to develop and strengthen the body
21. First aid procedures
22. Amount of sleep and rest a student needs
23. Necessity and importance of the medical examination
24. Physical fitness and health
25. First aid
26. Drugs and physical health and athletic performance

HEALTH ATTITUDES

Health attitudes refer to the health interests of persons or the motives behind health practices. All the health knowledge that can be accumulated will have little worth unless the student is interested and motivated to apply this knowledge to everyday living. Proper health attitudes, motives, drives, or impulses will cause a boy or girl to seek out scientific knowledge and utilize it as a guide to living. This interest, drive, or motivation must be dynamic to the point where it results in behavior changes.

The physical education program should be directed toward developing those attitudes that will result in optimum health. Students should have an interest in and be motivated toward possessing a state of buoyant health, feeling fit and strong, being well rested and well fed, having wholesome thoughts free from anger, jealously, hate, and worry, and possessing adequate physical power to perform life's routine tasks. If they have the right attitudes toward health knowledge, healthful living, and such health services as medical examinations, proper health practices will be followed. Health should not be an end in itself except in cases of severe illness. Health is a means to an end—it aids in achieving noble purposes and living an enriched life.

Another factor that motivates boys and girls to good health is the desire to avoid the pain and disturbances that accompany ill health. They do not like toothaches, headaches, or indigestion because of the pain or distraction involved. However, developing health attitudes in a negative manner, through fear of pain or other disagreeable conditions, is not as desirable as the positive approach to achieving proper health attitudes.

A strong argument for developing proper attitudes or interests centers around the goals the students are trying to achieve in life and the manner in which optimum health is an aid in achieving such goals. This is the strongest incentive or interest that can be developed in the individual. A great artist, an outstanding businessman, or a famed dancer is greatly benefited by good health. It is important that the study, training, hard work, trials, and obstacles encountered be met successfully. Optimum health will aid in the accomplishment of such goals. As Jennings, the biologist, pointed out, the mind can attend to only one thing at a time. If attention is focused on a headache or an ulcer, it cannot be satisfactorily focused on essential work that has to be done.

Some of the health attitudes that the physical educator can help to develop include an interest in the following:

1. Attaining and maintaining good health
2. Obtaining accurate scientific information concerning health
3. Forming proper nutrition and eating habits
4. Preventing accidents
5. Recognizing the roles of physical activity, sleep, rest, and relaxation in physical fitness
6. Separating health fact from fancy
7. Understanding one's physical limitations
8. Correcting any remediable body defects
9. Developing good health habits
10. Evaluating one's health habits and making needed changes
11. Understanding how one's body can function to utmost capacity

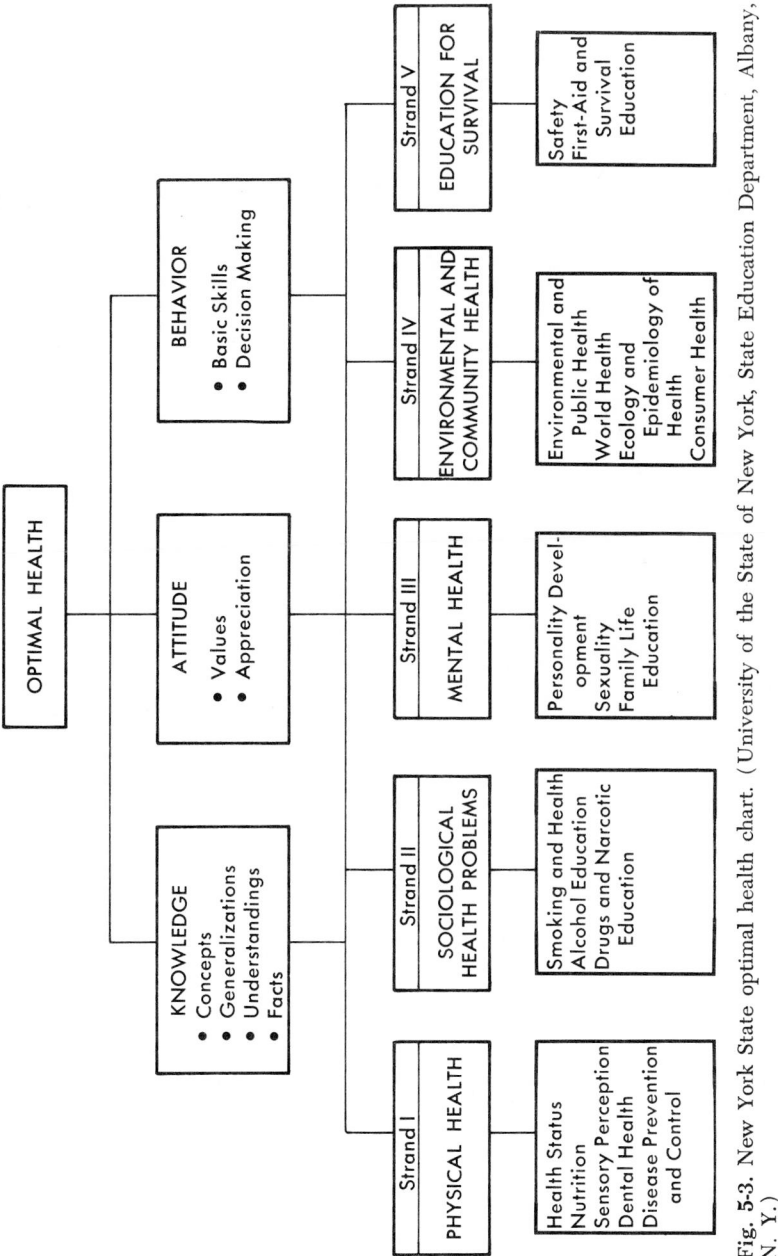

Fig. 5-3. New York State optimal health chart. (University of the State of New York, State Education Department, Albany, N. Y.)

12. Using the body in an efficient, graceful manner in sports activities and daily life
13. Mastering and enjoying a wide range of physical activities
14. Providing for play and large-muscle activities, as well as daily relaxation, in order to realize optimum achievement in physical and mental well-being
15. Knowing how various organic systems of the body work together
16. Acknowledging health responsibility as a member of a school, community, and family
17. Accepting reasonable responsibility in keeping the school, home, and community environment neat and clean
18. Participating in social and play activities with others
19. Being a good sportsman and taking failures and successes in stride
20. Learning to accept physical handicaps of self and others
21. Recognizing the effects of drugs, alcohol, narcotics, and tobacco on performance in physical activities

HEALTH PRACTICES

Desirable health practices represent the application to one's routine of living of those habits that are best, according to the most qualified thinking in the field. An individual's health practices will, to a large extent, determine his state of health. Harmful practices or habits, such as failure to obtain proper rest or exercise, overeating, overdrinking, and oversmoking, as well as the failure to observe certain precautions against contracting disease, will often result in poor health.

Knowledge does not necessarily ensure good health practices. An individual may have at his command all the statistics concerning the dangers of speeding on the highway; yet this information is useless unless it is applied. The health of an individual can be affected only as he applies that which is known. At the same time, knowledge will not usually be applied unless an incentive, interest, or attitude exists that impels its application. It is important, therefore, to see the close relationship that exists among health knowledge, health attitudes, and health practices. One contributes to the other.

Listed below are a few health practices with which every physical educator teaching at the secondary school level should be especially concerned:

1. To prevent the spread of infection, insist that each member of an athletic team and/or physical education class have an individual towel and drinking cup, and personal articles of clothing.
2. To prevent the spread of infection (such as colds, influenza, mumps, and measles), do not allow students to exercise or engage in a strenuous workout while an infection is still resident.
3. Give proper first-aid treatment promptly to floor or mat burns or other abrasions and wounds suffered in physical activity.
4. Have a physician present at all interscholastic contests in which the injury hazard is great.
5. Do not allow a player to reenter a game following a severe injury, particularly when unconsciousness or injury to the head or spine has occurred.
6. Work closely with the medical adviser and health department in all matters that are medical in nature, such as treating infected wounds. Honor all excuses from physicians.
7. Maintain a sanitary environment in the locker and shower rooms, gymnasium, swimming pools, and other facilities of the physical education department.
8. Insist on clean clothing, towels, and so on for all types of physical education activities.
9. Discuss with physicians, the medical society, nurses, and other qualified persons the school policy that should govern excuses from physical education for health reasons.
10. Encourage students with colds and other illnesses to remain home.
11. Make the health and welfare of stu-

Fig. 5-4. Maui High School, Hamakuapoko-Paia, Hawaii.

dents the primary considerations in planning all physical education and athletic programs.

12. See that students have adequate medical examinations if they participate in any of the various phases of the physical education program.

13. Conduct an athletic program in which contests are adapted to the physical capacities and other needs of the student.

14. Plan the playing seasons for athletics so that they will be of a reasonable duration, with no postseason contests. Make sure that players are well conditioned before competition is conducted.

15. Do not require girls to participate in the same highly organized and competitive athletic experiences as boys, and omit from their program heavy lifting, jumping from high places, and other activities that require hard landings in a vertical position.

16. Encourage all boys and girls to receive proper sleep, rest, and nutrition and to develop other desirable health practices essential to good physical performance and sound health.

17. Do not include boxing as part of the physical education program.

18. Be qualified in first aid.

19. In planning classes, allow time to permit change of clothing and showering.

20. Provide an opportunity for each student to participate in physical education class and the intramural sports program.

21. Give appropriate guidance to community groups sponsoring organized competitive athletics.

22. Offer a wide variety of activities based upon students' interests and needs.

23. Group students for participation on the basis of their abilities and needs.

SELECTED METHODS OF TEACHING HEALTH KNOWLEDGE, ATTITUDES, AND PRACTICES

Some methods of teaching health information to students are as follows.

Discussions. The classroom, gymnasium, athletic field, and other places where students gather offer many desirable moments for presenting and discussing important health information.

Example. A teacher's example is a very powerful method.

Films and other visual aids. Many excellent health films are available from state departments of health, voluntary health agencies, universities, and professional associations.

Reading assignments. There is a considerable amount of health material available, in pamphlet form as well as in book form. Bucher's high school physical education text, entitled *Physical Education for Life,*° contains several chapters on health matters relating to the physical education program. By being selective, a teacher of physical education can assign readings that will give meaning to the health principles he or she is trying to impart.

Speakers. The school doctor, team physician, outstanding community personality, professional sportsman, or other person can be brought in from time to time to accent the importance of health.

Special projects. Health Day, Physical Fitness Week, Clean-up Week, Work Day,

-----
°See Selected Readings.

and other projects can be utilized to focus attention on various aspects of health.

Awards. An award in the form of a letter, certificate, or other form of recognition can be given to the healthiest student or to the boy or girl who ranks highest on the physical fitness tests, on a health knowledge examination, or the like.

Experiments. An actual experiment such as feeding two rats different diets will work wonders in putting across health information to students.

PRINCIPLES TO KEEP IN MIND IN FURTHERING HEALTH OBJECTIVES

1. Physical activities should be included in the program only as the pupils' health status warrants. This means that such factors as students' strength, organic or functional disorders, muscular development, physical disabilities, and coordination, as ascertained through medical examinations, are taken into consideration.

2. All students should participate in the physical education program.

3. Class size should be sufficiently small to permit effective instruction and actiivty.

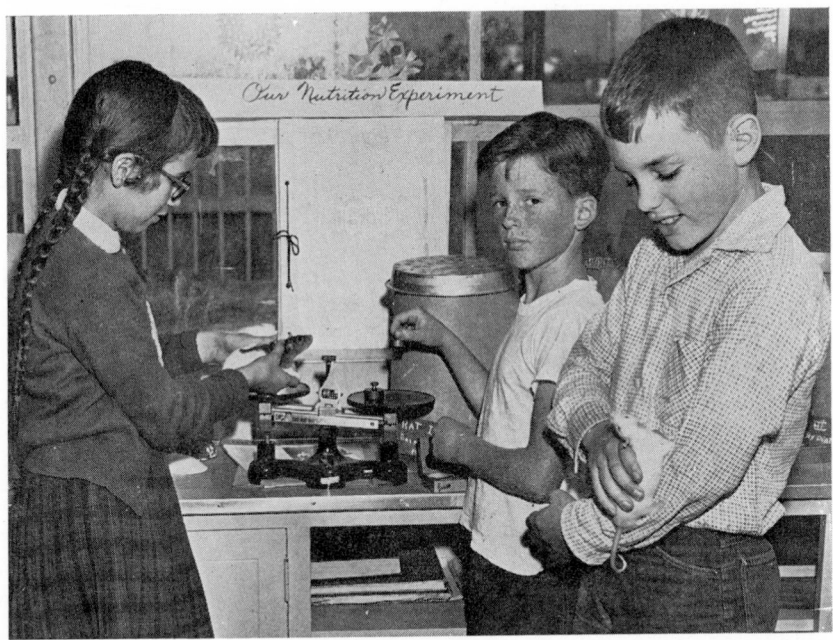

Fig. 5-5. Health experiment in nutrition. (San Diego County Schools, San Diego, Calif.)

A general guide would be to enroll not more than forty pupils in a class.

4. Every precautionary measure possible should be taken to provide for safety and to prevent accidents.

5. The intramural, extramural, and interscholastic athletic programs should be laboratory periods for the class instructional program and should be conducted in the light of the welfare and health interests of those who participate.

6. Every school should have a well-defined plan that provides for the proper medical and health considerations of each pupil. This means that there should be well-thought-through policies governing procedures for prevention of disease, emergency care in event of accidents, environmental sanitation, medical examinations, and so on.

7. The physical education program should establish and enforce sound hygienic standards.

8. The physical education teacher should be sure that each student understands the impact of food, drugs, smoking, and the use of alcoholic beverages on physical performance.

9. Each teacher of physical education should have an understanding and an appreciation of the school health program and a desire to further the health of his or her pupils.

POINTS TO REMEMBER

1. An understanding of the relationship of physical education to the health of the student
2. An appreciation of ways in which the physical educator can contribute to the health of the student
3. Health facts that physical education can teach to students.
4. Health attitudes that physical educators can help to develop in students
5. Health practices that physical educators can help to develop in students
6. Effective techniques and means of presenting health information

CASE STUDY FOR ANALYSIS

Through a program of testing and observation, determine the amount of scientific health knowledge possessed by a high school boy and girl, their attitudes toward health, and the health practices that are a part of their daily routine. Analyze this health information in light of the contribution a physical educator can make.

EXERCISES FOR REVIEW

1. What are some of the outstanding objectives of any school health program?
2. What should each secondary school student know about his or her body?
3. What is the relationship of attitudes to health practices?
4. What are some methods of motivating high school boys and girls to develop good health practices?
5. Why is it better to use the "positive" approach in the teaching of health?
6. Discuss and illustrate five methods of presenting health information to students.
7. Prepare a list of basic principles essential to making physical education a dynamic force in furthering the health of secondary school students.

SELECTED READINGS

Bucher, Charles A.: Administration of health and physical education programs, including athletics, ed. 5, St. Louis, 1971, The C. V. Mosby Co.

Bucher, Charles A.: Physical education for life, New York, 1969, McGraw-Hill Book Co., Inc.

Bucher, Charles A., Olsen, Einar A., and Willgoose, Carl E.: The foundations of health, New York, 1967, Appleton-Century-Crofts.

Bauer, William W., and others: The new health and safety, Glenview, Ill., 1966, Scott, Foresman and Co.

Diehl, Harold S., and others: Health and safety for you, New York, 1970, McGraw-Hill Book Co., Inc.

Haag, Jesse H.: Health education for young adults, Austin, Texas, 1972, Steck-Vaughn Co.

Miller, Benjamin F., and Burt, John J.: Good health, personal and community, Philadelphia, 1972, W. B. Saunders Co.

National Committee on School Health Policies: Suggested school health policies, ed. 4, Washington, D. C., 1964, National Education Association.

Oberteuffer, Delbert, and Beyrer, Mary K.: School health education, New York, 1966, Harper & Row, Publishers.

Willgoose, Carl: Health teaching in secondary schools, Philadelphia, 1972, W. B. Saunders Co.

6 A RELEVANT PHYSICAL EDUCATION PROGRAM

In light of the changes taking place in our society, communities, students, and educatioral programs, what constitutes a relevant physical education program for today's secondary schools? One way to explain this is (1) to outline what a physical education program should do for each student, (2) to show what selected physical education programs are actually doing in practice, (3) to discuss the status of physical education nationally, and (4) to identify ways in which physical education programs can be more relevant to the world in which we live.

WHAT SHOULD THE PROGRAM DO FOR EACH STUDENT?

The physical education program should:

1. *Develop his physical powers,* for example:

Body awareness	Speed
Strength	Agility
Endurance	Balance
Muscular power	Accuracy
Coordination	Posture
Flexibility	

2. *Develop his skill in many activities*
   Movement fundamentals
   Fundamental activities—running, jumping, skipping, and so on
   Individual sports—tennis, golf, and the like
   Team sports—such as basketball, baseball, track and field
   Gymnastics—tumbling and apparatus
   Aquatics—swimming and diving
   Rhythmic activities—such as dance

3. *Help him to understand physical activity*
   Movement principles (role of gravity, force, and the like)
   Contribution of physical activity to physical health, for example:

   Weight control
   Muscle tonus
   Relief of nervous tension
   Relaxation
   Absence of fatigue
   Contribution of physical activity to mental health, for example:
   Contribution to a desirable body image (research indicates the attitudes and feelings of a person toward his body affect his personality development)
   Outlet for aggressions
   Release from tensions
   Contribution of physical activity to academic achievement—research indicates there is a correlation between motor development and academic achievement because of physical fitness, development of motor skills, better self-concept, and so on

4. *Provide him with a meaningful social experience*
   He experiences success in his play activities.
   He is recognized and has a feeling of belonging.
   He learns to play by the rules.
   He develops such social traits as honesty, sportsmanship, and reliability, which contribute to the development of a socially desirable personality.
   He develops respect for other members of his class.
   He develops respect for leadership.
   He contributes to proper group adjustments.

WHAT ARE SELECTED PHYSICAL EDUCATION PROGRAMS DOING FOR EACH STUDENT?

Two physical education programs are presented here in outline form and provide accurate representations of the nature and scope of these two programs. It should not be assumed, however, that all physical education programs that exist in secondary schools across the country are the same.

The physical education program in secondary school I

Objectives: To achieve physical fitness and to fulfill the needs of the student.

Activities:

SEVENTH AND EIGHTH GRADES: football, soccer, basketball, tumbling, apparatus, volleyball, wrestling, track and field, softball. The girls engage in all of these activities except football and wrestling. Girls, in addition, play speedball and participate in rhythms.

NINTH TO TWELFTH GRADES

BOYS: touch football, soccer, speedball, volleyball, archery, lacrosse, basketball, tumbling, gymnastics, wrestling, softball, track and field, tennis, physical fitness

GIRLS: volleyball, field hockey, archery, basketball, tumbling, gymnastics, track and field, physical fitness, softball

Provision for the handicapped: No provision for the handicapped.

Progression from grade to grade: No provision for progression.

Teaching techniques utilized: Each instructor given a free hand in determining what techniques will be used. Most instructors utilize demonstrations using the better students to do the demonstrating.

Instructional materials utilized: Films are used occasionally.

Budget: $71,251 for total physical education program, including athletics. Class instructional program has always received as much money as needed.

Tests: Teacher-made tests are given for various skill activities.

Physical fitness tests

President's Physical Fitness Test for seventh and eighth grades

Marine Physical Fitness Test for high school

Records: Only attendance records are kept.

The physical education program in secondary school II

Objectives: Physical fitness, skill, fun, and social development.

Activities:

JUNIOR HIGH SCHOOL:

GIRLS: soccer, lead-up skills, volleyball, field hockey, tumbling, apparatus, basketball, track and field, softball, tennis, archery, dance, badminton

BOYS: handball, tennis, soccer, flag football, basketball, volleyball, gymnastics, wrestling, dance, tumbling, baseball, track and field, tennis, archery, speedball, calisthenics, casting

Activities are offered on a seasonal basis; fall, winter, spring, and are repeated each year in seventh, eighth, and ninth grades (boys and girls).

HIGH SCHOOL:

GIRLS: field hockey, volleyball, modern dance, badminton, apparatus, tumbling, softball, archery, track and field, coeducational dance, trampoline, tennis, body mechanics, conditioning, golf

BOYS: handball, archery, tennis, badminton, volleyball, calisthenics, conditioning exercises, touch football, soccer, horseshoes, basketball, table tennis, trampoline, tumbling, wrestling, bowling, relays, apparatus, softball, track and field, golf, rifle, casting, coeducational dance

Activities are offered on a seasonal basis; fall, winter, spring, and are repeated each year in tenth, eleventh, and twelfth grades (boys and girls).

Provision for the handicapped: Special schools provided for mentally retarded and some physically handicapped children (cerebral palsy and so on); little provision for handicapped in regular physical education program.

Progression: Very little provision for progression except as activities are offered in a more advanced manner in higher grades.

Teaching techniques utilized: Lecture, demonstration, some team teaching.

Instructional materials utilized: Charts, bulletin board materials, films, music.

Budget: Athletic budget—approximately $100,000. Physical education supplies and equipment budget—$18,881.

Tests: Skill and physical fitness tests.

Records: Attendance and test records are kept.

WHAT IS THE STATUS OF PHYSICAL EDUCATION NATIONALLY?

The following facts, taken from some national surveys and appraisals of physical education programs, have appeared in the press:

Some forty million children are not getting a satisfactory program in physical education because:

Clearly defined goals are lacking.

There is too much stress on the skilled student.

Programs are not individualized (for example, handicapped students are being ignored).

Programs are not developmental in nature.

Programs lack progression from grade to grade.

There is poor instruction.

There is a lack of meaningful instructional materials (for example, audiovisual aids).

There is a lack of proper testing programs to determine what progress each student is making toward established goals.

Money provided in the budget is not apportioned properly among various components of physical education program (basic instructional adapted, intramural, and interscholastic athletics).

What is happening as a result of the problems that concern today's physical education programs?

Educators, including physical educators, are concerned about what they can do to upgrade programs—administrators want suggestions for better programs.

Students are becoming concerned about what value the programs have for them as individuals.

Taxpayers are becoming concerned about what programs cost and where economy measures can be instituted. As a result, in many cases programs are being cut back and personnel dropped.

Innovations relating to such things as voucher systems, differentiated staffing, self-paced instruction, and the like are being introduced.

The question that professional physical educators are asking is: "How can physical education programs be improved?"

HOW CAN PHYSICAL EDUCATION PROGRAMS BE IMPROVED?

An analysis of present-day physical education programs shows that they can be improved by:

Outlining clearly defined goals to be achieved by students at each grade level

Developing meaningful programs that are developmental in nature and that are characterized by progression from kindergarten through grade twelve

Individualizing programs for each student (normal student, physically handicapped, mentally retarded, poorly coordinated, culturally disadvantaged, and so on)

Utilizing effective teaching techniques (such as team teaching, independent study, student involvement, applying the techniques that promote motor learning)

Having sound instructional materials for each activity in the program (materials on activities graded according to skill ability, audiovisual materials such as records, films, materials on the human body such as charts on organic systems, posture, safety and first aid, physical education textbooks that can be placed in the hands of students, and the like)

Evaluating each student's progress toward established goals periodically (for example, utilization of valid and scientific tests of physical fitness or skill, sound grading system)

Having a meaningful record system (a record of each student's skill achievement, physical fitness, posture, physical defects, medical examinations, and so on) that follows him from kindergarten to grade twelve

Providing for a consulting service and in-service education of faculty (teachers and administrators having ready access to experts in all phases of physical education including curriculum development, testing, teaching techniques, instructional materials; furthermore, providing for periodic in-service workshops for teachers of physical education and coaches)

DEFINITION AND COMPONENT PARTS OF PHYSICAL EDUCATION PROGRAM°

Physical education is an integral part of the total education process and has as its

---

°Parts of this chapter have been adapted from material in Bucher, Charles A.: Administration of health and physical education programs, including athletics, ed. 5, St. Louis, 1971, The C. V. Mosby Co.

aim the development of physically, mentally, emotionally, and socially fit citizens through the medium of physical activities that have been selected with a view to realizing these outcomes. This is the definition of physical education that is recommended for this important field of endeavor.

• *Physical education should be an integral part of the total system of education.* Its value is determined by its contributions to the objectives of education in general. It is one part of the total educational process and, therefore, must contribute to the achievement of the objectives of general education.

• *Physical education should promote the optimum physical, mental, emotional, moral, and social development of each student as a contributing member of a free and democratic society.* It is concerned not only with training the physical self but with the mental, social, and emotional aspects of human development. Its worth is associated with such things as health, organic efficiency, character, and personality. It helps each pupil in the process of normal growth and natural development.

• *A study of needs and interests of students is essential in determining the type of program content and methods for a physical education program.* The program does not exist apart from the student. The program must be made to fit the needs and interests of students, not the students made to fit the program.

Components of the secondary school physical education program have been listed by many authors and under a variety of terms. The four components of the school physical education program used here are: (1) the basic instructional class program, (2) the adapted program, (3) the intramural and extramural programs, and (4) the interschool program.

THE BASIC INSTRUCTIONAL CLASS PROGRAM

Where sound basic instructional class programs of physical education exist, they have been developed on the basis of the physical, social, mental, and emotional needs of the students. A broad and varied program of activities, both outdoor and indoor, progressively arranged and adapted to the capacities and abilities of each student, is offered.

Following are some important consider-ations for the basic instructional class program of physical education at the secondary level for both boys and girls.

Instructional in nature

• *The physical education class is a place to teach the skills, strategy, appreciation, understanding, knowledge, rules, regula-*

Fig. 6-1. Oconomowoc Senior High School, Oconomowoc, Wis.

Fig. 6-2. Instruction should be basic and interesting.

tions, and other material and information that are part of the program. It is not a place for free play, intramurals, and varsity competition. It is a place for instruction. Every minute of the class period should be devoted to teaching boys and girls the skills and subject matter of physical education.

• *Instruction should be basic and interesting.* Skills should be broken down into simple components and taught so that each individual may understand clearly what he or she is expected to accomplish and at the same time how it should be done. Utilization of demonstrations, loop films, models, slide films, posters, and other visual aids and materials can help to make the instruction more meaningful and interesting.

• *Instruction should be progressive.* There should be a definite progression from the simple to the complex skills. Just as a student progresses in mathematics from simple arithmetic to algebra, geometry, and calculus, so in physical education the pupil should progress from basic skills and materials to more complex and involved skills and strategies.

• *Instruction should involve definite standards.* Students should be expected to reach individualized standards of achievement in the class program. A reasonable amount of skill—whether it is in swimming, tennis, or another activity—should be mastered, depending upon individual differences. Laxity and indifference to achievement should not be tolerated any more in physical education than in any other subject area in the curriculum. When boys and girls graduate from high school they should have met definite standards that indicate that they are *physically educated.*

• *Instruction should involve more than physical activity.* All physical education classes do not have to be held in the gymnasium where physical activity predominates. A reasonable proportion of class time, perhaps as much as 10% to 20%, can be devoted to discussions, lectures, independent study, working on learning packages, and meaningful classroom activity.

Good coaches often have chalktalks for their players, in which they study rules and regulations, strategies, execution of skills, and other materials that are essential to playing the game effectively. This same principle can be applied to the physical education class period. There is a subject matter content that the student needs to know and understand. Physical activity should not be conducted in a vacuum—for if it is, it has no meaning and will not be applied when the youngster leaves the class and school. As the student understands more fully the importance of sports and activities in life, what happens to the body during exercise, the history of the various activities in which he or she engages, and the role of physical activity in the culture of the world, the class takes on new meaning and physical education takes on new respect and prestige.

• *A textbook should be used.* Just as other subjects in the secondary school program utilize textbooks in their courses, so can physical education profitably use a textbook. Assignments can be made, discussions held, and tests given—all of which will provide the student with a much more meaningful learning experience. Physical education should not be a "snap" course. It has content, and knowledge and appreciation are to be gained from this subject just as they are, for example, in American history. Bucher has written a high school physical education textbook for student use —*Physical Education for Life.*°

• *There should be records.* Adequate records should be kept by the instructor to provide tangible evidence of the degree to which objectives are being met by the students. This means that data on physical fitness, skill achievement, knowledge of rules and other information, and social conduct—such as sportsmanship—should be a part of the record.

• *There should be homework.* It is just as reasonable to assign homework in physical education as in general science. There is much subject matter to be learned and

---

°See Selected Readings.

many skills to be mastered. If teachers would require their students to work on various activity skills and knowledge outside of class, there would be more time in class for meaningful teaching.

• *Each student should have a health examination before participating in the physical education program.* An annual health examination should be regarded as a minimum essential to determining the amount and nature of physical activity that best meets each student's needs.

• *The teaching load of physical educators should be determined not only by the number of instructional class periods assigned but also by the total number of activities handled by the teacher both in class and outside of class.* To do efficient work a teacher should have a normal work load —not an overload. Some professional standards have established that class instruction should not exceed five hours, or the equivalent of five class periods per day.

Required of all students

Physical education represents a need of every child, just as do English, social studies, and other school experiences. Physical education became part of the school offering as a required subject to satisfy such a need and therefore should be continued on the same basis.

All students should take physical education. No one should be excused. If a boy or girl can come to school, he or she should be required to attend physical education class. At the same time, this presupposes that a program adapted to the needs of *all* pupils is provided.

The student is compelled to take so many required courses that elective courses are limited, if not entirely eliminated. If physical education is not required, many students will not have the opportunity to partake of this program because of the pressures placed on them by the required courses. In addition, the student looks upon those subjects that are required as being the most important and the most necessary for success. If physical education is not on the required list, it becomes a

subject of second-rate importance in the eyes of students.

Various subjects in the curriculum would not be provided for unless they were required. This is probably true of physical education. Until state legislatures passed laws requiring physical education, this subject was ignored by many school administrators. If physical education were on an elective basis, it could be crowded out of the school curriculum in many communities. Either the subject would not be offered at all or it would have to be eliminated because of low enrollment.

Even under a required program, physical education is not fulfilling its potentialities for meeting the physical, social, and mental needs of students in most schools. If an elective program were instituted, deficiencies and shortages would increase, thus further handicapping the attempt to meet the welfare and needs of the student.

The physical educator should try very hard to convince administrators, school boards, and the public in general of the place of his special subject in the curriculum of the secondary school. Only as this is done will the subject occupy an important place in the school and become a required offering that is respected.

Daily period

On the secondary level there should be a daily period for physical education or, through flexible scheduling, a system that provides adequate time for a meaningful physical education program. Although this does not exist in many schools at the present time, it should be a goal toward which all leaders should work. The great amount of subject matter, skills, and activities to be covered and the need for regular participation in physical activities are two good reasons that a daily period is so essential.

Credit

Physical education should be given credit like the other major subject matter offerings. It is included in the curriculum because it contributes to educational outcomes. The credit is justified by the contribution physical education makes to the achievement of goals toward which all of education is working.

Variety of activities

Some physical education activities that should be covered in the secondary school are as follows:

> *Team games:* baseball, softball, basketball, touch football, volleyball, soccer, and field hockey (women only)
> *Dual and individual sports:* track, badminton, table tennis, deck tennis, handball, horseshoes, tennis, archery, golf, and shuffleboard
> *Rhythms and dancing:* movement fundamentals, social dancing, folk dancing, rhythms, square dancing, and modern dancing
> *Aquatic activities:* swimming, diving, lifesaving, scuba diving, water games
> *Outdoor winter sports:* skating, snow games, ice hockey, skiing, and tobogganing
> *Gymnastics:* tumbling, pyramid building, apparatus, rope climbing, and acrobatics
> *Other activities:* self-testing activities, relays, corrective exercises, camping, and outdoor education

In order to best meet the needs of the secondary school student, the types of activities should be wide and varied. The junior high and early senior high school programs should be mainly exploratory in nature, offering a wide variety of activities, with the team games modified in nature and presented in the form of lead-up activities. Toward the end of the senior high school years there should be an opportunity to select and specialize in certain activities that will have a carry-over value after formal education ceases. Furthermore, many of the team games and other activities should be offered in a more intensive manner and in larger blocks of time as the student approaches the terminal point of the secondary school. This allows for greater acquisition of skill in selected activities.

As a general rule, boys and girls at the secondary level, including both junior and senior high, can profit greatly from rhythmic activities such as folk and social dancing; team sports such as soccer, field hockey, softball, baseball, touch football, volleyball, and speedball; individual activities such as track and field, tennis, paddle tennis, badminton, hiking, handball, bowling, archery, and fly casting; many forms of gymnastics, such as tumbling, stunts, and apparatus activities; and various forms of

E. F. Marten, Seattle

Fig. 6-3. Fencing is a physical education activity that is gaining in popularity.

games and relays. These activities will comprise the major portion of the program at the secondary level. Of course, the activities should be adapted to boys and to girls as they are played separately or on a coeducational basis.

THE ADAPTED PROGRAM

The adapted program refers to that phase of physical education that meets the needs of the individual who, because of some physical, mental, or cultural inadequacy, functional defect capable of being improved through exercise, or other defi-

ciency, is temporarily or permanently unable to take part in the regular physical education program. The adapted program can correct faulty body mechanics, develop physical fitness, and provide a meaningful program of physical education for students who may otherwise not be able to benefit from such an experience. The word "adapted" is used here, although in many books and schools this special program is known by other terms, such as "corrective," "handicapped," "individual," "modified," "remedial," "atypical," and "restricted."

Health examinations such as medical or

Fig. 6-4. Rich Township High School offers a variety of activities for its students. (Rich Township High School, Park Forrest, Ill.)

physical fitness tests often indicate that some of the pupils are not able to participate in regular physical activity programs. The principle of individual differences that applies to education as a whole should also apply to physical education. Physical education leaders believe that as long as a student can come to school, he should be required to participate in physical education classes. Adherence to this tenet means that programs must be adapted to individual needs. Many boys and girls who are

Fig. 6-5. Posture rating chart—part of New York State Physical Fitness Test. (Courtesy Division of Health, Physical Education, and Recreation, State Department of Education, Albany, N. Y.)

recuperating from long illnesses or operations or are suffering from other abnormal conditions require special consideration in their program of activities.

It cannot be assumed that all individuals in physical education classes are normal.

Unfortunately, many programs are administered on this basis. One estimate indicates that one out of every eight students in our schools is handicapped to the extent that special provision should be made in the educational program.

Fig. 6-5, cont'd. For legend see opposite page.

Special provisions under an adapted type of program also need to be made for such students as the mentally retarded, the physically handicapped, the poorly coordinated, and the culturally disadvantaged in the secondary school population. Culturally disadvantaged students, for example, often have had only a limited physical education experience, either because their families have moved frequently or because they may have attended ghetto schools that did not have adequate facilities and staff for a sound physical education program.

Culturally disadvantaged students benefit from an adapted type of program because they have so often not had prior training in physical education activities, nor have they developed the fitness needed to cope with a regular physical education program.

An adapted physical education program can help these students develop the skills, fitness, and ability they need to find enjoyment and success in sports, games, and recreational activities.

Types of students in adapted program

Students having such atypical physical conditions as the following may profit from an adapted program: (1) faulty body mechanics; (2) nutritional disturbances (overweight or underweight); (3) heart and lung disturbances; (4) postoperative or convalescent problems; (5) hernias, weak and flat feet, menstrual disorders, and the like; (6) nervous instability; (7) poor physical fitness; (8) crippling conditions (such as infantile paralysis); (9) cultural disadvantages; (10) mental retardation; (11) disruptive tendencies; (12) poor coordination; and (13) gifted or creative minds.

Scheduling

There is a feeling among physical education leaders that scheduling handicapped children and youth in separate groups is not always satisfactory. Many educators who have studied this problem believe that the atypical child should receive his physical education along with the normal children and, in order to accommodate his handicap, that the program be modified and special methods of teaching used. In such cases, the administrator should be certain that the modification of the program is physically and psychologically sound for the pupil. Sometimes mental and emotional defects can be minimized if the teacher acquaints other pupils with the general problems of the handicapped child and encourages their cooperation in helping the child to make the right adjustment and maintain his self-esteem and social acceptance. There also seems to be a trend in secondary schools to follow an adapted sports program rather than to have a corrective type of program.

In the larger schools it sometimes has been possible to schedule special classes for children with certain types of abnormalities. This procedure has not always proved satisfactory, however, because of the financial cost and the feeling that boys and girls should be scheduled with normal children for social and psychological reasons. Therefore, including the handicapped in the same classes with other students has become a common practice.

In some smaller schools where there is a staff problem, students needing an adapted program have been scheduled as a separate section within the regular physical education class. In some cases group exercises have been devised, and pupils have been encouraged to assist one another in the alleviation of their difficulties. These methods are not always satisfactory, but according to the schools concerned, they are much better than not doing anything about the problem. In other schools atypical pupils have been scheduled during special periods in which individual attention can be given to them.

The procedure followed by any particular school in scheduling students for the adapted program will depend upon its educational philosophy, finances, facilities, and staff available and should be guided throughout by the needs of the students.

Principles underlying a sound adapted physical education program

1. A thorough medical examination is a prerequisite to assignment to the adapted program.

2. Through the conference technique the teacher can gain from the student much information concerning his or her interests, needs, limitations, and abilities.

3. The program of activities should be adapted to the individual and his or her atypical condition. Special developmental exercises, aquatics, and recreational sports can play an important part in most adapted programs.

4. There should be a periodic evaluation of student progress.

5. Complete records of each student should be kept. Such information as the nature of the handicapping condition, the recommendation of physician, special activities, interviews, progress, and other pertinent data should be recorded.

6. Excellent teacher-student-nurse-physician-administrator rapport is essential to an effective program.

7. The teacher of adapted physical education should work very closely with medical and guidance personnel.

8. Teachers of adapted physical education should have a sincere interest in handicapped students and should recognize the real challenge in helping them.

INTRAMURAL AND EXTRAMURAL ATHLETIC PROGRAMS

Intramural and extramural activities comprise that phase of the school physical education program geared to the abilities and skills of the entire student body. It consists of voluntary participation in games, sports, and other activities. It offers intramural activities within a single school and such extramural activities as "play" and "sports" days that bring together participants from several schools. It is a laboratory period for sports and other activities whose fundamentals have been taught in the physical education class. It affords competition for all types of individuals—the strong and the weak, the skilled and the unskilled, the big and the small. It also includes both sexes, separately and in co-recreational programs. It is not characterized by the highly organized features of varsity sports, including their commercialization, many spectators, considerable publicity, and stress on winning. It is a phase of the total physical education program that should receive considerable stress.

Relation to interschool athletics

Both intramural and extramural and varsity interschool athletics are integral phases of the total physical education program, which is made up of the required physical education class program, the adapted program, the intramural and extramural programs, and the varsity interschool athletics program. Each has an important contribution to make to the achievement of physical education objectives. The important thing is to maintain a proper balance so that each phase enhances rather than restricts the other phases of the total program.

Whereas intramural and extramural activities are for the entire student body, varsity interschool athletics are usually for students who have a greater degree of skill. Intramurals are conducted primarily on a school basis, whereas extramural and varsity interschool athletics are conducted on an interschool basis.

There is no conflict between these phases of the program if the facilities, time, personnel, money, and other factors are apportioned according to the degree to which each phase achieves the educational outcomes desired, rather than according to the degree of public appeal and interest stimulated. One should not be designed as a training ground or feeding system for the other. It should be possible for a student to move from one to the other, but this should be incidental in nature, rather than a planned procedure.

If conducted properly, each phase of the program can contribute to the other, and through an overall, well-balanced program, the entire student body will come to respect sports and the great potentials they have for improving physical, mental, social, and emotional growth. When a physical education program is initially developed, it would seem logical to first provide an intramural program for the majoriy of the students, with the interschool athletics program coming as an outgrowth of the former. The first concern should be for the majority of the students. This is characteristic of the democratic way of life. Although the intramural and extramural athletics program is designed for every student, in practice it generally attracts the poorly skilled and moderately skilled individuals. The skilled person finds his niche in the varsity interschool athletic program. This has its benefits in that it is an equalizer for competiton.

In junior high school

In the junior high school the main concentration in athletics should be on intramural and extramural activities. It is at this particular level that students are taking a special interest in sports, but at the same time their immaturity makes it unwise to allow them to engage in an interscholastic program. The program at this level should provide for all boys and girls, appeal to the entire student body, be well supervised by a trained physical educator, and be adapted to the needs and interests of the pupils.

The American Association for Health, Physical Education, and Recreation, the Society of State Directors, and many other authoritative and professional groups have gone on record in favor of a broad intramural and extramural junior high athletics program. They believe that it is in the best interests of youth at this age level.

The junior high school provides a setting for developing students' fundamental skills in many sports and activities. It is a time of great energy—and a time when physiological changes and rapid growth are taking place. Youth in junior high schools should have proper outlets to develop in a healthful manner.

In senior high school

At the senior high school level the intramural and extramural athletics program should develop its full potential. At this time the interests and needs of boys and girls require such a program. These students want and need to experience the joy and satisfaction that are a part of playing on a team, excelling in an activity with one's own peers, and developing skill. Every high school should see to it that a broad and varied program is part of the total physical education plan.

The program of intramural and extramural athletics for boys and girls should receive more emphasis than it now has at the senior high school level. It is basic to sound education. It is a setting in which the skills learned and developed in the instructional program can be put to use in a practical situation, with all the fun that comes from such competition. It should

Fig. 6-6. Intramural activities.

form a basis for the utilization of skills that will be used during leisure time, both in the present and in the future. Since this is the time when so many young people, especially girls, lose interest in physical activity, the intramural and extramural program can help to maintain such an interest.

Corecreational activities should play a prominent part in the program. Girls and boys need to participate in common activities. Many of the activities in the high school program adapt themselves well to both sexes. Play and sports days also offer a setting in which both sexes can participate and enjoy worthwhile competition together.

For girls

According to many leaders in the field, intramural and extramural athletics are preferred and emphasized for women over interschool athletics. These leaders point out that certain biological, social, and psychological characteristics of girls and women adapt better to this type of organization and program. The Division of Girls' and Women's Sports of the American Association for Health, Physical Education, and Recreation has stated that sports, when conducted in the right manner, contribute to such desirable outcomes as fitness for living and to the development of the most desirable and attractive qualities of womanhood, including many physical and mental as well as social qualities.

The program should be composed of a wide variety of team and individual sports and other activities that may be played among the girls themselves or in mixed groups. Girls have spearheaded the drive for sports and play days and thus these activities deserve special emphasis. There should be qualified women leaders directing all phases of the program, although men should work very closely with them and lend support and help at every opportunity. Women should officiate in their own activities. Every safeguard should be taken to protect girls from harmful practices. There should be no commercial ex-

ploitation or unfavorable publicity attached to the program.

Principles underlying sound intramural and extramural programs

1. The goals of the intramural and extramural programs must be consistent with those of general education and physical education.

2. The supervision of the intramural and extramural programs should be the responsibility of qualified physical education personnel.

3. The planning and conduct of the intramural and extramural programs should be based upon democratic principles and allow for participation by students as well as faculty.

4. The facilities of the entire physical education department should be available for the intramural and extramural pro-

Fig. 6-7. Interscholastic athletics in basketball. (Central Westchester League, New York.)

grams in order to permit a wide variety of activities and the maximum participation possible.

5. The units of competition in intramural and extramural programs should depend upon such factors as the size of the school, needs and interests of students, natural formation of groups within the school, and other considerations that will lend flavor to the competition.

6. Tournaments should be so conducted as to permit maximum participation of students.

7. Eligibility requirements should be designed to enable maximum participation of the student body and to protect the health and welfare of the participants.

8. Achievement can be recognized by some token of recognition, but awards should not become a primary motive for participation.

9. Officials should be well qualified so as to promote better play and maintain safety.

THE INTERSCHOLASTIC PROGRAM

Varsity interschool athletics have a definite and important place in senior high school. Whether they should exist at the junior high school level is controversial. Varsity interscholastic competition at the senior high school level can help players achieve a higher standard of mental, moral, social, and physical fitness, provided the overall objectives of physical education are kept in mind.

Varsity interschool athletics represent an integral part of the total physical education program. They should grow out of the intramural and extramural athletics program. Athletics, with the appeal they have for youth, should be the heart of physical education.

Varsity interscholastic athletics at the junior high school level

There has been considerable discussion in recent years on the advisability of varsity athletic competition at the junior high school level. The resolutions passed by some professional organizations and the

stands taken by leaders in the field point to the fact that highly organized interschool athletics programs are questionable as a part of junior high school programs.

There are two sides to the question of junior high school varsity athletics, and at times they both sound convincing. Opponents have offered facts to indicate that it is risky business to permit boys and girls to play varsity interschool athletics at this level of growth and development. Those who favor these activities have shown that programs have been conducted in a safe and sound manner.

Both sides would agree, it seems, that more research is needed to determine the right policy to follow. Probably educators would be on the safe side if they waited until more research has been conducted before encouraging this kind of participation. Above all, the following principles are basic:

1. The main object of athletics should be healthful participation and fun.

2. Every youngster should have opportunities to participate in a varied program of many physical activities and sports both in a physical education class and in intramural and extramural programs. These phases of the total physical education program should receive priority for the junior high schools.

3. Occasional competitive experiences in selected activities on an informal basis such as sports days and play days can be conducted with profit.

4. A complete medical examination is a prerequisite.

5. Proper leadership consists of persons who know and appreciate the physical and emotional limitations of youngsters, the fundamentals of first aid, the sport itself, and how to condition and train players for the activity. A certified physical educator should handle such activities.

Varsity interscholastic athletics at the senior high school level

The high school level is the logical place to start interschool athletics on a more highly organized basis. This is the place where youngsters may find an opportunity to experience exhilarating competition and test their skill against that of teams in neighboring communities.

The following principles should guide the program:

1. High school varsity interscholastic athletics should be voluntary in nature. All students who desire to be on a team should be allowed to play on the squad. In theory no one should ever be cut from the squad. Every attempt should be made to have sufficient junior varsity, or grade "B," "C," and other teams, so that any interested student will have the opportunity to participate at his level of ability.

2. Athletics should be conducted in out-of-school hours. The class period should never be utilized for practice.

3. Players should not be excused from physical education class. Programs may be adapted, but every player can receive some benefit from participating in the class program.

4. The interschool athletic program should be organized and administered with the needs of the participant in mind. What will benefit the spectator should never influence the program.

5. A wide variety of activities based on the needs and interests of students should be offered. The number of students that can be accommodated in a wide variety of sports and other physical education activities should be the basis on which an interschool athletic program is founded and developed.

6. The coach should be selected on the basis of his knowledge of the game, ability to teach, understanding of the participant, and character and personality. Some physical education preparation is an essential.

7. Through interschool competition the player should become physically, mentally, emotionally, and socially more fit.

8. One of the first requisites for every participant in an athletics program should be a medical examination to determine physical fitness and capacity to engage in such a program.

9. Everything possible should be done to provide for the safety of the participant.

10. Every school should have a written policy in regard to financial and other responsibilities associated with injuries. The administrator, parents, and players should be thoroughly familiar with the responsibilities of each in regard to injuries.

11. Some form of insurance plan to cover injuries should be in force in all schools.

12. For boys' programs the standards of the National Federation of State High School Athletic Associations should apply, and for girls' programs the principles established by the Division of Girls' and Women's Sports should apply.

13. Officials should be well qualified. They should know the rules and be able to interpret them accurately; recognize their responsibility to the players; be good sportsmen, and be courteous, honest, friendly, cooperative, and impartial; and be able to control the game at all times.

Girls' interschool athletics

The impact of the women's liberation movement is penetrating the world of sport. More opportunities are being provided for girls, making it possible for them to participate in more and different sports as well as on a higher competitive plane.

Two examples of the increased opportunities for girls in sport at the high school level are the action of the New Jersey State Interscholastic Athletic Association on one hand and the action in New York State on the other. In New Jersey it is now possible for girls to try out for varsity high school teams on an experimental basis. In New York the Commissioner of Education can determine in which sports girls can play with boys on high school teams.

The sports world that was formerly man's domain is now being shared with women. Understandably, this new development has brought forth strong "pro" and "con" feelings. Dr. Vera Skubic, of the Department of Ergonomics and Physical Education, University of California at Santa Barbara, is one who has taken a strong position for the affirmative side. She stresses that in a democratic society all students should have the opportunity to compete for a position on a sports team. If a rule or policy exists that prevents such practice, Dr. Skubic points out, it is unfair and discriminatory.

The question of extremely organized athletics for girls is extremely controversial. The problems of too much, too little, and what is a happy medium are frequently raised, with enthusiastic supporters on all sides of the issue. There seems to be a general consensus of opinion that athletics can render a valuable service for girls. The question arises as to what type of program can best render this service. Girls can develop a better state of total fitness, skills for worthy use of leisure time, and other desirable qualities and attributes, just as boys can. However, it must be recognized that girls are not boys. There are many biological, social, emotional, and other differences that must be taken into consideration.

The girls' program should be concerned especially with the individual sports and activities, as well as with team games. The women in charge and those doing the officiating should be qualified. Official girls' rules should be followed. The social aspects should be stressed; jumping and body contact should be limited or eliminated altogether. Health safeguards should be observed, seasons limited, and restrictions enforced on the amount of competition allowed any one girl. Publicity and commercial aspects should be controlled so that the girls are not exploited. The statement on policies and procedures of the Division for Girls' and Women's Sports should be an important reference and guide.

CHECKLIST FOR SECONDARY SCHOOL PHYSICAL EDUCATION[*]

The "Guidelines for Secondary School Physical Education," developed by the American Association of Health, Physical Education, and Recreation, are being utilized as the checklist for this chapter. Although these guidelines do not cover all the features stressed in this chapter, nevertheless they provide a significant checklist for determining the degree to which a secondary school has a relevant curriculum in physical education.

GUIDELINES FOR SECONDARY SCHOOL PHYSICAL EDUCATION: A POSITION PAPER

This publication provides a rationale for the development of a sound and comprehensive program of secondary school physical education. Prepared by a committee of the AAHPER Physical Education Division, it is a composite of statements, beliefs, and resolutions approved by the American Association for Health, Physical Education, and Recreation.

The philosophy and content included are intended to assist students, teachers, administrators, curriculum directors, school boards, and laymen in the organization and the conduct of a quality physical education program in the secondary school. The guidelines set forth here assume that secondary school students have had continuing and appropriate learning experiences in physical education through the elementary grades. Appropriate modifications may be necessary to reflect future changes in attitudes, knowledge, and practices.

Physical Education Division Committee to write a position paper for secondary school physical education

Frances M. Kidd (chairman)
Minneapolis, Minnesota, Public Schools
Theodore T. Abel
Pittsburgh, Pennsylvania, Public Schools
Lucille Burkett
Shaker Heights, Ohio, High School

Thomas Martin
Columbia, Southern California, Public Schools
Paul Smith
Shoreline Public Schools, Seattle, Washington
Frank R. Williams
Arizona State Department of Public Instruction

Foreword

The focus of attention and the subject of concern of this publication is the secondary school student. He has a difficult and demanding role. During his teenage years, he must learn to manage the highly sophisticated skills and techniques necessary to function as a contributing member of our complex society. Secondary students today are concerned, bewildered, confused, restless, keen, conscientious, and thoughtful. They are different from the young adult of former years in the degree of their awareness of problems, opportunities, and concerns. It is vital that we understand the teenage subculture which constitutes

[*]From Kidd, Frances M., and others: Guidelines for secondary school physical education, Journal of Health, Physical Education, and Recreation **42**:47, 1971.

such a large and complex segment of American life. In-depth investigation of this culture should lead both the student and the teacher to a discovery of what the student needs, feels, and cares about. This discovery—this common concern—brings identity to the problem and gives direction for the construction of learning experiences. The task is to develop and present activities in physical education that are functionally linked to the knowledge and attitudes of the secondary school student and his society. It is the linking of what he learns to what he feels and cares about that makes school meaningful to the student. Physical education in the secondary school, through its specific contribution, should provide:

A setting in which experiences will help each student enjoy physical activity, to feel good about himself, and to accept himself and others.

Opportunities for vigorous activities through which there may be alleviation of frustrations and tensions.

Many avenues for self-identification and for identification with sex and peer groups.

A variety of opportunities to develop self-confidence, individual initiative, and responsibility to self and society.

Experiences which recognize a diverse range of human talents and interests, facilitating the discovery of specialized abilities together with the acceptance of limitations.

An atmosphere which relates and integrates the individual with his total environment.

Special attention to differences in physical development and maturity of individual students.

An environment that supports the rules necessary for the concept of fair play and for the safety of the participants.

Opportunities for students with severe structural or functional handicaps to participate in special activities adapted to their individual needs.

Coeducational physical education experiences.

Attention to the use of books, periodicals, and audio-visual media as resource materials.

Knowledge and experience in activities which will encourage and assist the individual to maintain fitness throughout life.

Leadership opportunities for each student.

Secondary school physical education

Physical education is that integral part of total education which contributes to the development of the individual through the natural medium of physical activity—human movement. It is a carefully planned sequence of learning experiences designed to fulfill the growth, development, and behavior needs of each student. It encourages and assists each student to:

Develop the skills of movement, the knowledge of how and why one moves, and the ways in which movement may be organized.

Learn to move skillfully and effectively through exercise, games, sports, dance, and aquatics.

Enrich his understanding of the concepts of space, time, and force related to movement.

Express culturally approved patterns of personal behavior and interpersonal relationships in and through games, sports, and dance.

Condition the heart, lungs, muscles, and other organic systems of the body to meet daily and emergency demands.

Acquire an appreciation of and a respect for good physical condition (fitness), a functional posture, and a sense of personal well-being.

Develop an interest and a desire to participate in lifetime recreational sports.

The instructional program

The instructional program has as its foundation a common core of learning experiences for all students. This core of experiences must be supplemented in ways that serve the divergent needs of all students—the gifted, the average, the slow learner, and the physically handicapped. It must be geared to the developmental needs of each pupil.

The program should provide for a reasonable balance in those activities commonly grouped as team and individual sports, aquatics, gymnastics, self-testing activities, dance, and rhythms.

Sequential progression in the specific skills and movement patterns involved in the activities included in the above grouping is essential.

There should be opportunity for elective learning experiences within the required program.

The acquisition of knowledge and understandings related to the development and function of the human body, and to the mechanical principles of human movement is necessary.

Learning experiences (physical activities) should be designed to foster creativity and self-direction and to encourage vigorous activity which includes emphasis on safety procedures.

Physical fitness—agility, balance, endurance, flexibility, and strength—should be developed.

Experiences which reinforce the development of behaviors, attitudes, appreciations, and understandings required for effective human relationships are important.

Several opportunities should be offered for those students who find it difficult and uncomfortable to adjust to the regular program because of physical, social, or emotional problems.

The program should present basic skills which can be employed in a comprehensive intramural, interscholastic, and recreational program for all girls and boys.

Intramural/interscholastic

The instructional program, which has as its base the teaching of skills and knowledges, provides a foundation for comprehensive intramural/interscholastic programs wherein the opportunity for organized sports is available to all girls and boys. Intramural/interscholastic athletics makes available a laboratory period in physical education and should be encouraged and provided for all students.

Medical examinations should be required for all who participate in vigorous activities.

A physician's statement indicating the student's fitness for participation should be required following a serious illness or injury.

The program of intramural/interscholastic athletics should provide opportunities for participation in a wide variety of sports and activities for both girls and boys.

Competition should be as equal as possible, based appropriately on age, ability, height, weight, physiological maturity, and strength of participants.

The financing of the instructional, intramural, and interscholastic athletic programs for girls and boys should be provided by local boards of education.

Remuneration for additional teacher assignments (e.g., intramurals, clubs, interscholastics) should be financed by the local boards of education.

Teachers who provide leadership in the intramural and interscholastic athletic program should be enthusiastic and well-prepared and should possess technical competencies in these additional areas of responsibility.

Interscholastic athletic leagues or conferences should be confined to students in grades 7-12. Tackle football for boys should not be included in the junior high athletic program unless the kind of equipment, facilities, health supervision, coaching, and officiating that are necessary for optimum safety of the participant can be provided. Boxing as a competitive sport should be prohibited.

All secondary school interscholastic contests, including post-season games, should be under the jurisdiction of state high school athletic associations.

Opportunities for leadership and service should be made available for students.

The entire program of physical education (class instruction, adapted, intramural, ind interscholastic) should be administered by a qualified director of physical education.

The teacher

Qualified and dynamic leadership is essential to the implementation of an effective and comprehensive program of physical education in the secondary school. The key to the teaching-learning environment is a competent, concerned teacher. The teacher must be knowledgeable about growth and maturational patterns and be sensitive to student needs, desires, and concerns.

The program of physical education in the secondary school should be taught by qualified teachers whose certification in physical education is recognized by the state department of education.

Teachers of potentially hazardous activities (aquatics, gymnastics, skiing) should have specialized training to the extent that they are recog-

nized and certified by the national agencies associated with these sports.

Men and women coaches should be certificated teachers and possess a major or minor in physical education or state coaching certification. Interscholastic sports should be coached and officiated by the most qualified personnel.

Teachers and coaches should have training in emergency first aid and be knowledgeable in regard to school referral procedures.

Teachers of secondary physical education should become familiar with the program of physical education in the elementary schools and share in program planning whenever given an opportunity, to assure desirbale progression and sequential arrangement of activities, K-12.

Health protection and insurance

The health and safety of the individual should be paramount in every phase of physical education.

There should be periodic medical examinations to assist in determining the health status of all students.

Students participating in any phase of the physical education program should be required to have adequate insurance coverage.

It is essential for hygienic and safety reasons as well as to assure freedom of movement that all students change to prescribed clothing for participation in physical activities. Showering should be required after participation in vigorous physical activities.

The school should provide towels, soap, showers, and sanitary dressing facilities with adequate maintenance.

There should be supervision in the locker room to assure safety and orderliness.

Authorized school district transportation should be provided when needed for all instructional activities and intramural and interscholastic athletics.

Schools should have written policies and procedures for accident prevention, emergencies, reporting to the administration, immediate first aid, and notification of parents or guardian.

Scheduling/time allotment/class size

Scheduling, time allotment, and class size have a direct bearing on the health, safety, and extent of participation by students, on the type of activities that can be offered, and on the student outcomes which can be expected.

A daily instructional period of directed physical education should be provided for all secondary school students equivalent in length to that found in the regular school pattern.

Schools organized on other than the traditional schedule should provide physical education experiences for each pupil comparable in time to that allocated to other major courses.

The instructional program should be scheduled to allow for maximum participation and adequate time for each pupil to have an opportunity to gain the satisfaction that comes from achievement.

All students should be enrolled in physical education classes. Time should be scheduled in the physical education program for pupils handicapped by functional or structural disorders and those who find it difficult to adjust to the regular program.

Assignment to physical education classes should take into consideration sex, skill, maturation, grade level, and health status.

The pupil/teacher ratio should be the same for physical education classes as for other subject areas with variations possible depending upon the activity.

There should be no substitute for the instructional program.

The teacher's schedule should allow time for preparation and planning.

Facilities/equipment/supplies

Facilities, equipment, and supplies are of the utmost importance in conducting a comprehensive program of physical education in the secondary school.

Physical education facilities, supplies, and equipment should be provided for the instructional, intramural, interscholastic, and recreational programs in proportion to the needs, interests, and numbers of girls and boys to be served. This includes adequate and desirable shower and locker room facilities.

Each area of the physical education program should be provided with appropriate equipment and supplies in sufficient quantity to provide each student with an opportunity to actively participate throughout the entire class period.

Daily maintenance service of the gymnasium, locker room, swimming pool, and showers and regular maintenance of the outdoor physical education area must be provided for the health, general welfare, and safety of the students.

All equipment, supplies, and uniforms issued by the school should be periodically checked, reconditioned, and laundered to ensure proper sanitary condition and maximum safety for students.

In the planning of facilities, both men and women staff members on the instructional level should be consulted to ensure the optimum functional value of the teaching stations. It is recommended that 125 square feet of activity instructional area be provided for each student participating.

School and community facilities should be planned and used to supplement and complement each other in meeting the needs of the students and the community.

Community recreation programs conducted within a school facility should be under the supervision of school personnel, to assure the safety of students and the protection of facilities, equipment, and supplies.

Evaluation

Evaluation is a continuous process which is necessary for the improvement of learning experiences in terms of objectives and effectiveness of instruction. Self-evaluation by the student and the teacher is a part of the process. Evaluation should be utilized as one means of interpreting the program to pupils, school personnel, parents, and community. Schools should make certain that their offerings and procedures are consistent with the accrediting agency by which they are governed. Credit for each year of physical education in the secondary school should be granted for graduation on a basis equitable with other subject matter areas. Credit in physical education should count toward honor grades and be included in establishing class rank order. Standards for credit in physical education for graduation should reflect the same kind of quality as established by local school boards or state departments of education for other areas of instruction.

POINTS TO REMEMBER

1. A workable definition of physical education
2. The four components of the physical education program
3. Basic considerations in the required class physical education program
4. Nature and scope of adapted physical education program
5. Characteristics of intramural and extramural physical education program
6. Considerations for an interscholastic athletic program

PROBLEMS TO THINK THROUGH

1. Why is it essential to consider all four components of a program of physical education in order to best meet the needs and interests of all boys and girls?
2. Why is it that many schools do not have an adapted physical education program?
3. Why is it that many schools do not follow resolutions of professional associations in regard to interscholastic athletic programs?

CASE STUDY FOR ANALYSIS

Select a secondary school and make a careful study of its class, adapted, intramural and extramural, and interschool athletic programs. Make a list of commendable aspects of the school's physical education program and a list of points that are weaknesses and require attention.

EXERCISES FOR REVIEW

1. Define physical education.
2. Why must the class physical education program be instructional in nature?
3. What are some important considerations in developing an effective instructional class program?
4. Make a study of what four physical education leaders say are important characteristics of the class physical education program.
5. Debate the issue—Resolved: Interschool athletics should be banned from all junior high schools.

SELECTED READINGS

Barron, Alice A.: Report of the first DGWS national conference on girl sports programs for secondary schools, Journal of Health, Physical Education, and Recreation 42:14, 1971.

Bell, Mary M.: Are we exploiting high school girl athletes? Journal of Health, Physical Education, and Recreation 41:53, 1970.

Bucher, Charles A.: Physical education for life, New York, 1969, McGraw-Hill Book Co., Inc.

Bucher, Charles A.: Female sports barriers are crumbling (syndicated newspaper column), Washington, D. C., July 29-30, 1972, President's Council on Physical Fitness and Sports.

Bucher, Charles A.: Girls and women in sports: pros and cons (syndicated newspaper column), Washington, D. C., August 5-6, 1972, President's Council on Physical Fitness and Sports.

Geyer, Claudia: Physical education for the electronic age, Journal of Health, Physical Education, and Recreation 43:32, 1972.

Kidd, Frances M., and others: Guidelines for secondary school physical education, Journal of Health, Physical Education, and Recreation 42: 47, 1971.

Nelson, Wayne E.: Need we fear voluntary physical education? Journal of Health, Physical Education, and Recreation 43:63, 1972.

Report of an AAHPER Conference: Perceptual-motor development: action with interaction, Journal of Health, Physical Education, and Recreation 42:36, 1971.

Schochet, Michael: We can't remain just a high priced repetitive recreation program, Journal of Health, Physical Education, and Recreation 41: 24, 1970.

Singer, Robert N., and others: Physical education, an interdisciplinary approach, New York, 1972, The Macmillan Co.

Stanhope, Carolyn L., and others: The new physical education, Journal of Health, Physical Education, and Recreation 42:24, 1971.

Studer, Harold R., and others: Instructional technology, Today's Education 59:33, 1970.

7 DEVELOPING THE RELEVANT CURRICULUM

The physical education program in secondary schools will experience many changes in the years to come. Students will play an increasingly active role in determining the type of program that will best meet their needs and interests. This will be reflected in such innovations as more electives, where students select from groups of activities those in which they wish to specialize. In addition, there will be independent study, where a student may spend an entire semester working on some sport or other project. Furthermore, students will be permitted to take tests that, if passed, will provide exemption from part or all the physical education requirement.

The physical education program will become more instructional in nature. Physical education will emphasize involvement in community programs together with greater utilization of community resources in the organization and implementation of the curriculum.

The 1970's will see the extensive utilization of computers and measuring instruments to accurately group students in physical education classes according to abilities, traits, skills, physical fitness, and previous experience in physical education. Textbooks will be used in physical education classes as in other subject-matter fields. The movement emphasis will permeate the program throughout the school life of the student. The adapted program will receive much more emphasis. The program of physical education will be aimed at developing physically educated students, with a trend away from teacher-induced learnings toward student-motivated learnings. The conceptualized approach will be utilized with the identification of the most important concepts to be transmitted to the student. These concepts will define the domain of physical education and the most important contributions the field makes to human beings.

A well-developed curriculum is a prerequisite for teaching and learning and the key to successful daily programming. It requires much time and thought to construct an extensive course of study that encompasses the present and future needs of an ever-changing student body and community. However, it must be done if students are to pursue a relevant curriculum in physical education.

REDESIGNING THE CURRICULUM— WHAT ONE STATE IS DOING*

Physical educators were invited from various sections of New York State to a workshop on the concept of "Redesign of Physical Education." As part of the pre-

---

*The University of the State of New York, The State Education Department: Final report on the workshop on the concept of "redesign" for New York State physical educators held at Stamford, New York, October 11-13, 1970, Albany, November 20, 1980.

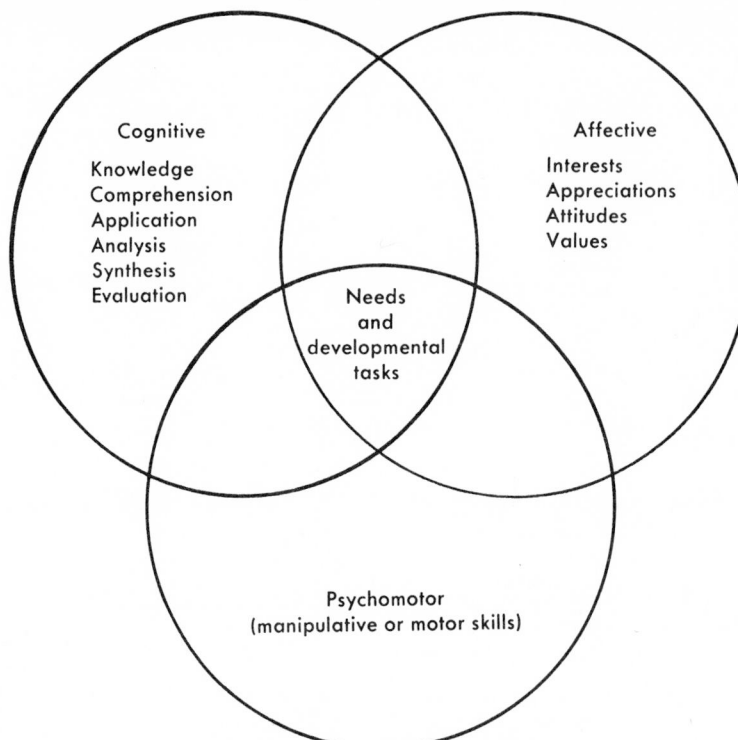

Fig. 7-1. Reinforce the curriculum in behavioral objectives. Note the interdependence of cognitive, affective, and psychomotor domains and their relationship to the learner's system of needs and developmental tasks. (From Tanner, Daniel: Using behavioral objectives in the classroom, New York, 1972, The Macmillan Company.)

liminary features of this workshop participants were asked two questions, the answers to which are particularly relevant to this chapter concerned with developing a curriculum in physical education. One question asked each participant was: "If I had the power to change my physical education program, the first problem that I would work on would be —." Some of the selected answers given to this question by physical educators indicate new directions for physical education:

Individualize learner goals

Relate physical education with the rest of the curriculum

Step up electives

Improve staff and student communications

Reevaluate objectives in terms of relevancy

Reinforce basic classroom learning through physical education

Eliminate repetitious content

Provide relevant course choices for each student

Meet needs of students

Reinforce the curriculum in behavioral objectives

Provide a more relevant curriculum

Develop program that is interesting to all students as well as enjoyable

Revitalize staff

Recognize individual abilities and offer challenges to each

Provide flexibility in program

Redesign entire curriculum

The second question that was asked of physical educators who attended this conference is especially pertinent to the development of a relevant curriculum: "What will be the characteristics of physical education in the 1980s?" Some selected answers to this question were:

Recreation oriented

Elective in nature

Less structured physical education classes

Greater use of resources in community

Stress on individuality

Growth of girls' interscholastics

Pupil planning

More coeducational activities

Individualized curriculum

Increased voluntary participation

New concepts in regard to facilities

Interdisciplinary curriculum

Use of audiovisual/television aids

Teacher-student/teacher-teacher/student-student planning

Involvement of community and student in planning curriculum

Emphasis on behavioral change in students

More guidance on an individual basis

Previous to the physical education workshop, experts in education had developed what they called "Redesign—the twenty-four characteristics of the New System of Education." These twenty-four characteristics were developed from the best thinking of experts in many educational disciplines, including educational psychology and philosophy, and specialists in innovative programs and learning resources. Many consultants assisted the New York State Department of Education in the process. One task of the workshop was to relate physical education to each of the characteristics of the "New System of Education." Since these characteristics have many implications for physical education programs of the future and for the development of a relevant curriculum, they are briefly stated here for the information of the reader:

1. The New System of Education (NSE) ensures that everyone in the community has the opportunity to be a student or staff member at any time during his life.

2. The NSE manages learning resources under its aegis and coordinates all learning experiences using community resources. Resources are continually added and subtracted.

3. The general community is encouraged to use educational facilities and resources. Facilities are open, convertible, and flexible; resources are easily available and responsive.

4. The NSE is self-renewing.

5. The NSE ensures that the organization is flexible and responds quickly to program needs.

6. The NSE is based on the best we know and is constantly searching for and implementing new ideas.

7. The NSE is continually evaluated at all levels by its own operations, as well as by outside resources.

8. Staff development is a continual, integral part of the program.

9. Staff members have a wide range of functions; different staff members perform different combinations of functions, which are constantly changing and evolving.

10. The NSE guarantees that decision-making power is in the hands of those who are affected by the decision.

11. The NSE sees that each student has an individual personal plan that is continually updated and changed as necessary to maximize his potential.

12. The NSE provides many alternate ways of attaining the goals of the students.

13. The NSE is continuous and open; a student may be in any program at any level in which he is capable of performing.

14. The NSE emphasizes processes rather than information.

15. The NSE emphasizes human values. Establishing a positive self-concept and a feeling of control over one's environment through active participation in decision making are major goals.

16. The NSE provides a range of learning experiences that emphasize direct, real, and relevant experiences.

17. The NSE emphasizes human interactions; equipment and facilities are means.

18. The NSE exists to serve the needs of people in the community. It is responsive to their needs and is held accountable; failure represents system failure only, not that of students.

19. The NSE is a zero-reject system (never excludes people).

20. The NSE functions full time, all day and all year, is available everywhere, and provides personal educational programs throughout the student's entire life.

21. The NSE has evolved by a process through which the community has gone.

22. The NSE has a stated set of goals translated into performance objectives and learning activities based on predictions about the future, extrapolation of the past, and designs based upon what pople would like their future to be as well as consideration of today's needs.

23. The NSE has a student population with widely diverse backgrounds.

24. The NSE has a carefully written plan, which describes it in detail.°

°The University of the State of New York, The State Education Department: Final report on the workshop on the concept of "redesign" for New York State physical educators held at Stamford, New York, October 11-13, 1970, Albany, November 20, 1970.

DEVELOPING THE CURRICULUM

A well-developed physical education curriculum is more than just a course of study or a program of activities. It is a statement of the philosophy behind the physical education program. It is a set of principles guiding the staff in all phases of classroom and extraclass instruction. It is a series of objectives and goals to be achieved by those who learn. It is the program, progressive in nature from year to year and season to season, providing the best opportunity for education to the majority of students as often as possible. It is the measuring rod beside which the achievements and accomplishments of students and staff alike may be evaluated. The curriculum is all these things—a culmination of the united efforts of the many people who serve to develop it.

Purpose

The purpose of a curriculum is to provide the best type of physical education program possible to students in a particular school situation. Nearly forty years ago William Ralph LaPorte headed a committee on curriculum research. His group formulated a practical program of physical education adaptable to wide variations of geographic and local conditions.* Since that time several types of curricula have evolved including *the core program,* consisting of units of study required of all students; *the elective program,* in which students select units of study according to personal preference; *the combined core and elective program;* and *the problem-centered program,* in which students and staff work out assignments according to the needs of the group. It is the task of a curriculum committee not only to determine the type of program to be presented but also to construct an appropriate progression of activities.

---

*LaPorte, William Ralph: The physical education curriculum, a national program, Los Angeles, 1937, University of Southern California Press.

The curriculum committee

The curriculum committee is usually established by the administrator of a school or superintendent of schools and is directed to develop or to revise the course of study. The head of the physical education department many serve as chairman of the group to develop or revise the physical education program, or the committee may select its own leader. Other members may include the physical education staff, a representative from the administration, such as a school principal, individuals from the health and recreation departments of the school and/or community, and selected classroom teachers from the elementary grades.

The size of the committee is variable and depends largely upon the size of the school and community to be served. The group may be further enlarged by visiting specialists or consultants in curriculum design who are called in to advise and guide the workshop meetings. In some school systems, developing a new curriculum may be labeled in-service education, and members serving on committees may receive credits toward salary increases for their participation. When university personnel are used as consultants for curriculum workshops, committee members may be able to receive graduate credits. Serving on the curriculum committee should be a very rewarding and enriching experience for both new and experienced teachers. Although completion of the study may require a full school year and after-school meetings, if a worthwhile program of physical education is the result, the entire school system and the community benefit.

Steps in curriculum development

Collection of data. Many facts and details should first be gathered by the committee to serve as a background or foundation upon which to build the new curriculum. Several factors influence a course of study, and they should first be identified, analyzed, and understood. To prepare for constructing a curriculum, therefore, subcommittees should be established to investigate the following areas:

The current program of physical education. The present program of physical education should be evaluated in terms of student achievements and progress. Specific weaknesses and strengths of the program should be identified and areas for expansion studied. Are students meeting or exceeding minimum physical fitness stan-

dards? Are more teachers or teaching stations needed at any level? These and similar questions need answering.

The needs of the students. A curriculum is successful only to the extent that the students benefit from it. They learn, they achieve, they develop, and they are better prepared to face the future as a result of experiences in physical education. Therefore, it is essential that the basic needs of

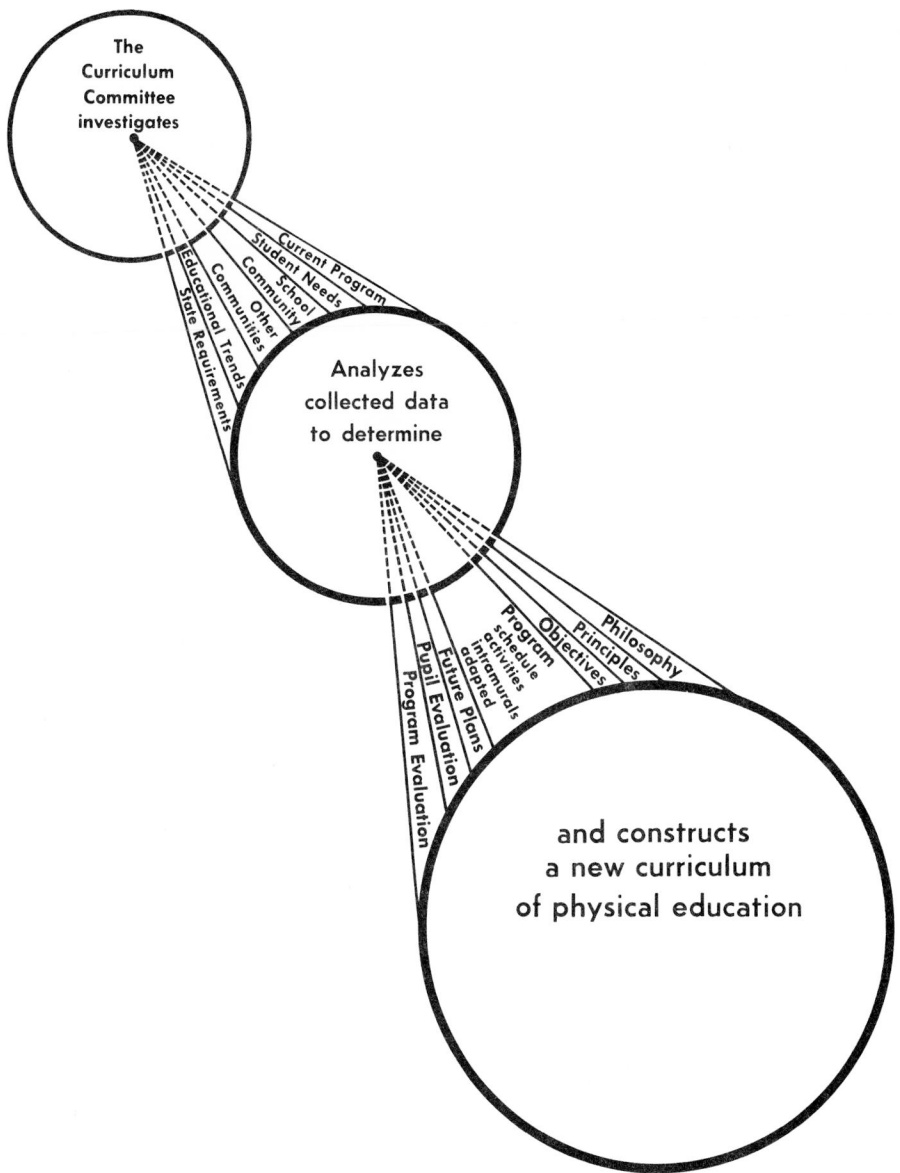

Fig. 7-2. Development of the curriculum.

the students be identified. Two areas require investigation in this respect. Current research findings related to adolescent growth and development should be studied, and a survey of student interests and attitudes should be taken. The results of these two studies of the needs of students should yield helpful information and background material.

The school's community. A curriculum should fulfill the specific needs of the school's particular community. It is essential to survey the community in terms of its prospective growth and change, school population expansion, and recreational needs. Similarly, it is important to survey community feelings in regard to the physical education program itself. Would the community approve construction of athletic facilities for increased interscholastic programs, for example? Is there a desire for adult recreation programs using school facilities? Is there an increasing need for other recreational activities? All these areas should be fully investigated before beginning the actual development of a curriculum.

The surrounding communities. The physical education curricula of schools in neighboring communities should be surveyed, as well as those of distant schools similar in size, geographic location, and climate. Much can be learned from the successes of others, and valuable ideas may be gained in this way. For example, if a course in scuba diving has been successful in other schools, the curriculum committee may want to consider such an activity in its own school program.

The current trends in society and education. A study should be made of recent trends in society and in the field of education in general, as well as in physical education. The latest techniques and methods of teachings, such as team teaching, learning packages, self-paced instruction, and programmed learning, should be considered. Research findings in relation to the learning process, grouping, and group dynamics should be studied. The identifica-

tion of learning theories and concepts regarding motor learning that are compatible with today's physical education programs should be given careful consideration. Information on improved equipment, new resource materials, new films, and new books and games should be collected. It is in this area in particular in which real stimulation and impetus may be found for changing a program. At the same time provisions may be made for program experimentation and research.

The state requirements. An investigation of state regulations and requirements should also be made to ensure acceptance of a new or revised curriculum. At the same time it should be determined whether any changes in state standards are anticipated or are in progress, in order to fulfill any future specifications that may be enacted.

When the subcommittees have completed studies in each of these six areas and have gathered as many facts and materials as possible, the committee as a whole should then be ready for the next step in curriculum construction.

Analysis of materials. The materials thus collected should be considered by the entire committee and serve as a basis for rebuilding the new curriculum. Recommendations of the subcommittees should be heard, and the committee as a whole should then determine the direction for the program and outline the present and future changes needed.

Development of the curriculum. When the data have been thoroughly analyzed and the committee has agreed upon the fundamental directions of the new curriculum, smaller working groups may again be appointed for the purpose of constructing the curriculum. Using the committee findings as a basis upon which to work, these new committees might prepare the following:

1. A statement of philosophy of the physical education department compatible with the school's philosophy of general education

2. A set of principles for teaching incorporating new methods, materials, and techniques for use at specific grade and/or ability levels

3. A set of goals and objectives for students at each grade level with provision for individual differences

4. An outline of class activities identifying levels at which new materials should be introduced, to ensure progression within the program

5. A schedule of classes, including suggested size of classes, time allotment, class sessions per week, and teacher assignments

6. An intramural and extramural program outlining activities to be included and standards for participation of boys and/or girls

7. An adapted program including methods of appraisal and referral and suggested time and types of activities for class sessions for each type of atypical condition

8. A prospectus for the years ahead suggesting additions needed in facilities and equipment and increases needed in the teaching staff and budget to accommodate innovations and expansion in the activities program and the school population

9. A synthesis of evaluation techniques covering individual record cards for students at different levels and methods of reporting and assessing achievement of objectives

10. A technique for the yearly evaluation of the total curriculum and staff, with suggested methods for revision of the curriculum when necessary

It should be noted here that a curriculum does not dictate to a teacher exactly what must be taught during a particular class hour. Rather, it serves as an overall guide for the establishment of the program within a school. It provides consistency, progression, and structure for the total physical education program, without binding or stifling the individual and collective creativity of the staff.

Adoption of the curriculum. After it has been developed, the committee as a whole should reconvene to amend and to adopt the curriculum, which should then be sent to the administration for approval and action. A curriculum of physical education should be revised as frequently as the need dictates.

SELECTION OF ACTIVITIES

The program of physical education consisting of activities such as team sports, individual and dual sports, rhythms, calisthenics, self-testing, and leisure-time and movement education activities should receive special attention. To provide students with a program consisting merely of popular team sports is neither adequate nor beneficial. Therefore, the following principles are offered as a guideline for determining the activities to be included in a balanced program of physical education.

Selected physiological principles for determining activities

1. The physical education program should provide ample opportunities for a wide range of movements involving the large muscles.

2. The facts related to human growth and development are important considerations in curriculum construction.

3. The differences in physical capacities and abilities found among students should be provided for in the program.

4. The physical fitness needs of students must be met by the physical education program.

Physiological characteristics are a major consideration in the selection of activities. It is necessary to understand the physical characteristics of boys and girls at all levels of growth and to meet them in selecting activities. The program must be rewarding for all levels of ability.

Selected psychological principles for determining activities

1. The physical education program should consist predominantly of natural play activities.

2. Activities should be selected in the light of the psychological age characteris-

tics of the student. For instance, the program should provide more coeducational activities for adolescents, because this type of program meets the needs and interests of this age group.

3. Activities that are valuable in providing an emotional outlet for the student are needed.

4. The selection of activities should provide for progression. In the junior high school the fundamentals of tumbling and apparatus work, along with simple stunts, may be taught. In the senior high school the student should progress to more advanced work and more challenging combinations.

5. The selection and placement of activities should allow for sufficient time for the skills to be learned reasonably well. It is better to learn three or four basketball skills reasonably well each year than to be exposed to ten in one year and not be able to perform any of them satisfactorily.

6. Activities should be taught so that each student develops a more desirable

self-concept and experiences a feeling of success.

7. Activities should be selected that best meet the seasonal drives of the students. Football is best taught in the fall, basketball in the winter, and baseball in the spring.

8. Psychologically speaking, the activities should provide a healthy outlet for boys and girls; they should be challenging, yet within the students' physical and mental capabilities. The aggressive student who is a problem to the classroom teacher can be placed in a gymnasium where he or she can run, hit the ball, throw, and be thrilled by the excitement of a close competitive contest. A constructive outlet for aggression can often be found on a football field, on a basketball court, or with a field hockey or soccer team. By wisely using the tools of the trade, the physical educator will have a positive effect upon students. There must be an opportunity to continually improve and develop knowledge and skills—that is, there must be a progression

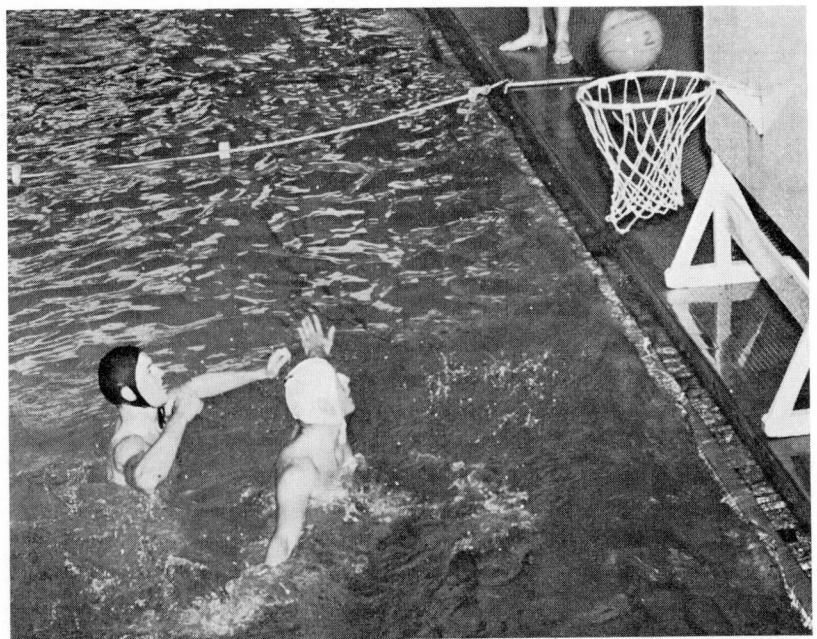

E. F. Marten, Seattle

Fig. 7-3. The curriculum should be rich in activities adaptable to use in leisure time.

that will keep interest high and develop abilities to a point where an activity can be enjoyed for the pleasure of doing it correctly.

Selected sociological principles for determining activities

1. The curriculum should be rich in activities adaptable to use in leisure time. For example, golf, tennis, and swimming should be in the program, if possible.

2. The activities should be selected for their possible contribution to the youth's training for citizenship in a democracy. The opportunity to participate in a team sport, select a captain, and be a member of a cohesive unit should be available with proper teacher guidance.

3. The curriculum should be suited to the ideals of the community as well as to its needs. It usually will be of value to include square dancing, swimming, or bowling in the curriculum to meet the interests and needs of a community.

4. The activities that are particularly rich in opportunities for individual pursuit, such as gymnastics, are especially desirable.

5. Activities that reflect nationwide interests should be provided in the program.

It is important to understand and have a working knowledge of popular American pastimes such as, baseball, football, and basketball, because of the values inherent in these team sports and because of their national recognition and acceptance.

6. The curriculum should provide opportunities for students to develop leadership qualities.

PLANNING THE TOTAL PROGRAM

The goals of physical education can be achieved only through the execution of a well-made plan. The teacher in the physical education program has the responsibility to set up the daily learning siutation in direct relation to overall objectives. This can be done only through careful and thoughtful planning of every physical education experience, so that it may be a purposeful one for each student and a step toward the attainment of the goals.

Planning the yearly program

The program of study for a single year is based on the overall curriculum, with specific objectives and activities selected according to the grade level. The program for the year must be exact and yet flexible enough to accommodate the changing

E. F. Marten, Seattle

Fig. 7-4

Fig. 7-5. Physical education class in archery. (Little Rock Public Schools, Little Rock, Ark.)

needs and abilities of the students. Steps in planning for the year include both selection of objectives and activities and evaluation.

Objectives. In planning the yearly program, teachers should select specific objectives from those outlined in the overall curriculum. Selection is based on the particular age group and developmental status of the class. A sub-objective of the goal of physical fitness, for example, may be the development of accuracy. A subordinate objective based on this factor may be the improvement of accuracy in the lay-up shot for basketball. Similarly, the methods of teaching activities should be selected specifically for the purposes of meeting these objectives. Plans must be flexible, however, since some students may already be proficient in the skills.

Activities. The activities to be included in a particular year of study are usually outlined in the overall curriculum. However, the teacher should determine the amount of time to be devoted to each activity, according to the needs and desires of the group. In schools that promote student planning, the teacher may base some decisions on the outcomes of discussions with students. For example, one class of ninth-grade girls may wish to study field

hockey exclusively in the fall, while another group may want to combine field hockey with tennis. However, the teacher must ultimately decide the program for the year, after considering such things as the seasons of the locality, the facilities and equipment available, and the size and needs of the group.

Evaluation. Methods of evaluating the year's work should be planned in advance. Student achievement and program content should be surveyed in terms of the established objectives. Procedures for evaluation are outlined in a separate chapter, but the teacher should realize that planning is an essential part of the yearly plan.

Table 7-1 shows a sample yearly program such as may be planned for a class of thirty-six ninth-grade girls meeting twice a week for forty-five—minute periods. Activities are listed under the particular goal for which they strive.

Planning the unit of teaching

A unit of teaching refers to the period of time during which a particular sport or activity is studied. The program for the year has several units of teaching, some scheduled for six weeks, eight weeks, and other amounts of time. The use of units in teaching physical education is of great im-

Table 7-1. Sample physical education program for thirty-six ninth-grade girls meeting twice weekly

Month and number of weeks		Physical fitness	Physical skills	Knowledge and appreciation	Social development
Sept.	3	Posture	Archery	Archery	Individual respon-
		Strength	Stance	Etiquette	sibilities in class
Oct.	4	Endurance	Technique	Safety	Program planning
		Speed	Hockey	Hockey	Group cooperation
Nov.	1	Agility	Dribble	History	Teamwork
		Accuracy	Drive	Rules	
		Balance	Dodge	Offensive and	
			Lunge	defensive	
			Tackle	strategies	
Total	8		Test	Test	
Nov.	3	Posture	Badminton	Badminton	Partnership
		Balance	Serve	Etiquette	etiquette
Dec.	3	Agility	Forehand	Doubles rules	Improve group re-
		Accuracy	Backhand		lationships and
			Volleyball	Volleyball	teamwork
			Single tap	History	
			Serve	Etiquette	
			Smash	Offensive and	
			Test	defensive	
				strategies	
				Rules	
				Rotation	
Total	6			Test	
Jan.	4	Endurance	Basketball	Basketball	Teamwork
		Speed	Passes	History	New groups
Feb.	2	Accuracy	Dribble	Offensive and	Leadership
		Balance	Pivot	defensive	
		Agility	Foul-shooting	strategies	
			Goal-shooting	Rules	
			Test	Notebook	
Total	6			Test	
Feb.	2	Strength	Modern dance	Modern dance	Group planning
		Endurance	Types of	History	Creativity
Mar.	3	Balance	movement	Noted	Cooperation
		Agility	Axial	performers	Leadership
		Posture	Swing	Values	
		Poise	Sustained	Purposes	
		Grace	Percussive	Test	
			Locomotor		
			Leaps		
			Skips		
Total	5		Turns		
Apr.	4	Strength	Stunts	Values of	Safety
		Endurance	Tumbling	training	consciousness
		Balance	Apparatus	Olympic	Leadership
		Agility	Parallel bars	performers	Group planning
		Posture	High bar	Safety	Cooperation
			Ladder	procedures	
			Rings	Spotting	
Total	4		Test		

Continued.

Table 7-1. Sample physical education program for thirty-six ninth-grade girls meeting twice weekly—cont'd

Month and number of weeks		Physical fitness	Physical skills	Knowledge and appreciation	Social development
May	4	Strength	Tennis	Tennis	Partnership
		Endurance	Forehand	History	etiquette
June	3	Agility	Backhand	Etiquette	New groups
		Speed	Serve	Doubles rules	Teamwork
		Accuracy	Volley		Leadership
			Softball	Softball	Cooperation
			Base-playing	History	
			Base-running	Rules	
			Batting	Scoring	
			Bunting	Base-playing	
			Catching	Test	
			Throwing		
			Fielding		
			Test		
Total	7				

portance to the quality of the learning experience. Unit teaching provides direction and structure to each class meeting, and the students recognize each session as being a distinct part of a whole. The physical educator; guided by the unit goals, offers progressive instruction for their attainment, and the students should be aware of the purposes of activities within the unit. In planning the unit of teaching the teacher must consider the specific objectives and activities to be included in the unit. Because this phase of planning is the basis for daily instruction and the learning experience itself, its importance must not be underestimated.

Objectives. Specific objectives established for the year form the basis of the sub-objectives in the unit plan. There should be sub-objectives relating to all four goals of physical education (see Chapter 4), for it is these sub-objectives obtained in the unit course of study that are the steppingstones to achievement of overall goals. Following is an example of the way in which objectives may be broken down for a unit: (1) *goal*—physical skill; (2) *objective*—to develop throwing power; (3) *specific objective (yearly plan)*—to improve pitching accuracy; and (4) *sub-objective (unit plan)*—to pitch fast balls over the plate. Sub-objectives would be

established for each of the four goals in this manner, with the age level and developmental needs of the students the determining factor in estimating accomplishment.

Activities. The choice of activities to be included in each unit of study should be made on the basis of the sub-objectives established. Certain principles should be kept in mind while planning the activities, in order to make the unit a complete series of learning experiences.

1. Provide a variety of learning experiences by using different types of activities (relays, games of low organization), techniques (drills, skull sessions), and materials (audiovisual aids, outside reading).

2. Provide activities that are appropriate to the needs, age level, and developmental achievements of the group.

3. Provide activities that are progressive in nature.

4. Provide flexibility in planning so that unforeseen interruptions and delays during the course of the unit do not hinder achievement of unit objectives.

5. Provide a definite form for the unit by introducing new skills and activities on a weekly basis or with each class session (depending upon the frequency of classes), so that students recognize progress within the unit.

Table 7-2. Sample basketball unit (six weeks)

	Physical fitness	Physical skills	Knowledge and appreciation	Social development
Week 1	Endurance Speed	Passes Dribbling	History Safety Rules: ball and line violations Assign notebook	New squads Discussion: leadership Elect captains
Week 2	Endurance Speed Agility	Review passes and dribbling New: reverse turn and pivot	Rules: footwork and fouls	Group responsibil- ity in drill practice
Week 3	Endurance Speed Accuracy Agility	Review pivot New shots: lay-up, chest, and one hand	Offensive techniques	Safety-shooting practice
Week 4	Endurance Speed Agility Accuracy Balance	Review shooting New: foul- shooting	Defensive techniques Planned plays	Teamwork Group planning
Week 5	Endurance Speed Agility Accuracy Balance	Review shooting Tournament	Etiquette in tournament Strategy Review rules	Continue group planning and teamwork
Week 6		Evaluation of skills	Written test Notebook due	Evaluation of so- cial cooperation Needs and plans for next unit

6. Provide activities that promote the greatest amount of participation for the greatest number of students by utilizing all facilities and equipment available.

7. Provide for appropriate ending activities in the unit: methods of evaluation based on predetermined, specific objectives, as well as some type of special, climactic activity such as a tournament, demonstration, performance, or similar presentation toward which the work has been building throughout the unit.

Table 7-2 is a sample unit taken from the yearly plan with its activities and subobjectives.

An alternative to the unit plan, called the day's order, is sometimes used. In this approach the program of activities varies from day to day. However, within a semester of teaching, the same amount of time would be devoted to each activity as in the unit plan. When scheduling problems prevail, this plan facilitates use of gymnasium space by more than one class, for one group could be working on basketball while the other class concentrates on trampoline or apparatus work at the sidelines.

Planning the daily lesson

The final step necessary in the planning phase of teaching is the actual lesson plan itself. This has as its basis the unit plan of objectives and activities but is a complete analysis of the step-by-step procedures to be followed during each class session. This plan is probably the most important one, because it represents the real contact with the students and what they should be learning. It therefore needs to be very carefully thought out from beginning to end, with many principles followed in selecting procedures and definite objectives established for attainment.

Objectives. Each lesson must have its

own set of definite objectives. Unless the teacher knows exactly what should be accomplished during the class period, the students will not know the daily objectives.

Procedures. An outline of procedures should be written down for each class meeting. The various methods of teaching and the progression from one type of activity to another need to be carefully worked out. The following principles for the daily lesson plan should be helpful in planning procedures for a single class period:

1. Provide maximum participation for all class members. When choosing a method of teaching, the physical educator should consider the size of the class, the facilities and equipment, and the time allotment and select those procedures that allow the greatest amount of practice for the most students.

2. Provide maximum instruction and supervision. The physical educator should select formations and drills that allow instruction for small groups and supervision for the entire class.

3. Provide for the safety of students. Group formations and game situations should be set up in such a way that students are protected from danger. This includes hazards both from stationary equipment and from adjacent practicing groups.

4. Provide for the health of the students. Methods of instruction should be selected in accordance with capacities of students in respect to overexposure, fatigue, and extreme heat or cold.

5. Promote student interest and enthusi-

Table 7-3. Sample daily lesson plan, based on the unit plan (Table 7-2, Week 2)

| Date: January 10 | Equipment: 4 basketballs |
| Class: Ninth-grade girls | Time: 45 minutes |

Objectives
1. To build endurance
2. To review passes and reverse turn
3. To introduce pivots
4. To discuss rules and strategy connected with the pivot
5. To improve participation in group discussion

Procedures	Organization	Time allowance (in minutes)
1. Change, roll call, and announcements	Squad formations	7
2. Warm-up exercises	Squad formations	5
Stretch, swing, flex, run in place		
Footwork (stop, start, slide)		
3. Review	Leader and line	2
Passes		
Reverse turn		
4. Introduce pivots	Leader and line	3
Demonstration		
Explanation		
Mimetics		
5. Drills	Shuttle formation	5
Dribble-pivot-pass		
Rest; discuss rules and strategy of pivot		
Dribble-pivot-pass over opponent		
6. Uses in game	Two squads play; others count pivots and reverses; alternate	10
7. Evaluation	Groups, informal	3
What has been accomplished?		
What are uses of pivots?		
What should be next skill studied?		
Why should all participate in discussions?		
8. Shower and dress		10

asm. The physical educator should strive, by varying the teaching patterns (games, drills, relays) and increasing the complexity of the work, to heighten student responses.

6. Provide for the growth and development of the students. The choice of methods should be dependent on the skill levels and accomplishments of the participants, and performances far above or below the estimated limits of their abilities should not be required.

7. Promote learning by proceeding from what is already known by the group to what is unknown. The students will thus be able to understand the relationship of new learnings to that which they have already learned.

8. Provide for self-evaluation by students of their abilities and for evaluation by the group and the physical educator of their daily accomplishments. In this way improvements and progress are recognized and advancement toward specific goals is kept in mind.

9. Promote carryover values and transfer of learning into daily life situations. Students who learn cooperation and good sportsmanship on the field or in the gymnasium, for example, need help in applying such learning to other experiences. The physical educator should make references to everyday situations to pave the way for application of these traits to daily life situations.

10. Promote creativity on the part of each student. Contributions of new ideas and theories from all the students should be sought by the physical educator. An atmosphere should be established in which all students feel free to express themselves.

One final note in regard to the daily lesson plan is concerned with flexibility. While it is essential that this plan should cover the full time allotted to the class and should be adhered to as closely as possible, the physical educator must be sensitive to the group's response to the procedures. If it is seen that the class tires quickly in a particular drill formation or that one of the

procedures is not successful, the physical educator should go on to a different phase of the lesson. It is always wise to plan more than the time allows, so that in such instances valuable time will not be lost for lack of organization or preparation. During the outdoor season, alternate daily lesson plans should be prepared for use indoors on rainy days. In this way no time is lost because of inclement weather.

A daily lesson plan drawn from the ninth-grade girls' unit on basketball is included as an example (Table 7-3).

ROLE OF STUDENTS IN CLASS PLANNING

The teacher of physical education should devote some thought to the role of students in program planning. How much opportunity should they have in planning their own course of study?

The answer to this question lies in the philosophy of the department concerning student creativity and free expression. It may be believed that students should share in many phases of the planning or that they should contribute only to planning within a single unit or part of a unit. Some measure of student contribution should be sought, however, because of the inherent values of increased motivation, understanding, and creativity it affords.

Motivation. When students assist in making plans for the class work, they are motivated and stimulated to participate to a greater extent. They believe that they have a share in the goals and have a genuine desire for their accomplishment.

Understanding. The discussions necessary to bringing out student suggestions require leadership and guidance from the physical educator. Some of the purposes of physical education might be pointed out to the students at this time to widen their understanding of the program as a whole. In this way their suggestions become consistent with their needs and with the goals of the program.

Creativity. Developing individual creativity is a goal of all education and one

Platnick's Photo Service, Hempstead, L. I.

Fig. 7-6. Promoting carryover values through swimming.

that should be included among the physical education objectives. Allowing students to contribute their own ideas and express their feelings is one way in which a creative atmosphere can be produced. While it may be more difficult to promote this type of rapport, it is indeed worthy of the attempt.

Problems. There are certain problems connected with student-teacher planning and the incorporation of the students' ideas into the program. In a large school where use of facilities is tightly scheduled and a prescribed regimen of activities must be followed, students would need to take these factors into consideration.

Another problem that arises in regard to student planning stems from the type of leadership offered by the teacher. There is

a real art to promoting good class discussion to bring out the contributions of all students and the physical educator must devote much time to planning key questions and ideas and to developing skill in this area.

INDIVIDUALIZING INSTRUCTION

After incorporating student suggestions into the program, the instructional phases of physical education may be further individualized with the inclusion of variable goals for individual achievement. Inasmuch as each student within a class has attained a certain level of ability in a particular sport, the goal for that student should be improvement of his own skill level. Therefore, the student needs freedom to work at his own level of interest and rate of speed. He should strive to improve according to developmental tasks laid out for him, based on previous record and performance. For example, in a skill such as pitching a softball or a baseball, proficiency levels for some students might indicate further practice to improve accuracy and speed, whereas other advanced students may need to advance to practicing various styles of pitching (fast ball, slow ball, inside and outside curves).

In terms of a prescribed curriculum, this may mean that some students are working on advanced skills earlier than suggested in the written guide. It must be remembered, however, that a curriculum is merely an outline, and individual development rarely follows a defined pattern. Therefore, freedom to explore and expand must be provided for.

When the teacher has completed all phases of planning—for the curriculum, the year, the unit, and the daily lesson—and has incorporated student ideas wherever possible, the time has come to carry out the plan.

THE CONCEPTUALIZED APPROACH

The process of education is undergoing a revolution in many areas of the curriculum. The sciences, mathematics, and languages especially are utilizing new teaching methodology and new technological devices and are drastically revising their curricula. Today's secondary school students are familiar with concepts and areas of knowledge that formerly were reserved for college-level courses.

Physical educators are well aware that they also must adapt physical education to the demands of this era. Physical educators have found that today's students require, and react well to, a conceptualized approach to physical education, and that this approach to teaching helps to stimulate curriculum reform in these areas.

Today's physical educators realize that the first task is to educate the student about his body and the scientific principles that control the use of the body and to educate

him to use his body effectively and efficiently. The conceptualized approach to the teaching of physical education helps students to better understand how their bodies move and why physical activity is so important in maintaining health and fitness. This approach to teaching physical education integrates the mental aspects with the physical.

In using the conceptualized approach, the teacher serves as a guide rather than a storehouse of information. Students learn, for example, the principles of body leverage, hip rotation, and foot and leg placement in throwing a softball by experimenting. The physical principles involved are best understood when they are ideated by the students themselves. This approach to teaching physical education depends upon the background of the physical educator and his willingness to place much of the burden for learning on the students themselves. This approach, however, also demands that the physical educator utilize a textbook geared to secondary school students and that each student be assigned readings and outside work based on the text and his related experiences in the physical education classroom.

The conceptualized approach to physical education helps students to understand why certain activities are selected for inclusion in the program and why such activities as physical fitness and the lifetime sports receive such great emphasis. This approach to physical education draws the student closer to the program and helps to make physical education activities a respected and pleasurable aspect of the school day.

PROJECTING PHYSICAL EDUCATION INTO THE FUTURE

What will physical education be like for the secondary school student of the future? Based on our knowledge of current advances in education and technology, some tentative projections can be made, but even these will be subject to change in the light of new events and discoveries.

The cost of education is constantly rising, and more and more students will need to be served by the secondary schools. More physical education facilities will have to be financed and built to accommodate these students, and teaching staffs will have to be increased. New materials, especially plastics, will probably be used extensively for gymnasium floors to reduce the constant need for refinishing and to save on maintenance costs. Synthetics will be utilized on outdoor surfaces to make them more usable for longer portions of the year. Geodesic domes will house multiple-use gymnasiums and auxiliary physical education rooms, and air-supported structures will provide additional teaching stations.

An increasing emphasis on research in physical education will lead to more scientifically formulated curricula. Much of the benefit from this research will result in better programs for the atypical student. The student in regular physical education classes will have a textbook, and he will utilize special audiovisual aids. He will be able to analyze his own performances through instant playback devices housed in physical education projection rooms.

Curricula in the secondary school will be broadened and increased, and students will be given a wider choice in the selection of activities. A wide variety of lifetime sports will be offered, along with physical fitness work, dance, and the usual variety of team and dual sports and activities. Portable pools will help to make swimming instruction a possibility for every student. There will be an emphasis on student-centered learning through the conceptualized approach, and the students will take on an increased responsibility for the program.

As physical education continues to assert itself in the secondary school curriculum, it will gain greater respect. This will help to decrease class size, to give classes a more homogeneous balance, to provide an individual program of physical education for every student, and to release the physical educator from the burden of non-teaching duties. The physical educators themselves will become more expert in their own field, will attend more in-service and graduate courses, and will be more knowledgeable about education in general. This will help physical education to gain full community respect and support.

Athletics will become more educational for both boys and girls. The current trend toward varsity-level competition for secondary school girls will continue and intensify, but these programs will be balanced by expanded intramural programs serving the needs and interests of all the students in the school. Intramurals for boys will also be expanded, but interschool competition will place a stronger emphasis on the individual and the effect of competition on him. Girls and boys will participate together in selected varsity sports.

As sophisticated communications and transportation media continue to make the world seem smaller, the international aspects of physical education will emerge. More and more students and physical educators will cooperate in international exchange programs, and Olympic and international sports and events will become vital parts of the secondary school program.

We cannot know or predict all the changes the future will bring. We may find that the philosophy and objectives of physical education will have to be drastically revised from year to year. Continued space exploration and reaching the moon may result in significant advances in the understanding of man's physiology and psychology that will affect our programs. Government-sponsored research and pilot physical education programs, changes in professional preparation, and revisions in general education will also have a profound effect on physical education, as will our need to serve disadvantaged students more meaningfully and our efforts to stablize domestic and world conditions.

BRINGING ABOUT CHANGE IN THE PHYSICAL EDUCATION CURRICULUM

If physical education is to grow and gain educational respect the traditional type of physical education must be evaluated carefully and alterations made in light of the changes taking place in society and general education. In order to bring about change, a discussion is provided that (1) looks at the catalysts that bring about curriculum change and (2) examines the ingredients essential to change.

Catalysts that bring about curriculum change

Changes occur in physical education curricula as they do in other areas of the school offering. There is usually a continuous list of myriad proposals for change. Each proposal should be considered on its own merits and put to the test of whether or not it has value.

What are the influencing factors in regard to change? A few associations, agencies, and individuals who produce change in physical education are discussed in the following paragraphs.

National associations and agencies. The President's Council on Physical Fitness and Sports is an outstanding example of one national governmental agency that brought about much change in programs of health, physical education, and recreation throughout the United States and the world. Through their speakers, publications, and communications media pronouncements, many changes have taken place in the schools and colleges of this nation. Physical fitness in some communities has become the overriding purpose of programs of health education and physical education, sometimes at the expense of the other objectives of these fields and a well-balanced program of activities.

Examples of other national associations and agencies that play a part in curriculum change are the National Education Association, the American Association for Health, Physical Education, and Recreation, the United States Office of Education, the Association for Supervision and Curriculum Development, and the American Medical Association.

State associations and agencies. As na-

tional organizations influence the curricula of our schools and colleges, so do state organizations. State boards of education or departments of public instruction, state bureaus, departments, or divisions of health and physical education, state education associations, citizens' committees, teachers' associations, and associations for health, physical education, and recreation are a few examples of organizations that influence curricula. Through the publication of syllabi, sponsorship of legislation, enactment of rules and regulations, exercise of supervisory powers, allocation of funds, and initiation of projects, organizations promote certain ideas and programs that initiate changes in schools and colleges.

Research. Research brings about change. As new knowledge is uncovered, more information is known about the learning process, new techniques are developed, and other research is conducted. Change eventually ensues if the research is significant, but the change may be slow in coming. It usually takes a long time for the creation of knowledge to penetrate to the grass roots, where it becomes part of an action program.

In the field of physical education, research on motor learning, the relationship of health and physical fitness to academic achievement, movement education, cognitive learning, physiological changes that occur in the body through exercise, smoking, ecology, and the relationship of mental health and physical activity represent a few examples of research that have or will have a bearing upon programs of physical education throughout the country.

College and university faculties. The leaders in education from the campuses of the nation who serve as consultants, write textbooks, make speeches, and are active in professional associations help to bring about changes in education in general and in the special field of physical education.

Social forces. Such social forces in the American culture as the civil rights movement, automation, mass communication, student activism, black studies, sports promotion, and collective bargaining through unions are a few of the movements sweeping the nation that have implications for curricula in schools and colleges. In addition, the social trends of the times involving attitudes toward sex, driving, alcohol, tobacco, drugs, and narcotics bring about curricula change. Times change, customs change, the habits of people change, and with such changes the role of educational institutions and their responsibilities to their society frequently change.

The ingredients essential to change

Change is a process that takes time. The steps through which change usually occurs are: *First,* the physical educators become aware of a needed innovation, for example, movement education in the elementary school. *Second,* as more and more people become interested in the innovation, an interest stage develops. Interest in movement education has been generated through experimental programs, workshops, writings and other means of communicating the idea to educators. *Third,* there is the evaluation stage, where physical educators determine the values that the change has for their programs—values that relate directly to the student and the goals of physical education. *Fourth* comes more extensive experimenting with the idea, and, finally, the *last step* is adoption. Movement education has gone through these steps in many schools systems with the change being adopted. However, many of the schools in the United States have not changed their program to incorporate movement education into their schools. Therefore, more change needs to take place not only in respect to movement education but also in many other areas.

Miller,* in her article entitled "A Man to Fill the Gap: The Change Agent," points out that each profession needs to bring about change to lessen the gap between what they know and what they practice.

---

*Miller, Peggy L.: A man to fill the gap: the change agent, Journal of Health, Physical Education, and Recreation 40:34, 1969.

Since there is a big gap between what we know and what we practice in physical education, change is needed and change agents are necessary to bring about the needed change. Miller defines the change agent as "a professional who has as his major function the advocacy and introduction of innovations into practice" or a professional person who tries to influence decisions that will bring about the adoption of new ideas. In bringing about change, the change agent, according to Miller, should be aware of seven principles. They are presented here in adapted form and related to physical education.

• *The change agent must be well informed as to the needs and characteristics of the client system.* The students and other human beings, such as the physical education staff in a school where it is desired to effect the change, are the client system. It is important for the change agent to base his plans on their needs.

• *The change agent must develop a close relationship between himself and the client system.* There must be a confidence in the change agent. A mutual trust and respect must exist between the client system and himself, for unless the client system has confidence in him, change cannot effectively be brought about.

• *The change agent must realize that change is not a unilateral undertaking but, instead, is a mutually cooperative affair.* The autocratic director of physical education who orders the innovation will never succeed. Change is a cooperative procedure between the change agent and the staff of his school system. As a result, there may be compromise and modifications, but the changes that are made will be more permanent and better accepted by the staff.

• *The change agent should enlist the support of key leaders in the client system.* Key leaders among the students in the school system and the physical education staff, as well as other persons, can help to ensure that the change is accepted by the client system and is adopted. Their involvement is essential in getting the entire student body and staff to accept the new development.

• *The change agent needs a well-developed plan and strategy for introducing change.* The plan for bringing about change in an organization cannot be a hit-or-miss affair. Foresight and planning must decide the timetable for moving from one step to the next in innovating change, for identifying the key leaders who in turn will influence others, and for formally approving the change. Also, the techniques to be used, the communications media to be solicited, the persons to be seen, the meetings to be held, and the information to be imparted must all be carefully planned out so that nothing is left to chance.

• *The change agent must be willing to change himself and to keep up with the times.* In order to be effective in bringing about change in others, the change agent must be a model of change himself. He must reflect an image of self-renewal and self-improvement. Such a person is needed in order to empathize with others and to be sensitive to the change process.

• *The change agent needs to help others to become change agents.* The change agent's success will be determined in large measure in how well he gets other members of a staff or organization to become change agents themselves. In so doing they will be abreast of the latest research findings in their field, have a recognition of the need for innovation, possess the ability to make wise choices as to what innovations will best help the client system, and be willing to try new ideas and practices.

POINTS TO REMEMBER

1. Curriculum planning is a group process.
2. The physical educator has a major responsibility in the formulation of a physical education program.
3. A curriculum guide for a school system is a set of minimum standards.
4. There must be understanding of the student and learning theories to produce a valid curriculum.
5. A curriculum study must fit the school system and the society in which it will operate.
6. Activities must be properly selected.

7. Evaluation is a never-ending process for a curriculum.
8. The daily plan, the unit plan, and the yearly plan are all outgrowths of the overall curriculum.

PROBLEMS TO THINK THROUGH

1. How detailed should a curriculum guide be in regard to length of time spent on an activity and items to be covered in a listed activity? Why?
2. Should there be room for initiative by the physical educator working from a curriculum guide? Why?
3. Compare two schools where the same activity may be handled differently. What may make it necessary to handle this activity differently?
4. Why is it important to understand the nature of the student in curriculum planning?
5. What administrative details would limit a curriculum?

CASE STUDY FOR ANALYSIS

Select a secondary grade level (boys or girls) and prepare, in outline form, a curriculum for one twenty-week semester. The school has separate gymnasiums for boys and girls, an outdoor turf area, two teachers for each class of sixty to eighty pupils, sufficient equipment and supplies for the largest class, and three periods of physical education weekly for each student. Analyze specific objectives, time allotment, activities, and fundamentals. Simulate a school situation by working in committee groups.

EXERCISES FOR REVIEW

1. What steps should be followed in the preparation of a curriculum?
2. How may a physical education teacher make his contribution to a curriculum study?
3. What principles should be considered in the selection of activities for a program?
4. Who may be a part of a curriculum study group?
5. Plan a six-week unit on badminton for seventh graders.
6. Plan a daily lesson within that unit.

SELECTED READINGS

Bucher, Charles A.: Administration of health and physical education programs, including athletics, ed. 5, St. Louis, 1971, The C. V. Mosby Co.

Bucher, Charles A.: Administrative dimensions of health and physical education programs, including athletics, St. Louis, 1971, The C. V. Mosby Co.

Bucher, Charles A.: Foundations of physical education, ed. 6, St. Louis, 1972, The C. V. Mosby Co.

Bucher, Charles A.: Physical education for life, New York, 1969, McGraw-Hill Book Co., Inc.

Bucher, Charles A., and Goldman, Myra: Dimensions of physical education, St. Louis, 1969, The C. V. Mosby Co.

Brameld, Theodore: A cross-cutting approach to the curriculum: the moving wheel, Phi Delta Kappan, March, 1970, p. 346.

Conant, James B.: The comprehensive high school, New York, 1967, McGraw-Hill Book Co., Inc.

Crosby, Muriel: Who changes the curriculum and how? Phi Delta Kappan, March, 1970, p. 385.

Curriculum for people, Today's Education 60:42, 1971.

Goodlad, John I.: Directions of curriculum change, National Education Association Journal 55:33, 1966.

Hermann, Don, and Osness, Wayne: A scientific curriculum design for high school physical education, Journal of Health, Physical Education, and Recreation 37:26, 1966.

Kidd, Frances M., and others: Guidelines for secondary school physical education, Journal of Health, Physical Education, and Recreation 42:47, 1971.

Metcalf, Lawrence E., and Hunt, Maurice P.: Relevance and the curriculum, Phi Delta Kappan, March, 1970, p. 358.

Shane, June Grant, and Shane, Harold G.: Cultural change and the curriculum: 1970-2000 A.D., Educational Technology, April, 1970, p. 13.

Silberman, Charles E.: Crisis in the classroom—the remaking of American education, New York, 1971, Random House, Inc.

The University of the State of New York, The State Education Department: Final report on the workshop on the concept of "redesign" for New York State physical educators held at Stamford, New York, October 11-13, 1970, Albany, November 20, 1970.

Toffler, Alvin: Future shock, New York, 1970, Random House, Inc.

Van Til, William: Curriculum: quest for relevance, New York, 1971, Houghton Mifflin Co.

Willgoose, Carl E.: The curriculum in physical education, Englewood Cliffs, N. J., 1969, Prentice-Hall, Inc.

8 INNOVATIVE PROGRAMS IN SECONDARY SCHOOL PHYSICAL EDUCATION

Webster's Dictionary defines the word "innovation" as the "act of introducing something new or novel . . . or a change effected by innovating. . . ." In other words, innovation represents a change in the way things are done. In the field of education it may represent an effort to bring about something new in respect to the substance, methods, materials, or some other aspect of education so as to provide experiences for students that are more relevant to the world in which they live.

Education in general is passing through an era when much innovation is taking place. Physical education is also concerned with innovation as it tries to develop programs more in tune with the times and the student of today. This chapter presents several innovative programs in physical education that are in operation throughout the country. Many of these programs are still in the early stages of development and thus their merit and worth have not been established. It is also recognized that many innovative practices that exist in many schools are not discussed in this chapter.

It is important for the physical educator, and particularly the new teacher, to know about innovative programs. This will broaden their knowledge, stimulate their thinking, and hopefully enrich their teaching and thus make their physical education programs more dynamic and meaningful to the students they teach.

Each of the innovative programs discussed in this chapter is presented only briefly. The purpose is to make the reader aware of some of the changes taking place in physical education throughout the country. The interested reader who desires more detailed information regarding these programs should contact the schools directly.

JUNIOR TEACHING AND RESOURCE CENTERS°
El Camino Real High School
Woodland Hills, California

Grades and students concerned: Tenth to twelfth grades.

Selected objectives: To provide an opportunity for selected high school students to experience being junior teachers in physical education classes grades one to nine.

To help students with leadership potential to become more familiar with the nature and scope of elementary and junior high school physical education programs.

To help students with leadership potential to understand the physical, social, and emotional needs and characteristics of children and adolescents.

To provide a teaching experience for students that may lead to full-time employment later on.

Selected features of the program: Students electing to serve as junior teachers receive five or ten credits.

Statement of Intent is completed by student who negotiates a contract with the teacher of physical education. Contracts are signed by students, parents, supervising teacher, and department chairman.

Junior teacher is involved in such duties as the interpretation of rules, assisting in testing for physical fitness, supervising activities, introducing various physical education activities, and helping students who are deficient in movement skills.

A staff member is assigned to each student teacher. The staff member's duties include holding seminars, conducting conferences, observing junior teacher, coordinating student's program, and evaluating results.

Resource center that contains such items as audiovisual aids and reference materials of various types is provided for junior teachers. There are also study and seminar accommodations.

°Adapted from material written by Carol Ghens for Secondary School Conference, Washington, D. C., 1972.

SKILL ACHIEVEMENT AND MODULAR SCHEDULING°
Poway High School
Poway, California

Grades and students concerned: Ninth to twelfth grades.

Selected objectives: To assist students in achieving proficiency in physical education skills.

To utilize modular scheduling in grouping students in accordance with their skill proficiency.

To help students enjoy physical education through competition with students possessing equal skill development to their own.

To further the physical fitness development of each student.

To provide individual instruction in skills for students who need and desire such help.

Selected features of the program: First, students are assigned to classes in skill area of their choice. Classes meet twice a week, with emphasis being placed on instruction.

Second, students are assigned to physical fitness laboratory. Testing is done periodically and records are kept on each student's progress.

Third, regularly scheduled competitive experiences or laboratories are conducted each Friday where each student competes with other students of similar skill level. Activities include badminton, volleyball, handball, touch football, basketball, and tennis. Since this program maintains that girls do not desire as much competition as boys, they are scheduled for skill classes on Fridays.

Fourth, there is an open laboratory period where students may receive individual instruction in the various skills. Performance standards have been developed for each activity in order to guide student

---

°Adapted from article by Welch, Ronald E.: Poway High School physical education program, organizational patterns for instruction in physical education, Washington, D. C., 1971, American Association for Health, Physical Education, and Recreation, p. 69.

achievement and permit better evaluation. Evaluation is done on the basis of three ratings: "outstanding," "satisfactory," and "unsatisfactory."

Computer scheduling makes it possible to schedule students for various phases of the physical education program according to their individual needs and interests.

Videotape recordings of students executing skills are utilized in aiding skill development.

Team teaching is limited to gymnastics.

Program is interpreted to parents via a student-parent handbook, articles, and an open house.

ELECTIVE PROGRAM*
Silverton High School
Silverton, Colorado

Grades and students concerned: Eleventh and twelfth grades.

Selected objectives: To make physical education more meaningful for students.

To give students a voice in curriculum development.

To provide for student choice in the selection of activities.

To provide activities for students outside the regular school day.

To capitalize on local environmental resources.

To provide activities that students may enjoy for a lifetime.

Selected features of the program: Physical education classes may consist of such activities as fly fishing in a river, weekend backpacking trip through an Indian reservation, cross-country skiing, or mountaineering.

Activities also include traditional team and individual sports, such as badminton, basketball, soccer, circuit training, volleyball, baseball, softball, and dance.

Program is coeducational and physical education activities are integrated into other areas of the general education program. For example, students on backpacking trip study federal aid to Indians and the way Indians live when they make a trip to an Indian reservation. Home economics is involved in arranging menus for trips, and shop classes help in making bows and arrows.

QUINMESTER PROGRAM*
Dade County Public Schools
Miami, Florida

Grades and students concerned: Seventh to twelfth grades.

Selected objectives: To provide a flexible physical education program for students.

To provide students with a choice of activities in which they wish to participate.

To provide self-contained nonsequential nine-week units of study.

Selected features of the program: School year is broken into five nine-week terms and students are required to be in attendance during any four of the five "quins" offered each year. Students who so desire may attend all five "quins" and thereby accelerate their graduation date.

Courses are written up in detail by instructors.

Students select courses in physical education in which they have special interest and/or need.

Physical education quinmester course offerings involve team sports, lifetime sports, rhythmic activities, and physical conditioning. Most courses are coeducational.

Although no specific course in the area of physical conditioning is required, it is recommended that physical fitness tests be given twice a year.

Quinmester curriculum may be viewed as a series of minicourses, each nine weeks in length and carrying one-quarter credit.

Thirty-seven schools are participating in the program.

*Adapted from material prepared and sent by George J. Pastor, Director of Physical Education, Silverton High School, Silverton, Colorado.

*Adapted from material sent by Robert F. Adams, Dade County Public Schools, and also from article by Rothstein, Hy, and Adams, Robert F.: Quinmester extended school year plan, Journal of Health, Physical Education, and Recreation 42:30, 1971.

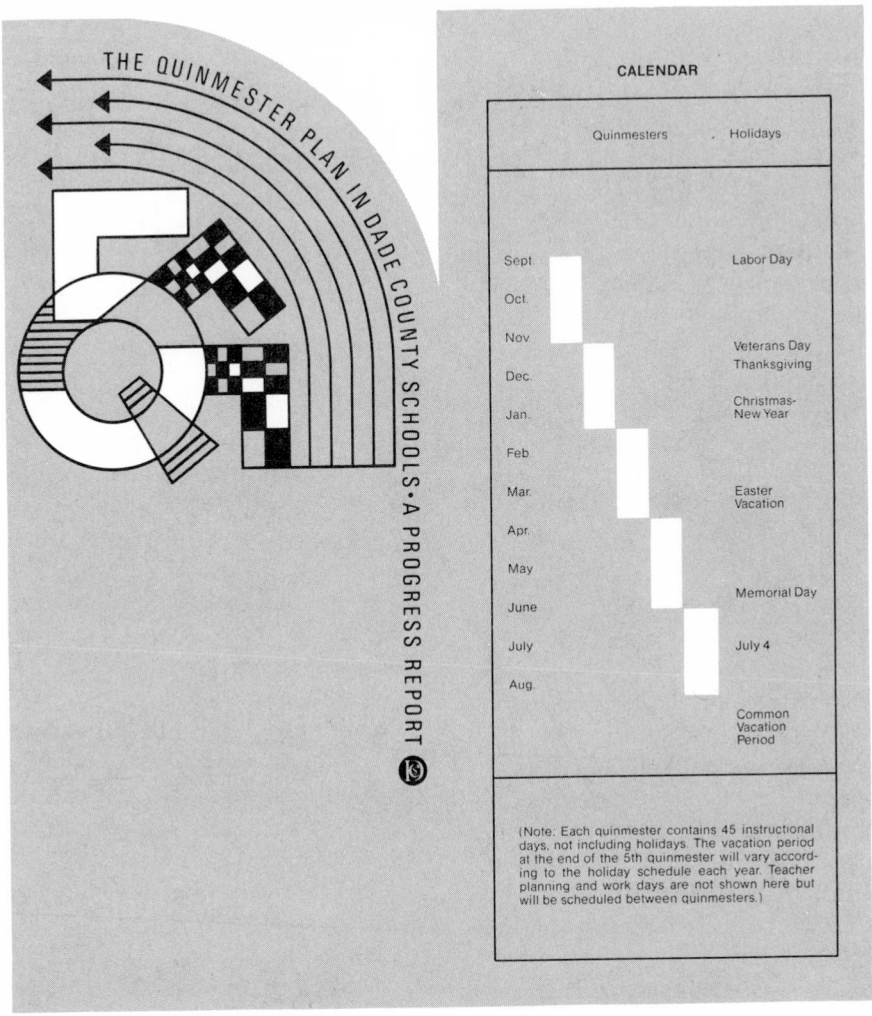

Fig. 8-1. Quinmester plan in Dade County Schools, Miami, Fla.

CONTRACTING*
Ft. Pierce, Central High School
Ft. Pierce, Florida

Grades and students concerned: Eleventh and twelfth grades.

Selected objectives: To facilitate the teaching of large physical education classes.

To enable students to pursue activities of their own choosing.

To assign grades to students in accordance with their achievement.

To inject new vitality into the physical education experience.

To utilize an objective procedure in evaluating physical education progress.

Selected features of the program: Students follow units of activity of their own choosing and report to class solely for the purpose of checking attendance.

Contracts are prepared on each activity that is offered in the physical education program. Each contract lists the requirements to be met by the student and the point value of each. For example, Contract 1 in a unit on bowling requires the student to bowl six games, keep score, list the reasons for keeping score, and identify the

---

*Adapted from letter and material sent by Barbara L. Fast and also from article by Fast, Barbara L.: Contracting, Journal of Health, Physical Education, and Recreation **42**:31, 1971.

symbols used in scoring. Each contract is valued at five points. This is multiplied by the difficulty rating, which ranges from one to five. The bowling contract thus has a twenty-point value. Materials are provided so that students can research assignments as needed.

When one contract is completed another one is made.

Student establishes his own pace and sets the schedule at which he wishes to fulfill the contract. Penalty and bonus points may be awarded.

Worksheets are kept on each student and provide a record of such things as contracts for each student, completion dates, point value, penalty and bonus points, and final score.

Grading system is as follows: 100 points, A; 90 points, B; 75 points, C; 70 points, D. No contract results in failure. If the contract is not completed it is returned to the student and pursued again.

FLEXIBLE MODULAR SCHEDULING ALLOWS FOR STUDENT CHOICE OF INDEPENDENT STUDY UNITS*
Ridgewood High School
Norridge, Illinois

Grades and students concerned: Junior and senior high school.

Selected objectives: To help the physical education program to be more enjoyable for the student.

To provide the student with a choice of activities.

To provide for independent study.

To provide for a carry-over of physical education values to adult life.

Selected features of the program: School utilizes flexible modular scheduling with twenty-minute modules in the school day. Classes may vary in length from one to five modules. The school is scheduled on a six-day cycle.

Physical education classes meet for three modules per day and four days per cycle. To allow for maximum utilization of facilities, class times overlap, with the overlapping time being used for dressing.

Physical education classes also meet for two modules in large groups per cycle. These classes meet in the auditorium and lectures, testing, and other activities are scheduled.

All students participate in physical education independent study projects (PEIS).

Independent study projects involve many of the traditional physical education activities such as basketball, baseball, and archery and also such activities as first aid, cheerleading, camping skills, outdoor recreation, personal defense, pom pom, and yoga.

In selecting independent study projects, students complete a special project sheet that lists their goals and objectives, procedures they will follow, safety precautions, and references and materials they will utilize in completing the project. Each project needs the approval of a teacher of physical education.

Students are graded on each project. Quarterly grades are arrived at as a result of a physical education team consensus.

PERFORMANCE OBJECTIVES*
Glenbrook North High School
Glenview, Illinois

Grades and students concerned: Ninth to twelfth grades.

Selected objectives: To provide achievement standards for students in each activity offered in the physical education curriculum.

To help students to better achieve the objective of education and physical education.

To provide a guide for students in respect to what is to be achieved in each activity in which they participate.

---

*Adapted from article by Sadowski, Gregory M.: Flexible modular scheduling allows for student choice of independent study units, Journal of Health, Physical Education, and Recreation **42:**25, 1971.

*Adapted from letter and material sent by Walter D. Sherman and from article by Sherman, Walter D.: Performance objectives, Journal of Health, Physical Education, and Recreation **42:**37, 1971.

Selected features of the program: Performance objectives were established for each grade level after the faculty evaluated the program in terms of its philosophy, the cardinal principles of education, health goals, and the objectives of physical education: organic, neuromuscular, emotional, social, and mental development.

Working committee prepared performance objectives for each activity in the four-year curriculum.

Examples of performance objectives for freshmen and seniors in one activity—basketball—include:

FRESHMEN: Dribble ten times with left hand and ten with right hand without losing control of ball while dribbling in the center jump circle.

During a thirty-second interval from any spot on the court make five baskets.

Demonstrate chest, bounce, and overhead passes across the free throw lane.

SENIORS: Execute a three-on-two drill.

Make four out of ten free throws.

Make eight shots in thirty seconds.

Demonstrate and show difference between man and defense zones.

Demonstrate and explain a scissors to the basket.

PARAPROFESSIONAL PROGRAM FOR PHYSICAL EDUCATION*
Old Orchard Junior High School
Skokie, Illinois

Grades and students concerned: Sixth to eighth grades.

Selected objectives: To enable teacher to provide more individual help to students.

To free teacher from clerical and nonprofessional details.

To enable teacher to utilize time for which he is trained.

To provide a better organized and meaningful physical education experience for students.

Selected features of the program: Each physical education class (usually seventy to eighty students) is assigned two teachers and one paraprofessional (assists teacher).

Teacher is responsible for all planning, teaching, and professional responsibilities such as handling discipline problems, teaching the various activities, and beginning and dismissing classes.

Teacher supervises work of paraprofessional who handles such responsibilities as refereeing games, keeping records, leading calisthenic exercises, administering make-up tests, supervising locker room, and getting equipment ready for classes.

Paraprofessionals are recruited through area universities and advertisements. Many graduate students in professional preparation for higher education programs are used as paraprofessionals.

Qualifications to become a paraprofessional include a demonstrated interest in students, willingness to go through an orientation and training period, noteworthy physical development, and possession of knowledge of various physical education activities.

Parents are kept informed regarding paraprofessionals. Parents, in turn, approve of their use in light of the more meaningful physical education program that is provided.

OPEN GYMS IN HIGH SCHOOL PHYSICAL EDUCATION*
Prairie High School
Cedar Rapids, Iowa

Grades and students concerned: Tenth to twelfth grades.

Selected objectives: To give students time to participate in physical education activities outside of the regular required program.

To provide students with additional time for personal instruction by staff.

To enable students to practice on skill

---

*Adapted from the article by Wright, Lee: Paraprofessional program for physical education, organizational patterns for instruction in physical education, Washington, D. C., 1971, American Association for Health, Physical Education, and Recreation, p. 63.

---

*Adapted from material sent by Gary Leeper, Prairie High School, and from article: Using open gyms in high school physical education, Physical Education Newsletter, September 15, 1972.

they have been instructed in during required program.

To provide an opportunity for students to engage in physical activity.

Selected features of the program: Modular scheduling provides each student with three one-hour periods of physical education within a six-day cycle.

Students may participate in all-girl, all-boy, or coeducational required classes.

Students are given choices of activities in which they desire to participate.

Required physical education classes meet at 8:15, 10:15, 12:15, and 2:15 each day. The remaining three hours of the school day are labeled as open gyms, at which time any student may participate in the physical education facility in any way that he chooses—all indoor and outdoor facilities are available to him.

Approximately 150 to 450 students participate each day in open gyms.

Other interesting features of Prairie High School program include electives, contract system for seniors that allows for independent study, periodic attitude test to determine attitudes of students toward physical education program.

SELF-DIRECTED LEARNING*
Eagle Grove Community Schools
Eagle Grove, Iowa

Grades and students concerned: Tenth to twelfth grades.

Selected objectives: To provide a program in gymnastics that the students decide for themselves is the best for them.

To permit students the opportunity to establish their own achievement objectives and to evaluate their own progress toward these objectives.

To permit students to work independently in the achievement of their physical education objectives.

To increase the enjoyment and learning potential of students in the physical education experience.

Selected features of the program: Girls

in Eagle Grove were given an opportunity to choose one of four alternatives in their gymnastics class relative to how it should be organized or taught, such as working entirely as a class unit, working in squads, working individually for a letter grade, or working as individuals in line with personally determined goals. All classes in the girls' physical education program selected the last approach.

In line with the individual approach each girl determined her present skills in gymnastics and then decided the goals she wished to achieve. Both of these items were recorded. Guidelines were established to assist students in selecting personal goals relating to skills needing development, pieces of apparatus to select, and the like.

After goals were selected and recorded girls proceeded to achieve these goals in the way they felt would be most effective and interesting for them. Resources such as films and books were available, other students in the class were asked to give help and assistance if requested, and the instructor was available for instruction and counsel as needed. Safety was provided for by encouraging each student to work with a partner and also to have spotters when necessary.

At the end of the unit each student completed a self-evaluation form. These evaluations showed that the girls enjoyed the experience of working independently, utilized the resources that were provided, found other students of great help in the learning experience, and appreciated having a say in the decision-making process.

LEARNING PROCESS BASED ON GOAL SETTING*
Framingham North High School
Framingham, Massachusetts

Grades and students concerned: Ninth to twelfth grades.

*Adapted from article by Geadelmann, Patricia L.: Self-directed learning, Journal of Health, Physical Education, and Recreation **42:**25, 1971.

*Adapted from material sent by and the article by Mathieson, Doris, and Driscoll, Sandra: Goal-centered individualized learning, Journal of Health, Physical Education, and Recreation **42:**26, 1971.

Selected objectives: To enable students to play an active role in determining what and how they are going to learn in the physical education class.

To involve students in the decision-making process.

To provide opportunities for students to become aware of their own human abilities and potential and to learn skills in accordance with these elements.

To help students to understand the worth of physical activity throughout life.

To help the student to function as a self-directed individual in assuming responsibility for meeting his goals.

Selected features of the program: Students are first helped to understand the decision-making process as it affects their learning and their goals.

In respect to goal setting, students are oriented to various activities and also to the steps relating to goal setting. (For example, they should know themselves, understand and be aware of what facilities and equipment are available, and be cognizant of other resources that can be utilized for learning.)

Students are given materials and guidelines and instructor assistance to help them in establishing their goals for the various activities, that is, they are encouraged to take a hard look at themselves, determine what they want to learn, delineate their goals, design a plan for meeting the goals, and develop a procedure for evaluating the degree to which their goals are achieved. The goals, plans, and the like that have been selected are written out and made a matter of record.

Class procedure includes such possibilities as solving problems relating to the activity (for example, in gymnastics—can you do a cartwheel?), working independently on goals they had set for themselves, attending a teaching lesson arranged by the teacher, reviewing posted unit charts, analyzing in written form the degree to which the students felt they had achieved their goals, and then setting new goals.

ELECTIVE PHYSICAL EDUCATION*
Stevenson High School
Livonia, Michigan

Grades and students concerned: Ninth to twelfth grades.

Selected objectives: To provide a physical education program that will be challenging to students.

To provide a program that has its own built-in self-motivation.

To provide a progressive well-planned sports and skill program.

To enable students to select skills they desire to learn in an activity rather than having the teacher require a set program of skills for the students to learn.

To help students accept responsibility for deciding how they will earn credits in physical education skills.

Selected features of the program: Physical education teachers reviewed the professional literature and prepared materials for each sport in the program, including elective sheets, lesson plans, guidelines, and schedules for marking periods.

Students are first introduced to the sport (introductory units) and then they have a day by day choice in what particular skills they wish to earn their credits. For example, in swimming the students may select particular strokes, dives, or swim for distance.

Girls are grouped according to ability in swimming and gymnastics. Depending on the degree of skill they possess, they proceed at a pace that meets their abilities and needs.

The introductory periods are designed to cover the skills that enable the student to participate in the game, even though his skill level may be deficient.

Activities covered include tennis, field hockey, self-testing activities, basketball, folk and square dancing, swimming, gymnastics, health, softball, track and field.

---

*Adapted from material sent by and article written by McDonald, Lois J.: An elective curriculum—day by day choices, Journal of Health, Physical Education, and Recreation **42**:29, 1971.

Students earn credits and are graded on the basis of their participation, performance, and written tests. Grades A to D are given and there are no failures—students who are not successful try again. Sheets are prepared for each of the activities offered in the program showing how credits are earned.

INNOVATIVE PHYSICAL EDUCATION THROUGH ELECTIVES*
Regina High School
Minneapolis, Minnesota

Grades and students concerned: Ninth to twelfth grades.

Selected objectives: To provide students with a choice of activities, both on and off campus, in which to participate as part of the physical education program.

To develop skills that will provide for the worthy use of leisure time during adult years.

To develop physical fitness.

To utilize the resources of the community in providing a more challenging physical education program for students.

To utilize modular scheduling as a means of arranging many different types of activities and a more meaningful program for students.

Selected features of the program: Physical education program includes traditional physical education activities such as volleyball, archery, gymnastics, basketball, tennis, softball, and track and field.

Physical education program also includes several off-campus activities including horseback riding, golf, bowling, skiing, roller skating, and swimming.

Off-campus activities are conducted in different settings throughout the community. For example, golf is conducted at one of the several clubs in the area, bowling at one of the local bowling lanes, and swimming at the Y.M.C.A. pool. Transportation is provided for students, although there is a small fee in some cases to cover costs.

Basic skills in off-campus activities are taught. For example, horseback riding classes are aimed at developing such things as an understanding of horses, knowledge of horsemanship, and so on. In so doing students take care of their horses including grooming, bridling, and saddling.

Additional aids used in instructional process include audiovisual aids and computer center. (In golf, for example, student can plan indoors and electronically measure yardage, select clubs, and sink putts on a screen.)

Computer scheduling has been carefully studied so that students can be scheduled into activities that meet their interests, needs, and abilities, plus meeting the school requirements in respect to the rest of the educational offering.

TRUMP MODEL SCHOOLS PROGRAM*
Edgewood Junior High School
Saint Paul, Minnesota

Grades and students concerned: Seventh to ninth grades.

Selected objectives: To adapt the Trump Model Schools Program to physical education including small and large group instruction, learning packages, and so on.

To motivate students to participate in physical activities on their own.

To develop a degree of self-understanding in each student in respect to activities in the program plus a recognition of the need for physical activity throughout life.

To provide for close teacher-student relationships.

To measure skill progress in terms of behavioral objectives.

To provide individual student assistance where necessary.

---

*Adapted from material sent and article written by Luck, K. Cash: Innovative physical education through electives, organizational patterns for instruction in physical education, Washington, D. C., 1971, American Association for Health, Physical Education, and Recreation, p. 80.

---

*Adapted and based on letter and materials sent by Jim Danner, Edgewood Junior High School, November 8, 1972.

EDGEWOOD JUNIOR HIGH SCHOOL PROGRESS REPORT
HEALTH, FITNESS, RECREATION DEPARTMENT
1972 - 1973 SPRING

STUDENT'S NAME _____

TEACHER-COUNSELOR _____   M F 7 8 9

Small Group Discussion Leader _____

This progress report lists the 3 year curriculum in the Health, Fitness, Recreation Department and is to be used by students, parents, and teacher-counselors as a basis for goal setting and pacing. The Curriculum Level Goal* is based on results from standardized achievement, ability, and departmental tests, past performances and teachers' observations.

Entry Date _____   Exit Date _____

COMPARISON OF GOALS AND PROGRESS

MARKING PERIOD	1	2	3	4	5	6	Final
Curriculum Level Goal*							
Present Curriculum Level							
Work Completed							
School Within A School							

Each marking period the work completed grade is based on: A—100 points or more, B—70 to 99 points, C—40 to 69 points, D—39 or less points.

SKILLS LEVEL (5 pts. ea.) _____
- ____ A5 Swim 25 yards
- ____ A6 Agility
- ____ A7 Cardiovascular
- ____ A8 Power
- ____ A9 Strength
- Participation Points ____

LEVEL I

BOWLING (4 pts. ea.)
- ____ X1 Getting Started
- ____ X2 Stance & Pushaway
- ____ X3 Approach
- ____ X4 Pendulum Swing
- ____ X5 Delivery
- ____ X6 Scoring
- Participation Points ____
- Level II ____
- Level III ____

CONDITIONING (5 pts. ea.) ____
- ____ G1 Jogging
- ____ G2 Circuit Training
- ____ G3 Isometrics
- ____ G4 Arm Curl
- ____ G5 Half Squats
- ____ G6 Military Press
- ____ G7 Dead Lift
- ____ G8 Bench Press
- Participation Points ____
- Level II ____
- Level III ____

GOLF (5 pts. ea.) ____
- ____ S1 Equipment
- ____ S2 Safety
- ____ S3 Grip and Stance
- ____ S4 Full Swing
- ____ S5 Half Swing
- ____ S6 Putting
- ____ S7 Scoring

GOLF (continued)
- ____ S8 Etiquette
- ____ S9 Game
- Participation Points ____
- Level II
- Level III ____

INDOOR HOCKEY (4 pts. ea.) ____
- ____ I1 Rules
- ____ I2 Dribbling
- ____ I3 Forehand Passing
- ____ I4 Backhand Passing
- ____ I5 Shooting
- ____ I6 Goal Tending
- Participation Points ____
- Level II ____
- Level III ____

RHYTHMS (4 pts. ea.)

BALLROOM

CONTEMPORARY

FOLK DANCE

SQUARE DANCE
- Participation Points ____
- Level II ____
- Level III ____

SOFTBALL (4 pts. ea.) ____
- ____ U1 Rules
- ____ U2 Throwing
- ____ U3 Catching
- ____ U4 Fielding - Fly Balls
- ____ U5 Fielding - Ground Balls
- ____ U6 Batting
- ____ U7 Pitching
- Participation Points ____
- Level II ____
- Level III ____

TENNIS (3 pts. ea.) ____
- ____ D1 Safety & Equipment
- ____ D2 Court
- ____ D3 Forehand Grip
- ____ D4 Forehand Drive
- ____ D5 Backhand Drive
- ____ D6 Serve
- ____ D7 Rules
- Participation Points ____
- Level II ____
- Level III ____

TRACK (4 pts. ea.) ____
- ____ V1 Running
- ____ V2 Starts
- ____ V3 Baton Passing
- ____ V4 Hurdling
- ____ V5 Long Jump
- ____ V6 High Jump
- ____ V7 Triple Jump
- ____ V8 Shot Put
- ____ V9 Discus
- Participation Points ____
- Level II ____
- Level III ____

SWIMMING (3 pts. ea.)

BASIC SKILLS
- ____ Y1 Bobbing
- ____ Y2 Rhythmic Breathing
- ____ Y3 Jellyfish Float
- ____ Y4 Front Float
- ____ Y5 Back Float
- ____ Y6 Flutter Kick
- ____ Y7 Back Glide
- ____ Y8 Front Glide
- ____ Y9 Front Glide & Flutter Kick
- ____ Y10 Back Glide & Flutter Kick
- ____ Y11 Overarm Pull
- ____ Y12 Back Stroke Pull

BEGINNERS
- ____ Y13 Front Crawl (8 yds.)
- ____ Y14 Front Crawl (16 yds.)
- ____ Y15 Front Crawl (25 yds.)
- ____ Y16 Basic Back Stroke

BEGINNERS (continued)
- ____ Y17 Changing Directions
- ____ Y18 Turning Over
- ____ Y19 Front Dive
- ____ Y20 Deep Water Skills
- ____ Y21 Elementary Rescues

ADVANCED BEGINNERS
- ____ Y22 Front Crawl (50 yds.)
- ____ Y23 Whip Kick
- ____ Y24 Elementary Back Stroke
- ____ Y25 Survival Float
- ____ Y26 Tread Water
- ____ Y27 Dive & Underwater Swim

SYNCHRONIZED SWIMMING
- ____ Y86 Front Crawl
- ____ Y87 Back Stroke
- ____ Y88 Sculling
- ____ Y89 Marlin Turn
- ____ Y90 Log Roll
- ____ Y91 Corkscrew
- ____ Y92 Tub
- ____ Y93 Oyster
- ____ Y94 Back Tuck Somersault
- ____ Y95 Front Tuck Somersault

SKIN DIVING
- ____ Y110 Fitting & Defogging Mask
- ____ Y111 Flooding Mask
- ____ Y112 Relieving Air Pressure
- ____ Y113 Fins
- ____ Y114 Snorkel
- ____ Y115 Breathing
- ____ Y116 Surface Swimming
- ____ Y117 Surface Diving
- ____ Y118 Swimming Underwater
- ____ Y119 Entering Water
- ____ Y120 Safety Written Test
- ____ Y121 Extra Credit Activities
- Participation Points ____
- Level II ____
- Level III ____

Level I Sign-Out
This student has completed Level I. With permission of the teacher-counselor, parent, and small group teacher, this student has signed out of HFR resource center.
- Date Excused ____ Teacher ____
- Date Reentered ____ Teacher ____
- Date Excused ____ Teacher ____
- Date Reentered ____ Teacher ____
- Date Excused ____ Teacher ____

LEVEL I
- Fitness ____
- Health ____

LEVEL II
- Aide ____
- GAA ____
- Health ____
- Intramurals ____
- Large Group ____

LEVEL III
- Health ____
- Interscholastic Athletics ____
- Large Group ____

COMMENTS:

HFR REQUIREMENTS: Each student shall finish Level I in the following areas over a three (3) year period of time. Students not attending Edgewood for the three year (7-8-9) period of time shall meet the requirements set by their HFR Small Group Discussion Teacher.

		Choose Two		Choose Two
☐ Archery	☐ Competitive Swimming or	☐ Basketball		☐ Flag Football
☐ Badminton	☐ Track	☐ Broomball		☐ Soccer
☐ Bowling	☐ Golf	☐ Floor Hockey		☐ Speedaway
☐ Broomball or	☐ Gymnastics	☐ Volleyball		**Swimming**
☐ Skating or	☐ Modern Dance (Girls)	☐ Water Polo		☐ Basic Skills
☐ Skiing	☐ Rhythms			☐ Beginner
☐ Health	☐ Tennis			☐ Advanced Beginner
	☐ Wrestling (Boys)			☐ Any other pool unit

Fig. 8-2. Edgewood Junior High School Progress Report, Health, Fitness, and Recreation Department. (Edgewood Junior High School, St. Paul, Minn.)

Selected features of the program: Large and small group instruction, learning packages, teacher-counselor relationship with students, and paraprofessionals constitute parts of the physical education program.

Students attend large group sessions once a week that are designed to orient, interest, and motivate them to participate in coming units of study involving various physical education activities.

Students attend a small group discussion once each week that is designed to build self-understanding, stimulate group dynamics, and broaden their understanding of health, physical education, and recreation.

Students attend three two-period sessions

Title: Wrestling—Head Lever

Level: I

Written by: J. Danner

Learning package no: J-6

Department: Health, Fitness, Recreation

Date: November 1, 1971

1. Behavioral Objective: On the mat you will put the Head Lever Ride on another wrestler holding tight to his wrist, driving your head into his arm pit, while driving from your toes.

2. Pretest: Satisfy the Behavioral Objective.

3. Do at least two of the things listed:
   A. In the resource center view the loop film "Head Lever."
   B. Practice the skill on the mat with another wrestler.
   C. Ask another student for a demonstration.

4. Tell the aide of work done.

5. Posttest:
   A. See a teacher's aide.
   B. Satisfy the Behavioral Objective.
   C. If you satisfy this behavioral objective, go on to another.
   D. If you cannot satisfy this behavioral objective, repeat the things listed.

of physical education laboratory each week where they learn skills presented in learning packages, each of which contains specific skills to be learned, behavioral objectives, the means of achieving objectives, and procedures for evaluating behavioral objectives.

All teachers engage in teacher-counselor role, with each teacher assigned to about twenty-five students or counselees. Both group and individual meetings are held where such items are covered as schedules, personal problems, school problems, and so on.

Five instructional aides (paraprofessionals) are assigned, one to each activity unit that is in operation. Aides have three major areas of responsibility: student control, skills testing, and individual student assistance.

INDIVIDUALIZED APPROACH TO LEARNING*
Omaha Public Schools
Omaha, Nebraska

Grades and students concerned: Fourth to twelfth grades.

*Adapted from material sent by and article written by Shrader, Robert D.: Individualized approach to learning, Journal of Health, Physical Education, and Recreation 42:33, 1971.

Selected objectives: To provide a student-centered learning experience in physical education.

To provide a learning continuum in physical education.

To provide an individualized physical education curriculum for students.

To make it possible for each student to regulate his own learning.

To convert the gymnasium into a learning laboratory.

To encourage students to assist other students in the learning process.

To have the teacher serve as a facilitator rather than as a presenter of learning.

Selected features of the program: Students are pretested to determine present status in respect to such items as skills, knowledge and understanding, and value domains (psychomotor, cognitive, and affective).

Each student is provided with an individual prescription (called a *phy-pak*) based on test results and his needs.

Each student works toward fulfilling his prescription as indicated. Self-testing and peer assistance are encouraged.

Each student meets with teacher for final evaluation of prescribed task.

Teacher determines whether task has been successfully accomplished based on

Fig. 8-3. Individualized approach to learning. (Omaha Public Schools, Omaha, Neb.; courtesy Robert Shrader.)

learning objective. Records are kept on student progress and new learning task (phy-pak) prescribed. If task has not been successfully completed, teacher offers suggestions regarding alternate ways in which learning objective can be achieved.

The phy-pak contract consists of nine parts: clarification of contract, what the prescription can do for the student, learning objectives, diagnostic test or pretest, learning tasks categorized into three parts (psychomotor, cognitive, and affective domains), learning activities, self-test, final test, and challenge activities.

INDEPENDENT STUDY OPTION*
Timberlane Regional High School
Plaistow, New Hampshire

Grades and students concerned: Twelfth grade—seniors.

Selected objectives: To enable students to develop lifetime recreational skills.

To permit students to choose activities in which they wish to engage.

To permit students the opportunity to develop skills at their own pace.

To individualize instruction.

To provide goal-centered learning.

Selected features of the program: Considerable freedom is given to students in the selection of activities if three requirements are met: there is a genuine interest in the activity on the part of the student, the activity has value for adult life, and the activity allows for a goal-centered learning experience.

Students may engage in activities on their own or in small groups.

Students may utilize school or recreational facilities and staffs in other agencies throughout the community.

Students interested in participating in independent study may make written ap-

---

*Adapted from material and article by Stanhope, Carolyn L.: Independent study option, Journal of Health, Physical Education, and Recreation 42:24, 1971.

plication and submit faculty recommendations supporting their application.

Student selecting independent study is expected to continue with that activity until the end of the quarter.

Two hours each week must be spent in practice.

Utilization of resource people and reference materials is encouraged.

Students meet with their faculty advisor at least once each week, at which time progress is evaluated and new goals are established.

Students participate in the final evaluation.

TOWARD THE TWENTY-FIRST CENTURY°
New York City Public Schools
New York, New York

Grades and students concerned: Ninth to twelfth grades.

Selected objectives: To enable students to become involved in planning their own program of physical education.

To help each student to become proficient in lifetime activities.

To utilize the resources of the metropolitan area as part of the physical education experience.

To help students and teachers to get to know each other better.

Selected features of the program: Program is only carried on in a few experimental schools at the present time but it is recommended for the entire New York City school system.

Program advocates career or satellite academies for training young people interested in physical education as a career.

Program endorses community involvement for credit in such areas as swimming pool aides, junior officials, recreational activities, day care counselors, problems in ecology, and so on for which the school would give course credit.

Program suggests a "cafeteria" of courses, with the student selecting on an elective basis various kinds of activities, including activities such as club ethnic studies related to physical education.

Program recommends work-study courses where students may work and earn.

Program suggests athletes could assist in after-school youth athletic activities, day care centers, and so on.

Program endorses broad exploration of recreative interests including camping, canoeing, winter sports, and riding.

Program endorses "minicourses" in addition to basic required courses.

Program encourages independent study, learning packages, and individual skill practice on the part of the student.

Program encourages wide use of resources throughout the community.

OPERATION SELF-IMAGE°
Junior High Schools
Schenectady Public Schools
Schenectady, New York

Grades and students concerned: Seventh to ninth grades.

Selected objectives: To improve the self-image of physically unfit and socially disadvantaged students.

To combine a physical fitness program with nutritious breakfast and lunch.

Selected features of the program: Boys in program were pretested and posttested in regard to their attitudes toward themselves and also toward their school, their attendance records, behavior ratings of teachers, and the national fitness test involving strength, visual acuity, ability, and orthopedic characteristics.

Program was conducted five days a week for one semester. Students reported at 7:00 A.M., class began at 7:15 with various exercises, followed by a circuit training program, showering, dressing, and breakfast.

Administrators, teachers, guidance coun-

°Adapted from The Association of Assistant Principals and Supervisors of Health and Physical Education in the New York City Public Schools: Toward the 21st century in health and physical education, New York, N. Y., 1972.

°Adapted from Mayer, Frank, and Grant, John: Operation Self-Image, Journal of Health, Physical Education, and Recreation 43:64, 1972.

selors, and workers in the cafeteria participated in the program.

Testing results showed that in general the physical fitness status of students and their attitudes toward themselves and school were improved. The administration of the school felt the experiment was a success.

NONGRADED CURRICULUM*
Athens High School
Athens, Ohio

Grades and students concerned: Ninth to twelfth grades.

Selected objectives: To provide a nongraded program in physical education for high school students.

To make it possible for students of similar abilities to meet physical education requirements in homogeneous groups.

To provide for the individual differences and interests of students.

Selected features of the program: Students are placed in classes according to level of skill achievement and physical maturity rather than according to their chronological age or grade level.

The AAHPER Physical Fitness Test Scores are used in determining in what phase students will be placed in the program. There are four phases: up to the twenty-fifth percentile, Phase 1; twenty-sixth to fortieth percentile, Phase 2; forty-first to seventieth percentile, Phase 3; and seventy-first to one hundredth percentile, Phase 4. If performance justifies, students can phase up or down at the end of each grading period.

Two years of physical education is required of all students. Elective activities are offered in junior and senior years. A student may start the two-year requirement cycle as a freshman, sophomore, or junior.

There are required and elective courses in the program.

Modular scheduling is utilized and this together with nongraded classes has provided for small classes, homogeneous groupings of students, additional class periods for additional work, clubs, and open laboratories.

POINTS TO REMEMBER

1. Society is changing and education, if it is to contribute to the society of which it is a part, must also change.
2. Physical education as a part of education must change to meet the needs of today's society and students.
3. Many innovative practices presently exist in schools throughout the United States. Physical educators should study the nature of such innovative practices and determine their value for their own physical education programs.
4. Student involvement is important.
5. Educational and physical education programs must be geared to the needs of the student.

PROBLEMS TO THINK THROUGH

1. What are the advantages and disadvantages of each of the innovative programs discussed in this chapter?
2. What constitutes a list of innovative practices that have greatest value for modern-day physical education programs?
3. How can change be brought about in a school system where a traditional physical education program exists?
4. What are the implications for physical education of innovations that are taking place in other subject matter fields in the educational program?

CASE STUDY FOR ANALYSIS

Select a school system where the faculty is steeped in tradition, where the age range of faculty is fifty to sixty-five years, where a formalized program of physical education is in operation that has been totally prescribed by the faculty, where the students do not play a part in the decision-making process, and where citizens of the community are very much concerned about rising educational costs and wonder whether the physical education program should be retained or whether it should be dropped as an economy measure. As an interested physical educator, describe what procedure you would follow in order to restore physical education as a valuable and important part of the school program so that the community would not question the worth of this activity.

EXERCISES FOR REVIEW

1. Discuss five major changes taking place in education today.
2. Compare education in 1900 with education today.

---

*Adapted from article by Burson, Robert: Non-graded curriculum and modular scheduling, organizational patterns for instruction in physical education, Washington, D. C., 1971, American Association for Health, Physical Education, and Recreation, p. 88.

3. Review the professional literature and identify school programs where you feel they are meeting the needs of students today.
4. What is the best way to bring about educational change?

SELECTED READINGS

Bucher, Charles A.: Administrative dimensions of health and physical education programs, including athletics, Saint Louis, 1971, The C. V. Mosby Co.

Bucher, Charles A.: Administration of health and physical education programs, including athletics, ed. 5, St. Louis, 1971, The C. V. Mosby Co.

Barnett, H. G.: Innovation: the basis of cultural change, New York, 1953, McGraw-Hill Book Co., Inc.

Journal of Health, Physical Education, and Recreation, September, 1971 (entire issue).

MacKenzie, Marlin M.: Toward a new curriculum in physical education, New York, 1969, McGraw-Hill Book Co., Inc.

Nixon, J., and Jewett, A.: Physical education curriculum, New York, 1964, The Ronald Press Co.

Willgoose, Carl E.: The curriculum in physical education, Englewood Cliffs, N.J., 1969, Prentice-Hall, Inc.

9 INTERPRETING THE RELEVANT PROGRAM OF PHYSICAL EDUCATION

Physical education has been the victim of the economy, taxpayers' rebellion, and fiscal pressures. Some budget officials and boards of education view physical education as a nonacademic subject and therefore low on the priority list when it comes to allocating money for new staff and equipment. Other educators have noted that with an austerity budget it is one of those extras they will have to do without.

Several months ago the city of Philadelphia decided to cut all extra curricular activities and reduce the physical education program requirement to the minimum mandated by state law. Fortunately, pressures exerted by responsible individuals and groups and a concerted effort to interpret the physical education program and its worth to students resulted in the programs being partially restored. As Edyth A. Fleming of the Philadelphia High School for Girls stated prior to an important meeting: "When Board of Education members meet with budget officials I hope they will be able to convince them that physical and mental conditioning go hand in hand and are equally necessary."

NEED FOR INTERPRETING PHYSICAL EDUCATION

There is an urgent need to interpret physical education to students, academic teachers and other educators, and the public in general. Accurate and significant facts need to be presented to these people so that they will understand the purposes and worth of our profession in the educational process as well as in their personal lives.

Physical education is a misunderstood profession. Surveys conducted among lay persons show that physical education is thought of as "calisthenics done to command," "athletics," "arms and legs and good intentions," or in terms of other misconceptions. Only as physical educators interpret their profession effectively will it be possible to obtain public support and to achieve its goals.

It is vital for teachers, students, parents, and the community-at-large to have a clear understanding of the important place of physical education in general education. This can be accomplished only where there is cooperation within the department, within the school, and within the community. A public that is not informed is not likely to lend its support to furthering physical education.

Teachers, to be effective participants in public relations, must be guided by well-thought-through, sound educational policies. This chapter concerns itself with policies and suggestions that will assist each physical educator to be an effective public relations worker, recognizing that it is his function not only to teach but also to interpret his program and its worth to the various groups of people that are consumers of his product and services.

THE PEPI PROJECT

The Physical Education Public Information (PEPI) project is one of the major efforts put forth by the profession to interpret physical education to the public. The project has identified some 600 coordinators for each of the nation's largest metropolitan areas who organize and interpret physical education in their own geographic area through such means as radio, television, newspapers, and other media.

The PEPI project was initiated on the premise that the tendency to curtail physical education programs can be reversed if people become aware of such basic values of physical education as:

Physical education is health insurance.

Physical education contributes to academic achievement.

Physical education provides experiences and skills that last a lifetime.

Physical education helps in developing a

PLAY AND YOUR CHILD'S REPORT CARD

By Charles A. Bucher
Consultant to the President's Council
on Physical Fitness and Sports

As a parent you want to help your child be a success in school. You spend long hours searching for material to be used in his reports, hire a tutor if he is lagging in arithmetic, sweat out the exams, and carefully scrutinize the report cards. You may even send a note to the principal and ask that he be excused from physical education so that he will have an extra period in the library.

Success in school, you sincerely feel, is filling the mind with historical facts, learning how to work with fractions, and developing a knack for writing compositions in English. Mastering these tasks, you have been led to believe, represents the formula for getting your child on the honor roll and into a prestigious college. As a neighbor of mine pointed out after seeing her son's report card: "I'm furious. My boy has three As, two Bs, and a D. The D is in gym and wrecks his average. He's not an athlete. It's not fair. It has only to do with his body—not his mind."

When well-intentioned parents ignore the physical aspect they are overlooking a vital part of their child's education, and ironically, may not be helping him to make that honor roll or get that much sought-after diploma from a first-rate college. They are oblivious to a proven fact—that their child's mind and body are dependent on each other for maximum achievement in school, as well as in life. In other words, the chances are that their children will get better grades in school if they develop some skill and are physically fit, than if they are uncoordinated and on the soft side.

More than a quarter of a century ago Lewis M. Terman, the famous psychologist from Stanford University, studied gifted children and found that physical weakness was rare among his bright subjects. Instead, most were fairly good physical specimens.

More recently, research conducted in Oregon among 9- to 17-year olds found positive correlations between achievement in school and such physical measures as weight, height, strength, and certain physical skills. A study in England revealed that most students above average in scholarship were also above average in physique. An examination of more than 33,000 children in St. Louis found that mental mediocrity was associated with physical mediocrity. Motor characteristics of 43 underachieving boys, ages 10 to 14, enrolled in the Psychology Clinic of the University of California at Los Angeles, were studied and one-half of the boys from 10 to 12 years old exhibited poor motor performance.

Other research studies have shown that children who repeated a grade in a certain school system were inferior in weight and height to those who were not held back. Physical performance and emotional development factors among nonintellectual considerations in another educational program were most significant in achieving academically in reading and arithmetic.

There are many factors that relate to scholastic achievement in school. Intelligence, the amount of time your child spends on the books, and how motivated he is to do well in his studies will most certainly play a very important part in determining how successful he is. However, these conditions in themselves will not entirely determine what grades he gets in English and social studies, his promotion from grade to grade, and other measures of scholastic achievement.

Physical factors also play a part in your child's scholastic achievement. Parents who encourage their child to be physically fit and to develop motor ability will be giving their boy or girl the best chance to succeed. Although physical fitness and skill cannot improve your child's intelligence, they will help his learning potential.

positive self-image and the ability to compete and cooperate with others.

PEPI has mobilized its efforts to get these messages across to the public, particularly taxpayers, students, teachers, administrators, school boards, parents, and funding agencies.

Coordinators have been carefully selected on the basis of their interest in the profession and in public relations, their reputation for working with people, and their ability to get the job done. All coordinators were required to attend several workshops in order to become oriented in the materials to be used, the procedure for obtaining time on television and radio, and other matters pertaining to the effective carrying out of their responsibilities.

Currently, PEPI is stressing that a "new" physical education exists, that physical education has changed, and that physical education is more relevant to the times through which the nation is passing.

For further information on PEPI and to help in this project, contact the American Association for Health, Physical Education, and Recreation offices in Washington, D. C.

AN EXAMPLE OF AN ATTEMPT TO INTERPRET PHYSICAL EDUCATION TO THE PUBLIC

Bucher has written many syndicated newspaper columns for the President's Council on Physical Fitness and Sports. The purpose of this effort is to interpret physical education so that it will receive greater public support in communities from coast to coast. An example of one of these columns is included in this discussion.

GENERAL PUBLIC RELATIONS POLICIES FOR PHYSICAL EDUCATION

1. Each school within an educational system should develop its own public relations program, which should be an integral part of the larger school organization.

2. Before attempting to foster good public relations between the school and the community, good internal public relations should be developed, involving students, teaching personnel, nonteaching personnel, and administrators.

3. The public relations program should recognize that there are many kinds of people to be reached, such as pupils, parents, alumni, physicians, and administrators, and that each group requires its own unique procedures and approach for effective results.

4. The public relations program should present an articulate philosophy of physical education that clears away the misconceptions and stresses the objectives and worth of the field through the presentation of scientific evidence.

5. The physical educator should recognize that how he relates to other individuals within and without the department has implications for the public relations program. Consequently, such factors as a pleasing personality and appearance, provision for a healthy physical environment, and harmonious relations with students and parents are very important.

6. Before using communications media, such as radio or television, advanced planning is essential.

7. Evaluation of the effectiveness of the public relations program and the attitudes of the various sectors of the public should be determined through a carefully planned research program.

PUBLIC RELATIONS IN PRACTICE

Fifteen school systems in New York State were questioned about their public relations programs for physical education. They cited these operational factors in the conduct of their program:

1. Each physical education department has an active public relations program in operation.

2. Definite policies are established to guide the public relations program.

3. Responsibility for public relations is shared by all members of the department, with the central authority residing with the director.

4. Many media are used to interpret the

program to the numerous groups to be reached.

5. Preparation and planning are essential in the use of all public relations media.

6. The total physical education program in action is recognized as being the most effective medium of public relations.

7. Effort is made to interpret to the public the correct facts concerning physical education.

The fifteen school systems surveyed were asked the question, "What message are you trying to convey to the public?" A compiled list follows of the answers given by the directors of the physical education programs:

1. The aims and objectives of the total physical education program
2. The value of the total physical education program
3. The importance of the program to the student
4. Recognition and achievement of all students in physical education classes and in intramural and extramural activities, and not just in athletics
5. The importance of the physical education program for each child
6. The efforts and energies that are directed toward giving each child a good program of physical education
7. The contributions of the physical education program to all children, not just athletes
8. The fact that even though interschool athletics receive most of the publicity, these activities do not receive priority in the program of physical education
9. The ability of the physical education program to enhance the health and welfare of the student

GROUPS NEEDING INFORMATION

Interpretation, or public relations, is basically concerned with communication. One person has defined it as getting the right facts to the right people at the right time and in the right way. Another has said it is doing good and receiving credit for it. One important consideration, regardless of definition, is to recognize that there are different kinds of people to be reached, and therefore different procedures and techniques are necessary in reaching these various groups. Six important groups that should be contacted are identified here.

Youth

Students in our schools who are exposed to physical education programs should be our best supporters. They should graduate from our schools and depart from our programs feeling that they have been very worthwhile, enjoyable, and educational experiences. They should believe that the subject of physical education needs support and should be recommended to other people. Students grow up to be presidents of boards of education, directors of banks, industrial chairmen, and other important citizens in our communities from coast to coast. The experience they have in physical education will help to determine how much they will support these programs as adults.

Colleagues

Faculty members in other subject matter areas are an important group to reach. The absence of coaches and other physical education personnel at faculty meetings and other academic gatherings frequently results in a lack of adequate communication and interpretation of the program to teachers of history, science, English, and other subjects. Physical education cannot expect to be considered an important part of the school educational program if the department is not represented at important meetings. Physical educators need the support of their colleagues. They should exploit every opportunity to reach these important educators, whether in faculty meetings or in informal discussions in the teachers' room.

Administrators

School administrators make decisions affecting physical education programs, determine budget allocations, approve facility allocations, and in many other ways help or hinder our professional progress. It is important to reach this powerful group and impress them with the contributions of physical education to the total education of the student.

Parents

Mothers and fathers should understand that physical educators contribute to their children's health and welfare. If they believe that their children are receiving a worthwhile educational experience in physical education, they will be strong supporters, but if they believe that it is a waste of time because of poorly planned programs, they may fail to provide their needed support.

Alumni

The alumni of a school can be a valuable asset to any physical education program, provided they are kept informed.

General public

Of course, the general public, consisting of business and professional people, taxpayers, and other citizens, are interested in their schools. Outstanding educational systems are marks of good communities. Therefore, it is important to interpret to the general public how physical education contributes to a strong educational program.

BASIC CONSIDERATIONS

Following are some basic considerations for reaching the various groups of persons noted above.

Studies and research. The results of investigations of various aspects of the physical education program, such as improvement in the students' physical fitness or skills, are excellent publicity material. These studies should help to place physical education on defensible ground as to its worth in the educational program.

Written material. Newsletters, reports, memoranda, brochures, and other forms of written material that have been accurately and neatly prepared are excellent media for reaching the various groups.

Sound departmental policies. If the department of physical education has given time and study to policies concerning excuses, uniforms, athletic participation, class participation, grades, and other important matters, the wide dissemination of such material will reflect efficiency and a well-functioning program.

Conferences. Student, parent, administrator, or teacher conferences are important avenues for explaining purposes of programs, indicating interests, eliminating problems, and planning projects.

Integrated programs. Planning interdepartmental programs is an effective educational and interpretive device. A folk dance festival, for example, that integrates the resources of the physical education, art, music, home economics, history, geography, and other departments is an excellent medium.

Involvement. "As you share you care" is a saying that has much merit. Administrators, townspeople, colleagues, students, and others can be involved in many aspects of the physical education program, ranging from athletics to a "careers day" project.

Internal considerations. Public relations should be considered internally before being developed externally. The support of everyone within the organization, from the top administrator down to the last worker, should be sought. Furthermore, such items as defining the purpose of the program, designating the person or persons responsible, considering the funds available, deciding on the media to be utilized, and procuring the wherewithal to carry on the program should be a first consideration.

Public relations plan. The public relations program should be outlined in writing, and every member of the organization should become familiar with it. The better it is known and understood, the better chance it has of succeeding.

Funds. There should be adequate funds to do the job. Furthermore, the person or persons in charge of the public relations program should be given freedom to spend this money in whatever ways they believe will be most helpful and productive for the organization.

Persons responsible. Individuals assigned to public relations responsibilities should modestly stay in the background, keep abreast of the factors that affect the program, develop a wide acquaintance, and make contacts that will be helpful.

Wide coverage. A good interpretative program will utilize all available resources and machinery to disseminate information in order to ensure adequate coverage.

Outstanding program. The program of physical education is the most important public relations medium. Good news travels fast but bad news spreads even faster. If the program is good, people will hear about it and, in turn, will give their support and help.

PRINCIPLES OF GOOD PUBLIC RELATIONS

C. O. Jackson, Professor Emeritus of the University of Illinois, lists the following ten principles that he believes are important to carrying out a good program of physical education:

1. *Begin with the best program* of health and PE that you can develop for your students in your situation. Existing time factors, facilities and equipment, aided by your initiative and ingenuity, will help.

2. *Use every opportunity* to acquaint fellow faculty members, other school personnel, with your plans, your special problems. Remember, a good listener makes greater progress, so be sympathetic to *their* problems.

3. *Take every opportunity to speak* to members of the community, individually and in groups, about your program. Talks before PTA groups, civic and fraternal organizations can be of real value in putting your ideas across.

4. *Dress, talk and act* like a respected member of both faculty and community. Your appearance, your personality are selling the program *and* your profession in your classes, at school, elsewhere in the community.

5. *Work with and through the administrator* in getting your ideas approved and accepted. Statements by leaders in education, and in medicine, and discussions of good programs in nearby schools can have nothing but good results.

6. *Sell the editor* of the local newspaper on the value of your program, the news value of the many releases you can give him. Discuss your problems with him, keep him informed of your progress. Even better, write up your problems in short, easy-to-read form for the editor or reporter. He will meet you more than half way if the "meat" of the story is easy to uncover.

7. *Arrange to use some of the educational time* on radio and TV for your program presentation. The complaint in many areas is that not enough such material is available to even meet requirements set up by the Federal Communications Commission.

8. *Carry on broader, more comprehensive programs* of intramurals, GAA, and recreation as an outgrowth of your in-class program of PE. This is a big step in doing something worthwhile for *all* students.

9. *Plan and carry out demonstrations*, athletic carnivals, play and sport days. Try an annual open house. Parents and townspeople are interested in what their children are doing—give them a good sample.

10. *Remember that good teaching* is the crux of good public relations. Your students are ambassadors of goodwill. If you challenge them, help them in your program, they and their parents will become your strongest supporters. Your program will grow and develop correspondingly.°

INTERPRETIVE MEDIA

Fifteen school systems were surveyed to determine what specific media were utilized by the departments of physical education in interpreting their programs to the various groups of people they were attempting to reach. The following media were listed:

Newsletter	Personal contact
School publications	Demonstrations and
Radio	exhibits
Television	Films
Newspaper	Pictures
Posters	Magazines
Letters to parents	Window displays
Public speaking	Brochures
Physical education	Sport days
program	Bulletin boards
Slogans	Professional associations

Some of the media that can be utilized effectively in physical education, along with general principles regarding their use, will be discussed briefly.

Slogans

The strength of a slogan lies in its emotional appeal—it is a distinctive phrase used to signify a purpose.

°From Jackson, C. O.: Ten principles of good conduct, Physical Education and School Athletics Newsletter, January 20, 1957, New London, Conn., Arthur C. Croft Publications.

Slogans should be informational, factual, colorful, appealing, and easily understood and remembered, and they should impel to action.

In addition, slogans should be timely, practical, personal, challenging, simple, based on truth, short, imaginative, and concrete.

They can be used in radio, television, speeches, songs, posters, letterheads, billboards, displays, rallies, exhibits, advertisements, and handbills.

Our nation's political history has been affected by slogans. A few examples: "Walk softly and carry a big stick." "Keep cool with Coolidge." "Make the world safe for democracy." "A chicken in every pot." "54-40 or fight." "Over the top." "Remember the Maine." "Taxation without representation is tyranny."

Slogans have noticeably affected our economic development. A few examples: "It's smart to be thrifty." "We will not be undersold." "What helps business helps you."

Products have used slogans effectively. A few examples: "I'd walk a mile for a Camel." "All the news that's fit to print." "Progress is our most important product." "The pause that refreshes."

Ways of life are reflected in slogans. A few examples: "A stitch in time saves nine." "Time and tide wait for no man." "He who hesitates is lost." "Spare the rod and spoil the child."

Slogans have been used successfully in health, physical education, and recreation. A few examples: "It pays to play." "Give your child's mind his body's support." "Cross at the green, not in between." "Brush today to check decay." "A sound mind in a sound body." "Health, energy, and power are yours." "Fitness—a basic goal of education." "You can't sit and be fit."

Posters

Posters should catch and hold the attention of the viewer.

Posters require an eye-catching design.

Posters should convey a message.

Color is one of the most important agents that help to convey a poster's messages if effectively used.

As a rule, posters should have a short, punchy, well-worded message.

Posters should be simple, interesting, attractive, and convincing and should leave a specific message with the viewer.

Posters should guide an observer's view from one part of the display to the other. This can be done through color, line, and various layout techniques.

Posters should be placed at eye level if possible.

Posters should have good balance, with essential features in the most prominent places.

Radio

A radio program should hold the listener's attention from start to finish. Many radio stations today broadcast little other than music and news. Programs must fit into such a pattern in order to hold the listeners rather than lose them.

Short programs are good. Very few persons turn on the radio today to listen to a dramatic play or a long discourse on some topic of the day.

The program should be informative and entertaining.

Language must be simple and direct—human interest and anecdotal material are always effective.

It is better to put depth into one idea rather than to cover many ideas and only scratch the surface of each.

Talk *with* rather than *to* the listener. Speak in the listener's terms.

Know your audience.

Consult with the broadcasters—producers, program directors, and so on. Find out the most effective methods for radio broadcasting.

Have a definite message in mind to put across to the public.

Be thoroughly familiar with the method to be used to relay the information: spot announcements, editorals, news broadcasts, reporting of school activities, panels, interviews, plays, quiz programs.

Determine the time of day at which the most receptive audience would be listening.

Publicize the radio program in advance. This can be done via advertisements, announcements on other broadcasts, school publications, and press releases.

Television

Explore the possibility of obtaining free time. The idea of performing a public service will influence some television station managers.

Consult television stations that are reserved for educational purposes.

Be prepared with written plans that can be put into operation immediately. Sometimes one must take advantage of opportunities for television time on short notice. Being ready may make the difference between acceptance or rejection for such an assignment.

Do not overlook the fact that television programming requires rehearsals, preparation of scenery, and other work.

Have boys and girls participate in the program. When youngsters are in the act, the attention of mothers, fathers, aunts, uncles, grandmas, friends, and so on is immediately attracted.

Motion pictures

One of the most powerful means of informing and enlightening the public in regard to physical education is the use of motion pictures.

Good pictures of daily class activity are tangible evidence of the worth of the program to parents and others. They are excellent for PTA groups, civic clubs, and the like.

Motion pictures usually receive better audience attention. The situation is not like that in television, where there is opportunity to change to another program.

Before making a film, analyze the poten-

Chester Studios, Inc., New York

Fig. 9-1. Physical education exhibition. (Yonkers Public Schools, Yonkers, N. Y.)

tial audience, the message to be conveyed, and other important items.

Survey the entire program of physical education in order to select the most significant and typical activities to be photographed.

Homemade film depicting daily operation of the school can be useful in interpreting the program to the public.

In a do-it-yourself operation, try to obtain some professional advice—perhaps from a photography club or a camera shop.

Use good equipment and material. Nothing is more annoying than watching a poorly planned movie that consists of shots that are blurred or not in proper focus, or going through an unpleasant experience with a projector that does not work properly.

Many films on physical education are available through professional organizations, college and university film libraries, commercial organizations, and state departments of education.

Fig. 9-2. Physical education demonstration. (Walt Whitman High School, South Huntington Schools, New York.)

Exhibitions and demonstrations

In physical education an exhibition or a demonstration can be a culminating school activity to show what has been accomplished in the program and what students have learned.

Exhibitions and demonstrations can focus public attention on a program and stimulate action in support of the program.

Exhibitions can take the form of bulletin board displays, showcases, scrapbooks, drawings, or posters to point up such subjects as physical fitness or some sport or skill. They can also be used to show how expert performers have acquired outstanding skill in a particular sport.

Demonstrations can utilize all the students regardless of skill and also present a picture of what actually goes on in day-to-day classes.

An exhibition, for best results, should be limited to one type of activity or purpose.

Exhibitions should be original, present facts, stimulate participation, provide new ideas, and create action.

Newspaper and magazine articles

Articles can be published in either local papers or periodicals or in national publications.

Articles should be factual, arouse and secure attention, contain human interest material, and be written in the language of the reader.

Magazines have many advantages since they have excellent color and layout, are read many times by different persons, reach a wide range of people varying in income and intelligence, and are found in many offices and homes.

Know the subject, the ideas to be put across, and the type of persons to be reached; then place the article in a suitable publication.

Newspaper material is often read hurriedly. Therefore, the style of writing must take this point into consideration.

Prepare all copy in typewritten form— neat, double spaced, and on one side of the paper only.

Ideas may be suggested to magazines and newspapers to be staff written.

Letters

Next to personal contact, correspondence is the best interpretive medium.

Letters can be direct, are economical, and may be adapted to any situation.

Letters should be individually typed. It is important to use correct grammar and spelling.

The message contained in the letter should be friendly, cordial, warm, courteous, sincere, enthusiastic, and natural.

Write your letters as though you were speaking to the individual in person.

Letters can be used to announce special programs, to indicate the necessary skills and understandings expected of students, to interpret the objectives desired to be reached, and so on.

Letters should be written in terms of the reader's wishes and needs.

Public speaking

Public speaking can be a very effective medium of interpreting. Through public addresses to civic and social groups in the community, public gatherings, professional meetings, and any organizations or groups that desire to know more about the work being performed, a good opportunity is afforded for interpreting the physical education profession to the public.

An effective job must be done in making a public speech, or it may result in poor public relations.

Know the subject to be discussed, have a sincere interest in the topic, and be enthusiastic.

Be direct, straightforward, and well prepared.

Give a brief presentation, and use clear and distinct enunciation.

Prepare an outline of the talk in advance. The talk should be well organized. Use correct English and have an interesting beginning and conclusion, as well as a theme or central point.

Professional associations

Professional associations on local, state, and national levels can do much to interpret physical education to the public at large.

Professional groups hold meetings to upgrade programs; prepare films, publications, and other materials; establish professional standards; sponsor radio, television, and other programs; publish articles in periodicals; and in many ways inform the community, state, and nation about the physical education profession. They deserve your constant support.

Professional organizations are valuable in reaching boards of education, the general public, colleagues in the profession, other teachers, pupils, and other groups.

SOME THINGS EACH PHYSICAL EDUCATOR CAN DO TO INTERPRET HIS FIELD OF PHYSICAL EDUCATION

Following is a brief list of ways in which the physical educator will personally be able to interpret to others the profession of which he is a part:

1. Join professional associations and help them to achieve their goals.

2. Attend faculty meetings after becoming a member of a school staff. Enter into discussions.

3. Become well informed about physical education as a professional field and about education in general.

4. Seek out school administrators, other members of the faculty, and the consumers of physical education's products and services. Help them to better understand the profession of physical education.

5. Understand the scientific foundations underlying physical education: the latest research and new trends and developments. Find out what the latest thinking is and translate it into action at the grassroots level.

6. Develop the best possible program of physical education. Have satisfied children and youth go out from the program.

7. Utilize every opportunity available to sell someone else on the worth of the professional field of endeavor. If the physical educator himself is sold, it will not be difficult to sell someone else.

8. Exploit every medium of communication to put the message across.

9. Think in positive terms. Think success, and the profession's chances of achieving great things will be better assured!

POINTS TO REMEMBER

1. Some of the basic principles underlying a sound program of interpretation and public relations
2. The various groups of people to whom the profession should be interpreted
3. A knowledge and understanding of the following interpretative media: slogans, posters, radio, television, motion pictures, exhibitions, demonstrations, newspapers, magazines, letters, public speaking, and professional associations
4. Some things that can be done to interpret the professional field of physical education

PROBLEMS TO THINK THROUGH

1. What are some of the common misconceptions about physical education? How did these misconceptions originate, and how can they be corrected?
2. What constitutes an adequate public relations program for a secondary school?

CASE STUDY FOR ANALYSIS

Choose some product that has gained national recognition, such as an automobile, cigarette, soap, and so on. Do an in-depth study to discover what techniques were used to promote it and to persuade the public to accept this product.

EXERCISES FOR REVIEW

1. Define the term "public relations."
2. What are the groups of people with which physical education is most directly concerned?
3. What are five principles to recognize in interpreting your profession to the public?
4. What do we mean by the statement, "As you share you care"?
5. Develop a slogan that can be used to promote physical education.
6. Prepare a poster to stress the importance of physical fitness.
7. Write a series of ten one-minute spot announcements for a radio station.
8. Write a letter that could be used to inform parents about the physical condition of their son or daughter.

9. What is the difference between an exhibition and a demonstration?
10. Write a five-hundred-word magazine article on the topic, "It pays to play."

SELECTED READINGS

American Association for Health, Physical Education, and Recreation: PEPI-GRAMS, a series of communications on the Physical Education Public Information Project, 1972.

Bernays, Edward L.: Public relations, Norman, Okla., 1952, University of Oklahoma Press.

Bucher, Charles A.: Administration of health and physical education programs, including athletics, ed. 5, St. Louis, 1971, The C. V. Mosby Co.

Bucher, Charles A.: Back to school—what kind of education is relevant? (syndicated newspaper column), Washington, D. C., September, 1972, President's Council on Physical Fitness and Sports.

Bucher, Charles A.: Foundations of physical education, ed. 6, St. Louis, 1972, The C. V. Mosby Co.

Bucher, Charles A.: Play and your child's report card (syndicated newspaper column), Washington, D. C., May, 1972, President's Council on Physical Fitness and Sports.

Caldwell, Stratton F.: Toward a humanistic physical education, Journal of Health, Physical Education, and Recreation 43:31, 1972.

Dapper, G.: Public relations for educators, New York, 1964, The Macmillan Co.

Geyer, Claudia: Physical education for the electronic age, Journal of Health, Physical Education, and Recreation 43:32, 1972.

National School Public Relations Association: It starts in the classroom, Washington, D. C., 1951, National Education Association.

Torpey, J.: Interpreting physical education for the public, Physical Educator 24:131, 1967.

PART THREE
THE TEACHER

10 BECOMING A TEACHER

Those who educate children well, are more to be honoured than those who produce them; for these only gave them life, those the art of living well. ARISTOTLE

A teacher who is attempting to teach without inspiring the pupil with a desire to learn is hammering on cold iron. HORACE MANN

It is the supreme art of the teacher to awaken joy in creative expression and knowledge. ALBERT EINSTEIN

The thing, above all, that a teacher should endeavor to produce in his pupils, if democracy is to survive, is the kind of tolerance that springs from an endeavor to understand those who are different from ourselves. BERTRAND RUSSELL

His [the teacher's] problem is to protect the spirit of inquiry, to keep it from becoming blasé from over excitement, wooden from routine, fossilized through dogmatic instruction or dissipated by random exercise upon trivial things. JOHN DEWEY

According to Unruh and Alexander,* the role of the teacher has changed considerably from past years, when it was mainly concerned with assigning tasks to students, imparting information, reciting, and testing. According to the authors, the teacher today is involved in such subroles as:

Diagnostician—analyzes the factors and conditions that affect the student's learning.
Decision-maker—involved in setting behavioral objectives, planning, and bringing about desirable change in the educational system.
Cooperator—works with such groups as students, other teachers, university personnel, parents, and lay committees.
Strategist—helps in planning the best type of educational program for each student as well as the overall curricula for the school.

*Unruh, Glenys G., and Alexander, William M.: Innovations in secondary education, New York, 1970, Holt, Rinehart and Winston, Inc., chap. 5.

Manager—manages, mobilizes, and utilizes various material and human resources that will enhance the student's learning, for example, audiovisual aids, learning packages, staff aids, and community experts.
Facilitator—contributes to the learning process for himself and students through such means as independent study, research, and experiences in the field.
Guide—works closely with the students in a friendly, warm relationship that promotes creativity and selects the right learning experiences.
Evaluator—evaluates and helps the student to evaluate the results of his and the student's efforts and learning experiences, including behavior changes and teaching effectiveness.

As can be seen from this delineation of a teacher's roles, there are many functions that he must carry out as well as many people with whom he must work. In addition to knowing the various subroles the teacher must play, the reader should also realize some of the selected new developments taking place in teaching.

SELECTED NEW DEVELOPMENTS IN TEACHING

Four of the significant new developments in teaching that the new teacher should be acquainted with are differentiated staffing, teacher aides, student leaders, and teacher accountability.

Differentiated staffing. Differentiated staffing means the assignment of personnel to different roles in terms of their training, abilities, career goals, aptitudes, and interests. The primary reason is to provide for a more individualized program and better service to students, to make greater use of teacher abilities, and to enable teachers to assume greater responsibilities and receive increases in compensation. Teachers have differentiated levels of responsibility and are paid accordingly.

Differentiated staffing recognizes the individual differences of teachers and how they can best be used to enhance student learning. In physical education there are many roles that teachers can fulfill.

Teacher aides. There has been greater and greater utilization of teacher aides. These assistants are sometimes known by different names such as "auxiliary personnel" and "paraprofessionals." Some of the tasks performed by teacher aides include clerical duties, such as recording grades, typing, and filing; nonclassroom duties, such as helping in lunchroom and playground supervision; assisting with large group instruction such as music and art; grading papers; assisting with small group instruction; helping in the preparation and use of instructional materials such as operating a projector; and performing work connected with the classroom environment, such as caring for bulletin boards.

Student leaders. Another development is the increased use of student leaders in schools. One reason for greater stress on such a practice today is the recognized need for more student involvement. Other reasons include the need to train leadership for the profession and the desire to render a greater service to students by providing them more individualized instruction from their better skilled classmates.

Student leaders may be utilized in several ways, such as class leaders, officials, committee members, supply and equipment managers, program planners, record keepers, office managers, and special events coordinators.

Teacher accountability. Most educational systems are giving increased attention to teacher accountability. The high cost of education and the rise in taxes to support this cost is causing the public, who pays the bill, to demand accountability in terms of what a teacher produces. The aim of such a movement is to develop objective standards as a means of improving school effectiveness. Among other things, it is designed to show which teaching and school methods have proved most effective in achieving specific educational goals. It will protect successful teachers against unfair criticisms by providing proof of their effectiveness; for those teachers who are not effective, it will indicate the additional training and help they need to become effective teachers.

It may help the prospective teacher to know the educational goals that the public thinks are important for them to accomplish. According to the Fourth Annual Gallup Poll of Public Attitudes Toward Education, as reported in the September, 1972, *Phi Delta Kappan,* the public wants children to achieve the following goals as a result of their education:

Education should help their children to get better jobs. 44%
Education should help their children to have beter human relations. 43%
Education should help their children to be financially successful. 38%
Education should help their children to be satisfied with themselves. 21%
Education should help their children to be mentally stimulated. 15%
Miscellaneous reasons. 11%

It will also be interesting to the reader to note that this Gallup Poll indicated that approximately three out of every four persons surveyed stated that they would be very happy to have their offspring take up teaching as a career. In other words, teaching is a very popular vocation today among all classes of people.

New teachers in today's modern secondary schools face tasks and responsibilities far different from those faced several years ago. Whereas previously a teacher worked alone to teach the students assigned to him, today's teacher may work with a team of several teachers and with many different groups. Whereas at one time a teacher had only one set of textbooks at his or her disposal, today there are films, television, cassettes, transparencies, computers, and programmed materials to assist in teaching. Once the teacher had to rely on subjective judgments to recognize pupils' attitudes, aptitudes, and interests, but today's extensive testing programs offer comprehensive guidance information instead. Yet these technological advances have not made the teacher's tasks in education any easier, for they have brought with them additional responsibilities. The teacher must learn how to operate specialized equipment. He or she must keep up with new materials being released and know when and how to utilize them appropriately.

Teachers presently graduating from professional institutions are being trained to meet these innovations in modern education. First of all, courses of study within their fields of interest are greatly specialized. For example, in physical education a prospective teacher may specialize in such areas as health, the dance, elementary school teaching, or coaching. Moreover, many institutions offer teacher-internship programs in which a student lives and teaches in a community while gaining first-hand teaching experience. Increased knowledge of child development and the learning process has made another substantial contribution to the training of today's teachers.

Yet these improvements in teacher training have not made the teacher's task any easier either, for administrators of modern secondary schools are expecting more productivity from their staff members. Administrators expect the teacher to keep abreast of the great advances in knowledge, application of the latest teaching methods, and utilization of modern equipment. Furthermore, administrators want increased professionalism through in-service workshops and advance study, plus increased commitments to their field through faculty associations and organizations.

Although the task of teaching has not become any easier, progress in education has brought benefits not only to students but also to the teachers themselves. Today's teachers now enjoy greatly improved standards and practices. Starting teachers' salaries, for example, have vastly improved from meager wages to an average of over

$7,000 per year. In some sections of the country, of course, the average starting salary is much higher. Furthermore, many schools now offer valuable fringe benefits in terms of retirement plans, medical and life insurance coverage, and tenure. Teacher organizations such as the National Education Association are developing increased powers to demand improved health standards for children and improved working conditions for teachers, such as lighter class loads, fewer nonteaching duties, and smaller classes.

Teaching is a demanding profession and an ever-changing one. A close look should be taken at the changing aspects of the teaching profession—the teacher's responsibilities within the department, to the school, and to the profession, keeping in mind specific relationships to physical education. However, the problems of personal qualifications, job application, and certification generally come first chronologically for those persons entering the profession. Therefore, these topics will be discussed first.

SOME RESPONSIBILITIES OF TODAY'S TEACHER

The role of the person who is teaching in the secondary school today is partially told in some of the highlights taken from a survey by the National Education Association's Research Division.*

8.3% of secondary school teachers are assigned to health and physical education.
14.7% of all teachers have loads that devote more than 50% of their time to duties outside their major field.
75.0% of all teachers have five or more unassigned periods per week.
The mean number of hours representing the weekly work load of teachers is 37.
180 days of teaching represents approximately the length of the school year for most teachers.
40.1% of the schools have team teaching, with 8.1% of the teachers as team members.
16.3% of the teachers have aides for themselves or are shared with other teachers.
98.8% of the teachers have male principals.

*The American public-school teacher, 1970-1971, NEA Research Bulletin **50**:3, 1972.

PERSONAL QUALIFICATIONS

The personal qualifications of the physical educator are an extremely important consideration. Administrators regard such characteristics as professionalism, promptness, and the ability to maintain control as attributes of primary importance, while students hold patience, understanding, and fairness as desirable qualities in a teacher.

There is no formula for a successful teacher to follow. The "coach" who is like a father to his boys may be as highly respected as the one who is a strict disciplinarian and dictator to his team. The woman physical educator who is highly organized and efficient may be as well liked as the young graduate who can participate with the girls.

Is being "highly respected" and "well liked" the key to successful teaching? Perhaps these characteristics are a part of the overall picture. Certainly maintaining discipline and imparting information well are equally important qualities for the teaching process. The personality traits exhibited by the teacher and the relationship established with the students are the vital links between the subject and its recipients. All four aspects of the teacher's character—physical, social, emotional, and intellectual—should be worthy of emulation by the developing adolescent.

Physical qualifications

The physical educator usually has many more students in classes than do other teachers. Close relationships with students develop through the intramural and interscholastic programs. Because of the number and type of these relationships between student and teacher, it is important that the appearance of the physical educator be worthy of respect and admiration from adolescents. Uniforms should be spotless and all clothing should be neat, clean, appropriate, and in good taste. The association of health, good hygiene, and cleanliness with physical education is so close that the instructor must represent these ideals to the students.

Fig. 10-1. The teacher should know the basic skills in physical education activities and be able to help his students master these skills. (Rich Township High School, Park Forest, Ill.)

The physical skills and abilities of the physical educator should be exemplary. In order to conduct satisfactory demonstrations and teaching lessons, teachers should be able to perform well in as many areas as possible. This does not mean that they must "star" in all events, but their background of basic coordinations should be well above average.

Social qualifications

Because of the many social objectives of physical education, it is important that the teacher be representative of mature social development.

As a person the teacher should meet people easily, mix well, and treat all individuals with respect and consideration. It is these qualities that the teacher emphasizes in the classroom, and the students should therefore be able to recognize them in the teacher.

As a leader the physical educator should strive to control but not dominate the group and to plan with but not for his students. In so doing the qualities of leadership that should be promoted are presented to the students, and they in turn may learn to lead well.

Emotional qualifications

It is important that every teacher be a stable, mature individual, well adjusted to life in his or her chosen occupation. This is particularly true of the physical educator. The nature and tenor of the work require an emotional control and a responsiveness that are not easily defined.

In order to establish effective teaching rapport, the teacher must have patience and understanding mixed with firmness and composure. To meet all the individual problems that arise daily with students— their maladies, their excuses, their upsets —the teacher must offer a sympathetic, understanding ear, indicating to the students a sincere interest in their personal difficulties. In handling the everyday occurrences in the classroom, the teacher should display firmness and quiet confidence, so

Fig. 10-2. The teacher should enjoy teaching. (Richwoods Community High School, Peoria Heights, Ill.)

that the students realize that the situation is well under control.

The many frustrations that beset the physical educator striving for winning teams and competitive excellence must be met with calm self-assurance. Administrative and community pressures should not become so strong that other teaching responsibilities are neglected or that self-concern replaces consideration for the students.

Intellectual and other professional qualifications

Intellectually, the physical educator needs many qualities that are equally important for him both as a teacher and as an influence on young people.

As a teacher the physical educator should be efficiently organized and able to maintain order in handling the myriad administrative details. An ability to express ideas clearly and distinctly both orally and on paper is also important, for students learn from what is imparted to them, and therefore materials must be intelligently presented. A professional manner and outlook enhance the profession itself in the eyes of the students, and this, too, becomes an important aspect of the teacher's personality. The image that a physical educator is a person of all brawn and no brains is slowly being overcome, and new teachers entering the field should further enhance this newer picture of the teacher as a real educator.

As an influence on young people, the teacher should have many interests both in and out of the field. This is important because it affords more opportunities for sharing the various interests of the students who are contacted daily. As a broader interpretation of physical education in its relationship to life is presented to the students, the physical educator is repected for more than just coaching abilities or professional skills. In this role of a counselor influencing students in their approach to life, the physical educator should have an outlook worthy of both respect and imitation.

Ideally, the physical educator should have a wholesome personality, sharing a deep knowledge and interest in the subject with students who are respected as people and led with sympathetic understanding. The personality that the teacher presents to the students may be as important as the material to be learned. Ideally, also, the physical educator should meet other qualifications and standards in addition to those of a personal nature. A discussion of these and their related problems follows.

PROBLEMS OF CERTIFICATION

Among the many problems encountered by any prospective teacher are those concerning the initial step of becoming properly certified. Often the confusion and red tape involved in finding appropriate information and determining personal status are so disheartening that the new teacher is bewildered before starting. The prospective physical educator is not different from other teachers in this respect, and knowing in advance about state requirements and qualifications can save a great deal of worry and frustration. Certification problems are complicated further by the continuous study and change of specifications.

Some of the newer approaches to teacher certification include a freer movement of qualified teachers across state lines, a simplication of the types of certificates issued, approved-program approach where the preparing college or university has its teacher-preparing program approved and then accepts the responsibility for training and certifying the teachers who pursue and graduate from said program, and basing certification upon a teacher's demonstrated abilities rather than upon courses he has taken in a collegiate program.

Certification requirements

All states have established minimum requirements that must be met by prospective teachers before they become legally certified to teach. These certification requirements in teaching correspond to similar requirements in other professions, such as the licensing of doctors and dentists after state or national examinations.

The certification of teachers serves several purposes. The regulations protect schoolchildren by ensuring a high quality of teaching, the employment of only superior and qualified personnel, and unifying teaching standards. The students therefore benefit from these requirements. For teachers, however, the task of meeting the varying state requirements complicates professional preparation and certification procedures.

There are nine general areas in which most states have governing regulations for teacher certification. While many states may agree on certain factors, they may disagree on others. The prospective teacher should therefore inquire directly of the state education department, division of teacher certification, for exact requirements. To summarize these nine general areas and the requirements presently established in the fifty states, the following information is presented.

Citizenship. More than one half the states have citizenship requirements or a declaration of intention clause. The teacher must be a citizen of the United States to qualify.

Oath of allegiance or loyalty. Approximately one half of the states do not require a loyalty oath for teacher certification. The others usually have a written statement that must be signed.

Age. The age requirement varies among states. The lowest minimum age is 17 years. In general 18 or 19 years of age is acceptable in states specifying a particular age. Some states have no stipulation in this regard.

Professional preparation. It is in this area that the greatest differences in state requirements may be found. Several states have particular courses that must be taken by candidates for certification. For example, in one state teachers must have studied American government and/or history; in another, state and federal government; and in still another, school health education.

Some of these special state requirements must be complete before the first year of teaching, while others may be fulfilled within a certain period of time.

Recommendation. A large majority of the states require a teaching candidate to have a recommendation from college or from the last place of employment.

Fee. A fee for certification, ranging from $1 to $15, is required in a majority of the states.

Health certificate. A certificate of general health is necessary in many states. Some states require a chest x-ray report instead of or along with this certificate.

Employment. Candidates from *other* states may need to have secured employment to become certified within some states.

Course of study. Besides the general areas of state requirements, there are basic and minimum regulations regarding the course of study that must be followed to qualify for specific certification in physical education. Again, the states disagree in their requirements of hours of study necessary within the subject of physical education.

Because of these curriculum differences and the variation between states in regard to the nine basic factors outlined, a certificate to teach in one state does not necessarily permit a teacher to teach in a different state. However, reciprocity among states in the same region of the country is a growing reality, particularly for graduates of an accredited teacher preparation program.

A further problem in certification presents itself where localities within a state have specific regulations governing selection of teachers. These are often more rigid than the standards established within the state itself. Detroit and New York City, for example, have their own sets of qualifications that must be met by their teachers, and many southern cities and states require high scores on the National Teacher Examinations. Local regulations usually involve such factors as teacher preparation and experience. An applicant may also be required to pass written and oral examinations for local licensing. Information regarding local teaching requirements may be secured by writing to the board of education in the city in question.

Prospective teachers should try to determine state and local regulations far in advance, if possible. In so doing they may guide their course of study in college to meet the requirements. They should then send in their records far enough ahead of time to become certified before accepting a position.

Types of certificates

The type and value of certificates issued by the states vary nearly as much as do their regulations. In some states, for example, there are merely two categories of certification, permanent and probationary, while another state may have twenty-two variations of certificates to issue. The certificate to teach physical education is generally limited to this special field of work, but its validity may be for one year (probationary) or for life. Some states grant temporary, provisional, or emergency certificates to teachers who do not fully meet all requirements, with the understanding that within a certain period of time the candidate will become fully qualified.

The value of the certificate again depends on state regulations. It enables the teacher to teach in any public school system within that state, except those where local standards require further qualifications. It may qualify the teacher to teach in neighboring states, depending on reciprocity agreements. It may also permit him or her to teach in private schools within the state, or at least in private schools seeking state accreditation.

The prospective teacher or the experienced teacher seeking employment in a different state should not let these differences in state requirements and qualifications become a hindrance. An inquiry to the state or local department of education should bring the necessary information in time to facilitate certification.

PROBLEMS IN JOB APPLICATION

Recent surveys and statistics indicate that teaching jobs will be much more difficult to obtain in the future than they have been in the past. Between now and 1980, for example, according to the U. S. Department of Labor, the nation may train more than four million elementary and secondary school teachers but there will be only approximately two million jobs. Declining birth rates, oversupply of teachers being trained, and a new array of educational hardware are some of the reasons for this projection. However, positions will still be open to those who are highly qualified and prepare themselves well for their responsibilities. Furthermore, there are many bright job opportunities in ghettos and poor rural districts, in teaching the handicapped, in early childhood education, in educational research, and in the federal Teacher Corps.

The next series of problems faced by the prospective teacher revolves around finding a job—writing a proper letter of application, having an interview, and attending to the similar details important in obtaining a teaching position. The superintendent who is forced to choose between two or more candidates for a physical education opening may allow his decision to rest on appearance, on spelling, or on the smallest of details. The applicant should therefore take great care in all phases of the process of finding and obtaining a position.

Letter of application

The prospective teacher usually hears of job openings through friends, the college bureau of appointments, an employment agency, and/or direct application by letter to a specific locale. The letter of application serves as an introduction to the prospective employer and should be carefully constructed to contain appropriate information.

In appearance the letter should be neat, typewritten, and grammatically correct. Pertinent details should be included concisely and yet in such a manner that the personality of the individual is conveyed to the reader. The employer wants to know about the applicant's educational background, experiences related to the field of education, and interests. Personal information such as age and health should also be included, together with names and addresses of references. If possible, the applicant should also state his availability for an interview.

In response to this letter of application the candidate should receive a letter stating either that there are no vacancies or that the position is open and an interview is desired. A printed application form is often included with the latter reply, and it should also be filled out neatly and carefully.

Interview

Interviews of teacher-applicants generally take place at the school itself, providing candidates an opportunity to see the school in action, or at the college of the graduating candidate. In the latter case a field representative of the school system usually interviews several candidates from the college, and a request from the superintendent for a school-visitation type of interview follows.

In either type of interview the prospective teacher should expect to ask and to answer questions of all types, for it is the purpose of the interview to allow the new teacher to learn about the school system, as well as to give the employer an opportunity to screen the applicant.

While the employer is questioning the applicant, he will be observing the teacher's bearing, outlook, speech, personal mannerisms, and general effectiveness as a person. Needless to say, the applicant should be prompt, well groomed, and neatly dressed for this occasion. The prospective teacher should be ready to answer in a concise and intelligent manner questions about any phase of teaching physical education. What is the most important attribute of a good teacher? What is the philosophy behind the inclusion of physical education in the school curriculum? What are some specific objectives of the program? How are the needs of the children determined? The range of possible questions is very broad, and the candidate can make little actual preparation for them other than to know and sincerely believe in the field of physical education.

The answers given by the applicant at the interview are not the only determining factor in obtaining employment. The employer may judge to some extent on the basis of intelligent questioning by the candidate about the type of education being offered in the school and the community's interest in school affairs. Inquiries about scheduling, class groupings, extramural duties, community activities, and school organizations indicate to the superintendent that the prospective teacher knows what is involved in a teaching position. At the same time the applicant is, of course, determining whether this particular school administration is genuinely interested in physical education and if this type of position is the most desirable and suitable in comparison to other available jobs.

There are several types of teaching jobs that the physical educator needs to consider. Is a large or small school system preferable? In a small school the teacher often has classes from grades one through twelve, while in the larger, multiple-building systems, a position may be limited to elementary, middle school, junior high, or senior high teaching. Is teaching in a large, departmentalized situation with several other persons a better position in which to start than one in which the teacher is entirely alone? These are questions that the teacher must settle in his own mind, in terms of his own personal preferences, after several school visitations and interviews have pointed out the differences.

Unfortunately, the prospective teacher does not always receive the position of first choice. A poor impression during the interview or a poor letter of application may make the difference. Other factors also enter into a failure of final appointment. Lateness of application or stiff competition for a high-salaried position may be a determining factor. The teacher seldom knows the real cause of failure.

Appointments are not generally made at the interviews themselves, for the board of education must give final approval, and the applicant should have additional time to think about such an important decision. Later the applicant may receive a letter from the superintendent saying that the position has been filled or with congratulations on his or her appointment and perhaps some type of contractual agreement.

Contractual agreements

Contractual agreements between employer and teacher vary in style, form, and content, but essentially they signify a promise of payment for services rendered. In some areas a single word or handshake is the only type of agreement used, while in other areas a formalized contract carefully specifying duties and assignments is required. Each board of education has its own particular method. However, the prospective teacher should inquire about certain aspects of the agreement in order to know exactly what responsibilities and fringe benefits are contained in it.

Term of employment. The initial contract is usually a provisional one, covering one year of teaching. In many schools there is a three-year or five-year provisional period for new teachers, and at the end of that time a more permanent type of contract may be issued. Some boards of education provide "tenure" for teachers, which means that following the provisional period teachers may be assured of a permanent position in their schools, if so desired.

Persons going into teaching should be aware that teacher tenure is under nationwide attack. For example, the Gallup Poll previously referred to indicates that the public in general does not like the idea of tenure—namely, 61% of them disapprove. For those who are parents and have children in school, 64% disapprove of tenure. Among professional educators 53% approve of tenure, 42% disapprove, and 5% have no opinion.

Responsibilities. In some instances contracts contain detailed outlines of teaching responsibilities, including, for example, the number of hours of intramural activities or the number of coaching assignments required of the teacher. These duties must be performed by the teacher if he enters into such an agreement, unless unusual circumstances permit exemption.

Release from a contract. Unusual circumstances, such as forced leave of absence or call to military service, may release the teacher from the total contract. This is possible in most cases by application to the board of education. The prospective teacher should realize, however, that except in these unusual situations it is not wise to break an agreement with the board of education. As professionals in the field of education, teachers are expected to be reliable and dependable people, with high ethical standards, and therefore able to live up to agreements.

Salary. Written agreements between teachers and employers usually indicate exact salary arrangements. In most schools a salary scale has been established, with definite regulations governing the placement of teachers on that scale. Years of service or merit usually determine increments in salary, although differentiated staffing is changing this practice in some places. Where years of service are used as a basis for raises in pay, teachers usually receive regular increments in salary. In schools where a merit plan is in effect, the better teachers usually receive higher pay on the basis of certain standards of teaching that have been established for evaluation of services. A third type of salary schedule has emerged from schools using the team teaching program. In this case the person or persons shouldering major responsibility for a course of study receive higher salaries.

Benefits. Some school systems also establish subsidiary teacher benefits that make them more desirable and attractive places in which to work. Sick leave policies and visitation days are examples of administrative consideration for teacher welfare. Provisions for sabbatical leave, health insurance, and retirement are also benefits that vary among schools and states. The new teacher should try to find out as much as possible about these fringe benefits for teachers in the particular school system offering employment.

When the prospective teacher accepts the appointment offered and signs the contractual agreement, if one is necessary, the benefits and terms are settled and the problems of job application cease. The teacher has now assumed new responsibilities and obligations that must be met. These responsibilities encompass the physical edu-

---

AN ACTUAL DAY IN THE LIFE OF ONE PHYSICAL EDUCATOR

Pre–First Period Activities
8:20   Sign in
8:20   Confer with other teachers
8:35   Set up and check equipment to be used that day

First and Second Periods—8:50-10:20 (double period for ninth graders)
Locker room supervision
Student leaders check attendance
Fifteen-minute exercise period in preparation for physical fitness test
Presentation of the skills and techniques involved in the sprint start
Individual practice—instructor and the student leaders check student progress
One-hundred-yard sprint—students demonstrate the skill that they have just learned
Shower and change clothes—locker room supervision

Third and Fourth Periods—10:22-11:48 (double period for tenth graders)
Locker room supervision
Student leaders check attendance
Fifteen-minute exercise period in preparation for physical fitness test
Review of the basic skills and techniques involved in the sprint start with student demonstration
Presentation of the basic skills and techniques involved in the long jump: the run, the gather, the take-off (float style in the air, hang style in the air, and the hitch-kick style in the air), and the landing
Student leader demonstration
Question-answer period on basic skills and techniques
Student individual practice with suggestions offered by instructor to improve individual performance
Shower and change clothes—locker room supervision

Fifth and Sixth Periods—11:50-1:10
Preparation of new skills for future presentation, review of new library materials, films, and so on, setting up skill scales for evaluation purposes, and preparation of written test questions on the activity being covered
Lunch

Seventh Period—1:11-1:53 (single period for twelfth graders)
Locker room supervision
Student leaders check attendance
Fifteen-minute exercise period in preparation for physical fitness test
Review of previous class instruction (beginning skill, the relay race, or intermediate skill, long jump)—student demonstration and explanation
Presentation of the basic skills and techniques involved in the shot put—8- and 12-pound shot puts are available
Individual student practice with suggestions offered by instructor to improve student performance
Question-answer period on the basic skills and techniques of this activity
Shower and change—locker room supervision

Eighth Period—1:55-2:40
Preparation period—continuation of activities begun in the fifth and sixth periods

cation department itself, the school faculty, the community, and the profession, and are equally important to a successful career.

RESPONSIBILITIES TO THE DEPARTMENT

Whether the school system is large or small, the physical educator has many responsibilities to the department, each of which is essential in administering a successful teaching program. These responsibilities demand the teacher's time and thoughtful consideration, but because they relate directly to the students, the results of the teacher's efforts are apparent.

In a large school

As one member of a team of physical educators, the individual instructor has definite responsibilities in relation to teaching regular classes, conducting the after-school program, and working with other members of the department. In all three areas these duties require constant cooperation and mutual understanding for a smoothly functioning program.

Teaching classes. Each teacher is officially in charge of the instructional program in assigned classes. This responsibility entails far more than just teaching or conducting classes, however. Some of the other duties entailed in class management are the following:

1. Program planning and evaluation
2. Grading and pupil evaluation
3. Testing
4. Motivating (through charts, diagrams, and the like)
5. Checking health problems
6. Counseling on student problems
7. Conferring with students and parents
8. Caring for shared equipment and facilities
9. Maintaining departmental standards in locker room, showers, and gymnasium
10. Keeping records

These duties are performed in cooperation with other members of the depart-ment, and the same or similar methods that have been approved for all are used. For example, one teacher would not keep one form of record on a student while another teacher in the same department followed a different system.

Conducting the after-school program. In addition to regular teaching responsibilities, the members of the department share in carrying out the many extra duties that are a natural component of the physical education program. Conducting an after-school program of intramural and extramural activities, as well as interscholastic athletics, involves many details, such as the following:

1. Coaching assignments
2. Scheduling games
3. Handling publicity
4. Scheduling facilities
5. Caring for uniforms and equipment
6. Arranging transportation
7. Handling finances
8. Checking custodial maintenance
9. Ordering awards
10. Keeping records

In a large school a single instructor would not be able to manage all these details alone. With the entire staff working together, however, a well-organized after-school program serving all the students may be effectively conducted.

Working with the staff. Conducting the after-school program is only one of the ways in which the members of the department cooperate. The director of the department usually considers the staff as a policy-making body that proposes and carries out progressive ideas. They plan together the direction the program will take and share with the administrator of the department the many details of budgeting, scheduling, making inventory, and so forth. In some schools the team teaching approach to physical education has been implemented. In this case the staff cooperates and coordinates all its efforts in order to capitalize on the special abilities of each of its teachers.

Cooperation promotes harmonious relationships among members of the department, and when disagreements or problems arise, they should be handled within the department itself. Ethical standards of conduct indicate that mutual support of colleagues be presented to outsiders and that individual problems of a member be taken to the department chairman, first, rather than to the principal or superintendent.

The new teacher should realize at the outset the nature of the role he must play as a member of a large school staff. Schools may differ in the actual delegation of the many responsibilities, but the teacher's obligation to share and cooperate remains the same.

In a small school

In a small secondary school it is customary for one man to be responsible for the teaching and handling of the boys' program and for one woman to take care of the girls' program. While such a situation simplifies the problems of group planning and departmental organization, the same administrative responsibilities outlined for a large school remain, and they must be carried out by these two individuals. Because the number of students served by the program is small, it is possible for one teacher to handle the many details involved in the teaching program and after-school athletics.

A new teacher will find that the job of teaching in a small-school situation requires much coordination between the boys' and girls' departments. The program of physical education is more effective if the instructional procedures and requirements of the two teachers are similar and methods of pupil evaluation agree. Also, their policies on intramural and interscholastic activities should be consistent, with schedules for the use of facilities for these programs mutually arranged.

When problems or difficulties develop between the two departments, concerning the sharing of facilities, for example, the two teachers should try to work out the solutions together. If the answers cannot be found, the teachers should both seek advice from the next higher authority. If there is no officially designated chairman of the department, the school principal would be the person to ask for guidance.

Working together effectively is of primary importance to a smoothly functioning program of physical education in a small-school situation. When the two teachers mutually assist and support each other in all phases of their work, this worthy objective is achieved.

RESPONSIBILITIES TO THE SCHOOL FACULTY

Beyond being a member of a physical education department, a teacher is also a member of a school faculty. This position carries with it many responsibilities related to administering a program of education for children. All teachers must share in this endeavor, which includes three general areas of obligation: upholding school policies, sharing mutual faculty responsibilities, and respecting the educational curriculum.

Upholding school policies

Administration of a secondary school program involves the establishment of well-defined policies concerning all phases of school life: the curriculum, school regulations, homework, activities, and sponsored functions. In most school situations teachers play an important part in regard to these policies.

In a democratically administered school system, the teachers share in the establishment of school policies. Decisions are formulated on the basis of group discussion and majority opinion. The physical educator should share with the other teachers in formulating policies at teachers' meetings.

School policies must be upheld by all members of the staff once they are determined. This includes the physical education teacher, who should not expect special privileges for members of varsity teams in respect to academic standards, for example, or request athletic considerations contrary to school regulations.

Sharing mutual responsibilities

In large and small school systems alike, the faculty shares many administrative duties. These are essential to a sound educational program, although they have no relationship to the school curriculum, and are a necessary component of school administration.

For example, there are many instances in which a teacher is called upon to act as a supervisor or sponsor of student activities. Teachers may be required to take bus duty or cafeteria supervision or to be responsible for noon-hour activities. Homerooms, study halls, club activities, and student council are all additional responsibilities, and the physical educator should expect to serve with the other teachers in any of these areas.

In many schools, faculty committees are established to study current educational problems, such as education for the gifted or elementary foreign language teaching. Committees to handle administrative details such as class scheduling, grouping, or safety may also be set up. Membership in these communities is usually voluntary, but all teachers are expected to serve in some capacity. While the conduct of the after-school program may make it difficult for the physical educator to attend committee meetings, every effort should be made to share in this phase of school organization.

Respecting the curriculum

Just as the physical educator should support the methods and procedures of his colleagues within the department, so should he or she uphold and respect those of the other teachers in all areas of education. The teacher should exhibit a geninue and sincere interest in all phases of the curriculum and respect the work and accomplishments of the other teachers.

In return, the physical educator can expect from other teachers similar respect and appreciation of the work being accomplished by the department. This regard should be deserved, however. Teachers in other subject areas do not necessarily evaluate the physical education program in the same manner that physical educators would. Instead of rating program content with which they are unfamiliar, other teachers tend to value the teacher's seriousness of approach to teaching, the manner in which the instructor fulfills educational responsibilities, the concern shown for student welfare, and general attitudes toward the profession.

The physical educator who meets all these responsibilities as a member of the teaching staff actually promotes appreciation for physical education as a profession.

There is one further obligation of physical educators that is directly connected with their particular field and deserves special mention at this time. Good working relations with members of the school custodial staff are of vital importance to the program and are clearly as important as relations with other teachers. The service of the custodians in gymnasium maintenance and in care of equipment adds significantly to the quality of physical education and should not be forgotten.

RESPONSIBILITIES TO THE PROFESSION

Membership in a profession such as physical education carries with it certain responsibilities that the new teacher should expect and accept. They are concerned mainly with professional advancement for the teacher and the growth of the profession itself.

Professional organizations

Professional associations are the media through which members mutually assist each other in achieving benefits for the group and promoting advancement.

As an educator, the physical education teacher should join the educational organizations available in his particular district or local area. This includes the faculty association, the local education association, and the country or district group, whichever organization has been formed. It is also considered the mark of a professional to join the state education association and the National Education Association. Membership in these associations is usually made available to the teacher through the school office at the beginning of each school year.

Physical educators should also join their own special local and state organizations and the American Association for Health, Physical Education, and Recreation. It is through these channels that the teacher is able to keep up with the latest advancements within the profession. There are also specialized organizations on the local level for coaches, women, or teachers of a particular activity. It is in these local, small groups that the greatest benefits are derived, for the members have the opportunity to know each other well and to share mutually in the problems and issues at stake.

Membership in these associations is made possible through literature sent to the school in each locale, in most cases. If not, teachers in neighboring districts are ready to provide the necessary information to newcomers.

Professional advancement

Membership in various associations is not the only professional responsibility of the physical educator. To reap the greatest benefits and to aid in advancing the profession itself, each member must make valuable contributions.

These associations are usually organized into committees that function in a particular area, such as planning, research, fitness, and publications. Working on these committees can be a very satisfying and rewarding experience, and one that should not be missed.

Even greater contributions to the profession as a whole can be made through research on problems in the field. Sharing results or findings on a particular method of teaching or testing is a real service to other members that should be willingly performed.

Personal advancement

Continued study for personal growth and development is another major responsibility of every member of a profession. In addition to individual study, the physical education teacher has two developmental paths open: in-service education and graduate study.

In-service education takes many forms within the school system and neighboring districts. It is found in individual and staff conferences and in workshops, clinics, and study institutes. Planning sessions, orientation programs, and interschool visitations are all phases of in-service education. Any opportunity in which teachers join together with associates to consider school problems is considered to be in-service education. Real values stemming from these sessions are seen when teachers change and grow together for the improvement of the school program and the profession.

Graduate study is the other method of personal, professional advancement. Some of the purposes of graduate study include the development of a higher degree of competence and the development of the ability to evaluate, interpret, and draw conclusions from the scholarly work of others.

There are several types of graduate degrees available to the physical education teacher.

1. Master's degree. A master's degree in physical education usually requires one year of study beyond a bachelor's degree. In some universities a thesis is part of the required program for a degree, while in other schools several related extra credits or a comprehensive examination is required in its place.

2. Doctor of philosophy, doctor of education, or doctor of physical education. The doctoral degrees usually require three or four more years of study. In the curricu-

lum for a doctorate a formal dissertation or document is a requisite.

Some institutions offer a professional or specialist's certificate for thirty hours of graduate work above the completion of the master's program.

The prospective teacher of physical education should realize that a professional attitude is another important responsibility that must be developed through associations and study programs with other professionals. In this way the teacher makes a valuable contribution to himself or herself and to the profession as a whole.

RESPONSIBILITIES TO THE COMMUNITY

Another responsibility of importance to the physical educator relates to the relationship established with the community. This is a two-way association, for the support a physical education teacher gains for the program depends largely upon the program itself and the way the citizens interpret it. The responsibilities of the physical education department in promoting this community relationship are three: presenting a sound program, joining community-sponsored activities, and supporting community standards.

Presenting a sound program

The physical educator is employed by a community's board of education to teach physical education in the finest manner possible. The program of physical education can be a comprehensive source of good public relations between a school and its community because of the many contacts that are a natural by-product of this program. It is in this field that an entire student body is excited by interscholastic competitive activities, and parents, too, share in these enjoyable events. Through the intramural programs, the demonstrations, and the testing program the parents become very much aware of and interested in the total program of physical education. The entire school administration benefits from a sound physical education program because of community interest; therefore, it is essential that the program be thoughtfully planned, presented, and evaluated.

Joining community activities

The physical educator has definite obligations to become a part of the community by joining selected community organizations, including the parent-teacher association. Furthermore, because of the close association between recreational activities

Fig. 10-3. The physical educator needs to involve himself with the community. (Lincoln High School, Yonkers, N. Y.)

and physical education, the teachers often are called to conduct evening programs and assist in sponsoring special events. While sharing in these activities the teacher has an opportunity to know the people of the community and what it is that they want from their schools. This is an advantage to the school, for it must serve its own particular community. At the same time the physical educator helps the school administration by serving as an interpreter of its philosophy to the community and helping the people understand what the schools are trying to do.

Serving the community in which they teach is a responsibility that must be met by all teachers. Good school-community relations are of primary importance to a school that is meeting the needs of its students. The physical educator must do his share by contributing in as many ways as possible, and the results will bring greater support to his program.

Supporting community standards

Throughout the many associations established with community citizens, the physical educator should support and honor the standards expected of teachers in that particular community where they are in accordance with high professional standards. It is important to remember that relating school gossip or information of a personal nature about a particular student does not earn respect for a teacher in the schools, but by wiser action the respect and status of teachers may be upheld in the community.

CODE OF ETHICS

The teacher is far more than just a teacher of physical education. His or her responsibilities extend to all relationships established with people, and all actions are governed in almost every area by a code of professional ethics. Many important principles in this code of ethics have been pointed out in relation to particular situations. The code of the National Education Association has been endorsed by the American Association for Health, Physical Education, and Recreation. This code represents the combined thinking of experienced leaders in the field and therefore should be respected. Furthermore, it provides a framework of guidelines for all professional physical educators, thereby guaranteeing the professional freedom it is designed to preserve.

The code consists of four principles. *Principle one* outlines the commitment to the *student* and indicates the cooperative, helpful, and professional relationship that exists between the student and teacher. *Principle two* outlines the commitment to the *public* and spells out the important role of educators in the development of educational programs and policies and their interpretation to the public. *Principle three* outlines the commitment to the *profession* and indicates the need to raise educational standards, improve the service to people, and develop a worthwhile and respected profession. *Principle four* outlines the commitment to *professional employment practices* and explains the importance of acting in accordance with high ideals of professional service that embody personal integrity, dignity, and mutual respect.

The code is designed to show the magnitude of the education profession and to judge teachers in accordance with the provisions of this code.

POINTS TO REMEMBER

1. Physical educators must fulfill personal and educational requirements to become certified to teach. These requirements vary throughout the states, as do the types of certificates issued.
2. Certain personality and character traits help make a teacher more effective in teaching and associating with students and colleagues.
3. A physical educator's relationship to the students is very important for effective teaching and guidance.
4. A physical education teacher's relationships with other teachers, the administration, the profession, and the community have an important bearing on the respect he earns for himself as a professional person and for his program.
5. A physical educator is governed by a code of ethics that protects him and other mem-

bers of the profession by suggested standards of behavior.

PROBLEMS TO THINK THROUGH

1. When is a teacher not a teacher?
2. What personal qualities are most important for a teacher of physical education—qualities that may not be as essential in teaching other areas?
3. With whom would a new physical education teacher discuss a disagreement relating to procedures in marking students (a) in a small school? (b) in a large school? With whom would he not discuss it?
4. In August a new teacher receives another job offer at a higher salary in a preferred locale. What course of action should be taken, if any?
5. What community clubs or agencies have a direct interest in the school physical education program? How would the teacher who lives outside the school's community indicate an interest in the activities of such groups?
6. An after-school intramural game conflicts with a special faculty committee meeting. The physical education teacher, as a member of this committee, must choose where his time will be spent. What factors enter into his decision?

CASE STUDY FOR ANALYSIS

The new physical education teacher has been asked by his experienced co-worker to help referee an important eighth grade intramural soccer championship game. The game ends in a tie, and rather than reschedule another playoff or play another quarter, his colleague rules that the team winning two out of three penalty kicks will win. The new teacher senses the keen disappointment felt by the team members with this ruling and does not agree with his superior's decision in this case. What, if anything, should he do?

EXERCISES FOR REVIEW

1. What specific information should be included in an application to a superintendent of schools? Write a sample letter.
2. Investigate the requirements for teaching in another state and determine in what ways these requirements are being met, if they are, and in what ways professional preparation may be lacking.
3. What questions may a candidate for a physical education position in a large school system expect to be asked during an interview with the administrator?
4. What school policies should this candidate inquire about during this interview?
5. A school system is planning to build a second junior high school and the administrator asks the physical education department to share in the formulation of plans for the physical education facilities. What steps would a new teacher take in order to offer real assistance in this project?

6. A new physical education teacher discovers that the community fathers run a highly competitive Little League program. If this teacher disagrees with the type of management the program is receiving, what procedures would he follow to combat this community enterprise?
7. List some outside interest and hobbies that would add to the professional growth of a physical educator.
8. In what areas of teaching physical education would further scientific research be particularly valuable?
9. In what ways does a professional code of ethics protect the teacher of physical education?
10. What responsibilities to the profession of physical education would be most difficult for a teacher to meet?

SELECTED READINGS

Batchelder, Richard D.: Unionism versus professionalism in teaching, National Education Association Journal 55:18, 1966.

Bucher, Charles A.: Administration of health and physical education programs, including athletics, ed. 5, St. Louis, 1971, The C. V. Mosby Co.

Bucher, Charles A.: Foundations of physical education, ed. 6, St. Louis, 1972, The C. V. Mosby Co.

Bucher, Charles A.: Physical education for life, New York, 1969, McGraw-Hill Book Co., Inc.

Coplan, Arlo H.: The ugly gym teacher, The Physical Educator 21:106, 1964.

Crawford, Wayne H.: Are you ready to teach? Journal of Health, Physical Education, and Recreation 36:87, 1965.

Davis, Hazel: Profile of the American public school teacher, National Education Association Journal 56:12, 1967.

Field, David: Bringing teacher and job together, Journal of Health, Physical Education, and Recreation 36:33, 1965.

Filbin, Robert L., and Vogel, Stefan: So you're going to be a teacher, Great Neck, N. Y., 1962, Barron's Educational Series, Inc.

Gallup, George H.: Fourth annual Gallup poll of public attitudes toward education, Phi Delta Kappan, September, 1972, p. 33.

Hanby, Kenneth R., and Belka, David E.: Beginning teacher tips in health and physical education, The Physical Educator 21:107, 1964.

Hillson, Maurie, and Hyman, Ronald: Change and innovation in elementary and secondary organization, New York, 1965, Holt, Rinehart and Winston, Inc.

Howe, Harold, II: A nation of amateurs, School and Society 94:448, 1966.

Hunter, Madeline C.: The agony and the ecstasy of teaching, National Education Association Journal 56:36, 1967.

Lieberman, Myron: Education as a profession, Englewood Cliffs, N. J., 1956, Prentice-Hall, Inc.

Melaro, Constance L., and Davies, Don: Comments on teacher certification, National Education Association Journal 55:18, 1966.

Morris, Van Cleve, and others: Becoming an educator, Boston, 1963, Houghton Mifflin Co.

The American public-school teacher, 1970-1971, NEA Research Bulletin **50**:3, 1972.

National Education Association: Conditions of work for quality teaching, National Education Journal **54**:33, 1965.

Stinnett, T. M.: The profession of teaching, New York, 1962, The Center for Applied Research in Education, Inc.

Unruh, Glenys G., and Alexander, William M.: Innovations in secondary education, New York, 1970, Holt, Rinehart and Winston, Inc.

11 THE BEGINNING TEACHER

According to the Fourth Annual Gallup Poll of Public Attitudes Toward Education, the major problems confronting the public schools listed in order of importance according to the sample surveyed, were: (1) lack of discipline, (2) inadequate financial support, (3) problems of integration-segregation, (4) difficulty associated with getting good teachers, (5) classes too large, (6) lack of interest on the part of parents, (7) inadequate facilities, (8) poor curriculum, and (9) drug use. Of all these problems, one of the most important is the need for good teachers. With good teachers many of the other problems will be solved.

As the day of birth is one of the most critical for the newborn baby, so is the first year of teaching one of the most critical for the newly trained teacher. The neophyte instructor has spent four or more years in college learning a great amount of theory from professors, talking about what to do when discipline problems arise with students, and discussing how to function with inadequate facilities. Now he or she finds himself or herself on the job in the classroom or gymnasium faced with a live and restless group of students. These boys and girls know that an inexperienced teacher is handling the class, and many seek opportunities to disprove all the theory that has been learned in four years of training. The big test has come. Will the beginning teacher be successful in meeting the challenge? Will the class be organized for effective instruction? Will the teaching techniques that have been mastered be equal to the practical situation that now exists? The answer to these and similar questions depends upon many factors, including whether or not the beginning teacher has been alerted to some of the problems that may arise and some of the procedures that may be followed in handling them. This chapter is aimed at helping the new teacher meet problems that are encountered the first year on the job. Although the problems of the beginning teacher are infinite, it is believed that many are common and that recommendations by experienced teachers will assist him or her in successfully completing the first critical year of teaching.

There is a high turnover rate of first-year teachers. While some teachers change jobs after the first year to improve their status, others leave the profession because of dissatisfaction and discouragement and because they have found the job of adjusting to the hard realities of teaching too difficult for them to master. Several research studies have been conducted to determine the reasons teachers give for job satisfaction or dissatisfaction. They include such items as teacher-administrator factors, physical conditions, teacher-community factors, teacher-faculty factors, teacher-student and teacher-parent factors, and salary and security factors. An example of such a study is one by Wey,[*] conducted several years

---

[*]Wey, G. W.: Why do beginning teachers fail? National Association of Secondary School Principals Bulletin 35:55, 1951.

196

ago but still true today, involving ninety-five beginning teachers who graduated from Appalachian State Teachers College. The research involved the identification of 2,537 difficulties encountered by the teachers. The three areas into which these difficulties were grouped were (1) difficulties related to personal characteristics, (2) difficulties related to instructional activities, and (3) difficulties related to community environment and relationships. Most of the difficulties pertained to (1) pupil control, (2) teaching assignment, (3) adaptation to pupil needs, (4) records and reports, (5) deficiencies in equipment, (6) teacher-principal relationships, and (7) personality.

According to a study conducted by the Research Division of the National Education Association,* the five major problems of teachers were identified as: (1) insufficient time for rest and preparation in the school day, (2) large class size, (3) insufficient clerical help, (4) inadequate salary, and (5) inadequate fringe benefits. Less stress was placed upon such problems as lack of public support for schools, ineffective faculty meetings, and poor administration.

It is readily evident from the research conducted that problems of beginning teachers are numerous and varied. It would be of great value to the new teacher to study each of these problems in as much detail as possible and the meaning they have in relation to adjusting satisfactorily to the job.

Many of the problems of teachers are "across the board" types of difficulties affecting all teachers regardless of subject-matter affiliation. However, the teacher of physical education encounters some problems caused by the nature of his or her special field of endeavor. Some of the more common problems of beginning physical education teachers that have been identified through research are associated with

---

*National Education Association; Teacher's problems, NEA Research Bulletin **46**:116, 1968.

the following:

Discipline
Facilities
Adjustment to the school
Class organization
Student hostilities toward the program
Methods of teaching
Legal liability
Numbers of students in class
Insufficient space
Equipment
Behavior problems
Introduction of new ideas and techniques
Intellectually inferior label associated with physical education
Program planning
Status
Role of physical education in education
Personal relationships
Interscholastic athletics
Budget
Scheduling
Grouping in classes
Time allotment
Insurance

Many problems of the beginning physical education teacher appear to recur over and over again and can be grouped into two classifications, personal and professional problems and administrative problems. Before discussing some of these problems it seems important to consider how selecting the right position and having a better understanding of the school, community, and job into which the new teacher is going will reduce or alleviate the problems.

ELIMINATING SOME PROBLEMS BEFORE ASSUMING THE POSITION

The teacher should carefully evaluate the position before accepting such a responsibility. Unfortunately, some teachers accept positions in schools and communities in which they do not fit or belong and, consequently, where problems are bound to arise. If one is going to be unhappy and ineffective on the job, it may be better not to accept such a position in the first place. The many complex factors related to proper adjustment on the job are usually associated with the nature of the person, the nature of the environment, and the interaction of the two. It is therefore important to the candidate for a teaching position to carefully weigh the available position and his or her abilities and personal characteristics for handling this position effectively. If this is done, many of the problems will be foreseen, and the qualities and preparation needed to handle them successfully will be evaluated realistically.

Advance considerations

Two advance considerations important to the beginning teacher before assuming the job are knowledge of the conditions of employment and pertinent factors about the school and community.

Knowledge of conditions of employment. It is imperative for the new teacher to understand the numerous details, duties, and responsibilities that he or she is about to assume, including a knowledge of classes to be handled, sports to be coached, clubs to be sponsored, homeroom assignments, study halls, length of the school day, after-school obligations, compensation to be received, salary schedules in force, sick leave, tenure, sabbaticals, health insurance, and other pertinent facts. Only as the teacher has a clear understanding of the responsibilities will he or she be able to prepare sufficiently, both mentally and physically, for the position. Information can be obtained from other teachers, mem-

bers of the administration, and/or school literature that contains pertinent school policies.

Lack of advance knowledge of unfavorable working conditions has caused many teachers to be unhappy in their positions. The following are some of the conditions most often mentioned:

1. Classes are too large.
2. The work week is too long.
3. The daily schedule is too long.
4. Clerical duties are excessive.
5. Community demands for out-of-school activities are too heavy.

In some studies it has been shown that the teacher is required on the average to spend approximately an hour each day in nonteaching, schooltime duties. Many school systems are attempting to minimize and will undoubtedly eliminate some of the unfavorable conditions. The beginning teacher should not become discouraged but should understand these problems and be prepared to meet them.

The importance of ample preparation and knowledge of conditions of employment cannot be overemphasized. Teachers who know and understand the conditions into which they are entering are less likely to be discouraged when they do not meet the optimum or theoretical standards they have been studying in college.

Fig. 11-1. Physical education classes should be of a size that will enable all students to actively participate in the scheduled activities. (Oconomowoc Senior High School, Oconomowoc, Wis.)

Pertinent factors about the school and community. A beginning teacher should have a thorough knowledge of the school and community of which he or she is a part. Items such as the following should be known: history of the school and community, traditions, curricular offerings, economic status, philosophy of education, industrial development, size, political structure, and problems and projected future growth. These factors will have implications for the type of students to be taught, the parents with whom the teacher will work, the community of which the teacher is to be a part, and the social, political, and educational climate within which the teacher must work. A more detailed analysis of the school and community are discussed in Chapters 1 and 2.

PROBLEMS OF BEGINNING TEACHERS CITED BY DIRECTORS OF PHYSICAL EDUCATION

A representative number of directors of physical education in school systems across the nation were surveyed to determine what they feel are the most difficult problems faced by beginning teachers. Since these administrators had an opportunity to observe beginning teachers as they embarked on their professional careers, their experiences should be of value in helping new teachers to have a good start. The thinking of these administrators may be summarized under the following headings: organization, teaching, teacher-student relationships, teacher-teacher relationships, and making adjustments.

Organization

Many of the problems of beginning teachers are caused by poor organization, which can easily be corrected. Some of the beginning teachers are not accustomed to moving large groups of students from one place to another and from one formation to another. They are not thoroughly familiar with the various methods of class organization for various activities. Sometimes they are poorly organized in respect to uni-

forms, lockers, towel fees, and many routine duties important to the efficient running of a physical education program.

Problems concerned with organization can be easily remedied if the beginning teacher will study them, become familiar with various types of organization, and ask questions and the help of experienced teachers.

Teaching

The beginning teacher is sometimes an excellent performer in various physical education activities, and it is hard for him or her to realize that some students have no idea how to throw or jump or perform other basic skills. Often too much time is spent in teaching games rather than teaching basic fundamentals and skills. Often the new teacher does not have the ability to completely involve the class in the activity. Sometimes there is a tendency to teach the units the teacher is interested in and does well and to minimize those in which he is weak.

The beginning teacher needs to put into practice the tools he or she has learned during undergraduate training. This includes presenting skills within the ability of the pupil, utilizing appropriate teaching techniques, making lesson plans, and, finally, recognizing one's own shortcomings in some areas of physical education and trying hard to correct deficiencies through in-service training.

Teacher-student relationships

Discipline and both personal and professional relationships are involved in teacher-student relationships. Students will frequently test the authority of the new teacher, and sometimes the teacher does not meet the test. Discipline problems may arise, and the teacher may fail to face them directly and, instead, refer the students to the principal's office. The teacher may expect too much from the students, the students may not be adequately motivated, or the teacher may show favoritism to certain students, especially athletes.

Fig. 11-2. Field hockey being taught at Hurst-Euless-Bedford Public Schools, Hurst, Tex.

The beginning teacher needs to establish rapport with pupils, which requires the ability to be both firm and pleasant, as well as consistent; to know boys and girls as human beings rather than just so many "numbers"; and to establish friendships with pupils without becoming "one of them." Establishing rapport in this manner requires further effort on the part of the new teacher if he or she is replacing another teacher who had been extremely well liked and respected by the pupils.

The beginning teacher should recognize that sometimes disciplinary problems are a result of the teacher's lack of planning and class organization. The teacher will be respected much sooner by boys and girls if he can handle the discipline himself rather than passing it on to the principal's office.

Teacher-teacher relationships

Physical education, including sports, tends to isolate teachers of physical education from the rest of the building and often from colleagues in other subject areas. As a result, some beginning teachers fail to realize the importance of participating in general building activities with all teachers, attending faculty meetings regularly, and becoming an integral part of the faculty.

From the very beginning the new teacher should become acquainted with other members of the faculty, work cooperatively with them, share committee responsibilities, attend faculty meetings, and be respected by all.

Making adjustments

The beginning teacher often finds facilities, staff, equipment and other conditions on the job to be far below his expectations and far from ideal. He should realize that teachers do not always have ideal situations in which to teach; in fact, very few of them do. Many are faced with poor equipment, limited facilities, changing weather conditions, and other substandard conditions.

The new teacher must adjust to the position, the school, other teachers, school policies, procedures, and routines. Regardless of the situation, the conditions that prevail should be accepted as a challenge to excellent teaching in spite of limitations. The teacher should follow through on the many duties, responsibilities, and "chores" for which he is responsible. He should make an adjustment to existing policies and to the curriculum, with its inherent demand for skillful budgeting of time. The teacher should recognize his responsibility to professional physical education standards and also to the students, faculty, and school of which he is a part.

Planning is necessary—even the teacher

of long experience needs at least a brief written plan as a protection against forgetfulness or wasting time. A teacher's responsibility involves actually teaching the student *how* to perform an activity or a skill; merely telling a pupil *what* to do or simply supervising activities in a gymnasium is not enough. Rules and regulations should be established and followed. Accidents may occur when rules are not followed. Exercising foresight will help to prevent problems and is preferable to trying to get out of predicaments. For example, the climbing ropes should be tied up before the class period starts so that it will be unnecessary to shout at the students who are swinging on them after class has begun. Finally, the teacher should practice a little self-evaluation each day and then faithfully try to eliminate weaknesses and expand on strengths.

SELECTED PROFESSIONAL PROBLEMS CITED BY BEGINNING PHYSICAL EDUCATORS

A few of the more common professional problems experienced by the beginning physical educator, with recommendations for meeting them, are the following: (1) discipline, (2) working effectively with colleagues, (3) lack of respect for physical education, (4) inequitable use of facilities, (5) problems peculiar to men and women physical educators, and (6) extra school assignments.

Discipline

Lack of discipline is one of the most common problems cited by beginning physical educators in the secondary school. Poor neighborhoods, parental neglect and indifference, overcrowded classes, student transiency, low economic conditions, and pampered children have been cited as contributing factors. Teachers have mentioned that some students are guilty of inattention, unpreparedness, smoking, drug use, cutting classes, refusing to follow instructions, talking, and many other infractions.

If a teacher is to be a success in his or her profession, classes must be conducted in an orderly manner, and the teacher must have the respect of the pupils. Part of the difficulty in regard to discipline problems may be caused by the youthful appearance of the teacher and the desire on the part of the students to test the new teacher.

Some beginning teachers are more sensitive than others about the reasons why discipline problems arise. For example, one teacher stated that poor planning on his part was quickly recognized by the pupils, causing many of his discipline problems. Another teacher noted that in some schools the beginning teacher must work three times as hard as an experienced instructor in order to establish proper student-teacher relations. A third teacher related that the previous teacher was not respected, which made it more difficult for him to work effectively. A fourth teacher made an excellent point when she said that she did not understand the boys and girls with whom she was working. She pointed out that she lacked knowledge of their stages of growth and development and therefore of what to expect at each age level. She recognized that this problem could be alleviated only by a thorough study and understanding of the physical, mental, social, and emotional characteristics of children and youth.

Experienced teachers have recommended many techniques that should be helpful to the physical educator in working with groups of students:

1. Be firm when first meeting a group. It is easy to relax after a good relationship has been established, but it is difficult to gain control over a group that has not known discipline.

2. Maintain poise with a noisy group. Call for silence and then wait for the order to be obeyed. If necessary, call to one or two individuals to be quiet. This will often have the desired effect on the class.

3. Use a whistle only when necessary. Blow it sparingly, but require attention whenever it is used.

4. Wait for silence before talking. A

murmur can multiply quickly if it is not stopped.

5. Know the pupils well in order to determine the best approach to each individual.

6. Maintain self-control. No situation should be allowed to deteriorate into a personal duel with the children.

7. Give all pupils a feeling of belonging. Show the boys and girls that they are all part of the group and will receive your interest and attention.

8. Be liberal in praise. Every child wants to be praised by the teacher, and accomplishment should be recognized.

9. Be friendly and relaxed. The atmosphere that the teacher establishes in class will be quickly copied by the pupils.

10. Be sympathetic. Show an awareness of the difficulty of the stunt or skill and encourage the child to continue.

11. Know the subject matter; have a sense of humor; have the courage of your convictions; work for challenging, exciting programs; and be consistent, fair, and democratic.

12. Know the pupils' interests, abilities, parental and family backgrounds, and achievements.

13. Make physical education activities interesting, meaningful, and vital.

14. Find out what the pupils' problems are and try to help them solve their difficulties.

Working effectively with colleagues

A problem frequently cited by beginning teachers is the problem of working effectively with other members of the department of physical education and with other faculty members. One beginning teacher commented that it was particularly difficult to gain the cooperation of older teachers because they were inflexible. Another teacher said that some colleagues do not cooperate because a new teacher is too ambitious and too much of an "eager beaver." Another teacher believed that physical education teachers are frowned upon as not being very scholarly. Finally, another

teacher commented that being young and inexperienced makes it difficult to adjust—one is looked upon more as a student than as a faculty member.

Probably the comment of one beginning teacher on this problem is the best advice that can be given. She said: "Whether or not you get along with colleagues depends upon you."

Human relations can be effective when a person is considerate, tries to help others, is not overly critical, listens to the advice of others, becomes a member of the team, and tries in every way to contribute effectively to the achievement of the goals of the organization.

It is important for the new teacher to understand that the experienced instructors have amassed practical knowledge in addition to their formal training, which places them well ahead of teachers just out of college. There are many techniques that can be learned from colleagues. The beginning teacher should watch closely and select the methods that can be of value.

The new teacher should try to follow accepted procedures and systems, fitting into the existing pattern as much as possible. Being willing to work, anxious to learn, and able to get along increases the possibility of obtaining quick acceptance by colleagues.

Another aspect of this problem is the distribution of the work load. There is the question of whether the new teacher should carry a heavier or a lighter load than the older teachers and do more or less committee work at first.

The new teacher should willingly accept assignments of teaching and nonteaching duties, but he should feel free to ask questions when there is some phase of the program or duties that is not clear. New teachers often run into difficulty because they are afraid to ask questions. They think this would indicate ignorance, and instead of seeking the answers, they blunder ahead, making mistakes and intensifying problems.

Each teacher is primarily responsible for

his or her own preparation for the job. There is also the responsibility of the administrator, however, to help prepare the new teacher for the experiences to be encountered. Some steps that administrators can take that in the opinion of their Association[*] would benefit a beginning teacher include those listed here:

1. To provide all the necessary pertinent information
2. To establish workshops for new teachers
3. To assign an adviser for each new teacher
4. To hold seminars for new teachers
5. To have new teachers observe excellent teaching
6. To demonstrate teaching techniques to improve skills

Lack of respect for physical education

Sometimes physical educators are referred to as "muscular women" or "muscle men" or given other uncomplimentary names. The effect of this situation is to separate these teachers from other teachers, who are considered educators. It is important to break down this stereotyped thinking. Only when administrators, colleagues, and the public, in general, understand the true purpose and philosophy of physical education will this thinking change.

Physical educators should be educators first. They should exemplify well-educated people. They should be interested in the total development of students, not just their physical development. Although the work may concern itself with the physical more than the work of other teachers, it should not deter them from an appreciation of the importance of giving high priority to the mental development of youngsters, recognizing that the physical is only a

means to an end. The end must be the education of the total child.

The dress of physical educators as well as their manners will help to support or disprove the sterotype. The working uniform should be restricted to the gymnasium. The teacher would not, of course, be expected to change clothes every time he leaves the gymnasium for a few minutes, but he should be properly attired for every school function, whether it is an assembly, a faculty meeting, or a conference, as well as for just going home. Furthermore, in all actions the physical educator should try to show that he or she is a well-mannered, cultured, educated human being who ranks on the same level with other educators.

Another major task for the teacher is to interpret the program of physical education wherever he or she goes. There is much misunderstanding in regard to the goals and values of the profession. All phases of the program—classes, adapted programs, intramural and extramural activities, and interscholastic athletics—should be interpreted correctly, together with their specific worth in the educational program for students.

The physical educator must be a professional person in every respect. This means joining local, state, and national organizations, recruiting outstanding personnel for the profession, continually seeking opportunities for self-improvement, being an effective teacher, continually keeping abreast of the latest developments and thinking in the field, and being a good public relations ambassador for physical education. If each physical educator would fulfill his responsibilities in these areas, physical education would soon be respected throughout the country.

Inequitable use of facilities

The use of the available facilities, according to many beginning teachers, seems to be a common problem throughout the country. Several beginning teachers point out that too often the women's department

---

[*]Commission on Staff Relations in School Administration, American Association of School Administrators: Staff relations in school administration, 33rd yearbook, Washington, D. C., 1955, The Association.

is asked to give up facilities in favor of the varsity interscholastic program. It may be that a separate gymnasium or field is not available for a girls' intramural program or that, because of the varsity schedule, the area is free only during the late afternoon hours or once a week. The equipment shared by both departments may also be divided inequitably. Finally, the budgetary allotments may be apportioned in such a way that the men's department obtains the lion's share and the women's department a bare minimum. The underlying causes may be the following:

1. There may be little administrative enthusiasm for the girls' program. Such a problem may take considerable time to correct, and the new teacher must work slowly and patiently to build up a more favorable administrative attitude. It may be that a solution can be reached by gaining the cooperation of the men's department. An effort should also be made to build up student and community interest in the girls' program. When interest is aroused, it may be possible to convince the administrator of the importance and value of the program, recognizing that the men's program should not suffer to accomplish the needed changes. The positive aspect of improving the women's program should always be emphasized. New teachers should be careful not to criticize another department.

2. Lack of understanding by the men's department may be apparent. Once again it is necessary to organize the best possible program and to stimulate interest among the girls. If the men's department is approached with an obvious understanding of the problems regarding time, space, practice, and other needs, but with some realistic suggestions, it may be possible to set up a schedule that can provide for all groups that need the gymnasium. As a result of the women's liberation movement, girls and women are having much more say in the administration of their own programs. This, in itself, will hurry the solution of many of these problems.

Problems peculiar to men and women physical educators

Men physical educators experience many different types of problems when beginning to teach. They may be required to take on additional responsibilities in the community, working with recreation, church, and various youth groups. If they are married, there are extra responsibilities that require additional funds when starting salary schedules do not adequately provide for family considerations. A beginning teacher may not be assigned teaching and coaching duties in accordance with his or her wishes.

There are many problems faced by the beginning male teacher, but the most common seems to be associated with an overemphasis on interscholastic athletics. The pressures involved in sports, when they are influenced by local newspapers, radio, television, community, and alumni, place undue importance on this phase of the physical education program. The physical educator wants to be an effective teacher in his regular classes and intramural activities but finds that community pressures often force him to spend a disproportionate amount of time on the interscholastic athletic program. Under such conditions the teacher should steer a steady course, realizing that he is associated with educational, rather than professional, athletics. The coach who puts a winning team above all else, tries to pressure teachers to keep boys eligible, teaches how to win at any cost, is rude to officials, is not completely honest, and closes his eyes to improper conduct will be a credit neither to his school nor to the profession of physical education. There are many valuable contributions that sports can make to the student, such as teamwork, skill, sportsmanship, respect for ability, and greater understanding of the value and place of sports in our society. These worthy goals must receive the main emphasis as the total physical education program for all students is kept in proper focus.

Women physical educators also have

many problems with which to contend during their first year on the job. Some of these, including inequitable use of facilities, have been mentioned. Other problems may involve her professional as well as her personal life.

Male physical education teachers frequently receive extra pay for extra coaching duties, but the time spent by female teachers with the girls' intramural and interscholastic programs sometimes remains unrecognized. When an unequal pay scale exists, the female physical education instructor—together with other teachers in the school who devote extra work to the band, orchestra, dramatic group, school newspaper, or other activity—should strive to impress the administration with the need for added salary benefits.

The beginning female teacher may find an obvious lack of interest in physical education among secondary school girls. The students may be more interested in dates and in their hair and their social obligations than in physical education. They do not want to become strong and athletic. If the girls' program is to have appeal to girls, characteristics of femininity should be fostered. Secondary school girls are interested in developing their feminine charms and their skills, not their muscles. The teacher should exemplify grace, poise, and femininity, along with fine coordination and body control, so that physical education can be recognized as developing such attributes of beauty. The personal appearance of the teacher, her attitude toward her work, and the appearance of her office and the locker room should contribute to the overall picture. Setting a feminine example attracts interest among students who may otherwise be lost to the program.

Personal problems may also confront the beginning teacher. If she is married, there is the problem of time to devote to the home. Physical education requires long hours, and home life may be neglected. Good planning and organization in the home as well as at school may relieve this situation. For the unmarried teacher, either

too much socializing in the evening or too much fretting about domestic problems may interfere with her work at school. The teacher who enjoys her work, however, finds that self-preoccupation disappears as soon as the morning bell sounds and that the problems of the students replace her own.

Not all the problems presented here will be faced by all new female teachers, but some of them will be present. The teacher who keeps in mind her responsibilities to her students, school, and profession, gets along with others, and does her best work should encounter little difficulty.

Extra school assignments

One of the most pressing problems facing beginning teachers of physical education is the extra duties required during the school day. It is not uncommon for the physical educator to be assigned to supervise a lunchroom period, to keep an eye on the entrance or exit where the students congregate, to handle traffic at school functions, to manage school dances, to monitor study halls, or to supervise the parking lot. Too often the number and type of such assignments place an unfair burden upon the teacher, sometimes to such a degree that they interfere with his or her primary responsibility as a physical educator. It is important, of course, to perform all duties to the best of one's ability. It is also reasonable to point out to the administrator in charge those instances when such assignments affect teaching, infringe upon hours that could be put to better professional use, or take an unfair amount of a teacher's free time.

SELECTED ADMINISTRATIVE PROBLEMS CITED BY BEGINNING PHYSICAL EDUCATORS

The beginning physical educator will encounter many problems that may be classified as administrative in nature. These problems involve administrative responsibilities and decisions of chairmen of departments, principals, superintendents of

Fig. 11-3. The physical educator is often required to take charge of planning special occasions as an extra assignment. (Walt Whitman High School, South Huntington Schools, New York.)

schools, and other persons who work in similar capacities in school systems. These responsibilities and decisions have important implications for the physical education program. Therefore, the teacher of physical education must be alert to the problems involved and continually interpret to those in administrative positions the philosophy, needs, and policies that are necessary if physical education is to make its greatest contribution to the students.

The administrative problems discussed in this section are encountered by many beginning physical education teachers, and they involve facilities, budget, scheduling, grouping of pupils, class size, time allocation, and legal liability.

Facilities

Considerable school construction is continually in progress and therefore many physical educators will be asked for their recommendations concerning facilities needed. Furthermore, as a specialist in this area the beginning teacher should know the basic facility requirements, adaptations that can be made to improve the program, and the best way to proceed in developing an adequate physical plant.

It is important that the beginning teacher know what a good physical education plant should contain in the way of standard equipment, adequate locker areas, and offices, including size requirements. This knowledge will be of help, especially if the plant is to be remodeled or enlarged or a new school is to be built. It is the responsibility of the physical educator to be able to work with the architects to make economical and sound suggestions. It is also important for the physical educator to know what is wrong with the existing plant so that he or she may take the necessary precautions when planning a program.

Gymnasiums and auxiliary facilities

The type, size, and number of gymnasiums should reflect the number of particiof alternating weeks can be spent in a classroom—discussing the rules, techniques, and strategy of sports; the value of physical education and physical fitness; leisure-time activities; and health instruction. It may also be possible to use some other indoor area for physical education when the gymnasium is not available.

Scheduling the physical education classes under such conditions presents problems. The number of students and of physical education classes per week, the length of periods, and the activities to be taught must all be considered in arriving at the best solution. It may be possible to schedule classes in such a way that when the boys of a class are taking physical education the girls are assigned to home economics, typing, or some other class program, and that when the girls are scheduled for physical education the boys are assigned to shop, mechanical drawing, and the like. This, again, would depend upon the school, the number of pupils, and scheduling difficulties.

Problem
No gymnasium is available.

Possible solution
In the event that no gmynasium is available, there is no great problem as long as the weather is fair. Classes may be held out-of-doors. When bad weather comes and classes move indoors, classroom periods might be used for discussions, as mentioned above. There are also some other areas that can be used for physical activity.

Multipurpose room (or large, uncluttered area). The multipurpose room is usually larger than a regular classroom. It has no permanent furniture, the ceiling is usually as a regular height, and the lighting fixtures are often without protection. It can be used for tumbling and apparatus work, relays, games of low organization, mimetics, testing, and other limited activities. At a nominal expense, the light fixtures and windows can be screened and the room used for additional selected activities.

Classrooms. It is possible to make use of an empty classroom or two for indoor physical activity if there is no multipurpose room available. There would not be enough room for running games, but there would be sufficient space for tumbling and apparatus work, for recreational activities such as table tennis, bat-back, and handball, and for some basketball where a goal-hi could be used or possibly a basket and blackboard permanently installed. With some ingenuity and modification, other activities may also be conducted.

Fig. 11-4. The beginning teacher should understand the physical education equipment needs for a good program.

pating individuals, the variety of activities to be conducted, the number of desired teaching stations, official court sizes, the number of spectators, and the need for enjoyable and safe activity participation. It is preferable for a gymnasium to be in a separate wing in the school building in order to minimize the possible disturbance to other classrooms, as well as to have the gymnasium readily available for after-school use without the necessity of opening the entire building.

Below are listed some facility problems, with suggestions for alleviating the difficulties.

Problem
Only one small gymnasium is available for use by both boys and girls.

Possible solution
One solution would be to alternate weeks in the gymnasium—one week for the boys and the next for the girls. During the spring and fall this would not present a great handicap because one group can be out-of-doors. During the winter months, it would be advantageous to have coeducational classes once or twice weekly. The remaining days

Other areas. It is also possible to practice track work in the hallways or in the basement areas.

A modified physical education program can be conducted without a gymnasium. An important consideration in the use of any area is to plan for the *safe* use of the facility, limiting activities to those that can be conducted without fear of accident. In such planning, it will always be necessary to take into account the features listed below.

1. Obstructions. Make provision to have obstructions covered, or establish a floor plan to avoid any activity near them. Be sure that the students are conscious of these obstructions.

2. Lighting. Secure larger bulbs or more fixtures, if needed, in order to provide sufficient light for the activity area.

3. Ventilation. Be conscious of temperature. Be sure that vents or radiators are covered or protected and that the students are made aware of them.

4. Composition of the floor. Consider those activities that would be applicable to wood, tile, or concrete floors and make selections accordingly.

Locker, shower, and drying areas

It is important that the physical education plant have adequate locker, shower, and drying rooms. Refer to the books at the end of the chapter for necessary and standard requirements.

Where their are insufficient locker facilities it will be necessary to work out a plan for their most efficient use. It is possible to have students double up or to assign certain grades permanent gymnasium lockers, while the other students have lockers only during their physical education period. It may be advisable to switch at some time during the year to equalize this advantage.

Dirty, dark, unpainted, unappealing locker rooms often can be brightened, cleaned, painted, and made more attractive. Where their is no locker room, it will be necessary to find an area that can be utilized for changing into gymnasium uniforms. This may be a vacant classroom, storage area, or lavatory. It is also possible to have the pupils wear their uniforms under their school clothes if there is no area available for changing. This should be the last resort, however, because it violates a basic use of the uniform. Students should be able to change out of sweaty or dirty clothes before returning to a classroom.

The problem of shower and drying rooms is very simple. Either there are facilities or there are not. If there are showers, it is important that they be used. If not, a dry rubdown should follow each activity period. In some cases perhaps a sponge bath may be feasible.

Special activity areas

There should be teaching stations in addition to the gymnasium for use in conducting many physical education activities. These may include rooms for remedial or adapted activities, apparatus work, weight lifting, wrestling, rhythms, squash, handball, fencing, or any other activities of particular interest. A recommended size for an auxiliary gymnasium is forty by sixty by twenty-four feet.

It is possible to convert regular classrooms for certain of these special activities. Some of these rooms would need special equipment—such as ladders, bars, ropes, pulley weights, or mats—in order to properly conduct the activities. Facilities needed will depend upon the interests, abilities, and desires of the students, as well as upon the comprehensiveness of the program, the availability of staff, and the accessibility of rooms.

Outdoor areas

When outdoor facilities are planned, it is highly desirable to have them located convenient to the gymnasiums and locker areas and also to have them available for year-round use by the community.

The size of outdoor areas will vary from ten to forty acres. On the junior high school level the facilities should be adequate for a girls' program of archery,

Fig. 11-5. Lincoln High School, Yonkers, N. Y.

volleyball, tennis, and hockey and a boys' program of soccer, touch football, baseball, speedball, softball, golf, and track. The senior high school field should also allow for field hockey, lacrosse, football, and baseball, as well as ample space for other activities in the regular physical education class.

When a school playfield is not available, it is still possible to have outdoor activities. Some schools may be in the vicinity of a park or recreational play area that would be satisfactory. It may be necessary to have double periods of physical education, to allow time for travel to and from this area. It will be necessary to receive permission from the school administration and the park or recreation department for the use of such space. Another alternate site may be the school parking area. It is possible that lines could be painted on asphalt and cars limited to a certain section in order to allow room for the physical activities. It may also be possible to use the school's grassy areas. As a last resort it may be necessary to use the street adjacent to the building. In such a case it would be essential to have the street closed, at least during school hours. No physical education class should be limited to indoor classes all year long.

An adequate physical plant can help in developing a good physical education pro-

gram. A poor plant, however, does not mean that there will necessarily be a poor program. In most cases it will be as good as the physical educator and the school administration want it to be.

The budget and PPBS

In the future the reader will hear the initials *PPBS* referred to more and more. These initials stand for planning, programming, and budgeting systems. In its totality the process involves comprehensive planning. It involves the instructional program and the resources needed to make the program an effective one. The program budget provides the machinery or plan for systematically relating the fiscal aspects of the operation to the accomplishment of the planned goals for which the organization exists. In other words, PPBS attempts to provide a system whereby the resources that are allocated are used in an efficient manner in the achievement of specific objectives. In this way the budget expresses in financial terms the operational plan of the organization.

In every school system, equipment and supplies are purchased each year for use in the schools. There are many things a teacher can do to secure the proper supplies and/or equipment needed for the program.

There are generally two sources of

money for physical education items: (1) the board of education and (2) organizations within the school.

An allocation from the board of education may consist of money allotted directly to the physical education department or given to the principal to divide among all the departments in the school. The usual procedure for using this money is for the teacher to requisition the needed items, obtain the principal's approval, and send the requisition to a central purchasing agent for processing and purchase. This procedure centralizes the purchasing power and often brings increased value for each dollar spent.

There is frequently some type of athletic association and/or other student organization that handles the proceeds from the sale of school general organization memberships, athletic contests, dramatic or music presentations, the school store, and other fund-raising affairs or activities. This money is used to support many of the school activities, as well as for the purchase of special supplies or equipment. It is a source of funds for items the central purchasing agent may not approve for payment out of tax money, as well as for special items that must be obtained quickly. The faculty adviser can explain the procedure for his particular school.

If the necessary funds are not available through these channels, there are still other means of obtaining equipment and supplies. The ingenuity of physical education teachers and pupils working together, with the cooperation of other teachers and the school administration, can solve many problems.

A small list of items that can be constructed at little or no expense in the shops or the backyard includes the following: starting blocks, hurdles, vaulting standards, crossbars, backboards, batons, chinning bars, a form of parallel bars, mat trucks, sideline markers, yardline sticks, goal flags, charging sled, and football dummies. It is also possible to call upon the home economics department to sew and clean uniforms and upon the art depart-

ment for publicity purposes. Special fund-raising drives can be organized, with the proceeds earmarked for specific needs. These may include a cake sale, a white elephant sale, or a dance.

Scheduling

The importance of proper scheduling cannot be overemphasized. A school that schedules physical education classes to meet the needs and interests of the students will usually have a good program.

Scheduling should be done according to a plan. The plan for scheduling should be based upon (1) the number of students taking the course, (2) the number of teachers available to teach the course, and (3) the number of rooms or teaching stations available. This plan should provide for early scheduling of physical education.

Since English, history, the sciences, mathematics, and physical education are required of all students, it seems logical to assume that these subjects should usually be scheduled first. Physical education and science laboratory periods should also be given particular consideration because there are usually fewer physical education teaching stations and science laboratories available than rooms for other subjects. If a sound progression in physical education is to be maintained, it is important that class size be approximately the same and that homogeneity by grade be a minimum prerequisite to scheduling. The physical educator should inform the administration of the sound reasons that make it important to give physical education early attention in setting up the school program.

In scheduling for physical education, every student should be included. This, of course, is based on the premise that the responsibility of the physical education department to adapt the program for the atypical child will be carried out.

Grouping

When considering how to group pupils for physical education, there are many problems that must be thought through before a decision is reached.

Platnick's Photo Service, Hempstead, L. I.

Fig. 11-6. Students will learn more readily in a swimming class if they are grouped homogeneously according to skill.

It is widely accepted that classes should be homogeneous. In physical education the real question is "homogeneous in what respect?" Various groupings can be made, depending upon the criteria used: grade, sex, age, health, physical fitness, ability, motor capacity, speed, strength, endurance, or interests, for example. The American Association for Health, Physical Education, and Recreation stresses the need for grouping students homogeneously, but the inability to scientifically measure such important factors as ability, maturity, interest, and capacity has been a deterrent to accomplishing this goal. The Association points out that the most common procedure for grouping today is by grade or class.

The ideal grouping plan will take into consideration all the factors that affect performance—intelligence, capacity, ability, interest, knowledge, age, height, weight, and the like. It is not administratively possible, however, to utilize all these factors in many schools.

Some form of grouping is essential to provide the type of program that will promote educational objectives and protect the student. On the secondary level the most feasible procedure appears to be to schedule classes by grade and then to organize subgroups within the regular physical education class. Classification within the physical education class can be based on such factors as age, height, intelligence, interests, motor ability, and motor capacity.

Size of classes

The size of physical education classes will vary greatly from school to school, and it may also vary from class to class within any one school. The number of pupils in each class has implications for teacher effectiveness.

Criteria to determine class size

When considering the size of classes, it is essential to consider the number of teaching stations, the supplies and equipment, and the size of the area, as well as the number of available teachers.

Many of the same principles that are applicable in an English class also apply in the gymnasium. Obviously, the effectiveness of both the English teacher and the physical education teacher will be seriously hampered if there is an excessive number of pupils. Individual attention is limited, and many children must "sink or swim" on their own. Organization of a large class takes more time, discipline may be a greater problem, and the administrative structure of the class must be more formal. Furthermore, there is less opportunity to help meet the individual interests and needs of the children.

In recommending proper class size to an administrator, the American Association for Health, Physical Education, and Recreation suggests that the number of pupils in a class should not exceed thirty-five.* LaPorte's committee suggests thirty-five as a suitable size for activity classes—and not more than forty-five. This group also recommends that the size of remedial and corrective classes should be twenty to twenty-five and should never exceed thirty.†

What to do with large classes

On the senior high school level, the problem of scheduling is a difficult one because students have individual programs. Each program is made to suit the individual student's needs. In the junior high school, it is sometimes a simpler process because of the block system, in which a group of students is scheduled as a unit and goes to different teachers as a unit.

One technique suitable for handling large classes is the use of student leaders. The effective use of trained pupils to assist in the management and organization of large classes can prove helpful. The students may be trained with a leaders' club that meets during a regular club period, after school, or both. With the assistance of these students it will be possible to institute an active squad work program. It will also be possible for the teacher to work with selected groups while the others are busy under the direction of their leaders. The responsibility for the class, however, always rests with the teacher. It is important for the teacher to oversee all activities, even though he or she may spend a major part of a class period with a particular group or groups.

Time

Standards for time allotment vary. In a survey of state requirements, the differences ranged from no specific time requirements for physical education, in some states, to minimum daily requirements. Many educators and administrators realize the importance of a minimum daily period of physical education.

The amount of time spent on physical education may vary from thirty to sixty minutes. When figuring the amount of physical education a student receives, the time needed for dressing and showering should be taken into consideration. For boys, this would be approximately five to seven minutes at the beginning of a period and about seven to thirteen minutes at the end of the period. It is usually necessary to add a few extra minutes for girls, particularly if hair must be dried. This means as little as fifteen to twenty minutes of actual activity on the gymnasium floor. In some situations, it may be advisable to have physical education on fewer days with longer periods. Considering a basic forty-five-minute period, the school that schedules five daily periods of physical education weekly may total as little as 125 minutes of physical activity per week. In the same school, by using two double periods each week, it is possible to have 150 minutes of physical activity while allowing the same amount of time for showering and dressing. Of course, with flexible scheduling it i

*American Association for Health, Physical Education, and Recreation: Administrative problems in health, physical education and recreation, Washington, D. C., 1953, The Association.
†LaPorte, W. R.: The physical education curriculum (a national program), Los Angeles, 1955, University of Southern California Press.

very easy to schedule classes with different lengths of time.

The time advantage that can be achieved by longer periods should be considered, even though the thinking of most educators is for a continuity that can be achieved only through a daily period of physical education.

Legal liability

A high school student who charged that he had been paralyzed as a result of negligence after an injury in a football game recently was awarded over $200,000. This is only one of many cases of legal liability that regularly occur in physical education programs.

With the growth in physical education programs throughout the country, there has been a resultant increase in the problems involving legal liability. The very nature of physical activity involves a certain amount of risk and hazard, and for their own welfare, teachers must be aware of their responsibility and liability for any accident.

Defining liability

A teacher's liability is "tort" liability; that is, it is "liability for personal or property injuries caused through the defendant's negligence. . . . Any tort action involves proof of four elements: that the defendant owed a duty to avoid unreasonable risk to others, that the defendant failed to observe that duty, that the failure to observe that duty caused the damage which occurred, and that damage in fact occurred to plaintiff . . ."*

Negligence. Negligence can be defined as something that a reasonable person would not do or the failure to do something that a reasonable person would do. There can be no legal liability unless there is negligence. Negligence must be shown. If one did not foresee a danger of accident as a reasonably prudent person should, there is negligence. Another condition demands an unfulfilled duty toward the injured person. Every teacher has such a duty because he or she is acting *in loco parentis* (in place of a parent).

Following are types of conduct* that constitute negligent acts:

1. Appropriate care is not used by the teacher. Example: An instructor permits a student to use the trampoline without stationing spotters.

2. The circumstances under which the activity is done creates risk, although it is done with due care and caution. Example: Two softball games are played on opposite ends of an area that is not large enough to permit overlapping outfielders.

3. The teacher is indulging in an act that involves an unreasonable risk of direct and immediate harm to others. Example: The physical education instructor places a boy at a certain position to mark where the shot put landed. The instructor puts a shot that hits the boy's head.

4. The teacher sets in motion a force, the continuous operation of which may be unreasonably hazardous to others. Example: A person, without justification, frightens a horse or dog that becomes uncontrollable.

5. The teacher creates a situation that is unreasonably dangerous to others because of the likelihood of the action of a third person or inanimate forces. Example: The instructor permits a student to ride a bicycle on a playground crowded with other pupils. The result is an injury to another student.

6. The teacher entrusts dangerous devices or instruments to persons who are incompetent to use or care for such instruments properly. Example: The instructor permits students to use fencing foils without supervision.

7. The teacher neglects a duty of control over third persons who, by reason of some

---

*From Fahr, Samuel M.: Legal liability for athletic injuries, Journal of Health, Physical Education, and Recreation **29**:12, 1958.

*Based on types of conduct that create unreasonable risks to others, from Harper, Fowler V.: A treatise on the law of torts, Indianapolis, 1938, Bobbs-Merrill Co., Inc., pp. 171-176.

incapacity or abnormality, he knows to be likely to inflict intended harm upon others. Example: The instructor fails to supervise and control the conduct of a boy who is a bully in the play area.

8. The teacher fails to employ due care to give adequate warning. Example: The instructor, although he is responsible for supervision, absents himself or herself from the area. In another example, a student is struck by a car when crossing the street between the gymnasium and the athletic field. Negligence is found because no crosswalk was provided, no safety instruction was given to the students, and no warning signs for motorists were posted.

9. The teacher fails to exercise proper care in looking out for persons who he has reason to believe may be in danger. Example: The teacher does not clear the students from the area directly behind the batter in a baseball game.

10. The teacher fails to employ appropriate skill to perform acts undertaken. Example: The teacher is unable to perform first aid when is should be administered.

11. The teacher fails to make adequate preparation to avoid harm to others before entering into an activity where such preparation is necessary. Example: The instructor permits students to use the horizontal bar without a mat underneath.

12. The teacher fails to inspect and repair equipment or mechanical devices used by others. Example: The teacher fails to inspect flying rings and other hanging equipment periodically.

How to avoid negligence. It should be obvious that the best way to avoid negligence is to use common sense and to insist upon safety rules at all times. Some necessary rules include the following:

1. Clear a playing area of all obstacles (equipment and obstructions).

2. Inspect all equipment regularly.

3. Lock up apparatus when it is not in use.

4. Have a health examination for all competitors.

5. Never permit a boy or girl who may be injured to participate.

6. Instruct in safety rules before permitting participation in an activity.

7. Employ spotters at all times.

8. Repair, remove, or do not use defective equipment.

9. Have ample insurance coverage at all times.

10. Never leave a class alone.

11. Always use protective equipment in contact activities.

12. Be sure the activity is suitable for the age level.

13. Do not force a student to participate in any activity that involves the hazard of personal injury.

14. Administer first aid when necessary.

15. Do not treat injuries.

16. Request, in writing, the repair of any hazardous conditions.

17. Insist that all participants wear proper uniforms at all times.

Defenses against negligence. In order for damages to be awarded, it is necessary for the plaintiff to prove that the negligence involved resulted in, or was directly connected to, the injury. The legal defense against such a charge may be any of the following:

1. Act of God. A condition occurs that is beyond the control of man.

2. Assumption of risk. When participating in an activity that involves certain risks, that individual assumes responsibilities for those risks. There is still, however, the responsibility for effective leadership and safe equipment and facilities.

3. Contributory negligence. The injured person does not act as a reasonably prudent person of his age should act. In this case the negligence of the teacher is canceled. Every person is expected to maintain a reasonable amount of self-protection.

4. Proximate cause of injury. The negligent act must be the direct and immediate cause of injury. If the negligent act was only indirectly or remotely concerned with the injury, the claim will be disallowed.

Teacher liability

Teachers are liable for their own negligence. The doctrine of *respondeat superior*

Fig. 11-7. The individual student assumes some risk when participating in physical education activities.

however, can relieve them of liability. This doctrine holds that employers are liable for torts of their employees committed within the scope of their employment. In Iowa, the State Supreme Court ruled that a teacher is not liable for charges while carrying on a government function, even though he is guilty of negligence. Some states, such as New York, New Jersey, and Connecticut, have "save harmless statutes," which permit the payment, out of school funds, for damages arising through the negligence of teachers or other employees of the school district.

Many teachers, particularly physical educators, purchase liability insurance from private companies. The American Association for Health, Physical Education, and Recreation has recently made available a policy that will protect its members from liability while engaging in any activity sponsored by the school or organization. The best means of avoiding any legal liability, however, is to make good use of the basic safety factors previously mentioned.

Insurance

Since schools require boys and girls to actively participate in physical education, they have a moral responsibility to protect them financially against injury. Staff members, because of the nature of their work and the need for protection against accidents and negligence, also need coverage. Some kind of insurance program should therefore be carried. Some factors to consider in such a protective insurance program are listed below.

1. All children and staff members should be covered in both class and out-of-class activities.

2. Prior to the selection of an insurance policy, a study should be made of school needs and problems, the various types of policies offered by different companies, and the insurance program that best meets the local situation.

3. Insurance policies should provide sufficient funds to cover doctor's fees, hospital expenses, x-ray examinations, dental care, and so on.

4. Commercial plans should be explored, together with athletic association plans and other plans. Although commercial plans may be more expensive, they may provide better coverage.

5. In many cases the nonallocated form of policy is the more desirable, since benefits will be paid up to a specific amount regardless of the type of injury, whereas an

allocated policy limits the benefits for each type of injury, such as a broken arm.

6. Staff members and other employees should also have insurance coverage.

7. The approved American Association for Health, Physical Education, and Recreation Income Protection and Public Liability Programs offered to members of the Association, in cooperation with Mutual Benefit Health & Accident Association, should be explored. Some of the benefits, as listed by the Association, are the following:

Rates are substantially lower than comparable coverage offered on an individual basis.

Disability benefits are doubled during hospital confinement.

Accident benefits are payable up to a lifetime, with house confinement never required.

Sickness benefits are payable up to five years, with house confinement required only during vacations or leaves of absence.

Eligible members may apply for coverage up to the age of sixty-five years.

POINTS TO REMEMBER

1. The possibility of avoiding many potential problems by investigating before accepting a position
2. The probability that discipline will be your major professional problem
3. Some problems directed toward the teacher as a member of the physical education department, not to him personally
4. The necessity of coordination between the male and female physical education departments
5. The need for the member of the physical education department to be an educator first
6. How to conduct a program when the facilities are limited
7. Sources of money for equipment and supplies and procedures for using the money
8. Why physical education classes should be scheduled early in developing the school's master plan
9. The need for homogeneity in physical education classes
10. Proper class size and how to subgroup for good instruction
11. Information regarding the legal liability of teachers

PROBLEMS TO THINK THROUGH

1. Why is the problem of acceptance of great importance to any beginning teacher?
2. How can one best prepare for the first day of teaching?
3. What do you anticipate as your greatest problem upon entering the teaching profession? Why?
4. Select any secondary school and determine how the facilities could be improved at a minimum expense. Use only the land and buildings available. What long-range major changes would you recommend?
5. How are supplies and equipment purchased in the school that you attend? Can the system be improved? How?
6. What are the advantages of having a physical education class containing students from the same grade?
7. Explain what a teacher should do when an accident occurs.
8. Compare the advantages of having five single physical education periods weekly with those of having two double periods weekly.

CASE STUDY FOR ANALYSIS

Unfavorable working conditions are causing many teachers to leave the profession. Some of these conditions relate to the size of classes, the length of the daily schedule and worksheet, and clerical duties and after-school obligations. Determine the degree to which adverse conditions prevail in a school system of your choice. Analyze factors that contribute to these conditions. How may the beginning teacher help to combat this problem?

EXERCISES FOR REVIEW

1. What are some techniques that are beneficial in working with large groups?
2. What school duties may be assigned to a beginning teacher?
3. Why is the orientation period important for good teaching?
4. Of what value are interscholastic activities to the student and the school?
5. How can the female physical education teacher avoid being labeled as the "girls' coach"?
6. What can the physical educator do if there is no gymnasium available in the school?
7. What areas can be used to change into uniforms in the absence of a locker room?
8. How can a physical education class have out-of-doors activities without a playing field?
9. What departments in the school can help to minimize physical education expenses?
10. What size should physical education classes be?
11. How may student leaders help the physical educator?
12. List ten negligent acts in physical education. Give an example of each.
13. What are the legal defenses against negligence?

SELECTED READINGS

Bucher, Charles A.: Administration of health and physical education programs, including athletics, ed. 5, St. Louis, 1971, The C. V. Mosby Co.

Bucher, Charles A.: Foundations of physical education, ed. 6, St. Louis, 1972, The C. V. Mosby Co.

Bucher, Charles A., and Reade, Evelyn: Physical education and health in the elementary school, ed. 3, New York, 1970, The Macmillan Co.

Gallup, George H.: Fourth annual Gallup poll of public attitudes toward education, Phi Delta Kappan, September, 1972, p. 33.

Hillson, Maurie, and Hyman, Ronald: Change and innovation in elementary and secondary organization, New York, 1965, Holt, Rinehart and Winston, Inc.

The American public-school teacher, 1970-1971, NEA Research Bulletin **50**:3, 1972.

Schooling, H. W.: Teacher-administrator relationships, National Education Association Journal **54**:32, 1965.

The University of the State of New York, The State Education Department, Newsletter of the Division of Teacher Education and Certification, No. 1, June, 1972, Competence Based Certification, Albany, N. Y.

Unruh, Glenys G., and Alexander, William M.: Innovations in secondary education, New York, 1970, Holt, Rinehart and Winston, Inc.

Van Til, William: Education: a beginning, New York, 1971, Houghton Mifflin Co.

12 THE PHYSICAL EDUCATOR AND TEACHING STYLE

Research studies have shown that the behavior and personality of one person when closely interacting with another person can have an effect on that person's behavior and personality. This is true of many human relationships that exist between individuals whether it be in a family setting or some form of business or other relationship. It is especially true of the relationship between teacher and student. The teacher's personality and behavior can affect the pupil's classroom behavior. Furthermore, since the personalities of teachers differ, it also follows that there are different teaching styles, with the result that the impact upon students is different.

Whereas in some occupations personality is secondary to accomplishing professional goals, such as in carpentry, for example, teaching success in great measure depends upon the style that the teacher uses with his or her pupils. Indeed, the teacher's personality and the way he behaves in the classroom, gymnasium, or playfield may be one of the most important factors in determining the outcomes accomplished from the physical education experience. The excellent teacher is not only one who has command of the skills, subject matter, and other requirements for his field of specialization, it is also the teacher who successfully transmits these skills and subject matter to his students.

Alexander M. Mood* points out that some authorities feel that about 10% of the teachers may be classified as being excellent, 10% as hopeless, and the other 80% as having varying degrees of competence and effectiveness. Mood goes on to point out that a characteristic of most excellent teachers is that they are sympathetic to students and deeply concerned about their welfare and interests. He further points out that research indicates there are some points that teachers should be aware of if they wish to do an effective professional job of teaching. These are presented here in adapted form:

• *The teacher should listen to what the students have to say and put it to use.* The teacher should pay attention to each question or comment no matter how trivial it may be. Each student should be given a feeling that he is participating in the learning process and has something worthy to contribute.

• *Each student should be provided with a sense of personal worth.* Teachers should go out of the way to instill in each student the feeling that he has some knowledge, skill, or attitude that is important and therefore deserves to be complimented.

---

*Mood, Alexander M.: How teachers make a difference, Washington, D. C., 1971, U. S. Office of Education, Department of Health, Education, and Welfare.

• *Each student should be imbued with a feeling of confidence, particularly in respect to his ability to learn.* The teacher must be very careful not to erode the student's self-confidence. This means that the teacher must understand that some student will learn faster than others and that students are also different in other ways that are affected by the learning process.

• *The teacher should not appear to be superior morally or intellectually.* If this does happen it builds up antagonism between student and teacher. Furthermore, students become overproctective of their egos.

• *Conflicts of interest with students should be minimized.* Students must be convinced that the teacher reflects goodwill toward them and therefore conflicts of interest should be reduced to a minimum. Although some conflicts will naturally exist—for example, attendance may be thought not to be necessary by pupils but important by teacher, and disruptive behavior cannot be tolerated—the teacher should aim at enlarging his community of interests with students rather than decreasing them.

• *Lecturing should be kept to a minimum.* Students learn more readily if they can grapple with questions and problems. Although this process is slower than having teacher expound the truth, it is generally agreed that it is more effective when the students do some thinking and themselves arrive at the answer.

• *The gymnasium, swimming pool, playground, or classroom should be characterized by a relaxed atmosphere.* Greater student participation and learning will take place in an open, relaxed atmosphere than in one that is rigid and formal.

• *Students should be kept active.* Physical movement is needed by all students throughout the school day—it will enhance the learning that takes place.

• *Genuine concern should be shown by the teacher for each student in the class.* Each student should be given the feeling and be convinced that the teacher cares about him as a person.

• *Individual students should not be permitted to fall behind.* Everything possible should be done to make sure each student makes progress and learns. The whole class should be aware of this feeling so that when a student starts to falter, not only the teacher but the whole class plays a part in seeing that the student learns and moves ahead.

• *Apathy and boredom should be combated.* These are deterrents to learning. Students should be kept interested and make the learning an exciting experience.

• *Teaching should be diversified.* A variety of methods such as films, slides, curriculum packages, programmed devices, and records should be used in teaching. The teacher must keep abreast of new teaching ideas.

• *Student participation should be encouraged in making learning attractive.* Students should be consulted about teaching and how to make it more interesting. Many of their experiments and ideas should be utilized.

• *The teacher should do the best type of teaching job possible.* Each teacher must do his very best job each day. Effective teaching is an important responsibility, and pupils should not be cheated.

• *Colleague interaction will help.* An exchange of ideas, discussion of problems, and joint ventures with other teachers are excellent ways to improve one's own teaching.

• *Grading systems should be questioned.* Grades create problems between teacher and student. If possible, they should not be used or at least the importance of grades should be minimized.

• *The teacher should be a model.* Setting a good example of what is right, honest, and scholarly is important to the learning process.

TEACHING STYLE AND METHODS AND MATERIALS

Courses in methods and materials in professional preparation curricula are typically concerned with instructing the future physical educator in how to teach a particular skill, how to correct student errors in skill performance, and how to direct the practice of a skill. Such courses may be said to be skill-centered. For example, the methods of teaching soccer are taught as a unit, and then the methods unique to other team, individual, and dual sports are taught as independent units. Methods and materials courses are also concerned with patterns of class organization for the teaching of a skill. The future physical educator learns how to teach the left-handed student, how to line the students up for instruction so that they do not face into the sun, and the most efficient methods of organizing a class for various drills and lead-up games.

Rarely do methods and materials courses consider the individuality and creativity of the teacher, and even more rarely do they take into account the individuality of the students to whom the methods will be applied. These courses do, however, serve an essential purpose as part of the professional preparation curriculum. They do introduce the future physical educator to effective methodology in both teaching and class management, and they do help to prepare for the student teaching experience. What methods and materials courses frequently do not do is to provide the future teacher with experiences in developing a system of teaching that is unique to himself.

DEFINITION OF THE TERM "TEACHING STYLE"

Teaching style and teaching methodology are two separate yet complementary phenomena. Teaching methodology is based on a standard philosophy of physical education and on the objectives of the physical education program. A physical educator's style of teaching is an expression of himself as an individual and is related to his personal philosophy and objectives. A physical educator adapts his methodology to his teaching style rather than the reverse.

We may thus define teaching style as an observable phenomenon that is an expression of the physical educator's individuality in relation to his stated philosophy and program objectives. Additionally, a physical educator's teaching style is reflected in his methodology of teaching and in his class organization and management.

Historically the term "style" was related to a pen or stylus. Later, it referred to handwriting and eventually to the quality and nature of a literary work. In the psychological sense, as it is used in this chapter, it refers to personality and to individual behavior. Specifically, it refers to the behavior of the teacher in the classroom, gymnasium, swimming pool, playground, or other setting where learning takes place. It encompasses the basic characteristics of teachers as reflected in their personalities, which have implications for their relations with students and their outlook toward learning and teaching.

Some persons have confused teaching style with teaching method. In respect to teaching method, we are referring more to the techniques and procedures used by the teacher in presenting certain subject matter or skills, such as textbooks and audiovisual aids, which are outside the range of personality structure. However, the choice of teaching method is of course influenced by a teacher's personality and behavior.

TEACHING STYLES

There are several types of teaching styles that have been identified by researchers in the field. Some of the more prominent of these styles are discussed for the reader. Hamachek* discusses four personality styles that are reflected in teacher behavior, which he points out were developed clinically by Shapiro.† These styles are the compulsive style, the suspicious style, the hysterical style, and the impulsive style.

---

*Hamachek, Don E.: Personality styles and teacher behavior, The Educational Forum 36:313, 1972.
†Shapiro, D.: Neurotic styles, New York, 1965, Basic Books, Inc.

Compulsive style

Hamachek refers to the teachers who possess this style as "living machines." They are rigid in their schedules and ways of behaving and thinking. A compulsive teacher might be one who is "dogmatic," "opinionated," or "bull-headed." He frequently does not listen to what a student is saying but, instead, spends his time thinking about what he is going to say in response. He is obsessed by detail, whether it be erasing the blackboards every night before he goes home, insisting that students perform a particular skill in exactly the way he demonstrates, or giving back to him in an examination the same information he initially passed on to them. He directs and tells students rather than interacting with them. He is not sensitive to the individual differences that exist among his students. He has limited interests. His classroom is devoid of a social tone—education is serious business, interpersonal dynamics are not a part of the learning process. It is very difficult for him to have "fun" with his students. The teacher with the compulsive style prescribes for his students in light of his own feelings and needs instead of in terms of the students' feelings and needs.

Suspicious style

The suspicious style is, according to Hamachek, a style that is characterized by some "paranoid-like" features. The teacher who has this type of style is often the one who feels the students are plotting against him. He has a guilty and tense feeling about many things that happen and imagines colleagues or other persons are trying to find out about his personal life, so he keeps a "wary eye" on them. Because of his suspicions he finds it difficult to let himself go and enjoy himself or his students. He sees very little fun in teaching and rarely laughs. Since he cannot accept or place trust in himself, he has difficulty in doing the same with others. Therefore he is reluctant to place faith in other people, whether it is a student or a colleague. Teachers who possess the suspicious style also are very conscious of those who possess power or postion and may have an antagonistic relationship with these authority figures. Such teachers are particularly wary of administrators who evaluate them. They feel that the principal or superintendent may evaluate their teaching, for example, in terms of their character or personal habits rather than in terms of their teaching performance.

Hysterical style

The teacher characterized by the hysterical style is different from the other styles discussed, particularly in respect to his being aware of the more colorful events that occur. In fact, the colorful events may be so highlighted by this person that the substance and fact of his teaching may be overlooked. In other words, the reactions of such a teacher may be more in terms of impressions than facts. Such teachers are easily influenced by other persons' feelings, prejudices, fads, and objects or circumstances that excite them. Their attention is captured not so much by the details and facts but by the headlines and sensational happenings that occur. They are the teachers who accentuate rumors about students and colleagues using drugs, engaging in sex, getting traffic tickets, or squandering money at the races. They are apt to think of students in terms of these emotional characterizations and judgments and, in turn, these may affect the manner in which they treat their students. It should be recognized that although the hysterical style may cause many teaching problems, it may also result in teaching behavior that is enthusiastic, colorful, and lively.

Impulsive style

The teacher who possesses this style is characterized by quick action that is unplanned and not carefully thought through. In such cases, judgment may be poor and reckless and result in poor decisions. In turn, these decisions may provide many disappointments. Such persons are unpredictable since behavior is often the result of whim or impulse. They usually are characterized by the immediate concerns of their own lives rather than permanent goals or values. As contrasted with the compulsive teacher, who critically evaluates a problem, the impulsive teacher acts on the spur of the moment, with initial impressions frequently becoming the basis for action.

Reflective style

Murphy and Brown* discuss a teaching style that is referred to as the "reflective" style. This is a style aimed at getting the students to think, analyze, reflect, and conceptualize. It encourages questioning and hypothesizing. The questioning and discussing take place in a climate of freedom and permissiveness, with the teacher serving as a guide rather than occupying a role of dispenser of the truth. There is a very warm, respected relationship between instructor and student that results in a high degree of motivation on the part of the student. The student experiences a feeling of freedom to discuss the subject in terms of his own attitude, experience, and opinion. He is not inhibited. The subject becomes interesting and exciting to students in the democratic atmosphere that is provided.

BASIC TEACHING STYLES

There are two basic kinds of teaching style: teacher-centered and student-centered. Although other styles have been discussed briefly, these two basic styles are discussed much more completely. Of course, there is some overlapping with previously discussed styles.

Teacher-centered style

The teacher-centered physical educator is often described as autocratic. He states his philosophy of physical education in terms of his personal relationship to his

---
*Murphy, Patricia D., and Brown, Marjorie M.: Conceptual systems and teaching styles, American Educational Research Journal 7:529, 1970.

profession and his personal conception of the goals of his profession in relation to his own teaching. His program objectives are stated in terms of what he wishes to accomplish as a teacher, and his evaluation is made in relation to what he has accomplished through his program. For example, the teacher-centered physical educator might list some of the daily objectives of a unit in basketball in the following manner:
1. To teach the dribble
2. To teach the hook shot
3. To teach foul shooting

The autocratic physical educator will evaluate the basketball unit as a successful learning experience if he has indeed taught the dribble, the hook shot, and foul shooting *and* has taught his class to perform these skills to a common standard. The satisfaction for the autocratic physical educator, then, is based not on student success but on teacher accomplishments in terms of teacher-centered objectives. The program evaluation is not derived from observing student success but rather from an analysis of the teaching and its effectiveness in terms of student learning.

The teacher-centered physical educator is somewhat of a perfectionist and expects that all his students will be able to perform a certain skill in the same way. He does realize that not all students have the ability to meet a single standard of performance, but his teaching is frequently geared to those students who can measure up to the physical educator's criteria for success. This teacher tends to feel that he has failed as a teacher when a student falls short of the expected goal. The teacher-centered physical educator strives to guide his students toward the response or action he views as being the correct one in any given situation. In a rules quiz, for example, all the students may correctly answer that there are nine players on a baseball team, They may not know why there are nine players or what the players' duties are, but they have given the correct response, and that accomplishes the goal.

The teacher-centered physical educator

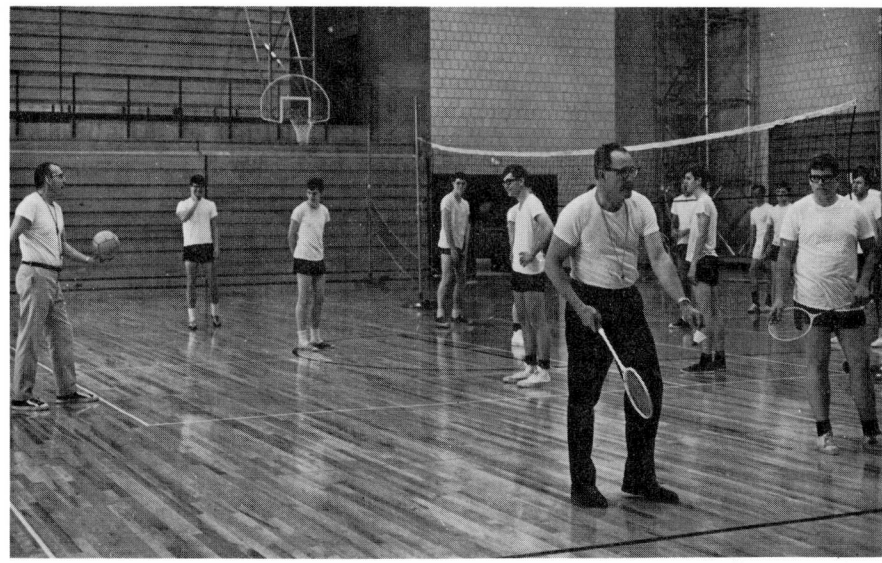

Fig. 12-1. Teaching style is an expression of one's personality. (Ames High School, Ames, Iowa.)

is generally a rather rigid individual, and his rigidity is transferred to the teaching situation. His classes tend to be dull rather than exciting, and his students are more often externally motivated by fear of failure than by an inner-directed desire to succeed. This physical education stylist is often the delight of supervisors and administrators because he demands excellent discipline and maintains tight control over his classes. It is difficult to be able to state accurately, however, whether or not the students in such classes derive any enjoyment from their physical education experience.

In a teacher-dominated physical education class, the instructor is most likely to follow tried and tested methodology rather strictly. This teaching stylist feels that only proved methods and techniques will work, and he resists innovation because he feels that it threatens his effectiveness as a teacher. He sometimes refers to educational innovations as fads that will not be fully accepted because their lasting value has not been demonstrated. A capsule analysis of this stylist would state that he has had one year of teaching experience that has been repeated "x" number of times.

The teacher-centered physical educator is less interested in the individual student than in the student group. He frequently views a class as simply a group of bodies that need to be physically educated. For this reason, the teacher-centered physical educator is less apt to know his students by name than to know them by their physical abilities. He frequently can describe accurately the tumbling, softball, or other skills of the fourth student in the second squad, but he may not know the student's name. His students often feel that they are less important to the teacher than the condition of the gymnasium floor, the cleanliness of the locker room, or the height of the grass on the playing field.

The teacher-centered physical educator is chiefly concerned with the cognitive areas of teaching and less often with the affective areas. He chooses the body of knowledge he will impart to his students and is interested only in their grasp of it as knowledge. He depends on observable motor skills and the scores on written and skill tests to tell him whether or not the knowledge is being absorbed. He is not particularly interested in whether or not his students appreciate, enjoy, or want to participate in certain physical education activities. The right of choosing the activities to be engaged in is reserved for the teacher, and the activity is taught for the sake of the activity.

The teacher-centered stylist feels that he must conform to the philosophy of the school administration, and this is frequently a traditionalist philosophy. Thus, the physical educator believes that it is also his duty to have his students conform, and he feels that this can be accomplished only through a traditional teaching style. In the gymnasium or on the playing field it is the physical educator who demonstrates new skills, and the students are expected to mimic the instructor's technique. Student evaluations are thus subjectively arrived at in relation to their ability to conform, not only in regard to techniques of performing skills but in the areas of behavior and attitude as well. The results of written tests are sometimes discounted if they diverge either way from the physical educator's subjective evaluation of the student.

This style of teaching physical education often helps to stereotype the field as one that stands apart from the rest of the school program. The teacher-centered physical educator is primarily concerned with his relationship to his own field only and tends not to keep abreast of changes in general education. He does not regard changes in general education any more seriously than he regards changes in physical education as being important to his own teaching and professional growth.

Intramural and interscholastic sports programs and physical education clubs are also influenced by the teacher-centered physical educator in much the same way as the class program is influenced. Often, the intramural and club activities offered are not decided on the basis of student need and interest but rather on the basis of what the physical educator thinks the students ought to have.

Under the teacher-centered approach, a student may be barred from joining clubs and intramural teams if he also has an interest in other school clubs and activities.

In some instances, a student whose band rehearsal makes him a few minutes late for a club meeting or game may find himself locked out of the gymnasium or locker room. The teacher-centered physical educator tends to theorize that the student cannot be seriously interested in the after-school program in physical education if he does not make the effort to arrive at the activity on time. This labels the student as a nonconformist in the eyes of the teacher and effectively drives the student away from after-school physical education activities. In some secondary schools, this lack of a cooperative relationship on the part of the physical educator with other school activities results in a marked failure of the intramural and club programs in physical education. Students will seek out and participate in those school activities that answer their needs and interest and that welcome them as individuals who have something to contribute.

With the teacher-centered physical educator, intramural teams in a rigid setting are frequently highly coached. Contests are instructional extensions of the class period rather than games played purely for enjoyment. The physical educator will supervise very closely, and at times he will remove a student from a game if he feels that the student is not "giving his all." He may also stop a contest to correct the skill errors of several players. Frequently, the physical educator will have formed the teams and appointed a captain for each without any student participation, and he will exercise the right to shift players from one team to another.

In varsity sports, the teacher-centered physical educator will dominate the game completely. The physical educator in his role as coach will decide all lineups and lineup changes and direct all game strategy from the bench. In a sport such as football, for example, the coach will send the plays in to the quarterback rather than letting the quarterback direct the offense. A game in which this kind of team goes on to victory is another example of guiding students to the response desired by the teacher. The victory serves as a proof, for the physical educator, of the worth of the teacher-centered style of teaching, but such a victory makes a questionable contribution to the physical, mental, emotional, and social growth of the players involved.

Student-centered style

The student-centered physical educator is sometimes thought of as a democratic teacher. The student-centered physical educator's philosophy is stated in terms of the relationship of physical education to the total educational field and its goals. He conceives of the goals of physical education as running parallel to those of general education. The student-centered physical educator's program objectives are stated in terms of student needs and interests, and his evaluation is based upon how well his program has succeeded in meeting those needs and interests. He might list some of the daily objectives of a unit in tennis in the following manner:

1. To be able to execute the forehand
2. To be able to serve
3. To be able to play a game of doubles

The student-centered physical educator will be pleased with this unit if, among the other basic tennis skills, his students can return the forehand shot into the playing court, serve well enough to keep the ball in play, and cooperate with a partner in playing a game of doubles. This physical educator is not satisfied with teaching minimal skills. Rather, he desires to have his students learn skills as well as they can so that they will find success and pleasure in physical activity. He does not attempt to develop champion players in a sport such as tennis, but he is instead concerned with the ability of his students to be able to play a recreational game of tennis, even if it is played on a beginning level. The student-centered physical educator does not expect or demand that all students attain a common level of skill; rather, he desires that each student attempt to reach his own potential. The satisfaction for this stylist is

based on student success in terms of student-centered objectives. The program evaluation is derived from an observation of student success and from an objective analysis of the teaching in relation to its ability to meet student needs and interests. This physical educator uses his evaluation as a guide to adaptations and modifications that might help him to meet student needs even more effectively.

The student-centered physical educator is especially cognizant of differences in student ability and avoids setting common criteria for skill performances. Instead, he prefers to devise charts or other devices that show the beginning, intermediate, and advanced level of performance for each skill or combination of skills. Each student can use these criteria to judge his own progress and performance and to attempt to move from the beginning to the more advanced levels according to his individual potential. Thus each student progresses at his own most comfortable rate and can thus find success that is meaningful to him as an individual. Because there are no artificial or induced standards toward which each student must strive, there is less chance for failure. The student-centered physical educator attempts to gear his teaching to each individual in the class rather than to any one similarly skilled group of individuals. The teaching is then on a more personalized basis, and there is a decided emphasis on remedial help for those who need it, as well as on coaching tips for those who are more advanced. The student-centered physical educator strives to help his students reach their own goals in regard to motor skill ability.

The student-centered physical educator is usually very flexible. In the teaching situation he will alter or adapt a lesson if he sees that it is not accomplishing its purpose. He will frequently make other on-the-spot changes if his class seems unusually tired or if a dreary day leads to student lethargy. He will devise unique games or activities that will help to rekindle student interest and enthusiasm, or he will place a unique

Fig. 12-2. Girls' swimming class at Ames High School, Ames, Iowa.

lesson in the program merely to provide a break in routine. His classes are exciting to watch, and his students are enthusiastic about the class because they find it stimulating and challenging. These students have an inner motivation to succeed because they are encouraged to operate as individuals and to succeed as individuals. This helps them to discipline their own behavior. At times, this physical educator is criticized by supervisors and administrators because the noise emanating from the gymnasium or playing field is interpreted as a lack of control on the part of the physical educator, rather than being recognized as the sounds of boys and girls responding enthusiastically to their physical education experience. Discipline is an undertone, not a fear-inducing characteristic of the class period.

The student-centered physical educator welcomes innovations because he feels that he is contributing to his students, to his profession, and to his own professional growth through the use of the latest techniques and methodology. He will, for example, adopt the principles of movement education, giving them an objective and sufficiently lengthy trial before accepting them as a permanent part of his program or rejecting them because they make a questionable contribution to his students. He judges innovations on student relevance rather than on how they relate to him as a teacher. This stylist also appreciates traditional methodology, but he does not view it as unchanging or unchangeable. Each new school year represents new techniques and methodologies to be tested, new activities to introduce, new individuals to guide through the physical education experience, new challenges to be met, and new personal experiences to be gained.

The student-centered physical educator is interested in each student as an individual and realizes that physical education makes a unique contribution to the individual that is made by no other phase of the school program. This physical educator knows each student by name and can accurately describe each student's physical education needs, interests, and abilities. He is interested in his students as whole human beings and willingly gives of his time for individual guidance and counseling. His students prize him as a teacher because they know that he views them as the most important part of the physical education program.

This physical educator attempts to teach his students to think for themselves, to be creative, to express themselves, and to ask questions. He is concerned with the cognitive objectives of physical education, but he is also especially concerned with the affective objectives. He is vitally interested in having his students become aware of the values of physical activity and the varieties of physical activity. He wants them to enjoy and appreciate physical activity, to seek out new activities, and to participate in them on their own. This teacher employs a conceptual approach to physical education so that his students will be able to base their knowledge of physical activity on scientific understanding. When new activities are introduced or new units initiated, the students understand the value of, and need for, that activity, aside from the fact that the activity is required by a syllabus.

The student-centered physical educator believes in a balance of activities presented in a logical progression, but he also very strongly feels that his students should be able to select the activities that appeal to them. Rather than dictating the activity for each unit, the physical educator will present his students with a list of several activities that will fulfill the same student needs as indicated by their motor ability and physical fitness test scores. If there is more than one teacher, the class may be divided into two interest groups. If there is only one teacher, the class may decide to select one activity, or the classes may be so arranged that two activities can be covered.

Some student-centered physical educators will extend the number of class periods allocated to a unit in order to assure meeting the needs and interests of the students.

The student-centered physical educator is also interested in conforming to administrative dicta, but he does not view this as a hindrance to his program or to his desire to utilize the latest thinking in physical education. Before adopting any new method or technique that might be viewed as radically different, he will present his plan to his superiors for approval, showing how he hopes that the innovation will make the physical education experience more meaningful for his students. This physical educator further realizes that there are many alternatives in teaching and is willing to test any alternative that seems pertinent and logical. He also knows that his performance of a skill is not necessarily the best way for his students to perform it. He takes variations in body build, flexibility, strength, endurance, and experience into account and enlists students to demonstrate a variety of techniques for their fellow classmates. This helps his students to understand that there is more than one acceptable technique in performing a skill.

Student evaluations, for the student-centered physical educator, are based on many objective measures. He does not believe that a single grade should be given to a student, especially when the grade is expected to include skill, attitude, and behavioral outcomes. This physical educator prefers to evaluate his students in a written, comprehensive statement that is more meaningful than a letter or number grade. Some secondary schools have permitted their physical education staffs to devise a separate physical education evaluation form based on just such a statement and including places for noting test scores and other factors. Such evaluation forms give a total picture of student progress.

The student-centered physical educator is interested in his own field as well as in the other areas of the curriculum. He reads professional journals and attempts to understand the changes being made in general education. He views education and physical education as dynamic, and he is aware of their many interrelationships and interdependencies. Through his reading and meetings with other professionals, he strives to grow as a teacher in conjunction with the growth of education and physical education as professional fields of endeavor.

Intramural and interscholastic sports, as well as physical education clubs, are student-centered when the physical educator is student-centered. The intramural and club activities offered are directly related to student needs and interests. There are frequently different programs for students in different grades. For example, in the fall season ninth-grade girls may be offered soccer and speedball, while senior girls may be offered field hockey and lacrosse. Similarly, ninth-grade boys may have programs in soccer and track events, while there is a touch football and field event offering for senior boys.

The student-centered physical educator wants his students to be interested in all phases of the school program. He will work cooperatively with the art, drama, or music teachers to plan a schedule of after-school events that will not conflict, or he may set aside a special day for students whose diversity of interest makes cooperative scheduling difficult.

Intramural teams are organized by the students under the supervision of the physical educator, and captains are elected by the vote of team members. The games are played for their recreational value, regardless of the skill levels of the various players. While the intramural program is considered to be an extension of the class program, it is regarded not as a teaching-learning situation but as an opportunity for each student to practice his skills and to enjoy the use of them in an activity of his own choosing. Team lineups, substitutions, and the conduct of the intramural games will be student-directed. The teacher will

supervise, but he will never control or dominate the games.

Varsity sports will also be student-directed. Although the physical educator will be directly responsible, as coach, for the overall administration of the team, the players themselves will take the most important role. Lineups, lineup changes, and game strategy will evolve from a dialogue between the players and the physical educator. Additionally, the quarterback in football or the catcher in baseball will have the responsibility for calling the game plays, with the physical educator suggesting plays only when the situation demands it. In victory, the glory belongs wholly to the players, and in defeat they will have learned invaluable lessons that will lead to future victories. The student-centered approach makes a definite contribution to the physical, mental, emotional, and social growth and development of the students and athletes in such a program because student initiative is the keynote.

Teacher-centered style versus student-centered style

Both the teacher-centered physical educator and the student-centered physical educator are equally knowledgeable about their subject matter. It is only their *approach* to teaching this subject matter that really differs. While the subject matter is the prime focus of the former, the latter focuses on the student in the teaching-learning situation.

Neither style of teaching is perfect, nor is either free of disadvantages. Both styles have their merits, and both have been used successfully by many different teachers of many different subjects. Each style has been described from a puristic, theoretical point of view so that differences would be more easily recognized and understood, but it must be remembered that teachers tend to borrow elements of both styles and incorporate them into their own unique teaching systems.

In practice, physical educators may shift from style to style, depending on the particular lesson. In teaching team and dual sports, the physical educator may use an approach that is closer to the teacher-centered style, and he may do this for a variety of reasons. For example, he may have a class, or several classes, that have not developed the maturity required for a student-centered approach, or the physical educator may want to teach a skill and have only a limited amount of time. This same physical educator may find that these same classes benefit most from the student-centered approach when its use is limited to such creative-expressive activities as dance, tumbling, gymnastics, swimming, and other individual sports. It is also possible to use the teacher-centered style during one part of a class period and the student-centered style during another part of the same class period.

A physical educator may use the teacher-centered style in his class program and in a varsity coaching situation but prefer the student-centered style for the intramural and club program, or the reverse may be true. Any number of combinations of teaching style may be observed in the individual physical educator, depending upon the activity, the needs of the students, and the physical educator's assessment of the most appropriate style for the situation.

The two teaching styles are not exclusive, and they do overlap. A physical educator may, in fact, state his objectives and goals in student-centered terms, yet instruct through the teacher-centered style. However, the predominating style in use at the time will be readily identifiable to the observer.

PHILOSOPHY AND TEACHING STYLE

There are five major philosophies that influence education, educational thought, and teaching style. These philosophies are idealism, realism, pragmatism, naturalism, and existentialism. The ability to understand the key concepts of these philosophies and to relate these concepts to education helps a physical educator to articulate a philosophy of his profession and guides him in developing a teaching style that reflects his personal philosophy.

Idealism and teaching style

Idealism is a heritage from the ancient Greek thinkers and philosophers. The idealist places universal ideas at the center of the universe and says that these ideas represent absolute and universal reality. Further, the idealist believes very strongly in man's powers of reasoning and intuition.

In regard to education, the idealist feels that the quest for knowledge is inner-directed and that the creativity and thought processes of the student are personal to him. The role of the teacher is to supply a learning atmosphere and mold the mind of the learner.

The idealist regards physical education as more than a purely physical experience. He expects the physical education program to provide opportunities for mental, social, and emotional growth as well. The idealist would strongly support a physical education program that encouraged student initiative and creativity and furthered his intellectual attainment. Having the student understand the *why* of the activity would be approved. The teacher would be looked upon as the possessor of all culture and worthy of emulation by the student. The emphasis would be centered upon seeing how nearly the pupil could achieve the ideal.

Realism and teaching style

Realism as a philosophy took hold as an entity during the late nineteenth and early twentieth centuries, although its roots are as old as those of idealism. The realist places the laws of nature at the center of the universe and supports the scientific method as the best way of seeking and gaining knowledge.

Mathematics and science are, to the realist, the core of the educative process. The educative process as a whole is thought of as a system of learning how to acquire knowledge, acquiring knowledge, and putting knowledge to use. The role of the teacher is to be objective in methodology, testing, and student evaluation. The development of standardized tests was influenced by the philosophy of realism.

The realist values physical education because he feels that the physical education experience helps the student to learn to adjust to the world. The outcome of the activity in terms of student adjustment is of prime importance to the realist. He would prefer a scientifically formulated program that follows a logical sequence. However, any activities offered in the program would have to be justified as valuable on the basis of scholarly research. He would require that student evaluations be derived from the results of objective tests. The realist would approve of a physical education program that had a teacher strong in scientific procedures.

Pragmatism and teaching style

Pragmatism is considered to be an American philosophy in its modern concept. The word "pragmatism" was first used in the 1800's, the approximate time this philosophy began to evolve out of its earlier form, which was known as experimentalism. Pragmatism is the philosophy associated with John Dewey.

The pragmatist is a flexible man who believes in change, in man's integration with his world, and in the scientific method. The pragmatist places experience at the center of his universe because he feels that man cannot know, or prove, anything that he has not personally experienced.

Dewey said that experience is the key to learning and that the problem-solving method gives the student the experience he needs in order to learn. The pragmatist stresses individual differences between students and demands a student-centered school. The role of the teacher is to inspire, guide, and lead the student through a variety of problem-solving activities.

The pragmatist demands a physical education program that meets the needs of the individual student. A wide variety of activities, with emphasis on creativity, is of prime importance. Rigidity and formality, which are inherent in drills and exercises, would not receive the approval of the pragmatist. He believes in providing activities that arise from the interests and experiences of the student and in adapting the activity to the student. He also prefers that students sample innovative activities, that they be involved in deciding curriculum content, and that they participate as equals in program planning.

Naturalism and teaching style

Naturalism is the oldest philosophy known to the western world. It shares many of the concepts of realism and pragmatism because it has had a strong influence on the development of these philosophies.

The naturalist places at the center of the universe only those things that exist in actuality. In other words, only material or physical things have significance. The naturalist values society as a whole but is more concerned with each man as an individual.

Naturalist thought has influenced the development of the educational philosophies of realism and pragmatism. The naturalist desires a student-centered school in which the educational process is geared to the growth, needs, and interests of each individual student. The problem-solving method is important to the naturalist, who feels that the role of the teacher is to guide the student through the process of investigation by the use of example and scientific demonstration.

The naturalist believes in a wide variety of physical activity and in vigorous exercise. All activities in his program must be geared to the student as an individual rather than as part of a larger group. The program should follow the natural pattern of the student's growth and development.

Existentialism and teaching style

Existentialism emerged as a philosophy in the late nineteenth century but did not receive significant recognition until after World War II. Existentialism is a thoroughly modern philosophy.

The concept of the individuality of man forms the core of existentialism. The existentialist believes that each man guides his own destiny, determines his own system of values, and occupies a place that is superior to that of the society at large.

The existentialist says that education is an adventure in the discovery of self and that the schools must be totally student-centered so that the individual student will not be hindered in his attempts at discovery. The existentialist advocates that the student be given full freedom to learn what he is interested in learning at the time he is interested in learning it. The student selects not only the subject matter but the method through which learning will take place. Norms, standardized tests, and group tests would be entirely eliminated in favor of an individual evaluative process. The role of the teacher is to monitor the learning environment and to supply the needed tools and opportunity for learning, as well as to serve as a stimulus for the student.

In regard to physical education, the existentialist would prefer a balanced and varied program that has something for everyone. Additionally, the existentialist would prefer that each student have freedom in the choice of activities and that he be responsible for disciplining himself, guiding his own learning, and evaluating his own progress. The teaching approach most preferred by the existentialist is that of the physical educator who is completely student-centered.

DEVELOPMENT OF A TEACHING STYLE

A teaching style develops gradually and is unique to each physical educator because of the myriad individual variations and shadings that may be applied to a style. There are various influences, however, that affect the development of an individual's teaching style. Two of the most important influences are the undergraduate professional preparation program and the student-teaching experience. A third influ-

Fig. 12-3. Boys' physical education class at Ames High School, Ames, Iowa.

ence is the philosophy of the school system in which the beginning teacher matures.

Influence of the undergraduate professional preparation program

It is in the undergraduate years that the future physical educator first explores the nonactivity aspects of physical education. Courses in the history and philosophy of education, psychology and other of the behavioral sciences, and physical education, in principles and practice of physical education, and in organization and administration of physical education form a foundation of understanding and comprehension of the breadth and depth of the field. Through such courses the future physical educator begins to form a personal philosophy of physical education. He is often required, as an adjunct to these courses, or in methods and materials courses, to formulate a series of objectives for physical education, to plan course outlines and curriculum content, and to write lesson plans.

The philosophy and teaching style of the undergraduate instructors have a profound influence on the development of the student's teaching style. In general, a department will decide upon how the students in that department are to write their objectives and construct the lesson plans that will carry out these objectives. The decision may dictate student-centered terminology or teacher-centered terminology, or some kind of compromise terminology. However, the point is too infrequently made that there is more than one way of writing objectives and that there is more than one style of teaching that will carry out the objectives satisfactorily. Experience in teaching gained in methods courses further influences and reinforces the dictated teaching style. It is this method of phrasing objectives and this style of teaching that is brought to the student-teaching experience.

Influence of the student-teaching experience

The student-teaching experience is often described as the culminating experience of the future physical educator's undergraduate preparation. This culminating experience is at times a traumatic one for the student teacher, but it is an invaluable experience because it provides an opportunity for further development of, or drastic modification in, teaching style.

Not all the master teachers associated with a particular undergraduate school will state their objectives or design their lesson plans in exactly the same way. There may be many variations, and the student teacher who has begun to develop a student-centered style may find that his master teacher advocates a rigidly teacher-centered style. These stylistic differences can be a source of friction between the student teacher and the master teacher. It is typically the student teacher who adapts his teaching style in order to gain the approval of the master teacher and in order to ensure a favorable evaluation at the end of the student-teaching experience.

The master teacher has an obligation to the student teacher but an even stronger obligation to the students being taught. Secondary school students are adaptable, and a change in teaching style at the beginning of a new unit will not have a detrimental effect on the students. A change in the middle of a unit could be less than beneficial. It is of no value to the student teacher to follow the example of the master teacher without question. Conferences between the two individuals can open doors to understanding, however, and may result in an enjoyable and worthwhile experience for both the master teacher and the student teacher.

Influence of the philosophy of the school system

The beginning teacher may or may not have a well-defined teaching style, depending upon the strength of his undergraduate experience and his willingness to express himself as an individual in the teaching situation. The initial weeks of full-fledged teaching give the beginning teacher an opportunity to evaluate further his undergraduate and student-teaching experiences.

In a one-teacher department, the beginning teacher will be free to test both teaching styles and to make adaptations, modifications, and compromises. Where there are several teachers in a department, the probationary teacher may be required to adhere to a preferred departmental style. In either case, the philosophy of the school system as a whole will give the beginning teacher clues as to how much innovation he can attempt.

The beginning teacher may find that he is free to innovate and to teach by any style he wishes. He may find that he must shift his teaching style frequently until he finds a style that he considers most comfortable and to which his students react best. An experienced teacher, too, will modify and change his teaching style from time to time as student needs and interests change.

IDEAL TEACHING STYLE

There is no one ideal teaching style. Each physical educator may find that the suitability of a particular teaching style depends on the circumstances and the teaching situation.

Teaching style must be the physical educator's unique expression of his role in relation to the role of his students. The value system of the students balanced against the value system of the physical educator will help to influence the choice of a teaching style.

Teaching style should be viewed as dynamic rather than static. As student needs change and as the profession of physical education grows, the teaching style should be adapted to keep abreast of this growth and change. Fear of attempting the new and untried impedes the professional growth of the physical educator, but a willingness to be flexible enhances the physical educator as a professional member of a professional field of endeavor.

The kind of teacher a person becomes will depend upon the kind of person he is. These two factors cannot be separated because they are so closely interwoven and related. The student-teaching experience, *as well as the actual teaching experience that comes later on, should reflect this important concept. The methods and materials used are important. However, it should never be forgotten that the process of teaching is never more important than the person who is doing the teaching. It is not only necessary for the prospective teacher to know about personality theories, it is even more important to know about his own personality.*

POINTS TO REMEMBER

1. The teacher should be able to exercise his individuality and creativity.
2. The student should be able to exercise his individuality and creativity.
3. A physical educator's style of teaching is an expression of himself as an individual.
4. Teaching style is an observable phenomenon.
5. The teacher-centered physical educator is often autocratic.
6. The student-centered physical educator tends to be democratic.
7. The physical educator's philosophy of education influences his teaching style.
8. There is no ideal teaching style.

PROBLEMS TO THINK THROUGH

1. How can methods and materials courses be changed so that they take more cognizance of individual teaching styles?
2. How closely aligned are teaching style and teaching methodology?
3. How can the area of affective learning take place more effectively under the teacher-centered style?
4. How can we objectively evaluate teaching style in terms of student need?
5. How can we justify the teacher- or coach-dominated activity or sport in terms of contributions to student creativity and initiative?
6. How can a physical educator determine whether his teaching style is unique to himself?

CASE STUDY FOR ANALYSIS

A student teacher finds that his teaching style and that of his master teacher are directly opposite. The student teacher feels that he is obligated to follow the example set by the master teacher, but he wishes to test his own theories, methods, and style of teaching. He hesitates to assert himself because he fears that he may be given a poor evaluation as a result. What steps should he take to resolve his dilemma?

EXERCISES FOR REVIEW

1. What are the characteristics of the teacher-centered style?

2. What are the characteristics of the student-centered style?
3. Under what circumstances should a physical educator change his teaching style?
4. How do the individual philosophies of education influence teaching style?
5. What factors help to determine the development of a teaching style?
6. Show why it is true that teaching style is dynamic rather than static.

SELECTED READINGS

American Association for Health, Physical Education, and Recreation: Becoming a better teacher (special journal feature), Journal of Health, Physical Education, and Recreation 32:17, 1961.

Bruner, Jerome S.: Toward a theory of instruction, Cambridge, Mass., 1966, Harvard University Press.

Conant, James B.: The education of American teachers, New York, 1963, McGraw-Hill Book Co., Inc.

Durant, Will: The story of philosophy, New York, 1961, Washington Square Press, Inc.

Fischer, Louis: Teaching style and religion in the classroom, The Educational Forum 32:211, 1968.

Gage, N. L.: Can science contribute to the art of teaching? Phi Delta Kappan 49:399, 1968.

Hamachek, Don E.: Personality styles and teacher behavior, The Educational Forum 36:313, 1972.

Hyman, Ronald T.: Teaching: triadic and dynamic, The Educational Forum 32:65, 1967.

Joyce, B., and others: Conceptual development and information processing: a study of teachers, Journal of Educational Research 59:219, 1966.

Katz, Jeffrey M.: Seniors view their student teaching, Kappa Delta Pi Record 4:75, 1968.

Lemen, Mildred: Implications of the problem-solving method for physical educators, Journal of Health, Physical Education, and Recreation 37:28, 1966.

Mood, Alexander M.: How teachers make a difference, Washington, D. C., 1971, U. S. Department of Health, Education and Welfare.

Murphy, Patricia D., and Brown, Marjorie M.: Conceptual systems and teaching styles, American Educational Research Journal 7:529, 1970.

Shapiro, D.: Neurotic styles, New York, 1965, Basic Books, Inc.

Solomon, Daniel: Teaching styles and learning, Chicago, 1963, The Center for the Study of Liberal Education.

Washburne, C., and Heil, L. M.: What characteristics of teachers affect children's growth? Scholastic Review 68:420, 1960.

Webb, Dwight: Teacher sensitivity—affective impact on students, Journal of Teacher Education 22:4, 1971.

PART FOUR
TEACHING PHYSICAL EDUCATION

13 THE TEACHING-LEARNING PROCESS

The application of learning theories to teaching, particularly in respect to instruction in motor skills, has been one of the major emphases in physical education during recent years. For too long little attention has been paid to what kind of teaching takes place and how skills should be taught. At the present time, however, the research is being done with the findings applied to what is taught in physical education classes. Much of this emphasis, of course, emanates from the field of psychology.

The teaching-learning process implies a duality of effort between the student and the teacher. The student learns from all the factors in his environment, but it is the school that is primarily responsible for formal learning through the educative process. Teaching and learning are synchronized into a process that is ongoing, developmental, and dynamic in nature. The teaching-learning process has many phases, each of which is vitally important to the process of education.

TEACHING

Learning is generally defined as an observable change in behavior. Teachers attempt to bring about positive behavioral changes through their classroom involvement with the student. To enhance learning, a teacher strives to provide the student with a favorable classroom environment that is conducive to learning. Teaching carries with it a twofold responsibility: the structuring of the learning material, and the provision of a desirable learning atmosphere. The structuring of the learning material will be dealt with in depth in the next chapter. This chapter is concerned with aspects of the learning environment itself.

Nature of a favorable environment

If the teaching process is to be enhanced, several environmental factors need careful consideration. Each factor stems from basic individual needs and may be categorized according to four major areas of concern:

1. Physical needs
   a. Heat. Temperatures should be maintained within a comfortable range so that students do not become drowsy from too much heat or overstimulated from too much cold.
   b. Light. Proper lighting in all classroom areas protects and aids students' vision.
   c. Ventilation. Proper circulation of fresh air is important to the health and comfort of everyone in the classroom.
   d. Equipment. Equipment should be in safe condition, adequate to the number of students in the class, and of the proper size and weight for the particular age level.
   e. Facilities. Adequate and safe facilities are a necessity for proper conduct of classes.
2. Emotional needs—A positive approach should be maintained in the handling of students and their problems. The National Association for Mental Health lists several factors essential to good mental health that have significance in the school situation:
   a. Acceptance. The student should feel that he is accepted as a person of worth by his teachers and his peers.
   b. Security. The student should know what is expected of him as a person and as a student.

237

c. Protection. The student should not be made to feel that either his peers or his teachers have marked him as a failure or potential failure.
d. Control. The student should understand and abide by proper standards of good conduct and courteous behavior.
e. Independence. The student should feel that he has the freedom to express himself as an individual as long as he does not impinge on the rights of others.
f. Guidance. The student's efforts and successes need to be constructively criticized, praised, and recognized.
3. Social needs—Democratic group processes recognize both the larger group and the individual within the group.
a. Cooperation. Through cooperative efforts with his peers the student should feel that he is making an individual contribution to the larger group.
b. Competition. Through controlled competition with his peers the student should feel gratification in success, experience the adventure of competing, gain pride in accomplishment, and know the satisfaction that comes from wholehearted effort.
c. Grouping. Through grouping techniques students should be placed in groups where they will feel most comfortable and where they will be encouraged to work to their capacity.
d. Rapport. Good teacher-student relationships help the student to feel that he is respected as an individual.
4. Intellectual needs—Not all students' intellectual needs can be met in the same way, and not all students function best in a single kind of learning situation. Some students learn best in a democratic environment where they are encouraged to be creative through a problem-solving approach. These students have the maturity to be able to conceptualize knowledge and come to their own conclusions through personal discovery. Other students function best in a rather rigidly teacher-dominated situation because they are not as yet ready to help guide their own learning. A single classroom may contain either type of student, or students who alternate between the two systems, depending on the material to be learned. Only through a comprehensive knowledge of each student can the teacher determine how each individual learns best and adapt the teaching methods as the need dictates.

Creation of a favorable environment

The preceding discussion outlines the basic factors necessary for the creation of an environment in which learning may take place. Yet each of these components must be combined so that an effective teaching-learning atmosphere is created.

Fig. 13-1. Girl performing on rings at Guymon Junior High School, Guymon, Okla.

If, for example, each factor is present save one, the atmosphere will not be as conducive to the educational process as it might be. An overheated gymnasium, a poorly ventilated locker room, or a teacher who concentrates only on the students with high motor skill ability will each have a negative effect on the teaching-learning atmosphere. The physical needs, such as heating, lighting, and ventilation, are often only minor problems that can be corrected at once if difficulties arise. However, the social, emotional, and intellectual needs of the students need much more care and attention. The complexity of these needs and their interdependencies demand far greater consideration from the teacher and far more time and effort. Meeting these needs usually is possible only through the establishment of effective teacher-pupil relationships. Unless the teacher is willing to

Chester Studios, Inc., New York

Fig. 13-2. The teacher needs to provide for the safety of the student. (Yonkers Public Schools, Yonkers, N. Y.)

become sincerely involved with his students, effective learning cannot take place, no matter how ideal the physical environment may be. This genuine involvement with the student sets the teacher apart from the teaching machine and gains for him or her professional respect. Good teacher-student relationships provide one of the most vital keys to successful teaching and learning. This particular relationship is probably most noticeable in the physical education classroom or on the athletic field, where the physical educator is not only a teacher of skills but a counselor of students as well.

Effective teacher-student relationships

The establishment of effective teacher-student relationships is dependent directly on the individuals involved in the educative process. The teacher must enjoy teaching, be patient and firm, know the subject matter, and know the growth and developmental characteristics of the students, as well as their needs and interests. A survey of secondary school students revealed that the outstanding characteristic a teacher should possess is understanding.

Effective teacher-student relations are frequently a direct outgrowth of the style of teaching or type of classroom control utilized by the teacher. For example, two teachers in charge of similar teaching situations might exhibit totally different personalities and require entirely different behavioral characteristics from their students. While one teacher might be autocratic, demanding immediate and strict obedience to directions and commands, the other might be a more informal disciplinarian who expects a measure of self-control from the students. The first teacher described would demand respect from the students and would teach in a cold atmosphere, while the second teacher would command the respect of the students and maintain a warm relationship with them.

There are three major categories of classroom control that relate to the effectiveness of the teaching situation. Two have been briefly described in the preceding paragraph, but there is also the *laissez-faire* type of teacher who elicits still a different kind of control.

1. Autocratic control. The teacher dominates the classroom and the students, gives commands, and expects high standards to be met in regard to discipline.
2. Laissez-faire control. The students are given almost complete freedom within the classroom while the teacher simply observes or monitors the situation. Little is required in the way of discipline, and the class is frequently out of control.
3. Democratic control. The students share in all of the classroom processes and are expected to be able to exert some self-discipline.

The type of physical education teacher who fits each of these descriptions is familiar to most observers. The autocrat is the domineering, drill-sergeant type. The laissez-faire physical educator is the one who merely throws out the ball to let the students play as they will. The democratic teacher tends to listen to the students and share the planning for the class with them. Although learning does take place in all three situations, the democratic physical educator would be the one most likely to have developed the warmest rapport with the students and would be the most understanding of the students and their individual needs.

Individualized approach

At the present time in education, trends in all subject-matter areas point toward meeting individual student needs. Students are being offered opportunities for independent study and research and are taking a larger share in their own education and its direction.

Examples of individualized programming in physical education can be seen in a class where each student is given the freedom to work independently on the skills within an assigned unit, attempting to improve according to his own capacities and abilities. In a basketball unit, for example, some more highly skilled students might work on shooting ten consecutive

Fig. 13-3. Badminton class at Ames High School, Ames, Iowa.

foul shots, while students of lower ability might work at another basket on simply improving their shooting technique in order to make a single successful shot.

To accomplish this type of teaching, the teacher must have a comprehensive knowledge of each of the students in the program. He must know the students' needs, their interests, and their individual abilities. While this individualized approach requires greater effort on the part of the teacher, there are many rewards in terms of student learning and teacher effectiveness.

LEARNING

Learning is a change or alteration in behavior and in general depends upon three major factors: heredity, the home environment, and the learning opportunities provided by the school. One study of high school students indicated that their high academic standings were 70% attributable to heredity, while the home and the school contributed 30%.*

Heredity

Nature versus nurture as a contributing factor in personality development has long fascinated educators and psychologists. They are especially interested in the extent to which the genetic makeup of an individual affects the outcome of his developmental nature. Present-day knowledge has now reached the point where science feels that genetic makeup will someday be able to be altered so that individuals can be produced who have desired, predetermined characteristics. In their studies of the makeup of intelligence, psychologists are finding that it may be possible to control portions of the intellect through the administration of such agents as ribonucleic acid. The significance of these discoveries holds many implications for education and physical education. Teachers need to remain up to date on discoveries and advances in these

vital areas. Teachers need to know how these changes will affect the classrooms of the future and the physical abilities of the students of the future.

Home environment

Community and governmental agencies have long been striving to improve the environmental factors that serve as strong educational forces. Better homes, better jobs, better wages, and improved working conditions have been denied large segments of the population. In the typical middle-class home, books and conversation are a part of life and a way of life. In the homes of the disadvantaged, books are a rarity, and the home can be of little aid in preparing the child for school and an education. A few significant advances have been made in respect to the disadvantaged. Project Head Start, for example, was believed to be a help in preparing preschoolers for their first formal educational experience by offering the childhood experiences that are lacking in the home. Improved living conditions for the lower socioeconomic groups many someday in the future make these homes vital contributors to the educational process. Teachers need to realize that not all students come from homes in which education is a potent force and that not all students are prepared for the challenge of school.

The school

As time goes on, computerized education may bring about many changes in the structure of the school. Through computers, a student may be able to obtain references from sources across the country or retrieve information in a short period of time rather than spend hours of research in a variety of books and reference materials. The teacher may become more of a guide through the machine-controlled process, giving the praise, encouragement, and personal help that the machine cannot give. Some of these changes have already come about in school systems, but until computers are utilized on a national scale,

---

*Coyne, Walter A.: Presidental scholars, American Education 3:6, 1967.

the school will still depend on the teacher and his training and abilities. In spite of the move toward computers, the teacher will still be the center of the educational process, for it is the teacher who must decide what the machine can do for each student, and it is the teacher who must evaluate what the machine is doing for the student. It is also the teacher who provides the human factor upon which good teaching and learning will always depend.

The school must ask itself what vital conditions and characteristics of a learning situation most influence a student during the developmental years. By knowing these determinants the school can adjust and adapt to future educational developments in every curricular area. By knowing the determinants of learning, the school will better be able to meet its responsibilities to its students.

Learning process

Learning does not take place simply because the proper atmosphere exists or because the physical tools for learning, such as books, pencils, or athletic equipment, are available. In order for learning to take place, there must first of all be an individual who is motivated to learn, incentives that will increase the motivation, challenges that make reaching the learning goal an adventure, and continued effort on the part of the individual to overcome the challenges and arrive at the goal.

While all individuals are capable of learning, not all individuals learn at the same rate or in the same manner. Not all learners can be reached by a common methodology or teaching style. Many different kinds of learning styles have been identified, and learners tend to use each of these styles in varying degrees, depending on the material or concepts to be learned. Some learners are completely verbal-oriented, for example, while other learners succeed best when the problem-solving technique is used. Memorization, concept formation, and trial-and-error learning are other examples of learning styles.

The incentives offered for learning are vital to the educational process because they enhance motivation. Grades for achievement, placement in a higher ability group, and teacher praise and recognition are forms of incentives that are commonly used in education.

The challenges presented to the learner also help to increase the individual's motivation to solve a learning problem. If a learning task is too easy and the goal is reached without much effort on the part of the learner, very little real learning can take place. As the individual overcomes a variety of challenges that are set in his path and as he draws closer to his goal, he learns—that is, each individual's success in overcoming a challenge is a true learning experience. However, no challenge should be so difficult that eventual goal attainment is made an impossibility.

In order to learn and to retain what he has learned, the individual must put forth a continued effort in order to overcome the challenges in his path and in order to arrive at his goal. A learner may experience failure in his first attempts at learning, but as he continues to try, he will reach a successful response in a given situation. As the learner continues to put forth effort, he will continue to make more and more successful responses that lead to goal attainment.

THEORIES OF LEARNING

Psychologists have attempted to explain the phenomenon of learning and to answer such questions as how it best takes place and what the laws are under which it operates. The basic theories of learning, for purposes of discussion, may be said to be divided into two broad categories. The first category may be called the connectionist theories. These theories state that learning consists of a bond or connection between a stimulus and a response or responses. The second category may be called cognitive theories. Those psychologists that support these theories feel that the various perceptions beliefs, or attitudes (cognitions or mental images) that a human being has concerning his environment determine what type of behavior the human being will have. The manner in which these "cognitions" are modified by the experience that the human being has indicates the learning that takes place. The basic principles underlying the cognitive theories were developed by the Gestalt psychologists.

Thorndike's laws of learning

E. L. Thorndike, a psychologist whose theories of learning have had a great impact on educators and education, believed in a stimulus-response theory, or S-R bond theory. His laws of readiness, exercise, and effect have influenced educational programs.

Thorndike developed these laws that set forth the conditions under which learning best takes place. Because psychology is a relatively new science and because there are many contradictory views as to various psychological principles, laws of learning should not be regarded as the final word. However, they are working principles and, as such, deserve the attention of all physical educators who desire to seek the most efficient and effective ways of teaching.

Law of readiness. The law of readiness means that an individual will learn much more effectively and rapidly if he is "ready" —if he has matured to the point and if there is a felt need. Learning will be satisfying if materials are presented when an individual meets these standards. This law also works in reverse. It will be annoying and dissatisfying to do something when the individual is not ready. The closer an individual is to reaching the point of readiness, the more satisfying the act.

In physical education activities the teacher should determine whether the child is ready in respect to various sensory and kinesthetic mechanisms and in respect to strength in some cases. The teacher should ask such questions as: Does the student have the capacity, at this time, for certain skills? Does he have the proper background of experience? Is the material being presented timely? Should it be postponed until some future time, or is now the time to present

it? Most physical educators agree, for example, that athletic competition on an interscholastic basis should not be part of the program for elementary school children. The child is not mentally, emotionally, and physically ready for such an experience. There is also considerable agreement that fine-muscle activity should not play too pronounced a part in the program for young children. Instead, their program should largely consist of activities that involve the large muscles.

The law of readiness also has implications for the learning of skills. An adult has difficulty hitting a baseball, riding a bicycle, throwing a football, and performing other physical activities if he has not developed some skill in these activities during his youth. During youth, on the other hand, individuals can perform reasonably well in these skills without too much difficulty. They are at the proper maturation level for the learning of such skills, and their neuromuscular equipment has developed to a point where skills are learned more economically and effectively. They do not mind passing through an awkward trial-and-error period. Physical educators should bear this in mind and set as their goal the development in youth of many interesting and varied skills. In this way students will have the foundational equipment when they reach adulthood to engage in a variety of physical education activities that will provide many enjoyable hours of wholesome recreation.

Law of exercise. The law of exercise, in respect to the development of skills in physical education, means that practice makes for better coordination, more rhythmical movement, less expenditure of energy, more skill, and better performance. As a result of practice, the pathway between stimulus and response becomes more pronounced and permanent.

In many ways this law of learning is similar to the law of use and disuse. As a result of continual practice, strength is gained, but as a result of disuse, weakness ensues.

Learning in education is acquired by

doing. In order to master the skill of bowling, swimming, or handball a person must practice. However, it should be restated that practice does not necessarily ensure perfection of the skill. Mere repetition does not mean greater skill. Practice must be meaningful, with proper attention being given to all phases of the learning process. The learner, through repetition and a clear conception of what is to be done, steadily makes progress toward the goal he is attempting to attain. Repetition, however, should not be blind. It is during the process of "repetition" that learning takes place.

Law of effect. The law of effect maintains that an individual will be more likely to repeat experiences that are satisfying to him than those experiences that are annoying. If experiences are annoying, the learner will shift to other, satisfying responses.

This law of learning, as applied to physical education, means that every attempt should be made to provide situations in which individuals experience success and have a satisfying and enjoyable experience. Leadership is an important factor. Under certain types of leadership undesirable experiences would be satisfying. One coach might approve of hitting an opponent and make this an enjoyable experience. Under other coaches such an act would be an annoying experience because it would be condemned and would not be tolerated. Leadership is the key to good teaching.

Guthrie's contiguity theory

Edwin R. Guthrie* developed the contiguity theory of learning, which emphasizes the stimulus-response association. Contiguity means that a response that is evoked by a stimulus will be repeated whenever that same stimulus recurs. The strengthening of the connection between the stimulus and the response takes place in a single trial. Guthrie believed that since associa-

tions can occur with one trial and last forever, there is no need for anything like rewards or motivation to explain learning. However, although Guthrie holds that the full connection is established in one trial, it usually appears to take place gradually. This means that all stimuli cues are not always presented in the same manner, and for this reason many stimulus-response associations must be made. In every learning situation, for example, there are various combinations of stimuli that are presented and the correct responses need to be established for each situation. Guthrie holds that repetition and practice are essential in learning in order for the individual to become aware of the stimuli that will evoke the correct response.

In physical education we can apply Guthrie's theory to the learning of a skill such as the high jump. If a youngster desires to be proficient in this skill, he must make sure that his bodily movements are always the same each time he approaches the bar. The individual must be aware of all the surrounding stimuli such as the runway and position of the bar. The proficient high jumper will be one who has established a successful pattern for his movements and does not deviate from it. Even the slightest change in stimuli can evoke an incorrect response. The youngster who becomes distracted by the noise of the spectators finds it difficult to clear the bar if he has been used to practicing in complete silence. According to Guthrie's theory, this youngster should practice under conditions that he faces during actual competition, for in order to achieve his best performance he must be aware of all the stimuli that are present at the time of competition.

Hull's reinforcement theory

Clark L. Hull* sees learning as a direct influence of reinforcement. He has established his theory on the influence of need

---

*Guthrie, E. R.: The psychology of learning (revised edition), New York, 1952, Harper and Row, Publishers.

*Hull, Clark L.: Principles of behavior, New York, 1943, Appleton-Century-Crofts.

nd its reduction as the prime elements in learning. In his theory Hull emphasizes hat learning occurs when the individual dapts himself to his environment and that uch adaptation is necessary for survival. When needs arise the individual's survival s threatened, and the individual must act n a certain manner to reduce the need. The responses that the individual makes hat lead to the reduction of the need are einforced, resulting in habits or learning. According to Hull's theory, a stimulus auses a response that results in a need. The need evokes a response on the part of he individual, which reduces the need. The esponse that resulted in the reduction of he need is then reinforced, which develops habits or learning. Hull employed drive nd primary reinforcement in his early vork. Later he used ideas such as drive timulus reduction and secondary reinforcement.

Hull's theory emphasizes that habits or learning result from reactions set into motion by needs. In physical education the eacher plays an important part in satisfying the needs of the student. Teachers who xplain the psychological and sociological bases for participating in an activity may timulate students to a larger degree than hose who present the activity without any ationale. To elicit correct responses from tudents, the teacher presents material that s meaningful, and therefore lesson plans onsist of material important to the learner.

In Hull's theory the child learns by doing—drive reduction is a doing phenomenon. In physical education the child arrives at the solution to many problems through his own efforts. For example, the student practices the "kip" on the low bar and after many attempts becomes aware that he is not achieving success because of the position of his arms or other weakness. Upon discovering the correct position, the student epeats it over and over to reinforce it. The esult is the correct movement on the low bar. The habit is learned. Further repetition of the activity with the correct response eads to a feeling of satisfaction on the part of the student, for the need is no longer a problem.

One of the major implications of Hull's theory to physical education is his finding that practice periods that are extremely long or lacking in reinforcement inhibit learning. An example of this is the pole vaulter who practices hour after hour. After a long period of practice without any reinforcement, he finds it difficult to clear his usual height. However, Hull states that the inhibitions decrease after rest periods, and the next day the vaulter can again clear his accustomed height. Thus practice periods play an important role in determining the performance of an individual.

Skinner's operant conditioning theory

The main feature of B. F. Skinner's[*] operant conditioning theory is the fact that the stimulus that reinforces the responses does not precede it but rather follows it. In operant conditioning, behavior is elicited by the individual rather than the stimuli. In this theory of learning the individual organism first makes the desired response and then is rewarded. Reinforcement is contingent on the desired response. Skinner's main emphasis is that the individual repeats at a future time the behavior that has been previously reinforced. Behaviors that are not reinforced are not usually repeated. When the individual is rewarded, he elicits that behavior again. Extinction occurs when the behavior is no longer reinforced.

Skinner makes the point that since teachers cannot always wait for behavior to manifest itself, they must sometimes shape the behavior of the individual. In teaching any physical skill it is recognized that reinforcement is extremely valuable. For example, if the teacher desires that a student learn how to make the jump shot, he encourages the student to learn the proper form. When the student is shooting at the peak of his jump, in the correct manner,

---

[*]Skinner, B. F.: The behavior of organisms, New York, 1938, Appleton-Century Crofts.

the teacher indicates approval to the student. The student becomes aware of the proper form and continues to use it, because he knows the skill is being properly performed according to the teacher's standard.

Skinner has placed great emphasis on the use of audiovisual aids and teaching machines because of their reinforcement value. Since the teacher cannot reinforce the behavior of all children in a class, such machines may be useful, although some psychologists believe that they may interfere with the organization of materials into structural wholes. Through the use of such new innovations as the videotape replay, the student sees himself in action and discovers his deficiencies. Such devices prove beneficial in reinforcing learning in large classes where the teacher cannot cope with all the individual problems that arise.

Gestalt theory

The Gestalt psychologists such as Max Wertheimer, Kurt Koffka, Wolfgang Kohler, and Kurt Lewin are greatly concerned with form and shapes. Gestalt theory is more concerned with perception than learning. One of the most important Gestalt principles having implications for physical education is the whole method theory. This theory is based on the premise that a person reacts as a whole to any situation. The whole individual attempts to achieve a goal. Furthermore, the greater the insight or understanding an individual has concerning the goal he wishes to attain, such as paddling a canoe or guiding a bowling ball to a strike, the greater will be his degree of skill in that activity. An individual reacts differently each time he performs a physical act. Therefore it is not just a question of practice, as it would be if he performed it the same way each time. Instead, the more insight he has of the complete act, the greater his skill. The individual performs the whole act and does it until he gains an insight into the situation or until he gets the "feel" or the "hang" of it. Since insight is so important,

dependent conditions such as a person's capacity, previous experience, and experimental setup are very important considerations.

Psychoanalytic theory of learning

Psychoanalysis is genetic as well as dynamic theory. Learning is related to the psychosocial stages of development and must take into account that it is affected by unconscious forces and in certain cases leads to repression, fixation, and regression. All these unconscious forces are involved in a psychoanalytic theory of learning. Freud's theory stressed the importance of cognitive control in the development of a rational ego.

MOTOR LEARNING

The term "motor learning" is generally used in reference to the improvement of a motor performance or the development of a skill. For example, when, through practice, a golfer improves his putting skill, an archer improves his aim, or a pitcher improves his delivery, motor learning has taken place.

Movement is a fundamental aspect of human behavior, and skills may be categorized in several different ways. Two frequently used categories of skills are types of action and function.

Motor skills, as they relate to types of action, may be divided into fine versus gross motor skills or into sensory versus perceptual motor skills.

Fine motor skills are those requiring manual dexterity, such as typing, whereas *gross motor skills* involve large-muscle activity, as in running.

Sensory motor skills are those which develop as a result of the sensory cues (feeling, tasting, hearing, seeing, and smelling). Serving a volleyball would involve a sensory cue, for example. *Perceptual motor skills* are developed whenever the perceptual process is involved (judgments concerning speed, depth, and background information). In archery, both types of skill are involved, because cues of feeling and seeing are used, as well as judgments concerning distance and point of aim.

Motor skills may also be categorized according to their function in human existence. Whereas some motor skills are essential for normal existence (walking, self-care), others may be classified in terms of their self-improvement or educational values (reading, writing), and others are recreational in nature. Physical education skills would be classified generally in this latter division.

How does a student learn a motor skill? Is motor skill ability inherited or acquired? Is it transferable from one type of activity to another? Researchers are beginning to find answers to some of these questions.

Process of motor learning

Motor learning involves the establishment of pathways within the complex neuromuscular system of the human body. The very simplest human movement, such as clapping the hands, involves a pathway that may be divided into three distinct parts: the sensory, the connecting, and the motor neurons. These neurons form a neural pathway to bring about muscular innervation, making the hands come together. Neuromuscular skills are merely different sets of pathways that have been established through practice. The following questions immediately come to mind concerning the development of skill.

• *Are all skills acquired, or are some movements inherited?* Some movements may be categorized as inherited. For example, under normal circumstances, individuals walk, and they perform "swimming" movements in the water. Refinements of these motions can be acquired. Examples include hopping, skipping, and stroking in the water. Other inherited movements include those reflexes that are automatic and involuntary by nature, such as the knee jerk, eye wink, and breathing.

• *Once learned, are motor skills always remembered?* Retention of motor skills is dependent on many factors. Those skills that are easily acquired, are natural, are used frequently, or are "overlearned" usually remain with an individual for a long period of time. For example, riding a bicycle, swimming, skating, and throwing are rarely forgotten. The degree of perfection in performance may vary, but usually a well-refined skill may be reacquired in a relatively short period of time.

• *How much should a skill be practiced?* The amount of practice necessary to learn a skill depends on the individual, his quickness at acquiring the skill, and the degree of perfection desired. It has been found helpful to practice a motor skill in a series of a few attempts, followed by rest, and then to return to a series again. By distributing practice and rest intervals, neural pathways may be developed and stabilized.

• *What about injuries?* In injuries where muscle tissue has been damaged, usually rest will allow a return to normal functioning. In instances where nerve endings are damaged, new neural pathways may need to be established, and relearning may take a little longer.

A great deal remains to be learned about the importance of one other essential factor related to learning: that one vital element that pushes one student to learn and improve, while another student, given the identical set of instructions, under the same conditions, does not learn or improve. Some identify this basic ingredient as *desire*, whereas others label it *motivation*. In either case, it has been recognized as the most important factor in learning.

MOTIVATION

The place of motivation in the learning process is indeed distinctive. It has been described as "that which gives both direction and intensity to human behavior."* Recent studies of all types of students, from dropouts to overachievers, have led investigators to certain conclusions about the motivated student:

---

*From Frymier, Jack R.: Motivating students to learn, NEA Journal **57**:37, 1968.

1. Girls tend to be more positively motivated than boys.

2. Students from more favorable socioeconomic situations are better motivated.

3. Motivation to learn appears to be a fairly stable and constant phenomenon.

4. There can be too much motivation. We need optimal rather than maximal motivation.*

Recognizing these factors about motivation, the teacher must provide external motivation for those students who need it. Because styles of learning vary—some are visual, some aural, and others physical—the teacher must attempt to reach each individual student in class.

Sources of motivation vary and are generally found to be one of two types: intrinsic or extrinsic. Both play an important part in the teaching-learning process and need to be understood by the teacher.

Intrinsic motivators

Intrinsic motivators are factors found within the individual that prompt him to practice, review, and improve in any phase of learning. A sincere desire to learn, because of a genuine need to use the material or skill, is probably one of the greatest forces promoting learning. When a student strives to improve his own performance for his own sake—when he believes it is important to him personally to know how to swim or to play golf, for example—then he will be more likely to master the subject and retain his skills.

Intrinsic motivation brings about the more desirable type of learning, learning that will not be disturbed by the emotional tensions of competition or external stress. This type of motivation produces learning that in and of itself is its own greatest reward. The student recognizes his own improvement and is satisfied with the results of his efforts. The transfer of knowledge is more likely to take place when learning is self-motivated. The student who

drives himself to a better performance in one skill area, such as ball-handling, will probably do better in other ball games as a result. Transfer and retention of knowledge and skill are a vital aspect of any educational endeavor, and the teacher should strive to promote this type of learning.

How does the teacher foster intrinsic motivation to promote learning? Educators generally believe that students who share in the planning of their programs of study are more likely to have a greater interest in it. The goals and objectives students set for themselves are usually those that they will sincerely strive to attain. Teachers who establish goals and objectives that take into account the needs and interests of their students, and who allow students to share in their specific program planning, can surely expect greater and more effective learning to result.

Extrinsic motivators

While some students are perhaps more highly motivated from within, teachers realize that extrinsic motivational factors are not without value. Grades, awards, trophies, and point systems fall into the category of extrinsic motivators—factors that originate outside the individual. There are some students who will work hard just to earn the coveted "A" or the trophy that the school awards. When the student does this, learning takes place.

Pressure from the peer group may also be classified as an extrinsic motivator. The desire of adolescents to be a part of the team or a star on the athletic field promotes much learning in physical education.

A third extrinsic motivator is especially important for a teacher to understand and use. In simplest terms, genuine praise may do more to promote individual learning than all the ribbons or medals the school can provide. When a student knows he is performing correctly, several things happen: he continues to perform in the same manner, thereby creating a pattern of automatized movement in performing a skill, he feels pleased with himself, and he

---

*From Frymier, Jack R.: Motivating students to learn, NEA Journal 57:37, 1968.

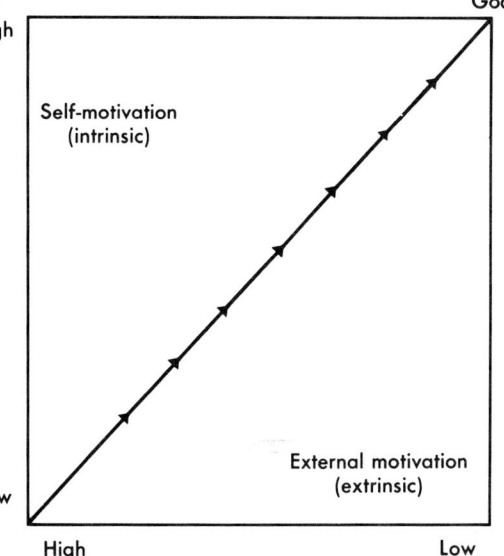

Fig. 13-4. Motivation.

develops a positive self-image that further promotes the learning process. Educators generally agree that punishment (fear or threat) in some way actually shatters the entire learning situation and disturbs the total teaching-learning process. This seems to hold true for every age level, in all subject-matter areas. Particularly, though, it is applicable to physical education, in which a confident self-image, plus a skilled performance (achieved through practice that has been guided by constructive criticism and praise), combine to help produce better physically educated individuals.

In connection with this discussion of intrinsic and extrinsic motivational factors, it is interesting to speculate about the aptness of Fig. 13-4. Assuming that individuals are motivated both from within and without in an inverse relationship, consider as ideal those students whose intrinsic motivation is so high that overall goals of education are nearly achieved. Students fall somewhere on this line as they approach this general purpose of education. It is for teachers in their role as planners, organizers, and motivators to move students upward on this ladder, or scale, toward effective behavior.

In the words of Congressman Winston L. Prouty:

> The mission of education ought to be to give each child the chance to work at his own level and to progress as far and as fast as his ability to learn permits.*

In summary, it should be remembered that students learn with or without stimulating material and with or without suitable environments. The source of such powers of learning is the internal motivational force. However, good teaching can further stimulate and enhance learning. Some learning may take place with little or no desire on the part of the student, but such knowledge does not remain with him long.

It is the teacher's responsibility to provide the motivational force in a suitable environment with stimulating materials. This is teaching.

PRINCIPLES AND CONDITIONS THAT ASSIST IN THE LEARNING OF MOTOR SKILLS†

Some of the major factors and conditions that promote the learning of motor skills are as follows:

• *Perception is important in motor learning.* Perception refers to the process of receiving and distinguishing among the available stimuli presented in any situation. It is essential in motor skill learning for an individual to perceive speed, distance, and shapes of objects. Deficiencies in any of these areas make the learning of motor skills more difficult. Various communication devices and techniques assist the learner in acquiring motor skills. Motion pictures, live demonstrations, knowledge of mechanical principles, and a realization and clear understanding of what is expected of the learner in performing a skill will be of particular value to beginners.

---

*From Prouty, Winston L.: Exceptional children —the neglected legion, NEA Journal **55**:25, 1966.

†Adapted in part from material in Bucher, Charles A.: Foundations of physical education, St. Louis, 1972, The C. V. Mosby Co.

• *Effective motor learning is based on prerequisite factors.* Such factors are strength, dynamic energy, ability to change direction, flexibility, agility, peripheral vision, visual acuity, concentration, an understanding of the mechanics of the activity, and an absence of inhibitory factors are essential to motor learning.

• *Skills should not be taught unless students have reached a level of development commensurate with the degree of difficulty of the skill.* Maturation is growth that takes place without any special training, stimulus, or practice—it just happens. It is closely associated with the physiological development of all individuals. Therefore the material must be adapted to individual maturation levels.

• *Each individual is different.* Teachers must be aware of the fact that individuals are different from one another and that these differences must be recognized if learning is to occur.

• *The learning curve is a consideration in motor learning.* Learning curves are not always constant, and they are different for each individual. The learning curve depends on the person, the material being learned, and the conditions surrounding the learning. Learning may start out with an initial spurt and then be followed by a period in which progress is not so rapid, or there may be no progress at all.

• *Learning takes place most effectively when the student has a motive for wanting to learn.* Motivation is an inducement to action. Usually the greater the motivation, the more rapid the learning. Motives should be of the intrinsic rather than the extraneous type. Rewards, awards, and marks should not be a means of motivating activity. The worth of the activity in itself should be the motive.

• *Learning takes place much more effectively when the student intends to learn.* If the student makes up his mind that he intends to learn a certain skill, if he arrives at the point where he sees a need for the skill, he is much more open to learning.

• *The student should know the goals toward which he is working.* Learning progresses much faster when goals are clear. The student should have a clear picture of what constitutes a successful performance. For example, if high jumping is being taught, the proper form and technique should be clearly demonstrated and discussed.

• *The student should receive feedback that indicates the progress he is making.* There are basically two kinds of feedback available to the student during the performance of a motor skill. Internal feedback is related to the concept of *kinesthesis*, while external feedback is related to the concept known as *knowledge of results*. Kinesthesis is associated with the feeling of the movement and has been recognized as being a conscious muscle sense. External feedback or knowledge of results is also extremely valuable to the student during and after the completion of a motor skill. Knowledge that one is progressing toward a set goal is encouraging and promotes a better learning situation.

• *Progress will be much more rapid when the learner gains satisfaction from the learning situation.* Satisfaction is associated with success. As the learner is successful in mastering a particular physical skill, his desire to learn increases so that he can experience additional success.

• *The length and distribution of practice periods are important considerations for effective learning.* Massed practice refers to long and continuous practice periods, while *distributed practice* refers to practice periods interrupted by rest intervals. There is some agreement that practice periods are most profitable when they are short and spaced over a period of time. The number of repetitions, such as shots at the basket or serves in tennis, should be considered as the unit of practice rather than the total number of minutes spent in the practice session.

According to some psychologists, when subject matter is very interesting and meaningful to the learner, practice periods may be made longer. Therefore it seems the length and spacing of periods should be adjusted to the class and material being learned.

• *As a general rule, learning is more effective when skills are taught as whole skills and not in parts.* In physical education it seems that the whole method should be followed when the material to be taught is a functional and integrated whole. This means that in swimming, which is a functional whole, the total act of swimming is taught. You learn to swim by using your arms and legs, and this can be taught as a whole. However, research indicates that complex skills should be broken down into their basic parts. In a complex sport such as football the game consists of blocking, broken-field running, tackling, passing, punting, and the like. In such a complex sport each of these skills represents a part of the whole that is football. However, they represent a functional and integrated whole by themselves and, as such, should be taught separately.

• *Overlearning has value in the acquisition of motor skills.* The initial practice in the learning of a motor skill is important in determining how long the skill remains in the possession of the learner. A partially learned skill does not remain in possession of the learner as long as one that is overlearned, that is, practiced until it establishes a pattern in the nervous system. If a skill is mastered and there is continual practice of the accomplishment, considerable time elapses before such a skill is lost to the learner.

• *Speed rather than accuracy should be emphasized in the initial stages of motor skill learning.* Physical educators are often required to make a judgment as to whether speed or accuracy should be emphasized in the initial stages of skill learning. Although some psychologists maintain that speed may lead in some cases to blindness in thinking, other researchers emphasize the speed factor. It would be desirable to be able to emphasize both speed and ac-

curacy; however, this is not always possible. In physical education many skills are carried on primarily by momentum, and according to some research, speed should be emphasized in the initial stages of such learning. At this stage an emphasis on accuracy interfers with the development of momentum needed to carry on the movement. In teaching golf and tennis skills that require momentum in order to be performed successfully, it is important to emphasize speed in the early stages of learning.

• *Transfer of training can facilitate the learning of motor skills.* Transfer of training is based on the premise that a skill learned in one situation can be used in another situation. For example, the student who knows how to play tennis takes readily to badminton because both skills require similar strokes and the use of a racquet. Most psychologists agree that positive transfer most likely occurs when two tasks have similar part-whole relations involved.

Physical educators must be aware of the concept known as *negative transfer*. Negative transfer occurs when one task interferes with the learning of a second task. For example, a young man being introduced to the game of golf for the first time experiences difficulty in swinging the club, because of his previous experience in another skill such as baseball. Perhaps you have heard the expression: "You're swinging the golf club like a baseball bat."

• *Mental practice can enhance the learning of motor skills.* Mental practice is the symbolic rehearsal of a skill with the absence of gross muscular movements. The physical educator should be concerned with the role of mental practice in skill learning. Research seems to indicate that although physical practice is superior to mental practice, mental practice is better than no practice at all. A combination of physical and mental practice is best.

• *A knowledge of mechanical principles increases the student's total understanding of the activity in which he is participating.*

A knowledge of mechanical principles that involve levers, laws of motion, gravity, and other factors are closely related to skill performance. Physical educators should be able to give their students sound rationale for the skills they are performing based upon a knowledge of basic mechanical principles.

• *Implementation of the principle of reinforcement will enhance learning.* One of the most fundamental laws of learning is reinforcement. In essence it means that the behavior most likely to emerge in any one given situation is one that is reinforced or found successful in a previous, similar situation. Therefore the best-planned learning situation will provide for an accumulation of successes. The reinforcement (reward) should follow the desired behavior almost immediately and should be associated with the behavior in order to be most effective.

• *Errors should be eliminated early in the learning period.* When instructing in such skills as field hockey and softball, the physical education teacher should attempt to eliminate incorrect performance as early as possible so that errors do not become a fixed part of the participant's performance. Inefficient methods, once learned, are difficult to correct.

• *The learning situation should be such that optimum conditions are present for efficient learning.* This means that distracting elements have been eliminated from the setting, the proper mental set has been established in the mind of the student, the proper equipment and facilities are available, the learner has the proper background to understand and appreciate the material that is to be presented, and the conditions are such that a challenging teaching situation is present.

• *A learning situation is greatly improved if the student diagnoses his own movements and arrives at definite conclusions as to what errors he is committing.* Self-criticism is much more conducive to good learning than teacher criticism. If the student discovers his own mistakes, they

are corrected much more readily than if they are discovered by someone else. A masterful teacher will develop teaching situations in which the student is led to self-criticism. This is a sign of good teaching.

SOME IMPLICATIONS OF RESEARCH FOR TEACHING SKILLS

The application of scientific research findings to program planning and the teaching of physical education activities is important. There is a gap between what is known and what is applied to teaching motor skills. Bell[*] has listed the results of some research and applied it to the teaching of selected physical education activities. A sampling of Bell's work is presented here in adapted form in order to show the implications of some research for the teaching of motor skills:

Archery: Four days per week of massed practice was shown to be better than two days of distributed practice.

Badminton: During the early stages of learning thirty minutes a day of distributed practice was found to be better than sixty minutes of massed practice per day, twice a week.

Basketball: Learning the foul shot improved as a result of mental practice in basketball.

Baseball: Knowledge of results helped to improve speed and accuracy in the baseball throw.

Bowling: Demonstration via the motion picture was of help if the learners had already had some practice.

Football: Mental practice in the football pass by reading an instruction sheet improved performance.

Golf: The whole method of practice (total swing) was superior to the part method.

Gymnastics: Videotape replay resulted in better performance.

Softball: Instruction in mechanical principles utilized in softball enhanced performance.

Swimming: The whole method of teaching was found to be superior to the part method.

Tennis: The best results were achieved where emphasis on speed and accuracy was the same.

Tumbling: No difference was found in the performance of two groups, one of which utilized motion pictures while the other did not.

Volleyball: A knowledge of mechanical prin-

---

*Bell, Virginia Lee.: Sensorimotor learning, Pacific Palisades, Calif., 1970, Goodyear Publishing Company, Inc.

ciples assisted in the performance of volleyball skills.

POINTS TO REMEMBER

1. A definition of learning
2. An understanding of the association theory
   of learning
3. An understanding of the Gestalt theory of
   learning
4. The differentiation between intrinsic and
   extrinsic motivation
5. The importance of readiness to learning
6. The value of rapport in the teaching-
   learning process

PROBLEMS TO THINK THROUGH

1. Of what value is a knowledge of theories
   of learning?
2. Why is there no one answer to the problems
   of how to teach?
3. In what situations, if any, would an autocratic type of classroom atmosphere be
   necessary? A laissez-faire type?
4. What types of motivational devices may a
   teacher use in handling special cases such
   as the obese? The awkward? The brilliant?
   The retarded? The handicapped?

CASE STUDY FOR ANALYSIS

After careful observation of three different
teaching situations, make a comparison in writing
of what has been seen in terms of the where,
when, what, who, and how of teaching. Pay
particular attention to the motivation of students
and the type of rapport established by the teacher.
What suggestions may improve the existing situation?

EXERCISES FOR REVIEW

1. What is learning?
2. Explain three types of teacher control prevalent in a classroom.
3. Define and explain several types of motivators.
4. What environmental factors enhance learning? Why?
5. Differentiate between the association theory
   and the Gestalt theory of learning, and apply each to teaching in physical education.

SELECTED READINGS

American Association for Health, Physical Education, and Recreation: Research Quarterly (entire issue), vol. 43, October, 1972.

Association for Supervision and Curriculum Development: Theories of instruction, Washington, D. C., 1965, The Association.

Bell, Virginia Lee: Sensorimotor learning, Pacific
Palisades, Calif, 1970, Goodyear Publishing
Company, Inc.

Biggie, Morris L.: Learning theories for teachers,
New York, 1964, Harper & Row, Publishers.

Biggie, Morris L.: Theories of learning, NEA
Journal **55**:18, 1966.

Blackie, John: How children learn, NEA Journal
57:40, 1968.

Bucher, Charles A.: Foundations of physical education, ed. 5, St. Louis, 1972, The C. V. Mosby
Co.

Cratty, Bryant J.: Movement behavior and motor
learning, ed. 2, Philadelphia, 1967, Lea &
Febiger.

Dawson, Kenneth E., and Norfleet, Morris: The
computer and the student, NEA Journal **57**:47,
1968.

Frymier, Jack R.: Motivating students to learn,
NEA Journal **57**:37, 1968.

Klotz, Donald: Make it simple! Iowa Journal of
Health, Physical Education, and Recreation,
April, 1971, p. 6.

Lockhart, Aileene: Conditions of effective motor
learning, Journal of Health, Physical Education,
and Recreation **38**:36, 1967.

National Association of Physical Education for
College Women and National College Physical
Education Association for Men: Motor learn-
ing, Quest, vol. 6, Spring, 1966.

Oxendine, Joseph B.: Generality and specificity
in the learning of fine and gross motor skills,
Research Quarterly **38**:86, 1967.

Oxendine, Joseph B.: Psychology of motor learning, New York, 1968, Appleton-Century-Crofts.

Ray, Henry W.: Freeing pupils from the sit-look-
listen syndrome, NEA Journal **56**:8, 1967.

Riessman, Frank: Styles of learning, NEA Journal
55:15, 1966.

Singer, Robert N.: Motor learning and human
performance, New York, 1968, The Macmillan
Co.

Smith, Hope M.: Motor activity and perceptual
development, Journal of Health, Physical Education, and Recreation **39**:28,1968.

Van Til, William: Curriculum: quest for relevance,
New York, 1971, Houghton Mifflin Co.

Vincent, William John: Reinforcement theory—
its implications for the teaching of gymnastics,
Physical Educator **21**:166, 1964.

14 METHODS OF TEACHING

Teaching causes a change in behavior (learning) through the relationship established between teacher and student. This relationship is the result of the preparation and presentation of materials in a manipulated situation, the *method* being selected by the teacher. The term "method," therefore, refers to the structuring of an educational setting in order that learning may take place. Methods include a variety of educational presentations, such as the lecture and the demonstration, each one appropriate for a specific teaching purpose. Selection of the appropriate method by the teacher during the preliminary planning stages of a unit is an important aspect of effective teaching.

The terms "methods" and "techniques" of teaching are frequently confused. *Methods* of teaching are ways of presenting material to students, while the *techniques* of teaching have reference to the tools or devices employed by the teacher to carry out successfully the method already selected. For example, if a demonstration of a skill has been planned as an introductory method, an appropriate technique might be a particular seating arrangement or lighting effect to be used during the demonstration. The technique makes the method more effective and enhances learning. Whereas methods are generalized approaches to the presentation of material, techniques are specific to circumstances in the particular class session and are developed through experience by a teacher over a period of time.

FACTORS AFFECTING THE SELECTION OF METHOD*

The proper selection of an appropriate teaching method involves consideration of several factors. While class size, equipment, and facilities merit some thought, these factors are more often considered in connection with organization of the class. Methods of teaching are determined by the nature of the activity itself, the particular purposes or goals to be achieved, and the age level and ability of the group.

Nature of the activity. The wide variety of activities included in a well-rounded physical education program necessitates utilization of different teaching methods, depending upon the nature or type of activity. Teaching an individual stunt such as a handspring requires a personal approach to improve an individual's performance, while teaching offensive team tactics requires total group knowledge. Therefore the selection of a method must take into account the nature of the activity. The nature of physical education activities may be differentiated in the following manner:

1. Team sports. Activities in which three or more players combine together to compete against a group consisting of a similar number of opponents. Scores are attributed to each group.

2. Individual and dual sports. Activities in which a single individual competes against a single opponent, or two players

---

*There are several innovative methods that may also be utilized. These can be found in Chapter 8, as well as in other chapters in the book.

Fig. 14-1. Girls' badminton class at Ames High School, Ames, Iowa.

Fig. 14-2. High school girls in dance. (New York City Schools.)

compete against two opponents. Scores of two players (partners) may be combined.

3. Rhythms. Activities in which a steady measured beat (vocal or instrumental) accompanies movement patterns, both axial and locomotor. Patterns may be performed singly, in pairs, or in groups.

4. Aquatics. Activities that take place in the water. These may be competitive, synchronized, instructional, or recreational in nature.

5. Gymnastic activities. Individual, self-testing activities in which tumbling skills and special apparatus are used. Individual scores may be totaled to determine team points.

6. Track and field activities. Individual self-testing activities in which running skills and speed are tested, as well as jumping and throwing power. Individual scores may be totaled to determine team points.

7. Winter activities. Activities that take place on snow and ice during the winter

months. These may be individual or team endeavors.

8. Games of low organization. Activities in which all individuals participate freely with a single purpose in mind, such as tagging another player or trying to hit him with a ball.

For the purposes of this chapter on methodology, activities will be categorized according to these distinctions.

Nature of the group goals. The nature of the group goals is an extremely important element to be considered in teaching methods. What do the students themselves expect to learn and achieve in a particular unit of work? In basketball, for example, they all want to play the game and to improve their skills only through playing. The creative teacher needs to develop exciting drills for skill practice, thus improving abilities of the individuals and upgrading game play while maintaining class enthusiasm.

Frequently the teacher needs to determine student objectives and goals for classwork. Providing an opportunity to hear students express their interests and desires will often bring out special individual hopes. Some girls may want to lose weight, and boys may want to improve game skill. Meeting these individual goals, revealed through democratic group processes, makes physical education a more meaningful experience for all.

Nature of the group. It is important to keep in mind the characteristics and interests of the students in the class. The differences between boys and girls, their physical abilities, their interests, and their attitudes all need consideration if teaching methods are to be appropriate. For example, on the junior high level, a variety of methods should be utilized to appeal to the students' widespread interests. Whereas a lengthy lecture would serve only to bore these younger students, it might be appreciated as a time-saver by older adolescents. The ability level of the students also needs clarification when methods are selected. Advanced students move rapidly through introductory and review sessions in a unit and should move on quickly into the advanced skills presentations.

In the discussion that follows, teaching methods are charted according to their appropriateness to the major areas of a physical education program. Methods are generally categorized according to phases within a teaching unit:

1. Methods of introducing the unit
2. Methods of improving physical skills
3. Methods of achieving social objectives
4. Methods of promoting intellectual learning
5. Methods of closing the unit

A section on definitions of terms follows the presentation of methods. Differentiation will be made for large and small classes to some extent, although this problem is handled in Chapter 19. Also, indications will be made of variations for boys and girls, for older and younger students, and for differing skill levels, whenever appropriate.

In schools where teams of teachers are organized, it should be pointed out that methodology as presented here remains unchanged. It is still the final presentation of material by an individual teacher that produces the causal relationship for teaching. Selection of methods may be the result of team consultation or of individual preference.

It should also be realized at the outset that teaching is an individual process; no exact pattern for teaching can be defined. A teacher must bring common sense and judgment plus knowledge and skills to the school situation and must combine these attributes to provide worthwhile learning experiences. Appropriate teaching methods can be selected by the teacher only in accordance with a particular school situation, and no outsider can prescribe that choice. Past experiences naturally aid greatly in making decisions about teaching methodology. New teachers should try out the various methods presented in this chapter to determine which are the most effective for them. They must evaluate their work and strive to improve their methods on the basis of each teaching experience, for only in this way does experience truly help to make better teachers.

METHODS OF TEACHING TEAM SPORTS

Team sports are the favorites of boys and girls and are taught extensively throughout the upper levels of a progressive program of physical education.

The values of football, softball, soccer, hockey, and the many other team sports are numerous. The physical skill and fitness benefits, the intellectual opportunities, and social organization all combine to make team sports an excellent educational experience.

Because of these inherent values and their widespread appeal, physical educators should strive to present team sports to students in a manner that will provide meaningful experiences to the greatest number. Thoughtful selection of methods will accomplish this end. There are certain teaching problems that are unique to this area of team sports, such as the different skill requirements of various positions and the complexities of annual rule changes. These and similar problems require special consideration.

Problems associated with the teaching of team sports

• *How should class time be divided between the teaching of game skills and actual playing of the game itself?* In teaching team sports the *whole-part-whole* approach is generally thought to be the most effective. This theory uses the word "whole" to include the entire picture of the game, and the word "part" refers to basic skills or elements that make up the total game. When a team sport is introduced to a physical education class, it is helpful during the first class session to provide an overall picture of the total game, perhaps through a demonstration game or film version. This should be followed by the selec-

tion of basic skills for practice, and then the skills can be used in game situations. As the unit progresses, individual skills may be stressed through drill practice for part of the period, with the closing minutes of the class being devoted to actual game play. The game situation should itself be a learning experience through proper coaching and suggestions from the sidelines.

An attempt should be made for all members of a class to experience the game situation, even though in large classes it is sometimes difficult to organize. When the importance of skills is understood in terms of their application to the game itself, students are more interested in improving them. Without adequate skills, the playing of the game becomes frustrating to students. Therefore, a teacher must carefully balance the introduction of skills and game play in classes, for the greater satisfaction of all the students.

• *How should skills that are specific to certain positions in a team sport (for example, pitching in baseball) be included in the unit?* At the junior high school level it is usually appropriate to teach students the fundamental skills essential to a particular sport. This provides each student with an opportunity to determine his own strengths and weaknesses and to appreciate the difficulties of all the skills required to play in sports. When more advanced skill progressions are introduced in high school, special groupings may be more meaningful, based on the interests and abilities of the individual.

• *How should theories of position play be presented and opportunities provided for students to play various positions?* Theories of position play should be presented with the use of such teaching aids as chalkboards, magnetic game boards, and films. It is particularly helpful to slow learners to have diagrams of football plays or basketball strategy outlined visually in front of them. Also, very large groups can be instructed efficiently and effectively with the use of these aids.

Opportunities to play in various posi-

Table 14-1. Methods of teaching team sports—baseball, basketball, football, hockey, lacrosse, soccer, speedball, volleyball

	Methods	Purposes	Group goals	Differences between large and small classes	Differences between boys and girls	Differences between age levels
Methods of introducing unit	Lecture Demonstration Verbal explanations	To introduce activity to entire class	To understand game as a whole	Less formal in small classes Easily adaptable to large classes		In junior high school, more time is needed for orientation but in small, short sessions
Methods of improving physical skills	Demonstration Performance: drill, mimetics, criticism Review Assignment Problem-solving	To improve physical skills, physical fitness	To improve skills related to game	Careful organization needed for most effective drilling in large classes (See Chapter 19)	Boys more interested in perfecting skills than girls	Progressive, from known to unknown
Methods of achieving social objectives	Problem-solving Discussion Supplementary team organization Verbal explanation	To promote safety consciousness, teamwork, cooperation, good sportsmanship	To develop team spirit, winning effort	In large classes good student leaders should be developed		In junior high school, teams and captains should be changed frequently
Methods of promoting intellectual learning	Lecture Verbal explanation Evaluation: oral, written Assignments Problem-solving Discussion Review	To teach history, rules, strategy, tactics, etiquette, related facts of sport	To understand rules of game and offensive and defensive strategy			Intellectual or associated learnings should be stressed with older high school students
Methods of closing unit	Supplementary special events: tournament between squads or classes Evaluation: skills, knowledge	To provide special opportunity for game play for everyone To measure progress of class	To have exciting tournament To measure progress	Use shorter time units in larger classes		

Fig. 14-3. Girls' physical education class. (Manchester High School, Manchester, N. H.)

tions should be provided, particularly at the junior high level, when specific sports skills are being developed. This may be done through squad assignments and position changes after short innings or baskets or after a specified number of downs or goals. For example, in baseball or softball, outfielders and infielders may exchange positions after each inning or after each out is made, if time is limited.

• *How should opportunities for creative thinking be provided?* The strategy and team play necessary in team sports provide the perfect media for allowing students the freedom to create new plays, new tactics for offensive and defensive positions, and new rules. Teachers should welcome such contributions and foster their application to game situations, rather than coaching every play.

METHODS OF TEACHING INDIVIDUAL AND DUAL SPORTS

A wide variety of activities is included in the area of individual and dual sports. Their values are numerous in terms of challenges to the individual to develop and improve physical skills, some of which will have later use in leisure-time activities.

Individual and dual sports have long been a part of the American way of life. Recent years have seen the mushrooming of business interests in some of these sports, to match the increase in leisure time being enjoyed by people in every walk of life. Of particular importance to physical educators has been the establishment of the Lifetime Sports Foundation. Through its research and financial resources, programs in five "lifetime" sports (archery, badminton, bowling, golf, and tennis) have been developed for the promotion of instruction in schools and communities. Working through state professional associations and utilizing physical educators, this foundation has sponsored clinics for teachers of these sports all over the country.

Recreational and combative activities, also included in this category, have been finding their place in physical education programs. Often some of these activities are included on an elective basis or as part of the coeducational program. Teaching must be structured on an individual basis in this area to be effective, and class organization is the key to success.

Table 14-2. Methods of teaching individual and dual sports—archery, badminton, bowling, fencing, golf, recreational sports, tennis, wrestling

	Methods	Purposes	Group goals	Differences between large and small classes	Differences between boys and girls	Differences between age levels
Methods of introducing unit	Lecture Demonstration Verbal explanation Discussion	To provide general understanding of total sport	To learn the game	Less formal in small classes		In junior high school, a brief acquaintance with many sports should be programmed
Methods of improving physical skills	Evaluation Performance: drill, mimetics, criticism Review Assignment Demonstration Problem-solving	To improve physical skills, physical fitness	To acquire skills and fitness necessary to play game for pleasure	Difficult to individualize instruction in large classes Use leaders Formalized instruction in large classes		In junior high school, only basic skills needed to play game should be introduced Advanced skills in high school
Methods of achieving social objectives	Lecture Discussion Verbal explanation Supplementary: team, squad organization Problem-solving	To promote safety consciousness, recreational skills, partnerships, co-operation, good sportsmanship	To learn to play with partner comfortably To learn spotting, safety techniques To do well in competition	Formal methods used in larger classes Easily adapted to small classes	Coeducational experiences may be provided in some of these activities	
Methods of promoting intellectual learning	Lecture Demonstration Verbal explanation Evaluation: oral, written Review Assignment Problem-solving Discussion	To teach history, rules, etiquette, game tactics, scoring, partner play, strategy	To learn strategies, scoring, etiquette, rules governing play for recreational enjoyment			Progressive, from simple to more difficult More extensive coverage in high school
Methods of closing unit	Evaluation: knowledge, skill Supplementary special events: tournament	To provide opportunities for scoring games, participation in games or meets, evaluation of progress	To try skills in game situation To measure self-progress To do well in competition	Tournament play will require longer time in large classes unless playing time is shortened		

Problems associated with the teaching of individual and dual sports

• *With limited equipment and facilities, how can individual sports be taught to large classes?* Basic instructional techniques can be provided to large groups simultaneously. For example, ninety students in a gymnasium might go through the motions of forehand stroking in tennis. Through mimetics and formalized instruction, a beginning can be made. However, individualized instruction and actual game play would probably be limited to one squad, and squads would need to rotate to the instructor's station, while in other areas squad leaders may organize related activities.

• *Should boys' and girls' classes be combined for instruction in individual sports?* There is no reason why boys and girls should not learn many of these recreational activities in combined classes. The skills involved in archery, golf, shuffleboard, and the like can be taught and learned in a coeducational setting, so that more efficient use can be made of the physical education staff. Social objectives can also be accomplished in this manner. At the junior high school level, where socializing techniques have not yet become as sophisticated as in high school, learning of skills might be impeded by mixed classes. Therefore, at this age level, coeducational classes might be more successful when recreational playing, rather than the learning of skills, is the purpose.

METHODS OF TEACHING RHYTHMIC ACTIVITIES

Because of the important values accruing to all participants, rhythmic activities should continue to be included throughout the secondary school program. The educational and recreational objectives of physical education find quick fulfillment in a well-conducted program of folk, square, and other dancing activities. The opportunities for creativity and the grace, poise, and balance required in modern dance are particularly appealing to girls. Other rhythmic activities, such as hoop work, rope jumping, and ball handling, are becoming increasingly popular for girls as a result of increased enthusiasm for gymnastics.

The magical force that rhythm provides to teaching makes it especially capable of bringing unity, cooperative effort, and satisfaction to even the largest classes.

Problems associated with the teaching of rhythmic activities

• *What should be done to improve motivation for folk and square dancing?* Secondary school students often profess a dislike for these activities, but in reality the boys and girls enjoy the opportunity of being together. Making classwork fast-paced and progressively difficult should help to keep their interest level high. The active, sincere participation and effective leadership of the boys' teacher will ensure the cooperation of the boys in the program.

• *To what extent should perfection in technique be developed in rhythmic activities?* Rhythmic activities should be performed to be appreciated. However, standards of perfection should vary in terms of the purposes of the group. Performance of folk and square dancing requires knowledge of foot patterns so that members of the square, set, or circle can keep pace with the group and not cause confusion. Perfection is not necessarily a goal, unless an exhibition is planned.

Skills involved in ball-bouncing routines and in hoop and rope work necessitate a higher degree of perfection for performance. The interaction of movements requires it. Similarly, the exhibition of creative modern dance routines requires additional practice toward perfection. However, rehearsals can be held during after-school hours if a special program is planned.

The degree of perfection sought compares inversely with the amount of material covered in teaching rhythmic activities. Whenever many folk and square dances

Table 14-3. Methods of teaching rhythmic activities—folk, square, social dancing, modern dance, rhythmic activities

	Methods	Purposes	Group goals	Differences between large and small classes	Differences between boys and girls	Differences between age levels
Methods of introducing unit	Demonstration Review	To introduce new movement patterns to be included in unit To review what is known	To understand what new movement will be encompassed in new unit			
Methods of improving physical skills	Demonstration Verbal explanation Performance: drill, mimetics Review Problem-solving Evaluation	To extend physical skills for improved responses To permit experimentation To determine present level of ability	To improve physical abilities for better usage To develop new movement, patterns, new responses	In large classes make appropriate use of space, alternate groups	Boys should strive to improve strength and power moves Girls should improve balance, grace, poise	
Methods of achieving social objectives	Supplementary groupings Problem-solving	To promote social co-operation To improve understanding of others	To work together co-operatively	Exchange positions of sub-groupings frequently Rotate groups in sub-groupings, if necessary	Some activities may be coeducational (folk, square, social dancing)	Change positions frequently in junior high school
Methods of promoting intellectual learning	Lecture Discussion Problem-solving	To learn historical, cultural background To provide problems for thoughtful solution To experiment with time, space, force	To study place of types of dance in cultures To develop new dimensions in terms of environment		Boys need to be motivated	In senior high school, new meanings and dimensions can be created in movement
Methods of closing unit	Evaluation Supplementary special events: exhibition	To determine progress of class To present program	To demonstrate dances that have been learned To participate in program			

are introduced to students, polished execution is apt to be sacrificed. A higher degree of skill and perfection would be achieved by a group that limits itself to a smaller number of routines for the purpose of exhibition.

METHODS OF TEACHING AQUATICS

The new high school complexes under construction today generally include swimming facilities, while older high schools are making use of the new portable swimming pools and air bubbles to provide aquatics in physical education. Teachers of physical education must be prepared to instruct some, if not all, water sports.

The aquatics program has many values. Physical exercise, endurance, and fitness, as well as techniques for personal safety, come immediately to mind. Moreover, the specialized skills necessary for synchronized swimming, lifesaving, and scuba diving are finding increased favor among today's adolescents. Surfing has captivated the interest of swimmers of all ages on both coasts, and the tremendous upsurge of interest in boating and recreational water sports has not only provided impetus to the acquisition of swimming skills but has created a responsibility for schools to educate students in all phases of aquatics.

Problems associated with the teaching of aquatics

• *With such a widespread differentiation in swimming skill, from rank beginner to lifesaver, how should instructional swimming be taught?* It is true that a wide variation of swimming skill is usually found in a physical education class, and since instruction in swimming skills has been established as the goal, the teacher should divide the group according to ability. The American Red Cross categories of swimmers are helpful for this purpose: beginners, advanced beginners, intermediates, swimmers, and advanced swimmers. Advanced swimmers could sometimes assist the teacher in teaching skill progressions to novices. Because water safety is of utmost importance, the teacher should seek all types of qualified assistance for lifeguarding purposes.

• *How should excuses from swimming class be handled?* This is one of the most difficult problems in teaching swimming. Colds in both boys and girls during the winter, the menstrual cycle of girls, plus their concern over getting their hair wet, continually interfere with the teaching program and necessitate special regulations for swimming class. Ideally, the program should be so interesting that the students do not want to miss swimming class. However, there are always some students who are less motivated toward swimming than others. Provision should be made for those excused from swimming activity to make up their class work after school on other days. During class they should assist as lifeguards, trying to learn through observation, and then help with towels and suits in the locker room.

Fig. 14-4. Rhythmic activity.

Table 14-4. Methods of teaching aquatics—swimming, synchronized swimming, recreational swimming (water polo), scuba diving, lifesaving, competitive swimming

	Methods	Purposes	Group goals	Differences between large and small classes	Differences between boys and girls	Differences between age levels
Methods of introducing unit	Evaluation Lecture Demonstration Verbal explanation Discussion	To divide group into ability groups To instill safety consciousness	To learn safety rules, personal safety skills in water			Some activities are too advanced for junior high school level
Methods of improving physical skills	Demonstration Performance: drill, critical analysis Review Problem-solving Evaluation: diagnostic skill tests	To determine present abilities To improve skills, fitness	To improve fitness, endurance, coordination, safety skills	Individualized instruction essential	Girls more interested in synchronized phases than boys	Watch for fatigue, cold in younger students
Methods of achieving social objectives	Lecture Supplementary: grouping Discussion Verbal explanation Problem-solving	To provide safety procedures To encourage participation, teamwork, cooperation	To create teamwork, group synchronization To acquire recreational skills			Instructional classes are generally not coeducational Lifesaving and other elective courses may be combined
Methods of promoting intellectual learning	Problem-solving Evaluation Assignments Discussion Demonstration	To create swimming routines To teach lifesaving knowledge, physiological dimensions To broaden interests in swimming	To learn synchronized swimming routine To learn how to care for others in water To learn about scuba diving equipment, methods	Problem-solving harder to use in large classes Assignments useful in large classes	Problems of buoyancy differences in boys and girls	In older groups stress physical laws and physiological principles of swimming
Methods of closing unit	Evaluation Supplementary special events: swimming meet	To measure progress in skills To evaluate progress in skills applied	To measure progress To participate in swimming meet or synchronized swimming program To go scuba diving on a lake			

• *Should activities such as synchronized swimming, scuba diving, and lifesaving be open only to advanced students?* The American Red Cross requires students to pass a preliminary test for admission into the standard lifesaving course. However, in the case of synchronized and competitive activities, the school should provide opportunities for interested beginners to learn these special skills. Advanced groups limited to swimmers of greater proficiency should also be established to further develop their talents and interests.

METHODS OF TEACHING GYMNASTICS

Interest in gymnastics has been steadily increasing in this country over the past decade. This has been evidenced by the addition in the curriculum of gymnastics for girls, by the development of gymnastic teams, and by the competitive meets scheduled on local, regional, and nationwide levels.

The teaching of gymnastics is usually

structured according to Olympic activity outlines, with tumbling providing the basis for learning more advanced skills and performing with apparatus. The teacher needs to devote a great deal of time to the development of good tumbling skills before introducing the trampoline, rings, parallel bars, and so forth. Particular attention needs to be paid to the establishment of good safety habits. From the outset of the unit, instruction should be offered in proper care and handling of mats, safety checks for equipment, and spotting techniques for partners. Rules for participants must be observed by all students if the unit is to meet with success.

Teachers should not overlook the valuable teaching assistance offered by the emphasis on, and publicity surrounding, the Olympics. Students can gain invaluable knowledge by watching taped versions of Olympic performers. Striving to compete within the limitations imposed by Olympic standards is also an excellent educational device.

Fig. 14-5. Gymnastics. (Guymon Junior High School, Guymon, Okla.)

Table 14-5. Methods of teaching gymnastics

	Methods	Purposes	Group goals	Differences between large and small classes	Differences between boys and girls	Differences between age levels
Methods of introducing unit	Lecture Demonstration (with aids) of individual activities simultaneously or in separate class periods Verbal explanation Discussion	To introduce various events in gymnastics	To learn about activities included in unit		Boys' events: rings, horizontal bar, parallel bar, vaulting, floor exercise, trampoline Girls' events: uneven parallel bars, balance beam, floor exercise, vaulting	
Methods of improving physical skills	Evaluation: physical skills Performance: drill, criticism Review Assignment Demonstration Problem-solving	To improve physical skills, physical fitness qualities necessary for performance	To acquire skills To improve physical fitness qualities	In large classes, smaller groups should be stationed with leaders at other activities	Girls tend to improve balance, poise, grace Boys need strength	Basic tumbling moves must be learned first
Methods of achieving social objectives	Discussion Demonstration Performance Supplementary: grouping Problem-solving	To learn safety techniques, spotting for each other To promote individual effort, teamwork	To care for safety of each other To do well in competition To cooperate	In large classes student leaders should assist with equipment and class organization		In junior high school, students enjoy working in pairs or small groups
Methods of promoting intellectual learning	Lecture Demonstration Problem-solving Verbal explanation Evaluation: oral, written	To learn about current champions To study principles of movement To motivate individual	To understand how to improve own performances To determine own capacities, try to improve			In senior high school, students should learn about physical laws governing balance, movement
Methods of closing unit	Evaluation: oral, written Supplementary special events: gymnastic meet, program	To measure progress To attempt competition or performance of events	To measure own progress To perform for others			

Gymnastics, with its variety of activities, provides opportunities to improve several important qualities and characteristics. Strength, balance, and control are very important when tumbling stunts are considered. For girls it is vital to point out the excellence in poise, grace, and beauty of movement that characterizes the balance beam and floor exercise routines. It is these very qualities that have helped to advance the popularity of gymnastics in recent years. The appeal that gymnastics has to the individual who wishes to try to improve himself cannot be underestimated.

Problems associated with the teaching of gymnastics

• *How can a teacher supervise various gymnastic activities effectively and simultaneously?* A teacher must give careful consideration to planning activities in gymnastics in order to keep safety first and foremost. A single teacher cannot supervise more than one activity at a time. Therefore, older students or students with advanced ability should be utilized whenever possible. If outside assistance is not available, activities should be coordinated in such a way that the instructor is free to supervise that activity that requires his personal attention, and other students should be able to lead running, exercises, or squad games that are less hazardous in nature.

• *How does a teacher motivate the poorly skilled students in gymnastic activities?* The student who is awkward, overweight, or in some other way unable to feel comfortable in gymnastics needs the special attention of the instructor. The very simplest tumbling skills and locomotor combinations should be acquired first, in order that the student may feel capable and satisfied. Simple floor exercise routines can be developed to enable that student to participate and then to improve.

METHODS OF TEACHING TRACK-AND-FIELD ACTIVITIES

Track and field, with its variety of events, has a widespread appeal to stu-

dents. Each participant will be able to find one or more activities particularly suited to him, either in field events or in running. Track and field is like gymnastics in this respect, as well as in terms of its demands on the individual to try to improve his own performance. In track and field the student is actually competing against himself, to better his own record in minutes or feet or inches. Success is therefore a measure of individual effort and work and an accomplishment of which to be extremely proud.

The values of track-and-field activities are numerous. Elements of physical fitness are an inherent aspect of track events (speed, endurance, strength, agility), and the benefits to the cardiovascular system are acknowledged by doctors as well as physical educators.

Here again the Olympics have added greatly to the significance of these activities and to our knowledge for improvement of performances. Teachers should take advantage of the information thus gained and should utilize all available data for motivational and educational purposes.

Problems associated with the teaching of track-and-field activities

• *How does one teacher supervise many track-and-field activities in one class period?* When activities are introduced to a large class, it is sometimes helpful to discuss each activity separately and to allow all the students to become acquainted with the teaching hints required for that particular skill. When all the events to be included in the unit have been covered, the teacher might suggest squad assignments at the various stations for practice, with leaders to assist.

• *Should all students learn to perform all events in track and field?* At the junior high school level it is generally a good idea to have all the students experience a wide range of events, as in track and field. Selection of specific skills to perfect might wait until the high school years, after determining those activities that seem to be best suited to the individual.

Table 14-6. Methods of teaching track-and-field activities

	Methods	Purposes	Group goals	Differences between large and small classes	Differences between boys and girls	Differences between age levels
Methods of introducing unit	Lecture Demonstrations (with aids) of individual activities simultaneously or at different class periods Verbal explanation Discussion	To introduce many track-and-field activities efficiently	To learn about activities		Girls' events may not include longer distances, hurdles, pole vault	In junior high school, should learn about all the activities included in this area Specialization in higher grades
Methods of improving physical skills	Evaluation: physical skills Performance: drill, mimetics, criticism Review Assignment Demonstration Problem-solving	To improve physical skill, physical fitness qualities	To acquire skills necessary for events To improve physical fitness qualities	In large classes individuals will need outside practice		In junior high school, there should be experimentation of various styles of performance, for example, styles of roll for high jump
Methods of achieving social objectives	Discussion Supplementary: grouping Problem-solving	To promote safety consciousness, teamwork, independent effort, group cooperation in competition	To learn safety procedures To do well in competition	In large classes use of group leaders necessary		
Methods of promoting intellectual learning	Lecture Demonstration Verbal explanation Evaluation: oral, written Review Assignment Problem-solving	To promote understanding of successful styles of movement needed for various activities, according to body build To study current record holders	To understand how to improve own performance through knowledge of physical laws, body types, and so on			In high school, students should learn about physical laws and forces behind successful patterns of movement

Table 14-6. Methods of teaching track-and-field activities—cont'd

	Methods	Purposes	Group goals	Differences between large and small classes	Differences between boys and girls	Differences between age levels
Methods of closing unit	Evaluation: oral or written, of knowledge, skill Supplementary special events: track meet	To measure progress To apply learning to competitive situation	To measure progress To utilize learning in competitive situations			

• *How can scores be recorded most effectively in large classes?* It is impossible for a single teacher to keep an accurate record of each individual in a large class. Therefore, squad leaders might be made responsible for recording performances, or individuals themselves might keep track of their own scores on individual record cards.

METHODS OF TEACHING WINTER ACTIVITIES

Winter activities can be classified as team sports (for example, ice hockey), recreational sports (for example, sledding and skiing), and even rhythmical activities (for example, figure skating). However, the elements of ice and snow add to the teaching situation rather unique problems needing consideration.

A basic groundwork of information, preliminary exercises, and land drills should be offered in preseason classes, in order that no time will be lost once appropriate ice-and-snow conditions exist. For example, in figure skating, mimetic practice of the difficult school figures, including correct shoulder and hip rotation, helps to clarify mental images of skills prior to execution on the ice. In skiing, practice of weight-shifting and edging is helpful. Safety information and tips on the care of equipment can be discussed in class lectures, and team strategies for ice hockey can be developed, with forwards and defensemen.

As soon as appropriate conditions exist, students should be allowed opportunities to try their skills on the slopes or the ice. Instruction will need to be individualized as much as possible by grouping students according to abilities and interests. These activities may easily be conducted on a coeducational basis, with the exception of ice hockey.

Problems associated with the teaching of winter activities

• *How can equipment be provided for students?* The nature of winter activities requires special equipment (for example, skis and skates) that precisely fits each individual student. Just as each student should provide his own sneakers for the gymnasium, so it seems logical to assume that students should try to obtain their own skates and ski boots, if possible. This is necessary both for safety reasons and for improved learning conditions. It is very difficult to try to learn to skate on skates that are too large or too small or on skis that cannot be properly adjusted to the boots. With the added danger of slipping and falling in these activities, a properly fitted ski boot or skate is essential. Because this equipment is expensive and requires special waxing and sharpening, winter activities are often optional parts of programs of physical education, to be enjoyed by those able to provide items essential for instruction.

Table 14-7. Methods of teaching winter activities—ice hockey, skiing, skating

	Methods	Purposes	Group goals	Differences between large and small classes	Differences between boys and girls	Differences between age levels
Methods of introducing unit	Lecture Discussion Demonstration Verbal explanation	To teach about care of equipment To determine goals for unit and each individual	To understand purpose of unit To select areas of interest			
Methods of improving physical skills	Verbal explanation Performance: mimetics, drill, criticism Evaluation: skill test Review Problem-solving	To teach basic skills involved in activities To improve performance	To improve abilities To enjoy recreational aspect of activities	Individualized instruction, if at all possible	Boys generally engage in ice hockey Girls enjoy rhythm, balance, grace, control of figure skating	
Methods of achieving social objectives	Supplementary: grouping Discussion	To promote group enthusiasm To teach safety skills, consideration for others	To get along with each other To learn how to watch out for others and care for them		Skiing and figure-skating classes should be coeducational	
Methods of promoting intellectual learning	Lecture Discussion Assignment Problem-solving	To teach about historical aspects, rules, growth, and development of sports	To learn rules of hockey To understand competitive regulations governing skiing and skating			
Methods of closing unit	Evaluation: skill tests Supplementary: program, competition	To provide opportunity to perform To evaluate progress	To perform in program or competition To evaluate self-progress			Competition scaled by age-level groupings

Table 14-8. Methods of teaching games of low organization

	Methods	Purposes	Group goals	Differences between large and small classes	Differences between boys and girls	Differences between age levels
Methods of introducing unit	These are supplementary activities (instruction would not be in units)					
Methods of improving skills	(Skills would already have been acquired) Performance	To provide practice for large numbers simultaneously	To play games	More adaptable in large classes		
Methods of achieving social objectives	Supplementary: grouping	To play together cooperatively for activity	To play for fun together	More adaptable for large classes		Highly popular in junior high school
Methods of promoting intellectual learning						Not challenging enough for senior high school
Methods of closing unit	None					

METHODS OF TEACHING GAMES OF LOW ORGANIZATION

In most circumstances, games of low organization are part of the elementary physical education program. However, there are certain occasions when they serve a distinct purpose within the secondary program.

It should be noted here that games of low organization involve any number of players in large-muscle activities. Rules and explanations are minimal, while activity level is optimal for all participants. Therefore, these activities are useful when the teacher desires a large segment of the class to enjoy activity while one squad is elsewhere receiving special instruction. Dodge-ball games, tag games, keep away, and mass soccer are types of activities requiring basic skills. Teams can be quickly devised to suit the needs of the situation, and activitiy can be started immediately. Fun and satisfaction are derived, and occasionally these, too, should be considered as important outcomes of the physical education program.

Problems associated with the teaching of games of low organization

• *How often should these be included in the program?* In the junior high school, games of low organization can be utilized frequently, for this age level still enjoys the freedom allowed in these activities. Older students in secondary school will lose interest more rapidly because of the lack of real challenge and lack of necessity for intellectual response. Occasional inclusion in the program will be successful, however.

Fig. 14-6. Swedish ball routine involving bouncing, throwing, and catching, with free movement of body. (Colorado Springs Public Schools, Colorado Springs, Colo.)

DEFINITION OF TERMS

Lecture. The lecture may be used frequently in physical education to present such topics as current events, history and development of a sport, rules, and etiquette. A lecture should be addressed to a group in such a way that all can hear and see the speaker. Preferably, it should be brief and to the point if the lecture is to be followed by active participation, because students are generally anxious to "get on with the game." However, a lecture in which a quantity of information is presented to a large class in an auditorium or a classroom setting becomes an advantageous and efficient use of time.

Demonstration. It is reasonable to expect a physical educator to demonstrate effectively most of the skills being taught. This does not imply expertness in every sport but a basic, sound background in fundamental skills. In addition to the teacher's demonstration, there are many excellent audiovisual instruments that are available and that enable the student to see a skill performed clearly and accurately. A well-illustrated high school physical education textbook can also be useful. (Bucher's high school textbook, *Physical Education for Life,* discusses and illustrates twenty different activities. See Suggested Readings at end of chapter.) When a skill is demonstrated before the class, certain important factors should be kept in mind:

1. The demonstration should be well planned so that all important points are firmly fixed in the teacher's mind.

2. The demonstration should be organized so that all students are able to see and hear well. If student assistants are used, they should know the purposes and procedures necessary to show effectively the particular skill under study.

3. All necessary equipment and materials should be on hand so that no time is wasted once the demonstration is begun and so that the time is used most effectively.

4. Helpful pointers for proper performance of the skill should be given. The skill should be analyzed according to its basic parts and then shown in its entirely. In teaching a new skill, emphasis should be on the right way to do it, not the wrong way.

A demonstration lesson may be in the form of an actual performance by a group, or a filmed or taped presentation of the subject may be given. The factors defined above are applicable to this situation as well as to a demonstration by a single individual.

Verbal explanation. In physical education verbal explanations are used extensively for introduction and analysis of skills. Whereas a lecture provides a formal, lengthy presentation of material, verbal explanations are generally brief, concise descriptions. Frequently this method is combined with a demonstration of a particular skill, prior to practice by the class, or it may be used in connection with rule discussions or settling squad disputes. By taking advantage of teachable moments for brief explanations about proper group cooperation and consideration, a teacher may promote genuine learning in social development.

The importance of the carefully chosen "word cues" in teaching should be stressed here. The creation of a correct mental image prior to physical execution of a movement sets the stage for the successful performance of the task. Telling students to use fingertips on a volleyball may produce the desired results, but describing the ball as a "hot potato to be tapped away quickly" might be more effective.

Discussion. In leading a discussion, the teacher will find that it is important to keep in mind the exact points to be stressed. Questions should be prepared in advance in order to guide the direction to be taken. All students should feel that their contributions are welcome, and the teacher should try to draw out opinions from students who may otherwise remain silent. Timing is another important consideration, for a discussion that drags on too long may lose its impact.

Discussions are often more effective than verbal explanations. By using thought-provoking questions and good discussion techniques, the physical education teacher can help the entire class to arrive at a greater understanding of learning experiences, such as team play and tactics, or to improve its attitudes toward health, safety, or exercising. However, worthwhile discussion demands time, whereas verbal explanation may be quite brief. The values derived for the students should be the determining factor if a choice must be made between these two valuable methods.

Performance. Performance is the backbone of physical education, because students learn by doing. Therefore, opportunities must be provided for students to participate to the fullest possible extent in the activities included in the program. Frequently, the *mimetic technique* is used when new skills are introduced prior to actual performance. This technique provides an opportunity to "get the feel" of a movement through imitation in a simulated experience. For example, the hockey dribble may be acted out with or without hockey sticks at the beginning of the unit.

Clever word pictures and rhythmic patterns assist students in kinesthetically feeling the desirable action. Mimetic drills may also be used as warm-up exercises at the beginning of a class period.

The use of *drills* is another valuable method of providing opportunities for performance of skills in physical education. Mastery of skills through practice and automatization is essential to satisfaction in game play, and the proper conduct of drills provides an efficient and effective teaching method.

Drills in physical education can be as dull as memorizing a multiplication table, or they can be nearly as much fun as the game from which they are derived. For real learning to take place they should be as interesting as possible, and this of course requires planning on the part of the teacher. The following principles are important when planning drill formations:

1. Drills should be an outgrowth of the game situation. This gives meaning to the drill. The students are not asked merely to kick a ball, for example, but are instructed to kick the soccer ball through the goal posts for a score.

2. Drills should allow maximum participation for all class members. A student has the opportunity to practice more frequently if the class is divided into many units, each of which is composed of a small number of students. For a teacher to make as many practice units as possible, all available equipment must be put to use. These two factors (the size of the class and the available equipment) must be considered when planning drills.

3. Drills should be interesting and fun. Adding the competitive element to a drill formation or scoring points for adapted techniques makes the drill much more fun while the student is trying to learn a skill.

4. Drills should allow for both individual instruction and total supervision. In setting up drill formations the teacher must remember his or her responsibility for the entire group and must therefore be able to supervise all working areas. At the same time, individual instruction should be given to students needing special help. Thus, in both instances proximity to the groups is essential.

5. Drills should be varied frequently to prevent boredom or loss of interest. Changing drill formations—for example, from the shuttle type to the circle—can be stimulating, which is necessary, particularly with junior high school students. However, every change must be planned so that time is not wasted unnecessarily in going from one lineup to another. For example, if groups are in four equal lines, it would be very difficult to set up three circles and wasteful to follow this change by going back to four units again. Groups should remain fairly constant, and formations should change smoothly from one to another.

6. Drills should not take the whole class period. Classes will lose interest in the perfection of skills if no opportunity to test them in the appropriate game situation is allowed.

7. Drills should progress from the simple to the more difficult. Drills should start with simple formations—either review old skills or practice new ones in simple form. When formations and patterns are changed, the skills should be made increasingly difficult or combined with other skills to maintain interest and utmost effort in participation.

The necessity of drills in teaching physical education is great, but for them to be most effectively used, they must be carefully and thoughtfully planned with all these factors in mind. Some teachers find it more satisfactory to teach one skill at a time, but others—feeling that good student leaders can direct skill practices—set up groups in order to provide for drilling on different skills at the same time. Under the direction of leaders, groups can rotate to different skill stations until all students have had practice within each assigned area. Such a procedure would depend, of course, upon the equipment and practice areas available, as well as upon effective leadership, but it would promote leadership and develop group responsibility and cooperation. This same division of groups may even be used on an elective basis, with students selecting the drill they need to practice most, and then rotating.

Constructive analysis. Constructive criticism of performance is another essential method of teaching for improvement of skills. Positive suggestions to students of ways in which they might change their batting stance or follow-through, to name two examples, have been found to be more helpful than negative statements of "No, not that way!" Personal, individual attention indicates the sincere interest of the teacher toward the student and helps to motivate him to improve his performances.

Evaluation. Evaluation becomes a method of teaching when it benefits the students by giving them an opportunity to measure their own progress and learning during a unit. Student evaluations may be accomplished through oral questioning, written tests, or physical skills and fitness testing. When tests are administered at the beginning and at the end of a unit, students are motivated to work harder for improvement. Students want to know the bases upon which they are judged; through testing they know what is expected of them and can rate themselves in comparison to their own previous scores. Testing and other methods of evaluation are discussed further in a separate chapter, but their usefulness as a method of teaching requires mention here. In connection with oral questioning as a method by which students profit from the class session, the following techniques for effective questioning should be understood.

1. Questions should be clearly stated so that they may be easily understood.

2. Questions should challenge the thinking of the students and require well-thought-out answers, not a mere "yes" or "no."

3. Questions should provoke contributory answers, not foolish responses.

4. Credit for a partially correct answer should be given. Sarcasm or ridicule should never be a teacher's tool for responding to improper answers.

5. Questions and answers should not be repeated by the teacher. The teacher should expect full attention from the group, so that such repetition is unnecessary. The teacher may, however, ask for a restatement of an answer by another member of the class to ensure complete understanding.

6. Questions should be directed to the class as a whole before an individual is called upon, in order to keep the attention of the entire class.

If these general suggestions are followed, a question period can be made a very worthwhile learning experience for all members of the class, even though they may not all have an opportunity to answer or contribute.

Assignments. Assignments, or homework, belong in a physical education program, and much learning can be accomplished if they are meaningful. For example, students who are weak in performance of some of their physical skills should be encouraged to devote additional time to improve and develop their abilities. This is especially true where daily physical education classes are not scheduled. The spending of valuable time in explaining rules and giving other information can be avoided if assignments using supplementary rule sheets or rule books are made. Some teachers may want to require notebooks on sports, sports personalities, or other outside reading, either as makeup work or as enrichment opportunity for students temporarily unable to participate, or for athletically gifted students. Students need to be aware of the wealth of material available today about all of their sporting interests, and they should share it with their classmates if time and opportunities permit.

Problem-solving. The problem-solving approach to teaching has received great impetus recently from the current emphasis placed on encouraging independent and creative thinking. In all educational pursuits the development of the initiative of the individual is sought, with opportunities being provided.

Physical educators are recognizing that students at the high school level can gain new insights into skill analysis, game situations, and especially movement experiences through this teaching method. It is felt that whenever freedom in movement permits personal recognition of a better way to perform a physical skill, such as throwing a ball for distance, after trials of many different ways, such a conclusion or result remains longer with the student. The permanent change in behavior is real learning because it is self-directed. The teacher's role in this method of teaching is one of setting up the situation and allowing freedom of experimentation. Students are led to experiment on their own and to think for themselves in answering a given problem. The problem may involve a physical skill, such as throwing a ball, or a game strategy, such as team plays for forwards shooting baskets or soccer goals, or it may involve the definition of movement in time and space as part of a creative experience in dance or movement education. The key to success with this method lies in the individual student's ability to feel free to experiment and to experience, and it is the teacher who provides this freedom.

Supplementary learning experiences. Other situations that cannot be classified as methods of teaching provide learning opportunities and expose students to learning experiences. One major source for students is their *observation* of the class and of their classmates' performance. It is recognized that little children learn more from each other, in swimming, for example, than from what they are told. In the same way, older students can learn by observing class details. A teacher can promote specific observations through directions to individuals. For example, in a basketball unit, where so often only a few players may actually participate in the game situation at one time, the remaining students may be instructed to analyze the players on the floor, or just one player, perhaps, in terms of floor mistakes, movement under the basket, ball-handling ability, or guarding techniques. A teacher promotes learning by following the class observations with discussions with the class as a whole.

Another supplementary learning experience stems from *team organization.* Opportunities for leadership and fellowship—for cooperating and working with others for the greater good—are the direct results of the squad or team setup used in physical education classes. By working with students and by managing teams, a teacher can improve social attitudes and promote attainment of social objectives. Differences in backgrounds of students, as well as cultural and racial distinctions, can be erased on the playing field or in the gymnasium, providing that the teacher works constructively toward this goal. *Special events* also provide supplementary learning. At the close of a teaching unit, competitive tournaments, demonstrations, and special presentations or programs by selected individuals permit additional learning. Often it is the inclusion of these special events which makes physical education one of the noteworthy features of a high school program. Students remember the tournament, the speaker, or the modern dance program, for example, that made the physical education class outstanding.

POINTS TO REMEMBER

1. Methods used in teaching physical education should relate specifically to the established goals.
2. Many different methods may be utilized in teaching classwork. Most of them may be combined or interchanged to provide variety in class structure, although some of them may be used only for accomplishment of specific objectives.
3. Certain principles underlie the choosing of methods in preparation for teaching a class, and these must be kept in mind for the development of an effective teaching situation.
4. The daily class in physical education is the most important factor in teaching and therefore must be carefully planned and

thought out in advance. Students may participate in planning this phase, as well as all phases of the program, if departmental organization permits.

5. The selection of methods depends on age level and developmental level of the class, as well as facilities and space, size, and time factors.

PROBLEMS TO THINK THROUGH

1. A new teacher of physical education, just added to the department, finds the year's program already formulated. In what ways can he or she (a) allow pupils to help in the planning within that program and (b) convince the department that cooperative pupil-teacher planning can be utilized in an overall schedule?

2. This same new teacher finds that, while the physical fitness and physical skills objectives are being adequately met, the other goals—knowledge, appreciation, and social development—are not being stressed by other members of the staff. In what way can he or she work for the attainment of these goals?

3. In what way can leaders be most effectively used in the instructional phase of the program?

4. How much use should be made of assignments, or "homework"?

5. How can a teacher emphasize the importance of students' evaluation of their own classwork?

6. Which goals of physical education have counterparts in the everyday living experiences of students, and how can a teacher ensure transfer of learning for them?

7. What place does motivation have in daily classwork, and how does a teacher promote it?

CASE STUDY FOR ANALYSIS

The newly appointed and only teacher in the girls' (or boys') high school department is responsible for teaching physical education classes three times a week to class groups ranging from twenty-four to forty-eight students. The administration has given the teacher a free hand to organize the curriculum, and no particular philosophy of education is expected to be followed.

Prior to his first class session this new teacher learns that previous course construction was entirely teacher-controlled. What introduction to class work should be given to the classes, and how would the classes be conducted for the first teaching unit? For later units? With what purposes in mind?

EXERCISES FOR REVIEW

1. Formulate three drills to be used in teaching beginning soccer that would be progressive and require little change-over time.

2. Devise a set of leading questions to be used in starting a group discussion on teamwork in basketball.

3. Outline the format of a softball (baseball) notebook to be assigned to tenth-grade students.

4. Write out an explanation of the foul-shooting technique.

5. Describe three mimetic warm-up exercises and appropriate commands related to tennis strokes.

6. Observe the teaching of a class and evaluate the methods used.

7. When ten or twelve students are playing a game of fullcourt basketball, in what way can the remaining students in the class be effectively and purposefully occupied?

8. Plan a series of review questions to be answered orally by a class studying volleyball.

SELECTED READINGS

American Association for Health, Physical Education, and Recreation: Organizational patterns for instruction in physical education, Washington, D. C., 1971, The Association.

Baley, James A.: Teaching the spike in volleyball, Journal of Health, Physical Education, and Recreation 35:57, 1964.

Bickert, Roderick Norman: Selected organizational values and characteristics of innovative and non-innovative school systems, doctoral dissertation, University of Iowa, 1967.

Borg, Walter R.: Ability grouping in the public schools, Madison, Wisc., 1966, Dembar Educational Research Services.

Bucher, Charles A.: Foundations of physical education, ed. 6, St. Louis, 1972, The C. V. Mosby Co.

Bucher, Charles A.: Physical education for life, New York, 1969, McGraw-Hill Book Co., Inc.

Goodlad, John I.: School, curriculum, and the individual, Waltham, Mass., 1966, Blaisdell Publishing Co.

Hertzke, George E.: A team-teaching approach to physical education, Athletic Journal 47:76, 1967.

Nixon, John E., and Jewett, Ann E.: Physical education curriculum, New York, 1964, The Ronald Press Co.

Rasch, Philip J., and Kroll, Walter: Safe wrestling, Journal of Health, Physical Education, and Recreation 36:32, 1965.

Santoro, Joel T.: Advantages of team teaching for physical education, Physical Educator 24:73, 1967.

Trump, J. Lloyd, and Georgiades, William: Doing better with what you have: NASSP Model Schools Project, National Association of Secondary School Principles Bulletin 54:106, 1970.

Vogelsinger, Hubert: Soccer, Journal of Health, Physical Education, and Recreation 37:31, 1966.

Wickstrom, R. L.: In defense of drills, Physical Educator 24:38, 1967.

METHODS AND MATERIALS FOR
TEACHING THE ATYPICAL STUDENT

In a recent annual report to Congress, the United States Commissioner of Education indicated that change is prevalent throughout the field of education and that federal monies are being provided to see that education for all students becomes a reality. The Commissioner particularly stressed the fact that increased educational opportunities should be provided the gifted and the handicapped.

During recent years much legislation has been enacted by Congress to meet the educational needs of the atypical student. This legislation has encouraged such things as stronger cooperative ties between school and community guidance services, interdisciplinary cooperation in educational programs, and pilot studies designed to improve the lot of the approximately seven million preschool and school-age handicapped children in the nation. Much of this legislation has implications for the adapted program in physical education. The Education Professions Development Act, for example, aimed at such things as improving the quality of professional teacher training programs, finding new and effective means of utilizing school staff, time, and instructional materials, and preparing educational personnel to better meet the needs of the handicapped.

The public attitude, as reflected in government action designed to provide equal education for all persons, has been changing. Today there is a strong feeling and a conviction on the part of the public that the handicapped child not only has a moral but a legal right to a sound education. This changing public opinion also carries over into the definition of the handicapped child. For example, in New York State the handicapped child is defined as one who can benefit from special services and programs because of mental, physical or emotional reasons. The American Association for Health, Physical Education, and Recreation interprets adapted physical education in terms of a physical activity program that is diversified and adapted to students with disabilities who have individual limitations and capacities.

The emphasis upon adapted physical education has resulted in many innovations in school systems in the United States and provisions for students with all types of handicapping conditions. A select few are listed here, particularly for the blind and visually handicapped, to indicate the nature and scope of such changes throughout the nation. It should be recognized, however, that adapted physical education programs are needed and exist for all kinds of handicapped students, including the mentally retarded, emotionally disturbed, culturally disadvantaged, and physically handicapped.

*Washington Irving Junior High School, Los Angeles, California.** Blind children

---

*Buell, Charles: The school's responsibility for providing physical activities for blind students, Journal of Health, Physical Education, and Recreation 41:41, 1970.

are provided a physical education program in which they participate in such activities as track and field, tug-of-war, weight lifting, combatives, rope skipping, basketball, and wrestling.

*Robert E. Lee School, Long Beach, California.** Blind children are enrolled and participate in the same activities as those offered normal children. The normal classmates assist the blind children in such activities as the fifty-yard dash and playing softball.

*Buena Vista School, Walnut Creek, California.** At this school when the blind student is at bat in softball, a batting tee is used. Other activities in which he engages are whoopla ball, folk dancing, tether ball, and flag football.

Fargo Public Schools, Fargo, North Dakota.† Visually handicapped students in the schools of this community meet with the regular physical education classes and engage in such activities as tumbling, self-testing activities, balance beam exercises, ice skating, relays, physical fitness tests, rope jumping, and conditioning exercises.

Physical education in the State of Michigan.‡ The program is designed to help each student to become aware of his potential. As such, he does not participate in those activities for which he is not physically fit. This goal applies to both handicapped and normal children.

Wheeling High School, Wheeling, Illinois.§ In the physical education program at this school blind students play softball with sighted classmates. Such modifications are made as roping off the diamond to guide the blind student when running

bases, sighted classmates giving signals to blind students to bat and to throw to a particular base, using a twenty-three-inch soft playground ball, and rolling rather than throwing the ball to the batter.

Other activities, events, and associations that have been organized and developed for the handicapped person on national and international levels include International Special Olympics for the Mentally Retarded, National Wheelchair Basketball Association, International Paralympics, Pan American Wheelchair Games, and National Mail-A-Graphic Bowling Tournament.

These innovative programs have many implications for physical education at the secondary school level. Educators are now in an era in which adapted physical education has come into its own and in which federal subsidy is extensive. Of course, the key to success of the adapted program, as is the case of all physical education programs, is the teacher. Particularly, in this special type of physical education, the teacher must be well prepared, dedicated, and sensitive to the needs of handicapped students.

THE CHALLENGE OF THE ATYPICAL STUDENT

A beginning physical educator soon discovers that the students in a single physical education class cannot accurately be said to form a homogeneous group. While all the boys or all the girls in a single physical education class may be in the same secondary grade and while all of them may fall within a certain narrow age range, they will not possess the same physical and mental abilities. Not all of them will have developed to the same levels of emotional and social maturity. A large majority of these students will fall into the classification "average," or "normal," for their age and grade. Other students will deviate considerably from their peers on a physical, mental, emotional, or social measure or on a combination of these measures. This latter group may be said to be atypical.

*Buell, Charles: The school's responsibility for providing physical activities for blind students, Journal of Health, Physical Education, and Recreation 41:41, 1970.

†Johansen, Gladys: Integrating visually handicapped children into public elementary school program, Journal of Health, Physical Education, and Recreation 42:61, 1971.

‡Buell, Charles: Physical education for visually handicapped children, Journal of Health, Physical Education, and Recreation 42:64, 1971.

§Bolt, Martha L.: Softball for the blind student, Journal of Health, Physical Education, and Recreation 41:40, 1970.

The atypical student in physical education presents a challenge to the teacher, for he may fall into any of several different categories. The culturally disadvantaged child is atypical, as are the physically gifted student, the creative student, and the awkward student with low motor ability. Atypical groupings also include emotionally disturbed students and mentally retarded students, as well as physically handicapped students. Each of these groups needs a strong and well-planned physical education experience. In schools where facilities and teaching personnel are available, adapted programs are developed especially to meet the needs of the atypical student. More often, the atypical student is thrust into a regularly scheduled physical education class. The physical educator must then be prepared to make both program and instructional adaptations to meet his special physical education needs.

It is a rare secondary school that does not have at least a few atypical students on its class rolls. It is a definite possibility that someday each physical educator may have to teach at least some students who fall outside the norm. Each physical educator should know how to best provide for the atypical student.

THE CULTURALLY DISADVANTAGED STUDENT

Culturally disadvantaged students have always made up a segment of the school population, but it is only recently that they have become a real concern to various communities and to the school serving these communities. It is a common error for the public to associate only the black child with cultural deprivation. Professional educators, especially, must realize that cultural deprivation crosses all color lines and ignores none of them.

The culture of poverty is especially apparent in the large urban centers. Ten years ago one in three city children was classified as culturally disadvantaged in estimates made by the Ford Foundation. At the present time an estimated 50% of the children living in cities are culturally disadvantaged. Many of the inhabitants of Appalachia, suburban communities, and isolated small towns and rural villages all across the United States are culturally disadvantaged.

Characteristics of the culturally disadvantaged student

The culturally disadvantaged student feels isolated from the mainstream of life. His home and neighborhood environment are negative influences that destroy his confidence rob him of a chance for success, and defeat any aspirations he may have. The goals of middle-class culture, as represented by the school, seem to be unreachable goals to someone who lives in the culture of poverty.

A culturally disadvantaged student may not achieve success in school because the cultural standards of the school and the home environment are usually inconsistent. Even schools in ghetto areas are staffed by teachers who represent the middle-class segment of society.

Fig. 15-1. Program for atypical students (Oconomowoc Senior High School, Oconomowoc, Wis.)

In a classroom situation the culturally disadvantaged student is unable to compete successfully scholastically, emotionally, or socially. Because reading and conversation have not been encouraged at home, he is severely restricted in his ability to communicate. He finds it extremely difficult to use logic or form concepts or to think in abstract terms. The culturally disadvantaged student is, for these reasons, often behind his proper grade level in achievement. He frequently attains low scores on intelligence and standardized tests because these tests are not designed to measure him accurately. As the culturally disadvantaged student continues to meet failure, he loses any motivation he may have had to achieve, and his levels of ambition and aspiration continue to decline.

Continual failure in the classroom negatively affects the school behavior of the culturally disadvantaged student. His short attention span, emotional instability, excitability, and restlessness often contribute to disruptive behavior patterns.

Educational needs of the culturally disadvantaged student

Many culturally disadvantaged students come from itinerant families. The children of migratory workers, in particular, will attend several different schools throughout the course of a single school year. Other culturally disadvantaged families are mobile because they constantly search for higher-paying jobs or better living conditions. This mobility further increases the educational deprivation of the culturally disadvantaged student.

Educational curricula for the culturally disadvantaged cannot be conventional middle-class curricula with conventional middle-class objectives and goals. The teacher cannot employ traditional middle-class methodology and impose middle-class standards of discipline. The traditional and conventional approaches to education do not help the culturally disadvantaged student to rise out of his poverty; they only succeed in driving him deeper into his narrow existence.

Many authorities have criticized the unrealistic educational atmosphere to which the culturally disadvantaged student is systematically exposed. On the elementary school level, especially, it is pointed out, reading books and textbooks illustrate and espouse a way of life that is totally alien to the culturally disadvantaged. It is further noted that if the student does indeed continue his education in a secondary school, the curriculum choices offered are really only weak attempts to resolve long-standing educational inequities. On the secondary school level the culturally disadvantaged student is sometimes arbitrarily channeled into a terminal vocational program, without regard to his hidden potential for seeking a higher education and a professional career.

Educators are constantly seeking to adjust curricula or to introduce innovative curricula that will better serve the culturally disadvantaged. As yet, definitive answers as to how a curriculum can realistically meet the needs of culturally disadvantaged students have not been found. However, educators have been able to identify three broad curriculum designs in secondary education for the disadvantaged. These three educational patterns may be termed remedial education, curriculum adjustment, and methodological modification. These patterns are not mutually exclusive.

Remedial education is a genuine need of the disadvantaged, but an entire secondary school curriculum cannot be based on such a program. However, many communities are engaged in out-of-school remedial education through such a program as Upward Bound.

Curriculum adjustment involves a slowing down of the educational pace. Curriculum content is identical for all segments of the school population, but classes made up of disadvantaged students spend proportionately greater amounts of time in each subject area. A regularly paced class will cover a unit of work in mathematics, for example, in many fewer class periods than will a slower-paced class of disadvantaged students. In these latter classes, discipline is very rigid—a concession to the teacher but not necessarily the most conducive atmosphere for the students. This slower method of teaching makes a questionable contribution to the disadvantaged student. It does not guarantee that educational or vocational needs are being met. However, it does allow the student to move into regularly paced classes when his ability permits and to move more slowly in those courses where he needs to increase his confidence and knowledge.

Methodological modifications are nothing more than the extreme adaptation of existing standard courses or specially designed standard courses. This educational technique is sometimes known as "tracking." When this method of educating disadvantaged students is adopted, the curriculum is made up almost entirely of vocationally oriented subject matter designed to prepare the student for the job market. Very few courses with a purely academic orientation are included in the programs, which may close the door on higher education. For example, courses in mathematics will be geared toward learning to make change, while courses in English will concentrate on writing a business letter or going to an interview. In the former there will be no attempt to teach the concepts of secondary school mathematics, such as algebra and geometry, and in the latter there will be no attempt to teach literature or theme writing. In some secondary schools, placement of a student in a program of this sort is undertaken in spite of the student's personal aspirations or untapped academic ability that might be revealed through exposure to a more academic curriculum.

These three systems may have more disadvantages than advantages, but they will be continued to be used until better methods are found to reach the needs of these youth in secondary schools. Culturally disadvantaged students do need vocational training, but they also need to be free to select courses that meet their individual needs and interests. The culturally disadvantaged student will not succeed educationally if all his courses are dictated or if he is confined by a tracking system or otherwise educationally isolated. The secondary schools must be as dedicated to educating culturally disadvantaged students as they are to educating the more advantaged segments of the school population.

The physical educator and the culturally disadvantaged student

In the physical education classroom the culturally disadvantaged student can be given an opportunity to meet success. Physical activity has a strong appeal for these youngsters, whether they are students in a school in their neighborhood or community or part of the student body in a school in an advantaged area.

The physical educator is the most important single factor in a secondary school physical education program for the disadvantaged. The physical educator must have a sincere interest in these students and must be willing to assume the responsibility for physically educating them. He should have an adequate background and special training in general education and physical education courses concerned with teaching the disadvantaged. These courses will help him come to a fuller understanding of the culturally disadvantaged student and the educational problems this student faces. The physical educator must have the ability to develop rapport with culturally disadvantaged students so that he can better respect, understand, and help these students. The physical educator must be able to provide an enriched program that will help to motivate the culturally disadvantaged student to make the best use of his physical, intellectual, and creative abilities.

The physical education program and the culturally disadvantaged student

The school physical education program frequently is the only supervised physical activity program for the culturally disad vantaged student. These students usually do not have a neighborhood recreational facility available and must conduct their sports and games on unsupervised streets or in dangerously littered lots. The school physical education experience must be designed to afford this student the physical education and recreational activities that are denied him elsewhere.

• *The physical education program must be carefully tailored to meet the needs and interests of the students.* Culturally disadvantaged students enjoy vigorous activity as well as creative and self-testing activities. There must be a wide choice of activities offered so that these students can select not only those experiences they find pleasurable but also those in which they can find success. As fundamental challenges are met successfully, new challenges must be presented in a logical progression.

• *The physical education program must be designed to increase the physical fitness and motor skill abilities of the students.* The program should include activities that will help the students to increase their physical fitness levels. Lack of structured programs outside the school denies culturally disadvantaged students the opportunity to participate in a regular program of physical activity, which often prevents them from maintaining even minimal fitness levels. Motor skill abilities are also often minimal simply because some students may never have had the benefit of a good physical education program in school.

• *There must be provision for suitable competition.* Culturally disadvantaged students need and enjoy competition. Competitive sports and games must be a part of the class program, but time must also be alloted for the individual to compete with himself in order to raise a physical fitness test score or to improve in a skill performance. Intramural programs are an invaluable extension of the class program, and the culturally disadvantaged student should be encouraged to participate. Likewise, culturally disadvantaged students should be encouraged to seek membership on interscholastic teams.

• *The program must provide for carry-over interests.* The culturally disadvantaged students need to develop a background in the lifetime sports. Swimming, dancing, and tennis, as well as other recreational activities such as bowling, should be included among the lifetime sport activities offered.

• *Equipment must be carefully purchased to suit the program.* There should be records, a phonograph, and a variety of rhythm instruments. Culturally disadvantaged students enjoy rhythmical activities and find that they are successful in such areas as dance, gymnastics, and tumbling, where they can demonstrate their creativity and express their individuality. Many warm-up activities, as well as many games, can be done to a musical accompaniment.

• *The program must allow for each student to be treated as an individual.* Culturally disadvantaged students are especially conscious of their individuality, and the program should allow ample opportunity for self-expression and creativity. Teacher recognition and praise for the most minor accomplishment are of utmost importance to the continued success of these students.

• *The program should help to instill good health habits and attitudes.* Where possible, showers should be available to the students. Each student should be provided with an individual locker, and cleanliness and proper maintenance of uniforms should be required.

• *The size of classes should be so arranged that discipline is easy to maintain.* Secondary school physical education classes are frequently overcrowded, and discipline is a major problem. If possible, culturally disadvantaged students should not be in a large class because little teaching takes place and because the individual student becomes lost in the mass. These students need and want to follow firm, consistent, and appropriate disciplinary standards. As much as any student, they must know what is expected of them and should be made to conform to the standards. However, any disciplinary standards imposed must relate directly to the students. Artificial standards will result in a total lack of discipline.

• *The physical education program should attempt to instill values that will extend into the classroom situation.* Through the activities of physical education, culturally disadvantaged students can obtain a release of tension in an acceptable way. They can also learn, from the give and take of sports, how to get along with others and will become more aware of the needs, abilities, and talents of their classmates. If these experiences are provided in the physical education class, at least some of the lessons will be transferred to the academic classroom.

• *The program should be correlated with the general education program of the school.* Through physical education activities much general educational knowledge and many such skills and abilities can be enhanced. Through folk dances, for example, it is possible to acquaint the student with the dress and customs of various cultures. This knowledge will help a class in history to become more interesting to the student and will help him to develop pride in his own culture. Through a sport such as baseball, mathematics can be brought to life. The students will be able to see the relationship between mathematics and its uses for such practical purposes as determining baseball batting averages, computing team won-lost percentages, and understanding angles so that this knowledge can be applied to laying out a baseball diamond.

THE PHYSICALLY HANDICAPPED STUDENT

The physically handicapped student may have a temporary disability, such as a broken arm, or he may be in a postoperative stage of recovery. Other physically handicapped students suffer from more permanent disabilities, such as blindness, deafness, or irremediable orthopedic conditions. The range of physical handicaps extends from minor to major in severity and directly affects the kinds and amounts of participation in physical activity.

Whatever the disability, a physical education program should be provided. Some handicapped students will be able to participate in a regular program of physical education with certain minor modifications. A separate, adapted program should be provided for those students who cannot participate in the basic instructional program of the school. The physically handicapped student cannot be allowed to sit on the sidelines and become only a spectator. He needs to have the opportunity to develop and maintain adequate skill abilities and fitness levels.

There are about three million children and youth between the ages of four and nineteen years in the United States who are physically handicapped in varying degrees. About 500,000 of these handicapped individuals are of secondary school age. These figures are based on estimates made by the Bureau of the Census through its ongoing United States National Health Survey. Many authorities feel, however, that accurate statistics have not as yet been made available and that the number of physically handicapped youth may be somewhat higher than these estimates. Further, these surveys sometimes classify mental retardation under the broad category of physical handicaps.

Many of the more severely handicapped secondary school children attend special schools where their unique needs can be met by highly trained staff members. The remainder are enrolled in the public secondary schools. It is this latter group with which the physical educator must be especially concerned.

Characteristics of the physically handicapped student

The presence of a physical handicap does not mean that the student also has a mental handicap, although this is sometimes true. Physical handicaps may stem from congenital or hereditary causes or may develop later in life through environmental factors, such as malnutrition, or from disease or accident. Sometimes negative psychological and social traits develop because of the limitations imposed on the individual by a severe physical handicap.

A physically handicapped student is occasionally ignored or rebuffed by classmates who do not understand the nature of the disability or who ostracize the student because his disability prevents him from participating fully in the activities of the school. These attitudes toward handicapped persons force them to withdraw in order to avoid being hurt, which results in their becoming further isolated from the remainder of the student body. Some experts have noted that the limitations of the handicap often seem more severe to the observer than they in fact are to the handicapped individual. When this misconception occurs, the handicapped student must prove his abilities in order to gain acceptance and a chance to participate and compete on an equal basis with his nonhandicapped classmates.

The blind or deaf student or the student with a severe speech impairment has different problems from those of the orthopedically handicapped student. The student who is partially sighted, blind, deaf, or impaired in speech cannot communicate with great facility. The orthopedically handicapped student is limited in the physical education class but not necessarily in the academic classroom. The student with vision, hearing, or speech problems may be limited in both the physical education classroom and the academic classroom.

Educational needs of the physically handicapped student

Physically handicapped students in general have the same academic needs, interests, and abilities as do their nonhandicapped peers. While special arrangements must be made for students who have speech, hearing, or visual disabilities, these students are capable of competing successfully in the classroom atmosphere.

Physically handicapped students need preparation for vocations, technical schools, or college. They can contribute to the school through participation in social and service activities. They are far less limited in the general education program and activities of the school than in the physical education program.

The physical educator and the physically handicapped student

There is a lack of physical educators who are specifically trained to teach the physically handicapped. School systems find that the cost of providing special classes taught by specially trained physical educators is prohibitive. Where there are no special classes, the physical educator must provide, within the regular instructional program, those activities that will meet the needs of the handicapped student. Further, placing the physically handicapped student in a regular physical education class will help to give him a feeling of belonging. This advantage is not always possible where separate, adapted classes are provided.

To be able to provide an adequate program for physically handicapped students, the physical educator needs special training. Advanced courses in anatomy, physiology, physiology of activity, and kinesiology are essential, along with special work in psychology and adapted physical education. The professional preparation curriculum should also include courses in movement education and body mechanics.

The physical educator must have an understanding of the physical disability of each handicapped student and must be aware of any psychological, social, or behavioral problems that may accompany the disability. The physical educator must know the capacities of each handicapped student so that he can provide him with an individualized program.

The physical education program and the physically handicapped student

No two physically handicapped students will have the same limitations in regard to the activities of the physical education program. Under no circumstances can the physical educator diagnose the disability and prescribe a physical activity program.

This must be accomplished by the student's physician. The physician's recommendations for students whose conditions have been previously diagnosed should be followed. If in the course of the year the physical educator observes that a student seems to have some kind of physical handicap that is not noted on the record cards of the school, the physical educator must refer the student to his family physician or the proper agency through the normal administrative process of the school. After the disability has been medically diagnosed and activity recommendations made, it becomes the responsibility of the physical educator to provide the proper program.

Some handicapped students will be able to participate in almost all the activities that nonhandicapped students enjoy. Blind students, for example, have successfully engaged in team sports where they can receive aural cues from their sighted teammates. Some athletic equipment manufacturers have placed bells inside game balls, and the blind student is then able to rely on this sound as well as on the supplementary aural cues. Ropes or covered wires acting as hand guides also enable the blind student to participate in track-and-field events. Still other activities, such as swimming, dance, calisthenics, and tumbling, require little adaptation or none at all, except in regard to heightened safety precautions.

In general, deaf students will not be restricted in any way from participating in a full physical education program. Some deaf students experience difficulty in activities requiring precise balance, such as balance-beam walking, and may require some remedial work in this area. The physical educator should be prepared to offer any extra help that is needed.

Other physically handicapped students will have a variety of limitations and a variety of skill abilities. Appropriate program adaptations and modifications must be made in order to meet this range of individual needs. The following general guidelines are helpful in physically educating the physically handicapped on the secondary school level.

• *Cooperate with the physician in planning each student's program.* The physician is the individual most knowledgeable about the history and limitations of a student's handicap. He is therefore in the best position to recommend a physical activity program for the student.

• *Test the motor skill ability and physical fitness levels of each student.* The student's abilities and levels of fitness should be tested in areas where medical permission for participation has been granted. This will not only ensure a proper program for the individual but will help in placing the student in the proper class or section of a class.

• *Keep the program under constant evaluation.* Careful records should be kept showing the student's test scores, activity recommendations, activities engaged in, and progress through the program. In this way, the physical educator will know whether the program is reaching its objectives, the student will be able to discuss his progress with the physical educator, and the school health team and the student's physician will be able to be kept up to date on the student's progress and needs.

• *Keep the adapted and regular programs as similar as possible.* Where the two programs are totally divergent, the physically handicapped student is isolated from his classmates. When the programs are as similar as possible, the handicapped student can be made to feel a part of the larger group and will gain self-confidence and self-respect. Similarity in the programs will also effectively serve to motivate the physically handicapped student.

• *Provide challenges for the student as he progresses.* Physically handicapped students need the challenge of a progressive program. They welcome the opportunity to test their abilities and should experience the fun of a challenge and the success of meeting it.

• *Provide time for extra help.* Handicapped students should be given an opportunity to seek extra help and extra practice after school hours. During this time they can benefit from more individualized instruction than is possible during the class period.

• *Select activities on an individual basis.* Although several handicapped students in a single class may be able to participate in several activities in common, they may not have a common interest in these activities. The fitness level of each student and his ability, recreational needs, sex, and age, as well as his interests, will help to determine the activities the student will engage in pleasurably.

• *Adapt the activity to the student rather than the student to the activity.* The student's disability determines the activities in which he can participate. Therefore, any modifications or adaptations that are made must be made in the activity.

• *Provide safe facilities and safe equipment.* Safe facilities and safe equipment are essential in any physical education program. Extra safeguards must be taken when a physical education class includes physically handicapped students.

• *Provide suitable extraclass activities.* Experts feel that physically handicapped students are placed in an unduly hazardous situation when they engage in highly competitive activities. Intramural and club programs should be provided, but they must be of such a nature that physically handicapped students can enjoy them in a safe, controlled atmosphere that precludes the danger of injury.

THE MENTALLY RETARDED STUDENT

There are special schools in many states that serve mentally retarded students either on a residential or a day-care basis. Public secondary schools also offer specially designed curricula and employ teachers who have the comprehensive background and training needed to teach in programs for the retarded. In some public schools, special physical education classes are offered for these students, while in still other schools, mentally retarded students partic-

ipate in the regularly scheduled physical education classes.

Mental retardation can be a result of hereditary abnormalities, a birth injury, or an accident or illness that leads to impairment of brain function. There are degrees of mental retardation ranging from the severely mentally retarded, who require custodial care, to the educable mentally retarded, who function with only a moderate degree of impairment.

Each year in the United States more than 126,000 babies are born who have some degree of mental retardation. At present, there are more than seven million mentally retarded children and adults in the United States.

Many agencies are conducting research in the field of mental retardation in an attempt to discover the causes of mental retardation, the nature of mental retardation, and the methods through which it may be prevented. Some agencies are operating innovative training schools for mentally retarded students. The Joseph P. Kennedy, Jr., Foundation is spearheading much of the research concerned with mental retardation and is also a leader in providing camping and recreational programs for the mentally retarded. The Kennedy Foundation has also sponsored training programs for teachers of the mentally retarded. The United States Government has sponsored an experimental physical education program for the mentally retarded at the Austin State School in Austin, Texas. This program is cooperatively conducted by a staff of special education teachers, specially trained physical educators, vocational rehabilitation technicians, and architectural engineers. A special program and special equipment have been designed especially for use with the mentally retarded. Climbing devices, obstacle courses, and unique running areas, as well as a swimming pool, are part of the special facilities. The objectives of this program include social and personal adjustment, as well as the development of physical fitness, sports skills, and general motor ability.

Characteristics of the mentally retarded student

Mentally retarded students show a wide range of intellectual and physical ability. The experts seem to agree that a mentally retarded child is usually closer to the norm for his chronological age in physical development than in mental development. Some mentally retarded students are capable of participating in a regular physical education class, while others have been able to develop only minimal amounts of motor ability. In general, the majority of mentally retarded students are two to four years behind their normal peers in motor development alone.

Despite a slower development of motor ability, mentally retarded students seem to reach physical maturity faster than do normal boys and girls of the same chronological age. Mentally retarded children tend to be overweight and to lack physical strength and endurance. Their posture is generally poor, and they lack adequate levels of physical fitness and motor coordination. Some of these physical problems develop because mentally retarded children have had little of the play and physical activity experiences of normal children. The problems of some mentally retarded youngsters are further multiplied by attendant physical handicaps and personality disturbances.

A mentally retarded student does not have the ability to think in the abstract or to remember isolated facts well. A short attention span, a tendency to overreact emotionally, and a low threshold of irritability also contribute to the classroom problems of the mentally retarded student. While not all mentally retarded students have the same personal characteristics, some of them also tend to be very restless, destructive, and impulsive.

Educational needs of the mentally retarded student

Mentally retarded students need a sound foundation in educational skills. Many of them will seek, and be able to hold, jobs at the conclusion of their secondary educa-

tion, and there must be vocational training courses for them. Girls in particular need and enjoy courses in home economics, while both boys and girls benefit from instruction in money management and the techniques of using the telephone and writing acceptable letters.

While special classes are usually conducted in many subject areas of the school curriculum, it has been found that the mentally retarded student can join with his peers in some subjects. Vocational and shop courses, art, music, home economics, and physical education are a few of the subjects in which mentally retarded students can find success outside of the special class. Likewise, the mentally retarded student can enjoy intramural activities and school clubs and can contribute to special events, school committees, and service organizations.

The physical educator and the mentally retarded student

The mentally retarded student requires a physical educator with special training, special skills, and a special brand of patience. Such a student lacks confidence and pride and therefore needs a physical educator who will help him to change his negative self-image. The physical educator must be able to provide a program designed to give each student a chance for success. The goals of the program cannot be so high that they are unreachable.

The physical educator must be ready to praise and reinforce each minor success. He should be capable of demonstrating each skill and giving simple and concise directions, and he must be willing to participate in the physical education activities with the students. Discipline must be enforced and standards adhered to, but the disciplinary approach must be a kind and gentle one.

The physical educator must be especially mindful of the individual characteristics of each mentally retarded student. Students who need remedial work should be afforded this opportunity, while students who can succeed in a regular physical education program should be placed in such a class or section. Above all, the physical educator must remember that he cannot proceed with a class of mentally retarded students in the same manner as he would proceed with a class of students with average intelligence and physical ability.

The physical education program and the mentally retarded student

Most mentally retarded students need to be taught how to play. They are frequently unfamiliar with even the simplest of childhood games and lack facility in the natural movements of childhood, such as skipping, hopping, and leaping. They are often seriously deficient in physical fitness and need work in postural improvement. Further, mentally retarded students find it difficult to understand and remember game strategy, such as the importance of staying in the right position, and cannot relate well to the rules of sports and games.

The majority of mentally retarded students need a specially tailored physical education experience. For those who can participate in a regular physical education class, care must be taken that these students are not placed in a situation where they will meet failure. In a special physical education class, the mentally retarded student can be exposed to a variety of physical education experiences. Physical fitness and posture improvement, along with self-testing activities and games organized and designed according to the ability and interests of the group, will make up a vital part of the special program. In such a class, activities can be easily modified and new experiences introduced before interest wanes. Research has indicated that specially tailored physical education classes can help mentally retarded students to progress very rapidly in their physical skill development.

Physical education can make a very positive contribution to the mentally retarded. Not only must the program be a suitable one, but the physical educator must also be adequately prepared and emotionally and intellectually dedicated to teaching these students.

• *The program should provide opportunities for increasing physical fitness.* Mentally retarded students do not usually initiate play experiences or seek out physical activity. Lack of a regular program of physical exercise, as well as lack of understanding of the need for such a program, means that the mentally retarded student may be lacking in physical fitness. A sound program that includes physical fitness activities can help these students to become more physically fit.

• *Provide a background of basic motor activities.* Movement education is especially suited to mentally retarded students. These students have often not engaged in the natural play activities of childhood and need to develop their gross motor skill abilities in order to be able to find success in some of the more sophisticated motor skills.

• *Provide a wide variety of self-testing activities.* Mentally retarded students enjoy even the smallest success in physical activity. Giving such a student an opportunity to compete against himself will help him to gain confidence and pride in accomplishment.

• *Provide a carefully structured, progressive program.* Mentally retarded students have the same physical activity needs as do normal students. A progressive program will help to interest and motivate them in a variety of physical activities.

• *Provide opportunities for competition in games of low organization.* Mentally retarded students enjoy the give-and-take of competition, but any competition must be geared specifically to their needs and abilities. The experience of competing will aid in the development of desirable social traits.

• *Introduce new activities at the beginning of a class period.* Mentally retarded children tire easily and have a short attention span. New activities will be learned more easily and will be enjoyed more be-

AAHPER-KENNEDY FOUNDATION

SPECIAL FITNESS TEST

for the

mentally retarded

A manual explaining the purpose of this test, administrative procedures, and how to record and use the results is available from:

AAHPER
NEA PUBLICATIONS—SALES
1201 SIXTEENTH STREET, N.W.
WASHINGTON, D. C. 20036

($1.00 per copy)

It presents graphs showing changes in the performance of retarded children with age, national norms for educable retarded boys and girls 8 to 18 years of age, and suggestions for improving their physical fitness.

It is highly recommended that anyone using this test obtain a copy of the manual.

Special Fitness Record Forms (score cards) are also available (5¢ each)

---

1. FLEXED ARM HAND

—horizontal or doorway gym (about 3½" dia.) bar adjusted to aproximately the student's height.

—overhand grasp, pull chin above bar and hold as long as possible

—may use stool or tester may lift to position

—score is time *in seconds* from when he hangs unaided until his chin touches or falls below bar.

2. SIT-UP

—student lies on back, fingers interlaced behind head, legs extended. Partner holds ankles down

—sit up, touch elbow to knee and return keeping fingers behind head.

—"curl up," no pushing off with elbows, back flat on mat each time.

—score is *number of* complete sit ups *in one minute*

3. SHUTTLE RUN

—2 lines, 30 feet apart, 2 blocks of wood (2" x 2" x 4") behind far line.

—on "GO!" student runs down, picks up one block, runs back and *places* it behind starting line, runs down and picks up second block, runs back and *carries* it across starting line

—score is time *in seconds to the nearest tenth* from "GO!" until he crosses finish line.

4. STANDING BROAD JUMP

—toes behind take-off line with feet several inches apart

—bend knees and swing arms backward

—jump by extending legs and swinging arms forward

—score is distance *in feet and inches* from take-off line to back of heel *nearest* take-off line

5. 50-YARD DASH

—starter raises hand, says "READY?—GO!" and sweeps hand down to signal timer who stands at finish line

—any starting position may be used

—score is time *in seconds to the nearest tenth*

6. SOFTBALL THROW FOR DISTANCE

—12" softball thrown from between two parallel lines, six feet apart (see figure)

—must be thrown overhand

—score is distance *in feet* from *point* of throwing to *point* of landing

7. 300-YARD RUN-WALK

—if indoors, six times around 50' x 25' course

—if outdoors, three times up and back a 50-yard shuttle course

—walking permitted but object is to cover distance in shortest possible time.

—score is the elapsed time *in minutes and seconds*

STANDARDS FOR AAHPER SILVER AWARD

(Qualified by achieving the standard on any five test items)

GIRLS

Age	Flexed Arm Hang (sec.)	Sit-Ups (no.)	Shuttle Run (sec.)	Standing Broad Jump (ft.—ins.)	50-yd. Dash (sec.)	Softball Throw (ft.)	300-yard Run-Walk (min.-sec.)
8	5	13	15.0	3' 1"	11.3	27	1:34
9	6	15	14.2	3' 4"	10.5	34	1:33
10	8	18	13.3	3' 10"	9.3	41	1:23
11	7	18	12.9	4' 0"	9.1	46	1:23
12	5	19	12.2	4' 3"	8.8	56	1:18
13	5	18	12.3	4' 6"	8.9	57	1:16
14	6	20	12.1	4' 6"	8.7	63	1:15
15	5	20	12.0	4' 6"	8.6	65	1:20
16	5	21	12.1	4' 8"	9.0	67	1:18
17	4	20	12.5	4' 9"	9.0	62	1:22
18	7	20	12.2	4' 9"	9.0	61	1:20

BOYS

Age	Flexed Arm Hang (sec.)	Sit-Ups (no.)	Shuttle Run (sec.)	Standing Broad Jump (ft.—ins.)	50-yd. Dash (sec.)	Softball Throw (ft.)	300-yard Run-Walk (min.-sec.)
8	7	16	14.0	3' 4"	10.5	43	1:33
9	8	17	13.1	3' 10"	9.9	58	1:24
10	8	20	12.6	3' 11"	9.2	66	1:20
11	11	22	11.9	4' 6"	8.9	80	1:15
12	12	24	11.6	4' 10"	8.3	95	1:12
13	10	25	11.3	5' 0"	8.2	104	1:10
14	13	26	11.0	5' 3"	8.0	112	1:07
15	12	31	11.2	5' 9"	7.5	137	1:01
16	17	29	11.1	6' 1"	7.3	154	0:59
17	17	30	10.6	6' 2"	6.9	159	0:56
18	25	31	10.6	6' 6"	7.1	159	0:57

STANDARDS FOR AAHPER GOLD AWARD

(Qualified by achieving the standard on any five test items)

GIRLS

Age	Flexed Arm Hang (sec.)	Sit-Ups (no.)	Shuttle Run (sec.)	Standing Broad Jump (ft.—ins.)	50-yd. Dash (sec.)	Softball Throw (ft.)	300-yard Run-Walk (min.-sec.)
8	10	18	13.8	3' 8"	10.1	33	1:28
9	11	21	12.9	3' 9"	9.1	46	1:24
10	13	25	12.1	4' 5"	8.8	52	1:16
11	12	24	11.9	4' 8"	8.4	65	1:15
12	10	24	11.5	4' 11"	8.1	71	1:09
13	11	22	11.6	4' 10"	8.3	72	1:10
14	12	25	11.3	5' 1"	8.2	86	1:08
15	11	25	11.0	5' 1"	8.0	84	1:12
16	11	24	11.2	5' 3"	8.1	82	1:11
17	11	24	11.7	5' 3"	8.2	81	1:13
18	10	24	11.5	5' 3"	8.5	84	1:11

BOYS

Age	Flexed Arm Hang (sec.)	Sit-Ups (no.)	Shuttle Run (sec.)	Standing Broad Jump (ft.—ins.)	50-yd. Dash (sec.)	Softball Throw (ft.)	300-yard Run-Walk (min.-sec.)
8	11	20	12.6	3' 9"	9.4	57	1:23
9	13	23	12.1	4' 5"	8.9	73	1:17
10	16	26	11.8	4' 8"	8.5	81	1:13
11	19	27	11.1	5' 1"	8.2	99	1:08
12	19	30	11.0	5' 4"	7.9	114	1:05
13	19	30	10.8	5' 6"	7.7	125	1:04
14	22	30	10.4	5' 11"	7.4	142	1:00
15	26	34	10.7	6' 4"	7.1	159	0:58
16	29	34	10.2	6' 9"	6.9	181	0:55
17	29	35	9.8	7' 2"	6.3	176	0:51
18	39	36	9.9	7' 1"	6.5	187	0:52

STANDARDS FOR KENNEDY FOUNDATION CHAMP AWARD

(Qualified by achieving the standard on all seven test items)

GIRLS

Age	Flexed Arm Hang (sec.)	Sit-Ups (no.)	Shuttle Run (sec.)	Standing Broad Jump (ft.—ins.)	50-yd. Dash (sec.)	Softball Throw (ft.)	300-yard Run-Walk (min.-sec.)
8	14	22	13.0	3' 10"	9.6	36	1:26
9	16	25	12.4	4' 1"	8.8	58	1:19
10	16	29	11.9	4' 8"	8.5	59	1:12
11	17	27	11.5	5' 0"	8.2	75	1:13
12	14	28	11.1	5' 4"	7.8	82	1:06
13	14	25	11.2	5' 1"	7.9	81	1:07
14	16	27	11.0	5' 6"	7.8	95	1:04
15	15	27	10.6	5' 6"	7.8	94	1:06
16	14	26	11.0	5' 7"	7.9	97	1:05
17	13	27	11.1	5' 6"	7.9	98	1:10
18	13	28	11.2	5' 8"	8.1	93	1:09

BOYS

Age	Flexed Arm Hang (sec.)	Sit-Ups (no.)	Shuttle Run (sec.)	Standing Broad Jump (ft.—ins.)	50-yd. Dash (sec.)	Softball Throw (ft.)	300-yard Run-Walk (min.-sec.)
8	15	22	12.4	4' 1"	9.1	61	1:22
9	19	27	11.9	4' 9"	8.6	85	1:14
10	21	29	11.4	4' 11"	8.2	89	1:08
11	24	29	10.9	5' 4"	8.0	108	1:05
12	25	32	10.7	5' 6"	7.5	123	1:03
13	25	33	10.5	5' 10"	7.5	140	1:00
14	32	34	10.1	6' 4"	7.1	151	0:56
15	33	36	10.3	6' 9"	6.9	181	0:56
16	37	38	9.9	7' 0"	6.5	188	0:52
17	34	38	9.6	7' 5"	6.1	187	0:49
18	49	38	9.7	7' 4"	6.3	204	0:49

For boys and girls who achieve the CHAMP standards on all seven test items and engage in at least 30 hours of sports and recreational activity.

Fig. 15-2. AAHPER—Kennedy Foundation Special Fitness Test for mentally retarded.

fore fatigue sets in and while interest is still high.

• *Provide for a choice of activities.* This will help the mentally retarded student to feel that he is important. Further, if a choice of activities is offered, motivation, morale, and discipline will remain higher.

• *Provide for lifetime recreational skills.* These skills are essential for any student, but mentally retarded students, especially, need to learn the value of recreation. Through specially designed intramural and club programs, additional recreational experiences can be introduced.

• *Stress positive health and safety habits.* Provide each student with a locker and require that proper care be taken of the physical education uniform. Where possible, provide time in the program for showers. Stress should be placed on the relationship between health and physical activity. Safety must be constantly stressed in all activities and must be related to other phases of the school program.

• *Keep accurate, up-to-date records.* Records will help in guiding the student and in assessing his abilities and limitations. The students' parents are also interested in their progress, and keeping them informed of gains will help to establish good public relations. Accurate and complete records will be invaluable to the student's guidance counselor, the school health team, and the student's personal physician. Complete records will also help the physical educator in making an objective evaluation of the program.

THE DISRUPTIVE STUDENT

The disruptive student may suffer from deep-seated emotional disturbances, or he may simply be in need of guidance and counseling to help him resolve less serious problems that lead to his disruptive behavior. Some students who dislike school will be disruptive in classes even though there is no serious emotional problem involved. In any case, the disruptive student presents special problems for the physical educator,

who must be concerned not only with teaching but also with the safety of the students in the class.

A single disruptive student can have a disastrous effect on the conduct of a class as well as on the behavior of the rest of the students in that class. Effective teaching cannot take place when discipline deteriorates.

Characteristics of the disruptive student

Emotionally unstable students have difficulty in maintaining good relationships with their classmates and teachers. Some of their abnormal behavior patterns stem from a need and craving for attention. Sometimes the disruptive student exhibits gross patterns of aggressiveness and destructiveness. Other emotionally unstable students may be so withdrawn from the group that they refuse to participate in the activities of the class, even to the extent of refusing to report for class. In the case of physical education, the disruptive student may refuse to dress for the activity when he does report. These measures draw both student and teacher reaction, focusing the desired attention on the nonconforming student.

Emotionally unstable students are often restless and unable to pay attention. In a physical education class they may poke and prod other students, refuse to line up with the rest of the class, or insist on bouncing a game ball while a lesson is in progress. These are also ploys to gain attention, and the student behaves similarly in the academic classroom for the same reason.

Some disruptive students may have physical or mental handicaps that contribute to their behavior. Others may be concerned about what they consider to be poor personal appearance, such as extremes of height or weight, or physical maturity not in keeping with their chronological age. Still other disruptive students may simply be in the process of growing up and are finding it difficult to handle their adolescence.

Educational needs of the disruptive student

The disruptive student is in need of guidance and counseling. The school should not impose discipline on the disruptive student before the causes for his behavior have been ascertained. The school has many services available to it through which it can help the disruptive student. School psychologists can test the student, and social welfare agencies can assist by working with both the student and his family. Case studies of the student and conferences with all the student's teachers can be invaluable in determining his needs. The school health team will also have pertinent information to contribute, as will the student's guidance counselors. Conferences with the student also help to open the doors to understanding.

The school cannot take the responsibility for arbitrarily expelling or suspending the disruptive student without first carefully and comprehensively examining the causes for his behavior. Expulsion or suspension often serve to heighten the negative feelings of the student and make it more difficult to draw the student back into the life of the school.

The physical educator and the disruptive student

If the physical educator is faced with many disruptive students in a single class, he must first examine himself and his relationship to that class. The physical educator's rapport with the entire class, his relationships with individual students, his disciplinary standards, and his program will all affect student behavior to some degree.

If negative student behavior stems from some aspect of a student's personality, then the physical educator must take positive steps to resolve the problem so that teaching can take place. The physical educator must deal with each behavioral problem on an individual basis and seek help from the school personnel best equipped to give aid. The student's guidance counselor will have information that will be of help

to the physical educator. A conference with this individual may reveal methods that have proved effective with the student in the past. Further, the observations made by the physical educator will be of value to the guidance counselor's continuing study of the student.

The physical educator will find that not all disruptive students are continual and serious behavior problems, since students as well as teachers have their good and bad days. The physical educator should have a private conference with the student whose behavior suddenly becomes negative and try to understand why the student has reacted in a way unusual for him. Such a conference will lead to mutual understanding and often help to allay future problems with the same student.

Much of the physical educator's task is student guidance. In individual cases of disruptive behavior, the physical educator should exhaust all his personal resources in order to alleviate the problem before enlisting aid from other sources. Any case of disruptive behavior demands immediate action on the part of the physical educator to prevent minor problems from becoming major ones.

The physical education program and the disruptive student

A majority of secondary school pupils enjoy physical activity and physical education. They look forward to the physical education class as one part of the school day in which they can express themselves and gain a release of tension in an atmosphere that encourages it. For this reason, the student who is disruptive in the classroom is often one of the best citizens in the physical education class.

Physical education is in a unique position to help the disruptive student. Most students profit from the activities of physical education, and through their actions in this phase of the school curriculum it is possible for teaching personnel to gain many insights into student behavior.

• *Know each student by name and as an*

individual. Individual knowledge of each student is of utmost importance in physical education and in understanding individual behavior patterns. Recognizing a student's needs and problems early in the school year will help to prevent future behavior problems.

• *Be certain that students understand the behavior required of them.* While physical education classes are conducted in a less formal manner than classroom subjects, this does not mean that lower standards of behavior are acceptable. Students should know what the standards are on the first day of class and should be expected to adhere to these standards in all future classes.

• *Discipline must be firm and consistent.* When rules are rigid one day and relaxed the next, students will not know how to react. Discipline must be enforced in a firm and consistent manner for all students during all classes.

• *Discuss behavioral problems with the individual student.* Respect for the individual student is a necessity. No student likes to be criticized or embarrassed in front of his peers. When a student is singled out from a group and used as a disciplinary example, the atmosphere in the class will deteriorate. Respect for the student means maintenance of respect for the teacher. If disciplinary matters are handled on a one-to-one basis, rapport is enhanced.

• *Expect good behavior from all students.* If the disruptive student knows that the physical educator expects him to behave in a bizarre manner, he will react in just this way. Good behavior should be expected until the student acts otherwise.

• *Try to ensure that the disruptive student will be successful in the physical education class.* Constant failure only abets disruptive behavior. If a student is known to be hostile and disruptive, an attempt should be made to avoid placing him in situations where he feels inadequate and shows this in his behavior. If, for example, a disruptive student does not run well, he may still make a superior goalie in soccer, a position that would not require him to run.

• *Give praise as often as possible.* If the disruptive student has a special skill talent ask him to demonstrate for the class. This will give him the recognition and attention he needs. Give praise for a skill that is well performed and notice the minor accomplishments of the student.

• *Allow the student to help with equipment.* Make the position of equipment leader a reward rather than a punishment. See that each deserving student, including the disruptive ones, receive this honor when they merit it.

• *Welcome the disruptive student to intramural and club activities.* No student is going to participate in extraclass activities unless he really wants to do so. Set behavioral standards for these activities and open them to all students in the school who meet the standards. Acceptance into a club or participation on an intramural team may help the disruptive student gain self-respect and peer recognition and approval.

• *Keep the student's guidance counselor informed of his progress.* The guidance counselor should know of any progress made by the pupil. Too often these individuals are informed only of failures or increasing behavior problems. Progress in one area of the school curriculum may have a positive effect on progress in other areas of the curriculum.

THE POORLY COORDINATED STUDENT

Well-coordinated students are the bright lights of the physical education class. Often held up as examples by the physical educator, they find success easily and receive much individual attention because they respond well to instruction and coaching. There is another segment of the school population, however, that needs individual instruction even more—the awkward, uncoordinated students who are frequently left to learn skills as best they can.

The student with low motor ability is often ignored by the physical educator. He is unpopular with his classmates because he is considered a detriment in team sports.

He is undesirable as a partner in dual sports and therefore is often paired with equally uncoordinated and awkward partners. The student with low motor ability needs special attention so that he can improve his physical skill performances, derive pleasure from success in physical activity, and gain a background in lifetime sports.

Physical education makes special arrangements for the physically handicapped, the mentally retarded, and the athlete. Very little is done for the poorly coordinated student.

Characteristics of the poorly coordinated student

The poorly coordinated student exhibits a measurable lack of physical ability. Less often considered is the psychological effect of the student's physical inabilities. The poorly coordinated student who is not given special help in the secondary school often becomes the adult who abhors any physical activity and is reticent about participating in adult recreational activities.

Poorly coordinated students are usually placed in regular physical education classes when they have no mental or physical handicaps. The only concession made to their problem is through ability grouping in schools where facilities and personnel are adequate. Even then, ability grouping sometimes is used only to separate the "duds" from the "stars," thus increasing the poorly coordinated student's feelings of inadequacy. The poorly coordinated student may be held up to ridicule by fellow students as well as by physical education teachers, who tend to use him as an example of how not to perform a physical skill.

The poorly coordinated student will resist learning new activities because the challenge this presents offers little chance for success. The challenge of a new skill or activity to be learned may create such tension within the student that he becomes physically ill. In other instances this tension may result in negative behavior.

Poor coordination may be the result of several factors. The student may not be physically fit, he may have poor reflexes, or he may not have the ability to use mental imagery. For some reason such as a lengthy childhood illness, the poorly coordinated student may not have been normally physically active. Other poorly coordinated students will enter the secondary school physical education program from an elementary school that lacked a trained physical educator, had no facilities for physical education, or had a poor program of physical education. A single factor or a combination of any of them will help to retard motor skill development.

Educational needs of the poorly coordinated student

The physical education program frequently motivates students with specific problems to perform better in the academic classroom by offering an opportunity for success in physical activity. This process may work in reverse with the poorly coordinated student. A student's dread of his physical education class will have a detrimental effect on his ability to perform well in the classroom. Both his behavior and his academic achievement may be adversely affected.

When classroom performance declines, it is the classroom teacher who will become aware of the problem first. As with any other student problem, the first step in resolving that problem is a conference with the student and then with the student's guidance counselor. It may be only through such conferences that the cause of the problem is revealed and the physical educator made aware of his contribution to the problem. Unless the physical educator is made aware of the problem, steps cannot be taken to remedy it. Many problems of this nature in a single school cast shadows of doubt on the value of the physical education program, its philosophy, and objectives. If measures are not taken to adequately resolve the problems, poor relations will develop between the physical educator, the student body, the remainder of the school faculty, the administration, and the community.

The physical educator and the poorly coordinated student

The physical educator must understand child growth and development and formulate a physical education program that is based on sound principles of growth and development. A knowledge of adolescent growth and development and of adolescent psychology is also an essential prerequisite to teaching on the secondary school level. Additionally, the physical educator must be able to use his knowledge to select activities and devise progressions that are appropriate to the age and grade level of the students in the program.

In working with poorly coordinated students the physical educator must exercise the utmost patience. He must know why the student is poorly coordinated and be able to devise an individual program for him that will help him to move and perform more effectively. The physical educator must be sure that the student understands the need for special help and should try to motivate him to succeed. When a skill is performed with even a modicum of improvement, the effort must be praised and the achievement reinforced.

With a large class and only one instructor, there can be relatively little time spent with each individual. The buddy system, in which a poorly coordinated student is paired with a well-coordinated partner, often enables both students to progress faster. Immediate successes will not be forthcoming for the poorly coordinated student, and the physical educator must be careful not to push the student beyond his limits. An overly difficult challenge, coupled with the fatigue that results from trying too hard, may result in retarding, rather than accelerating, improvement. Any goal set for the poorly coordinated student must be an attainable goal.

The physical educator has a very definite responsibility to the poorly coordinated student. Poor attitudes concerning physical activity can too easily be carried over into adult life. If these negative attitudes can be reversed by the physical educator early in the student's secondary school career, the student may find that he will be motivated to develop abilities in several of the lifetime sports.

The physical education program and the poorly coordinated student

The objectives of the program for poorly coordinated students will not differ from the objectives of any physical education program, but the emphases will lie in different areas, and many activities will be modified or adapted as the need arises.

Before a program is devised, the status of the students will need to be known so that their individual abilities and needs can be identified. Physical fitness and motor ability testing must be ongoing phases of the program. Through the physical education program the students must come to realize that their special needs are being met because they are as important as the well-skilled students in the eyes of the physical educator.

• *Carefully weigh the advantages and disadvantages of ability grouping.* Separating students into ability groups may cause poorly coordinated students to feel that they are being pushed out of the way. If ability grouping is used, they must receive adequate instruction and a meaningful program and have equal access to good equipment and facilities.

• *Select the proper activities.* If a student has poor eye-hand or eye-foot coordination, he will not succeed in such activities as tennis or soccer. Activities must be chosen that suit the abilities of the students and at the same time help them to develop the needed coordination.

• *Offer a varied, interesting, and progressive program.* Work on improving fitness and self-testing activities should form only a part of the program. Games of appropriate level, rhythmics and dance, and such activities as swimming and archery will help to stimulate and maintain interest.

• *Offer a club program for all students.* Physical fitness clubs swimming clubs, and other clubs open to all students will benefit poorly coordinated students. If ability grouping is used in class, a common club program will help to remove the stigma of separateness.

• *Include competition in the program.* With carefully arranged teams and schedules in an intramural program, poorly coordinated students can be given a chance to compete on their own level. Preparation for intramural competition should be a part of the class program.

• *Include some activities of a coeducational nature.* Dancing in particular lends itself to coeducational instruction. When classes can be combined and coeducational instruction offered, poorly coordinated students have an opportunity to develop social skills.

• *Group students on a flexible pattern.* Different groupings for different activities will stimulate interest and provide students with a variety of partners.

• *Provide for upward progression.* Reassess the students periodically to see how they are progressing. When an adequate level of success has been attained in a particular activity, move the student into a faster-moving and more highly skilled group.

• *Involve the students in program planning.* Offer a selection of activities that will appeal to poorly coordinated students and guide their selections in relation to their abilities.

• *Provide for lifetime sports skills.* Swimming and dance are ideal for future recreational use. Poorly coordinated students need a background of lifetime sports skills to help them offset the tensions that will arise in their lives and receive the fullest enjoyment from life. Rather than attempting to develop championship-level skill, these students need to develop enough skill to be able to appreciate and engage voluntarily in physical activity.

THE PHYSICALLY GIFTED OR CREATIVE STUDENT

By what criteria do we judge the gifted or creative student in physical education? Is it the boy who captains the basketball team, the girl who scores the most goals for the field hockey team, the boy who wins a state gymnastics title, or the girl who aspires to a career as a professional dancer? Is it the student who decides to be a professional physical educator? The gifted or creative student in physical education has a combination of many qualities, the depth of each quality varying with the individual. Gifted and creative students in physical education are atypical because they also need a specially tailored physical education experience.

In this section we are not concerned with the secondary school student who is gifted intellectually. These students may also be gifted physically, but some intellectually gifted students have only low or average motor ability. We are concerned here with the student who is exceptional because of his or her motor skill abilities and who perhaps is also gifted intellectually.

Characteristics of the physically gifted or creative student

The physically gifted student is not the student who is a star athlete in one sport or activity. The physically gifted student has superior motor skill abilities in many activities and maintains a high level of physical fitness. He may be a star athlete, but in general he is simply a good all-around performer. In a game situation, he always seems to be in the right place at the right time.

The physically gifted student learns quickly and requires a minimum of individual instruction. He is usually enthusiastic about physical activity and practices his skills of his own volition. Any individual instruction he does require is in the form of coaching rather than remedial correction. The physically gifted student has a strong sense of kinesthetic awareness and understands the principles of human movement. The student may not be able to articulate these latter two qualities, but observation by the physical educator will reveal that the student has discovered how to exploit his body as a tool for movement.

The physically creative student also has a well-developed sense of kinesthetic awareness and knows how to use his body properly. This student is the girl who dances with ease and grace or who is highly skilled in free exercise. It is the boy who is the lithe tumbler or gymnast. These students develop their own sophisticated routines in dance, tumbling, gymnastics, apparatus, and synchronized swimming. They may or may not be extraordinarily adept in other physical education activities but are as highly teachable as are the physically gifted.

Educational needs of the physically gifted or creative student

The physically gifted student or the physically creative student may or may not exhibit similar extraordinary abilities in the academic classroom. A student who is doing very poorly academically may be the superior student in physical education, or he may be superior in all phases of the secondary school program.

For the academically gifted student, most secondary schools offer honors courses, opportunities to conduct independent research, or courses that lead to college credits. Where a student shows exceptional talent in physical education but none in the classroom, appropriate measures must be taken to discover, and perhaps remedy, the cause of this disparity. Exceptional students in physical education should be identified to the guidance personnel by the physical educator in a conference, since grade reports will reveal a superior mark only and reveal little of the student as an individual. Guidance personnel should be informed of these exceptional students as early in the school year as a reliable and valid judgment can be made.

The physical educator and the physically gifted or creative student

The beginning physical educator, especially, may find it difficult to teach a student who seems to possess many more physical abilities than the teacher. However, there is no student in a secondary school who knows all there is to know

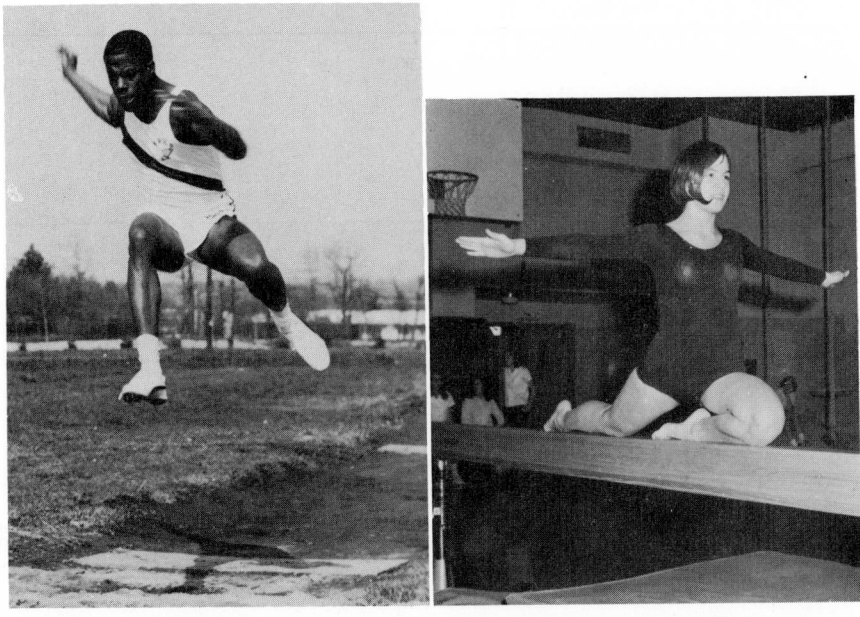

Fig. 15-3. The physical educator must meet the needs of physically gifted and creative students. (Left, Walt Whitman High School, South Huntington Schools, N. Y.; right, Mount Pleasant Senior High School, Wilmington, Del.)

about an activity. Students' knowledge is limited by what they have been taught or have learned on their own. Many experiences will still be new to them.

The physically gifted student or the physically creative student may not have attempted participation in a wide range of activities—he may have experienced only those activities offered in the school physical education program. Both the physically gifted and the physically creative student, as well as the average student, will be stimulated and challenged by the introduction of new activities. The creative student in dance may be introduced to a new kind of music, or the boy who is skilled on apparatus may enjoy adding new moves to his routines. The athlete may be a good performer, but he may need to become a better team player. He may rely on his superior skills rather than on a complete knowledge of the rules and strategies of sports and games.

The physical educator has a contribution to make to each student in the physical education program. The challenges presented by students of exceptional ability will help to keep the physical educator alert, stimulated, and enthusiastic about his teaching.

The physical education program and the physically gifted or creative student

A well-planned physical education program will be adaptable to the needs of all the students it serves. Before the program can be definitively developed, however, the specific needs, limitations, and abilities of the students in the program must be defined. The activities offered must be adapted to the needs of the students, since the students cannot be adapted to the program. Objectives are not achieved in the latter manner.

The exceptional student needs a structured program of physical activity, since this is a vital part of his mental, social, emotional, and physical development. Some schools have made it a policy to excuse athletes from the activity program

when their varsity sport is in season. This is a disservice to the student, especially when the varsity sport and the unit being taught in class are different. A student benefits from physical activity in a regular program. The physical educator can keep the interest of the exceptional student high by adopting some tested methods.

• *Develop a leaders' program.* This type of activity has proved valuable in many secondary schools. Leaders can assist the physical educator in innumerable ways and develop a sense of responsibility for the program because they are directly involved. Members of leaders' clubs have served as gymnastics and tumbling spotters in classes other than their own and can assist as officials in the class program and during intramural contests. Members of leaders' clubs still participate in the activities of their own class but at the same time receive the benefit of extra exposure to activities.

• *Utilize audiovisual materials.* Movies, filmstrips, loop films, and slides interest and benefit all students, but by watching these materials the exceptional student can compare his performance with those of experts, gain new insights into skills, and discover new techniques of performing skills.

• *Provide special challenges.* Textbooks in physical education are not in wide use in secondary school physical education programs. While all students could benefit from the use of a textbook, special outside readings, assignments, and research problems would provide an additional challenge for the exceptional student. Bucher has written a physical education textbook for high school boys and girls, *Physical Education for Life*, which should be especially helpful. (See Selected Readings at end of chapter.)

• *Encourage the exceptional student to assist in his own class.* Many of the highly skilled or creative students will be able to assist students who have low motor skill abilities. By working on a one-to-one basis, the amount of individualized instruction will be increased. The student with low motor ability will receive the special assistance he needs, and the gifted student will be helped to realize that not all students possess high levels of ability.

• *Assign the student to coaching responsibilities.* The exceptional student can assist in the intramural program by acting as a coach on a day when his team is not playing. Coaching a team will help the student to become more cognizant of the importance of team play, sportsmanship, and the need for rules. Such coaching, however, should be done under the close supervision of the physical educator.

• *Provide challenges within the program.* A skilled gymnast would not benefit from a beginning unit in tumbling. If his class is on this unit, the exceptional student might be assigned to work on advanced skills or on an advanced routine. A girl who shows great creativity in dance could be assigned to design a new dance or to devise some new steps.

POINTS TO REMEMBER

1. Every physical educator will at some time have atypical students in his classes.
2. There are many different categories of atypical students.
3. Physical education has a strong appeal for the culturally disadvantaged.
4. Physically handicapped students may exhibit a wide range of disabilities.
5. Some mentally retarded students can participate in regular physical education classes.
6. A disruptive student may affect the safety of a physical education class.
7. A poorly coordinated student may become a behavior problem if he does not receive special assistance.
8. The physically gifted or physically creative student can benefit from participation in regular physical education classes.

PROBLEMS TO THINK THROUGH

1. Should the objectives of physical education be the same for all secondary school students?
2. What is the advantage of having specially trained physical educators for special students?
3. What are the advantages and disadvantages of having special physical education classes for atypical students?
4. What special concern should physical education have for the student with average physical ability?

5. How can physical educators best plan a program for the resistive student?
6. What implications does ability grouping have for the atypical student?

CASE STUDY FOR ANALYSIS

You are a beginning physical educator in a medium-size secondary school and are the only member of your department. (There is one teacher for the boys and one for the girls.) On the first day of activity in the fall, you notice that one of your students is refusing to put on the physical education uniform. The remainder of your class is dressed for activity and ready to report to the playing area. What steps will you take to resolve this problem?

EXERCISES FOR REVIEW

1. What special responsibilities does the physical educator have for the atypical student?
2. How can the physical educator best adapt his program to the needs of the mentally retarded student?
3. What special physical education needs does the creative student have?
4. To what other resources can the physical educator turn when he needs assistance in understanding and working with the atypical student?
5. Through what means outside of the class program can physical education contribute to the atypical student?
6. What special challenges does the physically gifted student present?

SELECTED READINGS

AAHPER Project on Recreation and Fitness for the Mentally Retarded: Challenge, Washington, D. C., May, 1968, American Association for Health, Physical Education, and Recreation.

Activity programs for the mentally retarded, Journal of Health, Physical Education, and Recreation 37:24, 1966.

Auxter, David: Integration of the mentally retarded with normals in physical and motor fitness training programs, Journal of Health, Physical Education, and Recreation 41:61, 1970.

Blatt, Burton: Public policy with the education of children with special needs, Exceptional Children 38:537, 1972.

Bolt, Martha Lynn: Softball for the blind student, Journal of Health, Physical Education, and Recreation 41:40, 1970.

Bucher, Charles A.: Physical education for life, New York, 1969, McGraw-Hill Book Co., Inc.

Buell, Charles: Is vigorous physical activity feasible for blind children in public schools? Journal of Health, Physical Education, and Recreation 40:97, 1969.

Christensen, Dagney: Creativity in teaching physical education to the physically handicapped child, Journal of Health, Physical Education, and Recreation 41:73, 1970.

Conant, James B.: Slums and suburbs, New York, 1964, New American Library.

Daniels, Arthur S., and Davies, Evelyn A.: Adapted physical education, New York, 1965, Harper & Row, Publishers.

Debonis, Edith: The masters program in physical education with a specialization in physical education-recreation for the handicapped, Journal of Health, Physical Education, and Recreation 42:42, 1971.

Department of Health, Education and Welfare: Financial assistance programs for the handicapped, Washington, D. C., 1968, U. S. Government Printing Office.

Duggar, Margaret P.: Dance for the blind, Journal of Health, Physical Education, and Recreation 39:28, 1968.

Fantini, Mario D., and Weinstein, Gerald: The disadvantaged: challenge to education, New York, 1968, Harper & Row, Publishers.

Hilsendager, Donald R.: The Buttonwood Farms project, Journal of Health, Physical Education, and Recreation 39:46, 1968.

Pettit, Milton H.: Physical education for orthopedically handicapped children, Journal of Health, Physical Education, and Recreation 42:75, 1971.

Riessman, Frank: The culturally deprived child, New York, 1962, Harper & Row, Publishers.

Scarnati, Richard Alfred: Special Olympics, Journal of Health, Physical Education, and Recreation 43:49, 1972.

Tillman, Kenneth: Recreational activities reinforce learning experiences for the disadvantaged student, Journal of Health, Physical Education, and Recreation 43:32, 1972.

16 METHODS AND MATERIALS FOR DEVELOPING PHYSICAL FITNESS

The terms "physical fitness" and "fitness" have been defined and interpreted in many different ways during the past few years. There are some persons who believe that these terms refer only to body building and motor performance. Others, including most physical educators, prefer to think in terms of *total fitness* of the individual—physical, social, emotional, and intellectual fitness—and recognize this as the more valuable educational goal.

Physical educators have a very real responsibility to their students and the community in the area of physical fitness and its role in total individual fitness. Increased public awareness and curiosity about what is being done in the schools have forced teachers in this field to come up with concrete programs and answers. However, the public does not yet realize that physical fitness is but a part of the total fitness picture, and thus teachers have a dual educational role: explaining to students and to parents alike the overall story of total fitness and one of its components, physical fitness.

The current high level of interest in fitness is the result of a massive campaign sponsored by the President's Council on Youth Fitness, established first during President Eisenhower's administration and later changed by President Kennedy in 1961 to the President's Council on Physical Fitness. It is now known as the President's Council on Physical Fitness and Sports.

Under the leadership of such men as Shane McCarthy, Bud Wilkinson, Stan Musial, and James A. Lovell, Jr., the Council has attempted to raise the standards and level of physical fitness of people across the entire country. Their nationwide campaign reached out in many different educational areas, striving to accomplish the following:

1. To improve programs of physical education, with increased emphasis on physical fitness
2. To increase state leadership and supervision of physical fitness and sports programs
3. To increase the number of school personnel doing physical education work
4. To conduct regional clinics in physical fitness
5. To establish demonstration centers in schools where high-level fitness programs were organized
6. To develop adult fitness programs
7. To improve standards in Armed Forces testing and training programs
8. To publish pamphlets, booklets, and other resource materials
9. To inform the public and develop their interest in physical education through advertising in public media

Statistics indicate the remarkable effectiveness of the Council's work. Not only have physical education programs been improving, but the number of teaching specialists has increased, state supervision and leadership has been extended, and the physical fitness levels of students has substantially improved. Many states now have a governor's physical fitness council or commission. Fitness programs for cycling, swimming, jogging, and running specified distances have been developed, with badges and awards issued across the country to those who qualify.

Yet physical educators and Council members realize that only a beginning has been made. Other statistics indicate that much more has to be done—in the many states that do not yet have full-time people employed in the department of education to supervise the program, and in the nearly 40% of schools where no daily physical education classes are held for all students.

In March of 1968, President Johnson changed the Council's name to President's Council on Physical Fitness and Sports and located the Council in the Department of Health, Education and Welfare. This was done for the purpose of extending the scope of the Council and promoting sports and fitness in America.

TEACHING FOR PHYSICAL FITNESS

The task of teaching for physical fitness is a difficult one, particularly in regard to teaching adolescent students. The following reasons account for this:

1. Lack of interest. Adolescent girls are sometimes more interested in "feminine fancies" than physical pursuits, and boys often want to become star athletes without extensive effort.

2. Lack of understanding. Adolescents do not fully understand the term "physical

Platnick's Photo Service, Hempstead, L. I.

Fig. 16-1. Building physical fitness through swimming.

fitness" as it relates to their growth and development and their all-round health and total performance.

3. Lack of uniformity. Physical fitness is an individual attainment and cannot be achieved by a total group through an identical process.

Furthermore, the very nature of physical fitness requires maintenance. It is not a fact, like the multiplication tables, that once learned may be set aside. Physical fitness is a condition that must be maintained. Healthful attitudes toward fitness must be developed in students, along with an appreciation for its significance.

Achievement of physical fitness is another difficulty, for fitness itself varies in relation to the individual's personal requirements. The scholar needs physical skills different from those of the football player and therefore requires a different level of fitness. However, the basic components of fitness—such as good posture, desirable health habits, and social, emotional, and mental well-being—are necessary for all. It is the responsibility of the physical education teacher to promote the development of these components to their fullest degree. Students must be made aware of their need for physical fitness and led toward achievement of this goal. This should be done through both the instructional and the noninstructional phases of the total physical education program.

INSTRUCTIONAL PROGRAM

There are many methods and techniques useful for teaching adolescents in the area of physical fitness. The instructional program itself should contain definite steps for appraisal, guidance, and testing throughout the school year, and related discussions, assignments, and studies should be included for special emphasis.

Teaching methods and techniques*

Appraisal. The appraisal of physical fitness in secondary school is an important

---

*See also Chapter 20 on Evaluation.

teaching method that serves many purposes. Appraisal of fitness provides the teacher with a picture of the fitness level of each student and the overall school population. These data may then be helpful in determining individual student needs and the needs of the total program. Statistics on speed, accuracy, and other components of fitness should be used throughout the year to aid in program planning and to promote fitness. (See Chapters 20 and 21.)

The process of appraisal should be very beneficial for the student. It should provide an understanding of the true nature of fitness. Having endurance, efficiency, and coordination enough to complete satisfactorily the everyday tasks required in high school should be recognized as one of the fitness objectives. Students also need to recognize that physical fitness is not the same for each individual, and this attitude may be promoted through the appraisal process. Furthermore, appraisal helps to motivate students toward improvement of their own physical abilities. Instead of mistaking physical fitness for mere muscular strength, they see that exercise is necessary for proper growth and development and healthy resistance to disease.

Many materials have been developed for appraisal of physical fitness. They will be discussed in greater detail later in the chapter. However, it should be noted here that some of the physical fitness tests include norms, or scoring scales, for evaluation of physical performance. These are helpful in student appraisal, because they offer a more precise technique for comparing scores of students of the same age, height, and/or weight. Students, too, prefer to picture their own test results in terms of the achievements of hundreds of their peers, instead of just their classmates.

Norms do not provide the total picture in the assessment of physical fitness, however. A physical education teacher should be cautious in applying norms since these scores vary according to the basis used for their development (age, height, and so on). One study indicates that both physique (height and weight) *and* developmental level (accelerated, normal, or retarded growth pattern) are important determinants in physical performance levels. Norms that do not consider the overweight factor, for example, may be scaled too high for accomplishment by such persons.*

A study of 7,600 boys and girls, ten to eighteen years of age, analyzed the relationship of age, height, and weight to performances in the California Physical Fitness Test. Results brought about recommendations that *age* be used as a basis for test norms, for steady progress was shown by students each year in nearly all test items.†

Obviously, more research is needed in this area of testing physical fitness and establishing norms for guidance. The physical educator should recognize the limitations while taking advantage of the values.

Guidance. The teaching program should provide an opportunity for individual guidance of students in the area of physical fitness. This may be done in connection with the appraisal program, with individual conferences scheduled for each student to discuss personal problems and weaknesses. When a teacher is able to offer this personal attention to each student and can suggest exercises and methods of improvement, the boy or girl consciously puts forth effort to improve.

Group guidance in the general aspects of physical fitness should also be included in the instructional program through a unit of study. For girls, stress should be placed on proper posture and good body mechanics in daily activities—that is, in standing, sitting, walking, lifting, carrying books, studying, and so on. By appealing to the girls' desire to be attractive and to develop balance, grace, and poise in movement, the teacher may motivate these students toward improved fitness. A unit for boys should stress increasing their achievement levels in strength, endurance, flexibility, accuracy, balance, and other physical traits. In this way they, too, are motivated toward improving physical fitness. A successfully taught unit should have carry-over value not only into daily life but also into college and later years, by developing a wholesome attitude toward fitness and its importance in effective living.

Guidance in physical fitness should not only be included as a unit of study for students but should also be emphasized in each class in the *daily* instructional program. The value of daily calisthenics and warm-up exercises should be stressed in terms of their role in developing physical fitness. A study comparing the physical fitness of Japanese children to boys and girls in Iowa showed that Tokyo children scored higher in nearly all motor performance tests. Furthermore, it was shown that Japanese students had longer and more frequent physical education classes in which to develop these skills.* Students in the United States must recognize the importance of daily workouts for developing and maintaining a high level of performance in physical fitness activities. Guidance of this kind is of utmost importance to students while in school, for then in later years, as they organize themselves for adulthood, exercise will form an integral part of daily living.

Testing. Testing should be a regular part of the total physical education program, and testing for physical fitness should be included as one phase of evaluation. The materials for testing different components of physical fitness are extensive. Many of the established tests have been developed for men because of the emphasis on physical training necessary for the armed services, but some are suitable for use with

*Wear, C. L., and Miller, Kenneth: Relationships between physique and developmental level to physical performance, Research Quarterly 33:4, 1962.

†Espenschade, Anna S.: Restudy of relationships between physical performance of school children and age, height and weight, Research Quarterly 34:2, 1963.

*Ikeda, Namiko: A comparison of physical fitness of children in Iowa, U.S.A. and Tokyo, Japan, Research Quarterly 33:4, 1962.

Record form for identification of physically underdeveloped pupils

Teacher _____   School year _____

Period or section _____   Date of lst test _____

School _____

Girls

Name of pupil	Modified pull ups ages 10-17; 8			Sit ups ages 10-17; 10			Squat thrust ages 10-17; 3			Remarks*
	1st test		Retest	1st test		Retest	1st test		Retest	
	Pass	Fail	Date passed	Pass	Fail	Date passed	Pass	Fail	Date passed	

*Enter here any conditions, e.g., obesity, posture, etc., that may affect physical performance.

Fig. 16-2. Record form for identification of physically underdeveloped pupils. (Courtesy Guymon Junior High School, Guymon, Okla.)

boys in secondary schools. A few tests have been adapted for girls and have comparative norms that are valuable in the secondary school program. One of the best tests for both boys and girls is the Physical Fitness Test Battery developed by the American Association for Health, Physical Education, and Recreation. The motivational and educational value of these tests should be recognized.

Discussion. Students in secondary school should have an opportunity to discuss various aspects of physical fitness as part of their instructional program. Related problems such as dieting, relaxation, and menstruation are topics that arouse much interest in girls. Narcotics and alcohol studies provide excellent learning possibilities for both boys and girls. Special studies in these and similar subjects related to physical fitness in everyday life should be a regular part of the instructional program.

Assignments. Homework assignments on fitness that are coordinated with the regular instructional program should be given. These assignments may be in the form of improving performance of particular physical fitness exercises such as push-ups or sit-ups, or they may be in the form of readings related to this particular subject. Studying about young girls and boys who have accomplished unusual feats in athletics is both interesting and inspiring to adolescents. In schools using teaching teams, wherein students have an opportunity to do independent research, the topic of physical fitness may well be a fitting assignment.

Bucher has written a physical education textbook for high school students entitled *Physical Education for Life.* It devotes considerable space to the subject of physical fitness and how it can be developed and maintained. (See Selected Readings at the end of the chapter.)

Other techniques. In order to emphasize physical fitness in the instructional program, there are a few supplementary techniques that are particularly helpful. The use of audiovisual aids is an excellent way to stimulate student interest. Bulletin boards, performance charts, records, and similar devices serve as reminders when displayed prominently. In addition, having the students conduct drills and take turns in leading the class permits personal experience in promoting physical fitness. Of most importance is making physical fitness enjoyable, for when students see that activities are fun, they will profit more fully from the instructional program.

Materials for teaching and testing physical fitness

At the present time the quantity of materials for teaching physical fitness continues to increase as a result of nationwide interest, fostered by the President's Council on Physical Fitness and Sports, and increased emphasis on health status, drugs, and medical care. Physical educators have found greater interest in and reception for their programs among parents and lay people and have found it an ideal time to expand and extend their programs and facilities.

There is a wealth of material presently available to teachers for use in physical education classes. Following are some of the better-known physical fitness test batteries and exercise programs that have been developed in the campaign for fitness.

1. *Youth Physical Fitness*—suggested elements of a school-centered program, President's Council on Youth Fitness, Superintendent of Documents, Washington, D. C.
Part One—A discussion of the current concept and foundations of physical fitness programs, including suggested standards for instruction and complementary programs.
Part Two—Suggested tests and activities and developmental exercises for boys and girls, grades four to twelve. Standards for different age levels are included with suggested test items, all of which have been adapted from the AAHPER test.
2. *Youth Fitness Test Manual,* American Association for Health, Physical Education, and Recreation, Washington, D. C., 1965.
This booklet contains explanations for the administration of seven suggested test items, together with percentile scores for boys and girls at different age levels.
The Association has also developed record forms for this testing program and special awards and emblems that may be presented to participating students.

3. *Vim*—A complete exercise plan for girls twelve to eighteen years of age, and

4. *Vigor*—A complete exercise plan for boys twelve to eighteen years of age, President's Council on Physical Fitness, May, 1964, Superintendent of Documents, Washington, D. C.

These booklets contain helpful hints and facts about fitness for youngsters and include a daily exercise plan suitable for them to follow.

5. *Adult Physical Fitness*—A program for men and women, President's Council on Physical Fitness, Superintendent of Documents, Washington, D. C.

This is an adult program for home exercising with which the teacher should be familiar.

6. *Royal Canadian Air Force Exercise Plans for Physical Fitness*—5BX, for men; 10BX, for women, Queen's Printer and Controller of Stationery, Ottawa, Canada, Revised, 1962.

This, too, is an adult home exercise plan with which the teacher should be familiar.

7. *Physical Fitness for Girls*, by William Hillcourt, and

8. *Physical Fitness for Boys*, by William Hillcourt, A *Golden Magazine* Special, New York, 1967, Golden Press, Inc.

There are many other materials available in the area of physical fitness. Many state departments of education have developed their own testing instruments (California, Oregon, Washington, Iowa, Virginia, New York), as have some cities (Tucson, Denver, Omaha, Louisville, Kansas City). A movie entitled *Why Physical Education?** which has been produced for use in junior and senior high schools, discusses physical fitness and total fitness as the goal of physical education programs.

Other films and materials related to physical fitness are listed here.

FILMS

Girls Are Better Than Ever (13½ min.)   Free
Modern Talking Picture Service
1212 Avenue of the Americas, New York, N. Y. 10036
Time of Our Lives (27 min.)   Free
Associated Films, Inc.
600 Madison Avenue, New York, N. Y. 10022
Badhe Chalo (11 min.) Express postage collect
Information Service of India
Film Section
3 East 64th Street, New York, N. Y. 10021
Rhythmic Ball Exercises (13 min.)   Free
Embassy of Finland

Why Physical Education? 16 mm., sound and color, 14 minutes, produced by Wexler Film Productions, available from Henk Newenhouse, Inc., 1017 Longaker Road, Northbrook, Ill.

Press Section
1900 Twenty-fourth St. N. W., Washington, D. C. 20008
Physically Fit (Don Schollander) (4½ min.) Free
Modern Talking Picture Service
1212 Avenue of the Americas, New York, N. Y. 10036
Focus on Fitness (19 min.)   Free
Eastman Kodak Co.
Audio-Visual Service
343 State Street, Rochester, N. Y. 14650

MATERIALS

Adolescent Years
  As Others See Us
  How Teens Set the Stage for Smoking
  Why Girls Menstruate
Fitness
  Physical Fitness
  Exercise and Fitness
  Safeguarding the Health of the Athlete
  Seven Paths to Fitness
  Tips of Athletic Training (vols. I-VI)
American Medical Association, 535 N. Dearborn St., Chicago, Ill. 60610

The physical fitness checklist included here is another helpful educational tool for teachers interested in this type of material for their students.

Chapter 18 contains other movies and records, listed according to manufacturers, that may be useful in the area of physical fitness. It should be noted here that the American Association for Health, Physical Education, and Recreation is an excellent source for all kinds of supplementary materials on fitness, as is the President's Council on Physical Fitness and Sports. Teachers should also investigate their own state departments of education, for not only have testing programs been initiated from their offices but also publications on courses of study, programs, and clinic suggestions.

A PHYSICAL FITNESS CHECKLIST

Medical aspects	Yes	No
1. Thorough dental and health examination each year	—	—
a. Fit heart and circulatory system, digestive system, nervous system, and so on	—	—
b. Proper body development, according to age and sex (height and weight)	—	—
2. Correction of remediable health defects—vision, hearing, overweight	—	—

Physical activity
1. At least one and one-half to two hours a day spent in vigorous physical activity, preferably out-doors — —
2. Adequate muscular strength and endurance* — —
3. After running fifty yards, heart and breathing return to normal rates within ten minutes — —
4. Average skill in running, jump-ing, climbing, and throwing — —
5. Control of body in activities in-volving balance, agility, speed, rhythm, accuracy — —
6. Skill in recreational activities—arts and crafts, bowling, danc-ing — —

Posture
1. When student is standing up-right, string dropped from tip of ear passes through shoulder and hip joints and middle of ankle. — —
2. When student is sitting in a chair, trunk and head are erect, weight balanced over pelvis, or trunk slightly bent forward. — —
3. When student is walking, slump-ing is avoided, body is in proper balance, and excessively waste-ful motions of arms and legs are eliminated. — —

Health habits
1. Rest: at least eight hours of sleep each night — —
2. Diet: four servings daily from each of the four basic food groups — —
   a. Meat, poultry, fish, and eggs
   b. Dairy products
   c. Vegetables and fruits
   d. Bread and cereals
3. Cleanliness
   a. Daily bath — —
   b. Teeth brushed after every meal
   c. Clean hair, nails, and cloth-ing — —
4. Abstain from use of tobacco and alcohol — —

Isometrics

Widespread attention has been focused on isometrics, an exercise system develop-ing one particular facet of physical fit-ness—strength. Physical education teach-ers should understand the principle behind isometrics and recognize its values and lim-itations in order to place isometrics in its

---

The school health or physical education teacher can help to determine proper standards.

---

proper perspective within the physical edu-cation program.

Definition. Isometrics is a series of exer-cises designed to develop strength in par-ticular muscle groups. In isometrics muscle groups are contracted against an immov-able force, or resistance, and "held tight" before relaxing after a count of six to ten. The tension produced in the muscles in-creases their strength through this isomet-ric contraction. Isometric contractions should not be confused with isotonic, or dynamic, contractions, in which the muscle groups work against a resistant force that is overcome, as in weight lifting.

Values. An important value of isometric exercise is conditioning. Through daily ap-plication of isometrics, muscles learn to work efficiently and effectively in perform-ance of activity. It is believed that in-creased muscular strength improves speed, power, and flexibility, all of which are im-portant components of body conditioning and fitness. For this reason, isometrics has gained in popularity not only in school programs but also in amateur and profes-sional athletics as well.* It is important, however, to evaluate carefully the equip-ment and literature that are on the market on isometrics.

Isometric exercises are also valuable in corrective, or remedial, programs of physi-cal education. Whenever a student has identifiable weakness in specific muscle groups, such as arm and shoulder muscles, isometric routines are particularly helpful.

Limitations. Certain limitations exist in the isometric program of exercise when it is applied to a school program of physical education. As has been previously stated, the value of isometrics lies in meeting *indi-vidual* needs for strengthening and condi-tioning. In large physical education classes it would be very difficult to individualize

---

*Some manufacturers have developed special ex-ercise kits, charts, and handbooks of isometrics. Bucher's book, *Physical Education for Life*, lists many excellent isometric and isotonic exercises for high school boys and girls. (See Selected Read-ings at the end of the chapter.)

this program sufficiently for instructional purposes.

Furthermore, while students may become motivated at first with this approach to exercising, enthusiasm may soon be lost if no tangible results are seen. Dynamometers, machines that measure strength, are not standard equipment in most schools, and students may not recognize the progress they are making without them.

Also, emphasis should not be placed merely on isometrics. Isometrics, like weight lifting, has specific values that should be utilized whenever possible, within the limits of proper programming for physical fitness.

OUT-OF-CLASS PROGRAM

The noninstructional program, which includes all activities held outside the regularly scheduled physical education class, is equally important to the promotion of physical fitness. The intramural and extramural activities, clubs, demonstrations, contests, and other activities all serve to focus student attention on physical pursuits.

Intramural activities

The intramural program should be available to as many students as possible. By providing an interesting and exciting program of intraclass games in a wide variety of sports and in an atmosphere in which all students believe their participation is welcome, the teacher is able to increase the overall interest in physical fitness and skills.

Extramural activities

A program of interscholastic competition serves to heighten the interest of boys and girls, and their efforts to make the honor squads or varsity teams also induce improvement in physical fitness.

Clubs

There are several clubs that may be sponsored by the physical education department to provide benefits for physical fitness. Cheerleaders, baton twirlers, drill team, gymnastics, tumbling, cycling, and physical fitness clubs all promote physical fitness. The avid interest that many students have in these types of activities should be developed. Leaders clubs and modern dance groups also play a role in the physical education program, and membership should be open to all interested students.

Demonstrations

Public demonstrations and performances by club participants, such as those of the modern dance group, not only improve the physical fitness of participants but also serve to increase the interest in and appreciation of these activities.

Contests and campaigns

Sometimes a special contest or campaign to promote good posture or a similar component of physical fitness is an excellent technique for arousing and enhancing interest in physical fitness. Student planning as well as participation in such events should be fostered to gain the most value from them.

Organizations

Organizations such as an athletic association, Hi-Y, or scouting and explorer troops may serve to promote fitness both among its members and on a schoolwide basis.

Outings

Field trips, clinics, and outdoor camping expeditions are very popular with students, and they provide fitness experiences not otherwise available. The physical education teacher should try to sponsor such events whenever feasible.

Awards

For students who have shown much improvement or have performed exceptionally well in specific areas of physical fitness, a ribbon or small award may be presented. The American Association for Health, Physical Education, and Recrea-

Fig. 16-3. Cheerleaders club. (White Plains High School, White Plains, N. Y.)

tion has special awards and certificates that may be given in connection with the administration of their physical fitness test.

Cosponsored activities

Much interest can be stimulated with coeducational activities sponsored by both the boys' and the girls' departments or with special events sponsored cooperatively with community organizations. The local Dads' Club or Chamber of Commerce is usually interested in physical fitness activities and willingly conducts field days, contests, and sports days. The physical education teachers should work with the leaders of these organizations to ensure proper management and supervision for the benefit of the students.

POINTS TO REMEMBER

1. The physical fitness goal of physical education requires special emphasis because of increased national concern in this area.
2. The instructional program of physical education should be geared to physical fitness through methods of teaching that include appraisal and guidance.
3. The additional teaching techniques of testing and assignments should stress physical fitness in the instructional program.
4. The noninstructional program should emphasize fitness through its many components.

5. Students in secondary school need to be guided in physical fitness to become aware of its importance to everyday living.
6. Students need to realize the individuality of physical fitness and should understand their own personal requirements in this area.

PROBLEMS TO THINK THROUGH

1. How can the results of the appraisal of physical fitness be most effectively used for the benefit of the students?
2. In a community that sponsors few recreational programs, how may the physical education department of the secondary school promote community-wide interest in physical fitness activities?
3. The administration of a secondary school is disturbed about students smoking on school property, contrary to regulations. Students and some members of the community are in favor of a student smoking lounge. In what ways may the physical education department help in solving this problem?
4. In a small secondary school there is only one teacher of girls' physical education and one teacher for the boys. Activities after school are therefore limited to the supervision and facilities available to these two instructors. How may an adequate intramural program be set up that would promote physical fitness for the greatest number of students?
5. What methods may be used to improve physical fitness in students scoring low on apprasial?
6. In what ways may individual personal guidance be offered to students needing special attention in physical fitness work?

CASE STUDY FOR ANALYSIS

The physical education department in a large secondary school plans to promote a yearlong campaign for physical fitness, not only for students in the school but also for the community-at-large. The administration has approved the idea and offered some financial assistance to back their campaign. What steps would the staff take in carrying out their campaign within the instructional program? In the noninstructional program? In the community? What special activities and events may be sponsored? In what ways may students become involved in the program?

EXERCISES FOR REVIEW

1. What are the advantages and disadvantages in running a physical fitness appraisal program more than once during a year?
2. What particular objectives should be established for a unit on physical fitness with eighth-grade girls? Boys?
3. What aspects of physical fitness should be stressed in team sports? Individual sports? Formal activities? Rhythms? Aquatics?
4. What exercises are particularly valuable for developing strength? Endurance? Flexibility? Balance? Other components of physical fitness?
5. What types of charts and diagrams would serve effectively to motivate students in physical fitness?
6. What current outside reading materials may be valuable homework for high school students?
7. In what ways may a leaders club assist the physical education teacher in testing and promoting physical fitness?
8. What types of awards would be appropriate for performances in physical fitness?
9. What topics for discussions in physical fitness would be of particular interest to high school girls? Boys? Both?
10. What are the advantages and disadvantages to choosing a "most physically fit" boy and girl?

SELECTED READINGS

American Association for Health, Physical Education, and Recreation: The growing years—adolescence, fifth yearbook, Washington, D. C., 1962, The Association.

American Association for Health, Physical Education, and Recreation: Fitness series, Washington, D. C., The Association.

AMA and AAHPER Joint Committee on Exercise and Fitness: Health problems revealed during physical activity, Journal of Health, Physical Education, and Recreation 37:6, 1967.

Athletic Institute: Exercise and fitness, Chicago, 1962, The Institute.

Brooks, Betty Willis: Views of physical fitness from four educational philosophies, Physical Educator 24:31, 1967.

Bucher, Charles A.: Foundations of physical education, ed. 6, St. Louis, 1972, The C. V. Mosby Co.

Bucher, Charles A.: Physical education for life, New York, 1969, McGraw-Hill Book Co.

Cooper, Kenneth H.: How to feel fit at any age, Reader's Digest, March, 1968.

Cureton, Thomas Kirk: Improving the physical fitness of youth, Monographs of the Society for Research in Child Development, Inc., Serial No. 95, Yellow Springs, Ohio, 1964, The Antioch Press.

Hillcourt, William: Physical fitness for boys, New York, 1967, Goldren Press, Inc.

Hillcourt, William: Physical fitness for girls, New York, 1967, Golden Press, Inc.

Hunsicker, Paul A., and Reiff, Guy G.: A survey and comparison of youth fitness, 1958-1965, Journal of Health, Physical Education, and Recreation 37:23, 1966.

Ponthieux, N. A., and Barker, D. G.: Relationship between socioeconomic status and physical fitness measures, Research Quarterly 36:464, 1965.

Ponthieux, N. A., and Barker, D. G.: Relationship between race and physical fitness, Research Quarterly 36:468, 1965.

President's Council on Physical Fitness and Sports: Adult physical fitness, Washington, D. C., U. S. Government Printing Office.

President's Council on Physical Fitness and Sports: Vigor, Washington, D. C., U. S. Government Printing Office.

President's Council on Physical Fitness and Sports: Vim, Washington, D. C., U. S. Government Printing Office.

President's Council on Physical Fitness and Sports: Youth Physical Fitness, Washington, D. C., U. S. Government Printing Office.

Steinhaus, Arthur H.: Fitness beyond muscle, Physical Educator 23:103, 1966.

Vitale, Frank N.: Individualized fitness programs, Englewood Cliffs, N. J., 1973, Prentice-Hall, Inc.

Weiss, Raymond A.: Is physical fitness our most important objective? Journal of Health, Physical Education, and Recreation 35:18, 1964.

Yarnall, C. Douglas: Relationship of physical fitness to selected measures of popularity, Research Quarterly 37:286, 1966.

17 AN INNOVATIVE PROGRAM OF MOVEMENT EDUCATION FOR THE SECONDARY SCHOOL

The traditional curricula of our secondary schools are currently being challenged by the students they serve. These traditional curricula are gradually being replaced by innovative and flexible educational experiences that attempt to meet the needs of the students. The new focus in secondary education is on individual creativity and individualized learning. Some subject areas of the secondary school curriculum utilize teaching machines and other technological hardware in an attempt to individualize the learning experience. These technological advances have helped to create many changes in the methodology of teaching.

Secondary school physical education programs are emphasizing the individual through comprehensive instruction in the lifetime sports and through a renewed concentration on all phases of the creative-expressive activities, such as dance and gymnastics. This increased awareness of the individual and of the individual's creativity has made education for movement a vital part of the newly developing curricula in physical education.

THE ORIGINS OF MOVEMENT EDUCATION

Movement education has been misunderstood, misinterpreted, and at times misused within physical education programs in the United States. Movement education is not a recent development, nor it is synonymous with dance. Movement education has been a part of physical education curricula in English schools for many years and is closely aligned with the *movement exploration concepts* integral to dance. Movement education as a foundational phase of the physical education curriculum can be traced historically to the theories of the dancer Rudolf Laban. After fleeing Germany for England during World War II Laban established an Art of Movement Center bearing his name. Like the kinesiologists, Laban was a student of human movement. He believed that each individual possesses inherent natural movements and felt that through rigid and formal exercises man loses his ability to move freely and easily. Conversely, Laban said, experiences in spontaneous and exploratory movement would help individuals to reach their potential for efficient and effective movement through increased kinesthetic awareness.

Prior to World War II, physical education in English schools stressed formal gymnastics. During World War II England revised both its educational philosophy and its educational structure. Courses and teaching methodology were updated, and education for movement was made the central focus of physical education programs. English children are educated in movement from the earliest school years.

313

When the concepts of the movement education approach to physical education reached the United States in the late 1950's, they were first included in basic instructional programs for women on the college level. However, courses entitled "Movement Education" bore little resemblance either to Laban's principles or to the movement education methodology developed in England. Rather, these first attempts to educate for movement were closely correlated with the objectives, techniques, and methodologies associated with existing courses called "Body Mechanics," "Movement Fundamentals," or similar titles. These early courses in programs for college women used movement as a tool primarily to reeducate the body. The system of movement education as developed in England uses the body as a vehicle for enhanced motor skill development, beginning with the natural movements of childhood as the foundation for all bodily movement.

Since 1960, many articles and books have been written and published in the United States that focus directly on movement education. Research is being conducted and several pilot programs in elementary schools are well under way. Through these media, professionals are developing an understanding of movement education and its proper application within physical education curricula in the schools of the United States. Further, a corps of experts in the specialized area of movement education is being developed, and these individuals are giving freely of their knowledge and experience to other physical educators. At the present time, these advances are helping to make movement education one of the most significant new trends in the field of physical education.

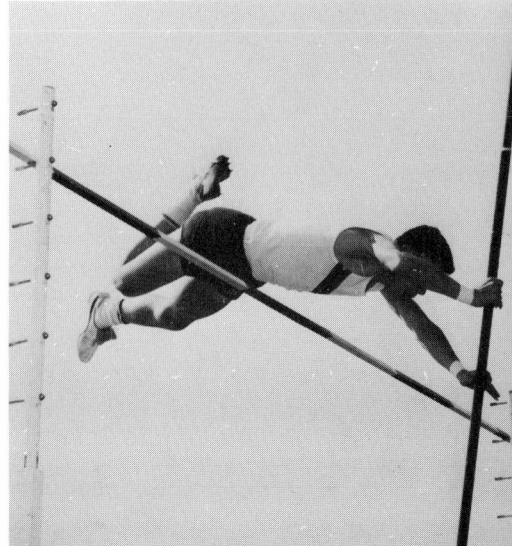

Fig. 17-1. Track-and-field events require adherence to basic movement principles in order to achieve best physical performance. (Walt Whitman High School, South Huntington Schools, N. Y.)

WHAT IS MOVEMENT EDUCATION?

Everything an individual does involves bodily movement of some sort. Movement education attempts to help the individual to become mentally as well as physically aware of these movements. Thus movement education is based on a conceptual approach to human movement. That is, the better the individual mentally understands a movement pattern, the easier it will be for him to develop physical skills. For example, softball is frequently a popular team sport that is taught on the secondary school level. Many girls and some

A comparison of movement education and traditional physical education concepts*

Movement education	Traditional physical education
A. The program	
1. The program is activity-centered.	1. The program is verbal-centered.
2. The program is student-centered.	2. The program is teacher-centered.
3. The program attempts to develop an intellectual awareness of the body.	3. The program attempts to develop skills oftentimes lacking in intellectual comprehension.
4. The program places an emphasis on the problem-solving method which includes exploration and discovery, based on the individual needs of the student.	4. The teacher serves as a model to be imitated by the students, and the method includes lecture and demonstration based on the needs of the group.
5. Repetition of problems leads to a greater variety of solutions.	5. Repetition of drills leads to an improved performance in motor skills.
6. Syllabus develops as each class period uncovers the needs of the individual that must be explored.	6. Syllabus often unrelated to previous learning experiences is presented to the students.
B. Role of the teacher	
1. In the learning process the teacher educates his students.	1. In the learning process the teacher trains his students.
2. The teacher is imaginative and creative in the methods he uses.	2. The teacher utilizes the traditional methods of teaching.
3. The teacher guides his students in the activities in which they are participating.	3. The teacher leads his students in the activities in which they are participating.
C. Role of the student	
1. Motivation for learning comes from inner self.	1. Motivation for learning comes from the teacher.
2. The student experiences the joy of his own natural movements and unique style.	2. Individual body types are not considered.
3. The student demonstrates his ability to reason logically and intelligently.	3. The student demonstrates his ability to take orders and follow directions.
4. The student demonstrates independence.	4. The student often lacks independence.
5. The student faces each new situation in an enthusiastic and intelligent manner.	5. The student oftentimes exhibits difficulty when confronted with new situations.
6. The student evaluates his own progress.	6. The teacher evaluates the student's progress.
7. The student develops at his own rate of progress.	7. Rate of progress is dependent upon the norm of the student development within the class.
8. Success is based on the student's goals.	8. Success is based on the teacher's goals.
9. The student competes with himself.	9. The student competes with his fellow classmates.
D. Class atmosphere	
1. There is an informal class atmosphere.	1. There is a formal class atmosphere.
2. Varied formations are used.	2. Set formations are used.
3. The teacher exhibits permissive behavior.	3. The teacher exhibits strict behavior.
4. Individual needs of the students are the determining factor in the allotment of time to be spent in any activity.	4. The completion of the subject matter is the determining factor in the allotment of time to be spent'in any activity.
E. Facilities and equipment	
1. The facilities are considered secondary to the need for a resourceful and creative teacher.	1. Facilities are of prime importance, although the need for a resourceful and creative teacher is recognized.
2. The equipment is created to meet the needs of the individual.	2. The individual must adjust to the equipment used.
3. The equipment is used in many different situations.	3. The equipment is limited in its use.

*From Bucher, Charles A.: Foundations of physical education, ed. 6, St. Louis, 1972, The C. V. Mosby Co., p. 347.

boys never develop the ability to throw well because of physical errors in the position of the throwing arm or errors in foot position. Through movement education, the position of each body segment in relation to the whole body is perceived by the student intellectually before the physical skill is attempted. When the student is intellectually aware of the position of his body as an entity, rather than considering his body to be made up of independent segments, physical skill learning is enhanced.

The experts do not agree on a single definition for movement education. They do agree, however, that movement education is dependent on physical factors in the environment and on the individual's ability to intellectually and physically react to these factors. Through movement education, the individual develops his own techniques for dealing with the environmental factors of force, time, space, and flow as they relate to various movement problems. The mental and physical skill development of the individual is of prime concern to the movement educator, rather than the common skill development of an entire class or group.

The nature and scope of movement education has been defined by several authors, two of whom are listed here. Felshin* lists five components in her classification, namely, human movement as (1) basic to human functioning and performance, (2) related to culture and society, (3) an esthetic experience, (4) a source of human meaning and significance, and (5) persistent and dynamic forms.

Mackenzie† identifies seven major classifications covering the nature and scope of human movement. These classifications include (1) movement forms (descriptions of sports), (2) mechanical principles of movement (body positioning), (3) structure and function of the moving human organism (body composition), (4) movement and the person (esthetic expression), (5) learning how to move (motor learning theories), (6) movement and health (therpeutic uses), and (7) movement and meaning (philosophical and sociological interpretations).

These classifications of the nature and scope of movement indicate clearly that physical education at all educational levels should be concerned with movement and involved with the study and development of an effective moving human organism.

THE UNIQUENESS OF MOVEMENT EDUCATION

How does the methodology of movement education differ from the traditional methodology of physical education? As much as physical education has traditionally been taught through structured classes, classes in movement education are also structured. It may seem that movement education is nothing more than a haphazard approach to traditional physical education in relation to skill teaching and learning, but this is far from the case. In many instances, movment education classes involve a more highly structured approach and demand more of the teacher in regard to concrete philosophy, sound objectives, logical progressions, and understanding of proper techniques and methodology, as well as creative ability.

Movement education employs the problem-solving approach. Each skill that is to be explored presents a challenge to the student. Learning results as the student accepts and solves increasingly more difficult problems. For this reason, the natural movements of childhood are considered to be the first challenges that should be presented to the student. Movement educators feel that adult problems in physical skill performance are the result of poor habits developed in early childhood. While most children spend their preschool years in uninhibited running, jumping, leaping, climb-

---

*Singer, Robert N., and others: Physical education, an interdisciplinary approach, New York, 1972, The Macmillan Co., p. 12.
†Mackenzie, Marlin M.: Toward a new curriculum in physical education, New York, 1969, McGraw-Hill Book Co., Inc.

ing, twisting, and other such vigorous activities, it is pointed out that these movements eventually become stereotyped. Students do not, on their own, explore a variety of movement patterns. Through movement education, boys and girls are encouraged to walk or run or otherwise move at different speeds, in different directions, and on different levels. They are encouraged to exploit physical obstacles, such as an inclined plane or even another person, and to incorporate them into unique movement patterns. The student gains confidence and enjoyment in the use of his entire body for movement and begins to develop an intellectual understanding of the capabilities of his body and how they differ from the capabilities of the bodies of others. These understandings, developed as physical skill develops, help to form a basis for more efficient and effective physical movement in later years.

Traditional physical education emphasizes the learning of specific skills through demonstration, drill, and practice. Movement education emphasizes the learning of skill patterns through individual exploration of the body's movement potential. These two approaches to skill learning are not in opposition to each other. Movement education does not supplant learning that takes place in traditional physical education programs. Movement education does help the student to develop a better foundation for the learning of the more sophisticated skills. Education in movement is the first step in becoming a physically educated person.

THE PLACE OF MOVEMENT EDUCATION IN THE PHYSICAL EDUCATION CURRICULUM

In the English schools, movement education begins in the first grade and is the sole vehicle through which physical education is taught in the elementary schools. In English secondary schools, girls continue to be educated in movement, but this is interwoven with the learning of specific sport skills. Secondary school boys concentrate on learning specific sports skills taught by traditional methods. However, both the boys and the girls have acquired a sound understanding of movement, and this knowledge facilitates their motor skill learning and performance.

Movement education teaches proper use of the body as a tool for movement. It is not concerned with the rules of specific sports and games, with the strategy involved in playing a game, or with teaching the mechanics of playing, for example, first base in softball or center in basketball. These areas of knowledge are the province of traditional methodology. Through movement education the student discovers the leverage, balance, force, and speed required to kick a soccer ball, dribble a basketball, execute a forward roll, or throw a softball. Through traditional physical education, the student learns the applications of these and other skills.

Particularly on the secondary school level, we find boys and girls who do not perform physical skills well. They may lack confidence, or they may not be motivated to perform well simply because they have never experienced the satisfaction of a well-performed skill. These uncoordinated boys and girls may be physically capable of a good performance but may not intellectually understand the physical criteria of a good performance. These students need to be educated and/or reeducated in movement.

Movement education should be an on-going part of physical education curricula. It should not be used as a short-term phase of the program included to bridge the changeover from indoor to outdoor seasons or to fill a gap of several lessons between different units of study. Movement education need not, on the secondary school level, fill an entire class period. It can be used during each class period to replace formal warm-ups or calisthenics. With careful and thoughtful planning on the part of the teacher, the principles of movement education can be used to introduce new sports skills or scientific concepts of skill perform-

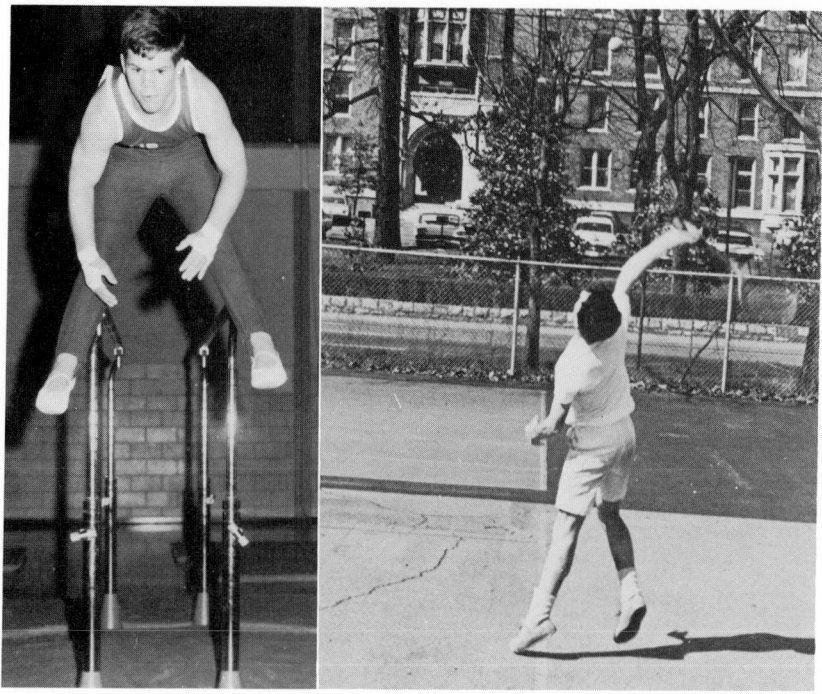

Fig. 17-2. Traditional physical education emphasizes the learning of skills through demonstration, drill, and practice. (Left, Mount Pleasant Senior High School, Wilmington, Del.; right, Peabody Demonstration School, George Peabody College for Teachers, Nashville, Tenn.)

ance, replacing demonstration and drill. In this way, teacher-directed learning can move toward student-conceptualized learning, thus enhancing not only the physical but also the intellectual objectives of physical education programs. Through the movement education method, students perform as individuals, and their performance depends in a large degree on their creativity and problem-solving ability.

THE ROLE OF THE TEACHER IN MOVEMENT EDUCATION

In traditional physical education programs, the physical educator explains a skill, demonstrates it, and directs student drill and practice. The teacher corrects errors in performance as the students strive to perfect the skill in relation to what they have seen and been told. The movement educator does none of these things.

A movement educator sets the problems and challenges for his students, guides the students through a thinking process, ob-

serves their attempts at solving the problem, and asks questions and stimulates their thinking through discussions of the problem. The movement educator improvises unique equipment where needed and avoids demonstrating or using formal patterns of class organization, such as circles, lines, or rows.

Whereas the physical educator sets the standards for the performance of a particular skill, the movement educator helps each student to become motivated to perform at his own peak of ability. Whereas the physical educator evaluates a student on the performance of a skill, the movement educator asks each student to evaluate his own performance and suggest his own ideas on how he can improve his performance. Whereas the physical educator tells a student that his headstand is unsteady because his head and hands are too closely aligned and shows the student the proper alignment, the movement educator asks the student to suggest how he might change the alignment of his body parts to stabilize his headstand. In this way, the student may attempt several unsatisfactory alignments before discovering the most stable one, but he will intellectually understand the physical adjustments he has made. This understanding will transfer to other skill learnings. The movement educator guides his students toward success by helping them to evaluate their own performance and by providing encouragement to each student as he or she seeks to solve a problem in movement.

Where traditional physical education methodology is speech-centered, movement education is activity-centered. The movement educator employs a problem-solving approach and allows the individual student to use his creativity to solve the problem. The movement educator neither dictates a solution to a problem in movement nor demonstrates the performance of a skill. Because there can be no stereotyping of a performance or imitation of the teacher's performance, the student is free to establish his own most comfortable movement patterns. The student is guided into using his body as the prime tool for movement rather than conceiving of his body as a force to be overcome before movement can take place.

MOVEMENT EDUCATION IN THE SECONDARY SCHOOL

Secondary school students can reap the benefits of movement education experiences whether or not they have been exposed to this method in the elementary school. Movement education lends itself to all phases of the physical education curriculum on all levels and can be adapted to use with all activities. The modification and adaptation of method will seem far stranger to the physical educator than to the student.

It would be difficult, if not impossible, to revert to the use of the natural activities of childhood in a secondary school situation. However, movement education can be employed on this level to introduce new skills,

and can be tailored to help in correcting performance errors in familiar skills. Further, most secondary schools offer units in dance. Dance and movement education depend both on the creativity of the individual and on his use of his body in relation to the time, space, force, and flow of a movement or series of movements. Both dance and movement education are often described as systems of nonverbal communication.

The techniques and methods peculiar to movement education are suited to use with secondary school boys and girls alike. If a unit in soccer is being introduced and the dribble or pass is to be learned, the teacher may ask his students to discover on their own how many different ways they can use their feet, with the exception of the toe, to propel the ball. The students are then given ample time to explore this problem. The teacher circulates from student to student, observing their progress. If the teacher should discover that a student persistently contacts the ball with the same foot, he will ask a question that will help the student to discover not only that he can use both feet but that there are advantages to be gained from doing so. At the end of the exploratory period, the teacher will call his students together and ask several of them to demonstrate the techniques they have discovered. Student evaluations and suggestions will be elicited, with the teacher guiding the discussion through questions. After this brief period, the teacher may ask the students to attempt to find out how they can keep the ball in motion while maintaining control of it. A third problem for the same class period may involve a problem in passing the ball back and forth with a partner over an increasing distance, while a final problem may be concerned with asking the students to discover how they can stop a rolling ball using their feet and legs only. Student demonstrations and discussions would follow each problem-solving period of the class time, and the class would be concluded by using these newly discovered

Fig. 17-3. Movement education is activity-centered.

skills in a teacher-created lead-up game. The use of relays would not be suitable since they emphasize competition between groups rather than focusing on the achievement of the individual.

The movement education approach also lends itself to apparatus activities. Freedom of use and movement on equipment, with appropriate regard to safety, can precede problems in mounting, using the piece of apparatus, and dismounting. This approach gives each student an opportunity to succeed, since no specific movement patterns are required or demanded. In teaching the use of the trampoline, for example, an initial problem might be to move across the trampoline in any way the students desire. Some may roll across, some may choose to bounce across, and others will go on all fours, while still others will create their own unique method. All these methods deserve teacher praise for a problem correctly solved. From this beginning, students may be asked to find out in how many different ways they can bounce on the bed of the trampoline. Through exploration and student demonstrations and discussions, use of the arms and legs for control and height will be better understood and perfected, leading to the learning of the proper use of, and skills unique to, the trampoline. Skill learning will thus have been guided by the teacher, but the skills

will have been discovered by the students themselves.

These two examples show how movement education can be used on the secondary school level to introduce new skills. Movement education can also be used effectively to perfect and improve performance in skills that have been learned previously. The physical educator begins with the observation stage and has the student suggest how he can improve his performance through the exploration of a variety of new stances, positions, or techniques.

Movement education on the secondary school level is an invaluable tool for use with the student who does nothing well in physical education. By being encouraged to explore skills rather than having to mimic stylized patterns, this student can attain a measure of success and become motivated to proceed and progress at his own pace.

Those secondary school students who have been educated in movement in their secondary school years will benefit from a continuation of this training. Further, they can be of inestimable aid to the secondary school physical educator who wishes to teach skills through the principles of movement education in situations where a majority of students have had no prior movement education experiences.

Movement education is not a panacea

that will make a highly skilled performer out of a student who is poorly skilled. It does offer a means through which the physical educator can assist the student in forming an intellectual concept of the skill to be performed or perfected. When corrections or adjustments are verbalized or demonstrated by the physical educator, the student need only attempt to mimic the physical movements, often totally disregarding any intellectual understandings that underlie the physical act.

Individual analysis of problem-solving situations is the basis for movement education. Rather than telling or showing students how to perform, the teacher guides the students through a series of possible responses as they seek solutions that are individually appropriate. In traditional physical education the teacher is a director, commander, and evaluator, while in movement education the teacher is a questioner, a guide, and an observer.

The high school boy and girl will find Bucher's textbook, *Physical Education for Life*, an informative resource on movement education. The basis of physical movement and its application to physical activities are discussed in detail in this book. (See Selected Readings at the end of the chapter.)

INNOVATIVE MOVEMENT EDUCATION CURRICULA FOR GRADES SEVEN TO NINE AND TEN TO TWELVE

Many curricula have been developed for movement education for the elementary school level; however, very few have been developed for the secondary school level. In exploring the possibility of including an innovative movement education program for the secondary school level in this text, we contacted Carol S. Rynbrandt, who has pioneered in developing a movement education curricula for grades seven to nine and grades ten to twelve for boys and girls who (1) have had an organized movement education experience at the elementary school level and (2) for those who have not. This curriculum represents an

outstanding contribution to the teacher of physical education in the secondary school who desires to utilize fundamental concepts that have proved so valuable and educational in the elementary school grades. The following introduction and movement education curricula for grades seven to nine and ten to twelve have been developed and written by Carol S. Rynbrandt* and used in this text with her permission.

Inherent to the successful implementation of this curriculum are an understanding and knowledge of the concepts of effort/shape—a qualitative, notational approach to observing, recording, and analyzing movement based on original concepts formulated by Rudolf Laban. Throughout the curriculum references are made to the elements of the effort/shape system, that is, weight, time, flow, and so on. (*A Primer for Movement Description†* is a valuable text on the effort/shape approach to movement.) Also needed is the belief that movement education is a creative and individualistic approach to learning about movement.

The following curriculum has been developed for both boys and girls, for boys as well as girls benefit from movement education. The values and aims are equally applicable to both sexes, for if within the curriculum a balanced choice of themes is offered to which both sexes can relate, then all students have the freedom of variety in response.

The curriculum is divided into four parts: (A) a program for students in grades seven, eight, and nine who have had no previous exposure to movement education; (B) a program for students in grades seven, eight, and nine who have had previous exposure to movement education; (C) a program for students in grades ten, eleven, and twelve who have had no previous exposure to movement education; and (D) a program for students in grades ten, eleven, and twelve who have had previous exposure to movement education. Previous exposure shall be defined as at least one year (two semesters) of classes.

PROGRAM A: mandatory—seventh, eighth, ninth grades

Class composition: All girls or all boys. For each sex, present movement situations that are especially appropriate.
Class organization:
   Unstructured, informal spacing of students.
   Teacher stands where she/he is visible by all students.
   Teacher should freely move about students during the class session.

---

*Assistant to Director of Education, Dance Notation Bureau, Center for Movement Research and Analysis, New York, N. Y.
†Dell, Cecily: A primer for movement description, New York, 1970, Dance Notation Bureau, Inc.

Possible class organization plans:

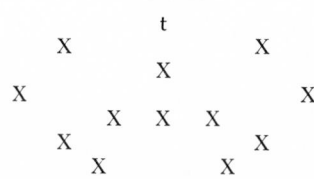

Semicircle

Scattered

Equipment and facilities:
1. Balls, jump ropes, medicine balls, hoops, wands, bean bags, inner tubes. THERE SHOULD BE ENOUGH EQUIPMENT SO THAT NO STUDENT WILL EVER HAVE TO WAIT TO USE SOMETHING.
2. Also benches, balance beam, mats, nets, and parachutes.
3. Record player, drum, gong, wood blocks, cymbals.
4. Spacious, well-lighted, well-ventilated room.

Content-materials°:

FIRST SEMESTER

1. Explore body movement possibilities—moving joints, fingers, limbs, different body parts. Especially be aware of movement elements of space, weight, time, and flow. Pose question—With what do we move?
2. Explore all aspects of space, and movement in space. Explore movement that is narrow, wide, high, low, on the diagonal. Again consider the four movement elements involved. Pose question—Where do we move?
3. Move with body parts other than legs. Explore twisting, stretching, bending, spiraling, contracting.
4. Work with the basic locomotor movements—walk, run, skip, jump, slide, hop, gallop.
   a. Vary speed of each of the above movements.
      1. Slow it down.
      2. Speed it up.
      3. Vary speed between slow and fast.
   b. Vary size, range of each movement.
      1. Make it small.
      2. Make it large.
      3. Make it narrow.
      4. Make it wide.
   c. Vary amount of weight exerted in each movement.
      1. Make it strong.
      2. Make it light
      3. Make it neither strong nor light.

°All suggestions listed under "content-materials" contain a breadth of material. Each suggestion should be subdivided and dealt with for a number of class sessions.

   d. Vary control of flow of each movement.
      1. Be very tense, rigid.
      2. Ve very loose, floppy.
      3. Be neither tense nor floppy.
5. Adapt movement to a partner.
   a. Follow the leader, changing quality, size, weight, flow.
   b. Contrast movement, move in opposition.
   c. Mirror movement.
   d. Mirror movement, but make a change a quality or element of the movement, for example, speed, size.
6. Move the arms and legs in unconventional manner.
7. Work to become aware of isolated actions, gestures.
8. Explore movement with objects—throwing, catching balls, hoops, wands, nets, inner tubes. How do objects affect one's movement?
9. Work with occupational rhythms: boys—sawing, cutting, chopping; girls—stirring, sweeping, washing. Explore movements, considering elements and qualities involved. Juxtapose qualities and abstract the movement.

SECOND SEMESTER

1. Work with particular shapes of movements—angles, curves, numbers, letters, the feeling between different shapes. Begin by shaping single body parts and sequentially add parts to involve total body.
2. Work with qualities of movement—swinging, percussive, sustained. Utilize lightness, flow, gravity, sharp and quick movement.
3. Explore movement in the three body planes—horizontal, vertical, sagittal. Use images of door, table, and wheel, respectively, to clarify planar concepts.
4. Work with interrelating to other people.
   a. Begin to sense group rhythm and pulse of movement.
      1. How does one's individual movement pulse differ from the group's movement pulse?
      2. How must one alter his movement to conform to the group rhythm and pulse?
   b. Begin to sense group quality of movement.
      1. How does the quality differ from an individual's quality?
      2. What must one do to conform to the group quality?
      3. How does one feel about conforming to the group?
   c. Sense the group's use of space.
      1. How does the group's use of space differ from the individual's use of space?
      2. Does one feel differently when moving in group space as opposed to individual space?
5. Work with ballistic, vibratory, and collapse qualities of movement. Develop movement phrases that include two or more qualities.

Once the above material has been covered, the class should review the concepts that they had difficulty grasping. Throughout the entire semester, the teacher should at all times consider the elements of space, weight, time, and flow of movement. The understanding of these concepts is the basis for all movement.

Throughout the semester the students, in some form, should, always be asking: How do I move? What do I move? Where do I move? Both teacher and student must know that in movement education there is never a wrong movement.

PROGRAM A: exemplary class session—moving with a partner

Specific objectives:
1. Develop an awareness of another person's movement.
2. Develop a deeper awareness of one's own movement through observing others and imitating their movements.
3. Strengthen student's sense for laterality of movement.
4. Develop kinesthetic sense of placement of body parts.

Concepts involved:
1. Movement is a visual art, and kinesthetic perception is enhanced by observing movement.
2. Each person is unique and has particular movement nuances.

Equipment and facilities: A spacious, well-lighted, well-ventilated room; phonograph.

Content-materials:
1. Have students select partner with whom they wish to work. Require that they choose someone they do not know very well.
2. One student is the leader and the other the follower. Leader starts moving simply, so that follower can replicate his movements. When "leading" is going well more complex movement may be tried, if desired. After three to four minutes students should be told to exchange roles. There should be no verbal conversation between the students.
3. The leader initiates movement and the follower mirrors his movement. Start with simple movement.
4. Change partners and repeat mirroring.
5. Incorporate big movements—jumps, hops, slides into mirroring.
6. Discuss what mirroring is and also what symmetry is.
7. With soft, slow background music ask students to move body parts symmetrically.
8. Ask the students to compose a short movement phrase using symmetry, while lying supine on the floor.
9. Each half of the class performs their movement phrase for the other half.

Teacher evaluation:
1. How well did the students grasp the concepts of mirroring and symmetry?
2. What didn't work?
3. How might you work with these concepts again?

4. What new ideas were realized for future sessions?

PROGRAM B: elective semesters—seventh, eighth, ninth grades

Specific objectives:
1. Promote creativity, sensory perception of movement, quick reaction, dexterity, and rhythmic sense.
2. Develop a consciousness of movement exploration.
3. Develop feeling for interrelationship of all body parts.
4. Discover where a movement starts and where it naturally progresses.
5. Capitalize on spontaneous, impulsive, emotional movement.
6. Experience success in movement.

Equipment and facilities:
1. Balls, jump ropes, medicine balls, hoops, wands, bean bags, inner tubes. THERE SHOULD BE ENOUGH EQUIPMENT SO THAT NO STUDENT WILL EVER HAVE TO WAIT TO USE SOMETHING.
2. Benches, balance beam, mats, nets, and parachutes.
3. Record player, drum, gong, wood blocks, cymbals.
4. Spacious, well-lighted, well-ventilated room.

Summary of approach:
1. Discovery of body's movement possibilities.
2. Movement utilizing inexpensive equipment.
3. Movement with partner and group.
4. Movement utilized in games and sports.

Content-materials (one semester):
1. Work with movement in group formation. Students discover elements requisite to group movement, themes that work well, and where the individual fits in the success of group movement.
2. Experiment with movement that is basic to sports activity—throwing, catching, striking. Abstract by changing flow, quality, time, weight, and use of space to see what happens to the movement and how its efficiency is affected.
3. Work with Laban's full-effort actions—press, dab, flick, glide, float, punch, slash, wring. (See *A Primer for Movement Description* for explanation.*) Each full-effort action combines the elements of movement in a different way. Have students explore various sport movement and everyday movements to discover where full-effort actions are used.
4. Work with objects and obstacles; use medicine balls, bean bags, hoops, wands, lightweight balls.
   a. Boys develop movement phrase using medicine ball or bean bags.
   b. Girls develop movement phrase using wands, hoops, or lightweight balls.
   Begin to concentrate on body rhythm and the effect of object on rhythm.

---

*Dell, Cecily: A primer for movement description, New York, 1970, Dance Notation Bureau, Inc.

5. Using a variety of musical instruments and a recorded music, combine movement with sounds and music.
   a. How does sound/rhythm affect and alter movement?
   b. Have students accompany movement with sound—that is, the movement dictates the sound.
   c. Have students move to sounds, rhythm, and music.
   d. Work with movement and music, so that both complement the other.
6. Work with the body rhythm inherent to sport skills; the rhythm of a run, a leap, a swing, a tennis serve, and so on. Emphasize that one really feel the movement's rhythm.
7. Contrast movement elements, light versus strong, quick versus slow, and incorporate them into the three body planes.
8. Explore one's kinesphere for near, medium, and far reach. Explain the kinesphere to students and discover what basic movement patterns take place in what part of the kinesphere. Analyze sports movements in the same way.
9. The culminating activity for the semester—a lecture-demonstration for the entire school or one class, depending which is most feasible and desirable. Demonstration would be comprised of the basic elements of movement; how, what, and why man moves; how movement can be abstracted; the "taking apart" of a sport skill; presentation of students' own creative solo and group movement phrases. Additional considerations might be the rhythm, the potential, and the freedom of movement.

PROGRAM B: exemplary class session—working with balls

Specific objectives:
1. To explore movement possibilities in working with a ball.

2. To discover to what extent the student can manipulate the ball and to what extent the ball forces the student to move in a certain way.

Concepts involved:
1. The body imparts energy, propels and stops objects.
2. Objects affect body movement.

Equipment and facilities: Soft rubber balls, assorted sizes, enough for each student to have one; a spacious, well-ventilated area

Content-materials:
1. Each student selects a ball.
2. The student investigates the ball very carefully; he explores to discover how it affects the way he moves.
3. The student explores to see how he can use the ball.
   How can he propel it with different body parts?
   How can he stop its movement using different body parts?
4. How can he best maintain a controlled movement with the ball?
5. Can he move the ball on the ground?
6. Can he move the ball in the air?
7. The students exchange balls, working with one of a different size or weight.
8. The students are asked to simulate movement without a ball.
9. Culminating problem: Comprise a movement phrase depicting how you most enjoy moving or manipulating a ball. Once the teacher has viewed the class as a whole, he would combine four or five students who have similar or contrasting movement phrases. These groups would then repeat their individual movement phrases as a group phrase for the other students.

Teacher evaluation:
1. How creative were the students in working with balls?
2. What size and weight balls seemed to work best?

Fig. 17-4. Movement education in New Zealand. (Department of Education, Wellington, New Zealand.)

3. What would you change if you were to present this session again?
4. Did the students enjoy moving?

PROGRAM C: mandatory—tenth, eleventh, twelfth grades

Class composition: Coeducational, equal number of boys and girls
Class organization:
Unstructured, informal, spacing of students (See Program A).
Equipment and facilities:
1. Balls, jump ropes, medicine balls, hoops, wands, bean bags, inner tubes. THERE SHOULD BE ENOUGH EQUIPMENT SO THAT NO STUDENT WILL EVER HAVE TO WAIT TO USE SOMETHING.
2. Also benches, balance beam, mats, nets, and parachutes.
3. Record player, drum, gong, wood blocks, cymbals.
4. Spacious, well-lighted, well-ventilated room.
Content-materials:
FIRST SEMESTER
1. Explore breathing and body relaxation. Present three-dimensional breathing, allowing breath to flow through entire body.

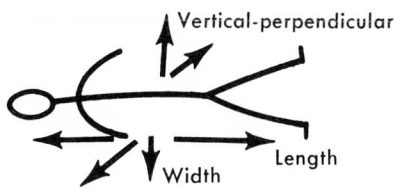

The following material is taken from Program A, for whatever age the class, all students must first experience the basic concepts of movement. The important point to remember is that method of approach does vary with different age groups. The content from Program A will be restated, but in a shortened form.
2. Explore body movement possibilities—joints, fingers, limbs.
3. Explore all aspects of space and movement in space.
4. Move with body parts other than legs—stretching, bending, twisting.
5. Work with the basic locomotor movements—walk, run, skip, jump, slide, hop, gallop. Vary speed, range, weight, and flow in each movement.
6. Adapt movement to a partner, follow, mirror, contrast.
7. Use the arms and legs in unconventional manner.
8. Work to become aware of isolated actions, gestures.
9. Explore movement with objects—throwing, catching balls, hoops, wands, nets, inner tubes, to see how movement is affected and altered by the objects.
10. Work with occupational rhythms: boys—sawing, cutting, painting, chopping; girls—washing, stirring, sweeping, typing.

SECOND SEMESTER
1. Work with particular shapes of movements—angles, curves, numbers, letters.
2. Work with qualities of movement.
3. Explore movement in the three body planes—horizontal, vertical, sagittal.
4. Work with interrelating to other people.
   a. Sense group rhythm and pulse.
   b. Sense group quality of movement.
   c. Sense group's use of space.
5. Continue to work with qualities of movement—ballistic, vibratory, and collapse qualities.

Methods:
Present situations that relate in some way to the students' other courses. Discuss gravity when working with weight, inertia when understanding movement flow, sociology when exploring group interaction. It is not the teacher's intention to get involved in the other course materials and so to view movement as secondary. But it is important that students realize that movement relates to all aspects of life. The class will be more meaningful if the teacher and students grasp basic movement concepts through an integrated approach.

PROGRAM C: exemplary class session—body relaxation, perception, and joint movement

Specific objectives:
1. To release tension in the entire body.
2. To clearly perceive body parts and joints and gain a better understanding of body make-up and movement potential.
3. To explore movement in each joint of the body.
Concepts involved:
1. The body is marvelously constructed.
2. Movement is the integrated working of the joints.
Equipment and facilities: A spacious, well-ventilated, well-lighted space.
Content-materials:
This session would transpire in the second half of the semester.*
1. Students are paired.
2. Student A lays on floor, in supine position, relaxed with eyes closed.
3. His partner, student B, slowly starts feeling student A's fingers, the joints of the hand, and wrist. Student B senses how the bones are connected and how the bones can move. As student B does this, he also is "shaking" out any tension that exists in the specific body parts of student A.
4. Following the hand and arm, student B continues to sequentially "shake-out" student A's other hand, arm, shoulders, head, back, chest, feet, ankles, legs, knees, hips, pelvis, until all body parts have been "shaken-out."
5. Student A should be completely relaxed,

---

*Session based on material provided by James Tyler, Instructor, New York University, Spring, 1972.

Fig. 17-5. Movement education in New Zealand. (Department of Education, Wellington, New Zealand.)

so that his body can be moved in any way —body parts will be very heavy.

6. Partners reverse roles. Throughout the "shake-out" the teacher should be directing the students and aware of their progress. This process should not be rushed and can take from fifteen to twenty minutes with each person.

7. Students are standing and are asked to begin moving only fingers in as many ways as possible.

8. After movement is flowing in the meta-carpals, wrist movement is added, then the elbow. It is an additive movement process incorporating all the joints of the body.

9. Once all joints are moving consecutively, the process is reversed until the fingers, which were the first to move, are the last body joints to stop moving.

10. In this session the students have experienced a state of total relaxation and also a total moving of body parts.

Teacher evaluation:

1. How successful was the session?
2. How did the students respond?

PROGRAM D: elective semesters—tenth, eleventh, twelfth grades

Specific objectives:

1. Promote creativity, sensory perception of movement, quick reaction, dexterity, and rhythmic sense.
2. Develop a consciousness of movement exploration.
3. Develop feeling for interrelationship of all body parts.
4. Discover where a movement starts and where it naturally proceeds.
5. Capitalize on spontaneous, impulsive, emotional movement.
6. Experience success in movement.
7. Continue to expand one's knowledge of movement.

8. Investigate the origin of movement education and the various approaches that exist.
9. Integrate movement experiences with other subjects in the school curriculum.

Equipment and facilities:

1. Balls, jump ropes, medicine balls, hoops, wands, bean bags, inner tubes. THERE SHOULD BE ENOUGH EQUIPMENT SO THAT NO STUDENT WILL EVER HAVE TO WAIT TO USE SOMETHING.
2. Also benches, balance beam, mats, nets, and parachutes.
3. Record player, drum, gong, wood blocks, cymbals.
4. Spacious, well-lighted, well-ventilated room.

Summary of approach:

1. Continual and fuller discovery of body movement.
2. Integration of movement education with other courses in the curriculum—history, biology, literature, sociology.
3. Discovery of "movement education" movement in sports.
4. Movement with partner and group.

Content-materials (one semester):

For those students who have had a maximum of two semesters of movement education, the content in Program B should first be presented and dealt with. Once that material has been covered, areas in which the students are weak should be reviewed, being presented from a different slant. There are endless possibilities of movement combinations that can be worked with if one considers the elements of movement, the qualities, full-effort actions, and so on. Also:

1. Work with more complex rhythmic patterns and motor coordinations. Beat a rhythmic pattern and ask students to devise movement phrase that complements the rhythmic pattern, and vice versa. Interchange gallops, skips, hops.
2. Build movement phrases from session to session.

3. Refine and alter old movement phrases.
4. Break down motor activities in sports. Discuss concepts, principles involved.
5. Allow students to suggest and initiate their own movement situations/problems.
6. Continue to utilize objects, obstacles, and music in different ways. Work to develop new effects.
7. Explore Laban's concepts of movement—effort/shape.
8. Investigate English and German systems of movement education.
9. Suggest research projects and books for reading dealing with any aspect of movement in which the students are interested.

Methods:

Encourage advanced students to pursue a particular movement interest or interest related to movement education. With some students, a contract curriculum might be worked out where the student would devise his particular course of study, pursue it, and at the end of the semester present a "product" representing his semester's work.

PROGRAM D: exemplary class session—group rhythm (ten to fifteen students)

Specific objectives:

1. To sense group rhythm.
2. To move as a group, as an integrated whole.

Concepts involved:

1. Individuals must adjust personal body rhythm in order to move as a group.
2. Group harmony requires some type of conformity for each individual involved.
3. Group movement affects individuals psychologically as well as physically, for example, movement pace, speed.

Equipment and facilities: Spacious, well-ventilated, well-lighted space.

Content-materials*:

1. Before the class begins any movement, they shall be instructed that they are to begin to walk, each at his own pace; they are then asked to begin to sense and adopt a group pace or walk, requiring that each person be very aware of everyone else in the group.
2. Once a group walk has been established, the group has been instructed to gradually speed up the pace to a run and at the same time use more space.
3. Once the group has established a group run, they are to decelerate to a walk, then to a very slow walk, and finally to a standstill. As this happens the group's use of space becomes smaller, so that when the pace is very slow, the group is also very close together. This may vary in time, taking from five to fifteen minutes.
4. Begin a new group experience with all students standing still. One student initiates a

walk or run. A second student begins to move at a different pace. The first student must adjust to the second student's pace. A third student begins to move and the first two students must adjust their pace to the pace of the third student. This process continues fairly rapidly until all students are moving. A group tempo is established that decelerates to a standstill.
5. Bring the students together and ask them what they thought of the experience. Talk about what group unity requires. Ask students to express any and all feelings concerning the experience or related group experiences.

Teacher evaluation:

1. How did the students respond?
2. Was a sense of group rhythm/tempo established?
3. If not, why?

Evaluation of movement education:

Class attendance—one fourth of grade
Objective evaluation—one fourth of grade
Student self-evaluation—one fourth of grade
Subjective evaluation—one fourth of grade

Objective evaluation, a written examination.

1. State elements of movement.
2. State qualities of movement.
3. What type of movement do you naturally find yourself doing?
4. List the three body planes and give an example of a movement in each one.
5. What type of movement is most difficult for you to do? Why?
6. (advanced) Explain what the kinesphere is.
7. (advanced) Execute eight full-action efforts.

Student self-evaluation, written or oral.

1. To what degree did you grasp the concepts of movement education as presented this semester?
2. Has your kinesthetic awareness of movement increased?
3. How would you rate your ability to execute the qualities and elements of movement?
4. What did and didn't you like about how the course was taught? How might it be improved?

Subjective evaluation, by the teacher.

1. Has the student's self-respect, self-worth, and self-control been improved, strengthened?
2. Is there a greater sense of kinesthetic awareness evident in the student's execution of movement?
3. Does the student think for himself?
4. Does the student recognize qualities and elements of movement in other students? To what degree can the student analyze movement?
5. Can the student improve his movement pattern by using another student's idea?

STUDENT EVALUATIONS IN MOVEMENT EDUCATION

In traditional teaching methodology in physical education, the teacher sets the

---

*Session based on material provided by James Tyler, Instructor, New York University, Spring, 1972.

Fig. 17-6. Movement education can be used on the secondary school level to improve performance in skills. (Left, Peabody Demonstration School, George Peabody College for Teachers, Nashville, Tenn.; right, Spartanburg Public Schools, Spartanburg, S. C.)

standards for the performance and evaluates student performance in relation to these standards. In the movement education approach to teaching physical education, standards may be applied to a skill performance, but the ways in which these standards are attained are quite different.

Every student in a movement education program sets his own goals, but because the students are reacting as individuals, they are not only directing their own learning but disciplining their learning as well. A skilled performance is thus judged not by a single standard for an entire class but by a series of standards that reflects the individual standards and differences of each of the members of the class. The physical education class becomes a laboratory experience in which the student is not only encouraged but given the freedom to test a variety of solutions to a performance problem before arriving at his personal answer to that problem. When a student is given such experiences, the satisfactions gained from a successful performance help to motivate him to accept increasingly more difficult performance challenges. Each student can experience success be-

cause each solution attempted is a step toward the personal goals set by the student. The movement education approach helps to eliminate the fear of failure and of ostracism or criticism for failure to meet a common standard. Students achieve on their own level and derive fun and satisfaction from their physical education experience.

Evaluations in movement education can be achieved objectively and realistically. Program objectives will be student-centered and student-achieved. For each activity within the physical education class program, including the team, dual, and individual sports and activities and physical fitness and dance units, there can be a movement education approach. Within this framework, student progress can be measured on an individual basis in a cooperative student-teacher effort. Written tests concerned with intellectual understanding of the scientific principles of skill performance can be employed. Physical skill tests designed to measure individual achievement, as well as physical fitness tests, can also be applied to the evaluative process. Students on the secondary school level are

Table 17-1. A progressive program

Area	Elementary	Junior high school	Senior high school
I. For developing skills	To develop movements necessary for basic sports skills (run, throw, catch)	To extend areas of basic skills in a wide variety of activities	To perfect techniques and capacities in basic skills
II. For physical skills	To understand basic components of physical fitness	To increase physical fitness levels through continued movement experiences	To improve and maintain physical fitness levels through movement experiences
III. For creative expression	To provide opportunity to respond freely to a variety of stimuli	To provide opportunity to experiment with many complex movements	To innovate and create new movements and new experiences
IV. For communicative experiences	To provide imaginative and dramatic opportunities	To provide more complex ideas for communication in terms of time, space, force	To innovate and create new relationships with environment
V. For understanding scientific principles	To understand basic function of balance and gravity	To develop greater understanding of forces of gravity in relation to static and dynamic movement	To understand physical laws governing motion, force, and balance as they apply to movement

capable of self-evaluation through student-teacher conferences. By combining these and other methods, a truer and more meaningful evaluation of each student's progress toward becoming a physically educated person can be derived. Total involvement of the student in all phases of the program will serve to enhance not only student achievement but the accomplishment of the program objectives as well.

MOVEMENT EDUCATION AND THE EXTRACLASS PROGRAM

Movement educators avoid group competition on the elementary school level. On that level, the student competes with himself to improve his own performance and understanding of it. Games are used, but the competitive aspects are eliminated as much as possible. Games are a means through which newly learned skills can be practiced and correct performance reinforced.

On the secondary school level, competition is a necessary part of many traditional programs. Students enjoy competition, and it serves as a stimulus to them. Within the regular class program, where movement education is employed, sports and games can be played competitively as soon as the students are satisfied that they have achieved sufficient skill ability to enjoy competition.

Intramural programs should be open to all students in a school. Participation in an intramural program should precede a student's membership on an interscholastic or varsity team. The movement education approach used in the class program will help each student to become more aware of the value of participating in sports and games of his own choosing outside the class program requirements. Students will also better understand the qualities needed for membership on the more highly competitive teams. Movement education programs help to complement and supplement the extraclass offerings of secondary school physical education programs.

POINTS TO REMEMBER

1. Movement education is a significant new approach to teaching secondary school physical education.
2. Movement education frees the individual student to work and progress at his own pace.
3. Movement education helps the student to better understand the physical laws that govern human movement.

4. Opportunities for creative expression and exploration are an invaluable aspect of movement education.
5. Physical skills are developed through an individualized problem-solving technique.

PROBLEMS TO THINK THROUGH

1. On what basis should a student be graded when the movement approach to teaching physical education is utilized?
2. Is the movement approach applicable for all the goals and objectives of physical education programs on the secondary school level?
3. Are movement education experiences equally vital for secondary school boys as well as girls?
4. Does the movement education approach offer a new means of motivating those secondary school students who are resistive to physical education?

CASE STUDY FOR ANALYSIS

A class of high school freshmen has scored low on initial physical fitness tests. The teacher has also observed that the students do not exhibit adequate levels of motor ability on a variety of skill tests. Intellectually, the class as a group expresses disinterest in and distaste for physical education. The first unit of instruction for these students will be track-and-field activities. How can the teacher interest and motivate these students as well as help them to improve their fitness scores and skill abilities?

EXERCISES FOR REVIEW

1. How does the problem-solving method of teaching help movement education to succeed?
2. In what ways can the area of dance contribute to movement education?
3. How does movement education correlate with traditional programs of physical education in secondary schools in the United States?
4. Compare the role of the teacher in traditional physical education with the teacher's role in movement education.
5. How can movement education help students to develop confidence in their skill performances?

SELECTED READINGS

Allenbaugh, Naomi: Learning about movement, NEA Journal 56:48, 1967.

Barrett, Kate R.: Exploration—a method for teaching movement, Madison, Wisc., 1964, College Printing and Typing Co., Inc.

Boyd, Barbara, and others: Whatever happened to basic movement skills? Journal of Health, Physical Education, and Recreation 37:21, 1966.

Brown, Margaret C., and Sommer, Betty K.: Movement education: its evolution and modern approach, Reading, Mass., 1969, Addison-Wesley Publishing Co.

Bucher, Charles A.: Foundations of physical education, ed. 6, St. Louis, 1972, The C. V. Mosby Co.

Bucher, Charles A.: Physical education for life, New York, 1969, McGraw-Hill Book Co., Inc.

Cratty, Bryant J.: On the threshold, Quest, vol. 8, Spring, 1967.

Diem, Lieselott: Who can? Frankfort, Germany, 1962, Wilhelm Lempert, Publisher.

Estes, Nolan: Encouragement for innovation, NEA Journal 55:30, 1966.

Hackett, Layne C., and Jenson, Robert G.: A guide to movement exploration, Palo Alto, Calif., 1966, Peek Publications.

Howard, Shirley: The movement education approach to teaching in English elementary schools, Journal of Health, Physical Education, and Recreation 38:31, 1967.

Kleinman, Seymour: The significance of human movement: a phenomenological approach, National Association for Physical Education for College Women Report, p. 123, 1962.

Lemen, Mildred: Implications of the problem-solving method for physical educators, Journal of Health, Physical Education, and Recreation 37:28, 1966.

Little, Billy Jean: Creativity in physical education, Physical Educator 24:75, 1967.

Locke, Lawrence F.: The movement movement, Journal of Health, Physical Education, and Recreation 37:26, 1966.

Mackenzie, Marlin M.: Toward a new curriculum in physical education, New York, 1969, McGraw-Hill Book Co., Inc.

Porter, Lorena R.: The movement movement, Today's Education 62:42, 1972.

Schurr, Evelyn L.: Movement experiences for children, New York, 1967, Appleton-Century-Crofts.

Smith, Hope M.: Introduction to human movement, Reading, Mass., 1968, Addison-Wesley Publishing Co.

Souder, Marjorie A., and Hill, Phyllis J.: Basic movement foundations of physical education, New York, 1963, The Ronald Press Co.

Sweeney, Robert T.: Selected readings in movement education, Reading, Mass., 1970, Addison-Wesley Publishing Co.

Wessel, Janet A.: Movement fundamentals, Englewood Cliffs, N. J., 1970, Prentice-Hall, Inc.

18 RESOURCES AND MATERIALS FOR TEACHING*

The use of teaching aids and materials is a method of teaching that supplements the learning process. Students who are not stimulated by other teaching methods may be motivated by films, charts, or other resource materials, and highly skilled students may broaden the scope of their knowledge by studying enrichment materials. Well-chosen teaching aids are of special value in teaching the culturally disadvantaged or other students whose formal experience with physical education has been limited. Acquaintance with the wealth of outside resources and information from which all members of a class may benefit is an invaluable aid in teaching, and the physical educator should make good use of such information.

In recent years considerable progress has been made in regard to teaching aids. The equipment and tools have been vastly improved and the resources and services greatly extended so that all schools may take advantage of these instructional materials.

In this chapter suggestions concerning valuable audiovisual aids, special aids, reading materials, outside resources, and sources of supplies are offered. The principles to be followed when using these materials are included at the beginning of the chapter to serve as a guide for the teacher in making proper use of them.

---

*See also Part Seven.

PRINCIPLES GOVERNING THE USE OF TEACHING AIDS AND MATERIALS

When selecting audiovisual aids or other resources and materials, the teacher of physical education should consider certain principles that make utilization of these aids effective and valuable. The similarity between these principles and those suggested in other methods of teaching should be noted, for the aim in each case is to create a worthwhile learning situation.

• *Materials should be carefully selected and screened.* The teacher should preview the materials to make sure they are appropriate for the unit and age level of the students and that they present information in an interesting and stimulating manner. For instance, a basketball slide film that is geared for boys would probably not be suitable for use in a girls' class.

• *Proper preparation of materials should be made.* The teacher should check all equipment that may be necessary for the presentation of materials, to make sure that it is in operating condition. Record players and movie projectors, in particular, need to be carefully checked before they are used.

• *The presentation of materials should be planned and integrated into the lesson.* Students should be properly introduced to the materials so that they know what to expect and so that they understand their relationship to the unit of study.

• *Materials should be presented to the stu-*

331

Fig. 18-1. The presentation of materials should be planned and integrated into the lesson being taught. (Hartsdale Public Schools, Hartsdale, N. Y.)

dents in a proper learning situation. Students should be located so that all may hear, see, and learn from the material being presented to them. They should realize that they will be held responsible for the information being presented.

• *Materials should be varied.* Different types of materials should be chosen for presentation to stimulate the varying interests of the students. A teacher using films or slide films exclusively does not take full advantage of supplementary materials available for widespread appeal.

• *Use of supplementary materials should be limited.* The teacher should place a reasonable limit on the use of extra teaching materials to maintain a balance between supplementary learnings and those gained from regular instructional materials.

• *Care should be taken to avoid excessive expenses.* A reasonable part of the instructional budget should be set aside for supplementary materials. This amount should be in accordance with the emphasis placed on this phase of the teaching program.

• *Records and evaluations of materials*

should be maintained. All supplementary materials should be carefully evaluated and records kept on file for future reference. This should save the unnecessary expense involved in reordering or duplicating materials and in maintaining outdated materials.

By following these principles the teacher is able to supplement learnings with materials that are valuable and interesting to the students.

A recent study by one of Bucher's students was concerned with current practices and trends in the use of audiovisual media for the teaching of motor skills in professional physical education programs. This study has implications for secondary school physical education programs in that it reveals the number of responding schools that offer or require a course in audiovisual media and techniques in their professional preparing programs.

The researcher developed and mailed a questionnaire that was returned by sixty-three physical education directors in a variety of colleges and universities. Of these respondents, five required a course in audiovisual media and techniques, while thirty-five offered such a course on an elective basis. A total of fifty-four of the individuals answering the questionnaire indicated that they felt that audiovisual media serve as a valuable supplement to instruction in the learning of motor skills.

The study also found that videotaping is increasing in use as an instructional tool. The audiovisual media used with the most frequency by the respondents in this study were, in order of frequency, 16 mm. and 8 mm. films, loop films, cartridge films, chalkboards, wall charts, slide films, filmstrips, and instructional television.

AUDIOVISUAL MATERIALS

Audiovisual aids and materials have become such an important part of physical education programs that space should be provided for a discussion of the use, types, and guidelines for such supplies and equipment.

A survey conducted by Bucher among about 100 schools and colleges found that more than half of them used some form of visual or audio aid in their programs. All of the persons surveyed felt that audiovisual media served as a valuable supplement to instruction in the learning of motor skills. The survey also found that videotaping is on the increase as an instructional tool.

Reasons for increased use of audiovisual materials

Some of the reasons for the increased use of audiovisual materials are:
• *They enable the student to better understand concepts and the performance of a skill, events, and other experiences.* The old cliché, "one picture is worth a thousand words," has much truth. The use of a film, pictures, or other materials gives a clearer idea of the subject being taught, whether it is how a heart functions or how to perfect a golf swing.
• *They help to provide a variety to teaching.* There is increased motivation, the at-

tention span of children is increased, and the subject matter of a course is much more exciting when audiovisual aids are used in addition to other teaching techniques.
• *They increase motivation on the part of the student.* To see a game played, a skill performed, or an experiment conducted before his eyes, in clear, understandable, illustrated form helps to motivate the student to engage in a game, perform a skill more effectively, or want to know more about the relation of exercise to health. This is particularly true in video replay, for example, where a student can actually see how he performs a skill and then compare his performance to what should be done.
• *They provide for an extension of what can normally be taught in a classroom, gymnasium, swimming pool, or playground.* Audiovisual aids enable the student to be taken to other countries, to experience sport events that occur in other parts of the United States, and to witness other events. All of these are important to physical education programs and the instructional program for students.
• *They provide a historical reference for the field of physical education.* Outstanding events in sports and physical education that have occurred in past years can be brought to life before the student's eyes. In this way the student obtains a better understanding of how the field of physical education plays an important role in American society and in other cultures of the world.

CLASSIFICATION OF RESOURCES AND MATERIALS

On the pages that follow, three categories of materials are discussed in terms of their purposes, problems, and specific resources. Suggestions are listed under *reading materials, audiovisual aids,* and *special aids,* and while these are recent and fairly inclusive listings, new types of materials are always being placed on the market. Teachers should be on the lookout for the very latest items available, as listed in journals, catalogs, and advertisements.

Fig. 18-2. Audiovisual aids. (Evergreen Park High School, Evergreen Park, Ill.)

READING MATERIALS

Purposes

To provide up-to-date information and enrichment materials on all aspects of the program.

Problems

To keep track of materials and assignments. A check-out system should be developed so that the teacher may know where materials may be located. In addition, some method of annotating particularly beneficial articles or resources should be devised, thus simplifying assignments.

Types

1. *Textbook.*
Bucher, Charles A.: *Physical Education for Life,* New York, 1969, McGraw-Hill Book Co., Inc.

The text for high school boys and girls provides information about physique, posture, physical skills, physical fitness, safety and first aid, and the body in motion. The book also includes basic instruction about twenty different sports and activities. Additional information is provided on the purchase and care of equipment. The textbook is both informative and motivating and is an excellent means of giving high school students a rich physical education experience.

2. *Magazines* (research, historical, educational, informational, or supplementary):
All-American Athlete, Dept. J., 801 Palisade Ave., Union City, N. J. 07087
Athletic Journal, Athletic Journal Publishing Co., 1719 Howard St., Evanston, Ill. 60202
The Coach, Lowe and Campbell Athletic Goods, 1511 Baltimore Ave., Kansas City, Mo. 64108
Coach and Athlete, 1421 Mayon St., N. E., Atlanta, Ga. 31324
Dance Magazine, 268 West 47th St., New York, N. Y. 10036

Journal of Health, Physical Education, and Recreation, 1201 Sixteenth St., N. W., Washington, D. C. 20036
Research Quarterly, 1201 Sixteenth St., N. W., Washington, D. C. 20036
Scholastic Coach, Scholastic Magazine, Inc., 50 West 44th St., New York, N. Y. 10036
U. S. Gymnast Magazine, P. O. Box 53, Iowa City, Iowa 52240
3. *Booklets, pamphlets, and catalogs* (educational and supplemental information about health, safety, and related areas):
American Association for Health, Physical Education, and Recreation, 1201 Sixteenth St., N. W., Washington, D. C. 20036
American School and University, Product Catalog File, American School Publishing Co., 470 Fourth Ave., New York, N. Y. 10016
The Athletic Institute, 805 Merchandise Mart, Chicago, Ill. 60654
American Medical Association, 535 N. Dearborn St., Chicago, Ill. 60610
Metropolitan Life Insurance Co., 1 Madison Ave., New York, N. Y. 10010
National Dairy Council, 111 N. Canal St., Chicago, Ill. 60606
Science Research Associates, 259 E. Erie, Chicago, Ill. 60611

AUDIOVISUAL AIDS

Purposes

To give information to a large group at one time in such areas as skill breakdowns, game play, techniques and rules of sports, and enrichment materials; to provide musical or other rhythmical accompaniment.

Problems

To keep an accurate and up-to-date file on current materials, with evaluative suggestions. Indi-

Fig. 18-3. Audiovisual aids. (Peabody Demonstration School, George Peabody College for Teachers, Nashville, Tenn.)

vidual file cards are helpful for this purpose. Large school systems and new schools generally maintain departments for audiovisual instruction, with personnel specifically hired for the maintenance, distribution, selection, and follow-up of all equipment and materials in this area.

Types

1. *Motion pictures.* Motion pictures for use in physical education classes are available in every area. They may be purchased in color or black-and-white or rented for nominal fees. Catalogs issued by film companies contain listings of films available for rental or purchase and generally include brief descriptions of the films themselves to help the teacher in making selections. Catalogs may be secured through the following:

Health, Physical Education, and Sports Films, Visual Aids Service, Division of University Extension, University of Illinois, Champaign, Ill. 61820

Educators Guide to Free Films, Educators Progress Service, P.O. Box 487, Spring Green, Wisc. 53588

Guides are also available for filmstrips and for tapes, scripts, and transcriptions.

The first is a catalog of films (see following partial listing) from all the various rental agencies, categorized by individual sports and related areas. Films may be rented through this university service.

The *Educators Guide* is an index of free films, listing names, titles, and companies where such films are available.

Other film companies that distribute educational films (whose listings would be found in the catalogs suggested above) include the following:

Association Films, Inc., 600 Madison Ave., New York, N. Y. 10022

Ideal Pictures, Inc., 321 West 44th St., New York, N. Y. 10036

Modern Talking Picture Service, 1212 Avenue of the Americas, New York, N. Y. 10036

School Film Service, 549 West 123rd St., New York, N. Y. 10027

A partial listing of films available for rental through Visual Aids Service, Division of University Extension, University of Illinois, Champaign, Ill. 61820:

Archery
  Archery for Girls
  Archery Fundamentals
  Archery Instruction and Safety
  Bows and Arrows
  Introduction to Field Archery
Baseball
  Baseball for Millions
  Baseball Instruction: Base Running
  Baseball Instruction: Batting and Bunting
  Baseball Instruction: Catching
  Baseball Instruction: First and Third Basemen
  Baseball Instruction: Outfielding
  Baseball Instruction: Pitching
  Baseball Instruction: Shortstop and Second Basemen
  Batting Fundamentals
  Batting Stars of Baseball
  A Boy, a Bat and a Baseball
  Catching Fundamentals
  Catching in Baseball
  Circling the Bases
  Democracy of Baseball
  Hitting in Baseball
  Infield Play at First and Third
  Lou Gehrig's Greatest Day (You Are There)
  Official Baseball
  Play Ball, Son
  Throwing in Baseball
Basketball
  Basketball for Boys: Fundamentals
  Basketball for Boys: Team Play
  Basketball for Girls: Fundamental Techniques
  Basketball for Girls: Game Play
  Basketball for Millions
  Basketball Fundamentals (second edition)
  Basketball Strategy for Girls
  Basketball Techniques for Girls
  Girls' Basketball for Beginners
  Official Basketball
  Play Championship Basketball
  This Is Basketball
  Understanding Basketball
Bowling
  American Bowls
  Bowling Aces
  Bowling Fundamentals
  Splits, Spares, and Strikes
Dance
  American Square Dance
  Canada Dances
  Dance Demonstration
  Dance Festival
  Dance Your Own Way
  Dancer's World
  Indian Dances
  Introduction to Dance
  Let's Dance
  Modern Dance

Social Dancing
Square Dancing
Football
Ball Handling in Football
Blocking in Football
Football Fundamentals: Blocking and Tackling
Football Kicking Techniques
Official Football
T Formation (Basic Plays)
T Formation (Open Plays)
Tackling in Football
This Is Football
Golf
Building Your Golf Swing
In the Rough
Pitch and Run—Pitching and Sand Shots
Play Better Golf, Part I (Fundamentals)
Play Better Golf, Part II (Advanced)
Putting
Welcome to Golf
Gymnastics
Advanced Tumbling
Beginning Tumbling
Gymnastics: Fundamentals and Techniques: Part I
Gymnastics: Fundamentals and Techniques: Part II
Gymnastics: Side Horse Exercises
Intermediate Tumbling
Rhythmic Exercises
Simple Stunts
Trampoline Fundamentals
Softball
Girls, Let's Learn Softball
Softball for Boys
Softball for Girls
Softball Fundamentals
Sports, Miscellaneous
Badminton Fundamentals
Fundamentals of Badminton
Fundamentals of Soccer
Handball Fundamentals
Soccer—Let's Play
Soccer for Girls (revised edition)
Speed-a-Way
Speedball for Girls
Table Tennis
Swimming and diving
Advanced Swimming
Anyone for Diving?
Beginning Swimming
Crawl Stroke
Diving Fundamentals
Dolphin Kick
Fundamentals of Swimming
Matt Mann's Swimming Techniques for Boys
Matt Mann's Swimming Techniques for Girls
New Magic of Swimming
Safe Swimming
Springboard and Front Approach
Springboard Diving
Swimming and Diving Aces
Swimming for Beginners
Tennis
Advanced Tennis
Beginning Tennis
Court Favorites (Tennis)

Fundamentals of Tennis
Technique of Tennis
Tennis—Elementary Fundamentals
Tennis—Intermediate and Advanced Fundamentals
Tennis for Beginners
Tennis Tactics
Tennis Techniques
Track and Field
Bannister Wins the Mile Run (You Are There)
Dashes, Hurdles, and Relays
The Discus
Distance Races
Fundamentals of Running
Fundamentals of Track and Field
High Jump
The Hurdles
Middle Distances
Pole Vault
The Relays
Running Broad Jump
Shot Put
The Sprints
This Is Track and Field
Volleyball
Fundamentals of Volleyball
Play Volleyball
Volleyball Drills and Techniques
Volleyball for Boys
Volleyball for Women
Volleyball Skills
Volleyball Strategy for Girls
Volleyball Techniques for Girls
Winter Sports
Introduction for the Art of Figure Skating
Ski Thrills
Wrestling
Scientific Unarmed Self-Defense: An Exposition of the Ancient Asian Esoteric Arts
Wrestling: Basic Skills, Part 1—Starting Positions and Takedowns
Wrestling: Basic Skills, Part 2—Escapes and Reversals
Wrestling: Basic Skills, Part 3—Breakdowns into Pinning Combinations

2. *Slide films.* Slide films have been developed for rental and purchase purposes on both a sound and silent basis.

A source of full-color slide films is The Athletic Institute, 805 Merchandise Mart, Chicago, Ill. 60654. To rent their slide films, contact must be made with Ideal Pictures, Inc., at one of their regional offices:

102 West 25th Street, Baltimore, Md. 21218
58 E. South Water St., Chicago, Ill. 60601
1840 Alcatraz Ave., Berkeley, Calif. 94703.

Slide films are available in sports, including beginning archery, beginning badminton beginning baseball, beginning bowling, campcraft, beginning fencing, beginning golf, beginning table tennis, gymnastics, beginning soccer, beginning softball, swimming, beginning tennis, track and field, beginning volleyball, and beginning wrestling, plus individual recreational sports such as fishing, ice skating, skiing, and judo. Excellent booklets accompany each of these slide films.

3. *Learning loops.* Several 8 mm. learning loops

may be purchased from The Athletic Institute. An 8 mm. loop film projector is also available directly from the Institute. These loops are an excellent device for specific instruction in skill performance. They are available in each individual event in track and field for men, track and field for women, gymnastics, and tennis.

4. *Loop movies.* Loop movies consist of several 16 mm. loops spliced together, end to end, for continuous projection. They are available for purchase from Champions on Film, 3666 South State St., Ann Arbor, Mich. 48104, with prices ranging between $20.00 and $50.00. These films cover such subjects as basketball, wrestling, swimming, baseball, golf, tennis, trampoline, and track.

5. *Television.* Although educational television (ETV) has met with widespread appeal at various age levels in all phases of the curriculum, its usage as a teaching technique in physical education is still rather limited.

Physical educators agree that the full potential of television has not been reached and recognize that recent developments in physical education, such as movement efficiency and sensory-perceptual experiences, contain concepts adaptable to television production.

6. *Videotape.* Videotapes are finding increased usage in many educational endeavors and are being recognized as an invaluable teaching aid in physical education activities. Several purposes illustrate the adaptability of this special type of recording device. It may be used in the following ways:

a. To videotape sports performances for later study with still frames, for closer analysis of action

b. To supervise several outdoor play areas from one location through a closed-circuit television monitoring device

c. To provide objective evaluation of an individual performance, such as diving or trampolining, through instant replay

d. To build up a school library of tapes for specific instructional purposes at later dates

These are only a few of the instructional possibilities of this versatile teaching tool. Its popularity will continue to increase because of its adaptability, the ease with which it may be operated, and its effectiveness. Current problems caused by tapes that fit improperly in some machines are being solved.

One source of equipment is Concord Electronics Corporation, 1935 Armacost Ave., Los Angeles, Calif. 90025, makers of audiotape recorders, videotape recorders, closed-circuit television, and communications products.

7. *Phonographs and audiotape recorders.* For extensive use in physical education classes, phonographs and audiotape recorders must be durable, portable, and provided with discrete volume controls. Transportation and storage of this valuable equipment may be a problem if safe closet space is not available relatively near the gymnasium. The following are examples of manufacturers:

Newcomb Audio Products Co., Dept. JO-10, 6824 Lexington Ave., Hollywood, Calif. 90028

Rheem Califone Corp., 5922 Bowcroft St., Los Angeles, Calif. 90016

8. *Records* (available in all speeds, some in unbreakable nylon materials, for teaching all rhythmic activities): Examples of sources are:

Canadian F.D.S., 605 King St., W. Toronto 2B, Ontario, Canada

Cheviot Corp., Dept. J-11, Box 34485, Los Angeles, Calif. 99034

Dance Record Center, 1159 Broad St., Newark, N. J. 07114

Dance Records, 1438 Springvale Ave., McLean, Va. 22101

Folkraft Records, 1161 Broad St., Newark, N. J. 07114

Freda Miller Records, Dept. J, Box 383, Northport, N. Y. 11768

Hoctor Records, P. O. Box 38, Waldwick, N. J. 07463

Honor Your Partner Records, Educational Activities, Inc. (formerly Square Dance Associates), P. O. Box 392, Freeport, N. Y. 11520

R.C.A. Victor Educational Records, 1133 Avenue of the Americas, New York, N. Y. 10036

Rhythms Production Records, Whitney Building, Box 34485, Los Angeles, Calif. 99034

Russell Records, P. O. Box 3318, Ventura, Calif. 93003

Stepping Stones, 2506 Overland Ave., Los Angeles, Calif. 90064

Windsor Records, 5530 J. Rosemead Blvd., Temple City, Calif. 91780

9. *Drum* (dance drum, bongo drum, and similar percussive devices). Drums are used extensively to provide rhythmical measures for creative activities. They should be kept in a dry place, for extreme dampness causes loss of tone. In such instances, placing the drum on a radiator for a few minutes restores tensity. The Fred Gretsch Mfg. Co., 60 Broadway, Brooklyn, N. Y. 11211, makes a handy dance drum at a reasonable price.

SPECIAL AIDS

Purposes

To provide graphic, illustrative material to students in an interesting and educational manner.

Problems

To find time to utilize displays effectively, to change displays for added interest, and to keep up to date with current events. Student assistants should be utilized to prepare and maintain the displays.

Types

1. *Charts, diagrams, and photographic materials* (for materials in several different sports):

Coordinated Program Chart Co., 2604 North Stevens St., Spokane, Wash. 99205

Division for Girls' and Women's Sports, American Association for Health, Physical Education, and Recreation, 1201 Sixteenth St., N. W., Washington, D. C. 20036

Easy Post, P. O. Box 425, Normal, Ill. 61761

Nissen Corp., 930 27th Avenue, S. W., Cedars Rapids, Iowa 52416

Physical Education Aids, P. O. Box 5117, San Mateo, Calif. 94402.

2. *Bulletin boards and chalkboards* (cork or beaver board, stationary or movable). These are excellent teaching devices, both for educational and motivational purposes. They should be colorful, interesting, neat, clear, uncluttered, and changed often. School administrators generally provide these materials.

3. *Magnetic boards* (blank-surfaced boards suitable for specific sports, such as soccer, football, or basketball, or all-purpose types of boards, suitable for all sports). These boards are excellent teaching devices for team sports. Although the initial expense ($19.00 to $50.00) seems rather steep at first, the lasting value of this item over several years makes it a worthwhile investment. A supplier of these boards is:

Jaconda Mfg. Co., Dept. HP, 5449 Hunter St., Philadelphia, Pa. 11931

OUTSIDE RESOURCES

Outside resources available to supplement the classroom teaching include professional personnel, community activities, and clinics.

PROFESSIONAL PERSONNEL

Purpose

To provide an interesting incentive to students by having a visiting professional demonstrate, teach, or discuss a sport or related experience.

Problems

To plan and organize for thorough effectiveness and safety. Preplanning with the guest is essential, and preparation with students allows them to gain more fully from the experience.

Types

The directors and personnel of professional organizations such as the National Golf Foundation, United States Lawn Tennis Association, and Amateur Athletic Association.

COMMUNITY ACTIVITIES

Purposes

To promote good public relations with the community and to provide additional activities for student participation.

Problems

To find time to plan and organize carefully the various details of the activities with community leaders.

Types

Recreational activities (tennis meets); PTA-sponsored special events and programs; benefit athletic demonstrations.

CLINICS

Purposes

To provide additional and valuable learning experiences to students attending these clinics, either as participants or observers. Taking an honor team, a leaders club, or an entire class to a special program of this type offers information and an opportunity for appreciation that they never forget because of the specialized nature of the experience.

Problems

Planning, organizing transporation, obtaining parental permission, and providing supervision of the students. In many schools definite procedures for taking students on field trips are outlined, and they should be carefully followed.

Types

Special games and programs put on by visiting professional clubs (basketball or football teams); special clinics sponsored by local or state teaching organizations; traveling college groups and community organizations.

MATERIALS FOR TEAM SPORTS

READING MATERIALS

National Federation of State High School Athletic Associations, 7 S. Dearborn St., Chicago, Ill. 60603:
   Official Football Rules (National Alliance edition)
   Football Case Book (Official Interpretations)
   Football Handbook
   National Basketball Rules (Federation edition)
   Basketball Case Book (Official Interpretations)
   Basketball Handbook
   Baseball Rules
   Baseball Case Book
   Baseball Umpires Manual
   Football Officials' Manual
   Basketball Officials' Manual
   Basketball Rules Simplified and Illustrated
   High School Football Rules Simplified and Illustrated
Division for Girls' and Women's Sports, American Association for Health, Physical Education, and Recreation, 1201 Sixteenth Street, N. W., Washington, D. C. 20036:
   Basketball Guide
   Field Hockey–Lacrosse Guide
   Soccer-Speedball Guide
   Volleyball Guide
   Softball Guide
Division of Athletics, AAHPER (above address):
   Speedball for Men

SLIDE FILMS (SOUND AND SILENT— FOR PURCHASE OR RENTAL)

The Athletic Institute, 805 Merchandise Mart, Chicago, Ill. 60654:
   Baseball (seven units)
   Basketball (seven units)

Basketball (girls; eight units)
Field Hockey (five units)
Soccer (three units)
Softball (eight units)
Volleyball (four units)
Student manual for each sport
Instructor's guide

SPECIAL CHARTS (TECHNIQUES)

Division for Girls' and Women's Sports, American Association for Health, Physical Education, and Recreation, 1201 Sixteenth St., N. W., Washington, D. C. 20036:
Basketball (twelve charts)
Softball (eleven charts)
Volleyball (eleven charts)

MATERIALS FOR INDIVIDUAL SPORTS

READING MATERIALS

Division for Girls' and Women's Sports, American Association for Health, Physical Education, and Recreation, 1201 Sixteenth St., N. W., Washington, D. C. 20036:
Archery-Riding Guide
Bowling-Fencing Guide
Tennis-Badminton Guide
Recreational Games and Sports
National Federation of State High School Athletic Associations, 7 S. Dearborn, Chicago, Ill. 60603:
Wrestling Officials' Manual

SLIDE FILMS (SOUND AND SILENT— FOR PURCHASE OR RENTAL)

The Athletic Institute, 805 Merchandise Mart, Chicago, Ill. 60654:
Archery (four units)
Badminton (six units)
Bowling (four units)
Campcraft (four units)
Cycling (eight units)
Fencing (four units)
Golf (six units)
Judo (six units)
Table Tennis (two units)
Tennis (six units)
Wrestling (five units)
Student manual with each sport
Instructor's guide
Lifetime Sports Education Project, American Association for Health, Physical Education, and Recreation, 1201 Sixteenth St., N. W., Washington, D. C. 20036:
Golf Group Instruction
Tennis Group Instruction
Gym-Bowl Instruction Kit
Gym-Bowl Teacher's Manual

SPECIAL AIDS
(TECHNIQUE CHARTS AND POSTERS)

Division for Girls' and Women's Sports, American Association for Health, Physical Education, and

Recreation, 1201 Sixteenth St., N. W., Washington, D. C. 20036:
Badminton (twelve charts)
Tennis (twelve charts)
Lifetime Sports Education Project, AAHPER (above address):
Golf Group Instruction (six posters)
Tennis Group Instruction (six posters)
Ideas for Badminton Instruction
Ideas for Golf Instruction
Ideas for Tennis Instruction
Harvard Table Tennis Co., 265 Third St., Cambridge, Mass. 02142:
Harvard Table Tennis Teacher (booklet)
Harvard Table Tennis Tournament (charts)
Fencing/Judo and Karate Equipment, Castello's, 30 East 10th St., New York, N. Y. 10003:
Catalog

MATERIALS FOR AQUATICS

READING MATERIALS

Division for Girls' and Women's Sports, American Association for Health, Physical Education, and Recreation, 1201 Sixteenth St., N. W., Washington, D. C. 20036:
Aquatics Guide

SLIDE FILMS (SOUND AND SILENT— FOR PURCHASE OR RENTAL)

The Athletic Institute, 805 Merchandise Mart, Chicago, Ill. 60654:
Competitive Swimming (three units)
Diving (three units)
Life-Saving (three units)
Skin and Scuba Diving (six units)
Swimming (four units)

SPECIAL AIDS

Division for Girls' and Women's Sports, American Association for Health, Physical Education, and Recreation, 1201 Sixteenth St., N. W., Washington, D. C. 20036:
Aquatics—Swimming and Diving Charts (eighteen)
Youngjohn Enterprises, Inc., P. O. Box 4522, Cleveland, Ohio 44124
Instructional swimming charts (eleven)
11×14 inch size
$23 \times 17\frac{1}{2}$ inch size
American Red Cross (local chapters)
Charts, skill sheets, instructional materials Free

MATERIALS FOR TRACK AND FIELD

READING MATERIALS

National Federation of State High School Athletic Associations, 7 S. Dearborn St., Chicago, Ill. 60603:
Track and Field Rules
Division for Girls' and Women's Sports, American Association for Health, Physical Education, and Recreation, 1201 Sixteenth St., N. W., Washington, D. C. 20036:
Track and Field Guide

SLIDE FILMS (SOUND AND SILENT—FOR PURCHASE OR RENTAL)

The Athletic Institute, 805 Merchandise Mart, Chicago, Ill. 60654:
Track and Field (nine units)
Track and Field (girls) (two units)
Student Manual
Instructor's guide

SPECIAL AIDS (AWARDS AND EMBLEMS)

American Association for Health, Physical Education, and Recreation, 1201 Sixteenth St., N. W., Washington, D. C. 20036:
Junior High School Emblems
Senior High School Emblems
Embroidered Emblem Patches (places in meet)
First place
Second place
Third place

MATERIALS FOR GYMNASTICS

READING MATERIALS

Division for Girls' and Women's Sports, American Association for Health, Physical Education, and Recreation, 1201 Sixteenth St., N. W., Washington, D. C. 20036:
Gymnastics Guide

SLIDE FILMS (SOUND AND SILENT—FOR PURCHASE OR RENTAL)

The Athletic Institute, 805 Merchandise Mart, Chicago, Ill. 60654:
Gymnastics (for girls and women) (four units)
Trampolining (three units)
Tumbling (three units)
Tumbling (advanced) (three units)
Student manual
Instructor's guide

SPECIAL AIDS (TECHNIQUE CHARTS)

Nissen Corporation, 930 27th Ave., S. W., Cedar Rapids, Iowa 52406:

Boys
Side Horse
Parallel Bars
Still Rings

Horizontal Bar
Long-Horse Vaulting
Free Exercise
Girls
Side-Horse Vaulting
Uneven Parallel Bars
Balance Beam
Free Exercise—Balancing and Beginning Tumbling
Free Exercise—Acrobatics and Intermediate Tumbling

MATERIALS FOR WINTER SPORTS

READING MATERIALS

Division for Girls' and Women's Sports, American Association for Health, Physical Education, and Recreation, 1201 Sixteenth St., N. W., Washington, D. C. 20036:
Outing Activities and Winter Sports
United States Figure Skating Association, 178 Tremont St., Boston, Mass. 02158
Figure Skating Educational Kit, by Mary Maroney

SLIDE FILMS (SOUND AND SILENT—FOR PURCHASE OR RENTAL)

The Athletic Institute, 805 Merchandise Mart, Chicago, Ill. 60654:
Ice Skating (four units)
Skiing (six units)
Student manual
Instructor's guide

MATERIALS FOR RHYTHMS

American Association for Health, Physical Education, and Recreation, 1201 Sixteenth St., N. W., Washington, D. C. 20036:
Selected articles on dance
Dance Production
Educational Activities, Inc., Box 392, Freeport, N. Y. 11520:
Keynotes to Modern Dance (course, records)
Musical Ball Skills (manual, records)
Rhythmrix (manual, records)
Dances Without Partners
Basic Popular Music

PART FIVE
CLASS MANAGEMENT AND CONTROL

19 CLASS MANAGEMENT

Effective class management is essential in every phase of teaching. It is perhaps even more important in physical education because of the nature of the equipment, facilities, and records involved and the larger class sizes that often exist. Because of the partial loss of class time needed for dressing and showering procedures, the remaining minutes must be put to the very best use if an effective teaching program is to result. This can be done only through efficient class management.

Class management, then, is synonymous with creating a teaching situation that is capable of achieving desired educational goals. From the point of view of the teacher, it means providing a climate and a setting that will result in effective teaching and learning, and for the student it means self-management and self-responsibility.

Class management includes attention to all the necessary procedures and routines that are a part of the daily instructional program. Roll call, excuses, and showers all require certain procedures to make the most efficient use of the time available.

Class management should not be confused with teaching method. The preparation of the setting and the organization of the class so that instruction takes place most effectively is the major concern.

The main purposes of good class management are as follows:

1. To make the most effective and efficient use of class time
2. To ensure the safety of the group through class routines and procedures
3. To provide a controlled classroom atmosphere in which instruction may take place
4. To promote self-discipline and self-motivation on the part of each individual in the class
5. To develop within the students a sense of responsibility toward themselves and toward each other
6. To enhance rapport between teacher and student that will promote learning
7. To create a group spirit in which each individual feels good within himself and feels comfortable with his group
8. To recognize and provide for the needs and interests of each individual within the group
9. To make the most effective use of the teacher's time and energy
10. To provide the most effective organization and arrangement of the class in order that instruction may be given and learning will take place

Effective class management is brought about through careful and thoughtful planning on the part of the teacher with the students. This mutual and cooperative planning should be the backbone of class organization so that students willingly maintain the standards they have established. Boys and girls understand and respect the mutual benefits derived and in a sense they manage themselves. When this happens it is class management at its best.

The teacher's role in developing this ideal type of class management is one of guidance and leadership during the planning periods and orientation of students at the beginning of the school year. Advance preparation, class orientation, and class procedures are the main areas with which the teacher must be concerned. These three topics will receive detailed attention in the first part of this chapter.

ADVANCE PREPARATION

Early preparation includes attention to the many details to which the physical education teacher should attend before school opens in the fall. The opening program, the equipment, the lockers, the records, and the schedule all need to be prepared. This readiness is a basic step to good class management, for it prepares the teacher in advance, and he or she is then able to devote full attention to the requirements of the students when they arrive.

Program planning

An outline of the program for the year should be formulated in view of departmental objectives. Plans for the opening unit and the first week of school should be drawn up in detail so that the teacher knows exactly what needs to be accomplished in the first meeting of all classes. In schools in which team teaching exists, the entire team should be involved in the planning. Of course, the program should remain flexible so as to provide for student involvement in the final plans.

Equipment and facilities

All equipment and facilities should be checked with the inventory that was made the year before. The teacher should make sure that all necessary repairs have been completed and that everything is ready and safe for use. This includes playing fields, gymnasiums, swimming pools, and other facilities. The special equipment needed for the first teaching unit, whether it concerns hockey, soccer, or football, should be taken from storage and placed in an appropriate place where it is easily accessible. The teacher will thus be prepared to make use of it as soon as the class is organized.

Locker room

Necessary preparations should be made in the locker room. A check to ensure that the lockers are clean and in working order will save much confusion. It is very frustrating to assign a locker to a student only to find that it does not work.

If there are bulletin boards in the locker rooms, they should be attractively prepared with appropriate pictures and materials. When the students come into the locker room and see these careful preparations, it will help to establish an atmosphere that is conducive to effective learning in physical education.

Class lists and records

The physical education teacher will find class lists very helpful. Preparing record files and grade books ahead of time saves confusion later on. It is usually quite difficult to find time to take care of these clerical duties once school has begun. There are always other urgent matters that require immediate attention, which means that sometimes paper work remains undone. The mental attitude of the teacher is greatly improved, too, when these details have been cared for beforehand, because he isn't burdened with thoughts of additional work that needs to be accomplished.

Schedules

Another detail that should be given attention before school opens is the teaching schedule. Any changes or errors that occur regarding teaching stations and assigned instructors should be provided for in advance of the initial class meeting. The scheduling of facilities should be cooperatively worked out by the men's and women's departments so that the instructional classes as well as the after-school program can be organized without delay. This includes games scheduled with other schools.

CLASS ORIENTATION

Proper orientation of each physical education class is important because it affects the outcome of the classwork throughout the year. It is during the first week of school that the students are introduced to physical education and are made aware of their personal responsibilities. This period of orientation also includes student registration, locker assignments, and group planning sessions and discussions.

Registration of students

Usually at the first class session some form of class registration is necessary. The information required and the form of registration vary, depending on the uses for which the registration is held. Customarily it is thought valuable to have on file the following items about each student:

Name
Address
Home telephone number
Age and birthday
Locker number and combination
Health status
Record of fee payments
Family physician
Activities (electives, intramural activities, honor teams)
Test scores and achievement records from previous grades
Awards, varsity letters

Only a part of this information is recorded during the registration period. Other factors regarding such matters as electives and awards would be reported later on. By maintaining a personal record of each student from year to year, an overall picture of his accomplishments is readily available.

The form on which information is recorded should be a printed card where appropriate details may be filled in. The cards may be used to call the roll until squad cards are made out (if this is the procedure), and then they may be filed in the physical education office.

Locker assignment

Another item of business that can be taken care of during the orientation period, when students do not yet have uniforms and sneakers available for participation, is the assignment of lockers. This routine procedure becomes difficult when combinations to built-in locks must be explained, but even in such instances no more than one class period should be necessary to accomplish this task.

Locker rooms are generally organized according to a regular pattern, with rows of lockers and benches arranged alternately. The room itself should be well lighted and ventilated and kept as clean as possible. There are different types of lockers used in school locker rooms: baskets, full-length lockers, half-size lockers, and combinations of baskets or small lockers. In each of these cases locks may be bulit in, with the teacher having a master list of combinations and a master key, or individual locks may be provided by the students. If students provide the locks, the teacher must keep an accurate record of students' locker combinations, for occasions arise when it is essential that the teacher have access to all lockers.

A major point to be kept in mind when assigning lockers is the spacing of class members. Aisles and sections must not be overcrowded, in order to guard against accidents and to facilitate dressing as rapidly as possible.

Lockers may be selected by the individuals in the class or specifically assigned by the teacher, but whichever method is used, it probably should be consistently followed by the teacher with all class groups. The choice of method depends on class size, locker room conditions, and departmental procedures that may have been established.

Group planning

The teacher may wish to devote part of one of the orientation periods to a discussion of the physical education program so that the students will understand the objectives and purposes of the program and have an opportunity to ask questions. The teacher should prepare in advance a general outline of points to be used in the discussion in order to ensure that all phases of the program are covered.

The extent of the discussion depends largely upon the course of action the teacher intends to follow. During the orientation a discussion of the year's program by the students may bring out suggested elective units or special requests in regard to the intramural and interscholastic programs. On the other hand, the teacher may use the time to introduce the program the particular class will be following, as determined by departmental requirements. The nature of the discussion will therefore depend on the degree of flexibility in program arrangement, as determined by the philosophy of the department in respect to student planning.

During the discussion period, time should be taken to determine, through class suggestion and selection, the rules and regulations that will be a necessary part of class organization. The students themselves should establish a code of conduct for the locker room, the showers, roll call, and other class situations in order to give them an opportunity to realize the need for such codes and hopefully to accept their own regulations more willingly.

The teacher must carefully moderate the discussion so that all individuals have an opportunity to express opinions and to ensure a constructive approach to the problems under consideration.

The orientation period may also be an appropriate time for the election or appointment of class leaders or captains. Valuable pointers on the qualifications of leaders may be brought out at this time.

CLASS PROCEDURE

Proper management of a class is brought about by giving considerable attention to many small details covering teacher and student behavior. The suggestions that follow govern various phases of a single class period except the actual instruction of the class. It is this class organization that is the key to promoting a valuable instructional period. Important factors in class procedure include locker room regulations, roll call, shower procedures, costume regulations, excuses, and preclass preparations.

Before class

When students come to a class in physical education the teacher should be completely prepared for them. Personally, the teacher should be properly dressed for class and stationed where students may easily locate him or her for advice or questioning. Plans for the class organization should be fixed in the teacher's mind, and all equipment should be in readiness.

The students should come to class in an orderly fashion, just as they proceed to all school classes. This businesslike atmosphere should continue throughout the dressing time.

Locker room regulations

Locker room regulations, determined and enforced by the class, should include the following:

Benches. Benches between lockers should remain clear of books and clothing to prevent these items from being crushed, pushed around, or lost. Benches are to be used to sit on while changing clothes.

Books. A special place should be set aside where students may place their books. Usually they may be placed on top of the lockers, provided the lockers are not too high. Such a location helps to prevent damage or loss to this important property.

Clothing. All clothing should be hung up neatly in long lockers, and shoes should be placed on the floor of the locker. This protects the clothing and prevents it from becoming dirty or damaged. Even where half-size lockers are used this regulation should be enforced as far as possible. Lockers should be closed and locked during class to ensure the protection of all belongings.

Valuables. Valuable jewelry and wallets should, of course, be locked inside a locker during the physical education class. Some teachers require all jewelry to be put away in this manner, thus preventing damage to or loss of the jewelry.

Lights. Locker room lights should be turned out when all students proceed to the gymnasium. A member of the class may be given this particular responsibility, or the job may be shared by many students during the course of the school year.

Routine. The routine followed by students within the locker room should be a matter of changing clothes in the quickest and easiest manner. Students should attend to the business at hand without any undue nonsense or fooling around. Loud and raucous behavior should not be permitted.

Time. The time allotted for changing clothes before class should be established by the students in the orientation week discussions. Customarily, five minutes is sufficient time for all students to change and proceed to their places.

Costume

The costume or gymnasium uniform may vary in style, shape, and color. The requirements governing its use, preferably established by the groups concerned, may also vary, from rigid to loose restrictions. The following considerations are pertinent.

Types of uniforms. Girls' uniforms range from one-piece gym suits with a skirt or short type of bottom to a two-piece outfit of blouse and shorts. Boys' uniforms are generally shorts and a T-shirt, perhaps marked by the school insignia.

Requirements. Besides determination of the basic outfit, there should be requirements concerning sneakers, socks, and sweatshirts for participants. Students are usually required to dress in these items for every class. Furthermore, all clothing should be clearly labeled with the owner's name, with either indelible ink, chain stitching, or name tags.

Improper preparation. Regulations may need to be established regarding students who do not fulfill all requirements concerning the prescribed uniform. Students should

realize their responsibilities in this matter.

Laundering. It is usually important to set definite time periods at which clean uniforms are required. For girls in classes meeting twice a week, a clean uniform is probably necessary every two or three weeks. For boys, the time period may have to be shorter. Effective means of checking on clean uniforms, probably during roll call, should be established to ensure enforcement of this requirement. Of course, if students can be impressed with the need for clean wearing apparel and thereby dress in this manner voluntarily, it is much better.

Roll call

A teacher is responsible for the group in his or her charge and should therefore keep an accurate record of attendance for each class session. Symbols are usually needed to denote excuses, absences, tardiness, and similar situations. Roll call can become a very complicated and time-consuming process and therefore needs careful consideration.

Methods. Teachers of physical education have devised various means of calling roll for the purpose of saving time and promoting efficiency. Some of the better methods are worthy of attention.

1. Number check. The students are assigned a certain number painted on the floor and must be standing on it when roll is taken. The numbers are painted, in order, along the sidelines of the gymnasium floor, and the teacher merely notes vacant numbers.

2. Number call. The students are given a certain number that they must call out at the appropriate time. Numbers not mentioned are then noted by the teacher as absent.

3. Roll call. The teacher calls out the names of all students and listens for their responses.

4. Squad call. Names of the students are checked according to organized squads, with leaders assisting the teacher by checking attendance.

Each of these methods has its own merits. However, the first suggestions are rather impersonal, and a more friendly atmosphere can be promoted through the use of the last method. Furthermore, the use of student leadership—while requiring more time on the part of the teacher for instruction and training—has the advantage of fostering leadership qualities.

Systems. There is no established rule about when class roll should be taken or what symbols should be used. It is customary for attendance to be taken at the beginning of a class period so that a report of students absent from class but not listed on the daily absence list may be sent to the office. This is an important function of every teacher. Offenders should be discovered as soon as they are found absent from any part of the school day. Besides fulfilling his responsibility for taking roll at the beginning of the class, the teacher will find proceeding from roll call formations to the next activity a convenient way of organizing the group for instruction. Taking roll in the middle of the period may interrupt drill practice, and sometimes there is not enough time at the end of the period, no matter how well the lesson is planned.

In regard to the use of symbols, most teachers develop their own systems. The main criteria that should be kept in mind are speed, clarity, uniformity, and exactness. If leaders are used, they must be able to understand the procedure and in the case of a teacher's absence the substitute should be able to interpret the system. Symbols most often required cover the following items:

Absence	Uniform cut
Tardiness	Suit
Excuse	Sneakers
Office	Not clean
Illness	
Observing	

Safety. Roll call is a very convenient time for checking on safety regulations. This important factor needs special emphasis in physical education, and it is at this point in the daily lesson that equipment rules and safety regulations can be reviewed. Each class member should know and accept his personal responsibilities for the safety of others.

Excuses from class

The problems concerning temporary and permanent excuses from class are always prevalent in physical education. Methods of handling these problems depend upon the size of the department, the department's philosophy, the facilities available, and the teacher.

Basic philosophy. A physical education program should include some kind of modified or adapted activities program for individuals who are injured, disabled, or recently recovered from illness. Limited activities under these circumstances should be prescribed by a physician and administered by the teacher. Because most physical education teachers understand the need for an adapted program, it is possible for them to carry out such instructions. When this type of program is in operation, there is no need for temporary or permanent excuses.

Methods of handling excuses. Temporary or permanent excuses from physical education class may be accepted by the teacher but should have the authorization of nurse or physician. This procedure channels health problems through health services, who are aware of health deficiencies. Some teachers send excused students directly to a study hall if they have no alternate program established within their classes and no adapted program is available. However, this is a questionable practice. Theoretically, students should participate in as much of the regular class activity as possible or in a program specially adapted to their needs. Whenever a particular activity is more than the student should undertake, he should have a specific assignment related to physical education. Students should be engaged in a purposeful activity. If it is possible to assign a remedial type of exercise, with permission of the physician, this should be done. Whatever course of action is taken, the teacher needs time and patience to motivate excused students to spend class time wisely and to help them achieve educational objectives.

Showers

The amount of time alloted for dressing at the close of the physical education class depends upon the shower requirement. Because of the health-teaching opportunity provided by a showering program, students should be encouraged to meet this regulation. Certain rules must be established in this regard, however, and procedures for enforcement set up. A well-run showering program requires certain restrictions for efficiency, safety, and consistency in their application. Towels, too, may become a problem unless properly handled.

In respect to the time necessary for efficient showering, twelve to fifteen minutes is the usual amount of time allocated. However, this can only be relative to the number of students in the class and the number of shower stalls available. Girls generally require a longer period of time to shower than boys, so this should also be considered.

Because of the danger of slipping on a wet locker room floor, students should dry completely in the drying area, which is usually constructed adjacent to the showers. If none exists, the teacher should designate a particular portion of the locker room, near the shower exit, "for drying only." In connection with safety, it is also essential that soap, deodorants, and other personal items be kept in unbreakable plastic containers.

The problem of towels can best be solved when the school provides them. Each student is then given a clean, dry towel that is returned at the end of the period. When students bring their own towels from home, they frequently allow them to mildew in the lockers, for lack of proper drying and cleaning. Squad captains should assist the teacher in the collecting and counting of towels, especially when towels are rented and the teacher is responsible for the exact

number of towels supplied by the rental company. If showers are required of all students, the teacher may find it of value to send students into the showers by squads. In schools where no individual shower stalls and dressing areas are provided, girls who are menstruating should be permitted to sponge off carefully at the sinks while partially dressed. In addition, a doctor's excuse from showering should be honored. All other students well enough to be in school and to participate in physical activity should be encouraged to take a shower.

Grading

Grading in physical education, as in any academic subject, is a very difficult matter. It should be kept in mind that the purpose of grading is to report an individual's progress both to that individual and to his parents. Each party should understand exactly what the grade represents if it is to have any real meaning and subsequent effect. It must be pointed out that a grade in physical education represents many different factors—not skill alone. For an extensive discussion of this topic, see Chapter 20.

Cumulative records*

Record keeping in physical education, as in every field of endeavor, is a time-consuming process. However, time devoted to this aspect of the program is well spent if the material collected is pertinent, useful, and up to date. Some of the main considerations regarding the records that should be kept are discussed in the following paragraphs.

The registration card referred to in connection with class orientation is the basic item to be included in the individual record file. Each year a new registration card is added to the file with up-to-date information. Other data that should be on file—either on the same card if there is room, or separately—should include such information as items concerning medical ex-

---

*See materials in Part Seven.

cuses, grades, skill accomplishment, attendance, grades, skill accomplishment, attendance, awards, and honors.

Records, efficiently kept from year to year, provide an accurate picture of an individual's growth and development and a meaningful basis for determining his particular needs.

Problems and interruptions

Flexibility in the management of classes should be a byword for all teachers but particularly for physical educators. Many unforeseen occurrences create interruptions in the established school routine, and the teacher who can remain flexible and adapt suddenly yet wisely is a real master. There are several types of interruptions that merit attention: assemblies, class outings, fire drills, and injuries. (Weather may sometimes cause an interruption if the teacher has not considered this factor when planning.)

Assemblies. In schools where a combination auditorium-gymnasium is used, assemblies become a major source of interruptions. Book week, the science fair, and special examinations are all held in the auditorium, in addition to the regular assembly programs. Even when assemblies do not interfere with the scheduled physical education classes, the chairs may have to be put up or taken down. In this event the physical education teacher must have alternate plans to follow: written work, textbook assignments, the use of audiovisual materials, or discussion. Fortunately, in good weather classes can be held outdoors.

Class outings or trips. When class groups are taken on special field trips or outings, the physical education teacher is often left with half a group. In this instance the regular classwork should be adapted to the smaller group.

Fire drills and shelter drills. Safety drills are essential in all schools, and regular, prescribed procedures should be followed when such drills occur during physical education class. Instructions are usually issued by the administration as to where the groups should exit. The teacher is responsible for his or her particular group and must see that orders are carried out. These drills can be a source of confusion, particularly when students are showering. The teacher should try to point out this difficulty to the principal so that the situation may be avoided.

Injuries. Injuries occur even where safety precautions exist. The teacher must be calm in following regular accident procedures. All instructions—to send for the nurse, carry out activity, or dismiss the class—should be given with unruffled authority, to prevent students from becoming unduly alarmed or excited and perhaps

Fig. 19-1. Girls physical education fencing class. (Oconomowoc Senior High School, Oconomowoc, Wis.)

from creating further danger because of thoughtless actions.

CHARACTERISTICS OF GOOD CLASS MANAGEMENT

Careful observation of a single physical education class should reveal to a large extent the degree of management the teacher has promoted. Thoughtful analysis of the conduct of the students and their application to the day's work should point out certain characteristics of good class management. The following questions provide a guideline for such an analysis:

1. How much time is used in locker room procedures before class? After class?
2. How much time is required to check attendance?
3. How much time is required for students to become organized into working groups?
4. Are the students properly prepared for participation?
5. Are the students motivated to improve and engaged in purposeful activity?
6. Do the students display eagerness? Enthusiasm? Cheerfulness? Attentiveness? Respect?
7. Are *all* students thoughtfully engaged in some form of activity related to the unit or classwork for that day?
8. Do the students display an understanding of the purpose(s) of the day's lesson?
9. Are the students aware of their responsibilities for the safety and welfare of the group?
10. How much time is consumed by the teacher in *repetition* of directions?
11. Is the teacher's attention constantly directed toward individual questioners and disturbing groups? Or is his or her attention directed toward the supervision of all groups and assistance to some?
12. Do the students reveal satisfaction from active participation in the class?

CONTROL

It was pointed out in the first part of this chapter that good class management sets the stage for instruction. The situation might then be described as teacher-controlled. In contrast, when routines and procedures are not understood and students do not know what is expected of them, confusion and chaos often are created. Discipline problems result from lack of control, a control imposed from without (the teacher) or within (the student). In either circumstance, instruction cannot effectively be carried on until proper controls are reinstated.

Incidence of discipline problems

Problems of misbehavior and violence have been increasing both inside and outside of schools. Juveniles have been found to be involved in more than one third of the crimes solved by the police in one year.[*] In studying misbehavior within schools, eight out of ten teachers who were surveyed reported confiscating weapons, and fourteen of those surveyed indicated violence had occurred in their schools. Furthermore, teachers indicated that misbehavior erupted in music, physical education, and activity courses more often than in other subject areas, generally because of overcrowded conditions. The median class size in junior high school physical education was 36.6, and in senior high school it was 38.8, higher than in any other subject.[†]

Discipline

It has been said that if education is changing behavior, discipline is controlling it for the purpose of education.

Methods of controlling behavior are many and varied, but the effectiveness of a single method may be determined only in terms of the resultant change. Was it a desirable change? Was the resulting change the one originally intended? For example, if, in handling a misbehavior problem, the

[*]National Education Association: Student behavior in secondary schools, Washington, D. C., 1964, The Association.

[†]National Education Association: Class size in secondary schools, NEA Research Bulletin **43**:1, 1965.

teacher wins the student's compliance but produces within him hatred for the activity, has the original goal been met?

Handling discipline problems

Self-discipline is a developmental goal for each individual, as are self-respect, self-control, and independence of thought, action, and deed. Ideally, the adolescent moves along a continuum toward selfhood, where fewer and fewer limitations need to be imposed from the external environment. Conversely, the less mature student requires discipline and controls from others to help him along the way.

The teacher must recognize the developmental nature of this goal and strive to handle discipline problems with consideration for the makeup of the individual and the scope of his actions. Most teachers prefer to handle misbehavior problems themselves, particularly when infractions are fairly mild. In cases where the degree of misbehavior is more severe, the teacher should follow school procedures already established for such circumstances. Reporting occurrences to the administration is the general course of action taken in most schools. Assignment to detention hall, removal from class, or dismissal from school may be necessary. Ultimately, however, dismissal merely removes the problem from the situation, rather than helping the student find ways to improve his behavior.

Corporal punishment

One of the most controversial issues in education today surrounds the question of using corporal punishment to solve discipline problems. Such action is allowed by some administrators but forbidden by others. Teachers should be aware of established policies in this regard and should not violate them under any circumstances. Should a teacher not be in agreement with a particular policy, it would be better for him to effect a change in the policy itself rather than to openly defy it. It is interesting to note that, in a survey of teacher opinion, over 58% of several hundreds polled responded in favor of corporal punishment, while 34% were opposed.*

Other techniques

Other, less severe techniques of handling discipline problems include written assignments, reading assignments, oral reports to the class, additional exercising, work tasks, makeup classes, and a failing grade. Weighing such factors as the age of the student, the seriousness of the infraction, and the number of infractions by an individual helps to determine the choice of technique. A teacher needs to be consistent in meting out penalties, but consideration of the individual case should be the strongest determinant. For example, if two boys are caught creating a disturbance of some kind and one of the boys is a constant troublemaker while the other is generally helpful, the resulting penalties might be different for each student.

The teacher also needs to keep in mind encroachments on his own time schedule each time penalties are determined. Having to read long dissertations (that may have been copied from a book) benefits neither the student nor the teacher, and having to stand around while students run additional laps wastes the instructor's time as well as breeds contempt for running in the minds of the offenders.

From this discussion it may be seen that no cardinal principles exist to guide a teacher in handling discipline problems. The burden remains with the individual teacher to be fair and effective while treating the student with consideration and respect. Humiliation, degradation, threats, and fear accomplish little toward motivating a student along desirable lines.

Prevention of problems

Just as the best defense is often described as a strong offense, so effective discipline might begin with prevention of problems. Students should not be given a chance to misbehave.

---

*National Education Association: What teachers think, Washington, D. C., 1965, The Association.

Ideally, students should not want to misbehave. The realistic teacher tries to prevent their even thinking about foolish behavior by making sure that (1) they are having too much fun, (2) they are too busy, (3) they are too much interested in what is going on, (4) they are working too hard to improve, and (5) they want to have a good educational record.

Under these circumstances control is enforced under the careful guidance of the instructor *through the students themselves.* Group discipline and self-discipline are in action here, rather than teacher-imposed regulations. Several keys to the development of this type of control may be deciphered here. Awarding of grades might be included as one of them, but for students who do not care about grades, and there are always a few, this factor would not be effective. (See motivation discussion in Chapter 13.) Effective planning and organization, as previously discussed, are certainly contributing elements to controlling the class session. However, the vital factor underlying the successful teaching picture can be found with the group itself. It is the power of the group that prevails. A creative teacher utilizes the dynamics of group interaction and the group process to reap benefits for each class member.

GROUPING

Current thinking in education reflects a widespread interest in the problem of grouping. There are many who feel that *age* continues to be the best determinant for class grouping. In another report from a junior high school principal, claims were made for the successful application of *height* as a measure of development, and therefore maturity, for grouping of students. For the most part, however, the trend seems to be toward ability grouping. It was the belief of Dr. James Conant, well-known educational authority, that groups should be homogeneous in all subject-matter areas except twelfth-grade American Government courses. In physical education, ability grouping has frequently been utilized in swimming courses, but grouping by skill level within other classes seems to be finding increased favor.

Methods of grouping. Several methods of grouping need study in terms of their advantages and disadvantages for physical education classes. It should be pointed out that methods of grouping can and should vary, depending on the teacher's purposes, the activity, the age group and size of the class, and the working units required for the course. The basic philosophy of the program also enters into consideration. The teacher needs to remember that successful teams or squads promote real enthusiasm and motivation in activities, and for this reason, appropriate grouping becomes a key factor in instruction. In a school in which teaching teams are used, groups may be selected according to activity, choice, need, or ability, depending on the unit of study. For example, in a very large high school in which 400 students are assigned to ten physical education teachers, groups would probably be divided on an entirely different basis from that which would be used in a small school in which only twenty-five students meet for class during a single period. At the junior high level it may be important to change groupings frequently to motivate and stimulate the students' changing interests. Many factors need consideration, and no single method of grouping answers the problems found in various teaching situations for physical education programming.

It is the responsibility of the physical education teacher to choose the method of grouping that is most appropriate to his or her teaching situation. Consideration must first be given to the desirability of possible *types* of groups as well as to the several *factors* that also determine the final selection of a method of grouping.

Types of groups. Methods of grouping may be classified according to the type of *control* that determines the selection of the group. Control may be in the hands of the teacher or the student, or it may be left to chance. Each type of grouping has its own particular advantages and problems, and each should be considered carefully by the teacher when he is grouping a class for instruction.

Teacher-controlled methods of grouping. In the teacher-controlled type of grouping the teacher determines the groups. Teams or squads are selected according to scores on fitness tests, according to a particular skill or ability such as basket-shooting or speed, or on the basis of some other single underlying factor, such as height or weight. The teacher then distributes students on different squads into either homogeneous or heterogeneous groups.

Homogeneous groups

Samples
1. Low, average, and highly skilled gymnasts
2. Slow, average, and fast runners
3. Tall, medium, and short students

Advantages
1. The teacher knows individual needs in the area under study.
2. The teacher can select teaching methods appropriate to the levels and abilities of a particular group.
3. Individual students feel at home in their group when the abilities of all are similar.
4. Opportunities for leadership are provided students in the low and medium groups that otherwise may not be available.
5. The teacher may control cliques of students through their distribution on teams.
6. Students formulate realistic assessments of their own abilities and may be motivated to improve.

Problems
1. It is an unrealistic classroom setup: groups are not generally composed of people of like ability.
2. There may be a lack of motivation and incentive among some students in the lower groups.
3. There may not be adequate leadership in low ability groups.
4. Teachers may have a difficult time finding opportunities to retest and change groups of students showing improvement.
5. Record keeping and evaluation of students may become complicated if groups change frequently within a unit.

Heterogeneous groups

Samples
1. Highly skilled students evenly distributed
2. Tallest players evenly distributed
3. Leaders evenly distributed

Advantages
1. The teacher controls the distribution of students of high, average, and low skills to make even teams.

2. The teacher may control cliquishness in the same manner.
3. Leadership in all groups may be assured.
4. Students of high ability are motivated to assist others on their own team, and those of low ability are motivated to improve.
5. Opportunities are provided for students to learn how to work together effectively with others.

Problems
1. Students dissatisfied with the group may be resentful and blame the teacher.
2. It is a very time-consuming method of grouping for the teacher because it requires much thought and preparation; well-balanced teams may not be the result.
3. A team or squad that does not perform well together immediately loses its spirit instead of trying harder to work together.
4. It is difficult to teach groups composed of different levels of skills.

Note: Schools presently engaged in the team-teaching approach have found teacher-controlled methods of grouping most helpful in dividing large classes into smaller study groups.

Student-controlled methods of grouping. In the student-controlled method of grouping, students select the teams. Captains previously elected by the class or appointed in some other manner select the members of their own teams. This may be done in front of the group or separately at a different time or place. Another method of grouping in this manner is to have captains select only part of their teams and allow the remaining students an opportunity to divide themselves evenly on teams of their choice.

Advantages
1. Captains are generally well-respected individuals and good leaders, for they have been elected by the group or otherwise selected for their abilities.
2. Initial selections by the captains generally provide an even distribution of highly skilled players to effect balanced teams.
3. Team spirit is promoted because players are generally pleased about being chosen or having an opportunity to select their own team.

Problems
1. Students waiting to be chosen by captains often feel left out and uncomfortable while hoping to be selected.
2. This is a time-consuming method if the entire class waits for teams to be selected.
3. The teams that result from this method are not necessarily balanced.
4. Cliques are not necessarily broken up by this method.
5. Some animosity may develop between students and captains.

Note: This method may be used most effectively to select teams for tournament games in ending a special unit of study, such as basketball or volleyball, especially if captains select entire teams without the class in attendance.

Methods controlled by chance. In this type of grouping, chance is the determining factor. Teams or squads are formed on the basis of homeroom groups or from numbers drawn from a hat. The system of lining students up and having them number off by "threes" or "fours" is frequently used. The line itself then offers a new factor of control, in that students may be lined up by alphabet, by height, or just haphazardly. The resulting teams are all heterogeneous in nature.

Advantages
1. Groups are realistic and competitive.
2. Skilled players assist others in their group.
3. Intraclass games and tournaments are usually interesting.
4. Students learn to play and get along well with all other students in their class.
5. Groups may be created and changed quickly and easily.
6. Many leadership opportunities are allowed if terms are changed often and if individuals are not allowed to serve as leaders a second time.
7. The teacher maintains standards of fairness and equality, because chance is the controlling factor.
Problems
1. It is difficult to meet the needs and interests of the individuals in these groups.
2. Teaching methods may not be appropriate for all students.
3. Teams may come out unbalanced, thereby hampering class tournaments and games.
Note: A teacher must vary methods used for selecting groups, for students are quick to catch on to repetitive methods. For example, if a teacher always divides groups by having students number off by fours, the students will soon begin to station themselves at intervals of fours as they line up.

These various methods of grouping have their advantages and problems. Before selecting the type of grouping most suitable to his or her teaching situation, the teacher needs to give careful consideration as to what is best for the students.

Other factors involved in grouping

• *How many squads or teams should be established?* The teacher should keep in mind the ultimate goal of providing the most practicing opportunities possible by creating the most groups according to equipment. The activity itself, the number of students, the number of teachers, and the facilities and teaching stations available are all determinants in answering this initial question. The samples given in Table 19-1 indicate the different numbers of teams that may result because of the difference in the situation, not the activity.

• *With which type of working groups may the objectives for physical development best be met in this unit?* Some units of study may require special groupings for drills, for example, forwards and guards in basketball, defensive and offensive players in football, and heavyweight and lightweight students in wrestling. Therefore, the teacher must determine whether heterogeneous or homogeneous groupings would be more suitable for the activity.

• *With which type of working groups may the objectives for social development in this unit best be met?* Teams providing opportunities for leadership and for establishing harmonious relationships may result from selections made by either teachers or students. Perhaps there are special cliques that need to be separated for a more smoothly functioning class, and the teacher may therefore prefer to control the groupings for a particular unit.

• *With which type of working groups may the objectives for intellectual development best be met?* Homogeneous groups may understand certain types of instruction more quickly when it is geared to each group's particular level. For example, rules

Table 19-1. Factors involved in grouping

Activity	Number of students	Number of teachers	Teaching stations and equipment	Squads/ members
Volleyball	48	1	2 courts 8 balls	4/12
	120	2	2 courts 8 balls	8/15
Basketball	60	1	6 goals 10 balls	6/10
	120	2	6 goals 10 balls	10/12

and historical development of games may be learned more quickly by groups of lower abilities when audiovisual aids (charts, magnetic boards, and the like) are utilized in teaching. However, lectures would probably be suitable in giving this information to other groups.

• *With which type of grouping may the objectives for emotional development in this unit best be met?* With a class of highly stimulated junior high school girls, for example, who are just being introduced to the game of speedball, squads may best be selected by the teacher in order to maintain calm and control. Then, at the end of the unit, the students may select teams for a tournament to climax the unit.

The teacher must weigh the answers to these questions before deciding which method to follow in grouping the class. The problem of heterogeneous versus homogeneous grouping in education has been and still is being argued from many different viewpoints. However, each teacher must determine the most suitable method in the existing circumstances.

SUMMARY

Good class management in physical education is the result of many factors. Planning, orientation, procedures, and grouping are all vitally important elements both for the prevention of discipline problems and for the promotion of instruction. Other contributing factors include the selection of class leaders and interaction between groups, which have intangible results yet promote the overall aim of education.

POINTS TO REMEMBER

1. There are certain preparations that should be made before school begins in the fall.
2. Methods of orienting a class to physical education work during the first week of school should be planned.
3. Students should participate in the formulation of codes of conduct in the locker room and gymnasium.
4. Methods and regulations should be established to minimize danger in the locker room when administering a shower program.
5. Methods and procedures for taking attendance should be efficient, clear, and concise.

6. Types of records kept in physical education should be purposeful, up to date, and complete.

PROBLEMS TO THINK THROUGH

1. What health items would it be important to include in an individual's record card?
2. To what extent should students participate in forming rules and regulations for class routine, and to what extent should the teacher's word be law?
3. Considering that the teacher is legally responsible for the students in his charge, should a leader or class assistant be responsible for taking attendance?
4. What reasons are in favor of having captains select teams openly, so that all members of the class know the order in which they are chosen? Against?
5. What should a physical education teacher do in a situation in which the school nurse sympathetically hands out excuses from physical education class too frequently?

CASE STUDY FOR ANALYSIS

In a large high school there are four men and three women physical education instructors teaching all pupils in grades nine through twelve. In the present situation no adapted physical education is taught except for the small amounts the individual teachers are able to give excused pupils in the regular class periods. How should a new teacher coming into this setup be prepared to handle excused students in his own class? How should he work to improve the situation? What materials and information would he need?

EXERCISES FOR REVIEW

1. Design an all-purpose registration card to be used for the orientation period and for permanent records.
2. Construct a list of regulations necessary for a locker room and shower setup and indicate what responsibilities could be given class leaders.
3. How many costume "cuts" should be allowed a student during each grading period before lowering his grade?
4. What key questions may be asked a group of students in leading a discussion to determine class standards?
5. What, assignments may be given to students excused from a basketball class, to be completed while observing class?
6. What are the advantages and the disadvantages of grouping a class of students into squads on the basis of skills?

SELECTED READINGS

Adams, Philip C., Jr.: Ability grouping in junior high school, Journal of Health, Physical Education, and Recreation 35:83, 1964.

American Association of School Administrators, Association for Supervision and Curricular Development, National Association of Secondary-

School Principals, and Department of Rural Education: A climate for individuality, NEA Journal 55:34, 1966.

Bettelheim, Bruno: Grouping the gifted, NEA Journal 54:8, 1965.

Bucher, Charles A.: Administration of health and physical education programs, including athletics, ed. 5, St. Louis, 1971, The C. V. Mosby Co.

Bucher, Charles A.: Foundations of physical education, ed. 6, St. Louis, 1972, The C. V. Mosby Company.

Bucher, Charles A.: Physical education for life, New York, 1969, McGraw-Hill Book Co., Inc.

Coffey, Margaret: Some unorthodox thoughts about showers, Journal of Health, Physical Education, and Recreation 37:29, 1966.

Committee on Exercise and Physical Fitness of the American Medical Association: Classification of students for physical education, Journal of Health, Physical Education, and Recreation 38:16, 1967.

Conant, James B.: The comprehensive high school, New York, 1967, McGraw-Hill Book Co., Inc.

Cratty, Bryant J., and Sage, Jack N.: Effect of primary and secondary group interaction upon improvement in a complex movement task, Research Quarterly 35:265, 1964.

Gnagey, William J.: Controlling classroom behavior, Washington, D. C., 1965, Department of Classroom Teachers, American Education Research Association, National Education Association.

Hall, J. Revis, Killebrew, Katherine, and Lewis, Nellie Mae: Personalizing instruction, NEA Journal 55:36, 1966.

Howard, Alvin W.: Discipline: three F's for the teacher, Education Digest 31:25, 1965.

Joyndt, Louis: Time savers, Physical Educator 21:159, 1964.

Muster, Karl W.: These techniques work for me, NEA Journal 56:16, 1967.

National Education Association, Research Division: Student behavior in secondary schools, 1964, Washington, D. C., 1965, The Association.

National Education Association, Research Division: What teachers think, Washington, D. C., 1965, The Association.

Nelson, Wayne E.: Take time to teach student leaders, Journal of Health, Physical Education, and Recreation 37:22, 1966.

Wolfson, Bernice J.: Individualizing instruction, NEA Journal 55:31, 1966.

PART SIX
EVALUATION

20 INNOVATIVE PUPIL EVALUATION AND GRADING

John is in the twelfth grade at Ft. Pierce, Florida, and is scheduled to take golf as part of his physical education requirement. In advance of taking the course he has signed a contract with his teacher that spells out in detail the work in golf that he must complete in order to earn a grade of his choice. For example, John knows he can earn ten points as part of the contract if he learns to swing a club properly, demonstrates proper technique to the instructor, and writes a short report that analyzes the sequence of movements to be followed in using the club effectively. Another part of the golf contract that is valued at twenty points requires John to read a book on golf and then write a summary and critique of the publication. There are other contract options that permit John to earn additional points. In order to get a grade of A in golf John must earn a minimum of 125 points. If he wants a B, he needs 100 points; a C, 90 points; and a D, 80 points. No completed contract receives a failing grade. If the quality is not acceptable, the contract time is extended.

Contract learning is an innovation that some school teachers are utilizing in various subjects in order to individualize learning and provide for students who have different interests and motivations. These teachers have described the "contract-for-grade" system as a way in which they can interact with students and where both have the opportunity to indicate their expectations for the course.

What the student accomplishes in the contract system depends entirely upon his own effort and how he applies himself. In physical education at Ft. Pierce, Florida, the sport's contracts are designed to be utilized by students on an individual basis and working at their own pace. The goal is not necessarily to create superskilled players but, instead, to have each boy and girl learn the basic fundamentals, rules, and etiquette of the sport and be able to participate in the activity with some degree of understanding and enjoyment.

In order to fulfill contract requirements, students frequently use as resources the school library, programmed texts, and other supplemental materials, teacher-student discussions, visual aids, the community, and consultants who are familiar with the subject. The teacher is on call to advise students during and after school hours. The sources of information for the students are as great as their imagination and ingenuity. Attendance is not always required. In some schools the students check in to class daily but thereafter are free to go where their resources are located.

Student reaction to contract learning has been favorable. For example, at Madison Consolidated High School in Indiana, students were asked to express their opinions. About 80% said they enjoyed contract better than traditional learning and wanted to use it again. Three out of every four students felt they learned more under the contract system than under methods

361

that had been in use in past years. Nearly nine out of every ten students liked the independent method of work, the opportunity to earn the grade they wanted, and the statement of exactly what must be done to be awarded a specific grade. Some representative student comments include: "You get the grade you want." "It gives the student a chance." "The system helped me more than the teacher." "I knew exactly what was required in order to get a certain grade." "It permitted me an opportunity to work at my own pace." "It places the responsibility upon the student and this is as it should be."

Contract learning is an innovation that school systems will want to consider as a possible method to personalize and motivate student learning.

Student contracting for grades in physical education is an innovative procedure where teachers of physical education are trying to make pupil evaluation more meaningful for the student. Other innovative procedures are also being used.

OTHER INNOVATIONS REGARDING EVALUATION

A physical growth report card has been used by the Abraham Lincoln High School in Philadelphia. The report card consists of ten different growth items broken down into physical components and personal characteristics. The physical components include muscle strength, muscle endurance, flexibility, cardiovascular endurance, and neuromuscular coordination. The personal characteristics include height, weight, and age, posture, muscle tone, health habits, and work habits. Although all of these components are not graded for each marking period, throughout the entire school year all do receive attention. By the end of the year a physical profile can be seen that shows the strong and the weak points of the pupil. A student receives a grade of A (exceptional), B (above average), C (good), D (poor), or E (very poor) for each component.

At Jessie M. Clark Junior High School in

Lexington, Kentucky, each member of the physical education class participates in the evaluation of other students and also rates himself. In addition, the teacher rates each student. Thus far, in practice there is much agreement among all three ratings. A conclusion reached by those who utilize this method is that the student feels more a part of the learning process and as a result is more concerned and plays a more active role in class.

At Framingham North High School in Framingham, Massachusetts, the members of the physical education class formulate goals they wish to achieve. Then they plan the steps by which they will achieve these goals, and, finally, they are rated on the degree to which the goals are achieved.

At Herricks Public School in Herrick, Long Island, New York, students also think through and write out the goals that they wish to achieve. They are told they should take a look at themselves, decide what they wish to achieve in physical education, define goals for themselves in light of their wishes, plan how to achieve these goals, and, finally, evaluate what they have accomplished. Student and teacher grades are averaged together in order to arrive at the final grade.

It would appear that evaluation and grades will continue to be used in our schools since the American society seems to demand them. At the same time, methods must be devised that will judge more accurately the work accomplished by students and, in addition, help the student to better understand himself and his accomplishments and the degree to which he is making progress toward desirable educational and personal goals.

EVALUATION IN PHYSICAL EDUCATION

Physical education teachers have the responsibility for evaluating the degree to which they are accomplishing professional objectives. This process of evaluation should cover two general areas: pupil achievement, which includes the progress report or grade, and program administration. In Chapter 21 details of the evaluation of program administration and teaching are discussed, whereas in this chapter the main topic is pupil evaluation and grading.

Evaluation of pupil achievement should determine to what extent program objectives are being met. Evaluation should reveal levels of student development toward each of the four major goals: physical fitness, physical skills, knowledge and appreciation, and social development. The results of this evaluation process should serve many purposes. Besides providing a basis for grading pupil progress, evaluation techniques should also provide essential information for the motivation, guidance, and grouping of students and for program planning and curriculum building.

Current emphasis on meeting individual needs has increased the importance of evaluation, particularly for the purpose of identifying exceptional children. In order for orthopedically handicapped, gifted, and retarded children to receive equal opportunities in education, special adapted programs, both in physical education and in general education, are being developed to meet their particular needs.

There are many techniques of evaluation that are useful in measuring pupil achievement. Selection of a particular instrument

depends on several factors, including time, facilities, and type and purposes of information sought. Physical education teachers must devise a program of evaluation suitable to the philosophy and objectives of their particular school situation and physical education program. However, at least a minimum program of evaluation should be instituted to fulfill the teachers' responsibilities in this area. Larson and Yocom* suggest that a minimum program of measurement and evaluation in physical education include the following:

A. Evaluation of pupil achievement
   1. Physical fitness
     a. Medical examination
     b. Physical fitness test
   2. Physical skills
     a. General test of motor ability
   3. Knowledge and appreciation
     a. Teacher-made tests
   4. Social development
     a. Observation
B. Evaluation of program administration (according to standards established by leading authorities)
   1. Class program
   2. Adapted program
   3. Interscholastic sports
   4. Intramural activities
   5. Administration
       Each to be evaluated
         in terms of:
     a. Activities

*Larson, Leonard A., and Yocom, Rachael D.: Measurement and evaluation in physical, health, and recreation education, St. Louis, 1951, The C. V. Mosby Co.

YOU EARN YOUR MARK IN PHYSICAL EDUCATION
(You earn **6** points a day for full participation)

Participation and Health	240 points
Skills (ability)	60 points
Knowledge of the Rules	20 points
Maximum Total	320 points

Grade	Range	Bonus Points—	
A	320 - 306		
B	305 - 286	Class Intramural Champ	10
C	285 - 261	Leader in Decathlon	5
D	260 - 241	Satisfactory Captain	10
F	240 - Below	Oiler Leader	15

Make-Up — 6 points a week on scheduled day.

Fig. 20-1. How a student earns his mark in physical education. (Richmond Union High School, Richmond, Calif.)

b. Leadership
c. Facilities
d. Equipment
e. Participation
f. Records
g. Research
h. Budgetary allotments

A more comprehensive program of measurement and evaluation would include several other testing techniques, such as sports skill tests, attitude and interest inventories, checklists, and questionnaires. The development of a program of evaluation for a particular school requires a great deal of thought and study on the part of the staff.

Methods and materials for evaluation of pupil achievement and various systems of reporting pupil progress are presented and discussed.

METHODS AND MATERIALS FOR EVALUATING PUPIL ACHIEVEMENT

An evaluation program of pupil achievement should be designed to determine level of achievement in relation to the four principal objectives of the physical education program. The following testing techniques, resources, and materials, plus methods of devising tests, are included for

PHYSICAL EDUCATION REPORT CARD
NASHVILLE CITY SCHOOLS

Pupil_____ School_____
Homeroom_____ Classroom _____ Year 19____ 19____

GRADE LEVEL	FALL					SPRING					YEAR'S AVERAGE
	1	2	3	Ex	Av	4	5	6	Ex	Av	

Items checked (✓) below need improvement

	1	2	3	4	5	6
Develops co-ordination						
Shows knowledge of rules						
Develops physically						
Strength						
Endurance						
Weight						
Participates						
Dress						
Playing						
Shower						
Attendance (Days absent from class)						
Conduct						

CODE
(Teacher may add plus or minus if she wishes)

A=90 - 100—Consistently does excellent work   C=75 - 81—Does fair work
B =82 - 89—Does good work   D=70 - 74—Low, but, passing
F =Below 70—Failing

Comments enclosed   Date_____ Date_____ Date_____
    Date_____ Date_____ Date_____

Teacher_____

(Front)

Fig. 20-2. Physical education report card. (Nashville City Schools, Nashville, Tenn.)

the physical education goal for which they are most suitable and applicable.

Organic development and physical fitness

Medical examination. A medical examination should be given to each student at least once a year by a competent doctor.

Physical fitness tests. Physical fitness tests should be given early in the school year and also in the spring. The results of such tests help determine the degree of fitness of the pupils, provide the teacher with a basis for student classification for instructional purposes, and indicate the progress of the students toward attainment of this objective. Several test batteries, such as the AAHPER Physical Fitness Test Battery,* have been devised for measurement in this area; they were discussed in Chapter 16.

Physical skills

Because a major portion of the physical education class is devoted to the teaching of skills, many skill tests in each of the

---

*Hunsicker, Paul: AAHPER physical fitness test battery, Journal of Health, Physical Education, and Recreation 29:24, 1958.

ATTITUDES AND PRACTICES	Items checked (✓) below need improvement					
	1	2	3	4	5	6
SOCIAL						
Uses self-control						
Is courteous in speech and action						
Co-operates						
Cares for property (incl. textbooks)						
Is considerate toward others						
Respects and obeys school rules						
WORK						
Makes good use of abilities						
Follows directions promptly						
Completes each task						
Works independently						
Uses initiative						
HEALTH						
Maintains personal cleanliness						
Maintains correct posture						
Obeys safety precautions						

PARENT'S SIGNATURE

1. _____

2. _____

3. _____

4. _____

5. _____

6. _____

(Back)

Fig. 20-2, cont'd. For legend see opposite page.

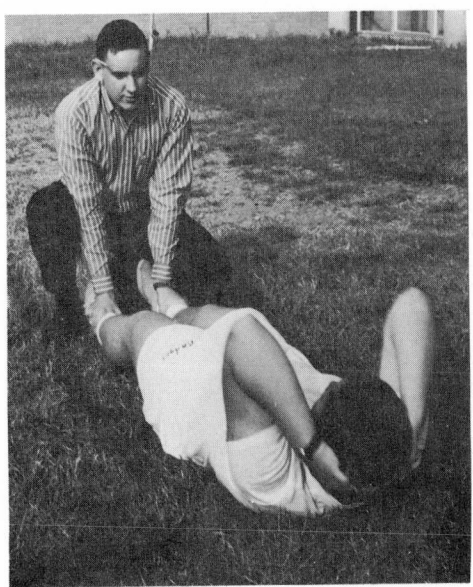

Fig. 20-3. A phase of the physical education testing program in Spartanburg Public Schools, Spartanburg, S. C.

various sports have been developed. They cover a wide range of age levels and grades in some sports, while in other activities there may be no suitable test available. General tests of physical capacity and motor efficiency have also been developed for evaluation of student performance and capacity.

Suggested general skills tests. Leaders in the field have devoted much time and research to testing *motor educability, motor capacity, physical capacity, motor ability,* and *motor efficiency.* These terms may appear at first to be synonymous with physical fitness. The beginning teacher should understand, however, that the work done in each of these areas is not to be confused with physical fitness testing. Some of the skill tests measure inherent aptitudes of pupils, while others measure achievement in basic motor skills. The beginning teacher wishing to use some of these tests should become familiar with the purposes of each—the following for ex-

Fig. 20-4. Physical skills need to be tested in physical education. Girls' trapeze skills. (Centennial High School, Pueblo, Colo.)

ample: (1) Rogers Strength Test,* (2) California Physical Fitness Pentathlon,† (3) McCloy's General Motor Ability and Capacity Tests,‡ (4) Larson Muscular Strength Test,§ (5) Illinois High School Physical Condition Test,* and (6) Indiana Physical Fitness Test for High School Boys and Girls.†

These are a few of the many tests available to the teacher of physical education for testing motor skills. Reference to the original works of the authors will provide directions necessary to the administration of these tests.

Suggested sports skills tests. Leaders in the field of physical education have devel-

*Clarke, H. Harrison: Application of measurement to health and physical education, Englewood Cliffs, N. J., 1967, Prentice-Hall, Inc.

†California physical fitness pentathlon, Bulletin of the California State Department of Education 11: 8, 1942.

‡McCloy, C. H., and Young, N. D.: Tests and measurement in health and physical education, ed. 3, New York, 1954, Appleton-Century-Crofts.

§Larson, L. A.: A factor and validity analysis of strength variables and tests with a test combination of chinning, dipping, and vertical jump, Research Quarterly 11:82, 1940.

*Illinois high school physical condition test and standards of performance, Bulletin No. 6, September, 1944, Office of Public Instruction, Health and Physical Education Department.

†State of Indiana: Physical fitness manual for high school boys, Bulletin No. 136, 1944, Department of Public Instruction.

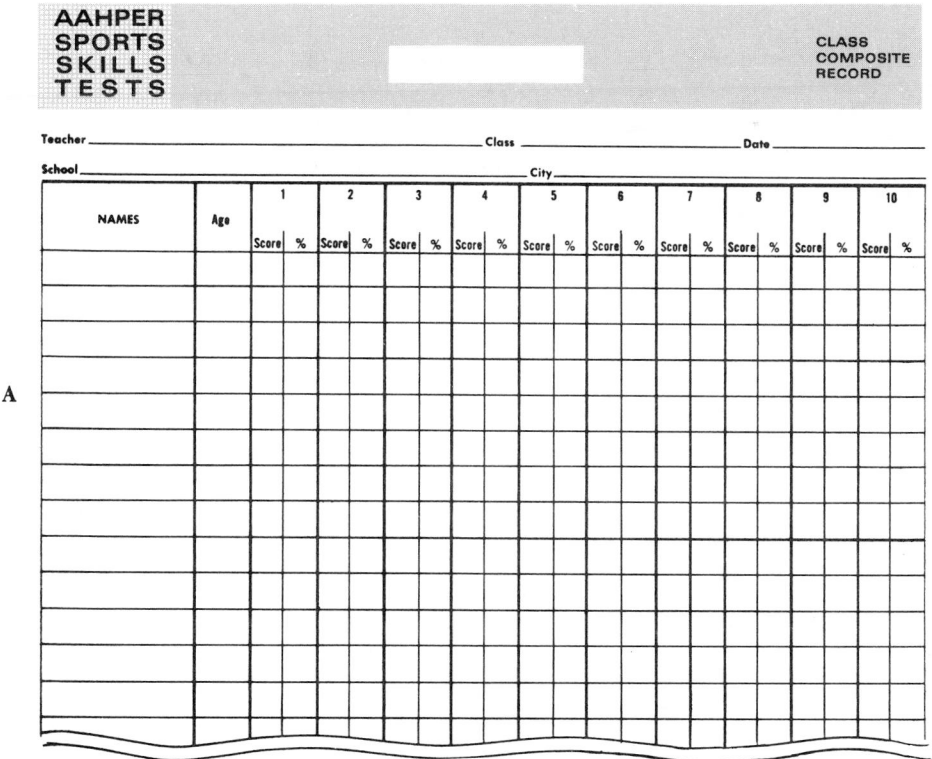

CLASS COMPOSITE RECORD

Continued.

Fig. 20-5. AAHPER Sports Skill Tests—class composite record. Shown on this and the following pages are the record forms for skill tests. The squad score card, **B,** is to be filled out as the test is given. Note that scores for the various test items are recorded in different ways. The class composite record, **A,** has space for recording the raw score and the percentile score, which is determined by using tables. (See Table 20-1.) The personal data sheet, **C,** has room for several tests; the profile, **D,** can also be used for several tests by using pencils of different colors.

| AAHPER SPORTS SKILLS TESTS | | | | | | *Softball* | | | | | SQUAD SCORE CARD |

Squad # 4   Teacher *Rachel Coyle*   Date *April 21, 1967*
School *Kennedy Jr. High School*   City *Rising Sun, Maryland*

NAMES	Age	1 Distance throw	2 Accuracy throw	3 Pitching	4 Speed throw	5 Fungo Hitting	6 Base Running	7 Fielding	8 Catching	9	10
1. *Joan Dean*	13	76	12001 30130 ⑪	00111 11111 ⑧	23.2 ㉑.4	01111 12121 00122 20101 ⑳	⑬.9 14.1	11001111 11011111 ⑰	10011010 00110061 ⑩		
2. *Ann Ryle*	13	80	00111 23022 ⑬	10221 12100 ⑩	㉒.6 22.9	11111 02211 21221 11102 ㉔	⑭.2 14.4	01111111 11011111 ⑱	11011011 0111006 ㉑ ⑪		
3.											
4.											
5.											
6.											
7.											
8.											

B

SQUAD SCORE CARD

Fig. 20-5, cont'd. For legend see p. 367.

oped testing instruments for skills in such sports as the following: archery, badminton, baseball, basketball, bowling, football, golf, gymnastics, handball, field hockey and ice hockey, riding, rhythms, figure skating, soccer, softball, speedball, squash, stunts and tumbling, swimming, tennis, and volleyball. Descriptions of these tests, including age level, equipment needed, and administrative directions, are given in one or more source books.*

Other suggestions for testing may be found in the individual sports rule books,

current literature, periodicals, and booklets on sports. In looking over these tests the teacher finds that certain basic skills necessary to the games themselves have been selected, and the testing procedures that have been devised for these skills are closely related to the game situation. Suggested methods for rating or scoring individual performances on a specified number of trials, as well as norms for grade level performances, are usually included. Limitations to the use of these tests exist, however, for in many instances too much time is required for their administration, their reliability or validity is questionable, or the norms listed may be for the college years. It is necessary to study these prepared tests carefully, therefore, to determine their suitability or adaptability to a particular teaching situation.

Perhaps the most significant develop-

*Clarke, H. Harrison: Application of measurement to health and physical education, Englewood Cliffs, N. J., 1967, Prentice-Hall, Inc.; McCloy, C. H., and Young, N. D.: Tests and measurement in health and physical education, New York, 1954, Appleton-Century-Crofts; Mathews, Donald K.: Measurement in physical education, Philadelphia, 1963, W. B. Sounders Co., Scott, M. Gladys, and French, Esther: Evaluation in physical education, St. Louis, 1950, The C. V. Mosby Co.

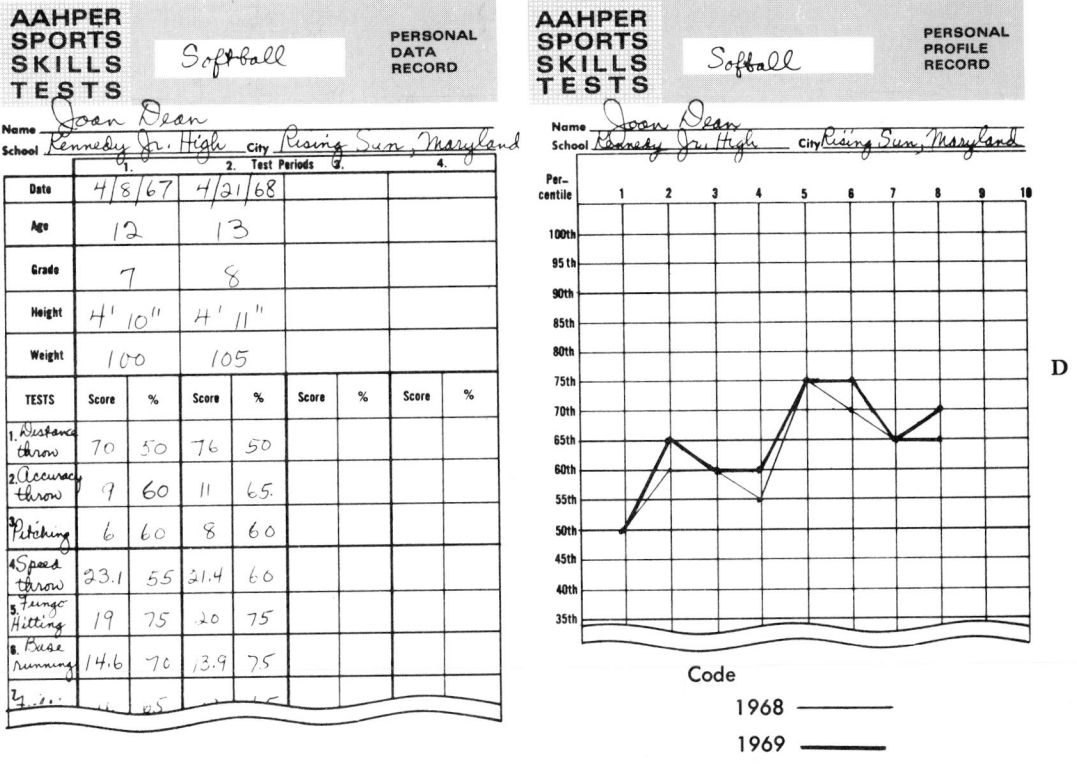

PERSONAL DATA RECORD   PERSONAL PROFILE RECORD

Fig. 20-5, cont'd. For legend see p. 367.

ment in the area of skill evaluation is under the sponsorship of the American Association for Health, Physical Education, and Recreation. Their Research Council has been working to devise tests and norms for effective evaluation of boys and girls, grades five through twelve, in physical education programs across the United States. This total project, which includes instructional manuals, will include skill tests for the following:

Archery	Lacrosse
Badminton	Soccer
Baseball	Softball
Basketball	Swimming
Field Hockey	Tennis
Football	Track and field
Golf	Volleyball
Gymnastics	

The sports skills test manuals are very helpful not only for testing purposes but for instructional pointers as well. Sample

class composite record forms, data forms, and profile forms (see Table 20-1) are available from the Association.

Teacher-made tests. When acceptable testing devices are not available, teachers may want to originate sports skills tests that are appropriate and accurate for their teaching situations. This is a long and involved process, but the following suggestions may be helpful when developing sports skills tests for personal use.

1. The sport should be analyzed to determine and select skills for measurement.

2. Special procedures should be devised for the administration of a test of a skill or skills.

3. A preliminary test should be administered to a group and a check made to see if those of acknowledged superior ability score higher than others in their performances.

Table 20-1. Softball throw for distance (girls)* (percentile scores based on age/test scores in feet)

| Percen- | Age | | | | | | | Percen- |
tile	10-11	12	13	14	15	16	17-18	tile
100th	120	160	160	160	200	200	200	100th
95th	99	113	133	126	127	121	120	95th
90th	84	104	112	117	116	109	109	90th
85th	76	98	105	109	108	103	102	85th
80th	71	94	98	104	103	98	97	80th
75th	68	89	94	99	97	94	93	75th
70th	66	85	90	95	93	91	89	70th
65th	62	81	86	92	88	87	87	65th
60th	60	77	83	88	85	84	84	60th
55th	57	74	81	85	80	81	82	55th
50th	55	70	76	82	77	79	80	50th
45th	53	67	73	79	75	76	77	45th
40th	50	64	70	76	72	73	74	40th
35th	48	61	68	73	70	70	72	35th
30th	45	58	64	69	67	67	69	30th
25th	43	55	62	66	64	63	66	25th
20th	41	51	60	61	61	60	63	20th
15th	38	48	56	57	58	56	60	15th
10th	34	43	51	52	54	51	55	10th
5th	31	37	43	43	49	45	50	5th
0	20	20	20	20	20	10	10	0

*From Softball for girls, skills test manual, Washington, D. C., 1966, American Association for Health, Physical Education, and Recreation, p. 37.

4. If the above check suggests validity, complete rating of the group should be made and the validity coefficient computed.

5. The test results should again be checked, this time against the rules of the game from which the skill was taken, with higher scores playing against lower scorers.

6. Retesting should be done on one group to compute the reliability coefficient.

7. The raw scores from the test should be converted to some type of comparable scoring system to make results most useful.*

A teacher following these procedures can be better assured that the results of the test are valid and reliable.

Other testing techniques. Sports skills tests are only one method of evaluating physical skills. In some types of activities there are no objective tests available for

*Stroup, Francis: Measurement in physical fitness, New York, 1957, The Ronald Press Co.

use, and more subjective measures must be made. There are also some skills that in themselves are difficult to measure objectively. Other techniques, such as teacher ratings and progress charts, must be used.

Teacher ratings are generally necessary in evaluation of the form used in completing a skill. For example, diving, ski jumping, and figure skating must be judged partially or totally on the basis of form. In addition, the form used in batting, shooting baskets, playing tennis or badminton, hockey dribbling, and swimming is important to the level of achievement and must be judged by teacher rating. The teacher should therefore determine a scale for judgment—one to five or one to ten—and establish specific standards for rating individual performance. When more than one judge is used, averages of ratings are computed and more acceptable results are obtained.

Teacher ratings are also necessary in the evaluation of creative movement or performance. Establishing certain criteria, or evaluative standards, provides a basis for rating on a predetermined point scale by the teacher or judges. Criteria such as use of space, use of body, use of focus, use of types of movement, and degree to which the given problem was solved should be developed by the teacher and explained to the students involved in the test.

Student progress in a particular skill is another factor that is sometimes difficult to measure. In some sports, such as bowling and archery, the scores themselves may be used to indicate improvement. The teacher can keep a record of scores on charts to measure individual progress. Charts are also useful in measuring progress, because keeping track of the number of baskets shot and missed or the number of goals attempted will result in an indication of performance skill and progress.

However, the performance of each individual must be assessed separately when charts are used to determine improvement for grading purposes. Some students may intentionally score low early in the season, in order to exhibit great progress when tested at the end of the unit. Also, several students may have identical progress scores, such as three more baskets on the second testing round. The teacher must then consider which student making a score of three evidenced greater improvement: the low scorer who managed to make three more baskets or the expert who scored high originally, yet still increased his score by three. Only by evaluating each student's performance can a teacher make proper use of charts in grading.

Knowledge and appreciation

In the area of knowledge and appreciation, tests differ from those of physical fitness and skills in that an intellectual process is involved, rather than a motor performance. Standardized written tests are available in some of the sports and may be found in rule books and source books of the various sports. Unfortunately, many standardized tests are limited to the college level. Teachers may therefore have to devise their own tests, using either the oral, essay, or objective form. In so doing, the teacher can make sure that the test covers assigned materials and that it is suitable for the age level being tested.

Principles of test construction. There are certain principles of test construction that should be followed when developing a knowledge test.

1. The items selected should cover the entire subject matter, with emphasis placed on the most important facets of the game.

2. The length of the test should be related to the time available for testing.

3. The test should be appropriately worded and geared for the age level to be tested.

4. Directions should be simple and clear.*

Techniques of testing. There are different techniques that may be utilized in test construction. True-and-false items, matching questions, sentence completion, multiple-choice, and diagrams, as well as short essays, may be combined to make an interesting and comprehensive examination of knowledge.

The following are a few suggestions regarding the wording of objective tests.

1. Questions or test items should be worded so as to avoid ambiguity and triviality.

2. Statements should be simple and direct, not tricky, involved, or based solely on opinion.

3. Words such as *never, always, none,* or *all* should be omitted in sentences requiring true or false answers.*

Knowledge tests are generally developed in objective form, but evaluation of appreciation requires other techniques. To determine attitudes and opinions in physical education, the teacher will find that short-answer questionnaires, opinion polls, and surveys are useful. These testing techniques are not designed to determine factual comprehension, as knowledge tests are, but to discover student preferences in the area of program content or their attitudes toward class conduct. Results of these tests, therefore, are not computed on an individual basis but are used to determine overall class opinions or estimations. Because of the personal nature of these testing techniques, the forms are, of necessity, teacher-made. Construction of these questionnaires or surveys depends on the information sought and the purposes to be surved.

Administration of tests. When a written test is administered, directions should be read aloud as well as written on the test paper. A few questions as to the timing or scoring of the test may be answered, but they should be limited. Following the signal "go," no further questions or talking should be allowed. Nothing is more discon-

---

*Stroup, Francis: Measurement in physical fitness, New York, 1957, The Ronald Press Co.

*McCloy, C. H., and Young, N. D.: Tests and measurement in health and physical education, New York, 1954, Appleton-Century-Crofts.

certing to the teacher or the students than unnecessary questioning. If directions are clear and the test well constructed, a satisfactory examination should result.

Social development

Social development is a goal of the physical education program that also requires evaluation, but unfortunately, it is one aspect that is often neglected by teachers. The social development of the adolescent is a complex process, as was pointed out in Chapter 4. However, various techniques of testing have been devised to measure some of its aspects: social adjustment, attitudes and interests, social efficiency, and social status.

Testing social adjustment. Measurements of social adjustment may be made through the administration of standardized inventories (such as the Bell Adjustment Inventory) that have been developed specifically for this purpose. Such inventories should be used cautiously, however, and the results regarded only as clues to or indications of adjustment problems. The guidance department of a large school system is probably better equipped to administer and interpret these tests, but the physical education teacher should be familiar with them. A list of some of the other tests for social adjustment includes the following: Science Research Associates Inventory, Minnesota Multiphasic Personality Inventory, Washburne's Social Adjustment Inventory, and the Bernreuter Personality Inventory. These tests are usually concerned with common adolescent problems or worries about the home, health, friends, and so on. Such tests or inventories are for general educational use, not for physical education personnel alone; therefore, the school psychologist or guidance counselor should be consulted in regard to this phase of testing.

Testing attitudes and interests. The guidance department should also be able to assist the physical educator in testing the attitudes or interests of adolescents. Attitudes may be measured in different ways.

As an example, three techniques are mentioned: (1) teacher evaluation (observation of students, with an anecdotal record being kept by the teacher), (2) opinion polls, and (3) rating scales. The physical education teacher should ask for the assistance of other teachers, and particularly of the guidance personnel, in this type of testing. Teachers work together because of a mutual interest in student problems, and sharing the test results promotes greater understanding among all concerned. This type of faculty cooperation would apply also to interest inventories such as the Strong Vocational Interest Blank or the Kuder Preference Record. The development of social interests, attitudes, and adjustment, while being a goal of physical education, is also a general educational goal, and testing them is the concern of the entire teaching staff.

Two scales developed specifically for testing attitudes in physical education are the Adams scales.* Students are asked whether they agree or disagree with such statements as "Physical education gets very monotonous," and "Physical education is my favorite subject."

Testing social efficiency. In regard to testing social efficiency, rating scales have been developed by leaders in the field of physical education specifically for use within the program. Three are listed.

1. The McCloy test consists of rating, on a scale of one to five, nine character traits.†

2. B. E. Blanchard devised a frequency rating scale for measuring character and personality in physical education classes.‡

3. O'Neel published a rating scale for

---

*Adams, R. S.: Two scales for measuring attitude toward physical education, Research Quarterly 34:1, 1963.

†McCloy, C. H.: Character building through physical education, Research Quarterly, October, 1930.

‡Blanchard, B. E.: A behavior frequency rating scale for the measurement of character and personality in physical education classes for boys, Research Quarterly, May, 1936.

high school boys in physical education classes.*

In these three tests, ratings of the frequency of behavior are measured by observer judgment. By referring to the original sources indicated, the teacher may learn the techniques of administering these tests for social efficiency.

Testing social status. Sociometrics is the measurement of social relationships as determined by use of a sociogram. The sociogram is useful in physical education as a method of teaching and of testing the social status of individuals in a class, team, or squad. The results of the sociogram point out the natural leaders in the groups and the outsiders trying to become members. When the device is used more than once with the same group, a comparison of the results indicates social growth or change. A sociogram may be taken, for example, by asking all members of a team to list two people whom they would most like to have as their friends, with their choices limited to a given group or team. Results may be pictured with arrows pointing to the names listed, as shown in Fig. 20-6.

It may be interpreted from the particular sociogram shown here that John is the strongest leader, with Bill following closely

behind. John, Larry, and Ed seem to form a rather small social clique, while Bill, who would like to join them, returns friendship with Fred only. It may be said also that Allen may be trying to break up this friendship and that Charlie, who was chosen by no one, would be happy with either Bill or Allen for a friend.

An indication of social development in such a group would be the movement of Charlie and Allen into an acceptable position in the group and the enlargement of the clique so that friendships are more spread out. A second sociogram would then show partial proof of social development and accomplishment through teamwork in whatever the group activity may have been. This is a simple technique of testing social development. It is useful as a tool in teaching because it indicates social interactions and points out possibly dangerous cliques, as well as those individuals who need assimilation into the group. The teacher, knowing this, can gear teaching to avoid social upsets and to improve social relationships.

Problems in evaluating student achievement

The testing of student achievement and the analysis of results necessary for their future application are essentials of the teaching program. For the new teacher, five main problems stem from this responsibility: (1) alloting time for testing, (2)

---

*O'Neel, F. W.: A behavior frequency rating scale for the measurement of character and personality in high school physical education classes for boys, Research Quarterly, May, 1936.

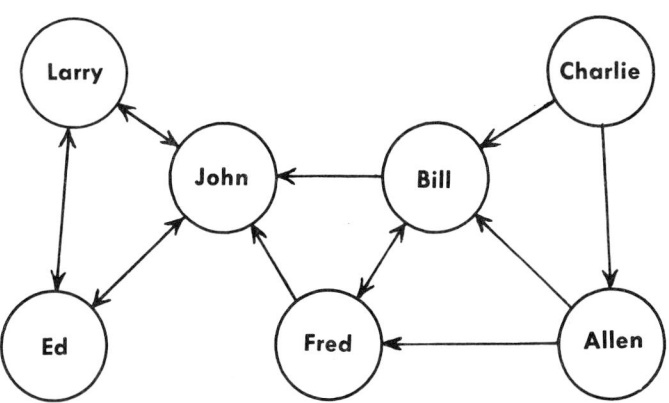

Fig. 20-6. A sociogram indicates social status.

selecting tests, (3) administering tests, (4) keeping records, and (5) using the results.

Allotting time. The time necessary for adequate evaluation of students' achievements must be set aside as a regular part of the teaching program. In situations where classes meet every day, one class period every other week may be devoted to testing. When classes meet only two or three times a week, the teacher should plan for evaluation procedures at least at the beginning and end of each unit of study in order to obtain accurate records of growth and progress.

Selecting tests. In selecting tests the new teacher should survey the available instruments to determine whether they are pertinent to his or her particular school situation. Proper selection of tests helps to overcome the problems of large classes, short periods, and individual rating needs. Because good organization and wise use of leaders also help to eliminate loss of valuable time, the beginning teacher should plan testing periods very carefully in order to make the most of them. Testing itself is a teaching method, with its promotion of good performances and its motivational purposes, and time taken for evaluation is therefore not wasted.

In selecting a test for administration to a class, the teacher should be concerned with five elements of the particular test: validity, objectivity, reliability, norms, and administrative feasibility. If the test is satisfactory in all these respects, the teacher may be assured that the results will be accurate.

Validity. The test should measure what it is supposed to measure. If the teacher is measuring balance, for example, the test should measure balance and not some other physical characteristic, such as speed or endurance.

Objectivity. The scoring of the test should be exact and well defined and as free as possible from personal opinion or subjective judgment. If two or more judges evaluate the performances of a class group, their answers or scores should be similar.

This is an important factor in testing, and it affects the students to a great extent. They recognize the value of exact scoring methods for particular performances and generally prefer them to scaled value judgments.

Reliability. The testing device should consistently produce the same results. If a test were repeated under very similar conditions with the same group, the results should be equivalent—with the better performers again scoring high and so on. Extraneous factors such as practice, distance, or time should not influence the results.

Norms. The test should have an accepted scale of performance scores normal for particular age levels and groups. Norms are useful for comparison of the achievements of one group with those of a similar group. Norms are valuable, however, only if they are based on a large population, which ensures a wide range of performance levels.

Administrative feasibility. It should be possible to administer a test to a class group without too much expense, loss of time, or other complication. It is logical to expect that testing student achievement consumes a reasonable amount of time, expense, and consideration. Evaluation should not, however, result in excessive loss of teaching time, to the detriment of the program. This factor often determines the feasibility of administration of a particular type of test. Taking into account class size, available equipment, and length of class periods may eliminate and otherwise sound testing device.

Making the selection of a testing instrument according to these five factors is necessary if accurate and worthwhile results are to be obtained. The teacher of physical education should take great care in surveying available tests before making a final choice.

Administering tests. The feasibility of administering a particular instrument of testing is not the only consideration involved prior to selection. Other factors unrelated to the test itself may become problems during test administration and therefore need to be anticipated by the teacher.

• *What provisions can be made in regard to changing climactic conditions?* For example, in a test for accuracy in archery or punting in football, wind direction and velocity may be a disturbing factor. Can retests be administered?

• *What provisions can be made for makeup testing of pupils who may be absent on the day the test is given?* Will time be set aside after school or during the regular class program to accommodate these pupils? Will the identical test be given, or will a substitute be used to prevent preparation on the basis of rumors or gossip?

• *What provisions can be made to correct errors made by student assistants, in timing, for example, or in scoring test results?* Will retesting solve this problem, or will the advantage of previous practice produce a higher score by the testee?

• *What provisions can be made for the maintenance of testing targets, line makers, and the like during the test administration?* Chalk lines frequently become blurred or erased during test administration. Can masking tape be used, or is it possible to assign a student leader the task of keeping lines or circles visible?

• *What provisions can be made for students who err throughout the entire test, either through a misunderstanding of the directions or through a lack of sufficient time?* Should such students automatically fail because of their unacceptable performances, or should they be allowed the opportunity to take the test again in the makeup period?

These are questions that the teacher must answer when administering tests, whether they be written or performance tests of student achievement.

Keeping records. The clerical duties attached to the testing program pose other difficulties. Records should be kept up to date and new test results constantly analyzed in terms of student progress and program planning for most effective use. The teacher must take time to do this if the true values of evaluation are to be realized.

In order to ease this difficulty somewhat, schools have been making use of community volunteers, or teacher-aids, to free regular teachers from these clerical duties, which consume so much time. The physical education teacher should investigate this possibility in regard to record-keeping. The form of the record itself may help to make the task less burdensome. Samples of such forms are included in the appendix materials at the end of the book. Some schools have been finding the use of IBM cards to be a real help in solving the problem of recording test results. The Evergreen Park Community High School uses this system to record physical fitness test results and to send reports home as well. A sample card is seen in Fig. 20-7.

It may also be helpful for the teacher to maintain a record file of evaluative tests used, adding comments concerning possible success or problems involved in their administration. This procedure would prevent repetition of testing with unsuitable instruments.

Using test results. The results of all types of tests of student achievement should be put to use if the process of evaluation is to have any direct value for the students. There are several ways in which this may be done, and the choice depends on the purpose of the particular test.

Tests administered at the beginning of a unit—whether skill, knowledge, or fitness tests—serve as prognostic devices to determine the needs of the group in relation to that specific activity. The teacher should interpret test results immediately and use them in planning the unit of study. Special groups may need to be formed on the basis of skills, or a special area of the activity may need emphasis because of a general weakness of the group. The motivational aspect of prognostic tests is also a valuable teaching tool.

Tests administered in the middle of a unit serve a diagnostic purpose, since results can indicate to the teacher those areas wherein teaching has not been sufficiently clear to make learning complete. The

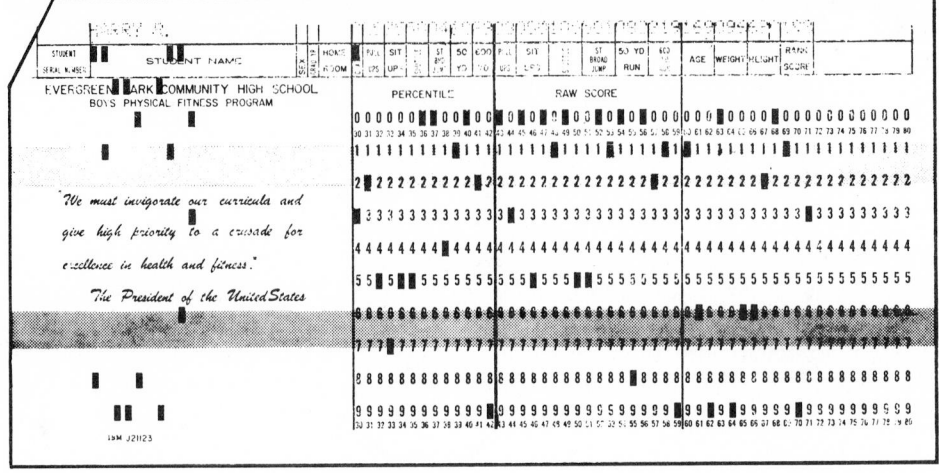

Fig. 20-7. IBM card used in Evergreen Park Community High School, Evergreen Park, Ill.

teacher then knows that the remaining class sessions need to include review and clarification of ideas to cement learning.

Tests at the close of a unit of study indicate pupil progress and achievement. When they are compared with preliminary tests, a vital measure of improvement and effort is obtained.

Evaluation of student achievement should do more than produce figures of present status. It should promote improvement of this status. This can be accomplished only through appropriate use of accurate test results.

Scores on all tests administered within a given unit, course of study, or semester should be averaged and combined with other determinants to equal a student's grade for that particular report period. The problems of using test results and developing a grading system are extremely important ones, and the physical education teacher must consider them very carefully and thoughtfully.

METHODS AND MATERIALS FOR GRADING

Grading in physical education is a complex process, for a single grade represents many different facets of pupil achievement, all of them important. In simplest terms, a grade is a teacher's (or teachers') estima-

tion of pupil status. It may take several different forms, it may be arrived at by many different techniques, and it may serve many purposes.

Purposes of grading

In general, a grade serves two primary purposes: it informs the student of his present status, and it also notifies the parents. Grades may also serve several subsidiary functions: (1) a motivational device for some students, (2) a guide to program planning and regrouping of students, because grades identify areas of strength and weakness in the curriculum and in the youngsters, and (3) a basis for counseling students, for abrupt changes in a student's grades would probably be indicative of problems. Unfortunately, grades are sometimes used as a threatening device to push or force students into activity, which is not a desirable purpose of grading.

Principles of grading

To be of real value, a grade in physical education should be developed according to certain well-defined principles:

1. It should be representative of an individual pupil's achievement in relation to the established objectives of physical education. Comparison of achievement with other students should be avoided.

2. It should be developed on the basis of all four objectives of physical education. Emphasis should be placed on physical skills and physical development to the same degree that these factors are stressed in the program of instruction.

3. It should be understood by the student. He or she should know its components, the method of derivation of the grade, and how the various items in the test were weighted.

4. It should be understandable to parents. It should be explicit enough so that the objectives of the program are clearly understood.

5. It should be expressed in the same manner as grades in other subject matter areas throughout the school. This not only facilitates record keeping and transfer of credits but also places physical education on the same level as other subjects.

6. It should be determined on the basis of several different evaluative techniques. Both subjective and objective measurements should be used.

7. It should be fair—a just estimation of the student's achievement and proper consideration should be given to other factors, such as improvement, effort, sportsmanship, and citizenship.

Methods of grading

There are several methods utilized in grading, not only in the field of physical education but also throughout the general educational complex in this country. Some examples include the following:
1. Letter grades: A, B, C, D, and E or F
    H, S, and U
    P and F
2. Numerical grades: 1, 2, 3, and so forth
3. Explanatory paragraphs
4. Checklists: often used to check weaknesses in such areas as effort, improvement, or citizenship

Problems in grading

In physical education the main problem is trying to arrive at a single grade that truly represents the pupil's achievement toward the various objectives. To what degree should performance and ability be weighted in relation to achievement in knowledge and social development? Some teachers believe that the former should have twice the value of the latter, because physical skills and development are the primary raison d'être of a program of physical education. Others believe that all four objectives should be considered equally. Another problem in grading centers around improvement. To what degree should improvement in skills affect the final grade? Should the student who has low motor ability but who shows real improvement in a sports unit be rated in the same manner as the highly skilled individual who merely loafs along throughout the unit?

A third question arises out of the procedures necessary in physical education class. Should credit for grading be given for having a clean gym suit, for being dressed for participation in every class, for showering, and for attendance? In addition, there is the problem of effort in physical education class. How does a teacher determine maximum effort, and is such effort accorded an automatic A? These are some of the questions the physical educator must answer before developing a grading system suitable for use in his or her school situation.

Dr. Lynn McCraw of the University of Texas proposes a plan for grading that offers some solutions to these problems (Table 20-2).

Ideally, the report card should be clear, concise, accurate, and explicit. It should show achievement in physical skills, general ability, social development, and all the objectives that were stressed throughout the program. Perhaps more than one grade is necessary to clarify the many facets of the program for the parents.

It is always revealing to discuss the problem of grading with the students themselves, to determine what elements they feel a physical education grade should

Table 20-2. Proposed plan for grading*

Components	Weightings	Instruments
Attitude in terms of Attendance Punctuality Suiting out Participation	5% to 25%	Attendance and other records Teacher observation
Skills in terms of Form in execution of skill Standard of performance Application in game situation	20% to 35%	Objective tests Teacher observation Student evaluation
Physical fitness with emphasis on Muscular strength and endurance Cardiovascular-respiratory endurance Agility Flexibility	20% to 35%	Objective tests Teacher observation
Knowledge and appreciation of Skills Strategy Rules History and terms	5% to 25%	Written tests Teacher observation
Behavior in terms of Social conduct Health and safety practices	5% to 25%	Teacher observation Student evaluation

*From McCraw, Lynn W.: Principles and practices for assigning grades in physical education, Journal of Health, Physical Education, and Recreation **35:**2, 1964.

encompass, and to allow them to estimate a grade for themselves. In a survey of high school girls, it was interesting to note that those whom the teacher rated A– or A ranked themselves only B or B+, while students whom the teacher ranked C+ or lower often rated themselves above the teacher's estimate. This typifies the attitudes of many students toward themselves: those who do little often think they deserve more, while those who put forth real effort rarely feel that they are deserving.

In a survey of eighth graders who were asked about the components of a physical education grade, the element cited with greatest frequency was effort. One astute remark made by an eighth-grade girl included the following observations:

> I think that physical education should be graded, but not on a scale, just by the level that one person can reach by himself. It is up to the physical education teacher to get to know her students and learn just how far their abilities go, and then grade each person on the basis of how much he or she is improving. This could probably best be

done by having a place on the report card where the physical education teacher can make a statement about the child's improvement.

The chart shown in Fig. 20-8 depicts another method by which various factors might be weighted in determining an individual's grade. Ability factors, such as physical fitness, game skills, and knowledge scores are included in percentages along vertical lines, while attitudes, adjustment, and improvement are diagrammed along the horizontal percentage line. If a student ranks in the fiftieth percentile in ability and in the eightieth percentile for his attitudes and effort, his final grade would be C+. On the other hand, a student with excellent physical skills and high ability who loafs during class period, putting forth little or no effort, would fall into the C range.

Grading in team teaching

Grading in schools using teaching teams for instruction has been a difficult problem

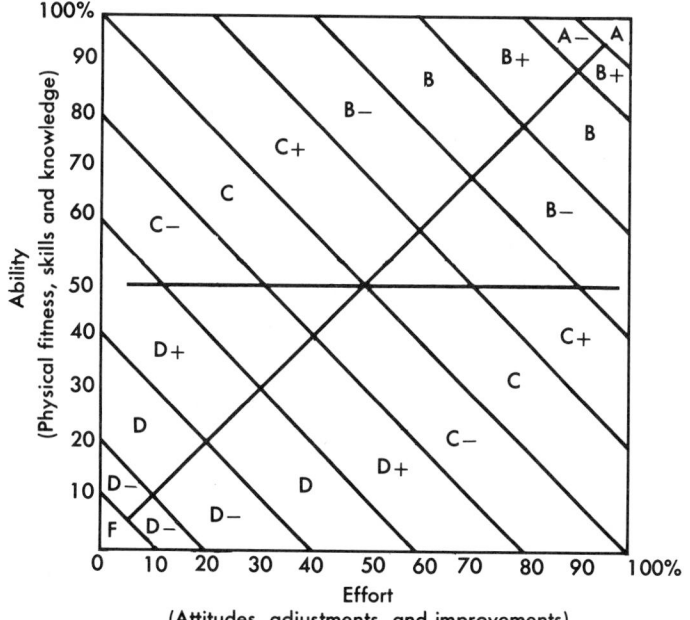

Fig. 20-8. Evaluation chart.

to solve. It has been found that members of the teaching teams must formulate criteria for grades together in order to provide consistency throughout the school. The master teacher in charge of a particular unit, such as volleyball, is responsible for all grades during that grading period, and the helping teachers turn their grades in to him for compilation. In this way a student accumulates several grades in many areas during one grading period. Teachers who have taught under this system seem to believe that it works out satisfactorily for everyone concerned.

POINTS TO REMEMBER

1. There are many important factors to be considered when selecting tests for evaluation, such as validity and reliability.
2. There are many types of tests useful in evaluating pupil achievement in the four goals of physical education.
3. Teacher-made tests of knowledge and skills must be constructed according to certain principles.
4. A system of grading should be developed on the basis of certain well-defined principles.
5. A grade should be a true measure of pupil status and should be expressed in a form

similar to that used in other academic areas in the school.

PROBLEMS TO THINK THROUGH

1. Should skill tests be administered both at the beginning of a sports unit and at the end? What factors should be considered in planning them?
2. Should a written knowledge test be given at the close of every sports unit?
3. When should physical fitness testing be done—at the beginning, middle, and/or end of the year?
4. Should tests of social development be given within a single sports unit? What type? At what other times of the year may they be given?
5. Under what circumstances may teacher-made tests be more valuable than standardized tests?
6. Of what value are tests of social interests and attitudes?
7. To what uses may the results of physical fitness tests be put?
8. A student of low motor ability would probably never be graded higher than a C in physical education class.

CASE STUDY FOR ANALYSIS

A high school physical education program consists of classes that meet twice a week. The department wishes to gather factual evidence that would point up to the administration the need for expanding the program and convince them of the value of a daily class in physical education. What evaluation techniques would be useful to promote this argument?

EXERCISES FOR REVIEW

1. Define validity of a test, and explain.
2. Define reliability of a test, and explain.
3. Devise a sample knowledge test of volleyball rules for seventh grade girls or boys.
4. Administer one physical fitness test item to a group and compare the scores with national norms.
5. Prepare a set of directions to be given orally before administering a written knowledge test to a class.
6. Select a specific skill essential to the game of basketball and devise a simple test for measuring its performance.
7. Look up a standardized skill test in one of the source books and evaluate its suitability for use in a nearby high school.
8. Make a sociometric study of a group or team presently established and evaluate the individual status of participants.

SELECTED READINGS

American Association for Health, Physical Education, and Recreation: Sports skills test manuals (archery, basketball, football, softball), Washington, D. C., 1966-1967, The Association.

Boyd, Clifford A., and Waglow, Irving F.: The individual achievement profile, Physical Educator 21:117, 1964.

Clarke, David H., and Clarke, H. Harrison: Research processes in physical education, Englewood Cliffs, N. J., 1970, Prentice-Hall, Inc.

Fabricus, Helen, Hanson, Dale, Singer, Robert, and Solley, William H.: Grading in physical education, Journal of Health, Physical Education, and Recreation 38:34, 1967.

Hunsicker, Paul: AAHPER physical fitness test batter, Journal of Health, Physical Education, and Recreation 29:24, 1958.

Johnson, Barry L., and Nelson, Jack K.: Practical measurements for evaluation in physical education, Minneapolis, 1969, Burgess Publishing Co.

Jorndt, Louis C.: Point systems-motivational devices, Physical Educator 23:19, 1966.

Larson, Leonard A., and Yocom, Rachael D.: Measurement and evaluation in physical, health, and recreation education, St. Louis, 1951, The C. V. Mosby Co.

Latchaw, Marjorie, and Brown, Camille: The evaluation process in health education, physical education, and recreation, Englewood Cliffs, N. J., 1962, Prentice-Hall, Inc.

Lawrence, Trudys: Appraisal of emotional health at the secondary school level, Research Quarterly 37:252, 1966.

Liba, Marie R., and Loy, John W.: Some comments on grading, Physical Educator 22:158, 1965.

McCloy, Charles H., and Young, Norma D.: Tests and measurement in health and physical education, New York, 1954, Appleton-Century-Crofts.

Mathews, Donald K.: Measurement in physical education, ed. 3, Philadelphia, 1968, W. B. Saunders Co.

Oliva, Peter F.: The secondary school today, Cleveland, Ohio, 1967, The World Publishing Co.

Oxendine, Joseph B.: Social development—the forgotten objective? Journal of Health, Physical Education, and Recreation 37:23, 1966.

Piscopo, John: Quality instruction: first priority, Physical Educator 21:162, 1964.

Smithells, Philip A., and Cameron, Peter E.: Principles of evaluation in physical education, New York, 1962, Harper & Row, Publishers.

Torrance, E. Paul: Rewarding creative behavior, Englewood Cliffs, N. J., 1965, Prentice-Hall, Inc.

Van Dalen, Deobold B., and Meyer, William J.: Understanding educational research, New York, 1966, McGraw-Hill Book Co., Inc.

21 TEACHER AND PROGRAM EVALUATION

Educators today are taking a very close look not only at programs but also at teachers themselves. Recent advances in education have necessitated the development of more accurate methods of rating teachers and their abilities. In this chapter the two important factors, teacher evaluation and program administration evaluation, are discussed.

TEACHER EVALUATION

Today's educational programs require a system of teacher evaluation that is in tune with the times. Appraisal should be carried out as a mutually desirable procedure for the purpose of helping both the student and the teacher. Emphasis should be placed upon such items as how effective the materials utilized are, to what extent the teacher understands the personalities of the students with whom he is working, and how well the teacher understands the subject matter of his field. Appraisals should be conducted by persons who are competent in this area. In a day of specialization it has been suggested that persons who are specialists in this area of evaluation should be the ones to evaluate teachers.

Reasons for teacher evaluation

Castetter* has outlined several reasons why evaluation of personnel is important

---

*Castetter, William B.: The personnel function in public administration, New York, 1971, The Macmillan Co., p. 232.

and necessary. These reasons are presented here in adapted form.

1. To determine whether a teacher should be retained. Administrators evaluate teachers to determine whether or not they make a desirable contribution to the school system where they are employed and whether they should become a permanent part of the faculty.

2. To determine the potential of a teacher. Evaluation can help in indicating the nature and scope of a teacher's potential to the school system.

3. To assign the teacher to responsibilities where the best performance will result. Through periodic evaluation it will be known where the teacher's abilities can best be utilized in the school system.

4. To improve the performance of the teacher. Evaluation can help the teacher to understand his weaknesses and strengths and how his weaknesses can be eliminated and his strengths utilized best.

5. To uncover abilities. Evaluation offers an avenue for determining teacher abilities that otherwise may go undected.

6. To serve as a guide for salary raises. Where salary raises are determined on the basis of merit and productivity, evaluation provides important information for these raises.

7. To identify important factors concerning program and students. Evaluation not only determines the teacher's effectiveness but also the desirability and effectiveness of the program and the reaction of students to the program.

8. To test the procedure by which the school recruits teachers. Teacher evaluation can assist in determining whether or not the recruitment procedure for new teachers is effective.

9. To provide motivation for teachers. A sound evaluation procedure can motivate teachers to do better work.

10. To improve the understanding between teachers and administration. Through an effective evaluation system teachers will be better able to understand the role and responsibilities of the administration and, in turn, the administration will better understand the role of the teacher.

11. To provide some basis for the transfer, promotion, or dismissal of teachers. Many objective facts must be mobilized if teachers are to be promoted, dismissed, or transferred in a just manner. Evaluation offers a means of obtaining some of these facts.

12. To motivate self-development. A very important reason for evaluation is to encourage the teacher to develop and become a better teacher.

TEACHER EVALUATION TODAY

Methods and techniques measuring teacher effectiveness and ability have been greatly expanded, and information concerning a teacher's personal history and growth has acquired greater importance, as evidenced by the bulging record folders filed in principals' offices.

Increased stress on the teacher and teaching has resulted from many factors. Educators today have recognized more and more the importance of the teacher-pupil relationship and therefore have been more concerned with the personality patterns of individual teachers. Then, too, with increasing emphasis upon teacher accountability, the effectiveness of teaching has assumed greater importance. Other factors, such as merit pay schedules and teaching team programs, have forced principals and supervisors to differentiate teachers in accordance with their productivity. Increased community pressures and criticisms of educational policies and procedures have brought about the need for greater professionalism among educators and, in turn, more effective appraisal of teachers and teaching has been encouraged.

Evaluation of teachers and their effectiveness involves several steps. As in other phases of evaluation, school systems vary in the extent and degree to which they fulfill this need. In general, however, a teacher's personal record file would include information regarding the following:

A. Personal status
   1. Health and physical status
   2. Intellectual abilities
   3. Social and emotional stability
B. Professional status
   1. History
   2. Experiences
   3. Teaching effectiveness
   4. Relationship with pupils
   5. Relationship with colleagues
   6. Relationship with the profession
   7. Relationship with the community*

The process of evaluation—that is, the actual collection of information—should encompass opinions from several sources. The teacher himself should be responsible for some self-evaluation; other sources are the administrator and colleagues.

Personal status

Health. A teacher should be in good health and physical condition. Some schools require periodic health examinations and chest x-ray films. The rigors of teaching demand a healthy, vigorous person, particularly in the field of physical education. However, physical perfection is not necessarily a requisite of any teaching position. There are countless handicapped persons who have been effective teachers in spite of their handicap. (A decade ago the New York City schools had a regulation stating that vision of all swimming teachers had to be nearly 20/20 and that no person wearing corrective lenses could be hired for this activity. However, this restriction has been lifted.)

---

*See Chapters 1 and 11.

Intellectual abilities. A teacher should be well educated, well read, and able to apply knowledge to everyday pursuits. Many schools require evidence of this ability, expecting prospective teachers to take the National Teachers Examination or the Teacher Education Examination Program. Other statistics are also used, such as college entrance examination scores and transcripts of college records.

Social and emotional stability. A teacher should be a well-adjusted person, finding contentment in his surroundings while making contributions to it. Administrators have several instruments and methods available to them for comprehensive appraisal of teachers' personalities. The Minnesota Teacher Attitude Inventory, the Minnesota Multiphasic Personality Inventory, and the Rorschach Test are some of the well-known tests that have been used. Other methods are observations, interviews, anecdotal records, and student opinion.

Professional status

Preparation. A teacher should have a broad knowledge of educational psychology and history and be particularly well schooled in the special subject matter of his choice. Administrators are particularly interested in the teacher's professional preparation and expect teacher-training institutions to make recommendations on the basis of fair and honest appraisal techniques. Grades in the major field and in student-teaching work may be of special importance.

Experience. A teacher should seek outside experiences that are both broadening and educational to expand the background brought to a teaching position. Administrators generally take a close look at all summer experiences, such as counseling and recreation work, as well as travels, in assessing a teacher's experiences. Past experiences in the teaching field are naturally important aspects that would also be studied.

Teacher effectiveness. A teacher should be able to apply knowledge and teaching techniques to the classroom situation and be able to communicate effectively with the students.

Methods of appraisal

Administrators have several methods of appraisal available for use in teacher evaluation.

New methods of appraisal

A survey conducted recently regarding administrator and teacher evaluation procedures in school systems enrolling 25,000 or more pupils and conducted by the Educational Research Service, sponsored jointly by the National Education Association and the American Association of School Administrators, indicates the following new approaches that are being utilized in the evaluation of teachers.*

Multiple evaluators. Instead of a teacher being evaluated by one or two persons, in some school systems the evaluation is taking on a multifaceted basis. Teachers are evaluated by a committee, students, subordinates, parents, and/or outside groups. The aim is for consensus evaluations, for example, among a committee or between the teacher and the evaluators.

Performance objectives. Objectives of desirable accomplishments are set by the teacher, administration, or both. Then the teacher is evaluated on the degree to which the objectives are achieved. For example, short- and/or long-range goals are set and stated in terms of measurable objectives. An example of a performance objective might be: "I will provide a special program for my students who are subpar physically." The teacher is then evaluated in terms of whether or not or to what degree this objective is achieved.

Multiple bases for evaluation. Some school systems feel that a combination of evaluation on the basis of performance objectives and also a procedure that lists predetermined characteristics of the effective teacher is best. In other words, the teacher

*Research Division, National Education Association: NEA Research Bulletin **50:**40, 1972.

is evaluated not only on the basis of whether he achieved certain objectives but also in regard to the degree to which he acquired the characteristics of a model teacher.

In-basket data. In this procedure a file is kept on various incidents that occur and details of teacher performance during the evaluation period. Such a file might contain notations on class observations, reports from students, complaints from parents, graduate courses taken, conferences held, and the like. Then, on the basis of all these items, the evaluation of the teacher takes place.

Traditional evaluation techniques

Observation. Administrators may make personal assessments of a teacher's abilities through periodic visitations to class. Criteria such as those listed in the chapter on class management would be helpful (control of the class, type of discipline used, attitude of the youngsters).

Student opinion. A periodic checkup of student opinions may be used to determine specific qualities of teaching. Students may be asked to rate teachers (one to four, or poor to excellent) on such factors as cheerfulness, preparation, discipline, and so on. The Morris Trait Index* is another survey that may be used by students.

Anecdotal record. An administrator may keep a file on problems that come to his attention as a result of a particular teacher's classroom activities. Complaints from students or teachers would fall into this category. (For example: Where was the teacher when those boys started that fight in the locker room? Or why are students always late to classes following gym class?)

Standardized instruments. An administrator may use one of several standardized evaluation charts to appraise teacher effectiveness. For example, Beecher's Teaching

Evaluation Record,* the Purdue Teacher Examination,† or the Ohio Teaching Record‡ may be used by the administrator himself, or he may request or require his teachers to file a self-evaluation sheet, such as the Haverhill Evaluation Inventory.§

Relationship with pupils. Administrators may take into consideration teacher-pupil relations. Requests for a particular teacher to serve as a chaperone or as a sponsor for a club activity might be indicative of that teacher's concern for students. Also, complaints from students and/or parents may be given due consideration by administrators.

Relationship with colleagues. An administrator may record a teacher's contributions at teachers' meetings, at workshops, or on voluntary committees. Holding an elective office in a faculty association, credit union, or committee would certainly be an indicator of status among one's associates and administrators would take note of this.

Relationship with profession. Administrators may become acquainted with a teacher's professionalism through his or her activities in local, state, and/or national organizations (committee work and office holding). Within the school an administrator may look for innovations and changes in teaching techniques and programming. He may also check a teacher's familiarity with the current literature in education.

Relationship with the community. Administrators recognize that good public relations are a vital force between a school and its community. Each teacher should foster good school-community relations. The teacher should show evidence of

---

*Beecher, Dwight E.: The evaluation of teaching backgrounds and concepts, Syracuse, N. Y., 1949, Syracuse University Press.

†Kelley, Ida B., and Perkins, Keith J.: How teach, Purdue Teachers Examination, Educational Test Bureau, Minneapolis, 1942, Educational Publishers, Inc.

‡Ohio Teaching Record, anecdotal observation form, ed. 2, Columbus, 1945, College of Education, Ohio State University.

§Haverhill Public and Vocational Schools: Evaluation inventory, Haverhill, Mass., The Schools.

---

*Morris, Elizabeth H.: Morris Trait Index L, Bloomington, Ill., Public School Publishing Co.

loyalty to the school and its administrative policies and practices—such as at PTA functions and board meetings—and he should be a loyal contributor to the community, working for its betterment through cooperation with and promotion of its interests, such as the Memorial Day Parade and the summer recreation program.

The appraisal practices set forth here are not intended to be an absolute formula. They are merely suggestions of possible practices that individual school systems may employ. Three other points should be emphasized in this regard:

1. Administrators generally evaluate all teachers in a similar manner. Physical education teachers should not expect special consideration because they have winning teams or bring in valuable gate receipts.

2. Consideration would naturally be given to length of experience in a particular school situation. The beginning teacher would not be expected to evidence the same degree of effectiveness or competency as the teacher with five or ten years of experience in that school.

3. Standards of evaluation are themselves indicative of the school's expectations. For example, submitting weekly lesson plans or not smoking on the job are regulations with which a prospective teacher may not wish to comply. A teacher who does not agree with the standards expected of him or her in a school situation would probably be more effective in another school system.

The National Education Association has published a booklet in which inferior and superior standards in all phases of school administration are compared. In the section on staff personnel policies and procedures, the following description is given of superior evaluation procedures:

Although special emphasis is placed upon probationary teachers, every professional employee is evaluated on a continuing basis and shares responsibility for such evaluation. The primary purpose of evaluation is looked upon as the improvement of performance and is in no way related to salary. The school system conducts in-service work-shops for the orientation and training of personnel responsible for evaluation, and takes this responsibility into consideration in determining work load and staff requirements. Procedures, evaluation forms, and guides are developed on the basis of co-operatively developed standards of performance and job descriptions. Criteria of evaluation are explicit, are written, and are made known to all staff members at the beginning of each school year. Criteria appropriate to each professional task are used for the evaluations. Each observation and evaluation includes a consultation between the staff member and the evaluator. Various techniques are used, including evaluations by more than one evaluator. Staff members sign and receive copies of written evaluations, and review and appeal procedures are in operation.°

PROGRAM ADMINISTRATION EVALUATION

Evaluation of program administration may be a yearly procedure, handled by members of the department for the purpose of curriculum organization, or it may be an examination of the whole school by a visiting team of specialists from the state department of education or professional association for the purpose of accreditation. The process of evaluation itself involves rating or judgment of the program according to selected criteria and standards. Standardized forms have been developed to evaluate various phases of the physical education curriculum. Excerpts from some of these forms that have traditionally been used are included in this chapter:

1. LaPorte health and physical education score-card no. II for junior and senior high schools and four-year high schools†
2. National Study of Secondary School Evaluation (1960): Evaluative criteria for boys' physical education (D-14) and Evaluative criteria for girls' physical education (D-15)‡

°From National Education Association: Profiles of excellence, Washington, D. C., 1966, The Association, p. 54.

†LaPorte, William Ralph: Health and Physical education score card no. II for junior and senior high schools and four-year high schools, Los Angeles, 1942, University of Southern California Press.

‡National Study of Secondary School Evaluation: Evaluative criteria, Washington, D. C., 1960, The Study.

3. Educational Policies Commission: Checklist on school athletics*

Where standardized tests are not available to judge program administration, criteria based on authoritative textbook sources or the judgment of experts in the field must be established.

The following are sample questions that may be formulated for teacher rating of program administration. They may either be answered poor, fair, good, or excellent, or be scored on a scale of one to ten. All areas of the program are listed, and questions are raised concerning the various factors.

Class program

1. Does the teaching program devote equitable time to team sports, individual sports, rhythms and dance, and gymnastic activities?

2. Are the available equipment and facilities adequate to allow maximum student participation?

3. Are reasonable budgetary allotments made for the class teaching program?

4. Are accurate evaluation procedures carried out and are worthwhile records kept?

5. Are minimal participation requirements met by all students?

6. Are students meeting proper physical education requirements in regard to dressing and showering?

7. Are proper safety measures taken in all activities?

8. Are opportunities for developing student leadership being provided in the class program?

Adapted program

1. Do adequate screening procedures determine all possible participants in this program?

2. Are adequate facilities, equipment,

---

*Educational Policies Commission, American Association of School Administrators: School athletics: problems and policies, Washington, D. C., 1954, The Association.

time, and space made available to the program?

3. Are proper supervision and instruction afforded each individual participant?

4. Is medical approval obtained for each individual's regimen of activity?

5. Do participants engage in some of the regular class work, as well as remedial classes, when advisable?

6. Are careful records and progress notes kept on each student?

7. Is the financial allotment to the program reasonable?

8. Does student achievement indicate the value of the program?

Intramural and extramural programs

1. Are intramural and extramural sports offered to all students in as many activities as possible?

2. Has participation in these programs increased during the past year?

3. Is maximum coaching supervision available to players?

4. Is adequate financial assistance given to this phase of the program?

5. Are accurate records maintained concerning the participants, their honors, award, and electives?

6. Does the reward or point system emphasize the joys of participation rather than stress the value of the reward?

7. Is equipment well cared for and properly stored to gain the most use from it?

8. Are competitive experiences wholesome and worthwhile for all participants?

Interscholastic program

1. Is financial support for this program provided by the physical education budget?

2. Is there equitable financial support for all sports in the interscholastic program?

3. Are interscholastic sports available to all students, boys and girls alike?

4. Are adequate health standards being met in respect to number of practices and games, fitness of participants, and type of competition?

5. Is competition provided by schools of a similar size?

6. Is the program justifiable as an important educational tool?

7. Are academic standards for participants maintained?

8. Are good public relations with the community furthered through this program?

Aquatics

1. Are maximum instruction and participation opportunities made available to all students?

2. Is superior care taken in cleaning and maintaining the pool area—with proper checks on water chlorination, temperature, and filter system?

3. Is adequate supervision by qualified personnel available at all times?

4. Are health standards of cleanliness and rules requiring freedom from infection enforced at all times?

5. Are proper safety regulations enforced at all times?

6. Does student achievement indicate the value of the program?

7. Are competitive swimming and diving events properly officiated and controlled?

8. Is swimming on the intermediate level a requirement for graduation?

Administration

1. Is the teaching staff well qualified and capable of carrying out the program?

2. Is the program run efficiently, with little loss of teaching time or space, and is maximum use made of facilities?

3. Are professional standards maintained as to class size and teacher assignment?

4. Is the departmental organization on a democratic basis, with all members sharing in the decisions?

5. Do members of the staff have a professional outlook, attend professional meetings, and keep up with the latest developments in the field?

6. In what areas have scientific tests and research been made for contribution to the profession?

These are just a few sample questions that may be used in evaluating program administration. The key to successful evaluation of this type lies in the follow-up steps for improvement.

Whenever possible, a standardized evaluation form should be utilized. A checklist developed by the New York State Department of Education is included here as an example.

PHYSICAL EDUCATION CHECKLIST*

Whatever method of program evaluation is selected, it should be realistic, functional, and continuous, in order to fulfill its major purpose of benefiting the students.

POINTS TO REMEMBER

1. Teacher evaluation is a growing responsibility of administrators.
2. Evaluation is a continuing process.
3. Steps involved in teacher evaluation encompass every aspect of a teacher's personal and professional status.
4. Program evaluation may be accomplished within a school system or by a visiting team of specialists.
5. All evaluation procedures must take into account special factors related to the particular community involved.

PROBLEMS TO THINK THROUGH

1. To what extent should self-rating procedures be included in a teacher's personal record file?
2. What is the primary purpose of program evaluation?
3. Should the teaching staff be informed of the methods of teacher evaluation in use within their school system?
4. For what reasons would test scores be evidence of effective teaching? For what reasons would they not?
5. Should a teacher be well liked by students in order to be an effective teacher?

CASE STUDY FOR ANALYSIS

A large new suburban high school is preparing for a visitation from the state accreditation committee. The physical education department is expected to collect concrete evidence of student achievement in all phases of the program. What materials would provide concise information for this purpose?

---

*From New York State Department of Education, Division of Health, Physical Education, and Recreation.

THE STATE EDUCATION DEPARTMENT
DIVISION OF HEALTH AND PHYSICAL EDUCATION

CHECK LIST FOR PHYSICAL EDUCATION

Education assumes a responsibility to pass on our cultural and social inheritance and to equip children and youth physically, mentally and emotionally for living in a changing world. This process involves (1) recognition of the needs of the individual in terms of the principles of pupil growth and development, (2) organization and administration of the curriculum for most effective use in the realization of its purposes as established by these needs and (3) continuous evaluation of the program to insure systematic progress toward the realization of the objectives of physical education and the purposes of education.

Physical education recognizes this concept of education and has a unique contribution to make in meeting these needs for the self-realization of the individual through the activities in its program. The beneficial effects of exercise and activity, however, are produced only when activities of the right type and amount are provided under qualified personnel. The methods and techniques used in the conduct of these activities need to be such that not only are these physical and organic needs met but opportunity is provided for growth in the development of social behaviors, habits, attitudes, emotional stability.

In order for individuals to function as contributing members of a democracy it is essential that they learn self-discipline in relation to the group through the development of those qualities which are essential to democratic living such as cooperation, leadership, fellowship, good sportsmanship etc. It is also essential that they develop (1) strength to be ready for tasks encountered in everyday routine and in emergencies, (2) stamina to continue necessary tasks without undue fatigue, and energy to participate in recreation activities after a day's work, (3) cardio-respiratory endurance for sustained effort in activities involving motion of the entire body, (4) agility to be able to make wide ranges of movement easily, (5) speed to be able to move rapidly when personal safety demands it, (6) control to coordinate body movement skilfully, (7) knowledge and skill in a wide variety of recreational activities to insure continued participation.

The check list has been prepared to help school officials and interested citizens' groups to judge their physical education programs in terms of the basic elements needed to reach the objectives stated above and to stimulate planning in terms of pupil needs and local conditions. It should enable communities to identify the strength and weaknesses of their physical education programs and to direct attention to areas needing further study and action for improvement. The check list is designed for such self-appraisal use. It is not for a report to the Department.

These elements are grouped under eight main headings:

Program activities	Personnel
Program planning	Facilities
Evaluating	Safety and sanitation
Scheduling	Budget

From New York State Department of Education, Division of Health, Physical Education, and Recreation.

I The program provides a broad variety of activities to serve all pupils.

   1 Informal activities such as singing games, simple circle games, creative activities (games of invitation and imagination) and games of hunting, fleeing and chasing type. Yes .... No ....

   2 Games of simple organization such as kickball, dodgeball, relays etc. Yes .... No ....

   3 Team games, such as basketball, volleyball, softball, soccer etc. Yes .... No ....

   4 Individual and dual games, such as badminton, tennis, horseshoes etc. Yes .... No ....

   5 Gymnastics, such as stunts, tumbling, apparatus. Yes .... No ....

   6 Rhythms and dancing, such as folk, square, social. Yes .... No ....

   7 Winter sports, such as skating, skiing, snowshoeing. Yes .... No ....

   8 Body mechanics and correctives. Yes .... No ....

   9 Swimming and water safety. Yes .... No ....

  10 Extraclass, interschool and intramural activities (boys and girls)

      a An organized extraclass program is provided for pupils in upper elementary grades. Yes .... No ....

      b All athletic activities are an integral part of the physical education program. Yes .... No ....

      c The intramural program is well organized and attractive to the extent that most of the pupils willingly participate. Yes .... No ....

      d Girls' interschool activities are limited to sports days, invitation games and other invitation activities. Yes .... No .... Girls' rules are used in the conduct of these activities. Yes .... No ....

      e Interschool activities for boys below the seventh grade are limited to sports days and invitation games. Yes .... No ....

II The program is planned in terms of community needs and of the growth and development needs of pupils.

   1 The purposes of education and objectives of physical education are used to guide planning. Yes .... No ....

   2 The activities are introduced at the appropriate grade and growth level. Yes .... No ....

   3 There is a written master plan which provides for progression and continuity in the instruction. Yes .... No ....

   4 Planning for the program is shared by administrator and staff. Yes .... No .... By staff and pupils. Yes .... No .... With citizens' groups. Yes .... No ....

III Provision is made for evaluating the program by determining the growth and progress of pupils.

   1 Records of pupil status and progress are maintained with reference to the following:

      a Physical fitness. Yes .... No ....

      b Knowledge and skill in activities. Yes .... No ....

      c Social growth and group relationships. Yes .... No ....

   2 Appropriate evaluative methods are used to determine pupil progress in the above-mentioned items.

      a Recognized standards. Yes .... No ....

      b Teacher-made tests or measures. Yes .... No ....

      c Anecdotal report. Yes .... No .... Teacher observation. Yes .... No ....

IV The school schedule provides for the following:

   1 A daily period of physical education instruction for each pupil. Yes .... No ....

   2 Pupils grouped for such instruction according to their grade or growth level. Yes .... No ....

Continued.

3 Classes of uniform size. Yes .... No .... Small enough to provide good working groups (a maximum of 40 pupils is recommended). Yes .... No ....

4 Additional classes for those who need remedial (corrective) work. Yes .... No ....

5 Restricted program for pupils physically unable to participate in regular program of activities. Yes .... No ....

6 Equitable scheduling of facilities between boys andgirls for both class and extraclass activities. Yes .... No ....

V Qualified personnel is provided to conduct a well-rounded program.

1 Sufficient personnel is provided to meet the class instruction and laboratory requirements in accordance with the needs of pupils as outlined in the Regulations of the Commissioner. (A physical education teacher for each 240 elementary or 190 secondary pupils is recommended.) Elementary: Yes .... No .... Secondary: Yes .... No ....

2 A qualified director (where there are five or more on the staff) or a department head (four or less on staff) is available to provide necessary administrative and supervisory services. Yes .... No ....

3 Continuous professional growth of staff is provided for through:

a Regular staff conferences. Yes .... No ....

b Attending general faculty meetings. Yes .... No ....

c Attending local, zone and state meetings and workshops. Yes .... No ....

d Recent graduate study in physical education and related fields. Yes .... No ....

e A well-equipped professional library. Yes .... No ....

f Professional visits to observe programs in other schools. Yes .... No ....

4 Girls' program is conducted by a woman teacher. Yes .... No ....

5 Additional faculty assistance is provided for intramural program.
Girls: Yes .... No .... Boys: Yes .... No ....

For interschool program.
Girls: Yes .... No .... Boys: Yes .... No ....

VI The physical education and recreation facilities permit a well-rounded program for all pupils.

1 Teaching station indoors for every 240 pupils enrolled. Yes .... No ....

2 Sufficient dressing space for largest class. Yes .... No ....

3 Dressing locker for each pupil in largest class. Yes .... No ....

4 A gymnasium storage locker for every pupil enrolled above the 4th grade. Yes .... No ....

5 At least one shower head for every five pupils in the largest class. Yes .... No ....

6 A well-drained, suitably located body-drying area. Yes .... No ....

7 Storage space for apparatus. Yes .... No .... Equipment and supplies. Yes .... No ....

8 Suitable office space for each physical education teacher. Yes .... No ....

9 A swimming pool. Yes .... No ....

10 Remedial (corrective) room. Yes .... No ....

11 All-weather paved area adjoining building for primary grades' use. Yes .... No ....

12 Separate apparatus and play area for smaller children. Yes .... No ....

13 Separate playing fields for Intermediate grades. Yes .... No .... Secondary girls. Yes .... No .... Secondary boys (class and intramurals). Yes .... No .... Interschool sports. Yes .... No ....

14 Court area for tennis. Yes .... No .... Badminton. Yes .... No .... Volleyball. Yes .... No ....

15 Area for archery. Yes .... No .... Horseshoe pitching. Yes .... No .... Golf instruction. Yes .... No ....

16 Shed or other building for the storage of outdoor equipment. Yes .... No ....

17 The elementary school is planned to function as a neighborhood center and the high school as a community center. Yes .... No .... This planning is shared with citizens' groups. Yes .... No .... Park officials. Yes .... No .... Planning officials. Yes .... No ....

VII Provisions are made for healthful and safe conduct of physical education activities.

1 A thorough annual medical examination is provided for all pupils. Yes .... No ....

2 All candidates for interschool teams are given a special examination at the beginning of each sport season. Yes .... No ....

3 Subsequent examinations within each sport season are given when needed. Yes .... No ....

4 All participants in the more vigorous sports are provided with adequate protective equipment. Yes .... No ....

5 There is a regular safety check on all equipment and apparatus. Yes .... No ....

6 Gymnasium floor is kept clear of apparatus and equipment when not in use. Yes .... No ....

7 Good care, proper use and orderly storage of equipment are provided. Yes .... No ....

8 Fields are properly maintained for maximum and safe use. Yes .... No ....

9 Clean and sanitary conditions prevail in all areas. Yes .... No ....

10 An appropriate towel service is provided. Yes .... No ....

11 Protection Plan or other accident insurance coverage is provided for the physical education classes. Yes .... No .... Interschool teams. Yes .... No .... Intramural groups. Yes .... No ....

VIII The physical education budget is adequate and there is an equitable distribution of funds between the different activities of the program.

1 The annual budget request for physical education is prepared on the basis of a careful inventory and the complete needs of the program to be provided for the school year. Yes .... No ....

2 Essential equipment is available for physical education. Yes .... No .... If not, the purchase of needed items is planned for. Yes .... No .... Available instructional supplies are satisfactory in quantity to permit maximum and simultaneous pupil participation in any one activity. Yes .... No .... The supplies provided permit instruction in a broad variety of activities. Yes .... No ....

3 Sufficient funds have been allocated for travel, protective equipment and other necessary expense in connection with: Boys' interschool activities. Yes .... No .... Boys' intramural activities. Yes .... No .... Girls' invitation games. Yes .... No .... Girls' intramural activities. Yes .... No ....

4 Funds are provided for attendance at professional meetings and conferences by staff members. Yes .... No ....

EXERCISES FOR REVIEW

1. Take a survey of at least ten people by asking them to list in order of importance the five most important qualities of a good teacher. Make a composite listing of these qualities.
2. Compare the complete evaluation instruments presented partially in this chapter and note differences.
3. Evaluate as completely as possible a high school in the college community.
4. Interview a teacher, and on the basis of that discussion, write a description of the teacher's personal and professional status. What key questions may be used?

SELECTED READINGS

Bookwalter, Karl W., and Bookwalter, Carolyn W.: Purposes, standards and results in physical education, Indiana University, 1962, Bureau of Educational Studies and Testing, School of Education.

Bucher, Charles A.: Foundations of physical education, ed. 6, St. Louis, 1972, The C. V. Mosby Co.

Brian, George: Evaluating teacher effectiveness, NEA Journal 54:35, 1965.

Castetter, William B.: Administering the school personnel program, New York, 1965, The Macmillan Co.

Castetter, William B.: The personnel function in educational administration, New York, 1971, The Macmillan Co.

Flippo, E. B.: Principles of personnel management, New York, 1966, McGraw-Hill Book Co., Inc.

Howsam, Robert B.: Facts and folklore of teacher evaluation, Education Digest 29:13, 1964.

LaPorte, William R.: The physical education curriculum, ed. 6, Los Angeles, 1955, College Book Store.

Larson, Leonard A., and Yocom, Rachael D.: Measurement and evaluation in physical, health, and recreation education, St. Louis, 1951, The C. V. Mosby Co.

Latchaw, Marjorie, and Brown, Camille: The evaluation process in health education, physical education, and recreation, Englewood Cliffs, N. J., 1962, Prentice-Hall, Inc.

Malone, Wayne C.: A checklist for evaluating coaches, Coach and Athlete 29:42, 1966.

National Education Association: Methods of evaluating teachers, NEA Research Bulletin 43:12, 1965.

National Education Association: What teachers and administrators think about evaluation, NEA Research Bulletin 42:108, 1964.

National Education Association: Evaluation of teachers, NEA Research Bulletin 50:40, 1972.

Simpson, Ray H., and Seidman, Jerome M.: Student evaluation of teaching and learning, Washington, D. C., 1962, American Association of Colleges of Teacher Education.

Smithells, Philip A., and Cameron, Peter E.: Principles of evaluation in physical education, New York, 1962, Harper & Row, Publishers.

Vander Werf, Lester S.: How to evaluate teachers and teaching, New York, 1960, Holt, Rinehart & Winston, Inc.

PART SEVEN
RECORDS AND FORMS FOR PHYSICAL EDUCATION

G A A Point System																
Name_____								Hr	R S R S Hr	R S R S						
	Year				Year				Year				Year			Remarks
	F	W1	W2	S	F	W1	W2	S	F	W1	W2	S	F	W1	W2	S	
Archery																	Awards Received
Badminton																	Award Date
Basketball																	1
Bowling																	2
Dance																	3
Field day																	4
Golf																	5
Hockey																	
Riflery																	
Saddle																	Responsibilities
Softball																	
Speedball																	
Swimming																	
Table Tennis																	
Tennis																	
Volleyball																	
Total																	
Grand Total																	☆ Received Trophy

TOURNAMENT DRAWINGS

ROUND ROBIN TOURNAMENT

In this simple but efficient method, each team plays every other team once with the final standing determined on a percentage basis.

The following formula will apply to any number of teams, whether the total is odd or even. With an odd number of teams there is the same number of rounds; with an even number of teams there is one less number of games than teams.

FOR ODD NUMBER OF TEAMS

Assign to each team a number and then use only the figures in drawing the schedule. For example, in a league with 7 teams start with 1, putting down figures in the following order:

7	6	5	4	3	2	1
6-1	5-7	4-6	3-5	2-4	1-3	7-2
5-2	4-1	3-7	2-6	1-5	7-4	6-3
4-3	3-2	2-1	1-7	7-6	6-5	5-4

Note that the figures go down on the right side and up on the left. No. 7 draws a bye in the first round and the others play as indicated. With an odd number of teams, all numbers revolve and the last number each time draws a bye.

FOR EVEN NUMBER OF TEAMS

With an even number of teams the plan is the same except the position of No. 1 remains stationary and the other numbers revolve about it until the original combination is reached. For example, with 8 teams:

1-2	1-8	1-7	1-6	1-5	1-4	1-3
8-3	7-2	6-8	5-7	4-6	3-5	2-4
7-4	6-3	5-2	4-8	3-7	2-6	8-5
6-5	5-4	4-3	3-2	2-8	8-7	7-6

Two things only must be remembered: (1) With an even number of teams, No. 1 remains stationary and the other numbers revolve. (2) With an odd number of teams, all numbers revolve and the last number each time draws a bye.

LADDER TOURNAMENT

```
TABLE TENNIS
1 _____
2 _____
3 _____
4 _____
5 _____
6 _____
7 _____
8 _____
9 _____
10 _____
```

In a ladder tournament the competition is arranged by challenge and the tournament requires a minimum of supervision. A player may challenge either of the two players above him in the ladder. If the challenger wins, he exchanges places with the loser in the ladder. All challenges must be accepted and played at an agreed time. Players draw for positions in the ladder; a starting and closing date for the tournament must be announced. Each player carries his handicap against all players, in case handicaps are used.

PYRAMID TOURNAMENT

The pyramid tournament is similar to the ladder tournament except the design allows for more participating and challenging. After the original drawings are made any player may challenge any other player in the same horizontal row. If he wins he may then challenge anyone in the row above, the two change places in the pyramid.

TOURNAMENT SCHEDULE CALCULATOR

Teams Entered	Byes Top	Byes Bottom	Single Elim. No. Games	Double Elim. No. Games	Round Robin No. Games
4	0	0	3	6 or 7	6
5	1	2	4	8 or 9	10
6	1	1	5	10 or 11	15
7	1	1	6	12 or 13	21
8	0	0	7	14 or 15	28
9	3	4	8	16 or 17	36
10	3	3	9	18 or 19	45
11	2	3	10	20 or 21	55
12	2	2	11	22 or 23	66
13	1	1	12	24 or 25	78
14	1	1	13	26 or 27	91
15	0	1	14	28 or 29	105
16	0	0	15	30 or 31	
17	7	8	16	32 or 33	
18	7	7	17	34 or 35	
19	6	7	18	36 or 37	
20	6	6	19	38 or 39	
21	5	6	20	40 or 41	
22	5	5	21	42 or 43	
23	4	5	22	44 or 45	
24	4	4	23	46 or 47	
25	3	4	24	48 or 49	
26	3	3	25	50 or 51	
27	2	3	26	52 or 53	
28	2	2	27	54 or 55	
29	1	2	28	56 or 57	
30	1	1	29	58 or 59	
31	0	1	30	60 or 61	
32	0	0	31	62 or 63	

(Round Robin Tournament, Ladder Tournament, and Pyramid Tournament from Athletic Field and Court Diagrams; courtesy Lowe and Campbell Athletic Goods, Kansas City, Mo.; Tournament Schedule Calculator courtesy Boys' Physical Education Department, New Trier Township High School, Winnetka, Ill.)

DOUBLE ELIMINATION TOURNAMENT

Two defeats eliminate an entry in this tournament. The losers in the first rounds move into the losers' bracket. The teams which advance farthest in either bracket meet each other in the final game. Should the winner of the losers' bracket defeat the winner of the first round bracket, the teams are rematched for the championship when one team will have lost two games.

Byes are distributed in the first round of the original elimination brackets as in a single elimination tournament, but in the first round of the losers' brackets byes must be arranged to avoid giving a second bye to an entry that has already had a bye. Also, at all stages of the losers' bracket, avoid pairing entries that have met in earlier rounds, if possible.

This type tournament is seldom used unless the entries are eight or less in number. If more than eight entries, double the process and the two winners meet for the title.

Formula for total number of games, with N representing Number of entries: 2(N-1)=Minimum Games to Play; 2(N-1)+1=Maximum Games to Play.

TYPES OF TOURNAMENT DRAWINGS

There are several different kinds of bracket arrangements that may be used in conducting tournament competition and the type of elimination is usually determined by several factors: (1) The type of activity. (2) The number of entries. (3) The amount of playing time. (4) Playing space and equipment. (5) Age of participants. (6) Officials available.

With a large number of entries it is sometimes desirable to run a combination tournament. For example: A double elimination—single elimination tournament. The winners of the double elimination brackets compete in a single elimination tournament to determine the ultimate champion.

Number of Byes. The first step before making a drawing for the bracket arrangement is to determine the number of entries.

When the number of competitors is 4, 8, 16, 32, 64 or 128, or any higher power of "2," they shall meet in pairs. When the number of competitors is not a power of "2" there shall be byes in the first round. For example: If there are 13 entries, a bracket of 16 with three byes is required. The purpose of having byes is to bring into the second round a number of competitors that is a power of "2." To determine the number of byes subtract the number of competitors from the next higher power of "2"; to determine the number of competitors in the first round subtract the number of byes from the total number of competitors. If the byes are an even number one half of them shall be placed at the top of the draw and one half at the bottom of the draw; if they are unevenly numbered there should be one more bye at the bottom than the top. The byes at the top half shall be the names first drawn. The next names drawn shall be placed in the first round. The byes in the bottom half are drawn last.

Seeding the Draw. It is a common practice to select the best teams or individuals and place them in the bracket so that they will not meet in the early rounds of the play. Two or more entries may be seeded—usually the four best are selected in a sixteen bracket and eight in a thirty-two name bracket. The seeded entrants are usually placed in the 1st, 5th, 9th, 13th, etc., bracket positions. The No. 1 and 4 seeded teams are generally placed in the first and fifth positions of the top bracket and the No. 2 and 3 seeded teams in the ninth and thirteenth positions of the lower bracket; or No. 1 and 3 in the upper with No. 2 and 4 seeded teams in the lower half.

CONSOLATION TOURNAMENT

There are two types in general use: The consolation type tournament is generally used only when the number of entries is 8 or 16. In No. I bracket arrangement only the losers in the first round of play compete for consolation title. In No. II, the losers in all the rounds except the final of the upper bracket compete for 3rd and 4th place.

In both tournaments every team plays at least two games before being eliminated.

SINGLE ELIMINATION TOURNAMENT

If the contestants are of equal strength or their strength is not known, have a drawing for positions in the bracket. If the strength is known, seed the best teams so they will not meet in the early rounds. Place the seeded entries in the 1st, 5th, 9th, 13th, etc., positions.

All BYES must occur in the first round of play. The total number of games played is always one less than the number of entries. To determine the number of games that the winner would have to play count the powers of two in the number of entries, e. g., with 32 entries the winner plays 5 games.

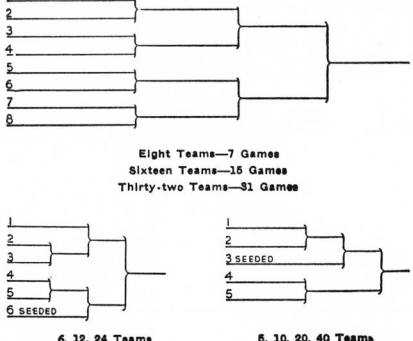

(From *Athletic Field and Court Diagrams;* courtesy Lowe and Campbell Athletic Goods, Kansas City, Mo.)

HEALTH AND ADAPTED PHYSICAL EDUCATION FORMS

The following forms and records have been selected from the authors' files. School systems across the country which developed these forms are to be commended for their work.

CODE:
- \+ Slight/Mild 1
- \++ Moderate 2
- \+++ Severe 3
- R Right
- L Left

Examining Doctor	GRADE	AGE	Forward Head	Head Tilt	Forward Shoulder	High Shoulder	Body Torque	Body List	Kyphosis	Scoliosis	Lordosis	Pelvic Tilt	Tibial Torsion	Knock-Knee	Bowleg	Hyperextended Knee	Pronation	Flatfeet	Obesity	General Faulty Posture	Psychological	Refer Private Physician	Special Class	Regular Class	SCHOOL / DATE / REMARKS
1.																									
2.																									
3.																									
4.																									
5.																									
6.																									
7.																									
8.																									
9.																									
10.																									
11.																									
12.																									
13.																									
14.																									
15.																									

:ma - 2/14/63:500

Health Service
HEALTH CONSULTATION REQUEST

Date_____19 __

We are requesting the examination of

_____   _____
Name   School

because of the following causes:

_____

_____

_____

_____
Signature

_____
Position

(Front)

The findings of our examination of the bearer are_____

_____

_____

_____

Recommendation_____

_____

_____

_____M. D.
Director of Health Service

(Back)

SPECIAL ADAPTATION FOR PHYSICAL EDUCATION PROGRAM

All pupils registered in the schools of New York State are required by the Education Law to attend courses of instruction in physical education. These courses are required to be adapted to meet the needs and/or improve his condition.

The physical education program is flexible, involving many forms of indoor and out-door activities. The following is a general list of activities included in the physical education program at the Rye High School during the school year:

___Football	___Touch Football	___LaCrosse	___Soccer
___Basketball	___Volleyball	___Softball	___Speedball
___Pole Vaulting	___Weight Lifting	___Baseball	___Wrestling
___Archery	___Tennis	___Apparatus	___Swimming
___Calisthenics	___Free Exercises	___Mimetics	___Self-testing Stunts
___Trampoline	___Tumbling	___Track	___Badminton
___Running Games	___Bowling	___Shot Put	___Golf
___Square Dancing	___Rhythms and Dances		___Social Dancing

THE EXAMINING PHYSICIAN WILL RECOMMEND THE ABOVE ACTIVITIES IN WHICH YOU MAY PARTICIPATE BY A (✓) MARK.

(Front)

TO THE EXAMINING PHYSICIAN: This pupil has come to you for
( )   Evaluation of a known condition
( )   Recheck of a known condition
( )   Care of a current condition

In order that we may best meet the present needs of this pupil, please fill out both sides of this card and return it to the SCHOOL NURSE TEACHER at the Rye High School.

Pupil's Name_____ Date _____

Findings:

This is to certify that I have examined the above pupil and recommend adaptation to the physical education program as indicated on the reverse side of this card for the period checked below.

	Weeks	Months	Indefinitely	School year
( ) No restrictions				
( ) Partial restrictions	___	___	___	___
( ) Total restrictions	___	___	___	___

Comments:

Signature of Examining Physician_____Tel. No._____
Note: This report will be attached to the pupil's school health record and a duplicate made for the physical education office.

(Back)

Adviser_____

Student_____

      Please report at the Nurse's Office as
soon as possible regarding:_____

_____

                       Thank you,

                   _____R.N.

                   _____R.N.

Date_____

GIRLS' GYM

      Please excuse_____,

adviser _____ from showers because

of _____

until _____

      She is under treatment _____. She is

not under treatment _____. Thank you.

                _____

Date _____

(Courtesy Girls' Physical Education Department, New Trier Township High School, Winnetka, Ill.)

_____Teacher_____

JUNIOR HIGH SCHOOL GROWTH RECORD

_____ School_____ Year _____ Date

HEALTH, SAFETY AND PHYSICAL EDUCATION	NOV.	JAN.	APR.	JUNE
1. Shows cooperative spirit				
2. Respects personal and public property				
3. Recognizes and accepts responsibility				
4. Is courteous				
5. Makes good use of time and materials				
6. Uses health knowledge				
7. Practices safety				
8. Shows skill in activities				
9. Shows leadership				

(Front)

Department of Physical Education
PUPIL EXERCISE CARD

Name _____Date_____Period_____

1. _____
2. _____
3. _____
4. _____
5. _____
6. _____
7. _____
8. _____
9. _____
10. _____

(Front)

HEIGHT AND WEIGHT CARD

Name_____ Teacher_____ Period_____

Grade _____

Date			Date										
Age			Weight										
Height			— + %										
Weight			Date										
Average			Weight										
— + %			— + %										

Remarks:

PHYSICAL EXAMINATION PERMIT

(This appointment must be kept. No excuse will be considered adequate.)

Adviser_____ Date_____

_____

is to be excused from class at_____ to have a physical examination.

Boys report to the training room in the gym. Girls report to the Nurse's Office, room 205.

Time student completed examination__

Released by:_____

Time student returned to class_____

Signature of teacher_____

_____

The teacher who receives this permit should return it to the adviser who should check to see that the time interval is reasonable.

(Courtesy Health Department, New Trier Township High School, Winnetka, Ill.)

DEPARTMENT OF PHYSICAL EDUCATION FOR GIRLS

Dear Parent:

       For many years, the Girls' Health and Physical Educa-
tion Department has had a policy to protect the eyes of those
girls who wear glasses. It has been our practice to ask the
girl to remove the glasses. However, if the use of the glasses
makes a great deal of difference, we ask the girl to protect
her glasses and her eyes by wearing glasses guards. Unfortunately,
since these guards are not things of beauty nor comfortable to
wear, we do have an occasional student who refuses to wear them.
In such instances we have taken particular care to explain the
reasons for the policy and why it is important. The answer
usually is that the student will take full responsibility for
any accident which might occur; obviously, however, this is no
substitute for protection.

       We want you to understand our policies in protecting
students' eyes and ask you to urge your daughter to cooperate
in wearing glasses guards for her own protection. You will
agree, we believe, that we have tried to take every precaution.

       We are sure that you understand our position and that
you will urge your daughter to take advantage of the protection
which is provided.

                         Yours very truly,

                         Instructor, Girls' Health and
                         Physical Education Department

NAME_____
Last   First

BODY MECHANICS INSPECTION CARD — GIRLS

School

Living with Parents?_____
(Yes - No)

Grade	B	A	B	A	B	A
Date (Begin. of Sem.)						
Age (Yrs. & Mo. - 14*)						
Height (Inches)						
Weight						
Average Weight						
— or + %						
Constipation						
Menses: Reg. - Days						
Dysmenorrhea						
Foot Inspection						
Swim. — Physician's Recommendation						
Current History (Illness, etc.)						
Physician's Recommendation						
Correction Needed						
Remarks						

PREVIOUS HISTORY
(Age or Date)

Menses Onset...................

Accidents, Operations,
Serious Illness, etc.

Feet						
Body Alignment						
Miscellaneous						
Posture Test Grade						

CODE: 1st Sem. — B = Blue Pencil
2nd Sem. — A = Red Pencil

DEVIATION FROM NORMAL — 1. Slight
(Red or Blue Lines & Marks)   2. Medium
3. Severe

(Front)

	B	A	B	A	B	A
Health Instruction						
First Aid Record						
Swim Test						
Physical Education Record						
Miscellaneous Record						
Assigned to: Class Instructor Period						
Withdrawn (Mo. & Yr.)						

Junior High Honor
Health Club

Notes:

(Back)

THE STATE EDUCATION DEPARTMENT
DIVISION OF HEALTH AND PHYSICAL EDUCATION

FORM FOR USE WHEN MAKING SPECIAL ADAPTATIONS
OF PHYSICAL EDUCATION TO MEET INDIVIDUAL PUPIL NEEDS

....*School*

To Dr .... *Family Physician*   *Date*.............................

Regarding the physical education activities of your patient...,

we shall appreciate your cooperation in filling out this blank and returning it at your earliest

convenience to.., principal of

....school.

All pupils registered in the schools of   are required by the Education Law
to attend courses of instruction in physical education.   These courses are required to be adapted
to meet individual pupil needs.   This means that a pupil who is unable to participate in the
entire program should have his activities modified to meet his needs and/or improve his condition.
Specific activities are provided for children who are below par physically and require special
attention for the following conditions:

(*Check the condition which applies to this pupil*)

.... Postoperative   .... Defective posture (functional)
.... Convalescent   .... Flabby musculature
.... Cardiac   .... Foot defects
.... Faulty nutrition   .... Others (specify)
.... Early fatigue

The following is a general list of activities included in the physical education program:

V	M	N		V	M	N		
....	....	.... Apparatus						
....	....	.... Athletics		....	....	.... Swimming		V=Vigorous
....	....	.... Dual combat		....	....	.... Recreational sports		M=Mild
....	....	.... Self-testing stunts		....	....	.... Marching tactics		N=None
....	....	.... Calisthenics and free exercises		....		.... Quiet games		
....	....	.... Mimetics		....		.... Corrective exercises		
....	....	.... Rhythms and dances		....		.... Rest		
....	....	.... Running games				....		

This is to certify that I have examined..
and recommend that he should participate only in the activities that are checked above for a
period of................weeks.

Remarks : ....

....

....   *Date*.............................
           Family Physician

NOTE.   This report will be attached to the child's school health record and a duplicate made for the
physical education office.

DEPARTMENT OF PHYSICAL EDUCATION FOR GIRLS

To the Examining Physician:

The administration of our high school wishes to cooperate with the family physician in its endeavor to provide the girls of the school with healthy and well-coordinated bodies. We feel that our physical education program is sufficiently flexible and broad enough in its scope to provide each student who is physically capable of attending school with some form of beneficial exercise.

There will naturally be some students in whom a period of rest alone is advisable. However, these should be extremely few in number. In our restricted physical education classes rest, relaxation, mild games, and posture work are stressed, and it is possible to adapt the work to the individual's strength.

Our department of physical education would greatly appreciate any suggestions that the physician has to offer and would welcome the privilege of conferring with him concerning the beneficial possibilities of their program in building the strength of his patient.

In order that the school may fulfill its purpose, we are asking all physicians whose patients are physically unable to participate in our physical education program or need their activity limited to fill out the accompanying blank.

We greatly appreciate your help and cooperation.

Yours very sincerely,

Superintendent

(Courtesy Girls' Physical Education Department, New Trier Township High School, Winnetka, Ill.)

DEPARTMENT OF PHYSICAL EDUCATION FOR GIRLS

Name_____, _____ Adviser_____
      (Last)   (First)

I have examined the above-named student and recommend that she be allowed
to participate only in those activities which have not been crossed out.

A. Strenuous	B. Intermediate	C. Mild
Basketball	Badminton	Archery
Field hockey	Baseball	Corrective or posture
Games--relay races	Corecreational games	exercises
Intramural swimming	Deck tennis	Restricted class
Lacrosse	Gymnastic exercises	Croquet
Lifesaving	Horeseback riding	Individual exercises
Rhythmic dancing	Recreational leadership	Modified games
Speedball	Social dance	Quiet social games
	Swimming	Relaxation
	Tennis	Table tennis
		Walking

If the condition of the above-named student is such at the present time
that complete rest is desirable during physical education classes, please
indicate this and the number of days for which the student should continue
in rest._____

Up to the date of_____, please restrict this student's activities as indicated above. She is under my care for_____.
                                                      (Ailment)

I would further like to suggest that the Department of Physical Education
could contribute to the well-being of this girl in the following manner:
_____

_____

                         Signed_____
                                   (Examining Physician)

                         Address_____

Date_____   Telephone_____

(Courtesy Girls' Physical Education Department, New Trier Township High School, Winnetka,
Ill.)

DEPARTMENT OF HEALTH AND PHYSICAL EDUCATION FOR BOYS

Student's name_____Address_____Telephone_____

Adviser_____

The range and latitude of the health and physical education program at our
high school is so varied that every pupil able to be in school should derive
benefit from some phase of this program. Daily classes of 40 minutes, with
about 15 minutes for undressing, showers, and dressing, leaves 25 minutes for
actual activity.

Please check (✓) either generally or individually the types of physical
education which you recommend for this pupil.

STRENUOUS( )	MODERATE ( )	MILD ( )
__ Basketball	__ Bag punching	__ Badminton practice
__ Boxing	__ Club swinging	__ Corrective exercises
__ Calisthenics	__ Practice hand ball	__ Free throwing
__ Hand ball	__ Running and walking	__ Horseshoes
__ Commando course	__ Shooting baskets	__ Playing catch
__ Rope climbing	__ Swimming (noncompetitive)	__ Swimming (recreational)
__ Running half mile	__ Table tennis	__ Tennis practice
__ Soccer	__ Tennis practice	__ Throwing at target
__ Swimming (competitive)	__ Tossing medicine balls	__ Walking
__ Tumbling--gymnastics	__ Touch football	__ _____
__ Wrestling	__ Volley ball	__ _____
__ _____	__ _____	__ _____

If the condition of this student is such at present that complete rest (re-
cumbent position in bed) is desirable during his physical education class
period, please indicate this and give the number of days he should continue
these supervised rest periods._____

If any other information should be given for the welfare of this boy, add same
here or feel free to call Mr._____ any school day at the high school,
Central 1-2400.
_____
_____

Up to the date of_____please restrict this student's activities as
indicated above. He is under my care for_____
_____

                              Signed_____
                                         (Examining Physician)

                              Address_____

Date_____   Telephone_____

(Courtesy Boys' Physical Education Department, New Trier Township High School, Winnetka, Ill.)

DEPARTMENT OF PHYSICAL EDUCATION FOR BOYS

_____ _____ _____ _____ _____
(Last name)   (First name)   (Adviser)   (Form secured) (Form returned)

Physician's <u>Partial</u> <u>or</u> <u>Complete</u> <u>Waiver</u> <u>for</u> <u>Swimming</u>

I have examined the above-named boy and recommend that his swimming be restricted as indicated below (please check):

The present required physical education swimming program for this boy includes every_____ within the following dates:_____

This boy may engage in STRENUOUS ( ) MODERATE ( ) MILD RECREATIONAL ( ) swimming, but

He should not dive. ....( )

He should not put his head under water. .....( )

He may swim but should wear a nose clip. ....( )

This boy should NOT participate in any swimming. ....( )

Please list any other restrictions and <u>reasons</u> for same with <u>time</u> involved so that a program may be arranged to his advantage.
_____
_____
_____
_____

Signed_____ Telephone_____ _____ Date_____
      (Physician)   (Exchange)   (Number)

To <u>Be</u> <u>Filled</u> <u>Out</u> <u>By</u> <u>Student</u>

Have you participated in swimming classes previously at this school?_____

Check below the approximate distance you are now capable of swimming:

None ....( )

One length of pool, 25 yd. ....( )

Two lengths of pool..........................( )

100 yd. or more ....( )

Signed_____
      (Student)

Note: Nonswimmers are often admitted to the pool from three to five times per week with individual help, resulting in rapid improvement. We live in an area where swimming is almost a "must" for fun, health, and safety. Don't miss this wonderful opportunity.

This form, properly filled out and signed, is to be returned to the BOYS' HEALTH OFFICE.

(Courtesy Boys' Physical Education Department, New Trier Township High School, Winnetka, Ill.)

GIRLS' HEALTH AND PHYSICAL EDUCATION DEPARTMENT

Name_____ Date_____

Homeroom_____ R_____ S_____

A notification has been received from the Health Service which specifies that your classification for participation in physical education and G.A.A. intramurals is the following:

Classification	Activity Requirements
_____ A	Regular physical education--no limitation in G.A.A. intramurals
_____ B	Regular physical education--no G.A.A. intramural participation without special permission from Health Service
_____ Special	Assigned to special class which does not have activities demanding strenuous or prolonged exertion--no G.A.A. intramurals without special permission from Health Service
_____ Rest	Assigned to rest in Health Service--no G.A.A. intramurals
_____ Dropped	No physical education; program changed, to report to homeroom--no G.A.A. intramurals without special permission from Health Service
_____ No physical education until further notice	Excused temporarily and to report to homeroom--no G.A.A. intramurals without special permission from Health Service

If your classification is anything except "A" you are not to participate in any G.A.A. intramural activities after school unless special permission is granted by the Health Service. This is your official and latest classification and is now in effect.

Chairman, Girls' Health and
Physical Education Department

PHYSICAL EDUCATION ACTIVITY, SKILL, AND SQUAD FORMS

The following forms and records have been selected from the authors' files. School systems across the country which developed these forms are to be commended for their work.

Co-Educational P. E.

| Last Name | First Name | | Period | Section | Standing |

INDICATE YOUR CHOICE (1 for first, 2 for second, etc.)

10th Grade	11th Grade	12th Grade
	Badm't'n & P'g P'g - _____	Archery - - - - _____
Dancing - - - - _____		
	Dancing - - - - _____	Badm't'n & P'g P'g - _____
Sports - - - - _____		Dancing - - - - _____
	Sports - - - - _____	
		Sports - - - - _____
_____ - - - _____	_____ - - - _____	Tennis - - - - _____
_____ - - - _____	_____ - - - _____	_____ - - - _____

Front

PHYSICAL EDUCATION DEPARTMENT

BASKET CARD

SCHOOL_____ HOMEROOM_____

BASKET NUMBER

(READ OTHER SIDE)   PUPIL'S SIGNATURE

PHYSICAL EDUCATION DEPARTMENT

PUPIL RECORD CARD

NUMBER_____ ROOM_____
BASKET_____ PERIOD_____
SQUAD_____   GRADE_____
NAME_____ (LAST) (FIRST) TEACHER_____
ADDRESS_____ (PRINT) TELEPHONE_____
PARENT'S NAME_____ (LAST)
AGE_____ HEIGHT_____ WEIGHT_____ CLASSIFICATION_____
YEARS MONTHS INCHES

DAILY RECORD — MAXIMUM 45 POINTS

DATES	1	2	3											TOTALS
45 40 35 30 25 20 15 10 5														

EVALUATION

ACTIVITY EVALUATION   HEALTH INSTRUCTION EVALUATION
ORIENTATION OR PROGRESS   OBJECTIVE OR SUBJECTIVE   TERM

SIX WEEKS   SIX WEEKS   SIX WEEKS   SIX WEEKS   SIX WEEKS   SIX WEEKS

(Front)

Back

IMPORTANT

1. Don't lose this card. Keep in wallet.
2. Report loss of card to Instructor immediately.
3. Don't lend card to anyone.
4. Always present card for equipment.
5. Remember! The roll is checked by this card.

TESTS

MAXIMUM SCORE 15   SELECT 3 SKILLS
(AVERAGE OR ABOVE: 5 POINTS; BELOW: 1 POINT)

SKILLS	TESTS	POINTS	SKILLS	TESTS	POINTS
PUSH-UP			FOUL SHOT		
PULL-UP			V. BALL SERVE		
SIT-UP (MIN.)			B. BALL THROW		
PASS (YDS.)			POT. RACE		
PUNT (YDS.)			40-YD. DASH		
GOALS (MIN.)			TENNIS SERVE		
ST. BRD. JUMP			GOLF PUTT		
SHOT (8 LBS.)			STEADINESS		
DASH (50 YDS.)			DEPTH PER.		
R. BRD. JUMP			REACTION		
GRIP—R. H.			FIELD VISION		
GRIP—L. H.					

SKILL TOTAL (MAXIMUM 15 POINTS)	
HEALTH TEST OR TEAM PLAY TOTAL (MAX. 40 PTS.)	
DAILY RECORD TOTAL (MAXIMUM 45 POINTS)	
GRADE TOTAL	

SPORTS PREFERENCES   SPECIAL COMMENTS

SPORTS	CHOICE 1	2	3
TRACK			
GOLF			
BADMINTON			
VOLLEY BALL			
SOFT BALL			
T. FT. B.			
TENNIS			
WRESTLING			
DANCING			
ARCHERY			
TABLE TENNIS			
BASKETBALL			
TUMBLING			
SHUFFLEBOARD			
HORSESHOES			
CROQUET			

(Back)

FORM NO. 246BX

Name...................................
(Last)   (First)   (Second)

(Adviser)

Home
Address................................   Home
(No.)   (Street)   (Village)   Tel. No.................

NEW TRIER TOWNSHIP HIGH SCHOOL
WINNETKA, ILLINOIS

BOYS' PHYSICAL EDUCATION RECORD

Name of { Parent*
          or
          Guardian* } ....
*Cross out one   (Last)   (First)   (Second)

Business Address.........................
(No.)   (Street)   (City)

(Name of Firm)   (Bus. Tel. No.)

Parent's
Occupation...........................   Family
          Physician.....................

Birth...........................   Place of
(Month) (Day) (Year)   Birth...........................
          (City)   (State)

How far can you swim? Check distance: Not at all ☐ 25 yards ☐ 100 yards ☐

YR.	DATES FOR ENTRANCE, ETC.	SEM.	PERIOD	CR.	REASON
FRESHMAN	ENT.	1			ADEQ. ABS. / MU'S.
		2			INADEQ. ABS. / ADEQ. ABS. / MU'S. / INADEQ. ABS.
SOPHOMORE	ENT.	1			ADEQ. ABS. / MU'S.
		2			INADEQ. ABS. / ADEQ. ABS. / MU'S. / INADEQ. ABS.
JUNIOR	ENT.	1			ADEQ. ABS. / MU'S.
		2			INADEQ. ABS. / ADEQ. ABS. / MU'S. / INADEQ. ABS.
SENIOR	ENT.	1			ADEQ. ABS. / MU'S.
		2			INADEQ. ABS. / ADEQ. ABS. / MU'S. / INADEQ. ABS.

	FRESHMAN	SOPHOMORE	JUNIOR	SENIOR
AWARDS INTER-SCHOL-ASTIC				
DATES FOR NOTES SEE BACK FOR DETAILS				

				S I G N A L S

LAST NAME	FIRST	SECOND	ADVISER		
				DUPLICATE NAME	WAIVER	WITHDRAWN
				RED	PURPLE	BLACK

ARE YOU READY FOR 7th GRADE PHYSICAL EDUCATION?

NAMES	SOCCER SKILLS	VOLLEYBALL SKILLS	FOLK DANCE SKILLS	SQUARE DANCE SKILLS	GYMNASTIC SKILLS	BASKETBALL SKILLS	TRACK SKILLS	SOFTBALL SKILLS	FOOTBALL SKILLS			

Name						Date of Birth			Date of Entry		

PHYSICAL EDUCATION RECORD — GIRLS

Address			New Address				New Address				
Grade	7	8	9	10	11	12	Grade	7	8	9	10	11	12
Teacher's Initials							Absences						
Citizenship							Excuses						
Preparation							Medical						
Class Work							Grade		COMMENTS				
Leadership							7						
Rhythms — Modern Dance													
Square & Folk Dance													
Social Dance							8						
Tap Dance													
Athletic Games — Basketball													
Field Hockey							9						
Soccer & Speedball													
Softball													
Volleyball							10						
App., Stunts, Tumb.													
Aquatics													
Archery							11						
Badminton & Tennis													
Adapted Activities							12						
Intramurals							Grade	7	8	9	10	11	12
Tests — Standing Broad Jump							Height						
Chins (Reg. or Mod.)							Weight						
Get up—Pick up													
Burpee							Final Gr.						

DEPARTMENT OF PHYSICAL EDUCATION
JUNIOR HIGH POINT CARD - GIRLS

NAME_____JUNIOR HIGH SCHOOL

			DATE	ATHLETIC ACTIVITY								SUMMER PLAYGROUNDS	LEADERSHIP									GRADE A IN P. E. CLASS	HEALTH								RUNNING TOTAL	GRAND TOTAL
				VOLLEY BALL	BASKET BALL	SOCCER	SPEED BALL	SOFT BALL	OTHER ACTIVITIES	OTHER ACTIVITIES	OTHER ACTIVITIES		GAA PRES.	GAA ASSTS.	COLOR CAPT.	SQUAD LEADER	MONITOR	OFFICIALS	TEAM CAPT.	CHAMPIONSHIP TEAMS	CHAMPIONSHIP TEAMS		ORTHOPEDICS	HONOR HEALTH CLUB	BEG. ARC	INTER. ARC	SWIMMER ARC	ADV. SWIM. ARC	J.A.R.C. LIFE SAVING		
CERTIFICATE																															
EMBLEM																															
CHEVRONS																															
LETTER																															
STARS																															
YR.	TCH.	GRADE																													
		7B																													
		7A																													
		8B																													
		8A																													
		9B																													
		9A																													

1000 POINTS_____

MEET _____ DATE_____ EVENT_____

FIELD EVENT REPORT CARD

JUDGE _____

SIGNED

NO.	NAME	AFF.	FT.	IN.	FT.	IN.	FT.	IN.	FT.	IN.	FT.	IN.	FT.	IN.	FT.	IN.	Best Effort FT.	IN.	PLACE

PHYSICAL EDUCATION RECORD

Name　　　　　　　　　　　　　　　　　　　　**Counselor**

Grade Year	Class	Per	Teacher	Health Finding	Date	Recommendation	Correction	G. A. A.

Remarks:

SENIOR SCHOOL GOAL SHEET

Pupil's Name ....

SKILLS — ATHLETIC AND GYMNASIUM (Boys)

Seventh Grade 19____ 19____	Eighth Grade 19____ 19____	Ninth Grade 19____ 19____
Gymnastic Skills Can do in good form—	**Can do in good form—**	**Gymnastic Skills** Can do in good form—
1. Forward roll _____	1. Handstand against wall _____	1. Spinning wheel _____
2. Backward roll _____	2. Cart Wheel _____	2. Hand spring _____
3. Head Stand _____	3. Handspring, with mat _____	3. Touch tow jump _____
4. Full squat _____	4. Forward roll, over 2 men _____	4. Forward roll — over 3 men _____
5. Double forward roll _____	5. Rope climb, using feet _____	5. Rope Climb — without feet _____
6. Walk balance beam forward _____	6. Standing rope jump _____	6. Fence vault shoulder high _____
backward _____	7. Running high dive Chest high _____	7. Running rope jump _____
7. Half lever rings _____	8. Support half lever parallel bars _____	8. Cut off on bars _____
8. Running high dive _____	9. Complete Pirouette _____	9. Cut off on rings _____
9. Travel on bars _____		10. Travel 7 rings _____
10. One leg squat _____	10. _____	11. Inverted push up against wall _____
11. _____	11. _____	12. Double knee circle horizontal bar _____
12. _____	12. _____	13. _____
		14. _____
Athletic Skills **Football**	**Athletic Skills** **Football**	**Athletic Skills** **Football — Accuracy**
Drop kick ____ ft.	Center ball — 5 yds. 5/6 _____	Drop kick 3/6 _____
Place kick ____ ft.	Center ball — 8 yds. 4/6 _____	Place kick 3/6 _____
Forward pass ____ ft.	Catch punts _____	Forward pass 3/6 _____
Punt ____ ft.	**Defensive formations**	Punt 3/6 _____
Basketball	7-2-2 _____	
Push pass _____	6-3-2 _____	**Basketball**
One hand pass _____	**Offensive Formations** Single wing back _____	Foul shot 5/10 _____
Bounce pass _____	Double wing back _____	Goal Shots 7 in 30 seconds _____
One hand bounce pass _____	T formation _____	
Push shot _____	**Soccer**	**Boxing**
Foul shot _____	Dribble and pass _____	Stance — on guard _____
Volleyball	**Basketball**	Shifting of feet _____
Serve _____	Properly executes Reverse pivot _____	Left lead to body, and guard _____
Return _____	Dribble and shoot _____	Left lead to head, and guard _____
Baseball	**Wrestling**	Box 2 — 1 minute rounds _____
Throws ball correctly _____	Standing position _____	
Catches ball correctly _____	Take-downs _____	**Track**
Track	Pinning holds _____	Run — 50 yds. 7 2/5 sec. _____
Start _____	Wrestle — 3 minutes _____	Running broad jump, 13' _____
High jump ____ft. ____in.	**Baseball**	Running high jump, 3'9" _____
Broad jump ____ft. ____in.	Bunt and run _____	Discus throw 50" _____
Shot put ____ft. ____in.	Run bases against time _____	Shot put (8 lb.) 28' _____
Baton passing _____	Accurate base throwing _____	Organizes and officiates at a team game _____
Sprint _____		
Distance _____		
Push ups _____	Time of running _____	Time of running _____
Push ups _____	Time of running _____	Time of running _____
Push ups _____	Time of running _____	Time of running _____
Push ups _____		

BP-1M-10-51

WATER POLO

REFEREE_____

TIMER_____ DATE_____

TEAM_____ Classification_____

NUMBER	NAME	POSITION	GOAL ATTEMPTS	GOAL ASSISTS	FOULS	GOALS			
						1st QTR.	2nd QTR.	3rd QTR.	4th QTR.
		LF							
		RF							
		CF							
		CB							
		LG							
		RG							
		G							
	TOTALS								

SCORE BY PERIODS	1st	2nd	3rd	4th

RUNNING SCORE _____

SCORECARD

GOAL SCORERS
1._____
2._____

PLACE_____

TEAM_____ Classification_____

NUMBER	NAME	POSITION	GOAL ATTEMPTS	GOAL ASSISTS	FOULS	GOALS			
						QTR.	2nd QTR.	3rd QTR.	4th QTR.
		LF							
		RF							
		CF							
		CB							
		LG							
		RG							
		G							
	TOTALS								

GOALKEEPER SAVES	1st	2nd	3rd	4th

1	2	3	4	5	6	7	8	9	10	11	12	13	14	15	16	17	18	19	20	21	22	23	24	25	26
1	2	3	4	5	6	7	8	9	10	11	12	13	14	15	16	17	18	19	20	21	22	23	24	25	26

(Front)

ENTRY BLANK AND ANNOUNCER'S FORM

DIVING ORDER_____ CLASSIFICATION_____

NAME _____

AFFILIATION _____

	GROUP NUMBER	DIVE NUMBER	TAKE OFF	DESCRIPTION	POSITION	BOARD	DEGREE OF DIFFICULTY
1							
2							
3							
4							
5							
6							
7							
8							
9							
10							

DIVING SCORING FORM

DIVING ORDER_____ CLASSIFICATION_____

NAME _____

AFFILIATION _____

	DESCRIPTION OF DIVE	JUDGES' AWARDS			TOTAL AWARDS	DEGREE OF DIFFICULTY	FINAL POINT
		JUDGE No. 1	JUDGE No. 2	JUDGE No. 3			
1							
2							
3							
4							
5							
6							
7							
8							
9							
10							

RECORDER_____ PLACE_____

(Back)

ACCIDENT FORMS

The following forms and records have been selected from the authors' files. School systems across the country which developed these forms are to be commended for their work.

GIRLS' HEALTH AND PHYSICAL EDUCATION DEPARTMENT

Re: Accident Report

Student injured_____ H.R._____

Date of injury_____ Time_____

Description of important details of accident:

Treatment or care by Health Service, if any:

Instructor or coach's follow-up:

(Signed)_____

(Use reverse side if additional space is necessary.)

STANDARD STUDENT ACCIDENT REPORT FORM
Part A. Information on ALL Accidents

1. Name: _____ Home Address: _____
2. School _____ Sex· M ☐; F ☐. Age: ____ Grade or classification: _____
3. Time accident occurred Hour _____ A.M., _____ P.M. Date: _____
4. Place of Accident   School Building ☐   School Grounds ☐   To or from School ☐   Home ☐   Elsewhere ☐

NATURE OF INJURY 5.			**DESCRIPTION OF THE ACCIDENT**

5. **NATURE OF INJURY**

Abrasion	____	Fracture	____
Amputation	____	Laceration	____
Asphyxiation	____	Poisoning	____
Bite	____	Puncture	____
Bruise	____	Scalds	____
Burn	____	Scratches	____
Concussion	____	Shock (el.)	____
Cut	____	Sprain	____
Dislocation	____		
Other (specify) _____			

DESCRIPTION OF THE ACCIDENT

How did accident happen? What was student doing? Where was student? List specifically unsafe acts and unsafe conditions existing. Specify any tool, machine or equipment involved. _____

PART OF BODY INJURED

Abdomen	____	Foot	____
Ankle	____	Hand	____
Arm	____	Head	____
Back	____	Knee	____
Chest	____	Leg	____
Ear	____	Mouth	____
Elbow	____	Nose	____
Eye	____	Scalp	____
Face	____	Tooth	____
Finger	____	Wrist	____
Other (specify) _____			

6. Degree of Injury: Death ☐ Permanent Impairment ☐ Temporary Disability ☐ Nondisabling ☐
7. Total number of days lost from school: _____ (To be filled in when student returns to school)

Part B. Additional Information on School Jurisdiction Accidents

8. Teacher in charge when accident occurred (Enter name) _____
   Present at scene of accident: No· _____ Yes: _____

9. **IMMEDIATE ACTION TAKEN**

First-aid treatment	____	By (Name): _____
Sent to school nurse	____	By (Name): _____
Sent home	____	By (Name): _____
Sent to physician	____	By (Name): _____
		Physician's Name: _____
Sent to hospital	____	By (Name): _____
		Name of hospital: _____

10. Was a parent or other individual notified? No.___ Yes.___ When._____ How·._____
    Name of individual notified: _____
    By whom? (Enter name): _____
11. Witnesses· 1. Name: _____ Address: _____
    2. Name· _____ Address: _____

12. **LOCATION**

Specify Activity		Specify Activity		Remarks
Athletic field	_____	Locker	_____	What recommendations do you have for preventing other accidents of this type? _____
Auditorium	_____	Pool	_____	
Cafeteria	_____	Sch. grounds	_____	
Classroom	_____	_____ shop	_____	
Corridor	_____	Showers	_____	
Dressing room	_____	Stairs	_____	
Gymnasium	_____	Toilets and		
Home Econ.	_____	washrooms	_____	
Laboratories	_____	Other (specify)	_____	

Signed: Principal: _____ Teacher: _____

(National Safety Council—Form School 1)   Printed in U.S.A. Rep. 200M—25302

REPORT OF INJURY OR ACCIDENT OCCURRING ON SCHOOL PROPERTY

School_____   Note: 5 reports should be made out:
                                    3 copies for Superintendent's
Date_____   office, 1 copy for Medical Office,
                                    and 1 copy to be kept at the school.
Time_____

Name of pupil_____   Age_____ Reporting Room_____

Address_____

Description of place where accident occurred:_____

State briefly but completely what happened, giving names of witnesses,
addresses and signatures, if possible:_____
_____
_____
_____

Description of injury:_____
_____
_____

By whom was aid rendered?_____

When and how were parents informed?_____

Disposition of case (home, hospital, etc.):_____

Method of transportation:_____

When was attending physician called?_____ At whose request_____

Name of physician:_____

                    Signature_____

SUBSEQUENT REPORT: By whom?_____ Date_____

When did pupil return to school duties?_____

Extracurricular activities of pupil:_____

        (a) Before accident:_____

        (b) After accident:_____

                    Signature_____

PHYSICAL EDUCATION TEST AND ACHIEVEMENT FORMS

The following forms and records have been selected from the authors' files. School systems across the country which developed these forms are to be commended for their work.

PHYSICAL FITNESS PENTATHLON

SCHOOL	
AVALON	POLY
DEWEY	WILSON
JORDAN	

LAST NAME · FIRST · IN

No.	Inst.	Pd.	Stand. Broad	Score	Rope Climb	Score	300 Run	Score	Bar Snap	Score		Score	Ht.	Wt.	Age	Exp.	Class	Total Score	Gr.
1																			
2																			
3																			
4																			
5																			
6																			
7																			
8																			
9																			
10																			
11																			
12																			

STANDARD PERFORMANCE

Class	Minimum	Average	Superior	Excellent
A	200	255	295	375
B	190	240	280	360
C	180	230	270	350
D	170	220	260	340

AVERAGE SCORE · **DATE**

Sophomore Yr.		
Junior Yr.		
Senior Yr.		

Decathlon Record Card

BOYS' PHYSICAL EDUCATION

Last Name   First   Initial   Date Enrolled   Grade

GRADE		AGE	WEIGHT	HEIGHT	SEMESTER	SHOT PUT	BROAD JUMP	DASH (75)	BASKETBALL	BASEBALL	FOOTBALL	ROPE CLIMB	CHIN UPS	SHUTTLE	STNDG BD JUMP	COLOR STANDARD	CHIN UPS	CROSS COUNTRY	JUMP - REACH	ROPE CLIMB	SHUTTLE	SIT UPS	INSTRUCTOR NAME:
10	F																						
	C																						
	S																						
	C																						
11	F																						
	C																						
	S																						
	C																						
12	F																						
	C																						
	S																						
	C																						

Medical Recommendations _____

PHYSICAL FITNESS
TEST RECORD
AND
REPORT CARD

....Age................

AAHPER YOUTH FITNESS TEST

FITNESS FOR YOUTH

PARENT'S SIGNATURE

#1 ....

#2 ....

NASHVILLE CITY SCHOOLS

Dear Parent:

The demand that vigorous exercise makes on the heart and other muscles and on the body systems such as lungs, nerves, etc., causes them to grow stronger.

A normal growing child is said to need from two to five hours of exercise every day. The school day is so crowded with other kinds of activity that only a small part of the day is given to physical exercise. Therefore, we are asking your help in giving additional exercise time to your child after school and on weekends.

Usually too many of the child's waking hours are spent sitting, while he eats, listens, reads, rides, watches, writes or waits. The child today is literally staging a sit-down strike right under our noses. You and your child's teacher by working together can provide the time and the activity necessary for the proper growth and development of your child. The teacher will teach the skills, stunts and games and with your encouragement, your child will practice these activities at home together with the active work assignments which we hope you will also provide for their proper development.

Let's work together to put an end to this "sit-down" strike and strengthen our children and the future security of our community and of America.

Respectfully yours,

Robert Dunkerley
Robert Dunkerley
Director of Physical Education

RD:jw

APPROVED: *Wm. Henry Oliver*
Wm. Henry Oliver, Superintendent
Nashville City Schools

PERSONAL DATA

	Trial 1	Trial 2
Age (in months)	_____	_____
Height (in inches)	_____	_____
Weight	_____	_____

	Trial 1 Date:		Trial 2 Date:	
	Raw Score	Precentile Score	Raw Score	Precentile Score
Pull-Ups (Boys)	___ ___	_____	_____	_____
Modified Pull-ups (Girls)	_____	_____	_____	_____
Sit-Ups	_____	_____	_____	_____
Shuttle Run	_____	_____	_____	_____
Standing Broad Jump	_____	_____	_____	_____
50-Yard Dash	_____	_____	_____	_____
Softball Throw	_____	_____	_____	_____
600-Yard Run-Walk	_____			

Teacher Comments: ....

....

....

Parent Comments: ....

....

....

PROFILE RECORD

Percentile — Pull-Ups or Bar Hang, Sit-Ups, Shuttle Run, Standing Broad Jump, 50-Yard Dash, Softball Throw, 600-Yard Run-Walk

Excellent 90-100

Good 65-89

Satisfactory 40-64

Poor 0-39

100 95 90 85 80 75 70 65 60 55 50 45 40 35 30 25 20 15 10 5

Plot your personal graph using the information on opposite page. Use a different color for each trial.

A CITIZENSHIP GUIDE SHEET

The selection shall be based on the service the pupil has rendered to the home room or to the school and on the general quality of his citizenship.

I. Attitudes of cooperation in the home room, classroom, and school
   A. Honesty
      1. Does not cheat during an examination
      2. Can be trusted to handle school funds
      3. Returns lost articles that he finds
      4. Tells the truth regardless of consequences

   B. Loyalty
      1. Does many important little jobs for the good of the school
      2. Behaves publicly in such a manner as to reflect credit to his school

   C. Dependability
      1. Works faithfully at everything he does
      2. Cooperates with teachers in and out of the classroom
      3. Willingly accepts assigned duties

   D. Sportsmanship
      1. Plays fair and square in all situations
      2. Takes defeat without making excuses
      3. Compliments others when they do well
      4. Keeps his temper even when competition is keen

   E. Conduct
      1. Obeys school rules
      2. Accepts deserved punishment without complaint
      3. Admits it when he has done something wrong
      4. Considers the good of the class and does not attempt to monopolize
         the teacher's time or class discussion

   F. Personal attitudes and self-improvement
      1. Makes new students feel welcome
      2. Shows respect to adults and classmates
      3. Has understanding and sympathy for weaknesses and failures of others
      4. Respects his own property, the property of others and of the school
      5. Does his schoolwork to his best ability

II. Activity and voluntary participation in home room and school activities
   A. Interest in service to the school through activities and clubs
   B. Support of home room activities such as parties, meetings, and intramural
      games
   C. Support of worthy causes such as Community Fund, Red Cross Drive,
      Christmas Project, etc.
   D. Support of school functions such as dances, plays, etc.

It is not expected that a pupil should have participated or excelled in all of the above items.

                    Citizenship Committee

NAME (Print)	Last		First				DATE OF BIRTH		Y	M	D	X
Date of Test												
GRADE												
AGE	y	m	y	m	y	m	y	m	y	m	y	m
WEIGHT		—		—		—		—		—		—
HEIGHT		—		—		—		—		—		—
$\left(\frac{Wt.}{10} + Ht.-60\right)$ MULTIPLIER	—		—		—		—		—		—	
PULLUPS		—		—		—		—		—		—
PUSHUPS												
ARM STRENGTH												
LIFT—BACK												
LIFT—LEGS												
GRIP—LEFT												
GRIP—RIGHT												
LUNG CAPACITY												
STRENGTH INDEX												
NORMAL S. I.												
PHYSICAL FITNESS INDEX												
Classification												

REMARKS

(Front)

Date						
SPECIAL NOTATIONS SCHOOL-MED. Examination						
CORRECTIVE DATA						
Weight-(Actual)						
" -(Chart)						
POSTURE						
FOOTBALL						
HOCKEY						
SOCCER						
BASKETBALL						
BASEBALL						
TRACK—FIELD						
TENNIS						
ARCHERY						
SOFT BALL						
HIKING						
SWIMMING						
TUMBLING						
HANDBALL						
BOXING						
CROSS COUNTRY						
TOTAL						
ABSENCES (Previous Year)						
LONG ILLNESS						
GENERAL SCHOLASTIC ACHIEVEMENT (Previous Year)						

(Back)

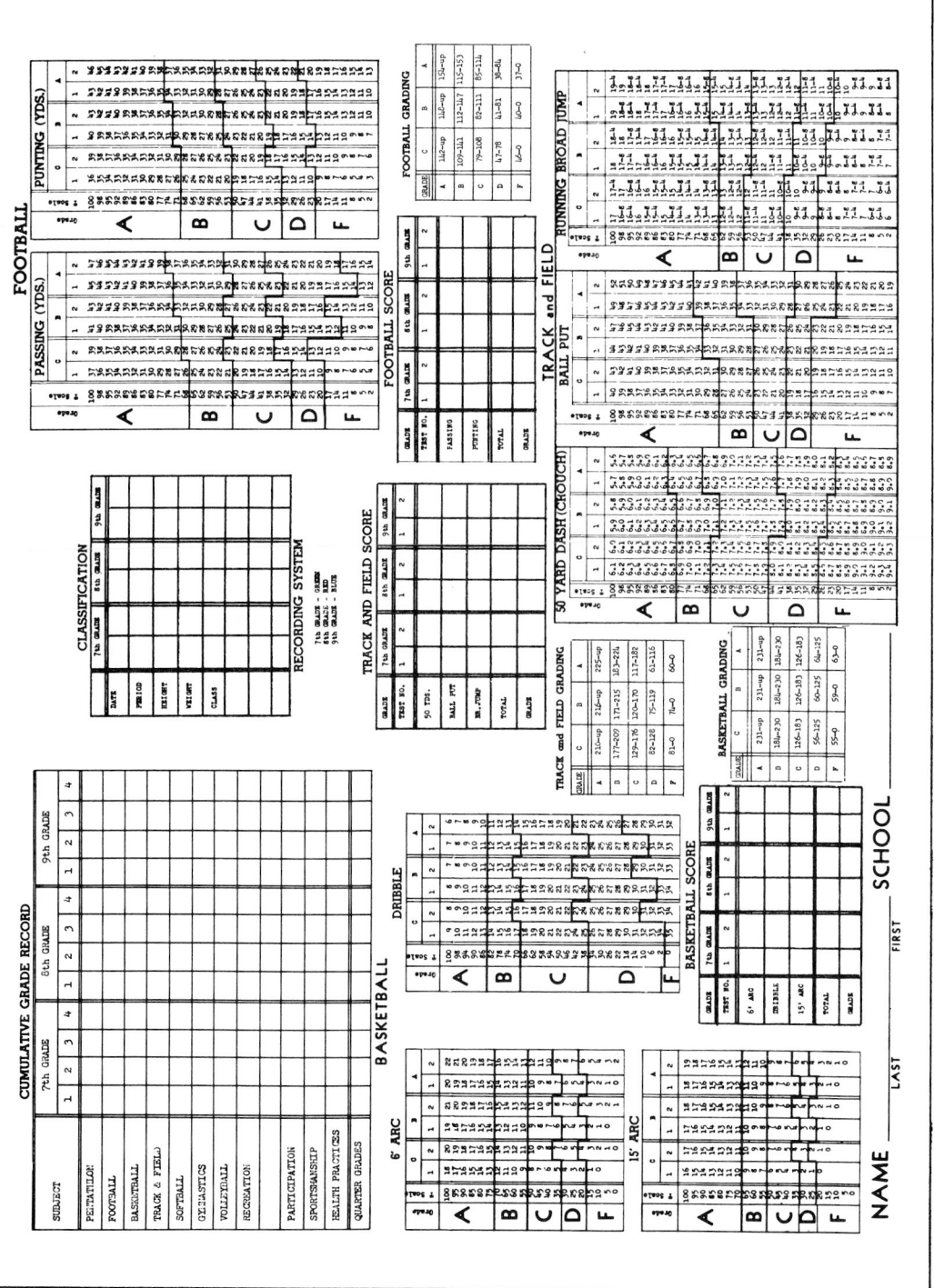

(Back)

SENIOR HIGH SCHOOL GOAL SHEET

7th, 8th and 9th Grades

Pupil's Name ....

PHYSICAL FITNESS — ATHLETIC PARTICIPATION

We believe that physical health is as important as mental health and that neither of the two can function to capacity unless the other is in proper balance. For this reason a definite program of physical education is carried on. This program is extensive for the majority, but intensive for the individual who has definite and specific needs. This sheet is an attempt to set forth in objective terms the physical fitness of the individual child so far as it can be measured and to give a record of the intramural sports in which he has participated.

Physical Fitness Index *

	Seventh Year 19........ 19........	Eighth Year 19........ 19........	Ninth Year 19........ 19........
Fall			
Spring			

NORMAL PHYSICAL FITNESS INDEX IS 1.00.

Posture * *

Fall			
Spring			

Intramural Participation

Football			
Speedball			
Soccer			
Basketball			
Volleyball			
Baseball			
Track			

* The Physical Fitness index is a number arrived at by a rather complicated formula which has been worked out over a period of years and through extensive research in children's physical abilities. It is an attempt to give, in one symbol, an expression of the physical tone of the individual. Since it takes into consideration many separate strengths, as well as height, weight and age, it is not only significant as regards the individual in comparison with people of his own structure, but it also gives an opportunity to discover any inherent weakness and to plan for its remedy. The members of the Physical Education Department will be glad to go into this matter in detail if you will call on them.

** Posture is stated as excellent, good or poor. This is done to bring to the individual's attention his habitual posture, for it is only by conscious effort that any change can be brought about. The members of the Physical Education Department will be glad to consult with you regarding this matter.

SENIOR SCHOOL

Department of Physical Education

Boys, Grades 10-11-12

Pupil's Name .... Teacher ....

Advisers: Grade 10 .... Grade 11 .... Grade 12 ....

Objectives of the Program:
1. To develop skills necessary for the satisfactory participation in the various sports, both group and individual.
2. To aid in the development of organic strength and physiological health through physical education activities.
3. To improve attitudes toward the social values of athletics, such as cooperation, fair play and self discipline.
4. To develop an attitude of awareness of desirable postural habits and practice.

	GRADE 10 — Date 19.... 19....	GRADE 11 — Date 19.... 19....	GRADE 12 — Date 19.... 19....
1st GOAL PERIOD	1. Football Skills — Completion of Skill Tests ...... 2. Soccer Skills ...... 3. Coeducational Activities ...... 4. P.F.I. Score (Self Evaluation Only) ...... 5. Preparation and Attitude	1. Football Skills (Senior Football Decathlon)...... 2. Soccer Skills ...... 3. P.F.I. Score (Self Evaluation Only) ...... 4. Preparation and Attitude	1. Football Skills (Senior Football Decathlon)...... 2. Soccer Skills ...... 3. P.F.I. Score (Self Evaluation Only) ...... 4. Preparation and Attitude ......
2nd GOAL PERIOD	1. Basketball Skills (Completion of Skill Tests) ...... 2. Gymnastics (Rings, Parallel Bars and Vaulting Box) ...... 3. Coeducational Activities ...... 4. Preparation and Attitude	1. Basketball Skills (Completion of Skill Tests) ...... 2. Gymnastics (Rings, Parallel Bars and Vaulting Box) 3. Preparation and Attitude	1. Basketball Skills (Completion of Skill Tests) ...... 2. Gymnastics (Rings, Parallel Bars and Vaulting Box) 3. Preparation and Attitude ......
3rd GOAL PERIOD	1. Tumbling ...... 2. Volleyball Skills ...... 3. P.F.I. Score (Self Evaluation Only) ...... 4. Preparation and Attitude	1. Volleyball Skills (Class Tournament) ...... 2. Gymnastics (Rope Jump, Ropes, Tumbling) 3. P.F.I. Score (Self Evaluation Only) ...... 4. Preparation and Attitude	1. Volleyball Skills (Class Tournament) ...... 2. Gymnastics (Rope Jump, Ropes, Tumbling) 3. P.F.I. Score (Self Evaluation Only) ...... 4. Preparation and Attitude ......

4th GOAL PERIOD	1. Track Skills
	    100 Yd. Dash ......
	    High Jump ......
	    Broad Jump ......
	    Shot Put ......
	 2. Softball Skills (Class Tournament) ......
	 3. Preparation and Attitude ......
	
	 Accumulated Points for Block "B" ......
		1. Track Skills
		    100 Yd. Dash ......
		    880 Yd. Dash ......
		    High Jump ......
		    Broad Jump ......
		    Shot Put ......
		 2. Softball Skills (Class Tournament) ......
		 3. Individual Sport Orientation (Golf and Tennis) ......
		 4. Preparation and Attitude ......
		
		 Accumulated Points for Block "B" ......
			1. Track Skills
			    100 Yd. Dash ......
			    880 Yd. Dash ......
			    High Jump ......
			    Broad Jump ......
			    Shot Put ......
			 2. Softball Skills (Class Tournament) ......
			 3. Instruction in Golf and Tennis ......
			 4. Preparation and Attitude ......
			
			 Total Points Block "B" ......
			 Yes ☐ No ☐

PHYSICAL EDUCATION ATTENDANCE AND EXCUSE FORMS

The following forms and records have been selected from the authors' files. School systems across the country which developed these forms are to be commended for their work.

P. E. EXCUSE

Last Name   (*Print*)   First Name   HR   Period

DATE: REASON   SIGNATURE

APPOINTMENT SLIP

Date........................... Room............... Range............... Seat.....................

....
Name

Please see me as soon as possible, or at...

Place............................... Signed...

Please bring this slip with you

ATTENDANCE CARD

Name _____   H.R._____ R____ S____

Address _____   Telephone _____

Parents/Guardians _____   Evanston _____
                                            or (City) _____

1st att.	1	2	3	4	5	6	7	8	9	10	11	12
2nd att.	1	2	3	4	5	6	7	8	9	10	11	12

1st Sem. Health Ed. _____

2nd Sem. Health Ed. _____

1st Sem. Physical Ed.	Med. Ex._____	**2nd Sem. Physical Ed.**
Period_____ Gym_____	_____	Period_____ Gym_____
Teacher _____	Feet:	Teacher _____
Suit - label	1 - OK___ I___ P___	Suit - label
Shoes - label	2 - OK___ I___ P___	Shoes - label
S. Shirt - label		S. Shirt - label

```
                                    |  TIME  )
           Time Issued              |  ISSUED )                              ┌──┐
═══════════════════════════════     |                                       └──┘
                                    |                                        Class
        PERIOD TARDINESS            |     PERIOD TARDY SLIP       ┌────────────┐
                                    |                            │            │
Name_____        |  NAME_____       │            │
                                    |                            │            │
Adviser_____  ┌──┐       |  ADVISER_____|___   └────────────┘
                         └──┘       |                              Issued by
Period_____          Class     |  REASON_____
═══════════════════════════════     |
                                    |  PERIOD_____
Issued )                            |
   by  )_____             |  This slip to be collected by the   TEACHER'S
                                    |  teacher and returned to the office.  SIGNATURE_____
```

(Courtesy New Trier Township High School, Winnetka, Ill.)

```
                          NEW ENROLLEE


          Date_____  Girls Phys. Ed._____
          Name_____          H.R._____
             Period_____
             Room_____  Teacher_____
             Feet checked_____  P.X. appt._____
             Cards:
                Attendance_____  Padlock_____
                Activity_____  Yellow_____
          Year_____  Credit_____

                                         Class List
```

CHANGE OF PROGRAM

Date _____ Girls' Phys. Ed. _____

Name _____ H.R. _____

    Periods — from _____ to _____

    Teachers — from _____ to _____

    Locker changed _____ Act. card _____

Drop _____ Note: _____

Left _____

Completed _____

Double _____

Make-up _____ Atten. _____ Class List _____

PHYSICAL EDUCATION EXCUSE

NAME ....

GRADE .... ADVISOR .... GYM PERIOD ....

DATES—EXCUSED FROM .... To ....

DOCTOR ....

REASON ....

....

NO PHYS. ED. ....

MODIFIED PROGRAM

      FULL PROGRAM EXCEPT COMPETITIVE SPORTS ....

      PARTICIPATION EXCEPT ....

SCHOOL SCHEDULE ADJUSTMENT, IF ANY ....

....

Name..
                        (Last)   (First)   (Second)
Home   Home
Address...Tel. No.........................
              (No.)   (Street)   (Village)

Name of { Parent* or Guardian* }
*Cross out one   (Last)   (First)   (Second)

Business Address...
                  (No.)   (Street)   (City)
If office is in large bldg. } Indicate— { ....
                                        (Name of Building)   (Bus. Tel. No.)
Parent's   Family
Occupation..Physician.................................
(Name of firm or institution with which connected)

Date of | Place of
Your | Birth ....
Birth | (City)   (State)

How far can you swim? Check distance: Not at all ☐   25 yards ☐   100 yards ☐

JUNIOR

CLASS 19	SEPT.	OCT.	NOV.	DEC.	19 JAN.	FEB.	MAR.	APR.	MAY	JUNE
M.										
T.										
W.										
TH.										
F.										

PERIOD ( )   CREDIT ( )   PERIOD ( )   CREDIT (

SENIOR

CLASS 19	SEPT.	OCT.	NOV.	DEC.	19 JAN.	FEB.	MAR.	APR.	MAY	JUNE
M.										
T.										
W.										
TH.										
F.										

PERIOD ( )   CREDIT ( )   PERIOD ( )   CREDIT ( )

WAIVER   WITHDRAWAL   RE-ENTRANCE

LAST NAME   FIRST NAME   ADVISER   S. NO.

ADVISER

FIRST NAME

LAST NAME

(Front)

(Courtesy Boys' Physical Education Department, New Trier Township High School, Winnetka, Ill.)

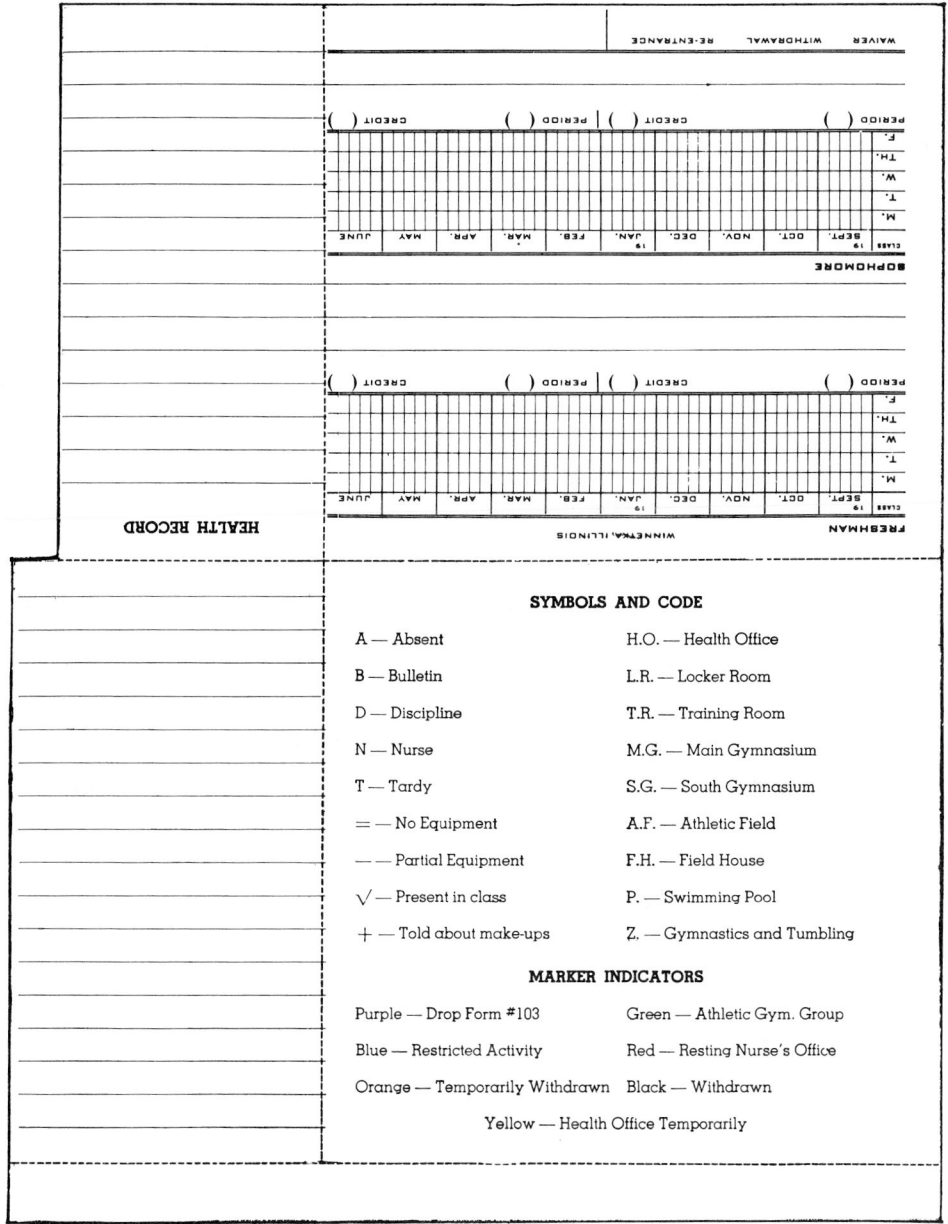

SYMBOLS AND CODE

A — Absent   H.O. — Health Office

B — Bulletin   L.R. — Locker Room

D — Discipline   T.R. — Training Room

N — Nurse   M.G. — Main Gymnasium

T — Tardy   S.G. — South Gymnasium

= — No Equipment   A.F. — Athletic Field

— — Partial Equipment   F.H. — Field House

√ — Present in class   P. — Swimming Pool

+ — Told about make-ups   Z. — Gymnastics and Tumbling

MARKER INDICATORS

Purple — Drop Form #103   Green — Athletic Gym. Group

Blue — Restricted Activity   Red — Resting Nurse's Office

Orange — Temporarily Withdrawn   Black — Withdrawn

Yellow — Health Office Temporarily

(Back)

(Courtesy Boys' Physical Education Department, New Trier Township High School, Winnetka, Ill.)

PHYSICAL EDUCATION EQUIPMENT FORMS

The following forms and records have been selected from the authors' files. School systems across the country which developed these forms are to be commended for their work.

Last Name						First							
Home Room			Locker			Lock			Phone No.				
Sport													
Checked Out						Checked In							
Belt	Jersey	Pants	Game Jersey	Nurmi Shirt	Helmet	Sweat Shirt	Sweat Pants	Socks	Shoes	Warm-Ups	Supporter Pads	Pads Hip	Shoulder

BOYS' PHYSICAL EDUCATION EQUIPMENT CARD

Boys Equipment Card

NAME:_____ ACTIVITY:_____ DATE:_____
       (LAST NAME FIRST)

ARTICLE	BLACK	ORANGE	WHITE
SHOES			
PANTS (PRACTICE)			
JERSEY "			
HIP PADS – SLIDE			
SHOULDER PADS			
THIGH PADS			
T SHIRT			
SUPPORTER			
SOCKS – STOCKINGS			
JERSEY (GAME)			
PANTS "			
WARMUP – JACKET			
WARMUP – PANTS			
HOOD			
HELMET – CAP			

HOME ROOM _____

AGE _____ HT. _____ WT. _____

YEAR IN SCHOOL _____

LOCKER # _____

TELEPHONE # _____

ADDRESS _____

_____

SIGNATURE:

_____

MISCELLANEOUS:

NEW TRIER TOWNSHIP HIGH SCHOOL - WINNETKA, ILLINOIS
BOYS' PHYSICAL EDUCATION DEPARTMENT

Report of Broken or Missing Equipment

_____ _____   1 2 3 4 _____
(Date) (Period)   (Class)   (Instructor)
    Broken --------------"X"   Missing --------------"O"

Badminton Racket - - - ( )   Soccer Ball - - - - - - - ( )
Basketball - - - - - - ( )   Speedball - - - - - - - - ( )
Handball - - - - - - - ( )   Table Tennis Ball - - - - ( )
Handball Gloves - - - ( )   Table Tennis Paddle - - - ( )
Softball - - - - - - - ( )   Tennis Racket - - - - - - ( )
Softball Bat - - - - - ( )   Touch Football - - - - - ( )
_____ - - - - ( )   Volleyball -- - - - - - - ( )

Student _____ Adviser _____

Remarks _____
_____
_____
_____

Form PE-11

HEALTH AND PHYSICAL EDUCATION DEPARTMENT

Annual Inventory of Physical Education Supplies and Equipment

Below is list of supplies and equipment for recording inventories. It is divided into two sections: supplies and equipment. The first refers to materials that are consumed in current use, and their service life is relatively short. The second refers to all articles that have permanent usefulness over a period of time and are not consumed or destroyed in their use. Check all supplies and equipment in both sections, adding any items that are not listed.

- -

Compiled by_____ School _____ Year _____

Supplies	Items on Hand	Add'l Items Rec'd	Total 1 & 2	New	Good	Poor	Dis- carded	Total 3 to 6
	1	2		3	4	5	6	
ARCHERY								
Arm Guards								
Arrows								
Bowstrings								
Bows								
Finger Tabs								
Quiver								
Target Faces								
Targets								
Target Stands								
BADMINTON								
Nets								
Presses								
Racquets								
Shuttlecocks								
BALLS								
Baseballs								
Basketballs								
Cage								
Footballs, junior								
Footballs, official								
Footballs, touch								
Golf, practice								
Golf, game								
Handball								
Hockey, practice								
Hockey, game								
Medicine								
Paddle Tennis								
Rubber Play Balls, large								
Rubber Play Balls, medium								
Rubber Play Balls, small								
Soccer								
Softballs								
Table Tennis								
Tennis								
Volleyballs								

Name_____Room_____
        First   Middle   Last

Locker_____Lock_____Date_____
        Number   Number

My signature above is in recognition of the agreement that in consideration of the free use of a school locker during this school year I agree to use the above-numbered lock on my duly assigned locker only, to keep my locker locked when not necessarily open, to maintain my locker in good condition, and to forfeit all rights to this lock if left at school after the close of examinations in June.

A lock may be redeemed by the school at the time the purchaser leaves school provided it is turned in by the person who originally purchased it from the school.

From whom was this lock purchased?_____

GIRL'S PADLOCK CARD

First Name)		(Middle Name)			(Last Name)

YEAR	ROOM-R-S	PERIOD	LOCKER	PADLOCK	COMBINATION

EQUIPMENT RECORD CARD
TO BE RETURNED TODAY

Name_____ Teacher_____ Period_____

No.	Article	No.	Article	No.	Article
	Archery, Arm Guard		Handball		Sponge Ball
	Archery, Arrow		Hockey Ball		Tape Measure
	Archery, Bow		Hockey Sticks		Table Tennis Net
	Archery, Glove		Jacks - Ball		Tennis Ball
	Badminton Racket		Jump Rope		Tether Ball
	Badminton Shuttlecock		Marbles		Timer (Stop Watch)
	Basketball		Pick-up Sticks		Whistle
	Bean Bag		Ping Pong Ball		
	Checkerboard		Ping Pong Paddle		
	Checker Men		Playground Ball		
	Chest Protector		10" 16"		
	Chinese Checkers		Quoits		
	Clip Board		Softball		
	Darts		Softball Bat		
	Deck Tennis Rings		Shin Guards		
	Dominoes		Shuffleboard Cue		
	Eye-glasses Guard		Shuffleboard Disc		
	Goal Guards		Shuttlecock		
	Golf Ball		Shuttle Loop		
	Golf Club		Soccer Ball		

EQUIPMENT ISSUE

Date...

I .... have

accepted school property ....

.... (write in article and its number)

and ag e to return it clean and in good condition or pay for said uniform.

Signed ....

H. R. #

Home Phone #   Home Address..

DEPARTMENT OF HEALTH AND PHYSICAL EDUCATION

Re: Lost Property Report

Student owner_____ H.R._____ R___ S___

Date of loss_____ Time_____ Period_____

List missing articles:

Description of known details:

Instructor's follow-up:

(Signed)_____

(Use reverse side if additional space is necessary.)

EQUIPMENT CHECKOUT RECORD

Player_____ Home Room_____

Address_____ Phone_____

Class_____ Height_____ Weight_____ Age_____

Parents Waiver_____ Examination_____ Insurance_____

Football   Cross Country   Basketball   Swimming   Wrestling

Baseball   Track   Tennis   Golf

	Out	In	Game Equipment	Out	In
Blocking pads			White jersey		
Shoulder pads			Maroon jersey		
Hip pads			White pants		
Thigh pads			Maroon pants		
Knee pads			Warm-up pants		
Helmet			Warm-up jacket		
Shoes			Stockings		
Practice pants					
Practice jersey					

I hereby certify that I have received the above-listed athletic equipment and will return same not later than the day following the last game of the season for the sport checked.

Signature_____

BOYS' PHYSICAL EDUCATION DEPARTMENT

Equipment Inspection

     Please write on this sheet the names of boys not wearing clean gym cloth-
ing. Also give the advisers' names. Thank you.

     Inspection may involve any day with special emphasis on each MONDAY. The
instructor should place his initials following the date of each recording.

Date	Instr. Init.	Boy's Name	Adviser	Dirty Clothes	Partial Equipment	Torn Clothing	*Borrowed Equipment

    *Borrowed equipment with or without owner's consent should always be
followed up with a discipline note.

(Courtesy Boys' Physical Education Department, New Trier Township High School, Winnetka,
Ill.)

BASKETBALL

Name_____ Address_____

Homeroom_____ Date_____ Phone_____

Medical_____ Permission_____ Insurance_____

Height_____ Weight_____ Age_____

Deposit received_____ Deposit returned_____

Equipment Issued	Equipment Returned

1. Game shirt
      White_____
      Purple_____

2. Game pants
      White_____
      Purple_____

3. Warm-up jacket_____

4. Warm-up pants_____

5. Reversible "T" shirt_____

6. Sneakers_____

7. Knee pads_____

8. Other_____

    _____

                          Signature_____

Remarks:

Dear Mr. and Mrs.

_____, who is in my _____ period class in physical education, has not:

_____ Bought her padlock and had her locker assigned

_____ Bought or presented her complete equipment-- regulation suit, tennis shoes, and sweatshirt

_____ Marked all her equipment with her first initial and last name (Markings should be embroidered above the pocket on the gym suit and in a similar place on the sweatshirt; name tapes are acceptable.)

Our equipment for physical education is as necessary as the textbook for English. Anyone is at a distinct disadvantage without required equipment. I am sure you will do all that you can to see that your daughter's deficiencies as indicated above are corrected at once.

Please feel free to call me about this or any other matter.

Sincerely,

Instructor, Girls' Health and Physical Education Department

MISCELLANEOUS PHYSICAL EDUCATION FORMS

The following forms and records have been selected from the authors' files. School systems across the country which developed these forms are to be commended for their work.

Athletic Permit

Name of Student ....

PARENTS' WAIVER

To Whom It May Concern:

This is to certify that my son/daughter.. (please write his/her name) has my permission to train for and participate in Athletic Honor Team Games / Tigerettes / Cheerleaders (underline particular activity) at White Plains High School. I assume for myself full responsibility should any accident occur to him/her either in training for such activity or in game performances, or in traveling to and from various schools where this activity is carried on.

Signature .... Parent

Date ....19......

Pupil's Name .... Gr ....

Permission is hereby given to .... to
                                        Pupil's Name
participate in the After-School Play Program for the

.... season. I understand (he) (she) will
        Fall, Winter, Spring

participate in .... on .... of each
                        Activity   *Days*

week from about .... to ....
                        Hour   *Hour*

Date ....
                                                        Parent or Guardian

Enrollment in this program is voluntary. However, once enrolled regular attendance
is expected unless prevented for reasons of health or family plans. The pupil is
expected to notify the activity supervisor of the reason for each absence.

Details of each season's program are given each pupil to take home in September
of each year. Another copy will gladly be sent on request.

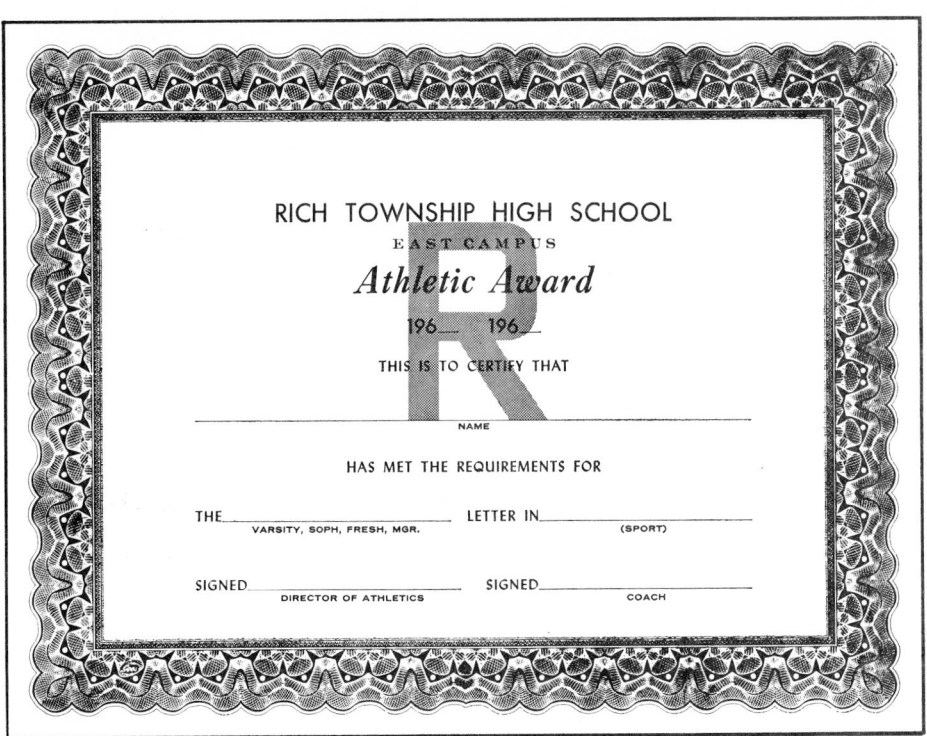

RICH TOWNSHIP HIGH SCHOOL
EAST CAMPUS

Athletic Award

196___ 196___

THIS IS TO CERTIFY THAT

_____
NAME

HAS MET THE REQUIREMENTS FOR

THE_____ LETTER IN_____
   VARSITY, SOPH, FRESH, MGR.   (SPORT)

SIGNED_____ SIGNED_____
      DIRECTOR OF ATHLETICS   COACH

DEPARTMENT OF PHYSICAL EDUCATION

Date_____ 19__

I am willing to have my son/daughter participate in the afterschool activities carried on by the Department of Physical Education. I hereby give my consent for _____, a pupil in the _____ School, to play _____ during the season of 19___. I shall not hold the Board of Education nor any of its employees responsible for the payment of any bills incurred because of accident or injuries to my son/daughter due to athletics or traveling to and from games or practice periods.

_____
Signature of Parent or Guardian

PHYSICIAN'S STATEMENT

I have examined _____
and believe that he is in condition to participate in any of the following sports.

Football	Baseball	Swimming	Obstacle racing
Soccer	Ice hockey	Tennis	Heavy apparatus
Basketball	Handball	Golf	Giant ball
Track and field	Volley ball	Badminton	Field hockey
Cross country	Canoeing	Tumbling	Speed ball

Signature_____M.D.

Date_____

SAMPLE RECOGNITION LETTERS

My dear Mike,

Physical Education has come pretty hard for you, Mike, but you've always been willing to tangle with it in a good try. Never have you sacrificed your fine sense of the neat and the appropriate to the false standards of haste or carelessness.

Your class and home room spirit has been fine too, Mike, and I want you to know that I appreciate it.

Yours sincerely,

Dear John:

I wish to commend you for your splendid work and fine cooperation. You have helped greatly in making our year successful.

It has been a real pleasure to work with you as a member of the intramural basketball team.

Sincerely yours,

Dear Bob:

It is a pleasure to send you this letter in recognition of the fine effort you have put forth in a subject which you have found very difficult.

May you always attack new problems with as much determination and may you become more and more successful in your physical education.

Sincerely yours,

G. A. A.

_____

has earned membership in the Girls' Athletic Association of

.... High School until _____

_____President

_____Secretary

She now has_____points toward_____

Certificate of Award

TO

_____

OF

_____

for Meritorious participation in

_____

SEASON_____

_____   _____
PRINCIPAL   DIRECTOR

BASIS FOR THE EVALUATION OF TEACHING SERVICES

I.   Teacher-Pupil Relationships (A teacher who works well with pupils)

1. Shows respect for the personal worth of each pupil
2. Seeks to understand pupil behavior before making evaluative judgments
3. Is sympathetic, kind, patient--yet firm
4. Respects confidences
5. Respects the individual differences in children and provides learning situations in his classroom to meet these differences
6. Gains the acceptance and respect of pupils

II. Evidence of Instructional Skill (A teacher who is effective in his teaching)

1. Is competent in the subjects he teaches
2. Uses a variety of materials and teaching techniques
3. Stimulates pupils to think critically
4. Adapts instructional methods and materials to the abilities and interests of individual pupils
5. Develops and uses effective techniques of evaluation
6. Makes extent and purpose of assignments clear
7. Maintains an attractive and stimulating classroom environment

III. Evidence of Classroom Control and Management (A teacher who controls and manages his class successfully)

1. Provides a well-controlled democratic environment
2. Enters into pupils' activities without dominating them
3. Encourages children to work to capacity without undue tension
4. Exercises care for the safety and health of pupils
5. Shows ability to organize
6. Is able to handle behavior problems without emotional upsets or emotional extremes

IV. Teacher-Staff Relationships (A teacher who works well with his associates)

1. Promotes good will among individuals and groups
2. Serves on committees and participates in other group projects
3. Carries his share of school responsibilities willingly and cheerfully; readily responds when called upon to assume extra responsibilities
4. Is alert to ways in which he can improve conditions in the school and helps others cheerfully
5. Goes through regular "channels" on matters affecting the welfare of associates or of the institution
6. Gains the respect of his associates
7. Is prompt and accurate with reports

(cont'd)

BASIS FOR EVALUATION OF TEACHING SERVICES (cont'd)

V.   <u>Services Other Than Classroom Instruction</u> (A teacher who **serves** outside of the classroom)

    1. Shows interest and takes an active part in the promotion of
student activities
    2. Sponsors student clubs and other extracurricular organizations
and activities
    3. Accepts responsibility for the guidance of students within his
sphere of competence
    4. Accepts his share of such assigned duties as yard or cafeteria
supervision, etc., and carries out these responsibilities
conscientiously
    5. Invites parent conferences; conducts them in a courteous and
helpful manner
    6. Shows interest in community activities
    7. Interprets constructively the objectives of the school **system** to
the community at large

VI. <u>Personal Characteristics</u> (A teacher who possesses the **personal**
qualities desired in teachers)

    1. Is careful of appearance--posture, grooming, **dress**
    2. Speaks in a well-modulated voice
    3. Is physically fit, appears healthy and energetic
    4. Possesses a good sense of humor
    5. Is free from excessive worry, fear, moods, and **false conceit**
    6. Shows mature control in handling emergencies
    7. Is interested and enthusiastic about his **work**

VII. <u>Evidence of Sound Professional Attitude and Desire to Strengthen</u>
<u>Abilities</u> (A Teacher who shows evidence of professional **growth**)

    1. Endeavors to improve in his classroom methods and **techniques**
    2. Avails himself of the opportunities offered to **improve by**
joining professional organizations, attending **workshops,**
summer school, professional meetings, and conferences; **keeps**
abreast of the professional literature
    3. Is willing to experiment with new ideas
    4. Respects the ethics of the profession
    5. Seeks assistance from principal and supervisor **when needed**

INDEX